The **Rough Guide** to

Goa

written and researched by

David Abram

with additional contributions from

Nick Edwards and Gavin Thomas

www.roughguides.com

Contents

Colour section 1

Introduction 4
Where to go 7
When to go 10
Things not to miss 11

Basics 17

Getting there 19
Arrival 23
Entry requirements 24
Getting around 26
Accommodation 29
Food and drink 31
Health 36
The media 40
Festivals 41
Sports and outdoor pursuits 43
Yoga and Ayurveda 44
Culture and etiquette 46
Shopping and souvenirs 48
Travelling with children 51
Travel essentials 52

Guide 59

1. Panjim and central Goa 61
2. North Goa 105
3. South Goa 157
4. Around Goa 207
5. Mumbai 229

Contexts 263

History 265
The religions of Goa 278
Environmental issues in Goa 283
Natural history 287
Goan music and dance 295
Books 299

Language 303

Konkani 305
Konkani words and phrases 305
Food and drink terms 307
Glossary of Hindi and Konkani words 310

Travel store 313

Small print & Index 319

Life's a beach
colour section
following p.112

The Portuguese legacy
colour section
following p.240

◀◀ Palolem beach ◀ Little Vagator beach

Introduction to Goa

A byword in India for "good times", Goa is where the country's elite come to party these days, and where hundreds of thousands of foreigners flock to escape the northern European winter. Its blissful climate (maximum daytime temperatures hover around 30 degrees from December until March) is one reason. The spectacular golden sand beaches spread along the state's palm-fringed coastline is the other – and there are plenty of them, from shimmering expanses that merge with the horizon to secluded coves backed by crumbling red cliffs. Goa's metamorphosis from remote Portuguese colony to international playground, however, owes as much to the distinctly hybrid culture of its inhabitants as to the state's natural assets. Nowhere else in the subcontinent will you find traditional Indian ways co-existing so peacefully and easily with those implanted by Europeans, and to this day a tolerant attitude to foreignness remains a distinctively Goan trait.

The explanation most often advanced for this is the longevity of Portuguese rule, which began in 1510 – well before the British gained their first toe-hold in India – and outlived the Raj by more than a decade. Goa's physical remoteness also played its part. Cut off from the rest of India by a wall of mountains and hundreds of miles of un-navigable alluvial plain, the colony remained aloof from the wider subcontinent for four and a half centuries, turning instead towards the sea and distant lands to evolve its own distinctive way of life. Not until 1961 was the colony finally absorbed into India; and it took a couple of decades more before the advent of mass

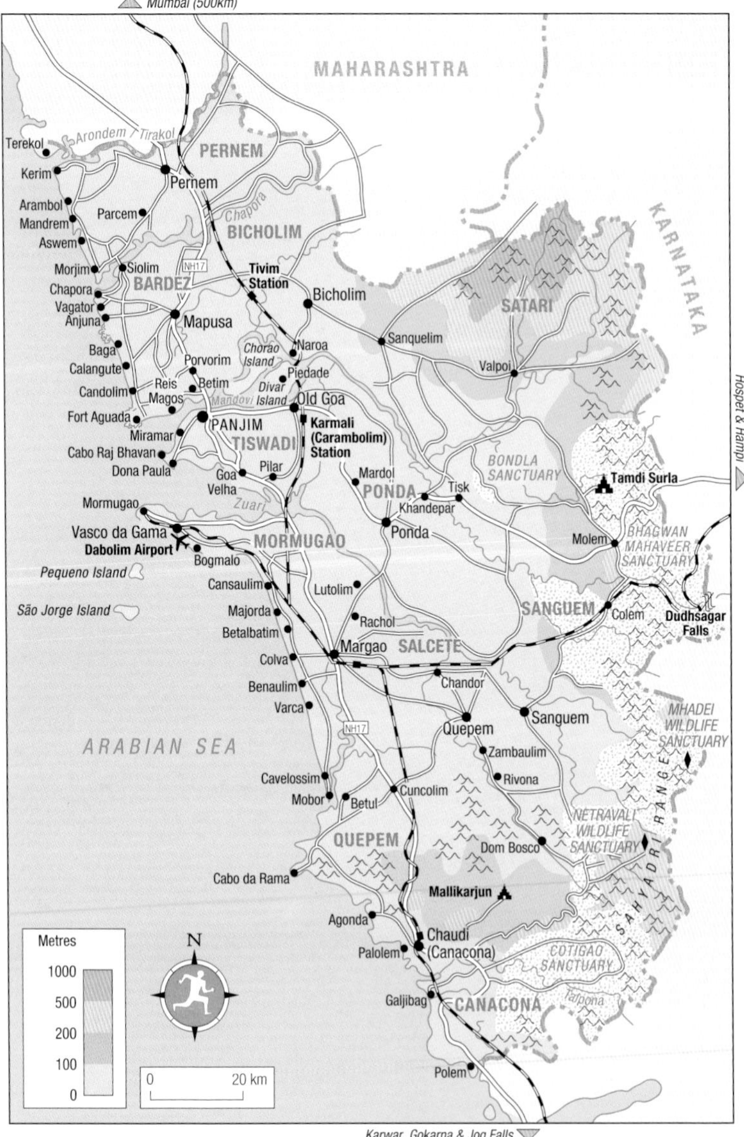

tourism – first in the form of the hippy trail and later with the package holiday boom – dragged Goa into the mainstream of Asian life.

These days, India's smallest state is anything but isolated. Two-and-a-half million visitors pour in each year, 375,000 of them foreigners who come to relax on Goa's glorious white-sand, palm-backed **beaches**. In mid-winter, while northern Europe hunkers down in the cold and damp, southern India's

Fact file

• Edged by 105km of coastline, Goa is 65km wide at its broadest point and covers a total surface area of 3700 square kilometres; you can drive from one extremity to the other in three and a half hours. Mumbai, the nearest large city, lies just under 500km north in neighbouring Maharashtra; bordering the state in the south and west is Karnataka.

• In March 2001 (the date of the last census) the population of Goa stood at 1,344,000, of whom 65 percent were Hindu, 29 percent Christian (Roman Catholics) and 5 percent Muslim. Around 10,000 immigrants arrive in the state annually.

• The literacy rate is currently 82.3 percent – relatively high for an Indian state. Gross domestic product (GDP) is in excess of US$3 billion – the highest of any Indian state, and two-and-a half times the national average.

• Konkani, granted official status only in 1987, is the mother tongue of most Goans, while Portuguese, the language of government until the end of the colonial era in 1961, is understood only by a tiny elite. English is most people's second language, spoken by nearly everyone in the towns and coastal resorts.

blissful tropical climate ensures six months of clear skies and warm seas.

The coast, however, is only a part of the picture. A short foray **inland** will take you into the state's real core: a patchwork of paddy fields, spice plantations and meandering rivers where church gables nose above the treeline and ferries are still the main mode of transport between villages. Once outside the Christian heartland, the polychrome traditions of **Hinduism** – the religion of more than two thirds of Goa's population – reassert themselves. Western dresses give way to vivid saris, and the priest's cassock to the coloured cotton *lunghi* of the temple Brahmin.

Sheltered by the sophistication of the resorts, it's easy to forget that workaday India may lie only a couple of fields away. In the past decade, Goa's **towns**, in particular, have been deluged by migrant workers from other states, many of whom live in shanty encampments on the outskirts and subsist on an average annual income that's far lower than the cost of a flight from Europe. Don't, however, let this deter you from venturing away from the beach. Exploring the less touristy areas inland – or across the borders

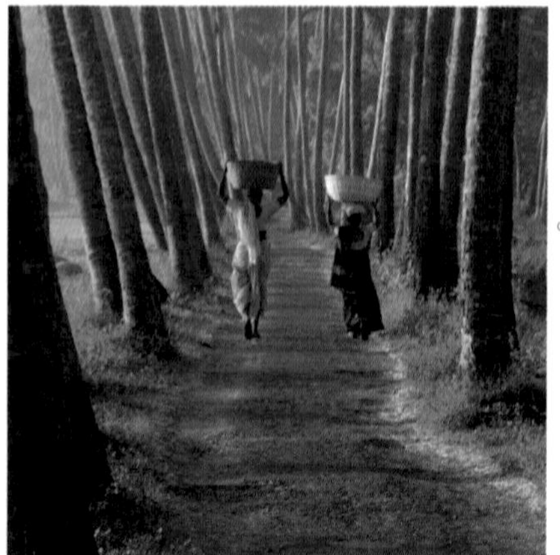

◀ Fisherwomen heading to market

▲ Basilica of Bom Jesus, Old Goa

into neighbouring Maharashtra and Karnataka – will yield some of the most memorable experiences of your trip, combining beautiful scenery with the chance to encounter a way of life that's a world away from the commercialism of the coastal strip.

Where to go

Where you stay in Goa will have a marked influence on your overall holiday experience, as the complexion of individual resorts varies greatly. An hour's drive from the airport, the stretch of coast immediately north of the state capital, **Panjim**, has emerged as the principal charter belt. Its three main centres – **Candolim**, **Calangute** and **Baga** – nowadays form an unbroken conurbation, with most of the comforts and amenities you'd expect of international resorts – and a beach jam-packed with parasols, cafés and sunloungers. New river bridges have stimulated a slow spread of package hotels northwards, but the area beyond Baga – around the villages and beaches of **Anjuna** and **Vagator** – remains the preserve of mostly longer-staying, independent travellers. Further north still, towards **Arambol**, the scene grows more alternative. Tourist accommodation there, with a few notable examples, is basic, pitched primarily at backpackers who stay for months, though this is changing fast.

South Goa, closer to the airport and with the town of **Margao** as its hub, has its own package tourist enclave centered on a string of ultra-luxurious resort complexes erected directly behind **Colva** beach, a 25-kilometre stretch of sand that's as spectacular as any you'll find in India. If you're travelling on a budget, the village to head for hereabouts is **Benaulim**, an ideal arrival point with inexpensive guesthouses and beach shacks, and plenty of Goan-Catholic character. It's been eclipsed in recent years, however, by **Palolem**, and neighbouring **Patnem** in the far south of the state. Picture-postcard bays of golden sand backed by swaying palms and jungle-covered hills, these beaches are undeniably idyllic and thus far free of concrete, but get correspondingly overwhelmed from November onwards.

Goan coconuts

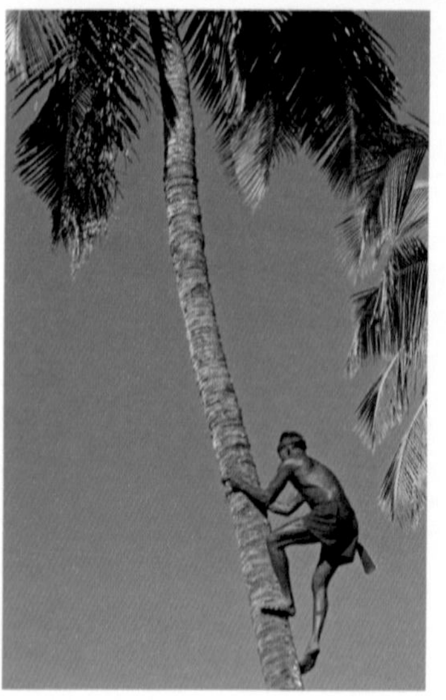

If you're lucky, the first sound you'll hear on your first morning in Goa will be the rustle of palm fronds. The ubiquity of the coconut tree (*cocos nucifera*) may be an essential part of the state's appeal as a holiday destination, but for the locals, it represents wealth, health and – most of all – hard graft. Goans consume something like 40 million coconuts per year (one per family every day), and the business of harvesting and looking after the trees comprises a way of life for one sixth of the population.

Coconuts find their way into virtually every Goan dish – from fiery fish curry to sticky sweet *bebinca* and *dodol*. The meat – or *copra* – yields a wonderfully rich oil for cooking, soap and cosmetics, while the seawater-resistant husk – coir – is spun to make nautical rope. The trunks provide building timber, and the leaves are plaited to make brooms or panels for shacks and hut roofs. The most characteristically Goan use of the coconut tree, however, is as a source of sap, which is distilled to make *feni* – a strong local liquor. Between six and eight thousand *toddi* tappers climb their trees two or three times daily to extract the juice. Most are poor by Goan standards and many suffer from alcohol problems, which explains why falling out of coconut trees is one of the most common causes of violent death in Goa.

For visitors, falling nuts are more of a worry. Keep an ear out for the tell-tale whack of a machete that precedes the crash to earth of harvested coconuts, and never fall asleep under a palm tree, no matter how cool it might feel.

▲ Aswem, North Goa

Visitors in search of space and calm tend instead to hole up further north at **Agonda** – a low-key resort offering a range of inexpensive accommodation, most of it in beach huts.

Foremost among the attractions away from the coast are the ruins of the Portuguese capital at **Old Goa**, 9km from Panjim – a sprawl of Catholic cathedrals, convents and churches that draws crowds of Christian pilgrims from all over India. The other essential excursions are to the **flea markets** at **Anjuna** (on Wednesdays) and **Arpora** (Saturday nights), where you can shop for Indian souvenirs or the latest designer party gear. Further inland, the thickly wooded countryside around **Ponda** harbours numerous **temples** showcasing Goa's idiosyncratic brand of Hindu architecture, while the *taluka* (district) of Salcete, around **Margao** in the south, is littered with wonderful **Portuguese mansions** (*palacios*). In addition, wildlife enthusiasts may be tempted into the interior to visit the nature reserves at **Molem**, in the far east of central Goa, and **Cotigao** in the south near Palolem, which both support fragile populations of rare animals.

With so many tempting beaches, markets, monuments and nature reserves within the state, it's no surprise that few visitors venture across the Goan border into neighbouring **Maharashtra** or **Karnataka**. But beyond the shelter of the Western Ghats, amid the plateau lands of the Deccan Trap, lie the remnants of several ancient capitals. Among these is one of the most exotic archeological sites in South India, the ruined city of Vijayanagar, or **Hampi**. Today, weed-choked palaces, temples and discarded statues are virtually all that remain of this once glittering metropolis, but a visit will give you a vivid insight into the extravagant art and culture of pre-colonial Hindu India, while the day-long train journey to the site is an adventure in itself.

For this reason, we've included a detailed account of Hampi in Chapter 4, **Around Goa**, which also features the highlights of the **Sindhurga district**, just north of Goa in Maharashtra, and the **Konkan coast**, the lush strip running south in the shadow of the Sahyadri Hills. Chapter 5 covers **Mumbai (Bombay)**, a hot, congested, upbeat city that is the arrival point for most international flights. Mumbai gets a pretty bad press, and most people pass straight through, but those who stay find themselves witness to the reality of modern-day India, from the deprivations of the city's slum-dwellings to the glitz and glamour of Bollywood movies – a stark contrast with Goa.

When to go

The best **time to go** to Goa is during the dry, relatively cool winter months between mid-November and late March, when daytime temperatures are perfect for lazing on the beach and the sea is warm. From the beginning of April onwards the heat and humidity begin to build, culminating in June, when a giant wall of black cloud marches landwards from the Arabian Sea. With the arrival of the **monsoon** proper, violent storms wrack the coast for days on end, and over the coming months 2.5m of rain falls. Not until October do the skies start to clear, and even then you can expect spells of intense humidity, grey skies, haze and occasional rain storms, alternating with bursts of strong sun.

For the past decade or so, the monsoons have spilled into November, shortening the tourist season. This has put the **peak period**, from mid-December to the end of January, under increased pressure. Finding a room or a house to rent at this time – particularly over the Christmas and New Year fortnight, when the tariffs double or triple – can be a real hassle in some resorts. So if you're travelling without pre-booked accommodation, it may be worthwhile reserving a room before you leave.

Average daily temperatures (°C) and monthly rainfall (mm)

	Jan	Feb	Mar	Apr	May	Jun	Jul	Aug	Sep	Oct	Nov	Dec
Average daily temperature												
Maximum (°C)	31.9	31.9	32.3	32.7	33.2	7/-1	29.0	28.7	29.0	31.0	32.0	32.0
Average monthly rainfall												
Rainfall (mm)	0	0	2	4	65	402	1331	376	211	169	10	2

things not to miss

It's not possible to see everything that Goa has to offer in one trip – and we don't suggest you try. What follows, in no particular order, is a selective taste of the region's highlights: idyllic beaches, outstanding monuments, delicious food festivals and great places to stay. They're arranged in four colour-coded categories, which you can browse through to find the very best things to see and experience. All highlights have a page reference to take you straight into the Guide, where you can find out more.

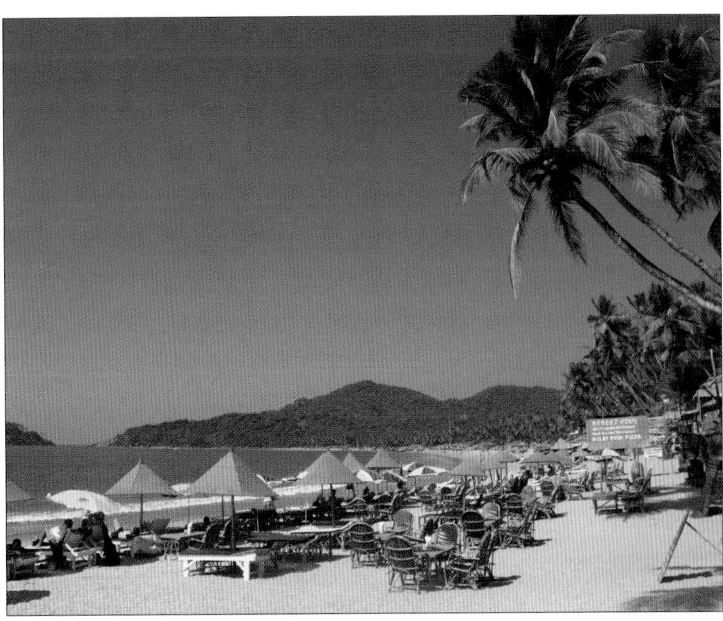

01 **Palolem** Page **195** • Far from secret, but still breathtakingly beautiful despite the hordes who winter here.

02 Mapusa market Page **108** • Goa's biggest fresh produce market: a riot of local sights, sounds and smells.

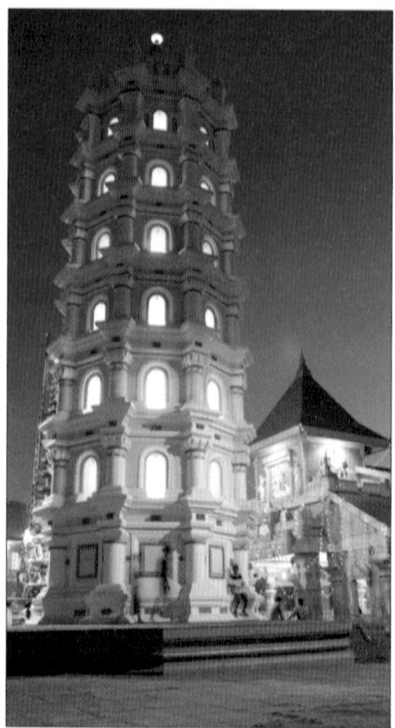

03 Hindu temples Page **98** • Goa has its own quirky hybrid style of Hindu architecture, with the best specimens around Ponda.

04 Arambol beach Page **154** • Hangout for Goa's long-stay hippy contingent, complete with holistic therapies and a wholefood bakery.

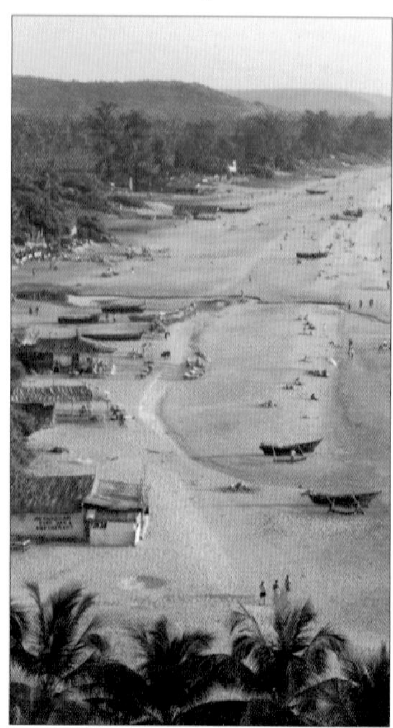

05 Heritage hotels
Page **30** • There's no better way to experience Goa's unusual period architecture than from the inside.

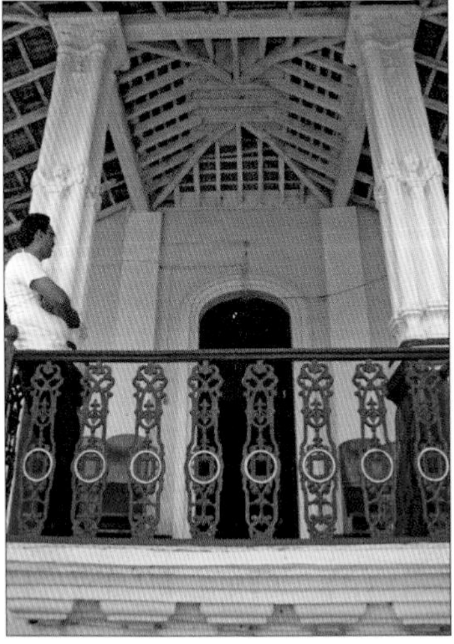

06 Colonial architecture
Page **72 & Portuguese legacy colour section** • Dilapidated eighteenth-century *palacios* and Baroque churches litter Goa's lush green hinterland.

07 Goan food Page **31 & Portuguese legacy colour section** • Goa's diverse historical influences have given rise to a superbly distinctive cuisine dominated by spices, seafood and coconuts.

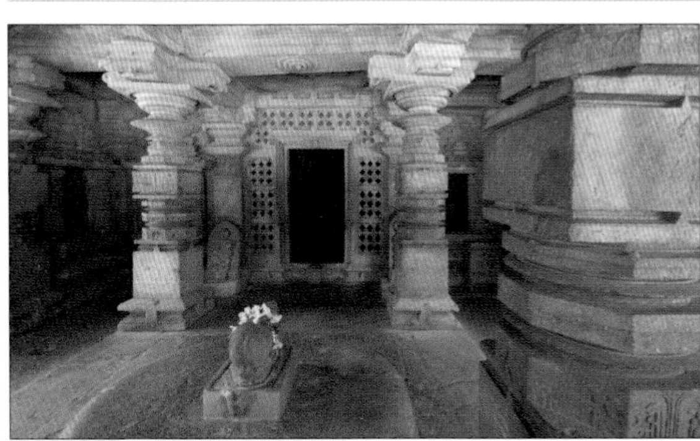

08 Tambdi Surla
Page **102** • Goa's last surviving medieval stone temple, marooned at an appropriately magical spot deep in the interior.

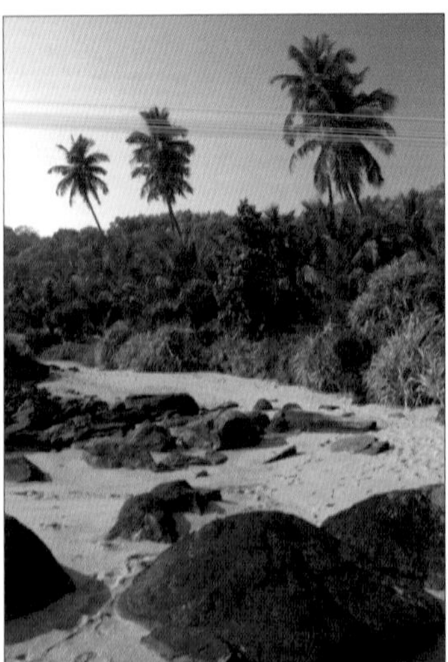

09 Gokarna Page **223** • Combine a taste of sacred Hindu India with some wonderful beaches at this crumbling pilgrimage town, a couple of hours' train ride south of Goa.

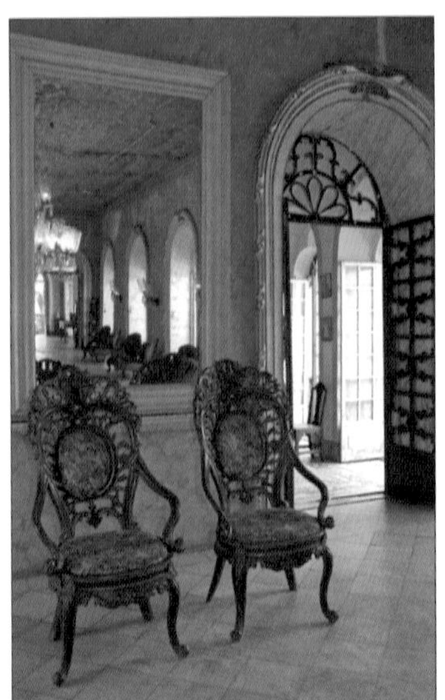

11 Menezes-Braganza house Page **169** • The state's most sumptuous colonial mansion, crammed with crystal, Chinese porcelain and carved furniture.

10 Hampi Page **242** • Monkeys scurrying over ruined temples, a sacred river and magnificent boulder landscapes, only a six-hour train ride inland.

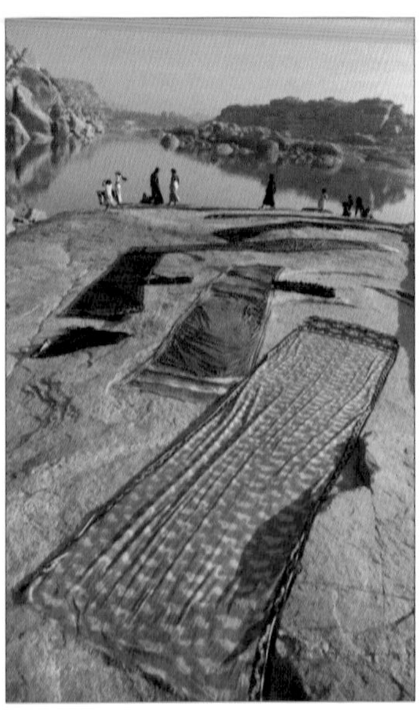

12 Spice plantations Page **96** • Cardamom, pepper, coffee and pineapples are just some of the exotic crops you can see being grown in the market gardens around Ponda.

13 Usgalimal carvings Page **172** • Hunting scenes and weird geometric shapes gouged into a river bend over 20,000 years ago.

14 Dudhsagar Falls Page **103** • Venture into the jungle-draped hills inland to see India's second-highest waterfalls.

15 Saturday night bazaar Page **132** • Cooler, in every sense, than Anjuna's flea market, and the place to chill on Saturday evenings.

16 Fontainhas Page **71** • Panjim's "heritage enclave" preserves the ambience of colonial times better than anywhere else in Goa.

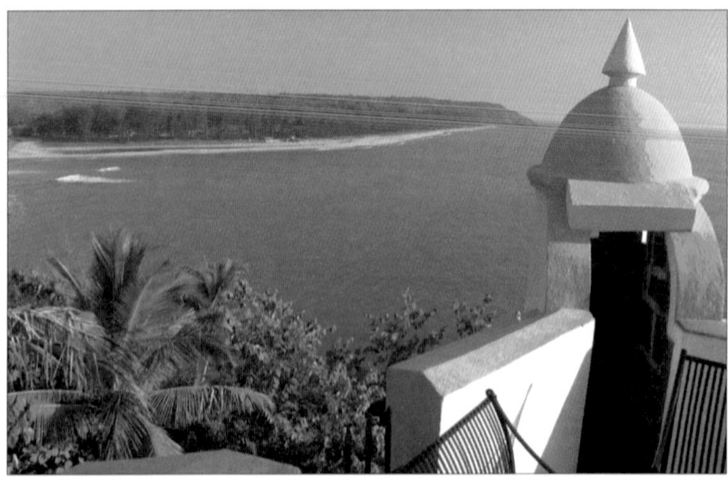

17 Terekol Fort Page **155** • Old fort in the far north that's been converted into a romantic heritage hotel, where you can wine and dine against a backdrop of sweeping sea views.

18 Benaulim Page **184 & Life's a beach colour section** • Watch fishermen hauling in their daily catch at this laidback resort.

19 Anjuna flea market Page **136** • Exuberantly colourful beachside bazaar (Wednesday only) showcasing tourist souvenirs from across India, at negotiable prices.

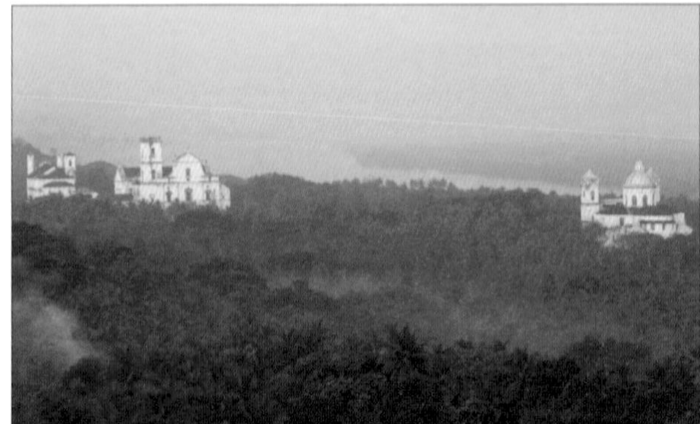

20 Old Goa Page **79** • Grand vestiges of the once-vast Portuguese capital include a campus of giant churches and the glass-sided tomb of St Francis Xavier.

Basics

Basics

Getting there 19
Arrival 23
Entry requirements 24
Getting around 26
Accommodation 29
Food and drink 31
Health 36
The media 40
Festivals 41
Sports and outdoor pursuits 43
Yoga and Ayurveda 44
Culture and etiquette 46
Shopping and souvenirs 48
Travelling with children 51
Travel essentials 52

Getting there

There are no direct scheduled services to Goa from anywhere outside India, but you can fly direct by charter from the UK. Otherwise, the best alternative is to catch a flight to Mumbai with a scheduled airline and pick up an onward service from there. Travelling to Mumbai from North America involves at least one or two changes of plane. From New Zealand or Australia, the quickest route is via Southeast Asia.

Airfares worldwide always depend on the **season**, with the highest being roughly November to March, when the weather in India is best; fares drop during the shoulder seasons – April to May and August to early October – and you'll get the cheapest prices during the low season, June and July, when Goa's beaches are wracked by monsoon gales and the weather is relentlessly wet and stormy. The most expensive fares of all are those coinciding with Diwali in November and over Christmas and New Year.

If India is only one stop on a longer journey, you might consider buying a **Round-the-World** ("RTW") ticket. Some agents offer "off-the-shelf" RTW tickets that will have you touching down in about half a dozen cities (Mumbai is on many itineraries); others will have to assemble one for you, which can be tailored to your needs but is apt to be more expensive. Figure on £850/$1600–£1500/$2850 for a RTW ticket including India, valid for one year.

Flights from the UK and Ireland

It takes between eight and a half and ten hours' flying time to reach Mumbai direct from the UK. However, most airlines route passengers through their hub city on the way, which adds significantly to the total journey time. You get what you pay for: economy airlines may offer rock-bottom fares from as low as £400 (or less), but you'll invariably find this means a long wait en route, as well as departure and arrival times at unsociable hours of the day. At the other end of the scale, a ticket costing upwards of £650 with British Airways or Air India should get you there non-stop from London by a more civilized hour. Flight-only deals with charters (see below) go for as little as £400 in low season, or around £550–750 over Christmas and New Year.

For the onward leg from **Mumbai to Goa**, most people book their internal ticket at the same time as they buy their international one. The fare – quoted at a higher dollar rate for non-Indian nationals – should cost exactly the same as it would if you bought it in India, although it's always worth checking (the airlines' published fares are listed on their websites; see p.22) as some unscrupulous agents will try to slap on mark-ups.

Note, however, that agents won't make bookings for the **low-cost airlines** that fly between Mumbai and Goa. Huge savings can be made if you buy a seat on **Kingfisher Airlines** (ⓦwww.flykingfisher.com), **Go Airlines** (ⓦwww.goair.in) or **Spicejet** (ⓦwww.spicejet.com).

Flying by charter from the UK

Given the hassles and extra expense involved with flying scheduled through Mumbai, it's easy to understand why most people travel to Goa from the UK by charter flights, even if they're not on a package holiday. Prices fluctuate greatly according to season and demand, but all in all, this invariably works out the most comfortable, convenient and cost-effective option.

At present, Monarch Airlines operates flights to Goa from **Gatwick** and **Manchester**. The flight time from Gatwick – including a refuelling stop of an hour in the Gulf – is around eleven and a half hours; add on 45 minutes for departures from Manchester.

Charter flights: rules and restrictions

The Indian Civil Air Authority imposes **three major restrictions** on travel by charter flight to Goa.

1. Charter tickets are valid for a maximum period of 28 days. If you wish to stay in India for longer, you'll have to fly scheduled to India and then catch a domestic flight via Mumbai or other Indian hub.
2. It is illegal to fly into India on a charter flight and out on a scheduled one, and vice versa. Indian travel agents do not always tell you this when you book, however, and are not liable should you be refused permission to board your flight.
3. Holders of Indian passports are not allowed to purchase charter tickets.

When hunting online for a **charter flight** ticket, the trick is to search for "holidays" rather than "flights". Indian aviation law prevents package companies who wish to sell off unused seats from advertising them as "flight only", which means the cheapest deals nearly always masquerade as packages, bundled with "dummy" or "bunkhouse" accommodation. However, there's nothing to stop you from purchasing one of these deals and ditching the accommodation voucher once you've arrived. It can still work out much cheaper than a scheduled flight via Mumbai, especially if you manage to pick up a last-minute bargain.

However, certain **restrictions** apply (see box above). One of these is a **limit of 28 days** to the maximum period for which any charter ticket is valid. Travellers who use charter flights to get to Goa and stay for longer than this typically throw away (or sell off) the return leg, and buy another when they decide to leave. You can do this through a number of reputable travel agents in Goa (for example Davidair in Candolim; see p.121) for £150–300, depending on demand (which peaks towards the end of March when most long-staying expats head home).

Flights from Ireland

There are no direct flights to either Goa or Mumbai **from Ireland**. However, BA flies direct to Mumbai from London, and several carriers, including Alitalia, Lufthansa and Royal Jordanian, fly there from Dublin, Cork or Shannon via their home capitals. Discounted fares hover at €600–750.

Alternatively, you could book a standard charter from one of the UK airports and catch a budget flight for the first leg from Ireland.

Flights from the US and Canada

If you live on the **East Coast** it's quicker to travel to India via Europe (at least eighteen hours' journey time), using Mumbai as a gateway, while from the **West Coast** you'll get there faster via the Pacific and Chennai (Madras). Either way, the trip is a long haul (at least eighteen hours from New York, or 22 hours from LA).

There are **direct flights to Mumbai** from New York, but flying from any other city in the US, or from Canada, involves changing planes at least once. Round-trip fares from New York to Mumbai start at around $1000. For the **onward connection** to Goa, allow roughly US$100/CDN$105.

Flights from Australia and New Zealand

There are no non-stop flights to India from either **Australia** or **New Zealand**; you have to make at least one change of plane in a Southeast Asian hub city. The choice of routes and airlines is bewildering, and most agents will offer you a combination of two or more carriers to get the best price. **Flying west**, the main, and cheapest, Indian gateway city tends to be Chennai (Madras), with Mumbai not far behind. As a rule of thumb, the best-value tickets from Australia are on departures from the east coast.

Flying **from New Zealand**, you'll get cheaper fares from Auckland than Wellington or Christchurch.

Package holidays

Goa ranks among the most affordable winter **package holiday** destinations in the world – for sun-starved northern Europeans, if not North Americans and Australasians. Depending on the kind of hotel you choose, a fortnight's break will set you back anywhere between £650 and £2500 (or more if you stay in a luxury five-star resort). Prices also vary according to the time of year, peaking between mid-December and mid-January, and lowering from late-March to mid-April when the charters stop. However, in the run-up to the busy Christmas–New Year period, there's often a brief fall-off in demand, and last-minute bargains from as low as £500 appear in travel agents' windows and on websites.

Bookings can be made directly via the tour companies, or through travel agents – the cost should be identical. As few retailers deal with all the different operators, however, it's a good idea to check online or phone around for a range of quotes. Worth a browse for detailed customer reviews of specific hotels and operators are Ⓦwww.holidays-uncovered.co.uk and Ⓦwww.tripadvisor.com. Finally, it's sensible to avoid half-board or all-inclusive holidays: in Goa it's much cheaper, and more enjoyable, to eat out than to stay in your hotel.

Flights from elsewhere in India

Since the advent in India of low-cost airlines, **domestic flights** to Goa have proliferated in number, and dropped considerably in price. You can nowadays fly there direct from a dozen or more Indian cities, and, with one change, from virtually every other civil airport across the country. Fares peak around the Christmas and New Year fortnight; at other times a lot of money can be saved by booking well in advance. A full rundown of carriers flying to Goa appears on p.22.

Six steps to a better kind of travel

At Rough Guides we are passionately committed to travel. We feel strongly that only through travelling do we truly come to understand the world we live in and the people we share it with – plus tourism has brought a great deal of **benefit** to developing economies around the world over the last few decades. But the extraordinary growth in tourism has also damaged some places irreparably, and of course **climate change** is exacerbated by most forms of transport, especially flying. This means that now more than ever it's important to **travel thoughtfully** and **responsibly**, with respect for the cultures you're visiting – not only to derive the most benefit from your trip but also to preserve the best bits of the planet for everyone to enjoy. At Rough Guides we feel there are six main areas in which you can make a difference:

- Consider what you're contributing to the **local economy**, and how much the services you use do the same, whether it's through employing local workers and guides or sourcing locally grown produce and local services.
- Consider the **environment** on holiday as well as at home. Water is scarce in many developing destinations, and the biodiversity of local flora and fauna can be adversely affected by tourism. Try to patronize businesses that take account of this.
- Travel with a purpose, not just to tick off experiences. Consider **spending longer** in a place, and getting to know it and its people.
- Give thought to **how often you fly**. Try to avoid short hops by air and more harmful night flights.
- Consider **alternatives to flying**, travelling instead by bus, train, boat and even by bike or on foot where possible.
- Make your trips "**climate neutral**" via a reputable carbon offset scheme. All Rough Guide flights are offset, and every year we donate money to a variety of charities devoted to combating the effects of climate change.

Airlines, agents and operators

International airlines

Aer Lingus Ⓦwww.aerlingus.com.
Air Canada Ⓦwww.aircanada.com.
Air France Ⓦwww.airfrance.com.
Air India Ⓦwww.airindia.com.
Air Pacific Ⓦwww.airpacific.com.
Alitalia Ⓦwww.alitalia.com.
American Airlines Ⓦwww.aa.com.
bmi Ⓦwww.flybmi.com.
British Airways Ⓦwww.ba.com.
Cathay Pacific Ⓦwww.cathaypacific.com.
Continental Airlines Ⓦwww.continental.com.
Delta Ⓦwww.delta.com.
EasyJet Ⓦwww.easyjet.com.
EgyptAir Ⓦwww.egyptair.com.eg.
Emirates Ⓦwww.emirates.com.
Etihad Airways Ⓦwww.etihadairways.com.
Gulf Air Ⓦwww.gulfair.com.
KLM (Royal Dutch Airlines) Ⓦwww.klm.com.
Kuwait Airways Ⓦwww.kuwait-airways.com.
Lufthansa Ⓦwww.lufthansa.com.
Malaysia Airlines Ⓦwww.malaysia-airlines.com.
Monarch Scheduled Ⓦwww.flymonarch.com.
Northwest/KLM Ⓦwww.nwa.com.
PIA (Pakistan International Airlines) Ⓦwww.piac.com.pk.
Qantas Airways Ⓦwww.qantas.com.
Qatar Airways Ⓦwww.qatarairways.
Royal Jordanian Ⓦwww.rj.com.
Ryanair Ⓦwww.ryanair.com.
SAS (Scandinavian Airlines) Ⓦwww.flysas.com.
South African Airways Ⓦwww.flysaa.com.
SN Brussels Airlines Ⓦwww.flysn.com.
Singapore Airlines Ⓦwww.singaporeair.com.
SriLankan Airlines Ⓦwww.srilankan.lk.
Swiss Ⓦwww.swiss.com.
Syrian Airlines Ⓦwww.syrianairlines.co.uk.
Thai Airways Ⓦwww.thaiair.com.
United Airlines Ⓦwww.united.com.

Domestic airlines

Air India Ⓦwww.airindia.com.
Go Air Ⓦwww.goair.in.
Indian Airlines Ⓦindian-airlines.nic.in.
Indigo Airlines Ⓦwww.goindigo.in.
Jet Airways Ⓦwww.jetairways.com.
Jet Lite Ⓦwww.jetlite.com.
Kingfisher Airlines Ⓦwww.flykingfisher.com.
SpiceJet Ⓦwww.spicejet.com.

Agents and operators

North South Travel UK Ⓣ01245/608 291, Ⓦwww.northsouthtravel.co.uk. Friendly, competitive travel agency, offering discounted fares worldwide. Profits are used to support projects in the developing world, especially the promotion of sustainable tourism.
STA Travel UK Ⓣ0871/2300 040, US Ⓣ1-800/781-4040, Australia Ⓣ134 782, New Zealand Ⓣ0800/474 400, South Africa Ⓣ0861/781 781; Ⓦwww.statravel.co.uk. Worldwide specialists in independent travel; also student IDs, travel insurance, car rental, rail passes and more. Good discounts for students and under-26s.
Trailfinders UK Ⓣ0845/058 5858, Ireland Ⓣ01/677 7888, Australia Ⓣ1300/780 212; Ⓦwww.trailfinders.com. One of the best-informed and most efficient agents for independent travellers.
Travel CUTS Canada Ⓣ1-866/246-9762, US Ⓣ1-800/592-2887; Ⓦwww.travelcuts.com. Canadian youth and student travel firm.
USIT Ireland Ⓣ01/602 1906, Northern Ireland Ⓣ028/9032 7111; Ⓦwww.usit.ie. Ireland's main student and youth travel specialists.

Package holiday companies

Blazing Trails UK Ⓣ01293/533338, Ⓦwww.blazingtrailstours.com. Escorted motorcycle tours of Karnataka's tourist highlights on Enfields, starting and finishing in Goa.
Cosmos UK Ⓣ0871/423 8422 5678, Ⓦwww.cosmos-holidays.co.uk. Beach breaks in two- to five-star resort hotels.
First Choice UK Ⓣ0870/850 3999 (or Ⓣ0870/757 2757 for flights only), Ⓦwww.firstchoice.co.uk. Standard resort packages, at a range of prices.
Hayes & Jarvis UK Ⓣ0870/366 1636, Ⓦwww.hayesandjarvis.co.uk. Two-week sun breaks in luxury hotels.
Highlife Holidays UK Ⓣ020/8238 5810, Ⓦwww.highlifeholidays.co.uk. Packages in a choice of four-star hotels.
Jewel in the Crown Holidays UK Ⓣ01293/533 338, Ⓦwww.jewelholidays.com. The UK's largest operator in Goa has on its books a wide range of holidays across the state, with optional extensions to Delhi, Agra and Kerala. Late-availability deals often drop below £750, and they're also a dependable source of flight-only tickets.
JMC UK Ⓣ0870/750 5711, Ⓦwww.jmc.com. Owned by Thomas Cook and affiliated to the airline of the same name, this big firm offers a wide range of package holidays to Goa at competitive prices.

Kuoni UK ⓣ01306/747737, ⓦwww.kuoni.co.uk. Standard resort-based packages, or longer tours of India.
Lazy Days in Goa UK ⓣ01202/484257, ⓦwww.lazydays.co.uk. Booking agency for quality accommo-dation in north and south Goa, ranging from one-bed apartments to country houses on private estates.
Olympic Holidays UK ⓣ0800 093 3322, ⓦwww.olympicholidays.com. Competitively priced packages in a range of hotels across the state.
SD Enterprises UK ⓣ020/8903 3411, ⓦwww.indiarail.co.uk. Package holidays, with disposable "bunkhouse" budget accommodation or stays in star-rated hotels.
Thomson Worldwide UK ⓣ0870/165 0079, ⓦwww.thomson-holidays.com. Fourteen-night deals, mostly in swish resorts.

Arrival

Goa is well connected to India's metropolitan cities by air, and with the Konkan Railway fully functioning, it's likewise never been easier to reach Goa by train from Mumbai and the southern states of Karnataka and Kerala. The train line over the Western Ghat mountains has also been upgraded in recent years, making the journey from inland Karnataka much quicker and more comfortable.

By air

Goa only has one civil **airport**: Dabolim, on top of a rocky plateau in the south of the state. It recently acquired a new terminal building, but is essentially still a rundown navy aerodrome, with the shells of old Russian military aircraft rotting outside camouflaged hangars, and construction workers and civilian ground traffic moving freely across the runway between flights. Less interesting are the **immigration formalities** for foreigners, which generally take upwards of one hour as ranks of khaki-clad officials scrutinize, stamp and recheck passports, disembarkation slips and customs forms. Be sure to hang on to every piece of paper you're given or you might be delayed.

In the **arrivals** hall, the State Bank of India has a painfully slow foreign-exchange desk, which opens to meet flights but isn't entirely dependable. If you use it, ask for an encashment certificate and carefully check the exchange rate (which is likely to be very poor), the condition of notes you receive and the exchange calculation. Alternatively, use the **ATM** immediately outside the main exit on the arrivals concourse.

Porters pester new arrivals from baggage reclaim onwards; you're entitled to use a trolley without their help, but may have to fight for the privilege. Coaches wait outside to whisk package tourists to their hotels, while other travellers head for the **pre-paid taxi counter**, which you'll find directly opposite the main exit doors of the terminal. Fixed fares to virtually everywhere in the state are displayed behind the desk; pay here and give the slip to the driver when you arrive at your destination.

By train

Goa has a string of minor stations on the **Konkan Railway**, but the main one for inter-state services, such as those arriving from Mumbai, Mangalore and Kerala, is at **Margao** (also known as "**Madgaon**"), in the south. It's well organized by Indian standards. Taxis and auto-rickshaws queue on the main concourse outside; to be sure of getting the correct fare, pay in advance at the booths to the right. Note that rates increase by fifty percent after 9pm.

Arriving in Goa on slower **passenger services**, you have a greater choice of places to alight. For Arambol, Mapusa and the beaches of north Goa, **Tivim** (Thivim) is the most convenient. Heading for Panjim (Panaji), get down at **Karmali** station, just outside Old Goa, 11km east of town. Palolem and the far south of Goa is most easily accessible from **Canacona**, on the outskirts of Chaudi (Chauri), a five-minute ride from Palolem beach.

By car

Road connections are slowly improving in the region, but the coastal routes can still be gruelling, especially at night, when most of the buses run. Worse still is the road over the mountains from Karnataka – the main Hubli–Ponda–Panjim highway – whose surface has been completely destroyed by over-loaded iron-ore trucks. So if you're travelling by taxi or rented car from Hampi or Hubli, and have any choice in the matter, avoid this road in favour of the much smoother and faster NH-63, which joins the main coastal highway NH-17 further south near the town of Ankola, in northern Karnataka.

By bus

Goa's four main interstate **bus terminals** are in Panjim (central Goa), Mapusa (north), Marga (south) and Chaudi (Canacona, near Palolem beach). Travelling between them by local buses is straightforward during the daytime, when services are frequent, but if you arrive late at night you might have to hole up in town, or at a nearby resort, and head off to your final destination the following day.

Entry requirements

Almost everyone needs a visa before travelling to India. If you're going to Goa to study or work, you'll need to apply for a special student or business visa; otherwise, a standard tourist visa will suffice.

These are **valid for six months** from the date of issue (not of departure from your home country or entry into India), and usually cost £30/US$75. You're asked to specify whether you need a single-entry or a **multiple-entry visa**, and as the same rates apply to both, it makes sense to ask for the latter just in case you decide to go back within six months. Note, however, that a ruling introduced in 2009 (in theory at least) prevents visitors on a tourist visa (or visas) from re-entering India within two months of their last visit except in exceptional circumstances and with pre-arranged clearance from your local embassy or consulate – although, again, whether or not this ruling is likely to be strictly enforced remains unclear at the time of writing. For details of other kinds of visas, check the websites opposite.

Visas in the UK, US, Canada and Australia are no longer issued by Indian embassies themselves, but by various sub-contractors – see the list opposite for details. The firms' websites give all the details you need to make your application. Read the small print carefully and always **make sure you've allowed plenty of time**. Applying in person it's possible to obtain your visa by the following working day – but don't bank on it; three to four working days is more common. **Postal applications** take a minimum of ten working days plus time in transit, and often longer.

Elsewhere in the world, visas are still issued by the relevant local embassy or consulate, though the same caveats apply. Bear in mind too that Indian High Commissions, embassies and consulates observe Indian public holidays as well as

Duty free allowances

Anyone over 17 can import into India two litres of wine or spirits, plus 200 cigarettes, or 50 cigars, or 250g tobacco. You may be required to register anything valuable on a tourist baggage re-export form to make sure you can take it home with you, and to fill in a currency declaration form if carrying more than $5,000. For full details, see Ⓦwww.cbec.gov.in/travellers.htm.

local ones, so always check opening hours in advance.

In many countries it's possible to pay a **visa agency** (or "visa expediter" – see list below) to process the visa on your behalf, which typically costs £60–70/$100–120, plus the price of the visa. This is an option worth considering if you're not able to get to your nearest Indian High Commission, embassy or consulate yourself. Prices vary a little from company to company, as do turnaround times. Two weeks is about standard, but you can get a visa in as little as 24 hours if you're prepared to pay premium rates. For a full rundown of services, check the company websites below, from where you can usually download visa application forms.

Visa extensions

It is no longer possible to **extend a tourist visa** in India, though exceptions may be made in special circumstances. In addition, new rules introduced in late 2009 now require that visitors travelling on a tourist visa must leave at least two months between visits to India. Thus, if your visa is about to elapse, it's no longer possible to pop over to a neighbouring country and then re-enter on a new visa a couple of days later.

Indian embassies, consulates and visa-processing centres abroad

Australia c/o VFS Global (Ⓦwww.vfs-in-au.net) which has offices in all states except Tasmania and NT; see website for contact details.

Canada c/o VFS Global (Ⓦin.vfsglobal.ca) which has nine offices countrywide – see website for details.

Ireland Embassy: 6 Leeson Park, Dublin 6 Ⓣ01/497 0843, Ⓦwww.indianembassy.ie.

Nepal c/o Indian Visa Service Centre (IVSC), House no.296, Kapurdhara Marg, Kathmandu Ⓣ01/400 1516, Ⓦwww.indianembassy.org.np.

New Zealand High Commission: 180 Molesworth St, PO Box 4045, Wellington Ⓣ04/473 6390, Ⓦwww.hicomind.org.nz.

South Africa High Commission 852 Schoeman St (corner of Eastwood St), PO Box 40216, Arcadia 0007, Pretoria Ⓣ012/342 2593, Ⓦwww.indiainsouthafrica.com; 1 Eton Road, Parktown, PO Box 6805, Johannesburg 2000 Ⓣ011/482 8484 to 9, Ⓦwww.indconjoburg.co.za; The Old Station Building (4th floor), 160 Pine St, PO Box 3276, Durban 4001 Ⓣ031/307-7020, Ⓦwww.indcondurban.co.za.

Sri Lanka High Commission: 36–38 Galle Rd, Colombo 3 Ⓣ011/232 7587, Ⓦwww.hcicolombo.org. Consulate: 31 Rajapihilla Mawatha, PO Box 47, Kandy Ⓣ081/222 4563.

UK c/o VFS Global (Ⓦin.vfsglobal.co.uk), which has offices in London, Birmingham, Manchester, Cardiff, Edinburgh and Glasgow – see website for contact details.

US c/o Travisa (Ⓦindiavisa.travisaoutsourcing.com), which has offices in Washington, New York, San Francisco, Chicago and Houston – see website for contact details.

Visa agencies

CIBT US Ⓣ1-800/929-2428, Ⓦwww.cibt.com; UK Ⓣ0844/736 0211, Ⓦwww.uk.cibt.com.

India Visa Office UK Ⓣ0844/8004018, Ⓦwww.indiavisaheadoffice.co.uk.

India Visa Company UK Ⓣ020/8582 1117 Ⓦwww.skylorduk.com/gle_visa.htm.

India Visa 24 UK Ⓣ0800/084 5037, Ⓦwww.indiavisa24.co.uk.

Travel Document Systems US: Washington Ⓣ1-800/874 5100, New York Ⓣ1-877/874 5104, San Francisco Ⓣ1-888/874 5100; Ⓦwww.traveldocs.com.

Visa Connection US & Canada Ⓣ1-866/566-8472, Ⓦwww.visaconnection.com.

Visa Link Australia Ⓣ03/9673 1500, Ⓦwww.visalink.com.au.

Getting around

Before Independence, the many rivers that drain Goa's coastal plain made getting around a stop-and-start affair. Nowadays, however, bridges have largely superseded the old estuary ferries, and the state is covered with surfaced roads. Served by fleets of white Maruti tourist minivans and clapped-out Goan buses, these connect all the major settlements and resorts on the coast with the three towns of the interior. To get away from your fellow tourists, though, you'll want to get off the main arteries and spend some time exploring rural Goa. The best way to do this is to rent some form of transport.

Motorbike/moped

Motorcycles and mopeds offer a great way to reach the state's remote beaches and cover long distances with relative ease. The downside, of course, is that two-wheelers can be perilous. Official records show that on average three hundred people die on two-wheelers each year in the state – a significant proportion of them foreign tourists. Before driving away, therefore, ensure the lights and brakes are in good shape, and be especially vigilant at night.

Motorcycles are available at most of the coastal resorts. Officially, you need an **international driver's licence** (IDP, type #1949, available through Post Offices, the AA or RAC in the UK) to rent and ride anything, but in practice a standard licence will suffice if you're stopped and asked to produce your papers by the local police.

All rented motorcycles in Goa should carry special **yellow-and-black licence plates**, which ensure you can ride free from harassment by traffic cops. Go for a cheaper bike with regular black and white plates, and you'll be pulled over with frustrating regularity. And make sure the owner keeps the vehicle's licence and insurance documents on the bike itself in case you're spot-checked. **Helmets** are also compulsory on the main highways. The owner of your rented motorbike should provide one, but it may not fit and isn't likely to be of the best quality so consider bringing one from home if you intend to do much riding.

Rates for motorbikes vary according to season, duration of rental and vehicle; and most owners insist on a deposit and/or your passport as security. The cheapest bike, a scooter-style Honda Activa 100cc, with automatic gears, costs around Rs200 per day. Easy to ride, it's perfect for nipping around the backlanes of Goa's beach resorts, but it has small wheels that don't ride the potholes well on the highway. Heftier Enfield Bullet 350cc bikes are also plentiful, costing Rs350–450 per day, although they are heavy and unwieldy, and have gear shifters and brakes on the opposite sides to normal – a potentially lethal source of confusion

Fuel is sold at service stations (known locally as "petrol pumps") in the main towns. In smaller settlements, including the resorts, it's also sold in mineral water bottles at general stores or through backstreet suppliers, but you should avoid them whenever possible as some bulk out their petrol with low-grade kerosene or industrial solvent. When riding in remote areas of the state where fuel stops may be few and far between, take a spare litre with you.

Most villages also have a **motorcycle-repair** garage, although in theory the person you rented your machine from should foot the bill for routine maintenance (including punctures, blown bulbs and any mechanical failures). Damage to the bike incurred during a road traffic accident, of course, has to be paid for by you. It is important you agree on such details with the owner before driving away; it's also a good idea to exchange mobile (cell) phone numbers.

Cycling

Indian-made, gearless **Hero bicycles** – ideal for a gentle jaunt along the hard sand but

Motorcycling in Goa: safety and sanity tips

For anyone used to the relative civility of roads in Europe or North America, traffic etiquette in Goa – or more precisely, the lack of it – can come as a rude shock. The golden rule if you want to come through the experience unscathed is to **expect the unexpected at all times**. Never allow your concentration to lapse for a second, even on apparently empty roads. Vehicles will frequently pull out of side lanes, at speed, without looking; oncoming traffic on the opposite side of the road will routinely overtake as if you don't exist; indication of any kind is rare, as is stopping at T junctions. Goan drivers will also not think twice about going the wrong way around a roundabout. And margins of error, generally, feel suicidally slim. Bear in mind, too, that none of this behaviour is regarded as in the least impolite – so follow the example of Goan drivers and keep your cool when someone else does something seemingly insane.

Hazards multiply at night. Speed breakers ("sleeping policemen") can appear in your path without warning, as can bullock carts, stray cows, dogs and cyclists without lights. Another bugbear is the fact that Goan drivers often forget to dip their headlights, or else align their dipped lights too high so that they dazzle oncoming traffic – which can result in you riding into an invisible pothole, or over an unfinished road edge.

Exercise due caution, however, and you'll end up remembering the joys of motorcycling in Goa more vividly than its dangers. By way of a reminder of why it's worth the risks, here's a list of the state's top biking roads.

Morjim to Arambol (North Goa) – dazzling coastal landscape, with plenty of places to pull over for a swim. See p.147.

Cabo da Rama to Agonda (South Goa) – the backcountry ride over Karmali Ghat, through cashew groves and dense forest, with views down the magnificent coast to the south, is sensational. See p.191.

Lutolim to Chandor, via Curtorim – a serene ride though one of the prettiest parts of the Goan hinterland, little changed in centuries. See p.167.

Palolem to Chandor, via the *ghat* road and Usgalimal – a true adventure, taking you through remote jungle to a prehistoric rock-art site, along a broken road with few villages. See p.204.

fiendishly heavy going over longer distances – may be rented in most towns and resorts. The going rate varies between Rs50 and Rs100 per day, and you could be asked to leave a **deposit**, or even your passport, as security. Lots of outfits in the resorts these days also offer more expensive 21-gear alternatives – worth investing in if you intend to cover longer distances or tackle any gradients.

Taxis

It's much more usual for tourists in Goa to be driven than to drive: car rental firms generally operate on the basis of supplying chauffeur-driven vehicles, while **taxis** are available at cheap daily rates. White six-seater **Maruti minivans** are the most common type of taxi nowadays. You'll also come across the occasional Ambassador (an Indian copy of the old Oxford Morris).

Rates are fixed by the government at Rs15/km but in practice, even for short journeys, you'll rarely be offered this. Drivers typically quote a grossly inflated fare, or a similarly high one listed on a board of "offical rates", which you then attempt to haggle down. If unsure, ask a member of staff in your hotel reception what the correct figure should be before approaching a driver.

Auto-rickshaws and motorcycle taxis

That most Indian of vehicles, the **auto-rickshaw** (also sometimes referred to as a "tuk-tuk" after its Thai lookalike) is the front half of a motor scooter with a couple of seats mounted on the back. Cheaper than taxis, and better at zipping in and out of

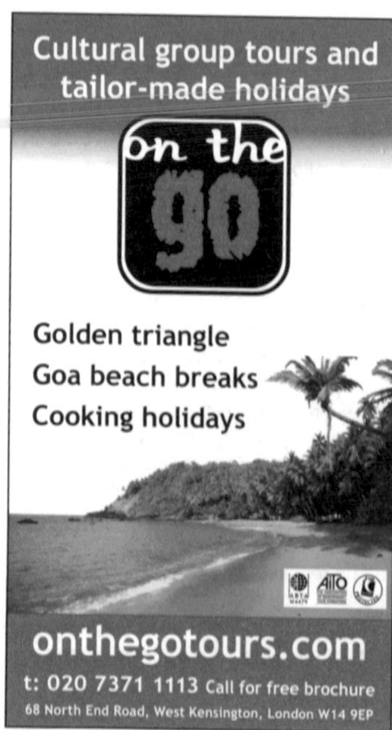

traffic, auto-rickshaws are a little unstable and their drivers often rather reckless, but that's all part of the fun. In Goa, they are painted black and yellow, and licensed rickshaw wallahs are obliged to wear a regulation-issue khaki-coloured jacket. The fares, by contrast, are far from uniform, and you'll have to haggle before you arrive at a reasonable rate.

For longer rides, Goa's unique pillion-passenger **motorcycle taxis**, known locally as "pilots", tend to be cheaper. Bona fide operators ride black bikes with yellow mudguards and white number plates. Fares should be settled in advance, and rarely amount to more than Rs50 for about a twenty-minute trip.

ferry

Crammed with cars, buses, commuters on scooters, fisherwomen and clumps of bewildered tourists, Goa's rusting, flat-bottomed **ferries** provide an essential service, crossing the coastal backwaters where bridges have not yet been built. They're also free for foot passengers (although a small fare is charged for motor vehicles) and run from the crack of dawn to late in the evening. A couple of services, such as the one in the far north of Goa to Terekol Fort, do not operate at low tide.

Rail

Many travellers arrive in Goa from Mumbai or South India by **train**, but if you fly direct and do not venture outside the state you may well never need to catch one.

A recently upgraded broad-gauge track runs east from Mormugao harbour, near Vasco da Gama, towards the interior, via Margao, linking up with the main Mumbai–Bangalore network on the far side of the Western Ghat mountains. The main reason you might wish to use it would be to visit **Hampi**, in Karnataka; more details of this service appear on p.213.

Bus

Cheap, frequent and running just about everywhere accessible by road, **buses** are by far the most popular mode of transport in Goa, at least for locals. Visitors not yet initiated into the joys of Indian public transport are unlikely to forget the experience. If you're lucky or catch the bus near the beginning of its route, you might get a seat. Otherwise, be prepared for an uncomfortable crush as more and more passengers squeeze themselves and their bags of shopping up the centre aisle. **Private buses** are particularly notorious for overloading. Conductors dangle out of the side doors chanting their destination with the rapidity of horseracing commentators.

One consolation for the crush is that **fares** are so low as to be virtually free by Western standards (just over Rs1/km). **Tickets** are generally sold by conductors on the bus itself – keep some small change handy for this – although the state transport company, **Kadamba**, sells them from hatches in the main bus stands. **Bus information** for specific destinations is given in the relevant account in the Guide section of this book. Note, too, that routes between Goa's main towns are served by frequent **non-stop services** on which you are guaranteed a seat; tickets are sold from separate hatches (look for the longest queues).

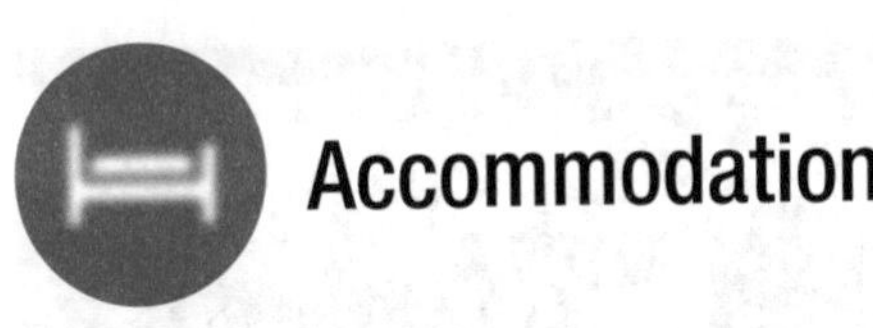

Accommodation

There are a vast number of beds for tourists in Goa, and most of the year you can rely on turning up pretty much anywhere and finding a room – if not in a hotel, then in a more modest guesthouse or hut camp. Only around Christmas and New Year, the state's peak season, are you likely to experience problems.

Costs vary enormously, depending on the level of comfort offered, but also the time of year and resort. If business is slack it's always worth haggling a little over the tariff, especially if you intend to stay for more than a week.

Inexpensive rooms and huts

Budget accommodation in Goa, catering mainly for backpacking tourists, ranges from dark little cells in old houses to little palm-leaf huts on the beach. Naturally, the further off the beaten track you get, the cheaper the accommodation; it's most expensive in Panjim, where prices are typically between 25 and 50 percent higher than elsewhere. In the more popular resorts such as Calangute and Baga, rates may double in peak season. At other times Rs500–750 (around £5.50–10/$8.5–15) should get you a decent double room or hut with a fan, window, attached shower-toilet and outside sitting space. Cold water and "bucket baths" tend to be the order of the day – not really a problem in the Goan

Accommodation price codes

All **accommodation prices** in this book are coded using the symbols below. The codes refer to the **cheapest double room in high season** (Nov to mid-Dec & mid-Jan to March), but not the peak period around Christmas, when hoteliers charge what they think they can get away with. Where hotels have a range of room options available this is shown by a spread of codes. Local taxes have been included in each case, unless specifically stated otherwise.

1. Rs300 and under. Very small, basic rooms in family houses, often with shared bathrooms.
2. Rs301–500. Bottom of the attached bathroom bracket, usually with a small veranda or balcony, but few frills.
3. Rs501–700. Modest but comfortable guesthouse accommodation; most beach huts also fall within this category.
4. Rs701–1200. Clean, comfortable ensuite rooms with a quiet fan and good-sized balcony.
5. Rs1201–2000. Upper mid-range hotel accommodation: spacious ensuite rooms with ample outside space, or luxurious huts at prime spots on the beach.
6. Rs2001–3000. Large hotel room, usually with TV, fridge and air conditioning. Some four-star hotels and luxury beach huts fall into this bracket.
7. Rs3001–4500. Swanky air-conditioned rooms or beachside chalets that come with most bells and whistles, including a minbar, TV, daily room cleaning and access to a pool.
8. Rs4501–7000. Grander than the previous category, but with essentially the same levels of comfort and new air-conditioning units. Most heritage places – period properties converted into hotels – fall into this bracket.
9. Rs7001 and over. Palatial air-conditioning rooms in smart resorts or designer boutique hotels, with a pool and usually a spa.

climate – but it's always wise to check the state of the bathroom and toilet before parting with any money.

Local opposition to construction in villages such as Palolem and Agonda in the south, and Arambol in the north, has created an accommodation shortage that some entrepreneurial villagers have got around by building Thai-style **palm-leaf** and **bamboo huts**. These are erected in November and taken down again before the onset of the monsoons. While some offer nothing more than scant shelter, others are equipped with comfortable sprung matresses, quiet fans, electric light, mosquito nets and individual bathrooms; the latter variety cost as much as, if not more than, equivalent-sized rooms during high season, but tend to be crammed far too close together, providing little privacy.

Mid-range hotels

Mid-range hotels in the Western mould, with reception areas, room service and a restaurant, nowadays account for the bulk of Goa's accommodation. Rooms in such places are frequently booked up en bloc by European package companies. However, a large number still rely mainly on walk-in customers. A spacious room, freshly made bed, decent mattress, fan, your own spotless (usually Western-style) toilet, balcony and hot and cold running water can cost as little as Rs1000 (around £14/$22). Extras that bump up the price include wide-screen plasma TV, fridges or minibars, and above all, **air conditioning** – abbreviated in this book (and in Goa itself) as a/c.

Upmarket hotels and resorts

Most of Goa's upmarket hotels are self-contained luxury **resort complexes** situated on or within easy walking distance of a beach, usually amid landscaped grounds and with their own swimming pools, restaurants, coffee shops, spas and sports complexes. You'll get a distorted impression of the area if you never venture beyond the walls of such hotels, which are often run by international chains and lie well away from any villages.

In a similar price bracket, but offering a totally different kind of experience, are the **boutique** and **heritage hotels** that have been proliferating across Goa in recent years. While the accent of the former is on interior design and exclusivity, the latter trade primarily on their historic architecture and ambience by offering accommodation in opulently converted old Portuguese-era *palacios*, often with period furniture and decor.

Long-term rentals and holiday lets

Houses are often rented by the month, or season. If you can get two or three people to share costs, and want to put down roots in a village or coastal resort, this is an option worth considering. However, the best places in hangouts frequented by long-staying independent travellers tend to be snapped up well in advance of the season. Seasonal lets also tend to be unfurnished, and you'll probably have to buy mattresses and cooking equipment.

To arrange **rental**, find a village where you want to stay and ask around. Rent varies from village to village, but you can usually pick something up in October or November for Rs20,000 per month; in villages dominated by Russian tourists, count on at least double that. Obviously, the more money you can pay up front and the longer you intend to stay, the less the house should cost.

For considerably more money, it is also possible to rent **villas**, serviced **apartments** or "**holiday cottages**" – more luxurious accommodation purpose-built for renting out to tourists. Such properties will be furnished, and come with modern bathrooms and other Western amenities such as fridges, gas cookers and the like. We've listed a few in this guide, but to get an idea of what's available, browse the following websites: Ⓦwww.aseascape.com, www.lazydays.co.uk, www.ownersdirect.co.uk and Ⓦwww.villa-vacation.com.

Food and drink

In keeping with the Konkani proverb "prodham bhookt, magi mookt" ("you can't think until you've eaten well"), food and drink are taken very seriously in Goa. They are also prepared and consumed at a typically laid-back pace, and you can expect to spend at least a couple of hours each day lounging at a table.

The overwhelming majority of places to eat in Goa are simple **shacks on the beach**, made out of palm thatch and bamboo poles, which their owners erect fresh each year after the monsoons. Prepared in rough kitchens to the rear, local seafood, fried or grilled with butter-garlic sauce and served with chips and a basic tomato salad, is their main stock in trade, along with bottles of Kingfisher beer. Shack menus also tend to feature pages of Indian, Chinese, and Continental (ie Western) specialities – though the exotic Italian or Mexican options rarely live up to their billing.

The reason for this is that shacks are these days nearly all staffed by young Nepalis and lads from less affluent Indian states who probably won't have seen a pizza or burrito in their lives until they stepped onto a Goan beach, and who tend to rely heavily on bottled sauces beefed up with "taste maker" (basically msg) to create flavours. Standards of hygiene and service, as well as cooking, can be hit and miss, with shacks changing personnel from one season to the next – which is why you won't find many reviewed in this book. Basically, follow recommendations from your fellow holidaymakers and when you find a good place stick to it. The best joints stand out because they're always busier than the competition – and crucially, their healthier turnover will mean food is prepared fresh each day rather than stored in refrigerators prone to power cuts.

For fine dining, star hotels offer swanky terrace or poolside restaurants, staffed by uniformed waiters and with trained chefs in the kitchen. They serve more or less the same range of dishes you'll find on the beach, though at much higher prices. In addition, popular charter resorts such as Baga, Calangute and Candolim also hold a wide choice of **high-end restaurants** where you can eat superb gourmet food in beautifully styled surroundings, all for a fraction of what you'd pay for such sophistication back home.

Goan food

If you come across a group of locals eating in a village café, chances are they'll be tucking into a pile of **fish curry and rice**. Goa's staple dish, eaten twice each day by most of its population, consists of a runny red-chilli and coconut-based sauce flavoured with dried fish or prawns, and served with a heap of fluffy white rice, a couple of small fried sardines and a blob of hot pickle. Cheap and filling, this is mixed into a manageable mush and shovelled down with your fingers, a technique that generally takes Westerners some time (and several messy faces) to master.

Goa is known primarily for its distinctive **meat** specialities. Derived from the region's hybrid Hindu, Muslim and Roman-Catholic heritage, these tend to be flavoured with the same stock ingredients of coconut oil and milk, blended with onions and a long list of spices, including Kashmiri red chillies. The most famous of all Goan dishes, though, has to be **pork vindaloo**, whose very name epitomizes the way Konkani culture has, over time, absorbed and adapted the customs of its colonial overlords. The dish, misleadingly synonymous in Western countries with any "ultra-hot curry", evolved from a Portuguese pork stew that was originally seasoned with wine (*vinho*) vinegar and garlic (*alho*). To this *vinho d'alho* sauce, the Goans added palm-sap (*toddi*) vinegar and their characteristic blend of Malabari spices. Pork was prohibited by the Muslims, but made a comeback under the Portuguese and now forms an integral part of the Christian-Goan diet, particularly at Christmas, when Catholic families prepare **sorpatel**, a rich stew made from the shoulders, neck, kidneys and ears of the pig.

For a glossary of Goan and Indian food see Language, p.307.

Goa is also one of the few places in India where beef is regularly eaten (as steak or minced and baked in pastry "patties"), although you're more likely to be offered chicken simmered in **xacuti** (pronounced "sha-koo-tee") sauce. This eye-wateringly hot preparation, traditionally made to revive weary rice planters during the monsoon, was originally vegetarian (in Konkani, *sha* means "vegetable", and *kootee* "cut into small pieces"), but is nowadays more often used to spice up meat of various kinds.

Not surprisingly, **seafood** features prominently in coastal areas. Among the most common varieties of **fish** are shark, kingfish, pomfret (a kind of flounder), barramundi, lemonfish, mackerel, sardines, sea bass and various kinds of snapper. These are lightly grilled over wood fires, fried or baked in clay ovens (tandoors), often with a red-hot paste smeared into slits on their sides. The same sauce, known as **rechead**, is sometimes used to cook squid. Shrimps, however, are more traditionally baked in pies with rice-flour crusts (*apas de camarao*), while **crab** and **lobster** are steamed or boiled and served whole. Another, more affordable, local delicacy that seafood lovers shouldn't miss are **tiger prawns**, as tasty and succulent in Goa as anywhere in the world. The same is true of **squid** (kalamari), although it has to be said that Goans tend to overcook it until it is rubbery and tasteless.

Rice and breads

In tourist restaurants, meat and seafood are generally served with chips and salad, but locally grown short-grain "red" **rice** is the main staple in the villages. In addition, the Portuguese introduced soft wheat-flour **bread rolls**, still made early each morning in local bakeries and delivered by cyclists, who announce their arrival with old-fashioned rubber honkers – one of the quintessential sounds of Goa. Restaurateurs mistakenly assume foreign visitors prefer Western-style spongy square loaves, so if you want to try the infinitely tastier indigenous variety, make a point of asking for **pao** (or *poee* in Konkani).

Another delicious Goan bread to look out for is **sanna**, made from a blend of coconut milk and finely ground rice flour that is leavened with fermenting palm sap (*toddi*). These crumpet-like rolls are steamed and served with pork and other meat dishes and are great for soaking up spicy Goan gravies.

Breakfast

Shacks and restaurants in the resorts all serve conventional Western buffet breakfasts of toast, jam, fruit juices and cereals, along with healthy tropical fruit salads, steeped in grated coconut and homemade set yoghurt (curd). The majority of Goans, meanwhile, habitually kickstart the day with **pao-baji**, a small plate of vegetables stewed in a hot, spicy, coconut-based sauce, into which is dunked a fresh bread roll, washed down with coffee. *Baji-pao* joints also invariably offer hot breakfast samosas, triangles of deep-fried maize flour stuffed with spicy potato and peas, and *batata-wada*, balls of potato masala rolled in light batter and fried.

Desserts

No serious meal is considered complete without a slice of the state's favourite dessert, **bebinca**. A festive speciality prepared for Christmas (but available year round), this ten-layered cake, made with a rich mixture of coconut milk, sugar and egg yolks, is crammed with cholesterol, but an absolute must for fans of solid old-fashioned puddings. The same is true of **batica**, another sweet and stodgy coconut cake that is particularly delicious when served straight out of the oven with a dollop of ice cream. If you find yourself in a traditional Goan village over Christmas or during one of the many religious festivals, you may also be lucky enough to taste **dodol**, the most prized of all local sweets. The reason you don't come across this gelatinous delicacy very often is that it requires a phenomenal quantity of fresh coconut milk and time to make. Typically, a team of three women will get through thirty or forty nuts, whose milk is mixed and boiled in a huge pot with *jaggery* for up to six hours without stopping. The goo has to be kept moving so that it congeals evenly, but the result is heavenly. It is traditional for Goans to send *dodol* made from family coconut trees to absent relatives working in the Gulf and elsewhere.

Indian food

If you get fed up with Goan-style fish and chips, **Indian** food is the next best option. Don't, however, expect the same kind of cooking you find in English-Indian curry houses.

South Indian-style snack bars – known as **udipi** or **"tiffin"** restaurants – are the most popular pitstops in Goan towns. Vegetarians, in particular, will find these simple canteens a welcome sight as the food they prepare is always "pure veg". The quintessential snack served in an *udipi* is the masala dosa – a crepe-like pancake made from a batter of ground, fermented lentil flour, griddle-fried and filled with a spicy mush of potato, mustard seeds, onions and chopped coconut. Each day from dawn onwards, they also serve hundreds of platefuls of lighter *iddli* (steamed rice cake) with **wada** (doughnut-shaped, deep-fried lentil cake) dipped in fiery *sambar* sauce and *chatni* (ground coconut and yoghurt, flavoured with mustard seeds and tamarind). The same side dishes accompany other popular South Indian snacks, such as *uttapams* (thick, soft pancakes made from partially fermented rice flour) and *parotta* (wheat-flour dough rolled into spirals, flattened and then fried in hot oil).

In India, the main meal of the day is usually served between 11.30am and 2.30pm and most restaurant menus will, at this time, feature a **thali**. Named after the stainless steel platter on which the meal is served and brought to you, a thali comprises four to six different vegetable, and one or two lentil-based, preparations, as well as raita or yoghurt. These are served in small individual bowls, arranged to one side of a large pile of rice, chapatis, a couple of runny sauces and poppadam. Usually a thali will also have a sweet.

To sample **North Indian** food at its best, you'll have to head for the upscale hotels, or a restaurant specializing in what is locally known as **Mughlai cooking**. Introduced to the subcontinent by the Persians, refined in the courts of the mighty Moghul emperors and now imitated in Indian restaurants all over the world, northern cuisine is known for its rich cream-based sauces, kebabs, naan breads and pilau rice dishes delicately flavoured with cloves, almonds, sultanas, cardamom and saffron.

The other popular northern style, elevated to an art form by the notoriously sybaritic Punjabis, is **tandoori**. The name refers to the deep clay oven (tandoor) in which the food is cooked. Tandoori chicken is marinated in yoghurt, herbs and spices before cooking. Boneless pieces of meat or seafood, marinated and cooked in the same way, are known as **tikka**, and may be served in a medium-strength masala, or in a thick butter sauce. They are generally accompanied by *rotis* or naan breads, also baked in the tandoor.

Fruit

Lying on the beach, you'll be approached at regular intervals by **fruit** wallahs carrying baskets of bananas, watermelons, oranges, pineapples and, from late March onwards, succulent mangoes. Once you've fixed a price, the fruit is peeled and sliced with a machete. It's safe to eat, but you may want to sluice it over with sterilized water to be doubly sure.

Fresh **coconuts** are the healthiest fruit of all. Their milk and meat are chock-full of vitamins, and a fair-sized nut will tide you over between breakfast and supper time if you're marooned on the beach. Itinerant vendors usually carry a couple, but in more off-track areas you're better off asking a *toddi* tapper to cut you one straight from the tree. Goans prefer to eat young green nuts, whose flesh is softer and milk sweeter. The top is hacked off and two holes punctured with the tip of a machete: you can drink the milk through these or with a straw. Afterwards, the fruit wallah or *toddi* tapper will crack the nut open so you can scoop out the meat.

Among the less familiar fruit, the **chickoo**, which looks like a kiwi and tastes a bit like a pear, is worth a mention, as is the water-melon-sized jackfruit, whose green exterior encloses sweet, slightly rubbery segments, each containing a seed. **Papayas** (best eaten chopped, with a drizzle of freshly squeezed lime juice) are also sold at most markets, and green **custard apples** crop up in fruit-sellers' baskets, although you'll probably need to be shown how to peel away their knobbly skins to expose the sweet yellow fruit inside.

Drinks

Pepsi and Coke are ubiquitous in Goa, along with their sweeter, less palatable local equivalents. You'll find fresh **fruit juice** on offer in the shacks, though always assume – unless they state otherwise on the menu or chalk board – that it'll be diluted with (untreated) well or tap water, or ice. Finally, the ultimate Indian heat busters have to be **lassi** – a mixture of curd and milk that is drunk with sugar, salted or mixed with fruit – and fresh **tender coconut**, whose refreshing, vitamin-packed milk you drink through a straw.

Bottled water

Bottled water is widely available and inexpensive in Goa. It generally isn't mineral water, but "packaged drinking water" originally from ground wells that's been filtered and chemically sterilized. In restaurants, you'll be offered a bottle at the start of your meal. Always check the seal before opening it, and bear in mind that different brands cost different amounts – Himalayan brand, for example, is proper mountain-sourced mineral water and can cost as much as wine.

Alcohol

Goa is synonymous in India with **alcohol**, which enjoys preferential tax status and is thus more easily affordable than elsewhere in the country.

Drunk in such prodigious quantities that it's become emblematic of the state is the local **beer**, Kingfisher ("The King of Good Times"). Fosters is also available, though it bears little resemblance to the stuff sold elsewhere in the world – a consequence of the **glycerine** and other preservatives added to beer.

Few visitors acquire a taste for the traditional Goan tipple, **feni**, but locally produced spirits, known by the acronym IMFL (Indian-made

Feni

Distilling was first introduced to Goa more than 400 years ago by Catholic missionaries. While the priests stewed up grape skins to make Portuguese firewater (*aguardente*), the locals improvised with more readily available substances such as coconut sap and cashew-fruit juice. The result, refined over the years to a rocket-fuel concoction known as **feni** (from the Konkani verb root *fen*, meaning "to froth"), has become the common man's tipple: a crystal-clear spirit that is, according to one aficionado, "to the Goan life what the sky is to a bird: a medium of limitless wonder and potential".

The most common variety of *feni* is made from coconut sap, or *toddi*. Three times each day, the *toddi* tapper shimmies up his individually numbered trees, which he normally rents from the local landlord on a share-crop basis, to release plastic seals bound around new shoots at the heart of the palm. The *toddi* then dribbles into a terracotta pot. At this stage it is slightly sweet, but by the end of the day the liquid becomes cloudy as it starts to ferment. *Urrack*, produced by boiling up the freshly fermented *toddi* and straining it through cotton, is rarely drunk. More often, it is distilled a second time, sometimes with cumin or ginger added as flavouring.

The juice used to make the stronger and more expensive cashew *feni* is squeezed from the yellow fruit of the *caja* tree, brought to Goa from Brazil 300 years ago by the Portuguese and now the source of the state's principal cash crop, **cashew nuts**. Once extracted, the juice is distilled in exactly the same way as its coconut cousin. However, cashew *feni* has a distinctly different taste, sometimes compared to Mexican tequila.

Both types of *feni* are drunk neat by local die-hards, but you'll find them a lot more palatable diluted with water, soda or a soft drink (lemonade and a twist of fresh lime works wonders with coconut *feni*). If you over-indulge, though, brace yourself for the Mother of All Hangovers the following morning.

Foreign Liquors), are generally palatable when mixed with soda or some kind of soft drink. Dozens of types of whisky are sold in bars, alongside Indian gin, vodka, rum and brandy; stick to big-name brands (such as Honeybee brandy and Old Monk rum) and you shouldn't go far wrong.

In addition to spirits, India produces several varieties of **wine**, grown in the temperate uplands of neighbouring Maharashtra and Karnataka. The industry is still in its infancy, but with the help of technologies and imported expertise, standards are steadily improving. That said, even the cheapest brands, such as Vin Ballet and Riviera, can easily double your restaurant bills. Still more expensive, and correspondingly easier drinking, are Grover's cabernet and white, and Chantilly. At the top end of the market are Grover's La Reserve, Sula Chenin Blanc and wines from India's foremost winery, Chateau Indage. The latter, while the best on offer, are comparable with cheap South American or Bulgarian wines you'd expect to pick up for less than £6 in the UK. Among **sparkling wines**, you've a choice between Marquise de Pompadour (a crisp, refreshing champagne made from a blend of Chardonnay, Pinot Noir and Ugni Blanc grapes), or Joie-Cuve Clos (a better-structured sparkling wine with a fruit-filled bouquet, not unlike Cava). Goan bars and restaurants also stock a variety of cheap **port**: Figueira's, Vinicola's and Golconda Ruby are the most popular brands. However, be warned that they all taste sickly sweet to the Western palate, are usually served chilled with ice and have been synthetically processed (thus prone to causing horrendous hangovers).

Foreign wine and spirits are on offer in upscale restaurants, and large supermarkets in Goa's resorts, though because the Indian government levies a duty of 250 percent on imported liquor, they cost an arm and a leg.

Health

Goa is one of the most salubrious states in India, and very few travellers fall seriously ill while they are there. However, it can be all too easy during healthy spells on the beach to forget that you are still in South Asia, and that normally innocuous things such as a salad, a rare steak or a drink mixed with untreated water can pose very real risks.

Precautions

When it comes to **food**, be wary of dishes that appear to have been reheated. Anything boiled, fried or grilled (and thus sterilized) in your presence is usually all right, though seafood and meat can pose real risks if they're not fresh; anything that has been left out for any length of time, or stored in a fridge during a power cut, is best avoided. Raw unpeeled fruit and vegetables should always be viewed with suspicion, and you should steer clear of salads unless you know they have been washed in purified water. The fruit-seller on the beach may have handled the peeled fruit, so make sure you douse your slice of pineapple or melon with safe water before eating it.

Be vigilant about **personal hygiene**: wash your hands often, especially before eating. Keep all cuts clean, treat them with iodine or antiseptic (a liquid or dry spray is better in the heat) and cover them to prevent infection.

Advice on avoiding **mosquitoes** is offered under "Malaria" on p.39. If you do get bites or itches, try not to scratch them: it's hard, but infection and tropical ulcers can result if you do. Tiger balm and even dried soap may relieve the itching.

Intestinal troubles

Some of the illnesses and parasites you can pick up in Goa may not show themselves immediately. If you become ill within a year of returning home, tell whoever treats you where you have been.

Diarrhoea is the most common bane of travellers. When mild and not accompanied by other major symptoms, it may just be your stomach reacting to unfamiliar food. With cramps and vomiting, it's more likely to be food poisoning. Either way, the problem

What about the water?

One of the chief concerns of many prospective visitors to Goa is whether the water is safe to drink. To put it simply, it isn't, even though you might see locals drinking it freely. **Bottled water**, available in all but the most remote places these days, is a much safer bet, though it has a major drawback – namely the **plastic pollution** it causes. Visualize the size of the pile you'd leave behind you after getting through a couple of bottles per day, imagine that multiplied by millions and you have something along the lines of the amount of non-biodegradable landfill waste generated each year by tourists alone.

The best solution from the point of view of your health and the environment is to purify your own water. **Chemical sterilization** using **chlorine** is completely effective, fast and inexpensive, and you can remove the nasty taste it leaves with neutralizing tablets or lemon juice.

Alternatively, invest in some kind of **purifying filter** incorporating chemical sterilization to kill even the smallest viruses. An ever-increasing range of compact, lightweight products is available these days through outdoor shops and large pharmacies, but pregnant women or those with thyroid problems should check that iodine isn't used as the chemical sterilizer.

should pass of its own accord in 24–48 hours without treatment. In the meantime, keep up your fluid intake by drinking plenty of water mixed with **oral rehydration salts** (commonly referred to as ORS, or called Electrolyte in Goa); they're available at all pharmacies, but it you can't get hold of them, use half a teaspoon of salt and three of sugar in a litre of water. While recovering from diarrhoea, it's also a good idea to avoid greasy food, heavy spices, caffeine and most fruit and dairy products. Indians swear by the restorative properties of black tea and lemon juice; some say bananas and papayas are also good, as is clear coconut water from green nuts. Drugs like Lomotil (Imodium) simply plug you up, undermining the body's efforts to rid itself of the infection, but they can be a temporary stopgap if you have to travel.

If symptoms persist more than a few days, you should see a doctor and get a stool test done for a more serious infection such as **bacillic or amaoebic dystentry**, or giardia. All of these common diseases respond quickly to antibiotics (available over the counter) as long as they're correctly diagnosed.

Bear in mind too that **oral drugs**, such as malaria pills and contraceptive pills, are likely to be largely ineffective if taken while suffering from diarrhoea.

Bites and stings

In addition to a range of tropical wasps and bees that can pack a hefty punch, you should keep an eye open for **snakes** while in Goa, particularly while crossing rice paddies. Descriptions of the four deadliest of the eight species of venomous vipers present in Goa appear in Contexts (see p.292). The best way to **avoid them** is to make plenty of noise while walking along country footpaths and across paddy ditches, and never poke around in holes or crevices in the ground; always use a flashlight and wear sturdy shoes (rather than flip-flops or sandals) if you go out at night. It's rare for people to be **bitten**, but if you are, the first thing you should try to do is identify the snake; this will make it easier for the doctors to decide which serum to inject you with when you arrive at the hospital, where you should go immediately: tie a tourniquet around the affected limb, releasing it for a minute and a half every quarter of an hour. Remember at all times (and reassure the person who's been bitten) that it is extremely rare to die from snake bites. The same applies to **scorpion** and **centipede** stings, and to **spider** bites; however, you should always try to identify whatever has bitten you.

Jellyfish won't kill you either, but you're more likely to be stung by one than by anything else. The larger specimens often have long dangling tentacles that will give a nasty sting if they get wrapped around you. The best thing to do after being stung is to bathe the wound in very hot water; the toxin that causes the pain breaks up at high temperatures. Antihistamine tablets (available at just about every pharmacy in Goa) also relieve the symptoms, as do anti-inflammatory painkillers such as Ibuprofen. In severe cases, jellyfish stings will leave slight scars that may last for up to nine months.

Heat trouble

The sun and the heat can cause a few unexpected problems. Before they've acclimatized, many people get a bout of **prickly heat** rash, an infection of the sweat ducts caused by excessive perspiration that doesn't dry off. A cool shower, zinc oxide (aka "prickly heat") powder and loose cotton clothes should help (avoid nylon and other synthetic fabrics that won't absorb sweat). **Dehydration** is another possible problem, so make sure you're taking enough liquid, and drink rehydration salts when hot and tired. The main danger sign is irregular urination (only once a day, for instance), but dark urine also probably means you should drink more water.

It's vital not to underestimate the burning power of the Goan **sun**: take particular care during your first week or two, and on days when there is a lot of high cloud around, which can make the sun seem deceptively benign. A light hat is a good idea, especially if you're doing a lot of walking.

Finally, be aware that overheating can cause **heatstroke**, which is potentially fatal. Signs are a very high body temperature without a feeling of fever, but accompanied by headaches and disorientation. Lowering the body temperature (with a tepid shower, for example) is the first step in treatment. If symptoms persist, seek medical advice.

HIV and AIDS

AIDS is still a relatively unknown quantity in India, and often regarded as a foreign problem, but indications are that HIV levels are rising.

Should you need an injection or a transfusion in Goa, make sure that new, sterile equipment is used; any blood you receive should be from voluntary rather than commercial donor banks. If you have a shave from a barber, make sure he uses a clean blade, and don't submit to processes such as ear-piercing, acupuncture or tattooing unless you can be sure that the equipment is sterile.

Vaccinations

No inoculations are legally required for entry into India, but diphtheria, typhoid and hepatitis A jabs are recommended for travellers to Goa, and it's worth ensuring that you are up to date with tetanus, polio and other boosters. Vaccinations for hepatitis B, rabies, meningitis, Japanese encephalitis and TB are also advised if you're travelling further afield in India, or working in environments with an increased exposure to infectious diseases.

Transmitted through contaminated food and water, or through saliva, **hepatitis A** can lay a victim low for several months with exhaustion, fever and diarrhoea. Symptoms by which you can recognize hepatitis include yellowing of the whites of the eyes, general malaise, orange urine (though dehydration could also cause that) and light-coloured stools. If you think you have it, get a diagnosis as soon as possible, steer clear of alcohol, get lots of rest – and try to avoid passing it on. More serious is **hepatitis B**, transmitted like AIDS through blood or sexual contact.

Typhoid fever is also spread through contaminated food or water, but is rare in Goa. It produces a persistent high temperature with malaise, headaches and abdominal pains, followed by diarrhoea.

Cholera, spread the same way as hepatitis A and typhoid, causes sudden attacks of watery diarrhoea with cramps and debilitation. Again, this disease rarely occurs in Goa, breaking out in isolated epidemics; there is a vaccination but it offers very little protection. Most medical authorities now recommend immunization against meningococcal **meningitis (ACWY)** too. Spread by

Dogs

Stray dogs hang around everywhere in Goa, especially on the beaches and outside café-shacks, where they scavenge for scraps. Stay in a village for any time and one is bound to latch on to you, but it's a good idea to avoid stroking them, no matter how in need of love they look. Quite apart from the rabies risk, most carry a plethora of parasites and skin diseases. Leaving your temporary pet, whose ribs will have disappeared after weeks of being well fed, can also be a wrench.

If you really want to improve the lot of Goa's stray dogs, get in touch with **International Animal Rescue**, whose volunteers and full-time vets care for dogs rescued from around Goa at their centre near Anjuna. Their work is entirely dependent on donations and sponsorship, most of which comes from tourists. Look out for their collection boxes around Baga and Calangute hotels, or call in person at the International Animal Rescue headquarters, **Animal Tracks**, in Assagao. Alternatively, visit their website at ⓦwww.iar.org.uk; background on the Goa centre and its work appears at ⓦwww.iar.org.uk/india/goa.shtml.

If you see a dog, or any other animal, urgently in need of veterinary care, you can contact IAR on ⓣ0832/255328, or take the animal direct to the centre by rickshaw or taxi. In South Goa, the **Goa Animal Welfare Trust** (ⓣ0832/265 3677, ⓦwww.gawt.org) performs an equivalent role, caring for strays and performing sterilizations to control canine numbers. Like IAR, they are grateful for donations, and welcome visitors to their centre in Bansai, near Chuchorem.

airborne bacteria (through coughs and sneezes for example), it is a very unpleasant disease that attacks the lining of the brain and can be fatal.

Rabies is widespread in Goa, and the best advice is to give dogs and monkeys a wide berth, indeed not play with animals at all, no matter how cute they might look. A bite, a scratch or even a lick from an infected animal could spread the disease; immediately wash any wound gently with soap or detergent, and apply alcohol or iodine if possible. If the animal might be infected, act immediately to get treatment – rabies is invariably fatal once symptoms appear.

Malaria

Malaria, caused by a parasite transmitted in the saliva of female **Anopheles mosquitoes**, is currently the number one killer in the developing world. Compared with the rest of India, its incidence in Goa is relatively small (around 15,000 cases and an average of thirty fatalities annually), but the region remains classified as a "High Risk" area by the WHO and precautions are advisable, especially if you plan to visit in the period towards the end of, or immediately after, the monsoon (Aug to early Nov), when outbreaks are fairly common. The disease has become endemic in more populated areas, notably (in order of the number of cases reported): **Panjim**, **Calangute**, **Margao**, **Colva** and **Dabolim Airport**. **Preventative tablets** (prophylactics) have to be taken according to a strict routine, covering the period before and after your trip (malaria has a variable incubation period of a few days to several weeks, so you can become ill long after being bitten).

The basic drug used is **chloroquine** (trade names include Nivaquin, Avloclor and Resochin), usually two tablets weekly, but Goa has chloroquine-resistant strains, and you'll need to supplement it with daily proguanil (Paludrine) or weekly Maloprim. **Malarone** is the newest addition to the armoury against the deadlier Plasmodium falciparum strain, and is increasingly prescribed for people travelling to areas of the world, like Goa, where chloroquine- and other drug-resistant forms of malaria are present. It is taken in tablet form once daily with food, starting two days before entering a malaria risk area and continuing daily until seven days after leaving the area of malaria risk.

Chloroquine and quinine are safe during pregnancy, but Malarone, Maloprim, Fansidar, mefloquine and tetracycline should be avoided**. Side effects** of anti-malaria drugs may include itching, rashes, hair loss and even sight problems, which is why many visitors choose to rely on less sophisticated methods of prevention.

The best way to avoid catching malaria, of course, is to make sure you **don't get bitten**. If there are mosquitoes around, sleep under a net – one which can hang from a single point is best (you can usually find a way to tie a string across your room to hang it from) – burn mosquito coils (available in most general stores) and use DEET-based repellent (an Indian brand called Odomos is widely available and effective). Though active from dusk till dawn, female Anopheles mosquitoes prefer to bite in the evening, so be especially careful at that time. Wear long sleeves, skirts and trousers, avoid dark colours, which attract mosquitoes, and put repellent on all exposed skin.

If you go down with malaria, you'll soon know about it. The fever, shivering and headaches are like severe flu and come in waves, usually beginning in the early evening. Malaria is not infectious, but can be dangerous and sometimes even fatal if not treated quickly, so at the first sign of serious symptoms, see a doctor and insist on a blood test if your temperature fluctuates.

Other mosquito-borne diseases

Another illness spread by mosquito bites is **dengue fever**, whose symptoms are similar to those of malaria, with the additional symptom of aching bones. There is no vaccine available and the only treatment is complete rest, with drugs to assuage the fever. Occurrences are pretty rare but tend to come in mini-epidemics; it's also worth noting that while first infections of the disease are rarely fatal, it can be life-threatening if contracted a second time. Moreoever, unlike malaria-carrying Anopheles, the mosquitoes that carry dengue bite during the day.

Japanese encephalitis, yet another mosquito-borne viral infection causing fever, muscle pains and headaches, has been on the increase in recent years in rural rice-growing areas during and just after monsoon, though there have been very few reports of travellers catching the disease and you shouldn't need the vaccine. The same is true of the African disease **Chikungunya**, a form of viral fever that has afflicted most parts of South India over the past few years. The name is derived from the Makonde word meaning "to bend" referring to the doubled-up posture that's a common symptom.

Doctors and hospitals in Goa

Pharmacies in Goa can usually advise on minor medical problems, and all doctors in Goa speak English. Basic medicaments are made to Indian Pharmacopoeia (IP) standards, and most medicines are available without prescription (always check the sell-by date). **Hospitals** vary in standard. The GMC (Goa Medical College), a twenty-minute drive south of Panjim on the national highway at Bambolim (Ⓣ0832/245 8700–07) is nominally the best equipped, but hopelessly over-stretched. Everyone who can afford it opts for treatment in one of Goa's many **private clinics**. These tend to be cleaner and more comfortable than state-run ones, but may not have the same facilities.

In Mapusa, the Vrindavan Hospital has a CT scan unit (essential for dealing with head injuries). For non-life-threatening orthopaedic injuries, Dr Bale's 24-hour surgery in Porvorim (Ⓣ0832/221 7709 or 221 7053), 4km north of Panjim on the main Mapusa road (NH-17), is also recommended. The hospital covering south Goa is the excellent Apollo Victor Hospital in Malbhat, Margao (Ⓣ0832/272 8888 or 272 6272). Ambulances can be reached by dialling Ⓣ102, but you'll usually get to hospital a lot quicker by flagging down a car or finding a taxi to take you.

Both private and state medical centres may require patients to buy necessities such as plaster casts and vaccines, and to pay for X-rays and diagnostic tests, before procedures are carried out. However, charges are usually so low that for minor treatment the expense may well be lower than the initial "excess" on your insurance.

The media

India generally, and Goa in particular, has a long history of literacy, and the media thrive at both local and national level. Wherever you stay, you won't be far from English-language newspapers, radio or television.

Newspapers and magazines

Goa has three English-language daily **newspapers**: the *Navhind Times* (Ⓦwww.navhindtimes.com), which tends to support the political establishment of the day, and the more independent *Herald* (Ⓦwww.oheraldo.in) and *Gomantak Times*.

These locally published broadsheets all dish up a uniformly dry diet of regional and national news, with very limited coverage of foreign affairs. If you want to read about what's happening in the rest of the world, visit the online editions of a **foreign paper** or **magazine** such as the *Guardian* (Ⓦwww.guardian.co.uk), *Time* (Ⓦwww.time.com) or *Newsweek* (Ⓦwww.newsweek.com).

Radio

The **BBC World Service radio** can be picked up on short wave, although reception quality is highly variable as the wavelength changes at different times of the day. In the morning, try 5965Khz (49m/5.95–6.20Mhz) or 9605Khz (31m/9.40–9.90Mhz); in the afternoon, 9740Khz (31m/9.40–9.90Mhz) or 11750Khz (25m/11.70Mhz). A full list of the World Service's many frequencies appears on the BBC website (Ⓦwww.bbc.uk/worldservice), where you can also listen to live broadcasts and archive material.

Television

The Indian government-run **TV** company, Doordarshan, which broadcasts a sober regime of edifying culture programmes and dull-as-dishwater soaps, has found itself unable to compete with the onslaught of mass access to **satellite TV** in Goa. Illegal use of cables ensures that one satellite dish can serve dozens of homes at an affordable price. The main broadcaster in English is Rupert Murdoch's Star TV network, which incorporates the BBC World Service, the Hindi-film-oriented Zee TV and a couple of American soap and chat channels. In the resorts, you'll also come across plenty of bars offering wide-screen Sky Sports.

Festivals

Goa abounds with all kinds of festivals and holidays – Hindu and Christian, national and local – and the chances of your visit coinciding with one are high. Religious celebrations range from exuberant *Zatras*, when Hindu deities are paraded around their temple compounds in huge wooden chariots, to modest *festas* celebrating the patron saint of a village church. Secular events are less common, although Carnival, which involves a cast of thousands, is the state's largest cultural event. Christmas also enjoys a high profile: travellers from all over South Asia converge on Goa for the Yuletide revelries, when local people traditionally consume prodigious quantities of pork, sweets and *feni* – the hallmark of most Goan festivals.

While Christian events follow the Gregorian calendar introduced by the Portuguese, the dates of Hindu celebrations vary from year to year according to the lunar cycle, with key rituals reserved for the full-moon (purnima) or new-moon (ama) periods. However, ascertaining exactly when any given temple is holding its *Zatra* can be difficult. If you're keen to see a major Hindu festival, ask for precise dates at the GTDC tourist office in Panjim (see p.68), as it arranges transport to most major events for pilgrims.

Public holidays

Republic Day (Jan 26). India's national day is marked with military parades and political speeches.
Independence Day (Aug 15). India's largest secular celebration, on the anniversary of its Independence from Britain in 1947.
Mahatma Gandhi's Birthday (Oct 2). A sober commemoration of Independent India's founding father.
Liberation Day (Dec 17). The anniversary of Nehru's expulsion of the Portuguese from Goa in 1961 is a low-key public holiday, with military parades and the occasional air force fly-past.
Christmas Day (Dec 25).

A festival calendar

Moveable dates

Ramadan The most venerated, blessed and spiritually beneficial month of the Islamic year during which Muslims may not eat, drink or smoke from sunrise to sunset, and should abstain from sex.
Id-ul-Fitr Muslim feast to celebrate the end of Ramadan.

January to mid-March

Festa dos Reis (Jan 6). Christians flock to Remedios Hill, Quelim (near Cansaulim, Salcete) for the state's main Epiphany celebration, during which three young boys, decked in brocaded silk and wearing crowns, ride to the hilltop chapel on white horses. Similar processions take place in the Franciscan church at Reis Magos, near Panjim (see p.113), and at Chandor (see p.168).

Bandeira (mid-Jan). Emigrant workers from Divar Island (see p.91) return home for the local patron saint's day, and march through the village waving the flags of their adopted countries and firing pea-shooters.

Shantadurga (Jan). A solid silver image of Shantadurga is carried in procession over the hills from Fatorpa to Cuncolim. The event, one of the most famous and well-attended religious festivals in the state, is known as the "Procession of the Umbrellas" because it is led by twelve colourful umbrellas carried on tall poles by youths smeared with red powder.

Carnival (Feb/March). Three days of *feni*-induced mayhem centring on Panjim (see p.75) marking the run-up to Lent.

Shigmo (Feb/March). Goa's version of the Hindu Holi festival – held over the full-moon period to mark the onset of spring – includes processions of floats, music and dance, in addition to the usual throwing of paint bombs; these can permanently stain clothing, so don't go out in your Sunday best.

Shivratri (Feb/March). Anniversary of Shiva's creation dance (*tandav*), and his wedding day. Big *pujas* are held at Shiva temples all over the state, and many Hindus get high on *bhang* – a milk and sugar preparation laced with ground cannabis leaves.

Mid-March to May

Easter (March/April). Christ's Resurrection is celebrated with fasting, feasting and High Mass held in chapels and churches across Goa.

Procession of the Saints (March/April). Twenty-six life-size effigies of saints, martyrs, popes, kings, queens and cardinals are paraded around Goa Velha (see p.77) on the first Monday of Easter week. This solemn religious event is accompanied by a lively funfair.

Igitun Chalne (May). *Dhoti*-clad devotees of Lairaya enter trances and walk over hot coals in fulfilment of thanksgiving vows. This famous fire-walking ritual only takes place in Sirigao, Bicholim taluka.

June–August

Sanjuan (June 24). Youngsters torch straw dummies of "Judeu", representing St John's baptism (and thus the death of sin).

Sangodd (June 29). Slap-up *sorpatel* (pork stew) suppers mark the *festa* of St Peter, the patron saint of fishers.

Janmashtami (Aug). Ritual bathing in the Mandovi River off Divar Island (see p.91), near Old Goa, to celebrate Krishna's birthday.

September–December

Ganesh Chaturthi (Sept). Giant effigies of the elephant-headed Hindu deity Ganesh, god of peace and prosperity, are displayed in elaborately decorated household and neighbourhood shrines.

Dusshera (Sept/Oct). A nine-day Hindu festival (usually with a two-day public holiday) associated with Rama's victory over Ravana in the *Ramayana*, celebrated with the construction of large effigies, which are burnt on bonfires with fireworks, and performances of Ram Lila ("Life of Rama") by schoolchildren.

Fama (Oct). Colva's miracle-working "Menino Jesus" statue (see p.178) is exposed to large crowds of pilgrims from all over Goa on the second Monday of October.

Diwali (Oct/Nov). Five-day "festival of lights" to celebrate Rama's and Sita's homecoming – an episode in the *Ramayana*. The event features the lighting of oil lamps and firecrackers, the giving and receiving of sweets and the hanging of paper lanterns outside Hindu houses.

Feast of St Francis Xavier (Dec 3). Tens of thousands of Catholics file past the tomb of SFX in Old Goa and attend open-air Mass outside (see p.88). All of Goa turns up, dressed to the nines, at some point in the week-long festival.

International Film Festival of India (late Nov to early Dec). India's answer to Cannes is an annual event in the capital, with films from all over the world screened in beachside parks, the local arts academy and the multiplex.

Christmas (Dec 24/25). Goan emigrants return home for the state's most important festival, which is celebrated by both Hindus and Christians. Missa de Galo, Midnight Mass (literally "cockerel mass" because it sometimes carries on until dawn), marks the start of festivities.

Sports and outdoor pursuits

Perhaps because of the innately laid-back nature of a beach holiday, outdoor sports don't feature all that prominently in Goa's resorts. That said, there are limited opportunities to try your hand at parascending from the cliffs in the north of the state, while a handful of outdoors companies are on hand to guide you into still wilder environments. The locals, meanwhile, have little time for any sport other than soccer – another enduring legacy of Portuguese rule.

Soccer

While the rest of India is cricket crazy, Goans are soccer mad. Impromptu knockabouts are played on beaches and local pitches all over the state when the heat of the day wears off, and National Football League (NFL) matches take place in Margoa's imposing **Jawaharlal Nehru Stadium**, regularly attracting crowds of 35,000 or more.

Goa boasts no fewer than three of the country's top soccer sides: Churchill Brothers SC, from Margao; Dempo SC, from Panjim; and Salgaocar SC, from Vasco. All of them play at the same (Nehru) stadium in Margoa during the official NFL soccer season, from mid-January until mid-May. Check out the local newspapers for previews of forthcoming matches. Tickets can be purchased on the day at the ground's admission kiosks.

Cricket

Margao's Nehru Stadium is also one of India's biggest cricket venues, and although the local Goan team isn't up to much, your visit might coincide with a national tournament or international test match, notices for which always appear in the state's daily papers.

Cricket may not be Goa's main sport, but its presence is inescapable, especially on big match days, when people gather round television sets in streets and bars to watch the climaxes of games. Players from the Indian team are media megastars in their own right, no more so than batting legend Sachin Tendulkar, from Mumbai, who has a holiday home in south Goa.

Volleyball and **beach cricket** are the two outdoor sports you'll most often come across, played with great gusto by the staff of shacks each evening around sunset time. Visitors are always welcome to join in.

Outdoor and water-sports

A few entrepreneurial expatriates in Goa have started up businesses offering **watersports** such as **kite surfing** and **windsurfing** – Aswem and south Arambol beaches are the main venues for these. Notices with contact details are usually pinned to the *Double Dutch* café's "Bullshit Info" board in Arambol (see p.155). Down in Palolem and Patnem, you can also rent catamarans for exploring the coast (see p.200) and sign up for guided **canyoning** trips to hidden waterfalls in the nearby hill forests (see p.200).

Visibility in the waters of the Goan coast isn't great, but two established **scuba-diving** outfits take clients to the clearer seas further south in Karnataka, where conditions are excellent and there is plenty underwater interest, including wrecks. For more, see p.43 and p.174.

Yoga and Ayurveda

Yoga is taught all over Goa, but the area between Anjuna and Arambol has become something of a heartland, attracting internationally famous teachers from India and abroad. In addition, dozens of little Ayurveda centres have opened in the resorts, offering traditional Indian herbal massages and medicines – though not all of them are staffed by qualified practitioners.

Outlines of what's on offer appear throughout the guide section, and on p.139 you'll find a dedicated box featuring holistic therapies and yoga outfits in north Goa. Most can enrol you at short notice, but some of the more popular ones need to be booked well in advance.

Yoga

The word "**yoga**" literally means "union", the aim of the discipline being to help the practitioner unite his or her individual consciousness with the divine. This is achieved by raising awareness of the true nature of self through spiritual, mental and physical discipline. Many texts and manuscripts have been written describing the practice and philosophy of yoga, but probably the best known are the *Yoga Sutras of Patanjali*, written by the sage Maharishi Patanjali in either the second century BC or the second or third century AD. He believed the path to realization of the self consisted of eight spiritual practices which he called the "eight limbs": these were *yama* (moral codes); *niyama* (self-purification through study); *asana* (posture); *pranayama* (breath control); *pratyahara* (sense control); *dharana* (concentration); *dhyana* (contemplation); and *samadhi* (meditative absorption).

Yoga styles

Many different forms of yoga have been popularized in the West, but broadly speaking they all focus on *asanas*, literally 'poses', which stretch, relax and tone the muscles of the body, and also massage its internal organs. Each *asana* is held to have a beneficial effect on a particular muscle group, and if practised regularly promotes suppleness and all-round health.

Iyengar yoga is one of the most famous approaches studied today, named after its founder, B.K.S. Iyengar, a student of the great yoga teacher Sri Tirumalai Krishnamacharya. His style is based upon precise physical alignment during each posture. With much practice, and the aid of props such as blocks, straps and chairs, the student can attain perfect physical balance and, the theory goes, perfect balance of mind will follow.

Ashtanga yoga is an approach developed by Pattabhi Jois, who also studied under Krishnamacharya. Unlike Iyengar yoga, which centres on a collection of separate *asanas*, Ashtanga links various postures into a series of flowing moves called *vinyasa*, with the aim of developing strength and agility. The perfect synchronization of movement with breath is a key objective throughout these sequences. Although a powerful form, it can be frustrating for beginners as each move has to be perfected before moving on to the next one.

The son of Krishnamacharya, T.K.V. Desikachar, established a third major branch in the modern yoga tree, emphasizing a more versatile and adaptive approach to teaching, focused on the situation of the individual practitioner. This style became known as **Viniyoga** (although Desikachar has long tried to distance himself from the term).

The other most influential Indian yoga teacher of the modern era has been Swami Vishnu Devananda, an acolyte of the famous sage Swami Sivananda, who established the International Sivananda Yoga Vedanta Center, with more than twenty branches in India and abroad. **Sivananda**-style yoga tends to introduce elements in a different order from its counterparts – teaching practices regarded by others as advanced to relative beginners. This fast-forward approach has proved particularly popular with Westerners, who flock in their thousands to intensive introductory courses staged at centres all over India.

Ayurveda

Ayurveda, a Sanskrit word meaning the "knowledge for prolonging life", is a five-thousand-year-old holistic medical system widely practised in India. It is thought to stem from the same period of Vedic philosophy as yoga, and places great importance on the **harmony** of mind, body and spirit, acknowledging the psychosomatic causes behind many diseases.

Ayurveda holds that the body is controlled by three **doshas** (forces), themselves made up of the basic elements of space, fire, water, earth and air, which reflect the forces within the self. The three *doshas* are: *pitta*, the force of the sun, which is hot and rules the digestive processes and metabolism; *kapha*, likened to the moon, the creator of tides and rhythms, which has a cooling effect, and governs the body's organs and bone structure; and *vata*, wind, which relates to movement, circulation and the nervous system. People are classified according to which *dosha* or combination of them is predominant. The healthy body is one that has the three forces in the correct balance for its type.

To **diagnose** an imbalance, the ayurvedic doctor not only goes into the physical complaint but also into family background, daily habits and emotional traits. Once a problem is diagnosed it is then prescribed a combination of **treatments**. These involve two distinct elements: first, the body is cleansed of toxins by a course of **panchakarma** – a five-phase therapy involving induced vomiting, enemas and the application of medicinal oils poured through the nasal cavity. Secondly, equilibrium is restored by herbal medicines applied using a range of different massage techniques. Other less onerous components, tailored for the individual patient, may include: *dhara*, where the oils are blended with ghee or milk and poured onto the forehead; *pizhichi*, in which a team of four masseurs apply different oils simultaneously; and, the weirdest looking of all, *sirovashti*, where the oils are poured into a tall, topless leather cap placed on the head.

Alongside these, patients are prescribed special balancing foods, and given vigorous full-body **massages**, or *abhayangam*, each day.

Where to go

Despite what the certificates displayed on their walls may suggest, few of the Ayurveda places in Goan resorts are staffed by fully qualified practioners. Standards of both treatment and hygiene vary greatly as a result, as do the prices – a significant factor if you sign up for a minimum three-week stint, as most places advise. Women travellers also sometimes complain of sexual harassment at the hands of opportunistic male masseurs; cross-gender massage is forbidden in Ayurveda, though the rule is routinely ignored in small, tourist-oriented centres. Dodgy oils that can cause skin problems are another risk you might be exposed to at a backstreet clinic.

The only sure-fire way to be guaranteed bona fide treatment is to go to a luxury **ayurvedic spa** attached to a star resort or heritage hotel, such as the **Pousada Tauma** in Calangute (see p.124). In Agonda, south Goa, the **Bioveda** camp (see p.193) is another reputable centre offering accommodation on the beach as well as quality Keralan-style treatment.

Wherever you go for your Ayurveda, however, the massages you receive should be regarded primarily as **rejuvenation** rather than cures. Proper Ayurveda strictly forbids patients from swimming in the sea or sunbathing, for example, as it can adversely affect a body temporarily weakened by strong, purgative herbs.

Culture and etiquette

Cultural differences extend to all sorts of little things. While allowances will usually be made for foreigners, visitors unacquainted with Goan customs may need a little preparation to avoid causing offence or making fools of themselves. The list of dos and don'ts here is hardly exhaustive: when in doubt, watch what the Goan people around you are doing.

Dress

The most common cultural blunder committed by foreign visitors to Goa concerns **dress**. People accustomed to the liberal ways of Western holiday resorts often assume it's fine to stroll around town in beachwear: it isn't, as the numerous stares that follow tourists who walk through Panjim, Margao or Mapusa shirtless or in a bikini top demonstrate.

Ignoring local norms in this way will rarely cause offence, but you'll be regarded as very peculiar. This is particularly true for women (see "Women", opposite), who should keep legs and breasts well covered in all public places. It's OK for men to wear shorts, but swimming togs are only for the beach, and you shouldn't strip off your shirt, no matter how hot it is.

Eating and the right-hand rule

Another potential faux pas has to do with **eating**. In Goa (although not, as a rule, in tourist restaurants), this is traditionally done with the fingers. Rule one is: eat with your right hand only. In Goa, as right across Asia, the left hand is for wiping your bottom, cleaning your feet and other unsavoury functions (you also put on and take off your shoes with your left hand), while the right hand is for eating, shaking hands and so on.

This rule extends beyond food too. In general, do not pass anything to anyone with your left hand, or point at anyone with it either; and Goans won't be impressed if you put it in your mouth. In general, you should accept things given to you with your right hand. It is also customary to wash your hands before and after eating.

Visiting temples and churches

Non-Hindus are welcome to visit Goan **temples** but you're expected to observe a few simple conventions. The most important of these is to dress appropriately: women should keep their shoulders and legs covered, while men should wear long trousers or *lunghis*. Always remove your shoes at the entrance to the main hall (not the courtyard), and never step inside the doorway to the shrine, which is strictly off limits to everyone except the priests (*pujaris*). Photography is nearly always prohibited inside the temple, but acceptable around the courtyard. Finally, if there is a passage (*pradakshena*) encircling the shrine, walk around it in a clockwise direction.

It's always a good idea to dress respectably when visiting **churches** and to leave a small donation for the upkeep of the building when you leave.

Other possible gaffes

Kissing and **embracing** are regarded in Goa as part of sex: do not do them in public. It's not even a good idea for couples to hold hands. Be aware, too, of your **feet**. When entering a private home – especially a Hindu one – you should normally remove your shoes (follow your host's example); when sitting, avoid pointing the soles of your feet at anyone. Accidental contact with one's foot is always followed by an apology.

Finally, always ask someone's permission before taking their **photograph**, particularly in or around temples. If you photograph a hawker, flower-seller or any other low-income itinerant vendor on the beach, it is not impolite to offer them a tip of, say, Rs20–50.

Women

Compared with other regions of India, Goa is an easy-going destination for women travellers: incidents of sexual harassment are relatively rare, and opportunities to meet local women frequent. At the same time, it is important to remember that significant cultural differences still exist, especially in those areas where tourism is a relatively recent phenomenon.

Problems, when they do occur, invariably stem from the fact that many Western travellers do a range of things that no self-respecting Goan woman would consider: from drinking alcohol or smoking in a bar-restaurant, to sleeping in a room with a man to whom they are not married. Without compromising your freedom too greatly, though, there are a few common-sense steps you can take to accommodate local feelings.

The most important and obvious is **dress**. Western visitors who wear clothes that expose shoulders, legs or cleavage do neither themselves nor their fellow travellers any favours. Opt, therefore, for loose-fitting clothes that keep these areas covered. When travelling alone on public transport, it is also a good idea to sit with other women (most buses have separate "ladies' seats" at the front). If you're with a man, a wedding ring also confers immediate respectability.

Appropriate **behaviour** for **the beach** is a trickier issue. The very idea of a woman lying semi-naked in full view of male strangers is anathema to Goans. However, local people in the coastal resorts have come to tolerate such bizarre behaviour over the past three or four decades and swimsuits and bikinis are no longer deemed indecent, especially if worn with a sarong. **Topless bathing**, on the other hand, is definitely out of the question. One very good reason to keep your top on is that it confounds the expectations of men who descend on Goa in large parties from outside the state expressly to ogle women, enticed by the prospect of public nudity.

Not surprisingly, the **beaches** are where you're most likely to experience **sexual harassment.** Your **reaction** to it is down to you. Verbal hassle is probably best ignored, but if you get touched it's best to react: the usual English responses will be well enough understood. If you shout "don't touch me!" in a crowded area, you're likely to find people on your side, and your assailant shamed. Touching up a Goan woman would be judged totally unacceptable behaviour, so there's no reason why you should put up with it, either.

Smoking

Goa stole a march on the rest of the world in 1997 when it imposed a blanket ban on **smoking** in public places. Although there's little police enforcement of this law, it has had a noticeable impact, and successfully eradicated cigarette advertising from the state.

Toilets

Most mid-range and upmarket hotels have **toilets** of the standard Western-style "sit-down" type, which are generally clean. In some budget guesthouses and bars, however, Asian facilities are the norm – these involve getting used to the squatting posture. Paper, if used, should go into the bucket provided rather than down the loo.

Rape

Rape is probably less of a danger in Goa than in most Western countries, but the number of sexual assaults on women travellers has seen a marked increase over the past decade. The few attacks on foreigners that have occurred have nearly all taken place at night, and after parties.

It therefore makes sense to take the same precautions as you would at home: keep to the main roads when travelling on foot or by bicycle; avoid dirt tracks and unfrequented beaches unless you're in a group; and when you're in your hotel or guesthouse after dark, ensure that all windows and doors are locked.

Indians instead use a pot of water and their left hand, a method you may prefer to adopt, but if you do use paper, keep some handy – it isn't usually supplied, and it might be an idea to stock up before going too far off the beaten track as it is not available everywhere. The old-style "pig toilets", which used, until a decade ago, to be a definitive feature of Goan-Catholic fishing villages, are getting rarer and rarer, and you probably won't come across one unless you venture to a bar on a remote beach where water is scarce.

Shopping and souvenirs

The streets and lanes of Goa's coastal resorts are glutted with handicraft boutiques and makeshift market stalls that offer inexhaustible shopping possibilities. You'll also be approached at regular intervals on the beach by hawkers selling everything from tropical fruit to bamboo flutes.

Where to shop

The most famous place to shop in Goa is the **flea market in Anjuna** (see p.136). Just about everyone with something to sell – whether a dog-eared paperback or a silver ankle bracelet – makes their way on Wednesday morning to the palm-shaded market ground, open on one side to the sea. Aside from the heat, its only drawback is that the prices tend to be high, but mostly because of the mad money some tourists are prepared to part with for trinkets.

On Saturday evenings, a couple of cooler **night markets** are held inland from Baga, attracting large crowds of holiday shoppers. The more appealing of the two is the one on the main Anjuna road at Arpora (see p.132), which has a good mix of Indian traders and expatriate Westerners selling designer party clothes, as well as fresh food stalls and live music.

For more down-to-earth local produce, try **Mapusa**'s wonderful **weekly market** on Friday mornings. Even if you're not buying, this is a great place to browse, with different streets given over to fish, meat, fruit, vegetables, spices, chouriço sausages and other typically Goan fresh produce.

The kind of **places not to shop** if you are bargain hunting are the posh Kashmiri handicraft boutiques, particularly those located in, or near, an upmarket hotel. Also, avoid going anywhere near a shop with a taxi driver. Cabbies in Goa make most of their money from emporiums who pay them **commission** for bringing customers, and then a percentage of the money they subsequently spend there. This, of course, is added on to the cost of whatever you're buying.

Bargaining

Wherever you shop (with the exception of general stores), you will almost always be expected to **haggle**. Bargaining is a matter of personal style, but should always be lighthearted, never acrimonious. There are no hard-and-fast rules – it's really a question of how much something is worth to you. Keep in mind, however, how much you want to pay.

Don't worry about initial prices. Some people suggest paying half or less of the opening price, but it's a flexible guideline depending on the shop, the goods and the shopkeeper's impression of you. You may not be able to get the seller much below the first quote; on the other hand, you may end up paying as little as a tenth of it – this is particularly true of beach hawkers. If you bid too low, you may be hustled out of the shop for offering an "insulting" price (a

Hawkers

Hawkers are a feature of beach life in even the most remote resorts, and you'll be pestered by a steady stream of them in the course of any day. The large majority are kids from Karnataka, flogging cheap cotton clothes, but you'll also come across Rajasthani girls with sacks of dodgy silver jewellery, buskers, painted bulls led around by their turbaned owners and, most distinctive of all, Lamani tribal women from Karnataka, with their coin necklaces, cowrie-shell anklets and rainbow-coloured mirrorwork.

Initially, this parade can be a novel distraction. The hawkers are usually polite and pleasant to chat with; and it is, after all, convenient to have a slice of melon or fresh pineapple cut for you just when you fancy one. Eventually, though, the constant attention will start to test your patience, and you'll find yourself experimenting with different ways to shake off the hawkers, who, given half the chance, will congregate in tight huddles around you. An "I've-been-here-a-while-already" tan helps, as does feigning sleep or burying yourself in a book.

Occasionally, however, one comes along who won't take no for an answer, in which case you'll either have to buy something (which will inevitably attract every other hawker on the beach) or else start shouting – neither is conducive to a peaceful time on the beach.

The best ploy if you're going to spend much time on the same beach is to hook up with one or two hawkers and always do "beesness" with them; that way, the others will more often than not leave you alone. And in case you start losing your temper, remember that the hawkers live off the few rupees' mark-up they make on the stuff they sell; they're not here out of choice, but from economic necessity.

typically Kashmiri ploy), but this is all part of the game, and you will no doubt be welcomed as an old friend if you return the next day.

Don't start haggling for something if in fact you know you don't want it, and never let any figure pass your lips that you are not prepared to pay. It's like bidding at an auction. Having mentioned a price, you are obliged to pay it. If the seller asks you how much you would pay for something, and you don't want it, then say so. And never go shopping with a tout, who will get a commission on anything you buy, which involves a higher price for you.

What to buy

Just about the only thing souvenirs on sale in Goa these days have in common is that they nearly all come from elsewhere in India, and cost a lot less than similar, or identical (imported) items would cost back in London or New York.

Goan goods

One exception to the dearth of authentically **Goan souvenirs** on offer in the resorts are **azulejos**, Portuguese-style painted tiles featuring "typical" Goan scenes and monuments. They're made in a small workshop in Panjim (see p.70) and sold at various emporia and lifestyle shops in and around the resorts, and at the Galeria Velha Goa in Panjim (see p.74).

Another typically Goan souvenir is a bottle of **feni** (see box, p.35), widely available in bars and liquor stores around the state.

Karnatakan goods

Among the most distinctive souvenirs are those touted by the Lamanis, an ethnic group from **Karnataka**. Easily recognizable by their multicoloured tribal garb, these hawkers are members of a minority community who traditionally lived by transporting salt across the Deccan Plateau. These days, the women and girls make most of the family money through the sale of **textiles** and cheap **jewellery**. Their rainbow cloth, woven with geometric designs and inlaid with cowrie shells or fragments of mirror and mica, is fashioned into shoulder bags, caps and money belts. while the jewellery is more traditional, made with coral beads, old Indian coins and low-grade silver. If you haggle hard and can put up with all the shouting and tugging that inevitably accompanies each purchase, you can usually pick up Karnatakan stuff at bargain prices.

Kashmiri goods

Forced to leave their homeland after the ongoing political unrest there killed off most of the tourist traffic, the **Kashmiris** are the most assiduous traders in Goa. If you get enticed into one of their shops, chances are it's a **carpet** they really want to sell you. Other Kashmiri specialities include **leather clothes**, **Himalayan curios** and lacquered **papier-mâché**, which they make into pots, little boxes and baubles for Christmas trees. The most relaxed places to check out the full range are the Anjuna flea market or Mapusa's Friday-morning market; venture into one of their little shops and you'll find it difficult to get out.

Other goods

Tibetan refugee traders have carved out a niche for themselves in the resorts selling reproduction **Buddhist curios** – prayer wheels, brass Buddhas, *tsampa* bowls or *thangkas* (religious paintings on cloth) – though few actually come from the mountains, and fewer still are actually antiques, as may be claimed. Their other stock in trade is **silver jewellery**, sold by weight. In principle, the price per gram is fixed (Tibetans claim they hate haggling), but in practice you can usually knock down the rate, which also varies according to how elaborate the piece is, and how much turquoise, coral or lapis lazuli has been added to it.

Handicrafts from the western Indian states of **Gujarat** and **Rajasthan** crop up in most souvenir shops. Beautiful block-printed and appliqué bedcovers are this region's forte, along with miniature paintings and elaborate mirrorwork textiles. You may also be shown gemstones from Jaipur, and elaborate silver jewellery, although it's never easy to tell fakes from the genuine articles.

The Night Market at Arpora (formerly Ingo's) is where you'll find designer **party- and beach-wear** made and sold by the village's Western population. Prices for items made by foreigners in local materials are much higher than they would be if sold by an Indian, for the obvious reason that the seller has a clear idea of living costs and lifestyles back in Europe; another reason is that the young Russians who nowadays pour into Goa seem to have bottomless wallets.

"Lifestyle stores"

Designer shopping features in Goa in the form of so-called "lifestyle stores", housed in elegant colonial-era buildings. They offer a mix of gorgeous authentic furniture, original art, traditional Indian textiles and household objects, all handpicked by their designer owners. Prices are sky high by Indian standards, in fact higher than you'd pay for similar or identical stuff in imported Asian arts shops at home, but you'll probably be tempted nonetheless; in any case, they make for enjoyable browsing.

Goa's main lifestyle stores are: **Sangolda** (see p.128), 4km inland from Calangute Church on the CHOGM Road; Wendell Rodrick's gallery **Cocoon**, midway between Calangute and Baga (see map, p.128); **Camelot**, on the way to Old Goa from Panjim; and **Casa Goa,** a little further up the same road.

Travelling with children

Parents are often put off the idea of travelling to Goa by the potential risks of a tropical climate, but provided you take some common-sense precautions, the region and its beaches provide a perfectly salubrious – in fact ideal – environment for families with little ones.

Goans adore kids and you'll be welcomed all the more warmly if you bring yours. The majority of tourists are either unmarried or of middle to retiring age, so the appearance of Western children always generates lots of interest and contact with local parents, especially if you stay in a small, family-run hotel or guesthouse.

The most obvious thing to watch out for is the Indian **sun**, which can roast young, sensitive skin at any time of the day or year. Come armed with sun hats and plenty of maximum-factor block, and keep skin covered as much as possible. Generally, the beaches are safe for kids to splash about in, but always be wary of a strong **undertow**, which can arise at certain phases of the tide even in relatively shallow water. Other hazards along the shoreline are fishermen's rejects, discarded from hand nets on the sand; and never allow your children to mess with washed-up jellyfish or sea snakes (especially the black-and-white striped variety) – they may not be completely dead.

Goan **dogs**, ubiquitous on beaches, are usually benign and friendly, but may not take kindly to the attentions of a toddler: bear in mind that if your child is bitten they'll have to have a rabies jab. Bites and stings, however, are less of a worry than the common mosquito and the concomitant risk of **malaria**. Always ensure your kids are well protected by prophylactic tablets, or at the very least DEET-based repellent in the evenings, and that they're well covered by a net throughout the night. Special small nets for babies' cots are sold at local markets and may be available through your hotel or guesthouse.

Formula milk and jars of **baby food** are available at supermarkets in the resorts, as are disposable **nappies**; you'll find international brands such as Pampers and Huggies, but they're not easy to get hold of away from the main towns. Staying in less developed coastal villages, you should come with enough stuff to see you through, and be prepared to cook for yourself as your kids may not take to the spicy meals prepared by Goan families. Rented houses nearly always have some kind of **self-catering** area, if not a fully equipped kitchen, though don't expect much more at the budget end of the market than a sink and worktop. Mid-range places should come with a decent-sized gas hob, pans, crockery and cutlery.

Most **hotels and guesthouses** will provide an extra bed for a small additional charge (usually less than 25 percent of the room rate). Bigger hotels are also likely to be able to provide cots, but check first (through your tour operator if you're on a package holiday).

> If your child should need **medical attention** at any stage, try to arrange an appointment with Dr Lily Sequeira, Goa's foremost pediatrician, who has a surgery in Panjim, contactable through the **Panjim Inn** ⓣ0832/243 5628.

Travel essentials

Costs

India, in spite of the present boom, is one of the least expensive countries in the world for travellers, and although the cost of living in Goa is far higher than most other regions, a little foreign currency still goes a long way compared with Europe and North America.

With provisions for tourists ranging from luxury five-star resorts to palm-leaf shacks, **what you spend** depends entirely on you. On a budget of as little as Rs1000–2000 (£15–30/$22–44 per day), it's possible to about scrape by if you stay somewhere basic, eat mostly in local places or simple beach shacks, and get around on foot rather than motorbike or taxi. Spending Rs2000–3000 (£30–40/$44–65 per day) per day will allow you to sleep in a spacious room or hut close to the beach, eat in tourist restaurants and get around by taxi or rented scooter.

On Rs3000–4000 (£40–55/$) per day, however, you should be able really live it up – go clubbing as often as you like, travel around by taxi or rented motorcycle, pamper yourself with an ayurvedic massage or two, and eat in fancy restaurants – though *not* stay in the smartest hotels, which typically cost Rs7000–15,000 per night for a double. To be spending more than Rs4000 just on just living expenses you'd have to be eating lobster and tiger prawns every night, splurging on souvenirs and renting air-conditioned taxis for long trips. Holistic therapies, yoga lessons and organized excursions are other things that can make a serious impact on your budget.

Costs vary considerably depending on where you are: basically, the more touristy the area, the higher the prices: for example, the price of a pineapple in Mapusa market inflates ten- to fifteen-fold between there and Calangute beach.

Crime and personal safety

While the vast majority of visitors to Goa never encounter any trouble, tourist-related crime is definitely more prevalent - and disparities in wealth more marked - than in any other part of the country. Theft is the most common problem – usually of articles left unattended on the beach or in rented houses. Don't assume your valuables are safe in a padlocked room or apartment, either.

Most people carry their passports and travellers' cheques in concealed **moneybelts**, but guesthouses and hotels often have some kind of **safe-deposit facility** where you can store your valuables, including laptops. It's also a good idea to make photocopies of your passport, visa and insurance documents in case they're lost or stolen.

Police

The Goan **police** – some wear blue berets, white shirts and blue trousers, others khaki – can be a major hassle for tourists. **Corruption**, which originally crept in as a reaction to low pay and late salaries but has since evolved into a form of institutionalized racketeering, is the root of the problem. Indeed, the pickings in India's premier tourist state are rumoured to be so rich that officers routinely pay small fortunes in the form of backhanders to be posted here. Over the past few years, some have even turned to old-fashioned robbery, the most publicized case being that of one Constable Digambar Naik, who was suspended for stealing £500 from a British tourist at Dabolim airport.

However, the way foreigners most often find themselves on the wrong side of the law is by **driving** around without a valid international driver's licence or helmet (see p.26). Even if

At the time of writing, the **exchange rates** were: Rs71 to GB£1; Rs46 to US$1; Rs44 to Can$1; Rs41 to Aus$1; Rs32 to NZ$1. Check ⓦwww.xe.com for up-to-the-minute rates.

The first call for any **UK nationals in trouble with the police** in Goa should be to British Consular Assistant Ms Shilpa Caldeira at her Tourist Assistance office in Panjim's Dempo Towers, near the Kadamba bus stand: ☎0832/243 8734.

you have both, though, the cop that waved you over will probably find another excuse to extract Rs100 or so baksheesh, usually for the absence of insurance papers.

Drugs

Cannabis, in the form of resin (*charas*) or dried leaf (ganja) may be consumed legally in many Indian states, but not in Goa, where all non-prescription narcotics are **illegal**. While a recent change in Goan law has downgraded possession of under 2g of any drug to an offence punishable by an on-the-spot Rs10,000 fine, if you're caught with any more than 2g, you'll be considered a dealer and liable to a ten-year prison sentence.

Should you find yourself arrested under the 1985 Narcotics Substances Act, the first thing you should try to do is bribe your way out of the situation as quickly and discreetly as possible. Don't underestimate the seriousness of your predicament. Goan police routinely accept backhanders, but for drugs offences the amount will probably run into thousands of dollars.

Should the situation escalate and you find yourself being formally charged in a police station, contact your nearest consul or high commission at the first possible opportunity.

Electricity

Generally 220V 50Hz AC, though direct current supplies also exist, so check before plugging in. Most sockets are European-style double round-pin but sizes vary. British, Irish, Australian and New Zealand plugs will need an adapter, preferably a universal one; American and Canadian appliances need a transformer, too, unless multi-voltage. Power cuts and voltage variations are very common.

Gay and lesbian travellers

Homosexuality is not generally accepted in Goa, and gay sex was only recently de-criminalized. It isn't surprising, therefore, that gay and lesbian life in the state is very low-key. The tourist scene is also straight-oriented, although one or other of the beach cafés at Ozran Vagator (aka 'Spaghetti Beach', see p.139) usually becomes a hangout for gay visitors during the season.

Insurance

In the light of the potential health risks involved in a trip to Goa – see p.36 – travel insurance is too important to ignore.

In addition to covering medical expenses and emergency flights, travel insurance also insures your money and belongings against **loss** or **theft**. Before paying for a new policy, however, it's worth checking whether you're already covered: some all-risks home insurance policies may cover your possessions when overseas, and many private medical schemes include cover when abroad. In Canada, provincial health plans usually provide partial **medical cover** for mishaps overseas, while holders of official student/teacher/youth cards in Canada and the US are entitled to meagre accident coverage and hospital in-patient benefits. Students will often find that their student health coverage extends during the vacations and for one term beyond the date of last enrolment.

After exhausting the possibilities above, you might want to contact a specialist **travel insurance company**, or consider the travel insurance deal we offer (see p.53). A typical travel policy usually provides cover for the loss of baggage, tickets and – up to a certain limit – cash or cheques, as well as cancellation or curtailment of your journey. Most of them exclude so-called dangerous sports unless an extra premium is paid: in India this can mean scuba diving, whitewater rafting, windsurfing and trekking with ropes, though probably not jeep safaris. Many policies can be chopped and changed to exclude coverage you don't need – for example, sickness and accident benefits can often be excluded or included at will. If you do take medical coverage, ascertain whether benefits will be paid as treatment proceeds or only after return home, and whether there is a 24-hour medical emergency number. When securing baggage cover, make sure that the per-article limit – typically under £500 – will cover your most valuable possession. If you need to make a claim, you should keep receipts for medicines and medical treatment, and in the event you have anything stolen, you must obtain an official statement from the police.

Internet

Goa's towns and resorts all offer plenty of **internet and email facilities** (charging Rs30–40 per hour) and most upscale hotels are wi-fi enabled.

Connection speeds vary depending on the time of day and equipment used. Generally speaking they're much slower than what you're probably used to at home, and prone to annoying crashes or (in quieter parts of the state) power failures. In busier centres, **broadband** (ADSL) is already the norm.

Laundry

In Goa, no one goes to the **laundry**: if they don't do their own, they send it out to a *dhobi*. Wherever you are staying, there will be either an in-house *dhobi*, or one very close by to call on. The *dhobi* will take your dirty washing to a *dhobi ghat*, a public clothes-washing area (the bank of a river for example), where it is shown some old-fashioned discipline: separated, soaped and given a damn good thrashing to beat the dirt out of it. Then it is hung out to dry in the sun and, once dried, taken to the ironing sheds where every garment is endowed with razor-sharp creases and then matched to its rightful owner by hidden cryptic markings. Your clothes will come back from the *dhobi* absolutely spotless, though this kind of violent treatment does take it out of them: buttons get lost and eventually the cloth starts to fray.

Living in Goa

You're not permitted to work in Goa on a standard tourist visa, but increasing numbers of foreign expatriates are living in the region on long-term business visas, earning a living as hoteliers, restaurateurs, travel agents and yoga teachers. Opportunities for meaningful **paid employment**, on the other hand, are few and far between due to the low level of local wages, which is why you don't find many foreign nationals waiting on tables or working behind bars.

However, a number of excellent **charities** operates in Goa and are well worth approaching if you'd like to offer your services as a **volunteer**. One that particularly impressed us was **Children Walking Tall**, a British-run operation that works with slum children in north Goa (Ⓦwww.childrenwalkingtall.com. CWT mount a valuable outreach programmes, and operates a drop-in centre, the Mango House, where local slum kids are provided with nutritious meals, extra-curricular tuition in art, crafts and computers, clothes for schools and a clean, secure environment in which to play. Volunteers of different ages and with different skill sets are vital to their year-round work – to distribute clothes and fruit in the slums, sort through donations, teach or organize fundraising events. If you think you can help, check the volunteering pages of their website.

Two other Goa-based charities worth singling out are the animal aid organization, International Animal Rescue (Ⓣ0832/255328, Ⓦwww.iar.org.uk/india/goa.shtml, based in the north of the state, and **Goa Animal Welfare Trust** (Ⓣ0832/265 3677, Ⓦwww.gawt.org) in south Goa. Both do sterling work with strays and mistreated animals, and welcome volunteers in the respective centres. Full background on their work and how you can help them in Goa appears on their websites.

Mail

Mail can take anything from six days to three weeks to get to or from Goa, depending on where you are and the country you are mailing to; ten days is about the norm. Most **post offices** are open Monday to Friday 10am–5pm and Saturday 10am–noon, but town GPOs keep longer hours, (usually Mon–Sat 9.30am–1pm & 2–5.30pm). **Letters** cost Rs20 to anywhere in the world, **postcards** Rs4–7 depending on the destination, though you'll have to stick the stamps on yourself as they tend not to be self-adhesive (every post office keeps a pot of evil-smelling glue for this purpose). Ideally, you should also have mail franked in front of you; stamps are sometimes peeled off and resold by unscrupulous clerks.

Sending a parcel from Goa can be a performance. First take it to a tailor to have it wrapped in cheap cotton cloth, stitched up and sealed with wax. Next, take it to the post office, fill in and attach the relevant customs forms, buy your stamps, see them franked and dispatch it. Surface mail is incredibly cheap, and takes an average of six months to arrive – it may take half, or four times that, however. It's a good way to dump excess baggage and souvenirs, but don't send anything fragile this way.

Maps

Made using a hand-held GPS device, the maps of the resorts and towns featured in this book are the **most accurate and up-to-date in print**, and detailed enough for navigating around the coastal strip. For trips into the interior by motorcycle, however, you may wish to print extracts from GoogleEarth (Ⓦearth.google.co.uk), whose coverage of the state's backroads is unrivalled by anything commercially available in India or abroad.

Money

India's unit of currency is the **rupee**, usually abbreviated "Rs" and divided into a hundred **paise** (pronounced pi-suh). Almost all money is paper, with notes of 10, 20, 50, 100, 500 and, recently, 1000 rupees: a few notes of 2 and 5 are still in circulation. Coins start at 10 paise and range up to 20, 25 and 50 paise, and 1, 2 and 5 rupees.

Banknotes, especially lower denominations, can get into a terrible state, but don't accept **torn banknotes**; no one else will be prepared to take them, though you can change them at the State Bank of India and large branches of other major banks.

Large notes can also be a problem, as change is usually in short supply. Many Indian people cannot afford to keep much lying around, and you shouldn't necessarily expect shopkeepers or taxi drivers to have it (and they may – as may you – try to hold onto it if they do). Paying for your groceries with a Rs100 note will probably entail waiting for the grocer's errand boy to go off on a quest to try and change it. Larger notes – like the Rs500 – are good for travelling with and can be changed for smaller denominations at hotels and other suitable establishments. A word of warning – the Rs500 note looks remarkably similar to the Rs100 note.

Carrying your money

The easiest way to access your money is with **plastic**, though it's a good idea to also have some back-up in the form of cash or traveller's cheques. You will find **ATMs** to withdraw cash at main banks in all major towns and resorts, though your card issuer may well add a foreign transaction fee, and the Indian bank will also levy a small charge, generally around Rs25.

Your card issuer, and sometimes the ATM itself, imposes limits on the amount you may withdraw in a day – typically Rs10,000–20,000. Note, too, that the first time you try to take money out after arriving in Goa your request may be refused – a standard security procedure aimed at preventing fraud. All you have to do is phone your bank or credit card's 24-hour line for the block to be removed.

Credit cards are accepted for payment at major hotels, top restaurants, some shops and airline offices, but virtually nowhere else. American Express, MasterCard and Visa are the likeliest to be accepted. Beware of people making extra copies of the receipt, to

UK nationals are entitled to apply for a **Flex Account** with the Nationwide Building Society (Ⓦwww.nationwide.co.uk), which gives you access to your money via an ATM with only a one percent transaction charge – lower than most high street banks – plus they offer better than average exchange rates.

fraudulently bill you later; insist that the transaction is done before your eyes.

One big downside of relying on plastic as your main access to cash, of course, is that cards can easily get lost or stolen, so take along a couple of alternative ones if you can, keep an emergency stash of cash just in case and make a note of your home bank's telephone number and website addresses for emergencies.

US dollars are the easiest **currency** to convert, with euros and pounds sterling not far behind. Major hard currencies can be changed easily in tourist areas and big cities, less so elsewhere. If you enter the country with more than US$10,000 or the equivalent, you are supposed to fill in a currency declaration form.

In addition to cash and plastic (or as a generally less convenient alternative to the latter), consider carrying some **travellers' cheques**. You pay a small commission (usually one percent) to buy these with cash in the same currency, a little more to convert from a different currency, but they have the advantage over cash that, if lost or stolen, they can be replaced. Not all banks, however, accept them. Well-known brands such as Thomas Cook and American Express are your best bet, but in some places even American Express is only accepted in US dollars and not as pounds sterling. Visa and American Express offer pre-paid cards that you can load up with credit before you leave home and use in ATMs like a debit card – effectively travellers' cheques in plastic form.

It is illegal to carry rupees into India, and you won't get them at a particularly good rate in the West anyhow (though you might in Thailand, Malaysia or Singapore). It is also illegal to take them out of the country.

Banks and forex bureaux

Changing money in regular **banks**, especially government-run banks such as the State Bank of India (SBI), can be a time-consuming business, involving lots of form-filling and queuing at different counters, so change substantial amounts at any one time.

Also in the main tourist centres, there are usually **forex bureaux**, which are a lot less hassle than banks, though their rates may not be as good. Outside **banking hours** (Mon–Fri 10am–2/4pm, Sat 10am–noon), large hotels may change money, usually at a lower rate, and exchange bureaux have longer opening hours. Hold onto **exchange receipts** ("encashment certificates"); they will be required if you want to change back any excess rupees when you leave the country.

If you are having **money wired**, many larger post offices act as agencies for Western Union (Ⓦwww.westernunion.com), while Moneygram's agents (Ⓦwww.moneygram.co.uk) include branches of Trade Wings and the Central Bank of India; agents are listed on their respective websites. Thomas Cook has an office in Panjim (see p.76).

Opening hours and public holidays

Standard **shop opening hours** in Goa are Monday to Saturday 9.30am to 7pm.

India has only four national **public holidays** as such: Republic Day (Jan 26, Independence Day (Aug 15), Gandhi's birthday (Oct 2) and Christmas Day (Dec 25). In addition, Goa has its own calendar of official holidays, including most major Hindu and Muslim holidays, plus the most important Sikh and Christian ones. Note that almost all banks, post offices, shops and businesses close on both national and Goan public holidays. For a complete list of festivals, including all those that are public holidays in Goa, see p.41.

Phones

Since the **mobile phone** revolution, privately run phone **international direct-dialling** facilities – **STD/ISD** (Standard Trunk Dialling/International Subscriber Dialling) places – have become a rarity in

Goa – too few in number, in fact, to be relied upon. The reason for this is that calls from them cost more than dialling from a mobile if you have an **Indian SIM card**. Visitors therefore nearly all bring their own phones these days, or purchase an Indian SIM to cover their trip. This is quick, cheap and relatively straightforward to do. **Mobile phone** shops and network outlets stock the cards. You must take along a photocopy of your passport (photo and visa pages), a couple of passport-style photos, fill in a form and pay a connection fee ranging from Rs25–250, depending on the dealer and network.

Coverage in Goa is best with Vodaphone, Airtel and Idea. Once your retailer has unlocked your phone, you pay for an initial charge card, which can be topped up ("re-charged" as it's known in Goa) at any one of thousands of outlets around the state; denominations range from Rs10–1000, though only by paying certain figures (for example Rs222 with Vodaphone) will you get the full amount in credits. Call charges to the UK from most Indian networks cost Rs2–3. Ask your card supplier to turn on the "do not disturb" option, or you'll be plagued with spam calls and spam texts from the phone company. Note also that if you're calling an Indian mobile number from outside the state where your own mobile is based (but not from abroad), you need to add a zero in front of the number.

Calling an Indian mobile or landline from a UK landline, you can save a lot of money by dialling via a company such as Ratebuster (ⓦwww.ratebuster.co.uk) or Best Minutes (ⓦwww.bestminutes.co.uk). No sign-up is required; just check the firms' websites for their access number for India, wait for a connection, then key in the Indian number you want to reach.

Card issuers

Emergency numbers for lost or stolen credit cards:

American Express ⓣ1800/419 1249 or 0124/280 1111

Diners Club ⓣ1800/112 484

Mastercard ⓣ000-800/100 1087

Visa ⓣ000-117/866 670 0955

Photography

Internet cafés and access points in most of Goa's resorts are these days equipped to burn photo files onto CDs. If your camera fails, forget trying to get it fixed in Goa. Your best bet would be to buy a new camera and card in Panjim, Margao or Calangute.

Traditional colour negative film is available in shops just about everywhere, and cheap by Western standards. When it comes to transparencies, however, you'll be limited to Fuji Sensia, if you're lucky.

Finally, beware of pointing your camera at anything that might be considered "strategic", especially Dabolim airport, and anything military, even bridges, stations and main roads. If you do, police are entitled to confiscate your camera on the spot. Remember, too, that some people prefer not to be photographed, so it's wise to ask before you take a snapshot of them – and only common courtesy after all.

International dialling codes

To call Goa from abroad, dial the international access code, followed by 91 for India, 832 for Goa, then the number you want.

To call abroad from Goa, dial the international access code (00), followed by the country code, then the area code (minus the initial zero if there is one), then the number you want.

	From India:	To India:
UK	ⓣ00 44	ⓣ00 91
Irish Republic	ⓣ00 353	ⓣ00 91
US and Canada	ⓣ00 1	ⓣ011 91
Australia	ⓣ00 61	ⓣ0011 91
New Zealand	ⓣ00 64	ⓣ00 91

Time

Goa is 5 hour 30 minutes ahead of London, 10 hour 30 minutes ahead of New York, 13hour 30 minutes ahead of LA, and 4 hour 30 minutes behind Sydney; however, summer time in those places will vary the difference by an hour.

Tourist information

The Indian government maintains a number of tourist offices abroad, whose staff are usually helpful and knowledgeable. Other sources of information include the websites of Indian embassies and tourist offices and travel agents (who are in business for themselves, so their advice may not always be totally unbiased).

In Goa itself, both the national and state-government run **tourist information offices**, provide general travel advice and hand out an array of printed material, from handy state maps to glossy leaflets on specific destinations. Government tourist offices are open Monday to Friday 9.30am–5pm and Saturday 9.30am–1pm; the main branch of **India Tourism** (Ⓦwww.incredibleindia.org) is on Church Square in Panjim (see p.68). This place operates independently of the information counters and bureaux run by the state tourism department, **Goa Tourism** (Ⓦwww.goatourism.org), and its sister organization, the local tourism-development corporation GTDC, who collectively offer a wide range of travel facilities, including guided tours, car rental and their own hotels.

Indian government tourist offices abroad

Australia Glasshouse Shopping Complex, 135 King St, Sydney NSW 2000 Ⓣ02/9555, Ⓔinfo@indiatourism.com.au.
Canada 60 Bloor St (West), Suite 1003, Toronto, ON M4W 3B8 Ⓣ1-416/962 3787, Ⓔinfo@indiatourismcanada.ca.
The Netherlands Rokin 9-15, 1022KK, Amsterdam Ⓣ020/620 8991, Ⓦwww.indiatourismamsterdam.com.
South Africa PO Box 412542, Craighall 2024, Hyde Lane, Lancaster Gate, Johannesburg 2000 Ⓣ011/325 0880, Ⓔgoito@global.ca.za.
UK 7 Cork St, London W1S 3LH, Ⓣ020/7437 3677. Ⓔlondon5@indiatouristoffice.org.
US 1270 Ave of Americas, Suite 1808 (18th floor), New York, NY 10020 Ⓣ1-212/586-4901-3, Ⓔny@itonyc.com; 3550 Wilshire Blvd, Suite 204, Los Angeles, CA 90010-2485, Ⓣ1-213/380-8855, Ⓔindiatourismla@aol.com.

Travel Advice

Australian Department of Foreign Affairs Ⓦwww.smartraveller.gov.au.
British Foreign & Commonwealth Office Ⓦwww.fco.gov.uk.
Canadian Department of Foreign Affairs Ⓦwww.voyage.gc.ca.
Irish Department of Foreign Affairs Ⓦwww.foreignaffairs.gov.ie.
South African Department for Foreign Affairs Ⓦwww.dfa.gov.za/consular/travel_advice.htm.
Safe Travel NZ Ⓦwww.safetravel.govt.nz/destinations/india.shtml.
US State Department Ⓦwww.travel.state.gov.

Travellers with disabilities

For travellers with **impaired mobility,** Goa can present major problems – at least, once you're beyond the confines of a resort hotel with luggage ramps and lifts. State-of-the-art wheelchairs and accessible toilets are virtually non-existent, and the streets of Panjim, Mapusa and Margao are full of all sorts of obstacles that would be hard for a blind person or wheelchair user to negotiate independently. Kerbs are often high, and pavements uneven and littered. There are also potholes all over the place, and very little room on roadsides. Few of the beach resorts have any kind of walkways for pedestrians, and in a wheelchair you'll struggle to keep out of the way of passing traffic – a particular menace along the Calangute–Baga strip.

On the positive side, you'll find Goans likely to be very helpful if, for example, you need their help getting on and off buses or up stairs. Taxis and rickshaws are easily affordable and very adaptable; if you rent one for a day, the driver is certain to help you in and out, and perhaps even around the places you visit. For more information about disability issues in India, check the Disability India Network website at Ⓦwww.disabilityindia.org.

Guide

Guide

1. Panjim and central Goa 61
2. North Goa 105
3. South Goa 157
4. Around Goa 207
5. Mumbai 229

1

Panjim and central Goa

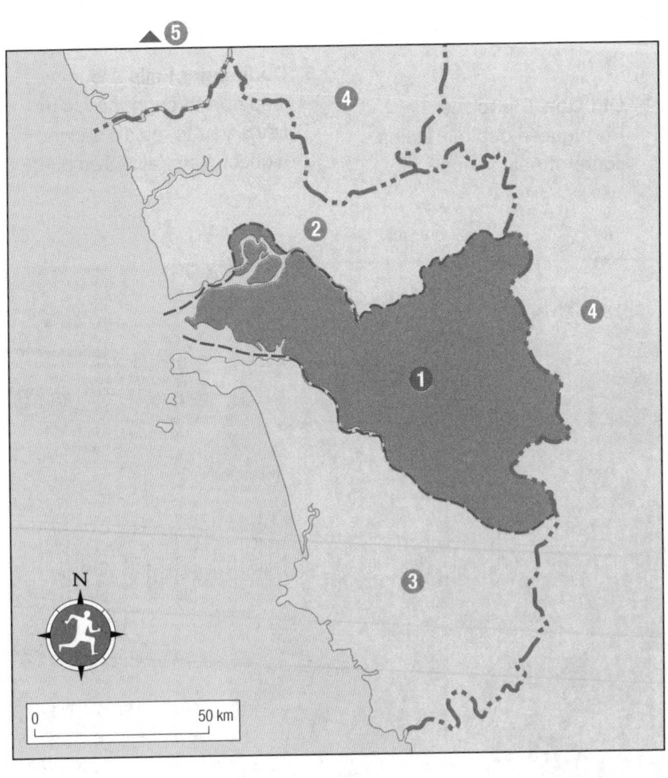

CHAPTER 1

Highlights

* **Fontainhas** The capital's Latin-influenced old quarter, lined by pretty nineteenth-century colour-washed houses, holds its own distinctively Portuguese atmosphere. See p.71
* **Panjim's Goan restaurants** Stick around town in the evening to sample traditional local cuisine at its spicy best. See p.73
* **Old Goa** The former Portuguese capital retains some of Asia's most imposing Baroque churches, as well as St Francis Xavier's incorruptible corpse. See p.79
* **Spice plantations** Star apples, nutmeg, cardamom, pineapples and mangoes are some of the exotic produce of the fruit and spice plantations reachable in an easy day-trip inland. See p.96.
* **Dudhsagar Falls** A bumpy jeep ride through the jungle takes you to India's second highest waterfalls. See p.103

▲ Dudhsagar Falls

1 Panjim and central Goa

The land wedged between the Mandovi and Zuari rivers, in the heart of coastal Goa, has been the region's most densely populated district since ancient times, from when its name, **Tiswadi** (meaning "land of thirty villages") derives. Bounded in the east by the Cambarjua Canal, the area is technically an island, whose remoter corners are still reached by river ferries more often than concrete bridges.

Known as the *Velhas Conquistas* ("Old Conquests"), this was the first territory to be colonized by the Portuguese, whose former capital at **Old Goa** remains the state's premier historical site. The ruined city's modern counterpart, **Panjim** – officially known by its Maharashtran name, Panaji – lies 10km to the west on the left bank of the Mandovi, its colonial-era houses and civic buildings well deserving a day away from the beach. More obscure remnants of the Portuguese hey-day reachable within half an hour of Panjim by road include **Pilar**'s seventeenth-century seminary and nearby **Talaulim**'s imposing parish church of Santana. **Divar Island**, directly across the river from Old Goa, harbours another wonderful crop of colonial villas and a stately hilltop church boasting a wonderful view up the Mandovi.

When the Portuguese conquistadors first annexed Tiswadi in the sixteenth century, many of the area's Hindu inhabitants fled east across the Zuari and Mandovi rivers to escape persecution. They took their deities with them, erecting new shrines among the hills of **Ponda** *taluka*, beyond the reach of the Inquisition. Architectural oddities fusing Hindu, Muslim and European Renaissance styles, many of these **temples** have survived to the present time and are an essential stop if you're heading inland to the **spice plantations** dotted around Ponda town. Press on further east still and the hills and jungles of the Western Ghat mountain range start to close in as you approach the **Bhagwan Mahaveer Sanctuary**, the wildest and most interesting of Goa's nature reserves. In addition to some dramatic scenery, the park boasts the spectacular **Dudhsagar** waterfalls and the last remaining medieval temple in Goa, the Mahadeva *mandir* at **Tambdi Surla**, in Sanguem *taluka*.

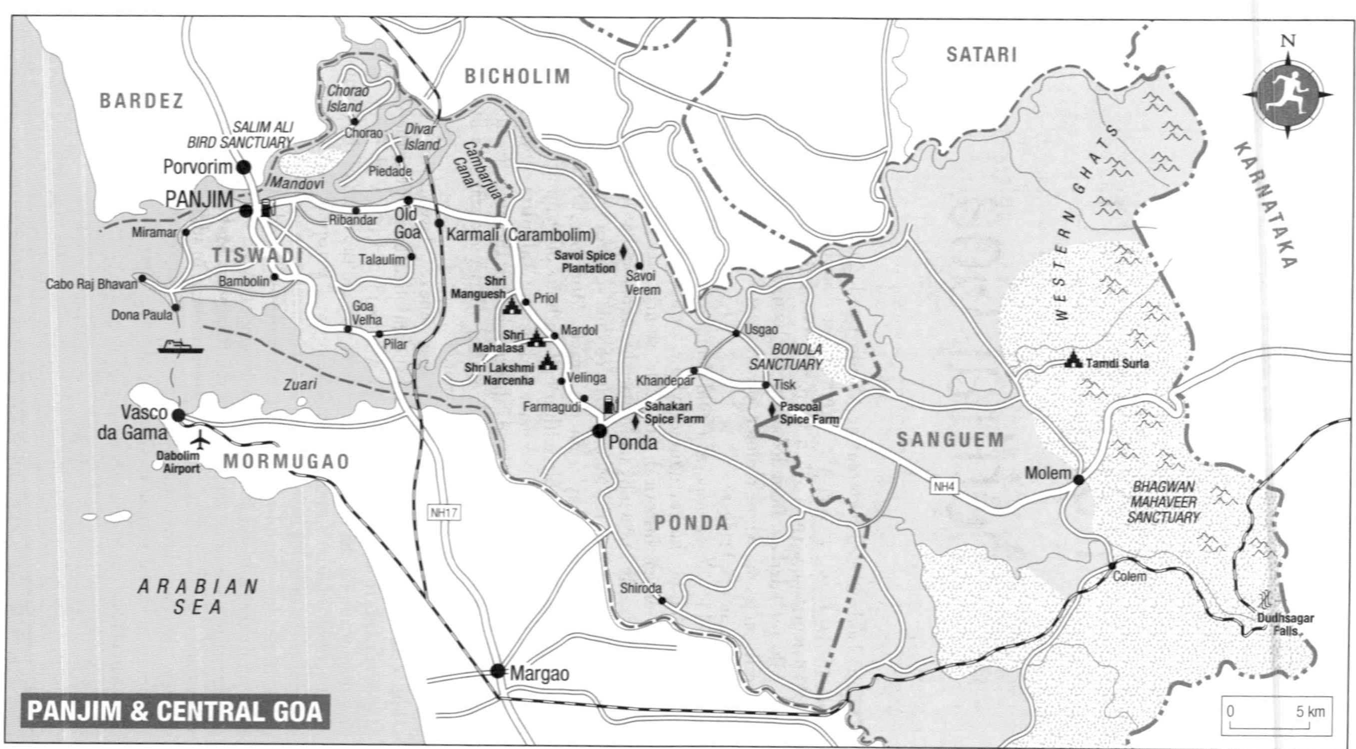
PANJIM & CENTRAL GOA
N
BARDEZ
BICHOLIM
SATARI
KARNATAKA
WESTERN GHATS
SALIM ALI BIRD SANCTUARY
Porvorim
PANJIM
Mandovi
Chorao Island
Chorao
Divar Island
Piedade
Cambarjua Canal
Miramar
Ribandar
Old Goa
Karmali (Carambolim)
TISWADI
Talaulim
Savoi Spice Plantation
Savoi Verem
Cabo Raj Bhavan
Bambolin
Shri Manguesh
Priol
Dona Paula
Goa Velha
Pilar
Shri Mahalasa
Mardol
Usgao
Shri Lakshmi Narcenha
Velinga
BONDLA SANCTUARY
Tamdi Surla
Zuari
Khandepar
Tisk
Farmagudi
Sahakari Spice Farm
Pascoal Spice Farm
Vasco da Gama
Ponda
SANGUEM
Dabolim Airport
MORMUGAO
Molem
NH4
BHAGWAN MAHAVEER SANCTUARY
NH17
PONDA
ARABIAN SEA
Colem
Shiroda
Dudhsagar Falls
Margao
0
5 km

Panjim

Stacked around a lush terraced hillside at the mouth of the Mandovi River, **PANJIM** (also known by its Marathi name, **Panaji**) was for centuries little more than a minor landing stage and customs house, protected by a hilltop fort and surrounded by stagnant swampland. It only became state capital in 1843, after the port at Old Goa had silted up and its rulers and impoverished inhabitants had fled the plague. Although the last Portuguese viceroy managed to drain many of Panjim's marshes and erect imposing public buildings on the new site, the town never emulated the grandeur of its predecessor upriver – a result, in part, of the Portuguese *hidalgos'* predilection for building their mansions in the countryside rather than the city. Panjim expanded rapidly in the 1960s and 1970s, without reaching the unmanageable proportions of other Indian capitals. Sights are thin on the ground, but the backstreets of the old quarter, **Fontainhas**, have retained a faded Portuguese charm, with colour-washed houses, Catholic churches and shop fronts sporting names such as De Souza and Fernandes.

While most domestic tourists base themselves here, many foreign visitors rarely see more of the town than the view from the Mandovi bridge as they cross en route to or from the airport, which is a pity. For although you can completely sidestep the capital when you're in Goa, it's definitely worth a visit – if only for a couple of hours on your way to Old Goa, 10km east.

Some history

The earliest mention of **Panjim** crops up in a Kadamba inscription, dated 1107, in which the settlement, then a handful of fishers' huts surrounded by dunes and swampland, is referred to as **Pahajani**, "land that does not flood". Recently, philologists have contested that the name may be derived from the Urdu *panch ima afsugani* – later corrupted by the Portuguese to *ponji* – meaning "five enchanted castles", a reference to the quintet of hilltop forts erected here by **Muslim invaders** during the fourteenth century. Boasting 55 cannons, these were installed to guard the mouth of the Mandovi River, along with a fortified waterfront palace erected by Yusuf 'Adil Shah, the first Sultan of Bijapur. However, the defences failed to repel the Portuguese, who took the forts prior to the main assault on Ela (Old Goa), after which the site was used as a military embarkation point and customs post.

The Dominicans founded a college here in 1584, and convents and *hidalgos'* houses sprang up in the seventeenth century, but Panjim remained little more than a scruffy colonial outpost of sailors and Kunbi fishing families until the lethal malaria epidemic of 1759. Leaving Old Goa to the mosquitoes, the then governor converted Panjim's waterfront Muslim palace into a splendid residence, and by the early nineteenth century the town had eclipsed its predecessor upriver. **Dom Manuel Port'e Castro** (governor 1826–35) was largely responsible for the transformation; he initiated the large-scale land drainage and construction project by which the town acquired most of its grand civic buildings, squares, schools and roads. **Nova Goa**, as it was then known, became the territory's capital in 1843. Given its (more politically correct) Marathi name, **Panaji**, in 1961, the town expanded rapidly after Independence. Today it's far and away the most important commercial centre in the state and the permanent venue for the prestigious **International Film Festival of India** (IFFI), the country's equivalent of Cannes, which takes place in late November.

Arrival and information

Until a little over a decade ago, most visitors' first glimpse of Panjim was from the decks of the old Bombay steamer as it chugged into dock at the now-defunct ferry ramp. These days, however, the town is usually approached by road – from the north via the huge ferro-concrete bridges that span the Mandovi estuary, or from the south on the NH-7, which links the capital with the **airport** at **Dabolim**

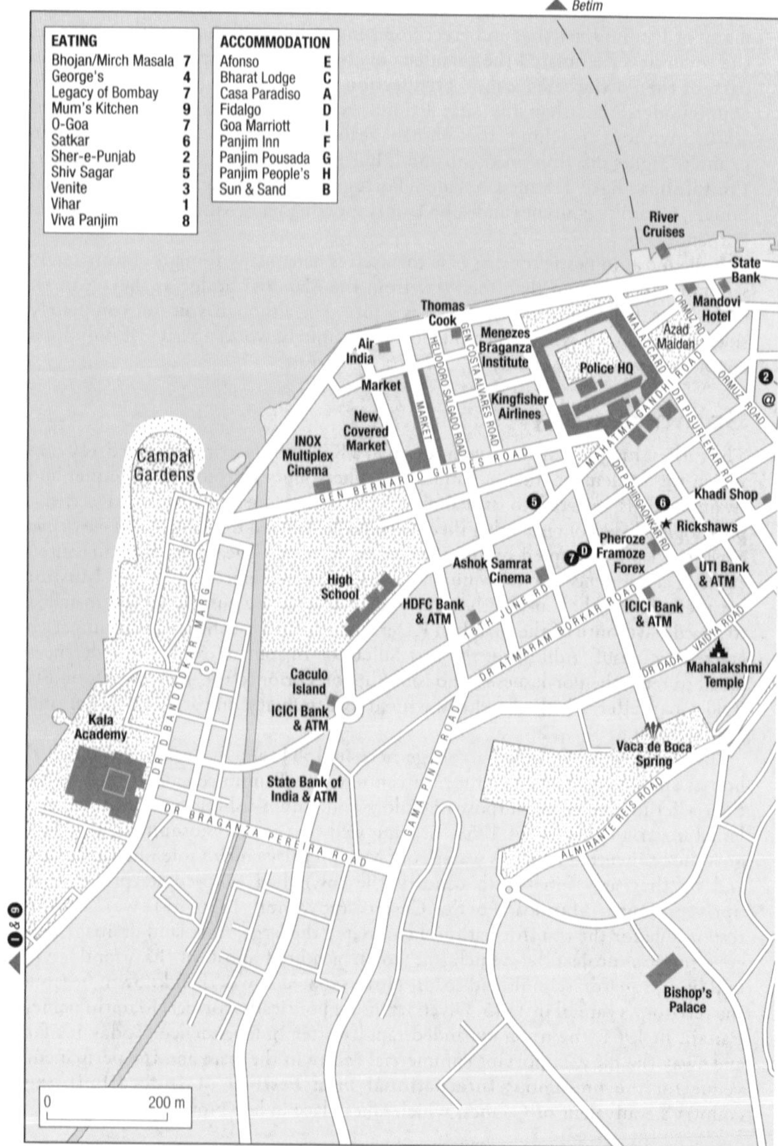

(see p.23), 29km south of Panjim on the outskirts of Vasco da Gama. Pre-paid taxis into town (45min; Rs550), booked at the counter in the forecourt immediately outside the airport's arrivals hall, can be shared by up to five people.

Arriving on the Konkan **Railway**, the nearest station to Panjim is Karmali (Carambolim), 11km east on the edge of Old Goa; buses and taxis (Rs250) queue outside to ferry passengers into town.

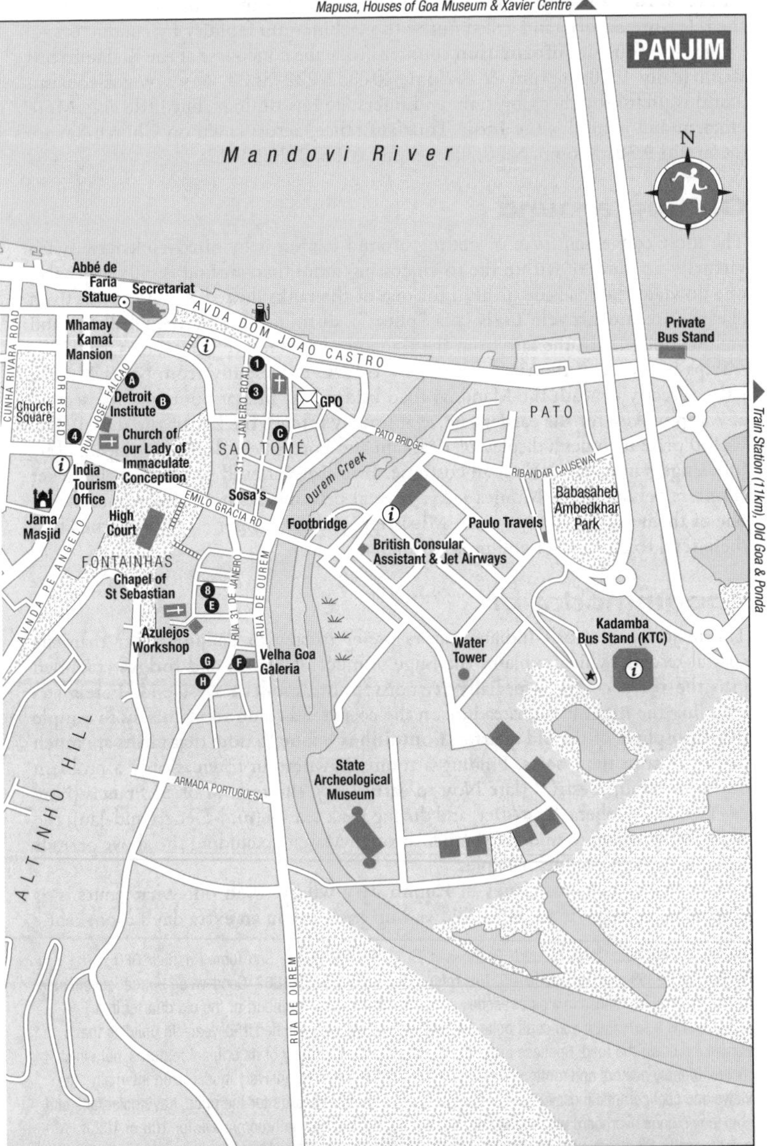

Long-distance government **buses** pull into Panjim at the town's KTC (Kadamba Transport Corporation) bus stand, 1km east of the centre in the district of Pato; private interstate buses arrive a short way further north at the new stand under the Mandovi road bridge. It takes around ten minutes to walk from here across Ourem Creek to Fontainhas, where the most appealing hotels are located. To reach the more modern west end of town, flag down a motorcycle taxi or jump into an auto-rickshaw at the rank outside the Kadamba station concourse (Rs30–50).

Local buses also arrive at the Kadamba bus stand. Destinations are written above the relevant platform and called out with machine-gun rapidity by conductors.

The Goa Tourism **information** counter inside the concourse at the Kadamba bus stand (daily 9.30am–1pm & 2–5pm; Ⓣ0832/222 5620, Ⓦwww.goa-tourism.com) is useful for checking train and interstate bus timings, but little else. More efficient and helpful is the **India Tourism** office, across town on Church Square (Mon–Fri 9.30am–6pm, Sat 9.30am–1pm; Ⓣ0832/222 3412).

Getting around

The most convenient way of getting around Panjim is by **auto-rickshaw**, with virtually no journey within the town costing more than around Rs50; either flag one down at the roadside or head for one of the ranks dotted around town. Even cheaper are **motorcycle taxis** (aka "pilots"), distinguished by their ballcaps and yellow mudguards; the fare from the Kadamba bus stand to Fontainhas is Rs30.

Trips by **boat** up the river are run by GTDC twice daily from Santa Monica jetty, directly beneath the Mandovi road bridge: the first at 6pm, and the second at 7.15pm. Aim for the earlier one, as it usually catches the last of the sunset. The Rs150 price includes a display of Konkani and Portuguese dance accompanied by folk singers in traditional Goan costume. **Bookings** should be made at the ticket counters behind Santa Monica jetty. Several private operators also run cruises – one of them on a jazzily lit, mock Mississippi paddle steamer – but be warned that these tend to be rowdier and more drunken.

Accommodation

The majority of Goa's Indian visitors prefer to stay in Panjim rather than the coastal resorts, which explains the huge number of **hotels** and **lodges** crammed into the town centre, especially its noisy, more modern west end. Foreigners spending the night here instead of on the coast tend to do so primarily to sample the atmosphere of the old quarter, **Fontainhas** – though note that tariffs are much higher than in the resorts. Finding a room anywhere in town is only a problem during the Film Festival (late Nov to early Dec), the festival of St Francis (Nov 24–Dec 3), Dusshera (Sept/Oct) and during peak season (mid-Dec to mid-Jan); the codes below apply to mid-November through March, excluding the above periods when prices can double or triple.

Note that **check-out times** in Panjim vary wildly. Find out what yours is as soon as you arrive, or a lie-in could end up costing you an extra day's room rent.

Afonso St Sebastian Chapel Square, Fontainhas Ⓣ0832/222 2359 or Ⓣ9764/300165. This refurbished colonial-era house in a picturesque backstreet is a safe bet if you can't quite afford the *Panjim Inn* down the road. Spotless attached rooms, friendly owners and rooftop terrace with views and cool ceramic mosaic floors – though someone's gone overboard with the textured wall paint recently. Single occupancy available. ❺

Bharat Lodge Sao Tome Rd, near GPO Ⓣ0832/222 4862. Good-value budget guesthouse, located at the heart of the old quarter in a terracotta-washed,150-year-old building that's retained many of its original features, but which has been extensively modernized internally. The rooms are large for the price, have quiet fans and good-sized bathrooms: ask for 106 or 102 if they're vacant. ❹

Casa Paradiso Ghanekar Building, Rua Jose Falcao ⓣ0832/222 6291, ⓦcasaparadisogoa.com. This guesthouse is the only mid-range place outside Fontainhas worth considering. The location, on a busy thoroughfare close to the Secretariat and Church Square, is none too inspiring, and there's no outside sitting space, but it is central and the rooms themselves spotless, with a/c and shiny ceramic floors. ❺

Fidalgo 18th June Rd ⓣ0832/222 6291, ⓦwww.hotelfidalgo-goa.com. Affordable, business-oriented four-star hotel in the bustling commercial end of town. Established in the early 1970s, it is a comfortable option for the price, with central a/c, a good sized open-air pool, ayurvedic spa, book shop and popular six-outlet "Food Enclave" on the ground floor (see p.73). ❼–❽

Goa Marriott Miramar beach ⓣ0832/246 3333, ⓦwww.marriott.com. Huge five-star out on the edge of town, facing the mouth of the Mandovi. Predictably formulaic, and not a great location for a package holiday (despite what the brochures might suggest), but large and luxurious, with all mod cons. From Rs11,000–20,000 ($235-430) per night. ❾

Panjim Inn/Panjim Pousada E-212, Rua 31 de Janeiro, Fontainhas ⓣ0832/243 5628, ⓦwww.panjiminn.com. Grand 300-year-old townhouse, managed as a homely heritage hotel, with period furniture, sepia photos, balconies and a veranda where meals and drinks are served. Their adjacent three-storey wing overlooking the river is in the same style, but with better views, while the *Pousada* annexe over the road has two lovely rearside rooms sharing a wooden balcony, itself surveying a secret courtyard. ❻

Panjim People's Rua 31 de Janeiro, Fontainhas ⓣ0832/222 1122, ⓦwww.panjiminn.com. Sister concern of the *Panjim Inn*, in a former high school opposite the original house (see above). It's more upmarket than their other two buildings, with new a/c units and large TVs in the rooms, themselves all huge, and fitted with antique rosewood furniture, gilded pelmets and lace curtains. The bathrooms feature the Sukhija family's trademark crazy-mosaic tiling. Tariffs mid-season start at around Rs8000 ($175) per night. ❾

Sun & Sand Bairo Alto Dos Pilotos, above Rua Jose Falcao ⓣ0832/240 0000, ⓦwww.sunnsandhotel.com. This modern business hotel, perched on the hilltop above the east end of town, has all the comforts you'd expect of a place where flight crews overnight, including a large pool, restaurant, Jacuzzi, health club, secure parking and wi-fi. But its greatest asset are the panoramic views over the rooftops of Fontainhas and the Mandovi River. Access is via a vertigo-inducing elevator. Tariffs from Rs7000–15,000 ($156–335). ❾

The Town

Panjim's few sights are all grouped in the east end of town. A good route stringing them together heads along the esplanade from the Secretariat to the **Menezes Braganza Institute**, and then south to Church Square via **Azad Maidan**, winding up with an amble through the old quarters.

Church Square

The leafy rectangular park opposite the India Tourism office, known as **Church Square** or the **Municipal Gardens**, forms the heart of Panjim. Originally called the Jardim de Garcia da Orta, after a famous sixteenth-century physician, it used to harbour a bust of Portuguese explorer Vasco da Gama, but this was pulled down after Independence, transferred to the museum in Old Goa and replaced with India's national emblem: three Ashokan lions mounted on an abacus decorated with a wheel, symbolizing "strength and unity in diversity".

Presiding over the east side of the square is Panjim's most distinctive and photogenic landmark, the toothpaste-white Baroque **Church of Our Lady of the Immaculate Conception** (Mon–Sat 9am–1pm & 3.30–6pm, Sun 10.30am–1pm & 6.15–7pm). Standing at the head of a criss-crossing laterite walkway, between rows of slender palm trees, it was built in 1541, when the town was no more than a swamp-ridden fishing village, for the benefit of sailors arriving here from Lisbon. The weary mariners would stagger up from the quay to give thanks for their safe passage before proceeding to the capital at Old Goa – the original home of the enormous bell that hangs from the central gable. The second largest in the state, the bell was salvaged from the ruins of the Augustinian monastery on Holy Hill

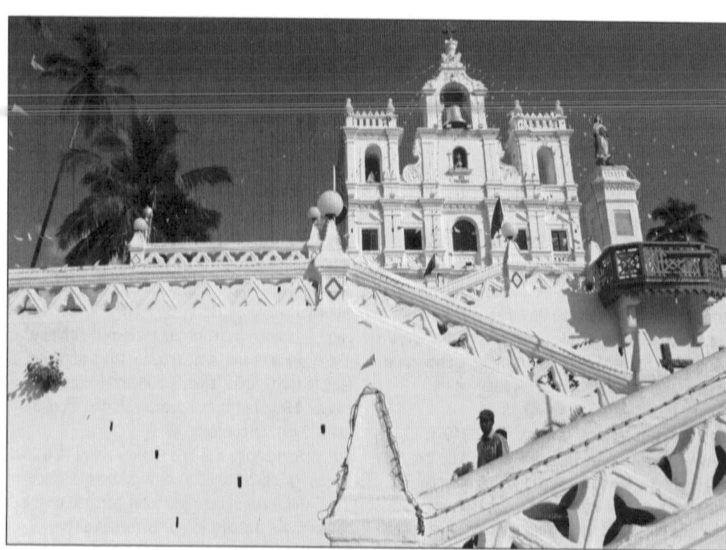

▲ Church of Our Lady of the Immaculate Conception

and installed here in a specially enlarged belfry, erected in 1871 at the same time as the steps. The interior of the church is dominated by a splendid gilt reredos dedicated to Our Lady.

North of Church Square

The road that runs northeast from the church, Rua José Falcao, brings you out at the riverside near Panjim's oldest surviving building. With its sloping tiled roofs, carved-stone coats of arms and wooden verandas, the **Secretariat** looks archetypically colonial. Yet it was originally the summer palace of Goa's sixteenth-century Muslim ruler, the 'Adil Shah. Fortified with 55 cannons and a saltwater moat, its defences did not, however, deter Alfonso de Albuquerque, whose troops stormed the building in 1510, then converted it into a temporary rest-house for the territory's governors, who used to overnight here en route to and from Europe. Following the viceroy's move from Old Goa in 1759, the palace – by this time known as the Idalcaon's Palace (from Adil Khan, a Portuguese corruption of 'Adil Shah) – became the official viceregal residence, which it remained until the completion of the even grander mansion at Cabo, near Vasco da Gama, in 1918. It now houses government offices.

An equally impressive edifice is the **Menezes Braganza Institute** (Mon–Fri 9.30am–1.15pm & 2–5.30pm; free), now the town's Central Library, which stands behind the esplanade, 1km west of the Secretariat past the Abbé de Faria statue. Among the colonial leftovers in this grand Neoclassical building are the panels of blue-and-yellow-painted ceramic tiles, known as **azulejos**, lining the lobby of the west (Malacca Road) entrance. These larger-than-life illustrations depict scenes from Luis Vaz Camões' epic poem, *Os Lusiadas*. The tone of the tableaux is intentionally patriotic (valiant Portuguese explorers being tossed on stormy seas and a nobleman standing defiantly before a dark-faced raja of Calicut), but the tale was, in fact, intended as an invective against the Portuguese discoveries, which Camões rightly believed were milking his mother country dry and leaving its crown easy prey for the old enemy, Spain.

Just south of the library building lies the parched grass square of **Azad Maidan**, fringed by tall trees and centred on a weed-choked pavilion of Corinthian pillars salvaged from the rubble of Old Goa. Built in 1847 to protect the huge brass statue of Alfonso de Albuquerque (now housed in the state archeological museum in Old Goa), the pavilion was made into a memorial to Goan freedom fighter Dr Tristão de Braganza Cunha after Independence.

Fontainhas and Sao Tomé

A palpable air of Portuguese *saudades* still hangs over the old quarter of **Fontainhas**, on the east side of town – a last bastion in India of Lusitanian culture. Amid its back *calçadas* and little red-tiled *praças*, elderly ladies in print dresses lean over balconies filled with bougainvillea plants and the chirping of caged finches, while violinists practise Villa-Lobos. Portuguese is still very much the lingua franca amongst the district's older residents – nearly everyone has relatives living in Lisbon.

Laid out on land reclaimed during the late eighteenth century by a Goan expatriate known as "the Mossmikar" (because he had amassed his fortune in the African colony of Mozambique), the neighbourhood comprises a dozen or so blocks of Neoclassical houses rising up the sides of **Altinho Hill**. Many have retained their traditional coat of ochre, pale yellow, green or blue – a legacy of the Portuguese insistence that every Goan building (except churches, which had to be kept white) should be colour-washed after the monsoons.

At the southern end of the district, the whitewashed **Chapel of St Sebastian** is one of many Goan *igrejas* to remain faithful to the old colonial decree. It stands at the end of a small square where Fontainhas' Portuguese-speaking locals hold a

Abbé de Faria

Next to the Secretariat stands a bizarre **statue** of a long-haired, haggard man glaring from his pedestal at the supine body of a woman, his hands stretched out towards her as if, in the words of Graham Greene, who saw it in the 1960s, he is about to "(pounce) like a great black eagle on his mesmerized female patient". Contrary to appearances, the portrait is not a scene from some lascivious nineteenth-century melodrama, but a memorial to one of Goa's more illustrious sons, the **Abbé de Faria** – priest, revolutionary and the founding father of modern hypnotism.

José Custodio de Faria was born in Candolim, Bardez, on May 20, 1756, the son of a down-at-heel seminarian and a local landowner's daughter. When this marriage ended in 1771, José's mother ran off to a nunnery, and his father took him to Lisbon, where the pair soon gained the patronage of the king, Dom José I. Faria senior eventually rose to become confessor to the king's daughter but fell out of favour in 1779, accused of whipping up sedition among Goan expats in Lisbon. José, too, was linked with the rebels and fled to Paris soon after.

While in the French capital, Faria developed an interest in the occult science of *magnétisme*, or **hypnosis**. Aided by his exotic dark skin, ascetic dress and Goan-Brahmin credentials, the young priest started up a course in a school hall on the Rue Clichy, attracting a large and predominantly female following, but his "performances" enraged the clergy and scientific establishment, who spread rumours that Faria was taking advantage of his women students and patients. These attacks on his reputation brought a premature end to his career and, in 1819, Faria died penniless – on the very day his now famous treatise on hypnosis, *De la cause du sommeil lucide* ("On the Causes of Lucid Sleep"), was published.

Faria's enduring contribution to the modern science of psychology is his insistence that hypnotic trances were not produced by body fluids, but by suggestion, which opened up the notion of the unconscious mind.

lively annual street *festa* to celebrate the Feast of Our Lady of Livrament in mid-November. The eerily lifelike crucifix inside the chapel formerly hung in the Palace of the Inquisition in Old Goa. Unusually, Christ's eyes are open – allegedly to inspire fear in those being interrogated by the Inquisitors. It was brought to Panjim in 1812, after the Inquisition had been suppressed in Goa, and installed in the Secretariat, finally coming to rest here a little over a century later when the viceroys had decamped to the Cabo. Mass begins at 6.45am.

A short way north of the chapel, just beyond the *Park Lane Lodge*, a flight of old laterite steps leads up Altinho Hill to Panjim's best-preserved nineteenth-century building, the **High Court of Mumbai in Goa**. Stripped of fancy pilasters, eaves, corbels and decorative frames, the edifice typifies the functional aesthetic that prevailed during the Pombal era, when Lisbon and the great Brazilian cities were rebuilt by the Portuguese.

Sao Tomé ward is the other old quarter, lying north of Fontainhas on the far side of Emilio Gracia Road. This is the area to head for if you fancy a bar crawl: the narrow streets are dotted with dozens of hole-in-the-wall taverns, serving stiff measures of sweet port wine and rocket-fuel *feni* under strip lights and the watchful gaze of colourful Madonnas.

The State Archeological Museum

The most noteworthy feature of Panjim's **State Archeological Museum** (Mon–Fri 9.30am–1.15pm & 2–5.30pm, Ⓦwww.goamuseum.nic.in; Rs10) at the far end of Ourem Creek, near the Kadamba bus stand, is its imposing size, which stands in glaringly inverse proportion to the scale of the collection inside. In their bid to erect a structure befitting a state capital, Goa's bureaucrats ignored the fact that there was precious little to put in it. The only rarities to be found amid the minor-league pieces of temple sculpture, hero stones and dowdy colonial-era artefacts are a couple of beautiful **Jain bronzes** rescued by Customs and Excise officials from smugglers and, on the first floor, the infamous Italian-style **table** used by Goa's Grand Inquisitors, complete with its original, ornately carved tall-backed chairs.

The Houses of Goa Museum

Across the Mandovi River, 5km from Panjim, the new hilltop suburb of **Porvorim** sprawls either side of the main Goa–Mumbai highway. A hectic ribbon development of car showrooms, truck stops and fast-food joints, it's an unlikely place to site a museum devoted to precisely the kind of cultural heritage that development such as this is gradually submerging. But just off the main drag, in the small hamlet of Torda, renowned local architect Gerard de Cunha and colleagues have set up the quirky **Houses of Goa Museum** (Tues–Sun 10am–7.30pm; Ⓦwww.archgoa.org; Rs25). Its general aim is to showcase the region's way of life as it used to be before the protective shield of Portuguese rule was lifted in 1961.

Appropriately enough, the triangular building itself resembles a modern ark, with themed displays divided between four levels interconnected by spiral staircases. The exhibitions are largely given over to domestic houses, pieces of which – from wonderful old doors and oyster-shell windows, to carved railings, ceramic tiles, furniture and masonry – are assembled to explain construction processes and changes in decor and style.

The Houses of Goa museum is most easily reached by taxi or auto-rickshaw. With your own transport, head north over the Mandovi bridge and keep going until you reach the big Alto–Porvorim Circle roundabout. Take a right here and follow the road until it forks, then bear left and head straight on for 750m or so, until you reach a second fork, where you bear left again: the museum is next to Nisha's Play School. By bus, you can travel as far as the Alto-Porvorim roundabout on any Panjim–Mapusa service from the Kadamba stand: get down at *O Coqueiro* restaurant, just north of the roundabout, then walk the remaining 2km, or jump in an auto if there's one hanging around.

Eating and drinking

In a week you could feasibly attempt a **gastronomic tour** of the subcontinent without straying more than five minutes from the centre of Panjim. Standards are generally high and prices much lower than in the resorts, while beer, *feni* and other spirits are available in all but the purest "pure veg" places. If you're unsure about which regional cooking style to try, head for the *Hotel Fidalgo* on 18th June Road, which hosts six different outlets, from Goan to Gujarati.

Bhojan/Mirch Masala *Hotel Fidalgo*, 18th June Rd. Authentic, pure-veg Gujarati thali joint, in the air-con restaurant complex of a popular upscale hotel. You won't eat finer Indian vegetarian cuisine anywhere in Goa. Rs140 for the works: five or six different vegetables, dhals, *papad*, rice and various traditional breads, plus fragrant milk sweets for desert. For equally superb non-veg, North Indian food (kebabs, curries, tandoori and the like) head next door to *Mirch Masala*.

George's Emilio Gracia Rd. This is a great little Goan-Catholic café serving proper local food at local prices, on cramped tables near the Immaculate Conception church. Grab a seat under a fan and tuck into calamari chilli fry, prawn-curry-rice, millet-fried fish fillets or one of the good-value seafood thalis. Most mains around Rs100.

Legacy of Bombay *Hotel Fidalgo*, 18th June Rd. Basically an upmarket *udipi*, only with bow-ties instead of grubby cotton tunics. Their menu features the usual dosas, South Indian snacks, *pao bhaji* and tasty spring rolls, as well as spiced teas and delicious lassis, but what sets this place apart is its stylish designer decor: the walls are lined with intriguing photographic montages of Mumbai.

Mum's Kitchen Dr D Bandodkar Marg (Panjim–Miramar Rd) ⓣ9011/095557, ⓦwww.mumskitchengoa.com. Rony and Suzette Martins, the owners of this great Goan restaurant in the suburb of Miramar,10min by auto from the centre of Panjim, collected old family recipes from mothers, grandmas and aunties across the state in an attempt to revive disappearing culinary traditions – not just the famous Catholic, meat-based ones, but also veggie rarities from the kitchens of Saraswat Hindus. The results are as authentic and flavour-packed as any you'll encounter in Goa. Try the smoky, Brahmin-style, *varan dal* made with ghee but no garlic or onions, or Rony's mum's own *haram mas*, tangy salted pork stew. Seafood lovers will also appreciate the seafood platter (Rs1750 for two). And save room for the house *bebinca*. Most mains Rs250–300.

Cookery course

If you're inspired by Panjim's cosmopolitan eating options to discover the secrets behind Indian cuisine, consider signing up for one of **Branca's Cookery Courses**, held daily at the Detroit Institute, near Panjim's Immaculate Conception Church. Classes are conducted in the kitchen of a traditional colonial-era house, under the watchful eye of a mother-and-daughter team. Instruction lasts from 10am until 1pm. You choose in advance from seven different courses (Indian, Goan, vegetarian, seafood, desserts, soups & snacks, bakery), and eat what you've created over lunch.

The "Indian" option tends to be the most popular, featuring different cooking styles and dishes from around the subcontinent, from Kashmiri pulao to Punjabi butter chicken, Bombay *pao bhaji* and *paneer makhanwalla.* But this is also a great place to place to pick up tips on Goan cuisine from a proper local chef with over twenty years' experience – and whose cheese puffs are the stuff of legend.

Courses typically cost Rs2500 per person, which includes all ingredients and lunch. Book in advance with Branca on ⓣ9822/131835, or via email: ⓔdetroitinstitute@yahoo.com.

O-Goa *Hotel Fidalgo*, 18th June Rd. Tasty Goan dishes – prawn curry, chicken *xacuti*, pork *sorpotel* – served on a poolside terrace in the heart of town. Their lunchtime "fish combo" meal (served daily noon–3pm; Rs200) is fantastic value, comprising several seafood and veg curries, with masala-fried clams and kingfish fillet, rice, waters and pickle.

Satkar 18th June Rd. Popular South Indian snack and juice joint. There's a huge range of dishes, including Chinese and North Indian, but most people go for their fantastic masala dosas and piping hot, crunchy samosas – the best in town.

Sher-e-Punjab Above Hindu Pharmacy, Cunha Rivara Rd, Municipal Gardens (Church Square) ⓣ0832/242 5657. This North Indian restaurant, an old Panjim favourite which recently had a major facelift, occupies a funky, glass-sided dining hall overlooking the square. The decor and a/c are state-of-the-art, but the flavours on offer are resolutely traditional. Steer clear of the Goan and Chinese menu – Mughlai is the thing here: chicken, mutton and *paneer* prepared in the tandoor or steeped in a rich, spicy, creamy sauces, which you scoop up with flaky naan breads. Mains only Rs150–210.

Shiv Sagar Mahatma Gandhi Rd. Smarter than average *udipi* café, it does a brisk trade with Panjim's middle classes for its consistently fresh, delicious pan-Indian food and fresh fruit juices. The northern dishes aren't so great, but their *udipi* menu is superb (try the delicious *palak dosa*, made with spinach), and their fiery *pao bhaji* is a real crowd puller on weekends. Child-friendly, a/c mezzanine upstairs. No alcohol.

Venite Rua 31 de Janeiro. With its wooden floors and tiny, candle-lit balcony tables, this touristy place in the old Sao Tomé district is one of the most atmospheric places to eat in Panjim. Continental and Goan seafood dishes dominate their somewhat overpriced menu (mains Rs200–300), but the down-at-heel, old-world ambience is why most punters eat here.

Vihar Around the corner from *Venite*, on Avda Dom Joao Castro. One of the best South Indian snack cafés in Panjim, and more conveniently situated than its competitors if you're staying in Fontainhas. Try their tasty rawa masala dosas or cheese *uttapams*. The only drawback is the traffic noise, so avoid it during rush hours.

Viva Panjim 178 Rua 31 de Janeiro, behind Mary Immaculate High School, Fontainhas. Traditional Goan home cooking – *xacutis*, vindaloo, prawn *balchao*, *cafreal*, *amotik* and delicious freshly grilled fish – served by a charming local woman, Linda de Souza, in a pretty colonial-era backstreet. This place should be your first choice for dinner if you're staying in Fontainhas.

Shopping

Top of your souvenir hunting list should be **cashew nuts**, sold in bulk from a string of stores along 18th June Road. Zantye's, available at several different outlets, are generally regarded as the best brand, but they've plenty of competition. The nuts themselves, which are the state's most lucrative foreign export after iron ore, come in various qualities and sizes, salted or plain, with and without shells, and are sold pre-packed at fixed prices. If you're not convinced of how delicious they are, ask for a small taster packet.

Goan **feni**, the ideal accompaniment for dry-roasted cashews, is also sold at numerous liquor shops along 18th June Road. Souvenir bottles tend to come covered in crazy shell confections, but you can buy the same stuff a lot more cheaply in plain plastic or glass containers.

As nearly all "Goan handicrafts" are imported, authentic artisanal items are thin on the ground. The only truly traditional Goan souvenirs available are **azulejos**, Portuguese painted tiles, which you'll find at a tiny workshop tucked down a sidestreet just outside the Chapel of St Sebastian in Fontainhas (see p.71). Nearby, next door to the *Panjim Inn* on Rua 31 de Janeiro, the **Velha Goa Galeria** houses an even bigger collection, displayed in a stone-floored, white-walled showroom. While you're in the area, have a nose around the lovely Geetanjali Gallery in the *Panjim Pousada*, opposite the Velha Galeria, which deals original **paintings** and **prints** by Indian artists.

Sosa's, a little air-conditioned boutique around the corner next door to the *Horseshoe* restaurant at E-245 Rua de Ourem, stocks the town's best selection of Goan **designer clothes**, ranging from glamorous ethnic frocks to loose,

Carnival

Panjim's chaotic three-day **Carnival**, held during late February or early March, was originally introduced in the eighteenth century by the Portuguese as a means to let off steam before Lent. It has been celebrated with gusto in Goa ever since, and now draws tens of thousands of revellers from around India and abroad. In recent years, however, the colourful parade forming its centrepiece has been the cause of controversy, as its organizers are accused of vulgarizing Goan culture for crude commercial gain.

The **origins** of Carnival date back to the hedonistic religious festivals of ancient Greece and Rome. Later, black slaves in the Spanish and Portuguese colonies infused it with a healthy dose of African panache. Known in Konkani as *Intruz* (a corruption of the Portuguese word *Entrudo*, from the Latin *Introito* meaning the start of Lent), Goa's version was grafted onto an indigenous tradition of local village festivals in which *khells*, or **satirical folk plays**, were – and still are – performed.

Following the centuries-old model, Panjim Carnival is kicked off on **Sabato Gordo** ("Fat Saturday") by the entry into the town of King Momo, who reads a decree ordering his subjects to forget their worries and "be happy". This unleashes three days of music, masked dance and general mayhem, accompanied by exuberant cross-dressing, mock battles fought with bags of sawdust or flour and water, and *assaltos*, or trick-or-treat-style raids on neighbours' kitchens.

Condemned by the Goan government as "colonial", the festivities were suspended following Independence but have enjoyed a revival over the past couple of decades, spurred on by injections of funds from local businesses, national liquor and cigarette manufacturers and five-star hotel chains. Such **commercialism** angers many Goans, who claim it runs counter to the spirit of Carnival, which traditionally inverts and satirizes the prevailing power structures. Worse still, in many people's eyes, is the gradual **vulgarization** of the event, which has become closely associated in the popular Indian imagination with licentious behaviour, particularly among local women. The prime propagator of this myth is Bollywood, which regularly includes scenes of seduction and sexual intrigue set against a Goan Carnival backdrop.

Over the past four or five years, other pressures have somewhat diminished the colours of Carnival – notably a **ban on alcohol** use by all participants. Notwithstanding, the main Saturday parade continues to draw large numbers of revellers to the Goan capital, while Goans all over the state avidly watch the event on television. However, if you plan to come to Panjim yourself, travel here for the day only, as hotels tend to be fully booked weeks in advance. And expect to get plastered in paint and sludge, hurled in balloon bombs by gangs of rowdy teenagers.

Portuguese-style cotton shirts. If they don't have what you want in your size, ask if they can arrange to have one made to measure.

The coastal resorts are full of young **tailors** who can run off baggy pyjama trousers and shirts on their old Singer sewing machines, but if you're after anything sturdier – such as Indian *kurtas* or suits – Panjim is a safer bet. One of the town's top stitchers (at least for men's clothes) is Chandu Tailors, down a small arcade (ask for the Sai Baba temple) opposite the National Cinema, just off Church Square. The best source of traditional Indian textiles is the nearby government Khadi Grammodyog, opposite *Rajdhani Hotel* on Dr Atmaram Borkar Road, which sells various kinds of hand-spun cotton for next to nothing and bolts of wonderful pure silk.

Other good buys in the town (although strictly speaking not Goan at all) are the wonderful tribal *dokra* (lost-wax) metal items, leather sculpture and textiles (mostly block-printed and batik) sold at Mrignayani in the Kadamba bus stand. Set up by the state government of Madhya Pradesh to provide employment for some of its poorest inhabitants, this emporium is run along the lines of an Oxfam shop, with recycled newspaper bags instead of plastic and strictly fixed prices.

Out at Ribandar, 5km east of town on the road to Old Goa, **Camelot** is a swish lifestyle emporium with a range of traditional Indian furniture and textiles, as well as expensive clothes by Indian designers such as Wendell Rodrick and Savio Jon. See p.50 for more on "lifestyle galleries". More stylish still, **Solar de Souto**, just before Old Goa on the main road, is of interest as much for the building that houses it as its stock: an ancient *palacio* alleged to be the only surviving mansion from the now lost Portuguese city. Exquisitely restored, it boasts a traditional inner pillared courtyard, galleries and cool café, in addition to a store selling Indian and Indo-Portuguese items for the home.

Finally, anyone suffering withdrawal symptoms from their local shopping mall should head for the road behind the *Mandovi Hotel*, where a handful of international retailers – Levi's, Benetton and Reebok among them – sell familiar products at lower prices than back home. The same applies to watchmakers, Titan, who have a swish outlet on 18th June Road, along with several pricey sunglasses manufacturers.

Listings

Airlines Indian Airlines/Air India, Dempo House, Dr D Bandodkar Marg ⓣ0832/242 8787 or 223 7826; Jet Airways/JetLite, Sesa Ghor, Patto Plaza, next to GTDC *Panjim Residency*, Pato ⓣ0832/243 8792; Kinghfisher Airlines Shop G-4, 5–6 Glass Tower, Swami Vivekanand Road, opposite Panjim Traffic Cell ⓣ1800/209 3030.

ATMs & Banks Nearly all the banks in town nowadays have ATMs, where you can make withdrawals using Visa or Mastercard; several are marked on the map on p.66. The most efficient place to change currency and travellers' cheques is: Thomas Cook, near the AirIndia/Indian Airlines office at 8 Alcon Chambers, Dr D Bandodkar Marg (Mon–Sat 9am–6pm, Oct–March also Sun 10am–5pm).

Bookshops The bookshops in the *Hotel Fidalgo* and the *Hotel Mandovi* stock English-language titles, including paperback pulp fiction and guides.

British Consular Assistant The British High Commission of Mumbai has a Tourist Assistance Office Panjim – a useful contact for British nationals who've lost passports, get into trouble with the law or need help dealing with a death. It's over near the Kadamba bus stand at 13/14 Dempo Towers, Patto Plaza ⓣ0832/243 8734 or 243 8897, ⓕ0832/664 1297, ⓔassistance@goaukconsular.org, ⓦwww.ukinindia.com. Outside office opening hours (Mon–Fri 8am–1pm & 2.30–4pm), you should contact the main British High Commission in Delhi (ⓣ011/2419 2100) which in theory has a duty officer on call 24/7.

Cinema Panjim's swanky new multiplex, the 1272-seater Inox, is in the northwest of town on the site of the old Goa Medical College, Dr D Bandodkar Marg ⓣ0832/242 0999, ⓦwww.inoxmovies.com. The complex screens all the latest Hindi blockbusters, and some English-language Hollywood movies; see the local press or their website for listings and booking details.

Hospital The state's main medical facility is the new Goa Medical College, aka GMC (ⓣ0832/245 8700–07), 7km south on NH-17 at Bambolim, where there's also a 24 hour pharmacy. Ambulances (ⓣ102) are likely to get you there a lot less quickly than a standard taxi. Conditions are grim by Western standards; relatives sleep on the wards to provide food for patients. Less serious cases can receive attention at the Vintage Hospital, next to the fire brigade headquarters in Panjim's St Inez district ⓣ0832/564 4401–05.

Internet access Most hotels and guesthouse offer internet access to guests. Otherwise, Cozy Nook Travels, at No 6 Municipal Building, 18th June Rd, has a fast ADSL connection.

Music and dance Regular recitals of classical Indian music and dance are held at Panjim's school for the performing arts, the Kala Academy in Campal (ⓦwww.kalaacademy.org), at the far west end of town on Dr D Bandodkar Marg. For details of forthcoming concerts, consult the boards in front of the auditorium or the listings page of local newspapers.

Pharmacies Hindu Pharma, near the tourist office on Church Square (ⓣ0832/222 3176) stocks a phenomenal range of ayurvedic, homeopathic and allopathic medicines.

Police The Police Headquarters is on Malacca Rd, central Panjim. In an emergency, call ⓣ100.

Travel agents AERO Mundial, ground floor, *Hotel Mandovi*, Dr D Bandodkar Marg ⓣ0832/222 3773; Travel Shop, 15 Trionara Appartments, 1st Floor, near Municipal Market ⓣ0832/2232020.

Moving on to Mumbai

If you're heading north to **Mumbai**, the quickest and easiest way is **by plane**. A couple of dozen flights leave Goa's Dabolim airport daily, with fares from as low as Rs1000 (or even less) if you book well in advance with one of the no-frills airlines – or as much as Rs30,000 on New Year's Eve. Try SpiceJet (ⓦwww.spicejet.com), IndiGo (ⓦwww.goindigo.in), Go Air (ⓦwww.goair.in), JetLite (ⓦwww.jetlite.com) or Kingfisher Airlines (ⓦwww.flykingfisher.com). Flying with Indian Airlines (ⓦindian-airlines.nic.in) or Jet Airways (ⓦwww.jetairways.com) will set you back more – typically around US$100 each way.

Four to five services run daily on the **Konkan Railway**, the most convenient being the overnight Konkan-Kanya Express (#0112), which departs from Margao (see p.161) at 6pm (or Karmali, near Old Goa, 11km west of Panjim, at 6.30pm), arriving at Mumbai CST (still commonly known as Victoria Terminus, or VT) at 5.50am the following day. The other fast train from Goa to CST is the Mandvi Express (#0104), departing Margao at 10.10am (or Karmali, at 10.37am) and arriving at 9.45pm the same evening. **Tickets** are most conveniently purchased online, through ⓦwww.cleartrip.com or Indian Railways' own, much less efficient site, ⓦwww.irctc.co.in. Alternatively, you can join the queues at KRC's hectic reservation office on the first floor of Panjim's Kadamba bus stand (Mon–Sat 8am–8pm, Sun 8am–2pm), or at KRC's main reservation hall in Margao Station (Mon–Sat 8am–4.30pm, Sun 8am–2pm; ⓣ0834/271 2780). Make your reservations as far in advance as possible.

The cheapest, though far from most comfortable, way to get to Mumbai is by **night bus**, which takes fourteen to eighteen hours, covering 500km of rough road at often terrifying speeds. Fares vary according to levels of comfort, and luxury buses arrive two or three hours sooner. Book Kadamba bus tickets at their offices in the Panjim and Mapusa (see p.108) bus stands (daily 9–11am & 2–5pm); private companies sell theirs through the many travel agents immediately outside the bus stand in Panjim, and at the bottom of the square in Mapusa. The most popular private services to Mumbai are those run by a company called Paulo Travels, who lay on a range of different services, from no-frills buses for Rs325/500 low/high season to swisher air-conditioned Volvo coaches with berths (which bizarrely you may have to share) costing Rs1200/1500. For tickets, contact their main office just outside the Kadamba bus stand, Panjim (ⓣ0832/222 3736, ⓦwww.paulotravels.com).

Goa Velha

Blink during the journey between Panjim and Dabolim airport on the NH-17, and you will probably miss **GOA VELHA**. Yet the village, dotted among the paddy fields 9km southeast of the capital, was, until the emergence of Ela (Old Goa) during the fifteenth century, southwest India's wealthiest city and busiest port.

Govapuri, or Gopakkapttana (later Gova), was founded in 1054 by the Kadamba ruler Jayakeshi I, who moved his capital here from Chandrapura – now Chandor in Salcete *taluka* – to exercise more control over the movement of maritime traffic through the busy harbour. Import duties and taxes creamed off this lucrative trade (in Arabian horses, Chinese silks and Southeast Asian spices) financed the construction of sumptuous palaces, temples and a well-planned city with its own charitable institutions. The period of prosperity survived two Kadamba rebellions, but not the arrival in Govapuri of the Sultan of Delhi's army in 1312. Following a lengthy siege – vividly described in the memoirs by the great Arab traveller, Ibn Battuta – the Goan kings fled back to Chandrapura. Thereafter, the city saw a series of bloody sackings as it changed hands between the Muslim Bahmani dynasty and the Hindu Vijayanagars. It was finally left to rot in 1470, after the Zuari River silted up and receded, leaving the harbour high and dry.

Precious little of ancient Govapuri remains in Goa Velha, save for the ruins of the original harbour walls, which are sometimes visible protruding through the mud of the estuary at low tide. However, if you pull off the highway just before entering the village (from the Panjim side), at the De Souza General Store, and follow the lane running into the *toddi* grove between the Kadesh Gas shop and mechanic's yard, you'll eventually come across the only *in situ* remnant of the once great city: a tubular, perfectly carved Kadamba **millstone** used for extracting coconut oil (the dynasty's chief export), which must have been too heavy, or too useful, to move; ask for the "*fatrar*".

Goa Velha's principal claim to fame these days is its **Procession of the Saints**, held on the first Monday of Easter week each year, when life-size effigies of saints, martyrs, popes, kings, queens and cardinals are paraded around the village. The tradition was instigated in the seventeenth century by the Franciscans as an attempt to reverse the decline in morals afflicting the colony, and by the eighteenth century a total of 65 statues, lavishly encrusted with gold and precious stones, were involved in the procession. Today, the number has fallen to fewer than thirty, but the parade remains a highlight of Goa's religious calendar, with devotees travelling from all over the state to receive the blessing of the figures as they pass. Festivities conclude with a candle-lit Mass outside St Andrew's Church in Goa Velha, presided over by members of the Third Franciscan Order.

Buses to Goa Velha run every fifteen minutes or so from the main KTC stand in Panjim; you can jump on any of the services bound for Margao and Vasco (other than the limited-stop ones) and get down on the highway.

Pilar

The seminary at **PILAR**, resting on the edge of a thickly wooded hill 12km southeast of Panjim and a couple of kilometres from Goa Velha, is one of two surviving theological colleges out of four founded by the Portuguese (the other is at Rachol). Established by the Capuchins in 1613, it was abandoned after the expulsion of the religious orders in 1835, but restored 22 years later by the Carmelites. Although it boasts a well-preserved seventeenth-century church and a small museum, the seminary, which is now run as a training college for Christian missionaries, isn't a particularly inspiring tourist destination, and most of its visitors come on pilgrimages. However, if you are passing on the nearby NH-17, the superb views over the Zuari estuary are worth a quick detour. Any of the Panjim–Cortalim–Vasco buses will drop you at the turn-off on the main road, from where it is possible to take a short cut through the modern wing of the seminary to a flight of old steps that lead up the hill.

The large 1950s-style college, run by the Mission Society of St Francis Xavier, occupies the site of an ancient Shiva temple, the Goveshwar *mandir*, from which the name Goa is believed to derive. The Konkani name for the hill itself was *rishincho mellavo*, or "meeting place of the holy men", suggesting this has been one of the region's most sacred sites for thousands of years. All that remains of the former Hindu shrine, however, is a stone-lined water tank, which now supplies the seminary orchards. Fragments of pottery and temple sculpture unearthed in the gardens or found submerged in the seminary wells are informatively displayed on the first floor in the small **museum** (Mon–Sat 8am–1pm & 2.30–6pm, Sun by request; free), along with a splendid *Simhalanchana*, the Kadambas' traditional lion emblem, a beautiful bas-relief of St Mary Magdalene carved in 1733 and featuring symbols of the four great Indian religions, and a copy of the first Marathi translation of the Gospels.

The **Church of Our Lady of Pilar**, next to the main car park down the hill, dates from the foundation of the seminary in 1613. Tombstones of Portuguese *hidalgos* line the floor of its old entrance porch, which opens onto cloisters decorated with original seventeenth-century frescoes, but the real highlight stands behind the main altar – a sumptuously carved Baroque reredos featuring a painted statue of Our Lady of Pillar.

Talaulim

Lost deep in the heart of Tiswadi *taluka*, **TALAULIM** village, 4km north of Pilar, would feature on few maps were it not for the enormous **Church of Santana** (St Anne) that looms from its northern edge. Boasting the most spectacular facade outside Old Goa, the church was founded in the sixteenth century after reports that a vision of the Virgin Mary's mother, St Anne, had appeared before local villagers in the form of an old woman with a hat and walking stick. In 1695, a much grander replacement was erected, modelled on the Augustinian Monastery in Old Goa, of which only a single ruined belfry now remains. Years of neglect have taken their toll on the building, but it's still an impressive sight. Rising in five stages, the mighty whitewashed facade is composed of a Baroque gable (featuring a statue of St Anne as its centrepiece), flanked by a pair of square towers and bristling with pinnacles, shell motifs and balustrades.

Talaulim is difficult to get to without your own **transport**, as buses from the capital only run every two hours. With a car or motorcycle, however, you can tie the Church of Santana into a neat loop with Old Goa, Pilar and Panjim, 7km northwest.

Old Goa

Soaring high above the palm canopy, the giant cathedral towers, belfries and domes of the former Portuguese capital, nowadays known as **OLD GOA**, are by far and away the state's most impressive historical monuments, and collectively one of the finest crops of Renaissance architecture in the world. In its heyday, *Goa Dourada*, "Golden Goa", 10km east of Panjim, was the largest, richest and most splendid city in Asia. With a population of around 300,000 in the 1500s (greater than either Lisbon or London at the time), it sprawled south from a grand civic centre and bustling port on the banks of the Mandovi River to within a stone's throw of the Zuari estuary, and west as far as Ribandar: a maze of narrow twisting streets, piazzas, ochre-washed villas and imposing Baroque churches.

These days you need a fertile imagination to picture Old Goa as it must have looked in the sixteenth and seventeenth centuries. The populous suburbs have disappeared without trace, reduced to rubble and reclaimed by the jungle, leaving a mere dozen or so churches and convents marooned amid the Archeological Survey of India's carefully manicured lawns. Granted World Heritage status by UNESCO, the site attracts busloads of foreign tourists from the coast and Christian pilgrims from around India in roughly equal numbers. While the former come primarily to admire the gigantic facades and gilt altars of Old Goa's beautifully preserved

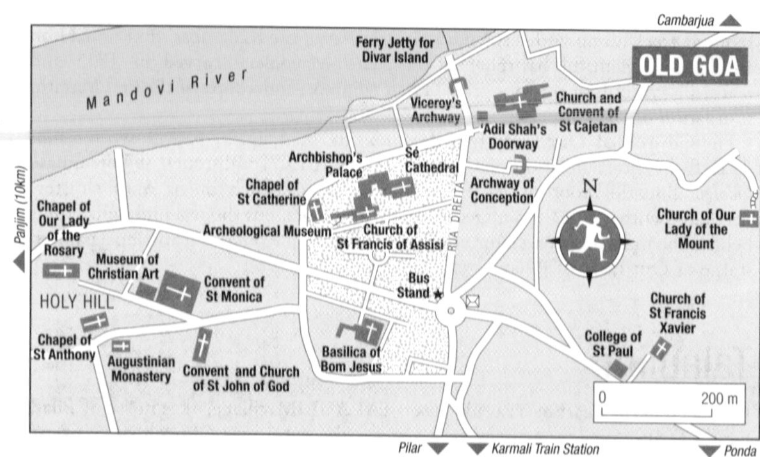

churches, the main attraction for the latter is the tomb of **St Francis Xavier**, the renowned sixteenth-century missionary, whose remains are enshrined in the **Basilica of Bom Jesus**.

For anyone staying at one of the nearby resorts, Old Goa is the obvious choice for a day-trip inland. Thirty minutes by road from the state capital, the site is served by **buses** from Panjim's Kadamba bus stand (every 15min; 30min); alternatively, hop into an auto-rickshaw (Rs120) or rent a taxi (Rs300–400).

Some history

The earliest recorded occupation of Old Goa was at the beginning of the twelfth century, when the local Hindu king founded a brahmin colony, or *brahmapuri*, here. Known as **Ela**, the settlement later expanded under the Vijayanagars, but was occupied by the Bahmani Muslims after they razed the former Hindu capital of Govapuri (now Goa Velha) further south. Eventually, Ela became the second city of the ruler of Bijapur, **Yusuf 'Adil Shah**, following the break-up of the Bahmani kingdom towards the end of the fifteenth century. Encircled by fortified walls and a deep moat, Ela's grandest building was the 'Adil Shah's palace, whose minarets once dominated the town, of which only a lone-standing doorway now remains.

Goa's fabled golden age began in 1510 with the appearance of the Portuguese. Commanded by **Alfonso de Albuquerque**, a squadron of warships moved in to mop up the remnants of a Muslim fleet it had previously engaged off Kerala, then seized the town to use it as a base for operations along the Malabar coast. The Portuguese were able to profit from the local trade in horses and spices, and as the wealth poured in, so did immigrants – by the end of the sixteenth century, some 2500 new arrivals every year replenished a population constantly depleted by disease. With them came missionaries from various religious orders, encouraged by the colonial government as a "civilizing influence" on both the natives and the famously licentious colonials. This process was hastened by the arrival in 1542 of **Francis Xavier**, and by the dreaded Holy Office, better known as the **Inquisition**, for whose trials and bloody *autos da fé* the colony later became notorious.

Beneath the outward gloss of piety, however, Goa was fast developing a reputation for **decadence**. Accounts by European travellers of the day record that adultery, drunkenness and sexual "laxity" were rife and records from the

Goan Royal Hospital show that by 1625, around five hundred Portuguese were dying here from syphilis and "the effects of profligacy" each year. Despite issuing edicts to crack down on the debauchery, the clerics themselves were far from innocent, keeping seraglios of black slave girls. A Scottish sea captain wrote sixty years later, in 1700, that the city was "a place of small Trade and most of its Riches ly in Hands of indolent Country Gentlemen, who loiter away their days in Ease, Luxury and Pride."

Easy wealth may have taken its toll on the colonizers' fortitude, but ultimately natural and economic factors rather than vice were to bring about Goa's decline. The original site was swampland, a perfect breeding ground for malaria-carrying mosquitoes. Bad drainage caused drinking water to become infected by raw sewage, and more than half the city's inhabitants died during the **epidemics** of 1543 and 1570, with a further 25,000 perishing in the first thirty years of the seventeenth century. To compound the health problems, the Mandovi started to silt up, preventing ships entering the harbour. Finally, after the Portuguese trade monopoly had been broken by the British, French and Dutch, **Viceroy Conde do Alvor** ordered the administrative capital to be shifted to Mormugao. This scheme was eventually dropped in favour of a move upriver to Panjim, but the damage to Old Goa had already been done, and most of the houses were demolished to provide masonry for the new capital. When the chronicler Abbé Cottineau de Kloguen passed through in 1827, he remarked with dismay that "nothing remains of the city but the sacred; the profane is entirely banished."

The architecture of Old Goa

Exuding the spirit of imperial self-confidence typical of its day, the architecture of Old Goa is resolutely European, inspired by contemporary Italian fashions rather than the indigenous traditions which it supplanted. The peak of the colony's building boom, in the early seventeenth century, coincided with the end of the Renaissance in Europe and the beginning of the **Baroque era**, with its predilection for twisting scrollwork, chubby winged cherubs, lashings of gilt and generally over-the-top ornamentation. In part, this shift was a reaction against the restrictive conventions of the past, but it also served the purposes of missionaries by providing awe-inspiring spectacles to impress new converts. You only have to step inside the Basilica of Bom Jesus to get some idea of the impact such splendour must have had on local people more used to modest monochrome stone temples.

The other architectural style represented at Old Goa is specifically Portuguese. Named after its principal patron, King Manuel I (1495–1521), the **Manueline movement** celebrated the achievements of the Portuguese discoveries by incorporating nautical motifs, such as anchors and ropes, into the buildings' design. Few examples of this style have survived, but you'll get a sense of it from the main doorway of the Church of St Francis of Assisi, next to the museum, or the Church of Our Lady of the Rosary on Holy Hill.

Although many of Old Goa's churches feature decorative details carved from **basalt** (reputedly brought to Goa as ballast in the ships that sailed from Lisbon, but more probably quarried at Bassein, near Mumbai), virtually all of Old Goa's churches were made of local laterite. As this porous red-brown stone eroded badly during the annual monsoons, a thick coat of lime whitewash, made from crushed clam shells, was traditionally applied over the top, and renewed after each rainy season. Nowadays, a far less appealing off-white paint is used, but the principle remains the same, as you'll see if you come here in September or early October, when the buildings are invariably still covered with streaks of black mildew.

Arrival and orientation

Arriving by **bus**, you'll be dropped off just south of the main square, which is flanked by the Basilica of Bom Jesus to the south, and the Sé Cathedral, Church of St Francis of Assisi and archeological museum to the north. The main highlights all lie within comfortable walking distance of here and can be seen in two to three hours. The logical place to start any tour of the site is at its northeast corner, where the Viceroy's Archway marks the traditional entrance to the city from the Mandovi riverfront. Head south from here along the **Rua Direita**, Old Goa's principal thoroughfare, and you'll pass the chief monuments in more or less chronological order, winding up at the Basilica, the spiritual hub of Old Goa. It's also well worth making an additional foray west to **Holy Hill**, site of some of the city's oldest and architecturally most important buildings, and east to the hilltop **Church of Our Lady of the Mount**, which commands the best view of the old city and its environs. However long you spend exploring the site, be sure to bring a sun hat and plenty of drinking water, as the heat and humidity can be ferocious. There is nowhere commendable to eat in Old Goa; for a snack or coffee, head a couple of kilometres back along the road to Panjim, where there's an excellent café in the lifestyle store, Casa Goa.

The site

Throughout its most prosperous period in the sixteenth and early seventeenth centuries, Old Goa could only be reached by river. This remains the most

The Goan Inquisition

Written histories of Goa are rife with accounts of atrocities committed by the Portuguese. None, however, compare with those perpetrated in the name of Christianity by the dreaded **Santo Officio**, or "Holy Office'. Better known as the Inquisition (from the Latin verb *inquiro*, "I inquire into"), the dreaded tribunal became the most brutal, systematic and macabre instrument of cultural bigotry ever devised by a European colonial power. As one eighteenth-century historian put it, "(the) Holy Office combined all that the ferocity of savages and the ingenuity of civilized man had till then invented."

The original targets of the Inquisition were not, as is often assumed, Hindus, but *Christianos nuevos* ("new Christians") – mainly Iberian Jews and Muslims who had been forcibly converted during the religious persecution of the medieval era, but who had since lapsed into their former faiths. Jews, in particular, had fled in large numbers to the new colonies of Africa, South America and Asia, where they had become the dominant mercantile community. It was to complain of their lax religious ways that Francis Xavier wrote to King Joao III of Portugal in 1546, encouraging him to dispatch the Holy Inquisition to Goa, which he duly did fourteen years later, in 1560.

By this time, the religious intolerance that had been making life difficult for the *Christianos nuevos* in Europe had also infected attitudes to local Hinduism in the *Estado da India*. Temple worship had been banned, shrines destroyed and Brahmin priests banished. With the arrival of the two Grand Inquisitors and their spies from Lisbon, however, the range of "crimes" for which one could be imprisoned broadened considerably. Substances and plants connected with Hindu ritual – turmeric powder (*haldi*), basil (*tulsi*) leaves, incense or marigolds – were banned, as was cooking rice "without salt"; wearing a *dhoti* or *choli* (sari top); selling arms or horses to Muslims; sodomy ("the unnameable sin"); and refusing to eat pork.

Goa being the most notoriously licentious and decadent European enclave in Asia, it wasn't long before the Inquisition's jails began to fill. Deep in the bowels of the Holy Office HQ (known to terrified locals as simply *Orlem Ghor*, "Big House"), suspects spectacular approach to the site, although the vast majority of visitors now travel up the Mandovi from Panjim by road, crossing a three-kilometre-long causeway, the **Ponte de Linhares**, built by slaves in 1633 and reputedly still the longest bridge in South Asia.

Originally, the riverbank was lined with the city's grandest *palacios* and mansions, which contemporary oil paintings show were painted a uniform white, with high-pitched terracotta-tiled roofs and austere fortified facades. Today, none of these remain, although you can get some idea of what they looked like from the Archbishop's Palace, described below, and the gorgeous Casa dos Colçao on the roadside at Ribandar (not open to visitors). Having docked at the main quay (now a barge refitting yard), new arrivals would enter the city walls via the **Viceroy's Archway**, the only fragment of the walls still standing. Made from a mixture of red laterite and green granite, the gate was erected in 1599 by Viceroy Francisco da Gama as a memorial to the his grandfather, the famous explorer Vasco da Gama, whose statue and coat of arms feature on the river-facing side. On the opposite facade, a Bible-carrying figure stands with its feet on the neck of a cringing native, symbolizing the victory of Christianity over "paganism".

Once under the archway, people would head along the Rua Direita (so named because it was allegedly the only straight street in town) towards the civic centre, passing the main bazaar, customs house, foundry and arsenal en route. Only sleepy palm groves line the road today, but when French adventurer François Pyrard walked down it after being shipwrecked in the Maldives in

would be tortured into confessing their heresy. Among the devices used for such purposes were, according to one record, "stretching racks, thumbscrews, leg crushers, holy water, burning sulphur, candles, quicklime and spiked wheels over which the victims were drawn with weights on their feet".

The only surviving first-hand account of the Goa Inquisition is attributed to a French physician named **Charles Dellon**, who found himself at the mercy of the Santo Officio in 1673, aged 24. In the end, his life was spared, but not before he'd endured one of the infamous **autos da fé** – literally "trials of faith" – staged every few years by the Inquisition. His blow-by-blow account of this ordeal, in which he and 150 others were paraded through the city before being told whether or not they would be burned to death, remains a spine-chilling read, not least for its depiction of the grotesque theatricality with which the whole event was enacted. Dellon records how, while the great bell of the Sé Cathedral tolled in the background, the accused were forced to march from Terreiro de Gales square to the Church of St Francis of Assisi, dressed in bizarre outfits of long black-and-white-striped robes, thigh-length yellow tabards and tall mitres daubed with ghoulish images and slogans.

Until 1774 – the point up to which detailed records survive – 16,176 people (an average of 75 per year) were arrested by the Goa Inquisition. The majority of these were Hindus, although of those condemned to death, 71 percent were *Christianos nuevos* of Jewish descent. Its activities were curtailed towards the end of the eighteenth century, but the Inquisition was not fully repealed until 1814, as part of a treaty between the Portuguese and British.

Few remnants of this gruesome chapter in Goa's history survive. The Palace of the Inquisition was pulled down during the shift of the capital upriver, and most of its written records incinerated in 1814. You can, however, sit at the old table used by the Inquisitors for their grim deliberations (see p.72), while the crucifix that formerly hung above it – rendered with open eyes to instil fear into the heart of the accused – can still be seen in a small chapel in Fontainhas, Panjim (see p.71).

1608, he was overwhelmed by the Rua Direita's cosmopolitan prosperity: "on both sides [are] many rich lapidaries, goldsmiths, and bankers, as well as the richest and best merchants and artisans in all Goa: Portuguese, Italians, Germans and other Europeans."

The Church and Convent of St Cajetan

The distinctive domed **Church of St Cajetan**, just south of the Viceroy's Archway, was erected between 1612 and 1661 by the Theatine Order. Sent to India by Pope Urban VIII, the priest-missionaries were refused entry to their original destination, the Sultanate of Golconda, and settled instead in Goa, where they built themselves this miniature replica of St Peter's in Rome, naming it after the founding father of their order.

Like St Peter's, the church's dome, the only one remaining in Old Goa, is partially obscured from below by an imposing Neoclassical facade, pierced by a Corinthian portico and flanked by a pair of square-turreted towers – the only concession made by the Italian architect to local Portuguese taste. Inside, the cross-plan of the building centres on a slab of stone concealing a well, thought to be a remnant of the Hindu temple that formerly stood on the site. St Cajetan is also renowned for its fine **woodcarving**, notably the decoration of the pulpit and the panels surrounding the high altar dedicated to La Divina Providencia. Behind this, a free-standing reredos rests on top of the crypt, where the embalmed bodies of Portuguese governors were once kept in lead coffins before they were shipped back to Lisbon. Forgotten for over thirty years, the last batch (of three) was only removed in 1992.

Adjoining this church is the **Convent of St Cajetan**, recently renovated and now used as a theological college for newly ordained priests. Immediately to its west, a lone-standing grey basalt **doorway**, raised on a plinth and reached by a flight of five steps, is all that remains of the once-grand Islamic **palace of 'Adil Shah**, ruler of Goa until the arrival of the Portuguese. Prior to the construction of the new viceregal Fortress Palace on the waterfront, the 'Adil Shah's building was occupied by the ruling viceroys. Thereafter, the Inquisition took it over, converting its

▲ The dome and twin campaniles of St Cajetan

basement into dungeons. It was here that the Inquisitor and his household lived and worked, while below, suspected heretics such as the Frenchman Dellon (see box, p.82) were held and tortured. This was also where the infamous Inquisitors' table that is now housed in Panjim museum originally resided.

Sections of the palace still stood when the governor decamped downriver to the swish suburb of Panelim in 1754, but these were eventually pulled down for use in the construction of Panjim. Ironically, the Muslim doorway may also have been made from plundered masonry. The decorative work on the lintel is typically Hindu, indicating that the stone must have come from an older temple erected nearby, although the scrollwork was clearly a later Portuguese addition.

The main square and Sé Cathedral

Old Goa's **main square**, originally known as the **Terreiro de Gales**, was formerly used for public hangings, cockfights and as a Portuguese military parade ground. These days, however, its well-watered lawns serve as a picnic spot for bus parties. A stern notice warns visitors (or more particularly "couples") not to "commit unholy acts" in the grounds, under threat of imprisonment or a hefty fine.

Dominating the square's north side is the mighty sixteenth-century **Sé Cathedral**, the episcopal seat of the Archdiocese of Goa and the largest church in Asia. Envisaged by its founder, Viceroy Redondo, as "a grandiose church worthy of the wealth, power and fame of the Portuguese who ruled the seas from the Atlantic to the Pacific", it took eighty years to build. Work on the interior was beset by financial problems and only completed in 1652, when Portuguese fortunes were already in decline. The shortfall was raised from the sale of land belonging to Goan Hindus who died without having converted to Christianity, while foundations were dug into the ruins of a mosque.

Although designed for the Dominican Order, the cathedral takes its cue from Jesuit architecture. The one typically Goan inclusion was the two square **bell towers** flanking the main facade. The campanile still standing on the south side – the other collapsed after being struck by lightning in 1776 – houses the largest bell in Asia, the legendary *Sino do Ouro*, or "**Golden Bell**". During the Inquisition, its tolling announced the start of Goa's gruesome *autos da fé*, held in the square in front of the Sé (now a lawn).

The main entrance opens onto an awe-inspiring **interior**, in which rows of huge pillars separate the broad barrel-vaulted nave from its side aisles. Ahead rises a magnificent reredos, deeply carved and layered with gold leaf. It features six painted panels depicting scenes from the life and martyrdom of **St Catherine**, to whom the Sé is dedicated.

The small shrine nearest the altar on the north wall, known as the Chapel of St Anne, houses relics of the Blessed Martyrs of Cuncolim, whose plucky mission to convert the Muslim court of Mughal emperor Akbar resulted in their execution. Also much revered is the **Cruz dos Milagres**, or "Miraculous Cross", two chapels further down, which pilgrims petition to cure sickness. Housed behind an opulently carved wooden screen, the cross, which allegedly grew from a braid of palm leaves planted in a rock by a local priest, stood in a Goan village until an apparition of Christ was seen hanging from it in 1619. The chapel next to the entrance (also on the north side) contains another famous holy object: the **font** that St Francis Xavier used to baptize new converts.

The Archbishop's Palace

Adjoining the Sé Cathedral, of which it is an exact contemporary, the **Archbishop's Palace** is unique as the last surviving civil building of colonial Goa's golden era. Now restored to its former glory by the Portuguese Fundaçao Oriente, its steeply inclined roofs and white facade perfectly embody the solidity and imposing strength of the so-called "chã" style of architecture, derived from military constructions of the day, of which the most extreme example was the Viceroy's Fortress Palace (Palacio da Fortaleza), which has since vanished without trace. Presenting their most austere aspect to the river, these two fortified palaces formerly dominated the skyline of the waterfront, appropriately enough for a city perennially under threat of attack. These days, the Archbishop's Palace, sandwiched between two of Old Goa's great churches, houses a missable collection of contemporary Christian art in the recently inaugurated **Kristu Kala Mandir** Art Gallery (Tues–Sun 10am–6pm; free) – not to be confused with the similar gallery at the St Monica Convent (see p.90).

The Palace's two grand **entrance porches** remain intact: the one on the right (as you look at the building) is original, complete with red decorative frescoes lining the side walls. During the Portuguese heyday, guards in blue livery would have stood on these steps, as they did in the viceroy's palace and most *hidalgo* houses. Inside, the two huge rooms originally served as an antechamber and audience hall for the archbishop. Both retain their exquisitely carved wooden corner **beams**, intricately decorated with designs of unmistakably Hindu origin.

The Church of St Francis of Assisi

The **Church of St Francis of Assisi**, sandwiched between the cathedral and archeological museum, dates from 1661 but stands on the site of an earlier convent church founded by Franciscans at the beginning of the sixteenth century. Elements of this first building were incorporated into the later one, probably to save money. They include the splendid Manueline doorway, whose heavy ornamentation stands out incongruously against an otherwise plain classical facade. Typical nautical themes include navigators' globes flanking the trefoil arch and a Greek cross above the royal coat of arms, which used to adorn the sails of Vasco da Gama's and other Portuguese explorers' ships.

The **interior** of the church is no longer used for worship, and has a much older and more faded feel than its neighbours. Sculpted tombstones of Portuguese *hidalgos* pave the floor of the nave, while the walls and ceilings are plastered with frescoes and floral patterns rendered in delicate green, pink, yellow and gold. Less successful, but still of interest, are the painted wooden panels lining the chancel next to the high altar, which illustrate the life and teachings of St Francis. The gilt reredos enveloping the east wall of the church centres on two large figures of St Francis and Jesus, beneath which are inscribed the vows of the Franciscan Order: "Poverty, Humility and Obedience".

The Archeological Museum

A wing of the old Franciscan monastery adjacent to the Church of St Francis of Assisi was converted in 1964 into Goa's main **Archeological Museum** (daily 10am–6pm; Rs5), which exhibits a modest selection of pre-colonial sculpture, coins and manuscripts, as well as Portuguese artefacts. Presiding over the main entrance hall is a huge sixteenth-century bronze statue of Alfonso de Albuquerque, the military commander who conquered Goa in 1510. The statue stood in Old Goa but was later shifted to Panjim's municipal square, where it remained until Independence in 1961.

The **first floor** of the museum is given over mainly to a collection of sixty paintings of Portuguese governors. Beginning with the 1527 portrait of Dom João Castro and ending with the right-wing Portuguese dictator Salazar, who was in power at the time of Goa's liberation, none possess much artistic merit, although they do provide a vivid account of formal dress over the centuries – much of it stiflingly unsuitable for the Goan climate. "A couple of generations in the withering heat of the Gangetic plains", wrote William Dalrymple when confronted with these paintings, "turned the great Mughals from hardy Turkic warlords into pale princes in petticoats. In the same way, by the end of the eighteenth century the fanatical Portuguese conquistadors had somehow been transformed into effeminate fops in bows and laces."

Hunt out the wonderful seventeenth-century oil paintings on wood of missionaries and *padrés* meeting sticky ends at the hands of Moluccan natives and wild Hindus, hung in the corner of the far gallery. The stairs near these lead to the monastery cloisters, renovated in 1707 and now the main **sculpture gallery**. Alongside a handful of Islamic inscriptions and hero stones stand several *sati* stones dating from the Kadamba period. These marked the spot where a widow committed suicide by throwing herself on her husband's funeral pyre. *Sati* was outlawed during the British Raj but still occurs – albeit very rarely – in more traditional parts of India, notably Rajasthan. A memorial to a martyr of a different kind is encased in the northwest corner of the courtyard. The centrepiece of this small shrine is a carved stone pillar from Chennai (Madras) in which a fragment of the lance that reputedly skewered the apostle St Thomas (who first brought Christianity to India) was once embedded.

The Chapel of St Catherine

The small but historically significant **Chapel of St Catherine** stands on a stretch of sloping ground immediately west of the museum, hemmed in by palm groves and dense vegetation. An inscription etched on one of its bare laterite walls recalls that the present structure was built in the seventeenth century on the spot where Albuquerque first entered the Muslim city, on St Catherine's Day in 1510. In fact, it replaced an older mud-and-straw church erected by the Portuguese commander as an act of thanksgiving soon after his victory. The building that superseded this was granted cathedral status by a papal bull of 1534, which it retained until the construction of the Sé. Architecturally, St Catherine's is important because its twin-towered facade provided the prototype for the Sé, and thus inaugurated a distinctively Goan style of church design.

The Basilica of Bom Jesus

Site of the world-famous mausoleum of St Francis Xavier, the **Basilica of Bom Jesus**, on the south side of the main square, is India's most revered and architecturally accomplished church, and the logical place to wind up a tour of Old Goa. Work on the building was completed in 1605, sixteen years after the Jesuits were first granted leave to construct a convent on the same spot. In 1964, it became the first church in South Asia to be promoted to a Minor Basilica, by order of Pope Pius XII, and today forms the main focus for Christian worship in the old colonial capital.

The design of the basilica is believed to be derived from the Gesù, the Jesuits' headquarters in Rome, and, with its idiosyncratic blend of Neoclassical restraint and Baroque extravagance, is typical of the late Renaissance, with a sumptuous **facade**, the most ornate in Goa, culminating in the intricately carved and disproportionately large central pediment at the top. This is dominated by the IHS motif, standing for *Iesus Hominum Salvator* ("Jesus Saviour of Men") – a feature of all Jesuit churches. Unusually for Goa, neither the facade nor the rest of the building is whitewashed.

Spanned by a stark, lofty wooden ceiling, the **interior** is positively plain compared with the facade, but no less impressive, dominated by a massive gilt altarpiece and a huge central statue of St Ignatius Loyola, founder of the Jesuit Order, accompanied by the Infant Jesus. As you pass through the main doorway, look for two blue plaques attached to the pillars beneath the choir gallery,

St Francis Xavier in Goa

Visit almost any church or Christian house in Goa, and you're certain to find an image of the state's patron saint, **Francis Xavier**, known locally, and with considerable affection, as "**Goencho Sahib**". The "Apostle of the Indies" was born on April 6, 1506, the son of aristocrats in Navarre, Spain. It was while studying in Paris in his late teens that he met fellow Basque nobleman and future mentor (St) **Ignatius Loyola** (1491–1556), who, after his ordination in 1534, recruited Xavier to be a founder member of the evangelical "Society of Jesus" (*Compañía de Jesús*) – later known as the **Jesuits.**

Around this time, reports were reaching the Lisbon court of the dissolute lifestyle led by Portuguese expatriates in Goa. The king, Dom João III (1521–57), appealed to the Jesuits for help to reverse this moral decline, and when one of the original candidates fell ill, Francis Xavier was asked to lead the mission. He and his delegation arrived a year later, on May 6, 1542, and immediately set to work saving the souls of Goa's wayward colonials.

Xavier founded several churches, schools, a university and printing press and ordained dozens of priests during his first five months. Then he sailed south to evangelize the Parava pearl-fishers of the Malabar Coast, where miracles such as curing the sick and raising the dead with a touch of his crucifix helped him notch up a staggering 30,000 conversions, before heading further east for Malacca and the Spice Islands.

Another brief spell in Goa was followed by two years in Japan, where Xavier tried unsuccessfully to convert the Shinto Buddhists. This was to be his last mission, for, on December 3, 1552, he died of a fever while trying to sneak into China. His body was buried on the deserted island of Sancian, near the mouth of the Canto River, coated with quicklime to hasten its decomposition. However, when the grave was reopened three months later, the corpse was in perfect condition. Reburied in Malacca, it was exhumed again after five months and found to be still incorrupt.

The arrival of Xavier's body in Goa, in March 1554, was greeted by a vast and euphoric crowd, but it was not formally enshrined in the **Basilica of Bom Jesus** until 1622. By this time, several bits of the corpse had been removed by relic hunters: his right arm had been dispatched to the pope in Rome (where it allegedly wrote its name on a pile of papers); one hand had gone to Japan and parts of the intestines to Southeast Asia. By far the most macabre mutilation, though, occurred in 1634 when a Portuguese noblewoman, Dona Isabel de Caron, bit off the little toe of the corpse's right foot. Supposedly, so much blood spurted into the woman's mouth that it left a trail all the way to her house and she was found out.

Once every ten years, the saint's body is carried in a three-hour ceremony from the Basilica of Bom Jesus to the Sé Cathedral, where visitors file past, touch and photograph it. During the last Exposition, in November/December 2004, an estimated 250,000 pilgrims flocked for *darshan* (ritual viewing) of the corpse, these days a shrivelled and somewhat unsavoury spectacle.

The mausoleum in the Basilica also becomes an object of mass pilgrimage on **St Francis Xavier's Day**, December 3. This is the most important event in the calendar of Christian Goa (after the Exposition) and every churchgoer comes at least once, togged out in smart new clothes. The atmosphere at the event is very special, and if you're in Goa at this time it's definitely worth making the trip to mingle with the crowds, listen to Mass being celebrated in Konkani and enjoy the funfair that springs up alongside.

commemorating (in Latin and Portuguese) the inauguration of the basilica in 1605. Midway down the nave on the north wall (opposite the sumptuously decorated main pulpit) stands a memorial to **Dom Jeronimo Mascarenhas**, whose will financed the construction of this church: its panels depict heroic episodes from his career as Captain of Cochin. Swathed in lush gold leaf, the gigantic **reredos**, filling the far end of the nave, remains the basilica's most arresting feature, with spiralling scrollwork, extravagantly carved panels, statues and pilasters illuminated for maximum effect.

The basilica's principal treasure, however, is to be found in the south transept, the **mausoleum of St Francis** (immediately to the right as you leave the Basilica through the door on the right of the main altar). This was installed in 1698, a century and a half after his death, gifted to the Jesuits by the last of the Medicis, Cosimo III (1670–1723), Grand Duke of Tuscany, in exchange for the pillow on which the saint's head was laid to rest. It took Florentine sculptor Giovanni Batista Saggini a decade to design and was made from precious marble and coloured jaspers specially shipped from Italy. Set in the base are four superbly crafted **bronze panels** illustrating scenes from the life of the saint. The huge silver casket mounted on the plinth contains what is left of the body, although it was not part of the Medici endowment but made earlier by Goan silversmiths in 1659. Its sides were originally encrusted with precious stones, but these have long since disappeared.

From the tomb, a corridor leads behind the main altar to the **Sacristy** (daily except Fri 9am–noon & 2–5.30pm), renowned for its beautifully carved wooden door and stone door jamb. On display inside are several chests containing clerical regalia, along with one of St Francis Xavier's toes, which fell off the corpse in 1890. Stairs lead from here, via a room full of garish modern paintings of "Goencho Sahib", to a first-floor gallery where you get a good bird's-eye view of the glass-topped casket and its contents.

The pillory

Goa's **pillory** formerly stood smack in the centre of the city's main square but now occupies a quiet site southeast of the basilica, overgrown with weeds in front of a mildew-covered concrete house. This pair of grey basalt columns, plundered from the ruins of a Hindu temple and mounted on a stepped plinth, once sported a set of iron rings to which criminals were bound, before being flogged and left to dangle for the edification of marketgoers.

The whipping post loomed large in the picaresque life story of one **Fernão Lopes**, a former Portuguese prisoner conscripted to fight with Albuquerque's original expeditionary force. Following the first rout of Muslim Ela, those soldiers who had acquitted themselves bravely in battle were given members of the 'Adil Shah's *zenana*, or harem, as a reward. Contemporary chronicles record that these men became known as *casados*, literally "married", and were subject to widespread derision and harassment for their relations with women deemed to be racially inferior. When clerics declared the alliances immoral, and the administration started arresting the Bijapuri women and handing them over to other men, some of the *casados* – including Lopes – defected to the nearby Muslim outpost at Banastarim, on the far bank of the Mandovi, in order to remain with their wives.

The move backfired, however, after Albuquerque's decisive counterattack of 1510, when Banastarim was captured. Included in the terms of the Muslim surrender was an agreement to hand over the Portuguese "traitors", who were swiftly tried and sentenced to torture by mutilation. The twenty or so *casados* were then lashed to pillories where they had their noses, ears, right hands and left thumbs removed. Half of them died from the wounds, but those who didn't were released and ordered out of Goa (one eventually made it all the way to Cochin, where he is said to have worked as a gravedigger).

Among the surviving *casados* was Lopes, whom the chroniclers surmise must have had a wife and child in Portugal, because at the first opportunity he set sail on a ship bound for Lisbon. He never made it, however. For reasons that have remained a mystery, Lopes jumped ship at the deserted island of **Santa Helena** (the St Helena of Napoleon's later exile) "...and refused to continue the journey". With clothes and supplies left for him on the beach by his companions, he holed up in a cave and somehow, with only four fingers on his left hand, managed to survive a year until a second passing ship dropped off a consignment of provisions, tools, seeds and chickens.

Over the next two decades, it became customary for Portuguese crews to pause at Santa Helena en route to the Indies to see how Lopes was faring – a tradition that over time blossomed into the full-scale colonization of the island. However, Portugal's own true-life Robinson Crusoe was not left to live out his remaining days in peace. Instead, he was seized and forcibly returned to Lisbon. He only returned to Santa Helena to die in 1546, after travelling to Rome to plead for absolution from the pope.

Holy Hill (Monte Santo)

If the heat still hasn't got the better of you by this stage, head west up the lane leading from the bus stand to take in the cluster of monuments on **Holy Hill**. Nestled amid thick vegetation, the first building encountered, to the left of the road, is the **Convent and Church of St John of God**, a late-seventeenth-century structure abandoned after the suppression of the religious orders in 1835. The **Convent of St Monica**, opposite, was at one time the only nunnery in the entire colony. Dating from 1601–27, it burned down in 1636, but was completely rebuilt the following year. These days, the triple-storeyed building looks the worse for wear, with weeds choking its buttressed walls and eroded Baroque stonework, but it is still occupied by nuns from the Mater Dei Institute. You can ask to be shown around the convent by ringing the bell at the main entrance; note the deeply carved Manueline-style reliefs here. Inside, cloisters and a sunken courtyard enclose a small octagonal garden called the **Vale de Lirio**. Although in a dishevelled state, the convent's church, next door, is also worth a quick look, mainly for its fine pulpit and the blue-painted azulejos near the altar. The **cross** behind the high altar is believed to be miraculous; it's said that in 1636 the Christ figure opened its eyes and blood dribbled from its crown of thorns. A row of enigmatic black-faced statues, known as the Black Virgins, once stood beside the main altar. For centuries, iconographers and liturgists argued about where they may have come from and how significant they were, until it was discovered that their black colour was ingrained soot from the countless candles that had been lit at their feet.

Next door to the convent church stands the **Museum of Christian Art** (daily 9.30am–5pm; Rs15). Its collection of antique Roman Catholic art objects ranges from large silver processional crosses to pocket-size ivory ornaments, damask silk clerical robes and some fine wooden icons, mostly dating from the seventeenth and eighteenth centuries. Among the quirkier exhibits is a mobile Mass kit, designed for Goa's missionaries and peripatetic Jesuit priests. Look out too for an unusual statue of John the Baptist wearing a tiger-skin wrap (in the style of the Hindu god Shiva).

At one time the grandest building in the colony, Holy Hill's melancholic **Augustinian Monastery**, opposite St Monica's, now lies in ruins, though the partially collapsed belfry remains one of the city's most distinctive sights. The monastery was founded when the Augustinians arrived in Goa in 1572, and was enlarged using a grant from the king of Portugal thirty years later. However, when the orders were expelled, the monastery and church were deserted and became derelict. The facade finally collapsed in 1942, but its bell was salvaged from the rubble and installed in Panjim's Church of Our Lady of the Immaculate Conception (via Fort Aguada), where it is still in use today.

Continue up the lane past the ruins and you'll soon arrive at the beautifully restored **Chapel of St Anthony**, commissioned in the fifteenth century by

Albuquerque and renovated by the Portuguese the year they were finally kicked out of Goa by Nehru. St Anthony is the patron saint of the Portuguese armed forces, which partly explains why the statue inside the chapel was granted the honorary rank of army captain. The painted figure used to be taken to the Treasury every year in a grand procession to collect its wages – a tradition discontinued by one of the governors, but quickly reinstated after he was nearly killed in an accident on St Anthony's Day.

To reach Holy Hill's most interesting monument, rejoin the path running in front of St Monica's church and follow it west as far as a small clearing. A plaque on the southwest corner of the **Church of Our Lady of the Rosary** records that from this vantage point above the Mandovi, Alfonso de Albuquerque followed the fortunes of the fateful battle of 1510. Erected by him soon after, in fulfilment of a victory vow, the original church was where St Francis Xavier preached on arrival here in 1542. Its successor, completed seven years later, is the oldest complete building in Old Goa, and the sole surviving church "Goencho Sahib" is likely to have visited in person. It also forms the state's best example of Manueline architecture, with unusual rounded towers, tall windows and rope mouldings. Its cruciform interior is unremarkable, except for the marble tomb of **Catarina a Piró**, believed to be the first European woman to set foot in the colony. A commoner (the *Nobilaria*, the Portuguese book of lineage, described her as an "ordinary woman"), she eloped here to escape the scandal surrounding her romance with Portuguese nobleman Garcia de Sá, who later rose to be governor of Goa. Under pressure from no less than Francis Xavier, Garcia eventually married her, but only *in articulo mortis* as she lay on her deathbed. Her finely carved tomb, set in the wall beside the high altar, incorporates a band of intricate Gujarati-style ornamentation, probably imported from the Portuguese trading post of Diu. Garcia's more modest gravestone lies in front of the main altar.

The Church of Our Lady of the Mount

Crowning a thickly wooded hilltop to the east of the city and restored to its former glory by the Portuguese Fundaçao Oriente, the **Church of Our Lady of the Mount** is one of Old Goa's least accessible monuments, but one well worth making the effort to see. The best time to **visit** is just after dawn, when the city's Baroque facades and bell towers are illuminated by the first rays of daylight. To get there, follow the Cambarjua road and turn right up a narrow lane when you reach a small bar. This motorable track winds up the hill, petering out at a car park, from where a flight of old steps runs the rest of the way (see map, p.80).

Our Lady of the Mount was one of three churches founded by Albuquerque after his victory over the Muslim ruler of Goa. The 'Adil Shah's army also mustered on this hilltop prior to their counter-assault on the city in 1510, as recorded by a plaque attached to the west wall of the church. Little of interest is to be found inside, but you could hunt around in front of the main altar for the tombstone bearing a skull and crossbones, which belongs not to a pirate, but to the Portuguese architect **Antonio Alvares Pereira**, who designed the original church.

Chorao and Divar islands

Marooned amid mangrove swamps, shifting sandbanks and waterlogged paddy fields in the Mandovi estuary, the islands of **Chorao** and **Divar** are rarely visited by tourists despite their proximity to Panjim. But if you want to get a taste of rural Goa and haven't time to venture far from the coast, a trip across the river en route to or from Old Goa is worth considering. Passing through a string of tranquil farming hamlets, their peaceful (and mainly flat) lanes are perfect for cycling.

A recommended route, looping from the Ribandar ferry jetty to the Shri Saptakoteshwar temple at **Naroa**, and back across Divar to Old Goa, takes a leisurely three to four hours by bicycle (or one and a half hours by motorbike) and makes a pleasant afternoon jaunt. Alternatively, nip across the Mandovi River from Old Goa to **Piedade**, Divar's largest village, to visit the hilltop **Church of Our Lady of Compassion**, whose terrace affords stunning views south over the former capital and upriver to Panjim.

Chorao Island

Most of the western spur of sleepy **CHORAO ISLAND**, reached by ferry from Ribandar, 5km east of Panjim (every 15min, 6am–10pm; Rs2), has been turned into the **Dr Salim Ali Bird Sanctuary**. Fringed by a dense wall of mangrove swamps, the roadless reserve, which you can only get close to by boat, is home to a healthy and varied population of coastal birds, as well as flying foxes, jackals and the odd crocodile. The grey-brown mudflats around the sanctuary are also a good place to spot one of the region's more unusual fish, the bulbous-headed mudskipper, which, as its name implies, can often be seen leaping through the silt.

Divar Island

Encircled by the Mandovi River, **DIVAR ISLAND** (from the Konkani *dev*, "god", and *vaddi*, "place") was an important religious centre in pre-colonial Goa, with one of western India's most powerful *Shivalingams*. This was smuggled to nearby Naroa, across the river, during the time of the Inquisition (when 1510 islanders were forcibly converted in a single mass event), but the church that now stands on its former hilltop site, together with the crop of elegant old colonial-style houses in the village below, warrants a short foray north from the ruins of Old Goa.

The island can only be reached by **ferry**: from the south via Old Goa's jetty (every 15min; free), or from the north at Naroa (every 20–30min; free). After crossing a flood plain, both roads converge on the island's main settlement, **Piedade**, with its rambling colonial-era houses sporting names like "Vivenda Fernandes" and "Saudades".

Fabulous views extend over Old Goa and the Mandovi from the open ground next to the **Church of Our Lady of Compassion**, rising from a hilltop above the village. Masonry from the Shiva temple that formerly stood here was incorporated into the first Christian structure erected on the site, reportedly seen by Albuquerque from his ship when he returned to Goa for the last time in 1515. But the only surviving traces of the Hindu occupation today lie within the chapel inside the adjacent walled **cemetery,** whose painted plaster ceiling and stone tracery window are thought to be Kadamba remnants.

Ponda

PONDA, 28km southeast of Panjim and 17km northeast of Margao, is the *taluka* administrative headquarters, but not somewhere you're likely to want to hang around. Straddling the busy Panjim–Bangalore highway, the NH-4, its centre is choked day and night with iron-ore trucks and lorries piled with Ponda's most famous export – Kingfisher beer – still brewed in the town.

If you are wondering why most of Divar's inhabitants seem to be women, this is because a large number of its menfolk work abroad. Every January, however, the prodigal sons return home to take part in the **Festa das Bandeiras** ("Flag Festival"), during which they parade around the village waving the flags of their adopted countries. The event is thought to derive from a much older pre-Christian harvest ceremony, in which villagers used to mark the limits of their territory by marching around its boundaries brandishing weapons.

Of the few visitors who stop here, most do so to see the nearby Hindu temples and spice plantations, or to take a quick look at Goa's last surviving sixteenth-century Muslim monument, the **Safa Masjid**, 2km west on the Panjim road. The only sixteenth-century Islamic monument in the region to have survived the excesses of the Inquisition, the mosque was built in 1560 by the Bijapuri ruler Ibrahim 'Adil Shah. It presides over a complex that once included extensive formal gardens and a large palace, but which now lies in ruins beside the highway. Without your own **transport**, the easiest way to get there is by auto-rickshaw from Ponda's main bus stand.

Capped with a more recent pointed terracotta tile roof, the rectangular **prayer hall** rests atop a high plinth, its whitewashed walls decorated with elegant Islamic arches. Surrounding the building are the stumps of several octagonal pillars where a covered courtyard once provided shade for worshippers. The interior, still in use, is plain except for the blind Bijapuri arches of the *mihrab*, or prayer wall, facing west towards Mecca.

Decoration around the sides of the **ablutions tank** mirrors that of the mosque next to it, suggesting that the two were contemporary. A superstition holds that it is dangerous to swim in the murky green water because of the hidden tunnels that are supposed to connect it with a smaller reservoir nearby. Some locals also claim that the Safa Masjid is connected by secret underground passages to a ruined hilltop fort 2km north of here, although none have yet been discovered.

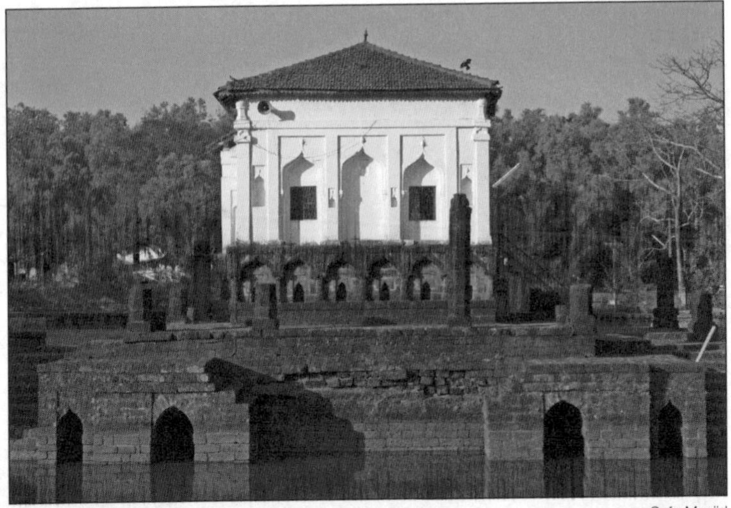

▲ Safa Masjid

Practicalities

Ponda is served by regular **buses** from both Panjim (via Old Goa), and Margao, and lies on the main route east to Karnataka. The town's Kadamba bus stand is situated in the middle of town on the main square, next to the auto-rickshaw rank.

If you find yourself stuck here and in need of a decent room, by far the best option in the centre of town is the anodyne, business-oriented *Hotel Sun Grace*, near the bus stand (Ⓣ0832/231 1238; ❹–❺), which has clean and pleasant rooms, some with air-conditioning, ranged on seven storeys, along with a restaurant and cafeteria. Decent **places to eat** are few and far between, but for a quick pitstop, the pure-veg *Bhonsle*, on the main drag just north of the market area next to the Saraswat Co-Operative Bank, is your best bet, serving a good selection of inexpensive South Indian-style snacks in clean surroundings.

Around Ponda

Scattered among the wooded valleys around Ponda are a dozen or so **Hindu temples** founded during the seventeenth and eighteenth centuries, when this hilly region formed a Christian-free buffer zone between Portuguese Goa and the Hindu-dominated hinterland. Although the temples themselves are fairly modern by Indian standards, their deities are ancient and revered both by local people and the thousands of pilgrims from Maharashtra and Karnataka, who travel here on special "*darshan* tours" to see them.

The shrines are concentrated in two main clusters: the first to the north of Ponda on the busy NH-4, and the second deep in the countryside around 5km west of the town. You would have to be an avid templophile to enjoy a visit to more than half a dozen in a day. Most people only manage the **Shri Manguesh** and **Shri Mahalasa**

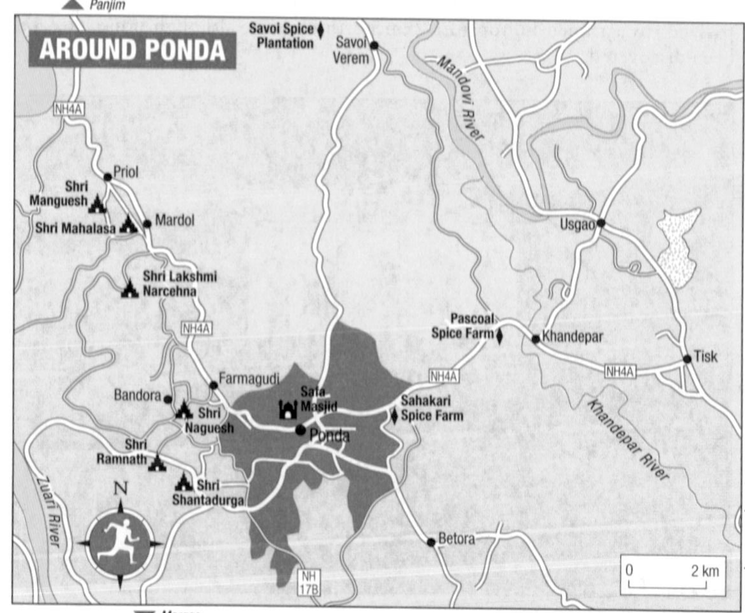

between the villages of Mardol and Priol; both lie a stone's throw from the main highway and are arguably the most interesting. Any of the regular **buses** that run between Panjim and Margao via Ponda drive past them. The others are further off the beaten track, although they are not hard to find on motorbikes: the locals will wave you in the right direction if you get lost. Ponda's auto-rickshaw wallahs also know the way, but expect them to charge for waiting time.

The Shri Manguesh temple

Shri Manguesh *mandir*, 9km northwest of Ponda near the village of **Priol**, is one of the largest, wealthiest and most visited temples in Goa. Its principal deity, a stone *Shivalingam*, was first brought here in the sixteenth century from its previous hiding place on the south bank of the Zuari River at Curtolim, although the present building was erected over two hundred years later. During the time of the Inquisition, devotees from the Old Conquests area used to creep across the Cambarjua Canal under cover of darkness to worship here, knowing that torture, imprisonment or worse awaited them if caught.

Emerging from the forest canopy at the foot of a steep hillside, the temple is approached via a raised walkway through waterlogged paddy fields – land given to the temple by the local raja in the eighteenth century. A flight of steps, lined by flower- and incense-sellers, leads to the main entrance, overlooking a large water tank whose ornamental brickwork is picked out with whitewash. The courtyard inside, hemmed in by modern *argashallas* (pilgrims' hostels) and offices, is dominated by a seven-storey *deepmal*, the most impressive lamp tower in Goa.

The temple itself is a kitsch concoction of Mughal-style domes, Baroque balustrades and pilasters piled around the sides of a grand octagonal sanctuary tower. Its principal deity, Shiva, in his beneficent form, Manguesh, presides over a silver shrine, flanked by a solid gold idol and lit by oil lamps.

The Shri Mahalasa temple

Like Shri Manguesh, the **Shri Mahalasa** temple (Ⓦ www.mahalasa.org/temples/mardol), 7km northwest of Ponda, originally stood in Salcete, but was destroyed in the sixteenth century during a siege by 'Adil Shah's Muslim army after a platoon of Portuguese soldiers had taken refuge in it. The deity survived, having previously been smuggled across the Zuari River to **Mardol**, where it was installed in a new temple. This has been rebuilt or renovated on several occasions since, the last time in 1993–95, when a shiny new *mandapa*, or pillared porch, was added and the courtyard paved with finest Karnatakan marble.

Crowned by rising tiers of red pyramidal roofs, the distinctly oriental Shri Mahalasa is noted for its fine woodcarvings, especially on the pillars supporting the eaves of the main *mandapa*, set above beautiful floral panels. Inside, an ornate ceiling spans deeply carved and brightly painted images of Vishnu's ten incarnations, or *avatars*. The presiding deity here is Vishnu's consort, the black-faced goddess Mahalasa (aka Lakshmi, goddess of wealth and prosperity), who peers out from her silver shrine, swathed in red and yellow silk.

Standing beside the seven-storey, yellow- and white-painted *deepmal* in the courtyard is an unusual brass **lamp pillar**. The column, erected in 1978, symbolizes the Hindu *Axis Mundi*, Mount Kailash, which the gods placed on the back of Vishnu's second incarnation, the tortoise Kurma (featured at the base of the pillar), prior to his epic plunge into the Primordial Ocean. The Preserver's winged vehicle (*vahana*), the half-man half-eagle Garuda, crowns the top of the pillar, whose oil lamps are lit every Sunday evening, after which the temple deity is processed around the courtyard in a palanquin.

Spice plantations

An essential ingredient in Goa's notoriously fiery cuisine, spices were one of the region's principal exports long before Vasco da Gama left the Malabar Coast with a *caravela* full of pepper in 1499. Nowadays, they are grown, along with other cash crops such as cashews, tropical fruit and areca nuts, in several large **plantations** around Ponda. Most package-tour companies offer pre-booked excursions to these farms (check out the excursion board posted in your hotel if you're on a package holiday), combining them with a visit to one or more of the Hindu temples nearby. Local independent outfits (such as Daytripper in Candolim; ⓣ0832/227 6726, ⓦwww.daytrippergoa.com) also run excursions out to the spice gardens (for Rs750–1000 per head), but you can go under your own steam more cheaply, travelling out by taxi or motorcycle.

The tours usually kick off with an introductory talk (and welcome drink of lemon-grass tea), followed by a stroll through the orchards. In keeping with a centuries-old system developed by strictly vegetarian Brahmin farmers, the plantations are divided into three tiers of terraces, stacked up a well-irrigated hillside. Planted at the top in the shade of flowering trees are coconuts, mangoes and jackfruit. Below these come breadfruit, star apples, banana trees, cinnamon and nutmeg; finally, at the bottom, are pineapple and cardamom. In what has become an obligatory photo opportunity, farm workers will also demonstrate how they harvest the areca nuts grown in huge quantities for use in *pan masala*. This involves swinging monkey-style from the top of one spindly tree to the next, brandishing a machete.

Of the four plantations lying within reach of Ponda, the **Sahakari Spice Farm** (ⓣ0832/231 2394, ⓦwww.sahakarifarm.com), just over 1km east on NH-4 (the main Margao–Belgaum–Hubli highway), is the closest to town. Its present custodians, the Sahakari brothers, have been working for more than 35 years to develop organic farming methods here, and the results are impressive, with large-scale compost heaps and methane gas production units (the latter used to fire up their own cashew *feni* stills). They also claim to be unique in Goa for growing vanilla and high-quality herbs for use in ayurvedic medicine, in addition to the usual range of spices, tea and coffee. The tours (Rs500 per head), which start with a traditional shower of marigold petals as you enter, are well organized and last an hour, ending with a slap-up banana-leaf thali. **Elephant rides** are offered as optional extras; visitors are encouraged to wash the tuskers in the plantation stream afterwards.

Ten minutes' drive further east along the main highway, the **Pascoal Spice Farm,** an award-winning twenty-acre organic farm, is an altogether less touristy experience than Sahakari, specializing in coconut, areca, cashews and pineapples. If you're travelling from north Goa, the **Savoi Plantation**, near the village of Keri, 15km north of Ponda, is quicker to reach. Once again, the one-hour tour (Rs500) is rounded off with a sumptuous thali of Hindu-Goan specialities (including delicious jackfruit curry) made from plantation-grown ingredients. Savoi also offers a couple of pleasant rooms in the form of village-style huts for around Rs1500 per double.

None of the plantations require advance booking; tickets can be bought on arrival.

West of the temple, a flight of steps drops down to a laterite-lined **water tank**, overlooked by a large sacred *peepal* tree. The opposite (east) gateway, leading from the courtyard to the main road, is surmounted by a pagoda-roofed musicians' gallery (*naubhat khanna* or *sonddio*), where the instruments used during Shri Mahalasa's *pujas*, Sunday evening promenades and annual *Yatra* are stored.

The Shri Lakshmi Narcenha temple

The secluded **Shri Lakshmi Narcenha** *mandir* at **Velinga**, 3km southwest of Mardol, is one of the more picturesque temples around Ponda. To find it, turn west where the main highway begins its climb up to Farmagudi, and follow the road for 1500m until it reaches Velinga village. The path to the temple starts at the top of the grassy square, in the centre of which stands a modern concrete shrine.

Transferred here from Salcete in 1567, the Lakshmi Narcenha *devta* housed inside this temple is Vishnu in his fourth incarnation as the man-lion Narashima, aka Narayan. However, his shrine and the brightly painted assembly hall leading to it (lined with images of Vishnu's various *avatars*) are of less interest than the beautiful water tank at the far end of the courtyard. Fed by an eternal spring, this is fringed by a curtain of coconut palms, and entered (from the opposite side) via a grand ceremonial gateway. Its stepped sides, used by locals as communal bathing - and *dhobi ghats*, are ornamented with rows of Islamic-arched niches. The squat tower behind is a musicians' gallery.

The Shri Naguesh temple

From the main intersection at Farmagudi, a narrow backroad winds sharply down the sides of a sheltered valley, carpeted with cashew trees and dense thickets of palms, to the **Shri Naguesh** temple at **Bandora**, 2km west of Ponda. This is one of the quietest shrines in the area, with an absence of crowds and knick-knack stalls that makes it all the more inviting. If you are working your way north, note that the temple can also be approached via the road that starts opposite the Shri Ramnath temple (see p.99).

Established at the beginning of the fifteenth century and later renovated by the Marathas, Shri Naguesh is older than most of its neighbours, although stylistically very much in the same mould, with the usual domed *shikhara*, or terracotta-tiled roofs (here surmounted by unusual elephant heads and with peacocks on the corners), and gaudy Goan decor. Lying in its entrance porch is a stately black **Nandi** bull, vehicle of the temple's chief deity, Shiva, here known as Naguesh. Once inside, your eye is drawn to the multicoloured woodcarvings that run in a continuous frieze along the tops of the pillars. Famous all over Goa, these depict scenes from the Hindu epic *Ramayana*, in which the god Rama (Vishnu's seventh incarnation), with the help of Hanuman's monkey army, rescues his wife Sita from the clutches of the arch-demon Ravana. After the great battle, the couple are reunited back home in Ayodhya, as shown in one of the last panels. The silver-doored **sanctum** (*garbhagriha*), flanked by subsidiary shrines dedicated to Lakshmi-Narayan (left) and the elephant-headed Ganesh (right), houses a Shiva *devta*. If you're lucky, you may see it flooded with holy water – a costly ritual performed to cure sickness. Opening onto the courtyard are a couple of accessory shrines. The one on the south side harbours a *lingam* carved with the face of Shiva – a rare form of the god known as Mukhaling. The temple **tank**, whose murky green waters are teeming with fish, is also worth a look, if only to hunt for the donatory inscription (on the wall beside the steps) recording the foundation of the temple in 1413.

The Shri Shantadurga temple

Standing with its back to a wall of thick forest and its front facing a flat expanse of open rice fields, Shri Shantadurga is Goa's largest and most famous temple, and the principal port of call on the region's Hindu pilgrimage circuit. Western visitors, however, may find its heavily European-influenced architecture less than exotic, and barely worth the detour from Ponda, 4km northeast. If you are pushed for time, skip this one and head straight for the temples further north at Mardol and Priol, see p.95.

From the row of souvenir and drinks stalls along the roadside, steps lead to Shri Shantadurga's main entrance and courtyard, dominated by a brilliant white, six-storey **deepmal**. The temple itself, crowned with a huge domed

Goan temples

Stick to the former Portuguese heartland of Bardez, Salcete and Tiswadi *talukas*, and you'd be forgiven for thinking Goa was exclusively Christian. It isn't, of course, as the innumerable brightly painted Hindu temples hidden amid the dense woodland and areca groves of more outlying areas confirm. The oldest-established and best-known **devuls** (from the Sanskrit word meaning "house of God") lie well away from the coastal resorts, but are worth hunting out. Apart from being some of South Asia's quirkiest sacred buildings, they are the main focus of religious life for the state's Hindu majority, offering the chance to experience at first hand traditions that have endured here for over 1500 years.

Goa's first temples were made of wood and mud-brick, and later of stone, during the rule of the Kadamba dynasty between the fifth and fifteenth centuries AD. Fragments of sculpture and masonry unearthed on the site of the ancient capital, Govapuri, suggest these were as skilfully constructed as the famous monuments of the neighbouring Deccan region. However, only one, the richly carved Mahadeva temple at **Tambdi Surla** in east Goa (see p.102), has survived. The rest were systematically destroyed, first by Muslim invaders, and later by the Portuguese. To ensure that the deities themselves did not fall into the hands of iconoclasts, many were smuggled away from the Christian-dominated coastal area to remote villages in the interior, which explains why the greatest concentration of temples in Goa today is among the hidden valleys of Ponda *taluka*, southeast of Panjim.

Architecture

The design of Goan temples has altered dramatically over the centuries, yet without ever ditching the four fundamental features of Hindu architecture. Symbolizing the Divine Mountain from which the sacred River Ganges flows into the world, the **sanctuary tower**, or *shikhara*, rises directly above the **shrine room**, or *garbhagriha*, where the *devta* is housed. This inner sanctum is the most sacred part of the building: only the strictly vegetarian Brahmin *pujaris* (high-caste priests) can cross its threshold, after performing acts of ritual purification. The **main shrine**, flanked by those of the two *pariwar devtas* (accessory deities) and surrounded by a circum ambulatory passage (*pradakshena*), is approached through one or more pillared assembly halls, called *mandapas*, which are used for congregational worship and ritual recitals of music and dance. When the halls are full, the crowds spill outside onto the *prakara*, or courtyard. Finally, adjacent to most temples you will also find a stepped **water tank**, or *tirtha*, in which devout worshippers bathe before proceeding to the shrine.

In addition to these basic components, Goan temples boast some unusual features of their own – some necessitated by the local climate, or the availability of building materials, others the result of outside influences. The impact of European/Portuguese

sanctuary tower, was erected by the Maratha chief Shivaji's grandson, Shahu Raja, in 1738, some two centuries after its presiding deity had been brought here from Quelossim in Mormugao *taluka*, a short way inland from the north end of Colva beach.

The **interior** of the building, dripping with marble and glass chandeliers, is dominated by an exquisitely worked silver screen, embossed with a pair of guardian deities (*duarpalas*). Behind this sits the garlanded Shantadurga *devi*, flanked by images of Vishnu and Shiva. According to Hindu mythology, Durga, another name for Shiva's consort, Parvati, the goddess of peace, resolved a violent dispute between her husband and rival god Vishnu, hence her position between them in the shrine, and the prefix *Shanta*, meaning "peace", that was henceforth added to her name.

architecture (inevitable given the fact that the majority of Goan temples were built during the colonial era, but ironic considering the Portuguese destroyed the originals) is most evident on the exterior of the buildings. Unlike conventional Hindu temple towers, which are curvilinear, Goan *shikharas*, taking their cue from St Cajetan's Church in Old Goa, consist of octagonal drums crowned by tapering copper domes. Hidden inside the top of these is generally a pot of holy water called a **poornakalash**, drawn from a sacred Hindu river or spring. The sloping roofs of the *mandapas*, with their projecting eaves and terracotta tiles, are also distinctively Latin, while the glazed ceramic Chinese dragons often perched above them, originally imported from Macau, add to the colonial feel. Embellished with Baroque-style balustrades and pilasters, Islamic arches and the occasional bulbous Mughal dome, the sides of larger temples also epitomize Goan architecture's flair for fusion.

Always worth looking out for inside the main assembly halls are **woodcarvings** and panels of **sculpture** depicting mythological narratives, and the opulently embossed solid silver doorways around the entrance to the shrines, flanked by a pair of guardians, or *duarpalas*. The most distinctively Goan feature of all, however, has to be the **lamp tower**, or *deepmal*, an addition introduced by the Marathas, who ruled much of Goa during the seventeenth and eighteenth centuries. Also known as *deep stambhas*, literally "pillars of light", these five- to seven-storey whitewashed pagodas generally stand opposite the main entrance. Their many ledges and windows hold tiny oil lamps that are illuminated during the *devta*'s weekly promenade, when the temple priests carry the god or goddess around the courtyard on their shoulders in a silver sedan chair known as a *palkhi*.

Near the *deepmal* you'll often come across an ornamental plant pot called a *tulsi* **vrindavan**. The straggly sacred shrub growing inside it, *tulsi*, represents a former mistress of Vishnu whom his jealous consort Lakshmi turned into a plant in a fit of spite. Hindus also regard a number of trees as auspicious, including the *peepal*, with its spatula-shaped leaves, and the majestic banyan, both of which can invariably be found in the temple courtyard, surrounded by circular pedestals, and bristling with red pennants and small shrines.

Yatras

The most spectacular processions of the year occur during the annual **Yatra** celebrations, when the temple *devta*, together with his or her two principal accessory deities, is hauled around the precinct in a colossal and ornately carved octagonal wooden chariot, or **rath**. The grand promenades, which attract large crowds of locals but few foreign visitors, are accompanied by cacophonic trumpet blasts and drumming from the temple musicians, whose instruments are stored in special galleries known as *sonddios*.

The Shri Ramnath temple

Thanks to the garishly outsize entrance hall tacked onto it in 1905, the **Shri Ramnath** temple, 500m north up the lane from Shri Shantadurga, is the ugly duckling of Ponda's monuments. The only reason you'd want to call in here is to view the opulently decorated silver screen in front of the main shrine, the most extravagant of its kind in Goa. Brought from Lutolim in Salcete *taluka* in the sixteenth century, the *lingam* housed behind it is worshipped by devotees of the Shaivite and Vaishnavite sects of Hinduism, Shri Ramnath being the form of Shiva propitiated by Lord Rama before he embarked on his mission to save Sita from the clutches of the evil Ravana.

Khandepar

Hidden deep in thick forest near the village of **KHANDEPAR**, 5km northeast of Ponda on the NH-4, is a group of four tiny free-standing rock-cut **cave temples**, gouged out of solid laterite some time between the ninth and tenth centuries AD. They are among Goa's oldest historical monuments but are also virtually impossible to find without the help of a guide or knowledgeable local: ask someone to show you the way from the Khandepar crossroads, where the **buses** from Ponda pull in.

Set back in the forest behind a slowly meandering tributary of the Mandovi River, the four caves each consist of two simple cells hewn from a single hillock. Their tiered roofs, now a jumble of weed-choked blocks, are thought to have been added in the tenth or eleventh centuries, probably by the Kadambas, who converted them into Hindu temples. Prior to that, they were almost certainly Buddhist sanctuaries, occupied by a small community of monks. Scan the insides of the caves with a torch (watching out for snakes), and you can make out the carved pegs used for hanging robes and cooking utensils; the niches in the walls were for oil lamps. The outer cell of Cave 1 also has lotus medallions carved onto its ceiling, a typically Kadamban motif that was added at roughly the same time as the stepped roofs.

The Bondla Sanctuary

Of Goa's four nature reserves, the **BONDLA SANCTUARY** (daily except Thurs 9.30am–5.30pm; Rs5, plus Rs50/100 for motorcycles/cars, Rs25 for cameras, Rs100 for video cameras), 52km east of Panjim on the border of Ponda and Sanguem *talukas*, is the least appealing. Encompassing a mere eight square kilometres of mixed deciduous and evergreen forest, its centrepiece is a seedy zoo whose cramped enclosures are guaranteed to disappoint animal and wildlife enthusiasts. On the plus side, Bondla is set amid some magnificent **scenery**. Draped with jungle, a spectacular ridge of hills rises to the southeast, roamed by herds of *gaur* (Indian bison), black-faced langurs, jackals, monkeys, wild boar, several species of deer, pythons, some gargantuan spiders and a handful of elusive leopards. The park is also a bird- and butterfly-spotter's paradise.

Approached from the west via the crossroad settlement of **Usgao**, Bondla's gates open onto a surfaced road which drops down to a parking area and café. Nearby, a small **Interpretation Centre** (daily except Thurs 9.30am–1pm & 2–5.30pm) gives a rundown of Bondla's flora and fauna, and displays natural curiosities, including a whale skeleton. Most visitors proceed from here to the **zoological and botanical gardens**, lured by the promise of elephant rides and the chance to ogle a captive lion or tiger, although its mangy macaques and big cats cooped up in pens are distressing, and you'd be better to head along the lane leading south from the car park. Fording several streams, this road is impassable during the monsoons, but at other times is a safe and scenic short cut to the more inspiring Bhagwan Mahaveer Sanctuary (see opposite) and the railhead for the Dudhsagar waterfalls at Colem, 25km southeast.

Practicalities

Unless you take a taxi, the easiest way to get to the park is to take a **bus** from Panjim or Margao to Ponda, and then jump into a taxi or auto-rickshaw for the remaining 13km. The Forest Department does lay on a minibus service to the sanctuary from the village of **Usgao**, 8km north of the highway, but it leaves at the early hour of 8.30am; check on ⓣ0832/261 0022 to make sure it's running.

Accommodation in Bondla is limited to the Forest Department's plain but pleasant *Tourist Cottages* (ⓣ0832/261 0022; ❸–❹), tucked away under the trees near the park gates, which consist of a dozen self-contained chalets. Rooms here can be hard to come by, especially on weekends and public holidays, so it's a good idea to make an advance reservation through the Forest Department's head office in Panjim, on the ground floor of Junta House (opposite the *Hotel Fidalgo*), Swami Vivekanand Road (ⓣ0832/222 4747).

Inexpensive Goan, Indian and Chinese **food** is available at *The Den* restaurant in Bondla, next door to the *Tourist Cottages*.

The Bhagwan Mahaveer Sanctuary

Bounded in the north by the mountains of the Karnatakan border, the **BHAGWAN MAHAVEER SANCTUARY** encompasses 240 square kilometres of semi-evergreen and moist deciduous woodland, broken with clearings of parched yellow savannah grass and the occasional mud and palm-thatched tribal village. The thick tree cover harbours a diverse array of **wildlife**. However, unless you are prepared (and equipped) to spend days trudging along unmarked forest trails, you will be lucky to see more action than the odd squirrel, as animal numbers were devastated by hunters and poachers during the colonial era. Since the creation of the sanctuary, many species have recovered, but the woods are still eerily quiet compared with reserves elsewhere in India.

Easily Bhagwan Mahaveer's most famous attraction, and an increasingly popular destination for tour groups, are the **Dudhsagar waterfalls** in the far southeast corner of the park, which can only be reached by a memorable jeep journey through some amazing scenery (see p.103). To get to Bhagwan Mahadev other well-known sight, you will need your own transport: the **Mahadeva temple** at Tambdi Surla, Goa's best-preserved ancient monument, lies at the dead end of a windy backroad, crouched at the foot of the Western Ghats. Also worth considering if you have your own car or motorcycle, and plan to spend a night or two in the park, is a visit to **Devil's Canyon**, a picturesque river gorge near Molem. Permission must first be obtained from the park warden, in the **Interpretation Centre** (daily 9.30am–5.30pm), 100m beyond the police checkpost, who will unlock the barrier and give you directions. The canyon itself is a popular picnic spot, particularly during the monsoon season, even though its river is rumoured to be infested with the ominously named "mugger" crocodiles. Another reason not to swim here are the notoriously treacherous and potentially fatal undercurrents. Around the end of the monsoons, if water levels are high, you may find the canyon closed to visitors as a result.

This far-flung corner of Goa is also the homeland of the **Dhangars**, whose traditional livelihood of semi-nomadic buffalo-herding is currently under threat from deforestation, forcing many to take up settled agriculture or migrate to the towns. Alcoholism is also something of a problem among the Dhangars, and the sight of men lying comatose by the roadside clutching an empty bottle is all too common in more remote districts of the park.

Practicalities

The main starting point for the Bhagwan Mahaveer Sanctuary is **Molem**, a fly-blown cluster of truckers' *dhabas*, chai stalls and liquor shops grouped around a crossroads, 28km east of Ponda on the NH-4. Only 10km from the Karnatakan border, this is also the site of a busy police and customs **checkpoint**, and the logical place to stock up on fuel if you are heading east by car or motorcycle; note that you are not technically allowed across the Goan border with a rented bike, although it is usually possible to baksheesh your way past the checkpoint. The nearest railhead is 5km south, at the village of **Colem**, served by four or five daily passenger **trains** from Vasco, Margao and Chandor; beyond Colem, the track remains closed pending the completion of conversion work. All **buses** bound for Belgaum, Hubli, Bangalore and Hospet (for Hampi) also stop at Molem, and there are several daily local services from Ponda. **Transport around the park** (which for most visitors means a return trip to Tambdi Surla, or to the train station) is limited to the handful of auto-rickshaws and jeeps that ply their trade on the Molem crossroads.

The only **place to stay** inside – or anywhere near – the sanctuary is the swanky *Dudhsagar Spa Resort* (Ⓣ0832/2612319, Ⓦwww.sandahotels.com; ❽), near the Molem checkpost, where you can combine trips into the forest with rejuvenating ayurvedic massages. Accommodation here comes in two forms: air-conditioned rooms with all mod cons or luxury Eco-Tents, complete with flat-screen TVs, minibars and huge bath tubs. Bicycles are available for hire, there's a tree-top platform for birdwatching and, if the humidity of the surrounding jungle isn't enough for you, a steam room to work up a sweat in.

Tambdi Surla

Six or seven hundred years ago, the Goan coast and its hinterland were littered with scores of richly carved stone temples. Only one, though, made it unscathed through the Muslim onslaught and the religious bigotry of the Portuguese era. Erected in the twelfth or thirteenth century, the tiny **Mahadeva temple** at **TAMBDI SURLA**, 12km north of Molem in the far northeastern corner of Sanguem *taluka*, owes its survival to its remote location in a tranquil clearing deep in the forest at the foot of the Western Ghats, which enfold the site in a wall of impenetrable vegetation.

Why the Kadamba dynasty, who ruled Goa between the tenth and fourteenth centuries, chose this out-of-the-way spot remains a mystery: no traces of settlement have been unearthed in the vicinity, nor did it lie near any major trade route. Yet the temple, dedicated to Shiva, was clearly important, built not from malleable local laterite but the finest weather-resistant grey-black basalt, carried across the mountains from the Deccan Plateau and carved *in situ* by the region's most accomplished craftsmen. Their intricate handiwork, which adorns the interior and sides of the building, is still astonishingly fresh and stands as a poignant memorial to Goa's lost Hindu architectural legacy.

Facing east – so that the rays of the rising sun light its deity at dawn – the temple is composed of a *mandapa*, or pillared porch, with three stepped entrances, a small *antaralhaya* (vestibule) and *garbhagriha* (shrine) surmounted by a three-tiered sanctuary tower, or *shikhara*. The tower's top section has collapsed, giving the temple a rather stumpy appearance, but the carving on its upper sections is still in good shape. As you walk around, look out for the beautiful **bas-reliefs** that project from the sides. These depict the gods of the Hindu trinity, Shiva (north), Vishnu (west) and Brahma (south), with their respective consorts featured in the panels above. In addition, bands of delicate carving pattern the sides of the porch, capped with an oddly incongruous roof of plain grey sloping slabs.

After a purifying dip in the river immediately east of the temple, reached via a flight of old stone *ghats* (sacred steps), worshippers would proceed to the main

mandapa for *darshan*, the ritual viewing of the deity. In its centre stands a headless Nandi bull, Shiva's *vahana* (vehicle), surrounded by four matching columns, one of whose bases bears a relief of an elephant trampling a horse – thought to symbolize the military might of the Kadamba dynasty. The building's finest single piece of stonework, however, has to be the intricate lotus motif carved out of the *mandapa*'s ceiling. Flanked by four accessory deities that include a damaged dancing goddess (left) and an elephant-headed Ganesh (right), the pierced-stone screen surrounding the door of the vestibule comes a close second. The shrine itself houses a stone *Shivalingam*, mounted on a pedestal.

To get to Tambdi Surla under your own steam, head north from the Molem crossroads and bear right when you reach the fork in the road after 4km. The next right turn, 2km further north, is signposted. From here on, the route is winding but easy to follow and very scenic, passing through a string of picturesque villages and long stretches of woodland. If you are coming from Ponda on the NH-4, note that it is quicker to approach Tambdi Surla via the hamlet of Sancordem: turn left off the highway 5km east of Tisk and carry on until you reach the fork mentioned earlier; again, signposts have been erected to guide visitors.

Despite its remoteness, Tambdi Surla sees large numbers of visitors, especially on weekends, when it becomes the target for numerous school trips – so if you want to enjoy the site's essential tranquillity come during the week. An additional threat to the peace and quiet of this forest area is the presence along the approach road of two "**jungle camps**" set up by rival outside entrepreneurs to lure groups of charter tourists from the north Goan resorts. Elephant rides are their main selling point, but they also employ the long-suffering tuskers to play afternoon football matches, dressing them in national team colours and giving them names like Beckham and Ronaldinho.

Dudhsagar Falls

Measuring a mighty 600m from head to foot, the famous **waterfalls** at **DUDHSAGAR**, near the easternmost edge of Sanguem *taluka* on the Goa–Karnataka border, are the second highest in India, and a spectacular enough sight to entice a steady stream of visitors from the coast into the rugged Western Ghats. After pouring across the Deccan Plateau, the headwaters of the Mandovi River form a foaming torrent that fans into three streams, then cascades down a near-vertical cliff face, streaked black and dripping with lush foliage, into a deep green pool. The Konkani name for the falls, which literally translated means "sea of milk", derives from clouds of mist kicked up at the bottom when the water levels are at their highest between October and December.

Overlooking a steep, crescent-shaped head of a valley carpeted with pristine tropical forest, Dudhsagar is set amid dramatic scenery, making the jeep journey there an unforgettable experience. On arrival at the falls themselves, spanned by an old viaduct, you'll probably be pestered by lads offering to show you the way to the river and to protect you from the monkeys that scamper around the place trying to pilfer food from picnickers. The path is steep and slippery in places, but you won't need a guide to find it: just head back along the rails from the train platform and turn right when you reach the gap between the two tunnels. After a fifteen-minute scramble, the trail emerges at a shady **pool** hemmed in by large grey-brown boulders – an ideal spot for bathing. If you want to escape the large groups that congregate here, clamber over the rocks a little further downstream, where there are a number of more secluded places to swim and watch the amazing butterflies and kingfishers that flit past.

A more strenuous way to while away a few hours before catching the jeep back is to climb to the head of the falls. This arduous hour-long hike is relentlessly steep and impossible to follow without the help of someone who knows the path, but well worth the effort for the superb views from the top.

Practicalities

The best time to visit Dudhsagar is immediately after the monsoons, from October until mid-December, although the falls flow well into April. Unfortunately, the train line, which climbs above the tree canopy via a series of spectacular cuttings and stone bridges, only sees three services per week in each direction (Wed, Sat & Sun; depart Margao 7.15am), none of them returning the same day. As a result, the only practicable way to get there and back is by four-wheel-drive **jeep** from **Colem** (reachable by train from Vasco, Margao and Chandor, or by taxi from the north coast resorts for around Rs1750). The cost of the onward thirty- to forty-minute trip from Colem to the falls, which takes you across rough forest tracks and three river fords, is around Rs1000–1250 per person; the drive ends with an enjoyable ten-minute clamber over the rocks, for which you'll need a sturdy pair of shoes. Anyone with a back problem should think twice about attempting this as few of the jeeps retain any suspension and the track is horrendously bumpy.

Finding a jeep-wallah is easy; just turn up in Colem and look for the "**Controller of jeeps**" on the opposite side of the tracks from the station. However, if you're travelling alone or in a couple, you may have to wait around until the vehicle fills up, or else fork out a ludicrous Rs4000 to cover the cost of hiring the whole jeep yourself. Alternatively, if you've travelled here **by motorcycle** you may – water levels permitting – ride to within easy reach of the falls: Enfields and Pulsars have enough clearance to ford the streams en route, but not Honda Activas and other small-wheeled scooters. Anyone who's ridden all the way to Colem on one of those, and is determined not to stump up the jeep fare, should follow the dirt track that runs alongside the main railway line for approximately 8km until it meets the jeep route, thus bypassing the stream crossings – local stallholders make this journey each day.Note that it can be difficult to arrange transport of any kind from Molem crossroads, where regular taxis are in short supply.

In recent years, GTDC, a number of resort hotels and some tour agents have also been offering Dudhsagar as an **excursion**. The all-in price of the trip, which starts at the crack of dawn and finishes around 8pm, usually includes the minibus or taxi fare to Colem, the jeep trip to and from Dudhsagar, guides and a packed lunch. If you rent a car, it's also possible to combine a visit to Dudhsagar with a detour to the Mahadeva temple at Tambdi Surla.

2

North Goa

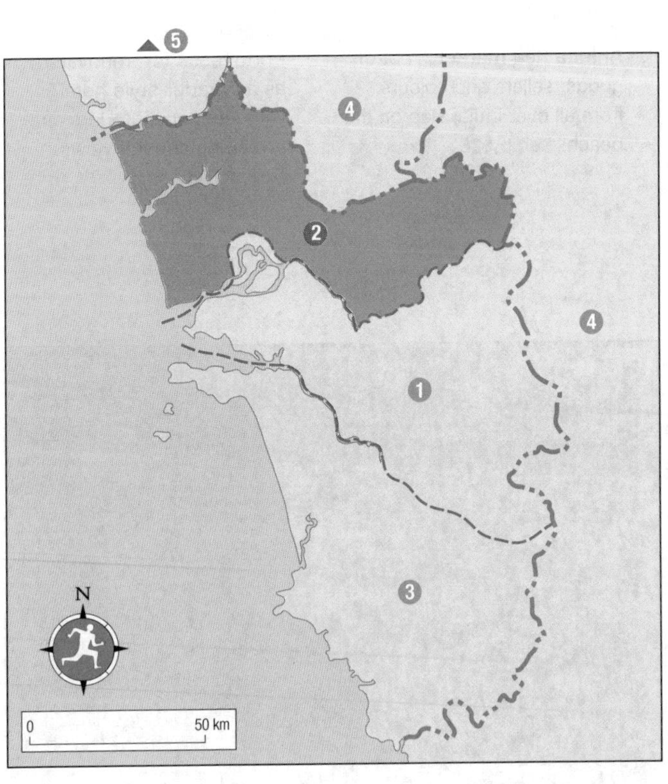

CHAPTER 2 Highlights

* **Boat excursions** Dolphin-spotting tours, backwater cruises and fishing trips all run off the north coast. See p.121
* **Saturday night markets** Far cooler in every sense than the flea market, and the best place for souvenir hunting. See p.132
* **Anjuna flea market** A riot of goods, sellers and colours from all over India, slap on the beach. See p.136
* **Aswem** North Goa's quietest stretch of coast – perfect for a sunset stroll. See p.149
* **Liquid Sky** Optimum venue for Goa Trance and dance, complete with sparkling sound system and an appropriately blissful view. See p.150.
* **Terekol** A historic Portuguese fort renovated as a parador-style hotel, with luminous interiors and sweeping coastal views. See p.156

▲ Saturday Night Market

2

North Goa

Beyond the mouth of the Mandovi estuary, the Goan coast sweeps **north** in a near-continuous string of beaches, broken only by the odd salt-water creek or rocky headland and by three tidal rivers – the northernmost of which, the Arondem (also known as the Tirakol), still has to be crossed by ferry. The most developed resorts in this district, known as **Bardez** *taluka*, all lie within a forty-minute drive of Panjim. Spread behind a seven-kilometre strip of golden sand, the **Candolim-Calangute-Baga** belt is, after nearly two decades of headlong development, firmly in the grip of tourism, its sand crammed nose-to-tail with sunbeds and shacks.

The alternative scene, meanwhile, gets into its stride at **Anjuna**, the next sizeable village up the coast from Baga. Scattered around paddy fields behind a white-sand beach, Anjuna is famous primarily for its Wednesday **flea market**, and the **trance music** scene that formerly held sway here. Since the 2YK clampdown by the Goan government, however, what survives of the state's vestigal party scene has drifted north along the clifftops to neighbouring **Vagator** and **Chapora**, where a couple of small dance venues keep the rave flame flickering in the shadow of a splendid laterite fortress.

Accommodation is thinner on the ground once you cross the Chapora River into the mainly Hindu *taluka* of **Pernem**. Development up here has been held in check by local planning laws, but has recently started to ribbon the coast road following the arrival in the area of large numbers of free-spending Russian tourists, most of whom congregate in the dunes backing **Morjim** beach – an important nesting site for marine turtles.

The impact of the rouble dwindles as you move north to the more culturally mixed resorts of **Aswem** and **Mandrem**, where a band of hut camps and shack cafés nestling under the palms forms the focus of a more sedate, family-oriented, holiday scene. **Arambol**, the largest coastal village in Pernem, also attracts the lion's share of visitors to the district – a mix of young Russians and Israelis, and yoga-centric northern Europeans. The beach here's broad enough to encompass the diverse crowd, and there's a lively café scene to keep you occupied in the evenings, with lots of live music on offer.

The **interior** of north Goa – through Bardez and Pernem to Bicholim and Satari *talukas* – harbours few sights likely to entice you from the coast, although the colourful Friday market at **Mapusa**, this area's hub town, definitely deserves a morning. Further east, the winding rivers and rolling hills harbour a string of old churches, temples and a single Portuguese fort (at **Corjuem**), all of which have been completely untouched by developments on the coast and make for a rewarding "off-piste" excursion.

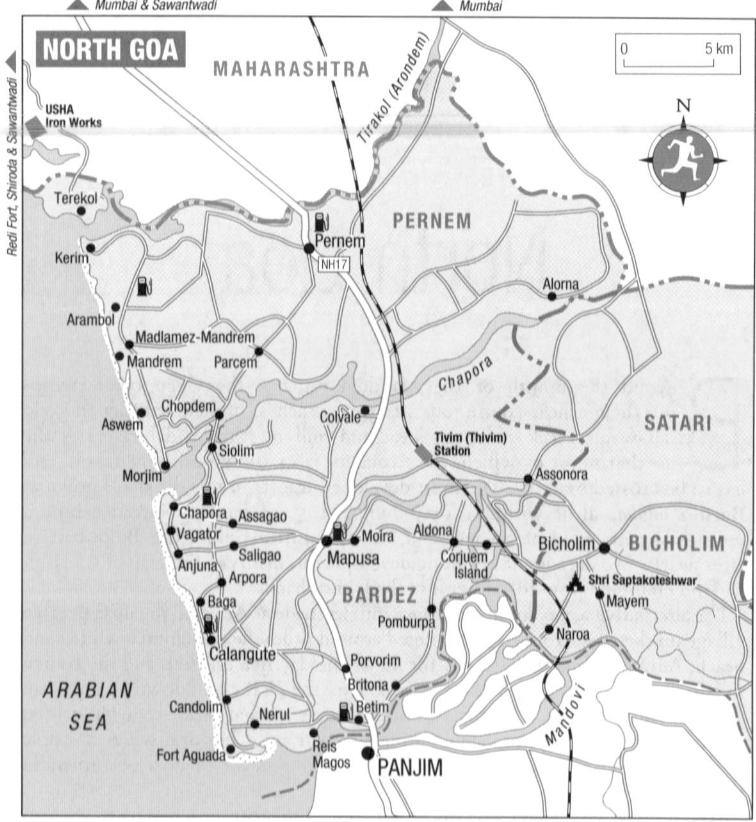

Also of historical interest is the Maratha fort at **Terekol**, at the northernmost tip of the state, from where you can continue north into Maharashtra (covered in Chapter 4 – see p.209). Just south of Candolim, the Portuguese fort at **Aguada**, whose imposing laterite battlements afford fine views up the coast, also warrants a side trip, while nearby **Reis Magos** boasts a sixteenth-century bastion and church dating from the earliest days of the Portuguese colony.

None of these sights should be considered unmissable, but getting to them via winding backroads lined with fragrant cashew bushes and paddy fields can be a lot of fun, yielding a strong sense of what Goa must have been like thirty or forty years ago.

Mapusa

With a population approaching 40,000, **MAPUSA** (pronounced "Mapsa"), the district headquarters and main transport hub of Bardez *taluka*, is the state's third largest town. A dusty collection of dilapidated modern buildings scattered around the west-facing slope of a low hill, the centre is of little more than passing interest in itself, although it does host the Goa's liveliest **market** (whence the town's name, which derives from the Konkani words for "measure", *map*, and "fill up", *sa*). Anjuna and Arpora's Saturday night bazaars may be better stocked with souvenirs, but this offers an altogether more authentic shopping experience, especially on Fridays, when locals from across Bardez Pernem come to buy and sell essentials, from fresh fish, fruit and veg to scooter parts and football shirts. The majority of stallholders are women from the surrounding villages, squatting in the shade of torn umbrellas. Local specialities to look out for include strings of spicy Goan sausages (*chouriço*), bottles of *toddi* spirit and the large green plantains grown in the nearby village of Moira.

For **books**, check out the excellent Other India Bookstore (Ⓣ0832/226 3306), hidden away behind Mapusa Clinic, which holds a vast range of titles relating to ecology, the environment and Goa in general; a full stock list is available online at Ⓦwww.otherindiabookstore.com.

Whatever you're looking for in Mapusa market, it's a good idea to arrive as early in the morning as possible to beat the heat; after 11am temperatures can be stifling.

Practicalities

Tivim (Thivim), the nearest **railway station** to Mapusa, is 12km east in neighbouring Bicholim district. Buses are laid on to link with arriving trains, but don't always show up; in which case jump in an auto-rickshaw or taxi.

Arriving by **motorbike**, bear in mind that traffic can be overwhelming on Fridays, and you should make a note of your registration number, as the bike parking areas along the main routes get filled with hundreds of lookalike vehicles by mid-morning, which can make it difficult to find yours again when you come to leave.

Buses drop passengers at the main Kadamba stand, just below the town's square, the **Municipal Gardens**, where there's a dependable petrol pump and ranks of motorcycle "pilots" touting for trade. If you're travelling in by taxi, ask to be dropped somewhere where you'll easily be able to meet up with your driver again afterwards, such as outside the Maruti temple or *GTDC Mapusa Residency*.

With Candolim, Calangute, Baga and Anjuna only a short bus or taxi ride away, there's no reason to stay in Mapusa, which is just as well as **accommodation** in the town in uniformally ropey. There are, however, plenty of good **places to snack** between bouts of shopping, the most famous among them *FR Xavier* café in the middle of the Municipal Market complex (opposite the banana section). Little changed since Portuguese times, it serves scrumptious veg patties and beef "chops" (rissoles), as well as spicy meals of fish, prawn and chicken curry, and other Goan standards such as *cafreal* and *xacuti*. Apart from the fresh fruit and juice bars dotted around town, the other commendable place to refuel is the inexpensive *Hotel Vrindavan*, on the east side of the main square, which dishes up Mapusa's best South Indian snacks – masala dosas, *wadas*, pakoras and the like – along with an impressive range of ice creams, sundaes and shakes.

Inland from Mapusa

The countryside rolling **east of Mapusa** towards the Western Ghats couldn't be more different from the coastal strip of Bardez. Clustered around whitewashed churches, villages of widely scattered Portuguese-era houses stand in the shade of areca palms and giant mango trees, overlooking slow-flowing rivers whose winding courses repeatedly challenge your sense of direction. This is where all those men and women you see riding scooters in formal wear through Mapusa

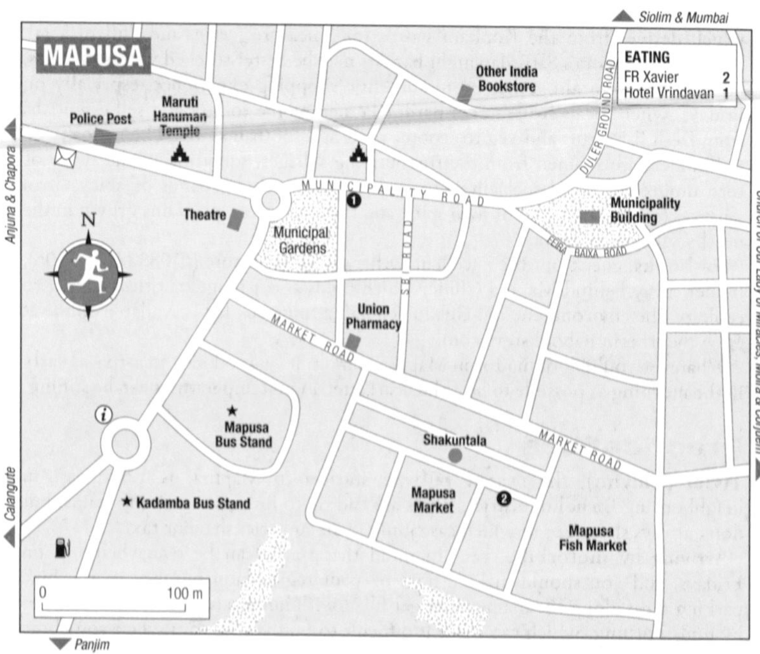

gratefully return to at the end of their working day. The new suspension bridge at Corjuem may well unlock its real-estate potential over the coming decade, but for the time being the area remains a sleepy backwater, full of traditional Goan character.

The route sketched out below begins in Mapusa and takes you in a wide loop through the villages of **Moira** and **Aldona** – both blessed with wonderful old churches – to the Portuguese fort on **Corjuem Island**. From there, you can either press on to Bicholim *taluka*, where the Shri Saptakoteshwar temple at **Naroa** houses one of Goa's most revered Shiva deities, or else backtrack and head south along the banks of the Mapusa River towards Panjim, stopping at a string of picturesque Christian villages en route.

Moira, Aldona and Corjuem

From Mapusa, finding your way to the road for the villages described below can be tricky. Start on the main drag running past the market from the bottom of the Municipal Gardens square and keep heading east (away from the centre), stopping periodically to ask the way to Moira, and you'll end up on the right track.

The first landmark, on the eastern fringes of town, is **Nossa Senhora de Milagres** (Our Lady of Miracles) church. Originally built on the site of a Hindu temple in 1594, it harbours three ornamental altar screens from Old Goa that are regarded as the most vivid of their period, painted in naive style. The church's other claim to fame is that in 1961, during the Indian army's "liberation" of Goa, its roof was blown off during an attempt to sabotage nearby Marby bridge.

The approaches to **MOIRA** take you through the large banana plantations from which the area's famous plantains originate; if you've been to Mapusa's Friday market you'll have seen the huge fruit, which become dark red-brown when ripe, piled in heaps. They were grown here centuries before the Portuguese erected the stately **Our Lady of the Immaculate Conception** on a prominent platform at the edge of the village in 1636. Like its neighbour in Mapusa, the church contains several treasures salvaged from Old Goa after the holy orders were expelled and the former capital was being dismantled piecemeal for building materials. In this instance, a massive bell (requiring the construction of a new belfry to accommodate it) and fine crucifix (installed in the adjacent mortuary chapel) were acquired from a seminary on Holy Hill.

ALDONA, 5km east of Moira, ranks among the prettier villages in Bardez, with dozens of houses with deep verandas spread over a hillside that falls away sharply to the Mapusa River. A new road bridge now connects it with its equally picturesque neighbour **CORJUEM**, where a compact little **Portuguese fort** made of pitted laterite rises from a hilltop overlooking the former colonial border. One of only two surviving inland forts, it protected Portuguese territory from attack by the Marathas and marauding Rane Rajputs in the early eighteenth century.

Inland hideaways

The deep **interior of Goa**, and the mountainous region lining the state's border with neighbouring Karnataka shelter **some gorgeous places to stay**, where you might wish to break a foray inland from the coast.

Part of the chic Casa chain of boutique hotels, **Casa Colvale** is the most alluring of the bunch. Situated in the village of Colvale, fifteen minutes' drive north of Mapusa on NH-17 (ⓣ0832/229 9021/28, ⓦwww.casaboutiquehotels.com; ⓽), it occupies an elevated position deep in the countryside, with an idyllic view of winding tropical rivers, coconut plantations and rice fields. Accommodation consists of two bungalows: the first, with four bedrooms, enjoys a 180-degrees panorama from the edge of a laterite cliff; the other, a five-bedroom house, sits on the riverbank below. Both are sumptuously furnished in contemporary style, with original Goan art on the walls, and have big verandas, plus access to a dreamy overflow swimming pool. The food is as wonderful as the setting, and there's a spa on site. Deluxe double rooms, with breakfast included, cost Rs9000–15,000 ($203–338) according to season.

Keep heading deeper still inland, as far as the former Portuguese border post of Corjuem (see p.111) and you'll come to **Panchavatti** (ⓣ9822/580632, ⓦwww.islaingoa.com; ⓽), dream home of British-Belgian expatriate Loulou Polak, who sold her art imports business in Brussels and built a palace here on a hilltop instead. For a change of scene from the stylish guest rooms, fitted with fine Indian handicrafts and textiles, you can lounge on a long, shady veranda extending the length of the building, where Hindu and Christian votive statues gaze out across rolling paddy fields and hills. There's a luxurious pool, in-house masseur and gourmet kitchen serving cuisine as hybrid as the architecture. Full board for two, including all meals, costs Rs10,000–12,000 ($225–270).

A resort hotel would have to be very special indeed to tempt you all the way into the heart of the mountains along the Karnatakan border, and **Wildernest** (ⓣ0934/111 2721 or 08314/207954, ⓦwww.wildernest-goa.com; ⓽) is exactly that. Swathed in rich old-growth forest, this self-styled "Eco-Resort" rests on a terrace at an altitude of 816m, looking across the tree tops and nearby waterfalls to the plains in the distance – a spellbinding vista best enjoyed while sipping a cocktail in the hotel's infinity pool. The rooms are environmentally friendly thatched structures built of acacia wood and other local materials, but fitted with huge glass windows, luxury beds and all the mod cons of a star hotel. Aside from the location, the main incentive to stay here is that *Wildernest* is well set up for hikes and wildlife-spotting expeditions into the surrounding hills; the hotel has its own resident guides. Rates are in the range Rs3500–7000 ($79–157) per double depending on the season.

Plans are afoot to give the building a facelift as part of a more general promotion of this area by the local tourism corporation; in the meantime, it remains one of Lusitanian Goa's most atmospheric architectural oddities, redolent of the era when this was a lonely outpost on a hostile frontier.

Naroa

Head straight across Corjuem Island and you'll eventually arrive at a second, smaller river bridge, from where the road continues west to **Mayem** village. A right turn here will, after around 5km, bring you to **NAROA**. Hidden in a wooded valley on outskirts, the **Shri Saptakoteshwar temple** shelters an aspect of the god Shiva in the form of a *lingam*. The deity has a long and turbulent history. Cast from seven separate metals ("an alloy of the unalloyable"), it is believed to have been made by seven sages, known as the **Saptarishis**, after Shiva himself had appeared to them at the end of a seventy-million-year fast. Patronized during the fourteenth century by the Kadamba royal family, the shrine housing it, at Narve on Divar Island, was demolished in 1560 by the Portuguese – its masonry plundered to build the church in Piedade – after which the *lingam* was used as a well shaft until a party of Hindu marauders managed to rescue it. The idol was then smuggled across the river to Bicholim, where it was installed in a brand-new temple revamped in 1668 by the Maratha rebel leader Shivaji.

With its shallow Mughal dome mounted on an octagonal drum, sloping tiled roofs, European-style *mandapa* (assembly hall) and tall lamp tower, the present structure is regarded by art historians as the prototype of the modern Goan temple. Its **interior** is plain by Indian standards. Vaulted arches line the marble-floored hall, entered beneath an equestrian mural of Shivaji, and although the wood-panelled shrine lacks the conventional embossed silver surround, its glaring-eyed golden *devta* is very fine.

From Naroa, it's possible to cross the nearby Mandovi to **Divar Island** (see p.92) and continue from there to Old Goa. Alternatively, backtrack to Aldona and head southwest along the banks of the Mapusa River via the route described below.

Pomburpa and Britona

The road running south from Aldona to Panjim rejoins the banks of the Mapusa River at **POMBURPA**, where the church of **Our Lady Mother of God** (Nossa Senhora Mãe de Deus) occupies a shelf cut into a low hill. If it's open, have a peek inside at the fantastically elaborate Rococo reredos, riddled with gold leaf, cherubs and scrollwork.

A ferry crosses here to Chorao Island (see p.91), but it's worth continuing on the main road southwest to see another wonderful church, **Our Lady of Rock of France** (Nossa Senhora de Penha de Franca), in the village of **BRITONA**. Rising dramatically up from the riverbank, its facade looks out across the confluence of the Mapusa and Mandovi rivers to Old Goa, whose belfries and domes are just visible in the distance. Listening to the waves slapping against the bottoms of fishing canoes moored nearby, it's not hard to picture the scene as it must have looked in the heyday of empire, with merchant vessels standing off mid-stream and the opposite banks lined by ranks of stately Portuguese mansions. The church's presiding Madonna – named after a mountain peak in Spain that was captured from the Moors during the Reconquest and which later became famous as the site of a vision – was traditionally carried on long voyages by sailors to protect their ship from danger. In times past, seamen would pray in the church before leaving Goa.

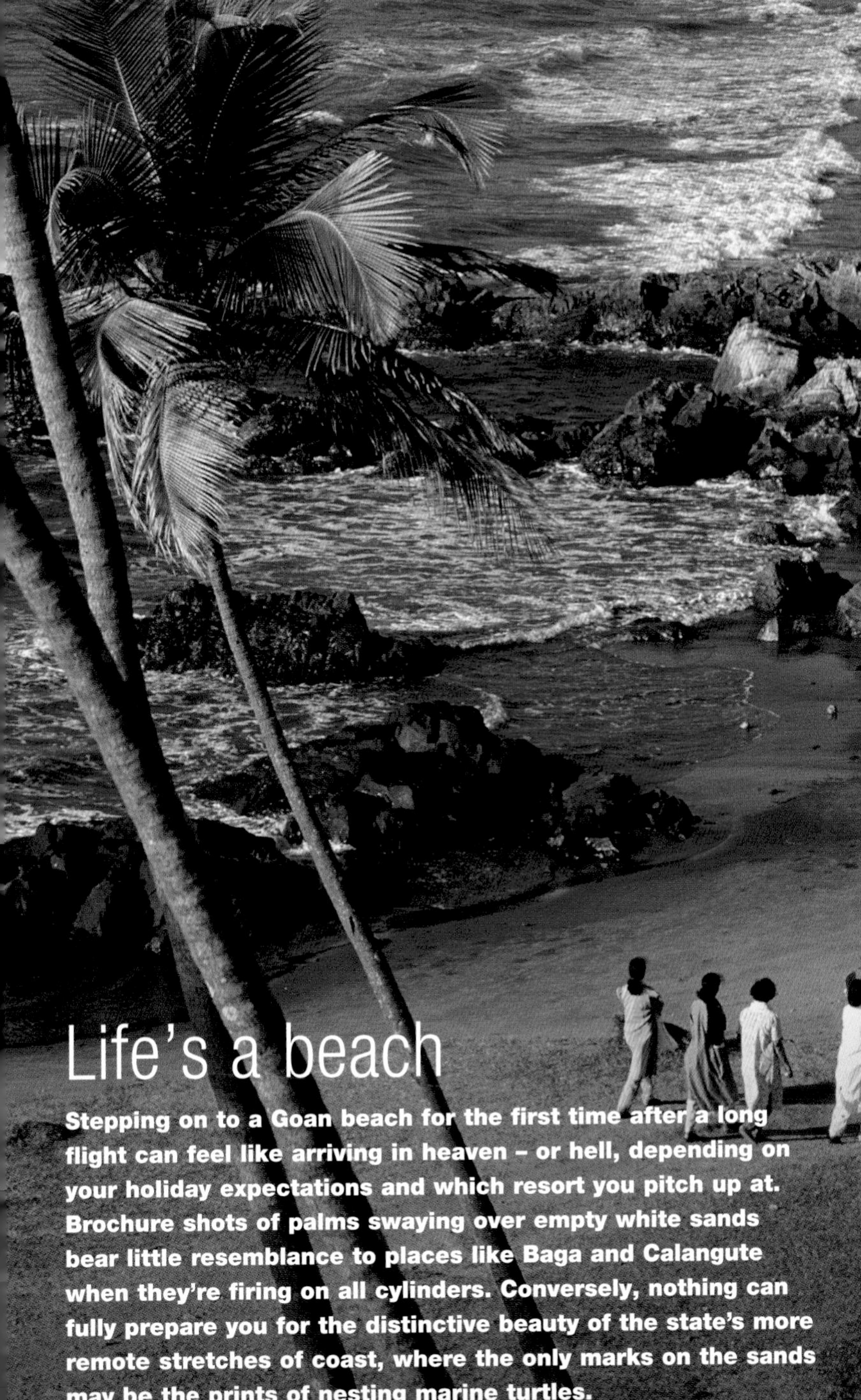

Life's a beach

Stepping on to a Goan beach for the first time after a long flight can feel like arriving in heaven – or hell, depending on your holiday expectations and which resort you pitch up at. Brochure shots of palms swaying over empty white sands bear little resemblance to places like Baga and Calangute when they're firing on all cylinders. Conversely, nothing can fully prepare you for the distinctive beauty of the state's more remote stretches of coast, where the only marks on the sands may be the prints of nesting marine turtles.

Fish drying ▲

Porter landing trawler catch, Colva ▼

Fishy business

One element common to all Goan beaches, however large or small, touristy or undeveloped, is **fishing**. Around 50,000 locals scratch a living from the shoreline's diminishing fish stocks, and their activities provide an endless source of fascination for visitors. Seemingly oblivious to the early-morning yoga sessions on Palolem beach, or the hard-core fitness routines of Russian tourists at Morjim, teams of men in shorts and cotton *tangas* file out of the palm groves to haul on coir ropes attached to huge nets. It's heavy work that lasts for over an hour, at the end of which their wives show up in vibrant red, orange and green saris to argue over who gets what, and then pile the catch into baskets which they carry home on their heads, while the men carefully coil the nets to dry on the sands.

Visitors are more than welcome to lend a hand (though don't expect to be offered a share of the spoils). If, however, you happen to be within eyeshot when the tide's on the turn, you'll be badgered to help heave fishing **boats** in and out of the water. Goan boats are splendid beasts, particularly the wooden outriggers lining Benaulim and Varca beaches. Made of rough mango and jackwood planks bound together with no more than coir, tar and painted prayers, they stand on the sands, staring impassively seawards as tourists cycle, jog and stroll past, and crows leave impertinent white streaks on their lovingly decorated, garlanded bows.

In-shore fishing is nevertheless a hard way to earn a living – and a dangerous one. Just how dangerous was underlined in November 2009, when three fishermen from Benaulim died after their boat was swept out to sea by a cyclone.

Beach traffic

Nod off for a second on any Goan beach these days and you can be sure your doze will be ruptured by the appearance of someone selling something, regardless of how much you appear to want it, or not: cheap cotton *lunghis*, baggy beach shorts, slices of watermelon, jewellery, a massage, hand-propelled helicopters that light up in the dark and talking drums are the most common goods on offer. But there are wackier sights too, such as itinerant magicians, slack-rope walking toddlers and outlandishly decorated sacred bulls led around by their turbaned, *shennai*-blowing owners.

The **hawkers** tend to wander home towards late afternoon, leaving the tourists and local fishermen casting lines into the surf to enjoy the sublime colours of the Goan sunset in relative peace. When darkness descends, the shack owners switch on their fairy lights, crank up their sound systems, and wait for sun-weary visitors to show up.

Unfortunately, the bright light spilling over the sands these days plays havoc with the local turtle population: hatchlings heading out to sea are often drawn off course by them. Electric light also masks one of the most magical features of Goa's beaches. Splash around in the inky sea on moonless nights, beyond the reach of the shacks' bright bulbs, and you'll be covered in glowing particles that explode into clouds when you move your arms quickly underwater. This **phosphorescence**, caused by a kind of luminous algae, is becoming inexplicably more rare: only once every six or seven years does it appear in such strength that entire waves glow a vivid green when they break at night.

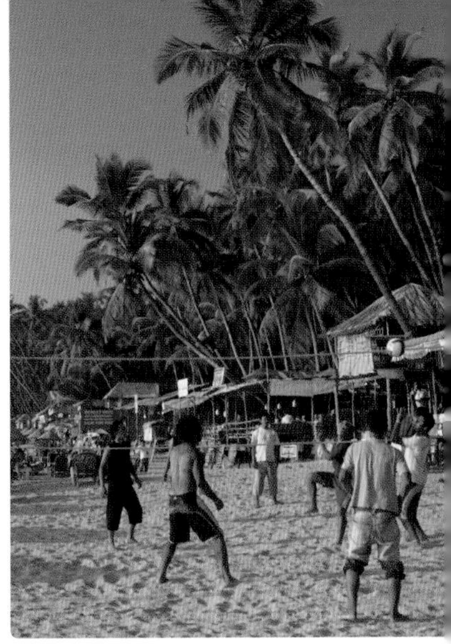

▲ Palolem beach

▼ Ice cream hawker, Benaulim beach

▼ Training prize-fighting water buffalo, Benaulim beach

Mandrem beach at sunset ▲

Isolated beach, South Goa ▼

Best hidden beaches

No Goan beach is truly deserted these days, but the following can come pretty close. Our list also includes a few off-track locations beyond the state borders, which you'll need your own transport to reach.

▸▸ **Paliem** (see p.154). Around the headland from Arambol in the far north, backed by a saltwater lagoon and a pair of red laterite bluffs.

▸▸ **Paradise** (aka "Shiroda") Beach. To the north of Redi fort in Maharashtra (see p.227), a five-kilometre stretch of soft white sand sweeps up the coast to a low headland. Easily reachable via NH-17, it lies just west of Shiroda.

▸▸ **Mandrem** (see p.150). The quietest stretch of beach south of Arambol; a huge swathe of white sand ending at a tidal creek you can wade across at low tide.

▸▸ **Cabo da Rama** (see p.191). Hidden away below the old Portuguese fort and its surrounding headlands are a couple of idyllic coves – hard to reach, but deserted on weekdays.

▸▸ **Khola** (see p.195). A secluded, tranquil bay just north of Agonda, where there's a small tent camp but little else.

▸▸ **Butterfly**. This pearl-white cove, tucked around the headland to the north of Palolem, is only reachable by boat. Its name derives from the exotic butterflies that flit over the waves.

▸▸ **Galjibag** (see p.203). A mile of empty sand and surf, and refuge of the endangered Olive Ridley marine turtle.

▸▸ **Polem** (see p.205). Remote beach in the far south, backed by palms. It could be nicknamed "smugglers cove", as its main source of income is ferrying moonshine *feni* to nearby Karnataka.

▸▸ **Half Moon** (see p.227). The last, and prettiest, in a series of coves carved from the steep laterite headland to the south of Gokarana, in neighbouring Karnataka.

Despite being only a stone's throw upriver from Panjim, Britona village has retained lots of old-world charm, with dozens of decaying Portuguese-era houses fronting the roadsides like discarded film sets. Occupying a converted seventeenth-century customs warehouse on the riverbank, the *Casa Britona* (Ⓣ0832/241 0962, Ⓦwww.casaboutiquehotels.com; ⑨) has rooms fitted with four-poster beds and opening onto a large rear terrace where, shaded by tall palm trees, there's a swimming pool and wooden dining deck jutting over the water and mangroves. However, the beautiful decor and prime riverine location comes at five-star prices: Rs7000–8000 ($158–180) per night depending on the time of year, rising to Rs13,000 ($293) over Christmas.

From Britona, you've only 3km of backroad left before the Mandovi Bridge and skyline of Panjim hove into view. A perfect extension to this trip is a visit to Gerard de Cunha's **Houses of Goa Museum**, only a few kilometres north at Porvorim (see p.72).

Betim and Reis Magos

The concrete road bridge across the Mandovi River linking Panjim with the north bank collapsed on July 5, 1986, killing several people and sparking off a heated row about corruption in the government and the construction industry. The disaster was doubly embarrassing for those responsible, as the bridge had been in use for a lot less time than it had taken to build. Its replacement fared even worse, falling apart before it was even finished. The present structures (there are now two), completed in 1992, look sturdy enough, but if you are not convinced, jump on the ferry (every 20–30min; Rs5) that shuttles between Panjim's old steamer jetty and the fishing and boat-building settlement of **BETIM**, 1km west of the bridge.

Reis Magos

Having wound past Betim and Panjim's smelly **trawler fishing dock**, the coastal road veers inland to **Verem** village, where a small Hindu tree shrine marks the turning to **REIS MAGOS**, 3km further west. It's not on a bus route, but you can get there easily enough by motorcycle taxi from the main road if you're not up to walking. Visible from across the river in Panjim, Reis Magos' **church** (Mon–Sat 9am–noon & 4.30–5.30pm) was built in 1555 and taken over soon after by Franciscan friars, charged with missionary responsibility for the colony at the time, who founded a small seminary here. Historians believe the original church was constructed on the ruins of an old Hindu temple, and the two bas-relief lion figures flanking the steps at the ends of the balustrades lend credence to this theory, being a typical feature of Vijayanagar temple architecture in the fourteenth and fifteenth centuries. A further indication of the site's former prominence is the Portuguese royal family's coat of arms, featured below the crucifix at the top of the gabled facade. Two viceroys are also buried inside the church: one at the west entrance, the other to the north of the nave. The better preserved of the tombstones, both still in crisp condition with their Portuguese and Latin inscriptions clearly legible, is that of **Dom Luis de Ataide**, renowned as the hero of the 1570 siege of Old Goa, in which a force of seven thousand defenders managed to keep an army of a hundred thousand Muslims (with two thousand elephants) at bay for ten months. The centrepiece of the church's elaborately carved and painted **reredos**, behind the high altar, is a multicoloured wood relief showing the Three Wise Men – or *Reis Magos*, after whom the village is named – bearing gifts to the Infant Jesus. Each year, this scene is re-enacted in the **Festa dos Reis Magos**, held in the first week of January, during Epiphany.

Crowning the sheer headland immediately above the church, Reis Magos **fort** was erected in 1551 to protect the narrowest point at the mouth of the Mandovi estuary. Like the Adil Shah's palace on the opposite bank, converted by the Portuguese after Albuquerque's defeat of the Muslims, it formerly accommodated viceroys and other dignitaries newly arrived from, or en route to, Lisbon, and in the early eighteenth century proved a linchpin in the wars against the Hindu Marathas, who were never able to take it. These days, the bastion, surrounded by sturdy laterite walls studded with typically Portuguese turrets, is used as a prison and not open to the public.

Fort Aguada

FORT AGUADA, the old Portuguese bastion on the headland dividing the Mandovi from Calangute beach, is the largest and best-preserved colonial citadel in Goa. Built in 1612 to guard the coast from attacks by Dutch and Maratha raiders, its name derives from the presence inside of several freshwater springs – the first

Forts

Crowning river mouths and hilltops along the whole length of the state, Goa's crumbling red-black **forts** stand as evocative reminders of the region's colonial past, dating from an era when this was a remote European trading post on the margins of a vast maritime empire. Laterite, the hard, heavily pitted stone used to build them, was quarried locally and proved an efficient foil for the heavy weapons being developed in the sixteenth and seventeenth centuries, at the high watermark of Portuguese power in Asia.

The castles of medieval Europe were no match for improved gunpowder and cast-iron cannonballs, so the Portuguese, under the guidance of an Italian architect, **Filipo Terzi**, strengthened Goa's defences by erecting forts with low, thick walls, filled with cushions of earth and built at an angle to deflect shot. The large, V-shaped bastions added to the battlements were designed both to deflect incoming fire and to give greater range to the huge Portuguese revolving cannons.

Inside, buildings were chiselled out of solid rock, and the level of the ground around them was lowered to give extra defensive height. Underneath, store rooms and arsenals were excavated, interconnected by a network of narrow tunnels and corridors; these are still visible in Fort Aguada. They often led to concealed safe moorings at sea level – essential supply lines in times of siege. The whole was then encircled by deep dry moats and ditches to waylay foot soldiers and cavalry, though the Portuguese most feared attack from the sea by their trade rivals, the British and Dutch. The latter did penetrate the Mandovi estuary in 1604, but it was from the land that the most decisive invasion of the territory came, sixty years later, when the army of the Hindu Maratha leader Shivaji poured virtually unopposed through a poorly defended interior border.

As the threat of attack diminished through the eighteenth and nineteenth centuries, the Portuguese forts gradually fell into disrepair, and today most of them, like the one at **Rachol** in Salcete, have been completely reclaimed by vegetation or their masonry plundered for building material. Only a handful of bastions remain intact, their walls, ditches and discarded cannons choked with weeds. Of these, **Fort Aguada** is by far the most impressive, with **Chapora** (see p.142), also in north Goa, a close second. Other forts worth visiting include **Terekol** (see p.156), in the far north of the state, **Corjuem** (see p.111), the only inland bastion left standing, and windswept **Cabo da Rama** in the south.

source of drinking water available to ships arriving in Goa after the long sea voyage from Lisbon. On the north side of the fort, a rampart of red-brown laterite juts into the bay to form a jetty between two small sandy coves; the gigantic cannon that once stood on it covered a blind spot in the fortification's defences. This picturesque spot, known as **Sinquerim beach**, was among the first places in Goa to be singled out for upmarket tourism, with the construction of the five-star *Fort Aguada Beach Resort* in the 1970s. Long the first choice of visiting VIPs, film stars and movie crews, it has nowadays somewhat fallen out of fashion, while the cove below it has virtually disappeared – eroded away, or so the locals claim, by changes in tide patterns caused by the hulk of the MV *River Princess*, marooned for more than a decade in the bay just offshore (see p.119).

The fort

The extensive ruins of the **fort**, formerly encircled at sea level by battlements (of which only fragments now remain), can be reached by road from the south end of Candolim (see map). En route you pass the palace of diamond and rubber tycoon Jimmy Gazdar, overlooking the bay (and prison) from the steep hillside. A monumentally kitsch pile of pink marble staircases, spiral pillars, follies and fountains, it was the brainchild of Goa's most famous architect, Gerard da Cunha. Visitors are not welcome.

From "Jimmy's Palace", the surfaced lane runs the length of the ridge to an impressive square-shaped **citadel**, joined to the anchorage, jetty and storehouses on the south side of the headland. Since World War II, these have served as Goa's largest prison, **Fort Aguada Jail**. Ringed by thick battlements, the heart of the fort directly above the prison was protected by two hundred cannons and a deep dry moat, which you still have to cross to get inside. Steps lead down from the middle of the courtyard within to an enormous vaulted **cistern** capable of storing ten million litres of fresh water.

The other unusual feature of the fort is a four-storey Portuguese **lighthouse**, erected in 1864 and the oldest of its kind in Asia. Scaled via a spiral staircase, the oddly stumpy structure surveys the vast expanse of sea, sand and palm trees of Calangute on one side, and the mouth of the Mandovi to Cabo Raj Bhavan and the tip of the Mormugao peninsula on the other. Superseded by a modern lighthouse only in 1976, it used to house the colossal bell salvaged from the ruins of the Augustinian monastery in Old Goa, which now hangs in Panjim's Our Lady of the Immaculate Conception.

In Aguada's **Church of St Lawrence**, on your left before the citadel on the road, the saint's statue presides over the high altar's reredos, clutching a model ship. Normally, the Portuguese erected churches outside their forts' battlements so as not to give the enemy a potential stronghold within firing distance of the inner defences, but Aguada was so sprawling it was deemed safe to site the shrine here. The overall design proved eminently successful: this was the only Portuguese fort in Goa never conquered during more than 450 years of colonial rule.

Candolim

CANDOLIM (from the Konkani *kandoli*, meaning "dykes" – a reference to the system of sluices used to reclaim the land from the nearby marshes) is the granddaddy of Goan beach resorts. More sedate and rambling than Calangute, it's retained its leafy edges, traditionally attracting a mostly ageing, northern European clientele content to watch the world go by over a beer glass from their

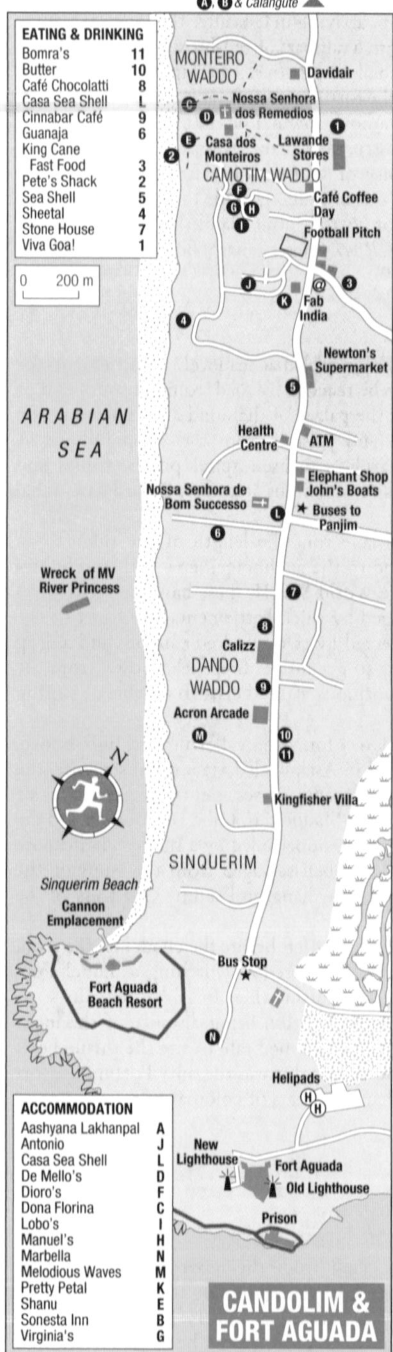

hotel (or timeshare) balcony. The mass arrival in recent years of young Russian charter tourists has definitely shaken the place up a bit, but the pace is still noticeably slower than further north along the beach – or least, it is once away from the main drag running through the village. Known as the CHOGM Road (after the "Commonwealth Heads of Government Meeting" for which it was upgraded in the early 1980s), Candolim's strip comprises an unbroken line of gaudily lit restaurants, shops and Kashmiri handicraft emporiums. Traffic flies down it at breakneck speeds during the day but dies off rapidly in the evening, when the fairy lights and clanking of local cover bands take over. By midnight it's invariably dead, save for a handful of downbeat bars, although over the peak Christmas and New Year period wealthy metropolitan Indians keep the cash registers ringing until sunrise.

Few independent travellers pitch up here, but Candolim has lots of pleasant **places to stay**, many of them tucked away down quiet sandy lanes and offering excellent value for money, making this a good first stop if you've just arrived in Goa and are planning to head further north after finding your feet.

Arrival and information

Buses to and from Panjim stop every ten minutes or so at the stand opposite the *Casa Sea Shell*, in the middle of Candolim. A few head south here to the *Fort Aguada Beach Resort* terminus; you can also flag them down from anywhere along the main drag to Calangute. Maruti **taxis** are ubiquitous. During the season, however, there is often a dearth of **motorcycles for rent**, in

Portuguese palacios in Candolim

Anyone with an eye for old **Indo-Portuguese architecture** will find plenty of inspiration among the shady palm groves of Candolim's outlying **waddos**, where several **palacios** recall the era when this ranked among the most affluent of Goa's villages. In the seventeenth and early eighteenth centuries, malaria and cholera decimated the population of the capital, forcing those wealthy families who could afford to buy land to build grand new houses in this more salubrious seaside district. Among them were the **Pintos**, a powerful dynasty infamous for fomenting a rebellion against the Portuguese in 1787. Marshalled by a priest called Father Couto, 47 disaffected clerics, soldiers and local grandees (including several Pintos), exasperated by the racial discrimination rife in the colonial hierarchy at the time, assembled in the Pintos' house to prepare a coup against the regime in Panjim. However, the Portuguese governor got wind of the impending revolution and dispatched troops to arrest the culprits, who were promptly shipped off for two decades of imprisonment in Portugal or – in the case of the lowly troops – hanged and quartered.

The house where the so-called **Pinto Revolt** took place collapsed long ago, but others dating from this period still stand and are well worth hunting out. In the north of Candolim, the **Casa dos Monteiros** is an outstandingly well-preserved, late-seventeenth-century rural *palacio*, of a kind that has virtually disappeared. The Monteiros, once among the richest and most influential families in Goa, were linked to the Pintos through marriage, and it is thought this house is similar to the one their in-laws lived in at the time of the 1787 revolt. It stands within a low enclosure wall, facing a small chapel, **Nossa Senhora dos Remedios** (Our Lady of Remedies), opened by a special papal bull in 1780. Divided by ornamental pilasters, the oyster-shell windows of the mansion's three facades are capped by beautifully proportioned triangular pediments, typical of the period but now extremely rare in Goa.

Candolim's other *palacio*, the **Casa dos Costa-Frias**, stands further south, not far from the Bosio Hospital, and also belonged to relatives of the Pintos. Built in the early eighteenth century, it boasts a wonderful whitewashed gateway with moulded Corinthian columns and a pediment crowned by a cross. The facade, the north side of which was recently renovated, is equally impressive, with a full set of sliding oyster-shell blinds, surmounted by elegant stone-carved scrollwork. Behind the house (facing the road), the family **chapel** too dates from the early eighteenth century, although the twisting pillars flanking its doorway hark back to the more exuberant Manueline style of the sixteenth.

Both of these *palacios* are still inhabited by descendants of their original occupants and are thus **not open to visitors**, but no one will mind you admiring them from outside the enclosure walls.

The one place in Candolim that's specifically set up for visitors to look around old houses is the wonderful **Calizz** folk museum (ⓦwww.calizz.com), near the Acron Arcade (see p.119).

which case search for one in Calangute. The nearest petrol pump lies 5km east on the main Panjim road, just beyond Nerul.

Accommodation

Candolim is charter holiday land, but if bookings are down you can pick up some great bargains here.

Inexpensive

Antonio Camotim Waddo ⓣ0832/248 9735, ⓣ98223/381214. Spacious and comfortable chalet rooms, some with kitchenettes, all with balconies, in a couple of large, modern, double-storeyed blocks between the road and the beach. It's situated in quiet, traffic-free neighbourhood well away from the strip, and efficiently run by the Pires family. ⑤

Lobo's Camotim Waddo ⓣ0832/329 0415. An old favourite budget travellers' haunt in a peaceful corner of the village, this is a notch up from *Manuel's* opposite, with larger rooms, long common verandas and very friendly owners. ❸

Manuel's Camotim Waddo ⓣ0832/248 9729. Small family guesthouse that's also been around for years and is welcoming, clean and cheap, although somewhat boxed in by other buildings. All rooms have fans and attached shower-toilets. ❸

Virginia's Camotim Waddo ⓣ0832/645 1069, ⓣ9923/640584. Another cheerful budget option, boasting better beds and furniture than the competition, as well as safe lockers in the attached rooms and relaxing bentwood chairs to lounge on. Try this place first – it's great value. ❸

Mid-range

Casa Sea Shell Fort Aguada Rd, near *Bom Successo* ⓣ0832/247 9879 ⓦwww.seashellgoa.com. Old-established former charter hotel near the Nerul road junction where you've a choice between standard non-a/c rooms or larger, newer and better-furnished ones with flat-screen TVs and a/c. Facing each other across a palm-shaded garden, both blocks offer accommodation that's spacious for the price, impeccably clean and well aired. Best of all, you get the run of a well-kept little pool around the back, picturesquely situated beside a chapel. If it's fully booked, ask for a room in the identical and slightly cheaper (but pool-less) *Sea Shell Inn* (ⓣ0832/248 9131 ⓦwww.seashellgoa.com) up the road ❹–❺

De Mello's Escrivao Waddo ⓣ0832/248 9650. One of the larger complexes in the dunes hereabouts, offering a range of differently priced rooms, all with nice balconies, and some of which occupy a pair of Escher-esque blocks in the garden. It's only a stone's throw from the beach and very quiet, and there's a pleasant little café for guests. ❹

Dioro's Camotim Waddo ⓣ0832/329 0713 or ⓣ9823/269376, ⓔdiorosgoa@yahoo.com. Very large, tiled, spotless rooms with huge balconies and fridges, in a quiet residential area well back from the main road and close to the beach. Good value for money, considering the space and comfort, even at Christmas; and they've a well-kept garden. ❺

Dona Florina Monteiro's road, Escrivao Waddo ⓣ0832/248 9051, ⓦwww.donaflorina.co.in. Large guesthouse in a superb location, overlooking the beach in the most secluded corner of the village. Its friendly owner, Jessie D'Souza, has added a breezy rooftop terrace with ceramic mosaic floors for guests to practise yoga on. Well worth paying a little extra for if you want idyllic sea views. The only catch is that there's no car access. ❹

Marbella Sinquerim ⓣ0832/247 9551, ⓦwww.marbellagoa.com. Individually styled suites and spacious rooms (from Rs3000) in a beautiful house built to resemble a traditional Goan mansion. The decor, fittings and furniture are gorgeous, especially in the top-floor "Penthouse" (Rs5500), and the whole place is screened by a giant mango tree. Unashamedly romantic and well worth splashing out on. ❼–❽

Melodious Waves Dando Waddo ⓣ0832/247 9711, ⓦwww.melodiouswaves.com. Twenty newish rooms with balconies in a quiet location, well back from the main road and two minutes through the dunes from a relatively peaceful stretch of beach. Tariffs reflect its proximity to the *Fort Aguada Beach Resort*, though are still good value. ❹–❺

Pretty Petal Camotim Waddo ⓣ0832/248 9184, ⓦwww.prettypetalsgoa.com. Not as twee as it sounds: very large, modern rooms, all with fridges, quality mattresses and balconies, and relaxing, marble-floored communal areas overlooking lawns. Their top-floor apartment, with windows on four sides and a huge balcony, is the best choice, though more expensive. ❹–❺

Shanu Escrivao Waddo ⓣ0832/248 9899. Good-sized, well-furnished rooms with narrow balconies right on the dunes, some of them with uninterrupted views of the sea. Ask the hospitable owners for #120 (or failing that #118, #111, #110 or #107). Breakfast is served in your room. ❹

Expensive

Aashyana Lakhanpal Escrivao Waddo ⓣ0832/248 9225, ⓦwww.aashyanalakhanpal.com. Über-chic boutique hidey-hole tucked away in the palm groves behind the north end of Candolim beach, whose famously stylish five-bedroom villa costs a whopping $11,000–17,000 per week but is, notwithstanding, often block-booked for whole months. More modest, and a perfect option for families, are their three secluded "casinhas". Tariffs ($2000/week) include the run of a fabulous diamond-shaped pool, lush garden, Ayurveda spa and the attentions of an army of staff. ❾

Sonesta Inn Escrivao Waddo ⓣ0832/248 9448, ⓦwww.sonestainns.com. A smarter than average package hotel, two minutes' walk from the sea, ranged around a large central pool. Most of the comforts of a four-star, but on a smaller scale, with rooms, suites and three-bedroom villas. ❼–❾

The beach and town

The **beach** itself, arching south towards Fort Aguada and (what's left of) Sinquerim, holds the usual rank of shacks, many of them established in the same site for decades, growing pricier the nearer they stand to the *Fort Aguada Beach Resort*. You can expect plenty of attention from masseurs and hawkers, but comparatively little from gawpers and day-trippers – those that do break bus tours here tend to do so in order to marvel at the hulk of the **MV River Princess** lurching in the shallows just offshore. A 240-metre-long iron-ore transporter, the ship ran aground here during a monsoon gale in June 2000. It belongs to one of Goa's richest tycoons, Anil Salgaonkar, who is still in dispute with the government over who should foot the bill for salvaging the wreck. Meanwhile, after several aborted attempts to refloat and tow it away in one piece, the *River Princess* sinks deeper into the sand each year – a surreal spectacle so close to India's flagship tourist beach.

The village also boasts a bumper crop of **old mansions** and traditional Goan houses (see box, p.117), some of the best of them in an award-winning folk and architectural museum called **Calizz** (daily 10am–7pm; Rs300; Ⓦwww.calizz.com), on the south side of Candolim near Acron Arcade (see map, p.116). Comprising five beautifully restored period buildings spread over a site of several acres, the complex showcases various styles of traditional Goan homes – both Christian and Hindu – from humble mud structures dating from pre-colonial times to a sumptuous Portuguese *palacio* with chapel attached. On display inside is an engaging array of antiques, furniture, religious icons and daily artefacts. The ticket price includes a 45-minute guided tour.

Eating and drinking

Candolim has an amazingly eclectic choice of **places to eat**, ranging from seafood shacks on the beach to the full five-star monty at the *Fort Aguada Beach Resort*. The British palate is particularly well catered for, down to greasy English breakfasts and Yorkshire-pudding Sunday lunches. Bear in mind that Calangute and Baga are also accessible from here.

Bomra's Souza Waddo, Fort Aguada Rd Ⓣ9822/149633 Understated, relaxed place, on a dimly lit gravel terrace by the roadside. From the outside you'd never know this was one of Goa's gastronomic highlights, but the food – contemporary Burmese and Kachin cuisine – is superb. The menu's reassuringly short; try their spinach wraps in fragrant *tahini* sauce for starters, and the beef in peanut curry or snapper with lemongrass, tofu and noodles for main. They also do fantastic *mojitos* and, for desert, delicious ginger crême brûlée.

Café Chocolatti Near Acron Arcade. Goa's answer to Juliette Binoche's "Vianne Rocher" (from the movie *Chocolat*), the British-raised owner of this delightful café in south Candolim, Nazneen, has conjured up a Mecca for chocoholics. Over a perfect cup of freshly ground coffee in the garden, you can indulge in gourmet Belgian-style truffles, tinged with chilli, mocca and orange, and crunchy almond-flavoured Italian biscuits. Plus there's a counter serving gift-wrapped takeaways.

Casa Sea Shell *Casa Sea Shell* hotel. This is the place to head for topnotch tandoori (from a real charcoal-fired oven) and North Indian dishes, although they also offer a good choice of Chinese and European food, served on a hotel patio next to an illuminated fountain. Excellent service and moderate prices. Don't miss the to-die-for Irish coffee.

Cinnabar Café Acron Arcade, Fort Aguada Rd. Hip new café, with Italian-style glass- and wood-panelled interior, stone vases and Indian curios, serving a mean cappuccino. Occasional DJs add to the ambience. Opens at 8am for cooked breakfasts.

Guanaja River Princess Lane. Step into Savio's quirky wood cabin for a proper choco-fest featuring flavours you won't find anywhere else, many of them derived from local, typically Goan ingredients such as mango, chilli, sour kokum and coconut. They also bake crunchy fresh croissants, biscuits and savouries (though the coffee isn't up to much).

King Cane Fast Food Bosio Hospital Rd, near the football pitch and covered market. Terrific little Goan snack cart, on the roadside in the market area, run by husband and wife team Salvador and Maria Barretto. Everyone comes for the spicy beef chilli fry, served in a bap like a burger, but the *sorpotel* (a pungent mix of pork cuts, offal, blood, *toddi* vinegar and spices) is knockout. Maria cooks it over four days, simmering the stew for 10min each day to bring out the flavours.

Pete's Shack Escrivao Waddo. This is one beach shack that deserves singling out because it's always popular and professional. Serves great healthy salads (Rs150–250), with delicious olive oil, mozzarella and balsamic vinegar. All the veg is carefully washed in chlorinated water first, so the food is safe and fresh. The same applies to their seafood sizzler and tandoori main courses. For dessert, try the wonderful chocolate mousse or cooling mint lassis. Their real pride and joy, however, is the loo – which must be the grandest on any Goan beach.

Sea Shell Fort Aguada Rd. A congenial terrace restaurant in front of an old colonial-era *palacio* decked with green fairy lights. Sizzlers, spaghetti bolognaise and beefsteaks are their specialities, but they do a range of seafood, Indian and Chinese dishes, as well as delicious cocktails. Not as pricey as it looks, either (most mains Rs250–350).

Sheetal Murrod Waddo. One of the few restaurants in Goa specializing in authentic Mughlai cuisine: the creamy, Persian-influenced style of cooking elaborated by the Mughal rulers between the fifteenth and eighteenth centuries in India. Served in copper *karais* by a team of snappy waiters dressed in traditional *salwars*, the menu features a long list of chicken, mutton and vegetarian dishes steeped in rich sauces. Try the wonderful *murg malai* (chicken in cashew-nut paste topped with cream) or equally delicious *dal mughali* (black lentils, kidney beans and small cubes of *paneer* with ginger). Count on Rs350–450 per head, plus drinks.

Stone House Fort Aguada Rd. Blues-nut Chris D'Souza hosts this lively, low-lit bar-restaurant, spread in front of a gorgeous bare-laterite Goan house. Prime cuts of beef and kingfish served with scrumptious baked potatoes are their most popular dishes. Blues enthusiasts should come just for the CD collection. Most mains under Rs300.

Viva Goa! Fort Aguada Rd, Candolim north. Succulent, no-nonsense Goan food fresh from the market – mussel fry, barramundi (*chonok*), lemonfish (*modso*) and sharkfish steaks fried *rechado* style in chilli paste or in millet (*rawa*) – served on a roadside terrace. Tourists are welcome, but it's essentially local food at local prices.

Shopping

Crammed with all those little holiday essentials – from sim cards to ayurvedic suncream – the Elephant Shop, on Chogm Road, is a Candolim institution, beloved especially of the resort's British contingent. There are two branches on opposite sides of the main drag, run by different sides of the same family. Russian tourists, meanwhile, do most of their shopping at Newton's – a huge Gulf-style supermarket stocking an unbelievable array of items, including Goa's most extensive range of wine and spirits – though its prices are far higher than those of the corner shops nearby.

The Delhi chain store, Fabindia, has opened a small store just north of Newton's; it's a great place to find handmade Indian textiles and bits and bobs for the home such as bedspreads, cushion covers and lampshades. Acron Arcade, on the south side of Calangute near Calizz, also holds outlets of Benetton, Reebok and other well-known brands, as well as designer jewellery and furniture. All of the above are marked on our Candolim map (see p.116).

Nightlife

Nightlife in Candolim revolves around sedate drinking in any number of the restaurants, bars and pubs lining the main strip and its side lanes. Few places stand out of the crowd, but *Butter*, at 242 Souza Waddo on the south side of the village towards Sinquerim, makes more of an effort than most, with a trendy lounge ambience and trademark giant saxophone on the roadside. Big-spending over-30s

Boat trips and cruises from Candolim

The waters off Calangute beach support a thriving population of dolphins, though you'll need to jump on a boat to see them. Run by a former fisherman, John's Boats (Ⓣ0832/562 0910, Ⓦwww.johnboattrips.com) have cornered the market in spotting cruises, thanks to their "No Dolphins, No Pay" policy – and British-safety-standard lifejackets. The four- to five-hour trips start at 9am from "John's HQ" on the main Chogm Road (see map, p.116), and cost Rs900 per head (includes food, drink and taxi pick-up from your hotel; book in advance). The same firm has also acquired a splendid **Keralan rice boat** in which they run two-day tours (with one night on board) around the backwaters of the Siolim River. This is a unique, highly recommended experience in Goa, taking you deep into the state's unspoilt interior, with wonderful views of the hills inland and the chance to spot abundant bird- and wildlife. Again, the price (around Rs5000 per head) includes all meals and transfers. Contact John's office for more details.

Budget alternatives to these tours, and a wide range of other excursions, are offered by British-run Daytripper (Ⓣ0832/227 6726, Ⓦwww.daytrippergoa.com), whose bright hoardings line the main road in Gaura Waddo, north of Candolim.

from Mumbai and Delhi flock in around Christmas and New Year to lap up the overpriced cocktails under giant trees wrapped with fairy lights. Unless, like much of the clientele, you're on air-kissing terms with the owner, count on an Rs1000 admission charge. A still more glamorous party scene takes place a short way further south: on the opposite side of the road from *Butter* stands **Kingfisher Villa**, Goa's most ostentatious mansion and the multi million-dollar home of Kingfisher beer and airline tycoon, Vijay Mallia. Pass here one night when he's hosting one of his famous parties, and you'll see gangs of paparazzi hanging around to snap photos of the Bollywood stars and other Indian celebs who glitter in and out of the huge gateway.

Listings

Beauty Parlours Pelifa's, down near the Acron Arcade, receives glowing references from readers. Pamper yourself Goan style. Men and women welcome.

Books Café Literati, on the southern edge of Calangute (see map, p.116), is one of Goa's best small bookstores, with a huge range of quality fiction and titles on India. They also run a funky little café where you can refuel between browses.

Classical Indian dance In Calangute, recitals of traditional Indian dance are also given on Tuesday evenings at the Kerkar Art Gallery, and there are evening performances of Keralan Kathakali.

Foreign exchange There are plenty of ATMs and places to change money in Candolim, but the rates offered for travellers' cheques by the banks and foreign exchange bureaux up in Calangute (see p.128), are more competitive.

Travel agent Davidair (Ⓣ0832/248 9303, Ⓦwww.com2goa.com), on the left side of the main road as you leave Candolim towards Calangute, has been established for nearly two decades and is very efficient. It's also one of the few agents licensed to sell charter tickets to Manchester and Gatwick, which it frequently does for as little as £200. Also recommended for Agra/Delhi excursions.

Calangute

CALANGUTE was, in Portuguese times, where well-to-do Goans would come for their annual *mudança*, or change of air in May and June, when the pre-monsoonal heat made life in the towns insufferable. It remains the state's busiest resort, but has changed beyond recognition since the days when straw-hatted musicians in the

Dead lucky?

Bob's Inn, midway between Calangute and Candolim, is not somewhere you'd associate with quickening heartbeats (quite the opposite in fact). But pulses must have raced in the bar the day photographs of its most notorious, recently deceased regular, "**Jungle Barry**", popped up on newspaper front pages all over the world. What at first seemed like a surreal joke turned out to be one of the most improbable scenarios imaginable: that hard-drinking, guitar-strumming Jungle Barry, with his tatty khaki shorts, long grey hair and beard and catatonic appearance, had in fact been none other than the aristocratic fugitive "Lucky" **Lord Lucan**.

First published in the UK's **Sunday Telegraph** in September 2003, the revelations were based on extracts from a book written by a retired Scotland Yard detective, Duncan MacLaughlin. Obsessed for years with tracking down the fast-living peer, who'd vanished in 1974 after his children's nanny had been found bludgeoned to death, MacLaughlin had been led to Goa by pictures he'd been shown of a boozy old hippy who ran "bush tours" out of *Bob's Inn*.

Many theories as to Lucan's whereabouts had been posited over the years. Some believed he'd been kidnapped by the IRA; others that he'd shot himself and had had a friend feed his remains to the lions in London Zoo. He'd variously been spotted in Melbourne, Mozambique, Dublin and San Francisco, and many other places besides, but no one had ever managed to provide incontestable proof of his fate.

The photographs shown to MacLaughlin did indeed suggest some resemblance in the distinctively arched eyebrows, hairline and lack of earlobes. But when the ex-policeman started to dig for more evidence, other coincidences started to pile up, such as Barry's reputedly posh English accent and his encyclopedic knowledge of vintage cars.

However, the *Sunday Telegraph*, who snapped up rights to MacLaughlin's subsequent book, was to rue its rush to print. No sooner had Jungle Barry's blurry mugshot appeared in the paper than a flood of people emerged claiming they recognized the man in the photos as one Barry Halpin, a well-known performer from the pubs and folk scene of northern England in the 1960s. Among them was the singer and comic Mike Harding, who reportedly laughed until he cried when he saw Halpin's face in the newspapers.

The whole episode still raises smirks in *Bob's Inn*, where it is regarded as a fitting coda to a life spent spinning long and unlikely yarns. Jungle Barry never lived long enough to witness his "outing" by the over-zealous former drug-squad officer, but would doubtless have enjoyed the notoriety if he had. His picture still hangs in the bar, where he is fondly remembered.

beachfront bandstand would regale smartly dressed strollers with Lisbon *fados* and Konkani *dulpods*.

Beach parties of a less genteel nature first started to become a regular feature of life here in the late 1960s. Stoned out of their brains on local *feni* and cheap *charas*, the tribes of long-haired Westerners lying naked on the vast white sandy beach soon became tourist attractions in their own right, pulling in bus-loads of visitors from Mumbai, Bangalore and beyond. Calangute's flower-power period, however, is decidedly long gone.

Nowadays, the owners of swish resort hotels look back on the hippy era with a mixture of amusement and nostalgia. They and their fellow Colongutis have paid a high price for the recent prosperity. Mass **package tourism**, combined with a huge increase in the number of Indian visitors (for whom this is Goa's number one beach resort), has placed an impossible burden on the town's rudimentary infrastructure. Each year, as another crop of construction sites blossoms into

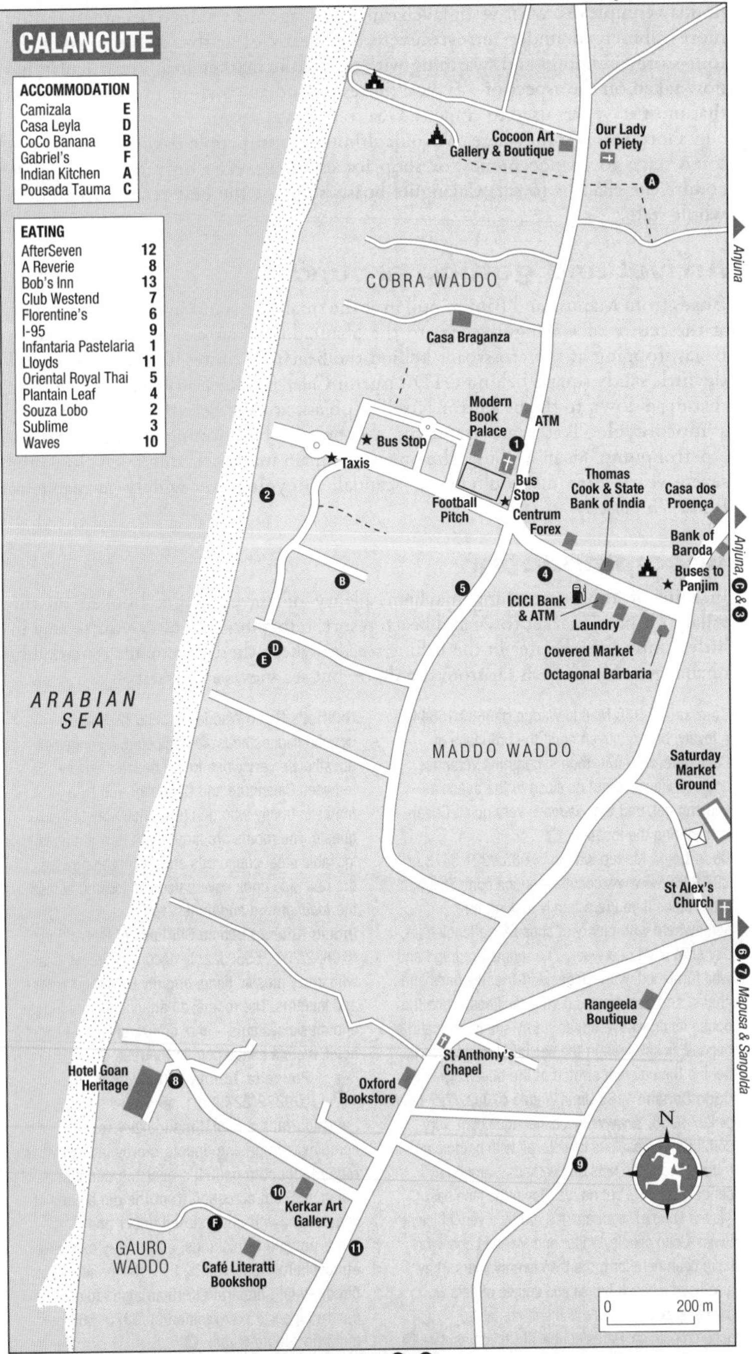
CALANGUTE
ACCOMMODATION
Camizala E
Casa Leyla D
CoCo Banana B
Gabriel's F
Indian Kitchen A
Pousada Tauma C
EATING
AfterSeven 12
A Reverie 8
Bob's Inn 13
Club Westend 7
Florentine's 6
I-95 9
Infantaria Pastelaria 1
Lloyds 11
Oriental Royal Thai 5
Plantain Leaf 4
Souza Lobo 2
Sublime 3
Waves 10
Baga
Cocoon Art Gallery & Boutique
Our Lady of Piety
Anjuna
COBRA WADDO
Casa Braganza
Modern Book Palace
ATM
Bus Stop
Taxis
Bus Stop
Football Pitch
Thomas Cook & State Bank of India
Casa dos Proença
Centrum Forex
Bank of Baroda
Anjuna, C & 3
Buses to Panjim
ICICI Bank & ATM
Laundry
Covered Market
Octagonal Barbaria
ARABIAN SEA
MADDO WADDO
Saturday Market Ground
St Alex's Church
6, 7, Mapusa & Sangolda
Rangeela Boutique
St Anthony's Chapel
Hotel Goan Heritage
Oxford Bookstore
N
Kerkar Art Gallery
GAURO WADDO
Café Literatti Bookshop
0
200 m
Candolim, Panjim, 12 & 13

holiday complexes, what vestigial charm the village has retained becomes steadily more submerged under ferro-concrete and heaps of garbage. Hemmed in by four-storey buildings and swarming with traffic, the market area, in particular, has now taken on the aspect of a typical makeshift Indian town of precisely the kind that most travellers used to come to Goa to get away from.

In short, this is somewhere to avoid, although most people pass through here at some stage to change money or shop for essentials. The only other reason to endure the chaos is to eat: Calangute boasts some of the best **restaurants** in the whole state.

Arrival and getting around

Buses from Mapusa and Panjim pull in at the small bus stand in the market square at the centre of Calangute, next to the Shantadurga temple. Some continue to Baga, stopping at the crossroads behind the beach en route. **Taxis** hang around the little sandy square behind GTDC's grim *Calangute Residency*, next to the steps that drop down to the beachfront itself. Also ask around here if you want to rent a **motorcycle**. Rates are standard; the nearest functioning **service station** ("petrol pump") is in Mapusa, the one in the main market having been closed for seven years after an adulteration scandal. **Bicycles** are widely available at Rs60–75 per day.

Accommodation

In spite of the encroaching mayhem, plenty of travellers get hooked on the village's mix of market town and beach resort, returning year after year to stay in little family guesthouses in the fishing *waddo,* where the life remains remarkably unchanged. Nowhere is far from the shore, but sea views are a rarity.

Camizala 5-33B Maddo Waddo Ⓣ9689/156449. A lovely, breezy haven amid the brouhaha of Calangute, with four rooms, common verandas and sea views. About as close to the beach as you can get, and the *waddo* is very quiet. Cheap considering the location. ❸

Casa Leyla Maddo Waddo Ⓣ0832/227 6478 or 227 9068, Ⓦwww.cocobananagoa.com. This is a great place if you're a family looking for somewhere with plenty of space for a longish let, say of at least one week. The rooms are huge and well furnished, with fridges, kid-friendly beds and chairs, and basic self-catering facilities, while the house itself, whose upper storey sits in the palm canopy, is set deep in the secluded fishing ward, behind the quietest stretch of the beach. ❺–❻

CoCo Banana 1195 Umta Waddo Ⓣ0832/227 6478 or 227 9068, Ⓦwww.cocobananagoa.com. Very comfortable, spacious chalets, all with bathrooms, fridges, mosquito nets and verandas, around a central garden – but no a/c. Down the lane past *Meena Lobo's* restaurant, it's run by a very efficient Swiss-Goan couple, Walter and Marina Lobo, who have been here for more than twenty years. They also have a beach house and couple of flats worth enquiring about if you'd like self-contained accommodation. Rates double at Christmas. ❺–❻

Gabriel's Gauro Waddo Ⓣ0832/227 9486, Ⓔgabrielsguesthouse@gmail.com. A congenial guesthouse very close to the beach, midway between Calangute and Candolim, run by a fantastic family who go out of their way to help guests. The rooms are large, with new a/c units, lockable steel cupboards and decent mattresses; the rear side ones have balconies looking across the *toddi* groves and dunes. ❹

Indian Kitchen Behind Our Lady of Piety Church Ⓣ0832/227 7555. Jazzily decorated guesthouse with crazy mosaic tiling, brightly patterned walls and lanterns. The rooms, all attached, have fridges and music systems – and, amazingly for a budget hotel, there's a little pool to the rear. ❹

Pousada Tauma Porba Waddo Ⓣ0832/227 9061, Ⓦwww.pousada-tauma.com. Small luxury resort complex, comprising double-storey laterite villas ranged around a pool. It's near the middle of Calangute, but screened from the din by lots of vegetation, with understated decor and repro-antique furnishings, and a very exclusive atmosphere preserved by five-star prices. Their big draw is a first-rate Keralan ayurvedic health centre (open to non-residents). $370–550 per night (including taxes). ❾

The beach and town

Calangute's scruffy **beachfront** is the number-one destination in Goa for tourists from other Indian states. The atmosphere here can get especially intense on weekend evenings, when huge crowds gather on the foreshore to frolic in the surf, wearing regulation straw hats and wet saris. In a curious reversal of former times, foreign visitors nowadays drop by to watch the Kingfisher-fuelled jamboree, attended by herds of snack sellers, trinket hawkers, ear cleaners and stray cows. If you're tempted, brace yourself for lots of rowdy attention from drunken men cavorting in their underpants – and innumerable photocalls.

The quickest route out of the melee is to head fifteen minutes or so south, towards the rows of old wooden boats moored below the dunes at Maddo Waddo (literally "toughies' quarter"; see box below).

At the other end of the village's social hierarchy, one of Calangute's wealthiest families in the early eighteenth century built an extraordinary mansion, the **Casa dos Proença**, which still stands just north of the market area, on the opposite side of the road from the Bank of Baroda. Its most distinctive feature is a wonderful tower-shaped veranda whose sides are covered in screens made from oyster shells (*carepas*). The gallery is surmounted by a grand pitched roof, designed to funnel the air entering the room through the windows and other openings towards the ceiling – an ingenious natural air-conditioning system that was in time adopted all over the Portuguese empire. Dating from the early nineteenth century, Calangute's other wonderful old *palacio* is the **Casa Braganza**, on the first lane north of the *Infanteria Pastelaria* café.

Another of Calangute's oddities is the old octagonal **customs post**, presiding over the crossroads at the centre of the market. During the Portuguese era, a string of these curious structures was erected along the coastal route to monitor trade and traffic and to deter smugglers. Only a few are left standing (at nearby Siolim and at Assolna in the south); this specimen now serves as a barber's shop (*barbaria*). One of the traditional pleasures of Calangute market (at least for men) is to have a shave or haircut inside it, watching the progress of your tonsure in the mirrors lining its eight walls.

Calangute's **covered market**, just off the main crossroads, is one of the state's busiest. With separate sections given over to fish, meat and vegetables, it's full of pungent Goan aromas and a great place for a wander. On Saturdays there's an even

What's in a waddo?

All large Goan villages are divided up into **waddos**, or "wards", which used to be inhabited by members of the same caste and were thus associated with different occupations. Calangute is no exception, and the names given to its various wards reveal glimpses of their pre-tourism past. **Gauro Waddo**, on the south side of the village, for example, derives from the Konkani for cattle, *gauri*; its residents reared cows and provided the village with milk. "Aggor" means "salt pan" and **Aggar Waddo** was the source of Calangute's salt, while **Porba Waddo** (*porob* is the word for "scribe" or "clerk") was where people came to have documents written and accounts formalized. **Cobra Waddo** has less to do with snakes than the production of coconut oil from tender coconuts, or *copra*. The names of other wards carry the imprint of more specific local events, such as when the Lobo family first came to Calangute from Carambolim (near present-day Panjim) on the backs of camels, or *untt* – whence **Umta Waddo**. The village even has its own rough neighbourhood, appropriately named **Maddo Waddo**, after the Konkani word for "toughies" (it's now the fishing quarter south of the main beachfront).

more colourful **open-air market** held on a plot behind Calangute church, next to the post office, 200m southwest of the main intersection.

St Alex's Church, five minutes' walk down the lane from the post office, is another important local landmark. With a facade dominated by a stately false dome, it boasts a splendid Rococo interior whose highlight is a particularly sumptuous pulpit covered in swirling gold leaf.

Eating and drinking

Ever since *Souza Lobo* opened on the beachfront to cater for Goan day-trippers in the 1930s, Calangute has been somewhere people come as much to **eat** as for a stroll on the beach, and even if you stay in resorts elsewhere you'll doubtless be tempted down here at some stage for a meal – whether in the famous *Plantain Leaf* South Indian canteen in the main bazaar, or one of the swankier restaurants on the outskirts. For other options in the area, see the accounts of Baga (p.130) and Candolim (p.117).

A Reverie Near *Hotel Goan Heritage*, Gauro Waddo ⓣ9823/174927 or ⓣ9326/114661. Extravagant gourmet restaurant under a grand terracotta-tiled canopy. Both the menu and ambience are as about decadent as Goa gets, but the prices remain within reach of most budgets (around Rs1000 per head, plus drinks). The dishes are all original (verging on eccentric in some cases), and beautifully presented: try the smoked French duck with truffles and spiced berry sorbet, or home-cured beef with mustard ice cream; and there's warm chocolate pudding for dessert. Reservations recommended.

AfterSeven Gauro Waddo, midway between Calangute and Candolim, down a lane leading west off the main road, between the Lifeline Pharmacy and a small chapel ⓣ9226/188288. Superb gourmet restaurant, in a quiet garden setting, which had to change its name from *After Eight* following threats of legal action from Nestlé (they've had to start opening an hour earlier too). The menu offers mainly sophisticated continental dishes, such as camembert soufflé (Rs295), and special char-grilled fillet steak, served with blue cheese or Béarnaise sauce (Rs350). They also claim to offer Goa's longest wine list. Reservation recommended.

Florentine's 4km inland from St Alex's Church at Saligao, next door to the Ayurvedic Natural Health Centre. It's well worth making the trip inland to taste Florence D'Costa's legendary chicken *cafreal*, made to a jealously guarded family recipe that pulls in crowds of locals and tourists from across north Goa. The restaurant's a down-to-earth place, with prices to match, serving only chicken, some seafood and vegetarian snacks.

I-95 Behind the Art Chamber, Castello Vermelho, 1.115 A Gauro Waddo, ⓣ0832/227 5213, ⓦwww.i95goa.com. Alfresco fine dining devised by a dynamic young Indian team. The food's refined Continental cuisine: meat and seafood come grilled on lava stones, which lend a deliciously smoky aroma. Try the kingfish *darne*, with *roesti* potatoes and lemon-herb butter, or the pan-seared chicken breasts stuffed with rocket and apricots. For veggies there's a wonderful forest mushroom and red-onion risotto. And their bread-and-butter pudding is sublime. Count on the best part of Rs1000 per head for three courses, plus drinks.

Infantaria Pastelaria Next to St John's Chapel, Baga road. Roadside terrace café run by *Souza Lobo's* that gets packed out for its stodgy croissants, freshly baked apple pie and traditional Goan sweets (such as *dodol* and home-made *bebinca*). Top of the savoury list, though, are the prawn and veg patties, which locals buy by the boxload.

Lloyd's South Calangute, nr the turning for Kerkar Art Gallery. This inconspicuous little roadside joint, which stays open until 4am (or later), is where the local restaurateurs and Delhi expats chill out after hours. Sample the char-grilled steaks and spicy barbecued chicken, and you'll understand why. They also do knock-out Goan specialities – choriço chilli fry, pork *sorpotel*, and eye-watering fiery shark *amotik* – rustled up fresh each day by the owner's mum. Cold beers and local prices.

Oriental Royal Thai Two minutes' walk south off the main crossroads on the beach road, at the *Hotel Mira* ⓣ0832/329 2809 or ⓣ9822/121549. Fabulous Thai cuisine prepared by master chef Chawee, who turns out eighteen house sauces to accompany choice cuts of seafood, meat and poultry, as well as plenty of vegetarian options. Be sure to try their signature dish, *soom tham* (papaya salad). At around Rs700–800 for three courses, it's good value for cooking of this standard.

Plantain Leaf Market area. The best *udipi* restaurant outside Panjim, if not in all Goa, where waiters in matching shirts serve the usual range of delicious dosas and other spicy snacks in a clean, cool, marble-lined canteen. To the accompaniment of relentless background *filmi* music, try their definitive *iddli-wada* breakfasts, delicious masala dosas or the cheap and filling set thalis (Rs65).

Souza Lobo Beachfront. A Calangute institution, even though the food – served on tablecloths by legions of fast-moving waiters in loud Hawaiian shirts – isn't always what it used to be. Stuffed crab, whole baby kingfish and crepe Souza are the house specialities. Most main dishes cost Rs200–300.

Sublime 1/9-A Grande Morod, Saligao, 5km inland from Calangute market, ⓣ9822/484051. Indian-American chef Salim (aka Chris) earned a cult following with his previous restaurant in Anjuna. Its successor is bigger and more glamorous, with rose petals on glass-topped tables, and waiters in gold-trimmed *lunghis*. But the food, if anything, is even better, comprising a short, focused menu that's simple and stylish. Mains include balsamic beefsteak on a feta gratin, and fish fillet pan-fried in crunchy macadamia nuts with sweet-potato and maple-syrup mash. For starters, the ginger-battered squid is hard to top. Count on Rs600–800 for three courses, plus drinks. And reserve ahead.

Waves Kerkar Art Gallery. Sophisticated fusion cuisine, prepared by German chef Orlando Leykauf, and served in a beautifully decorated garden. Seafood and steaks dominate the dinner menu, which features some original creations as well as crowd-pleasing Continental standards. If you're feeling adventurous try the chicken breast with fresh coconut and saffron cauliflower, or lamb chop in tangy tamarind and port sauce. As well as à la carte, they also offer a good value three-course set menu for Rs450, including Orlando's signature leek soup.

Nightlife

Calangute's **nightlife** is surprisingly tame for a resort of its size. All but a handful of the **bars** wind up by 11pm, leaving punters to prolong the short evenings back at their hotels, find a shack that's open late or else head up to Baga (see p.128).

In the opposite direction, *Bob's Inn*, between Calangute and Candolim, is a famous old bar, renowned above all for its eponymous owner, who claims with some justification to have been Goa's first hippy. He was certainly around when the flea market started up, and was instrumental in organizing some of the legendary parties of the 1970s, as were several of his regulars. Seated around the long wooden table in the middle of the bar, under a portrait of Goa's most famous hippy, "Jungle Barry" (see box, p.122), the ageing heads love to do nothing more than reminisce about the good old days, between bouts of backgammon and serious drinking.

Meanwhile, the present generation party with a bit more fizz at a hilltop site in the Mollem Bhat Valley, 4km inland at Sangolda, near Saligao. With a dance-floor surrounded by jungle, rooftop pool and chillout areas, **Club Westend** (2–3 times weekly 9pm–4.30am; ⓣ0832/324 6727) is one of Goa's few bona fide dance venues. Admission fees fluctuate around Rs500–600, the music is dominated by trance, and the clientele is mostly 20-something Russians. Since the club's chief competitor in Arpora was forced to close in 2008, the queues and crowds here have started to become an issue, but there's really nowhere else worth bothering with south of Vagator. It's usually open on Tuesdays, Fridays and Saturdays; check in advance for precise days and details of international DJs.

Finally, for a more serene evening out, check out Tuesdays at the **Kerkar Art Gallery**, in Gauro Waddo at the south end of Calangute (ⓣ0832/227 6017, ⓦwww.subodhkerkar.com), which hosts weekly **classical music and dance** recitals from 6.45 to 8.30pm, held in the candle-lit back garden. The little concerts, performed by students and teachers from Panjim's Kala Academy, are kept comfortably short for the benefit of Western visitors, and are preceded by a short introductory talk. Tickets, available in advance or at the door, cost Rs300.

Listings

Art and lifestyle galleries The Kerkar Art Gallery (Mon–Sat 9.30am–7pm; free), at the southern edge of Calangute, exhibits and sells original paintings, sculpture and crafts by local Goan artists. Further north on the Baga road, the Cocoon Art Gallery is a smart boutique with designer clothes by Wendell Rodricks and hand-painted azulejos. The Rangeela Boutique, on the southeast edge of Calangute, is another small, chic designer outlet specializing in floaty white outfits and spangly flip-flops. It occupies the ground floor of a gorgeous old Goan house painted purple and white (with a matching auto-rickshaw parked outside). For quality ethnic Indian furniture, textiles and traditional ornaments, head 4km east of Calangute on the CHOGM road to Sangolda (Mon–Sat 10am–7.30pm), housed in a magnificently restored 200-year-old *palacio*. Alongside Sangolda stands another must-see studio in an old Portuguese-era mansion, where artist-designer duo Yahel Chirinian and Doris Zacheres exhibit extraordinary lighting sculptures and other installations.

Banks and exchange Thomas Cook has a branch in the main market area (Mon–Sat 9.30am–6pm), where there's also an efficient ICICI Bank with 24-hour ATM. Private currency changers on the same street include Wall Street Finances (Mon–Sat 9.30am–6pm), opposite the petrol pump and in the shopping complex on the beachfront, who exchange both cash and travellers' cheques at bank rates. At the Bank of Baroda (Mon–Fri 9.30am–2.15pm, Sat 9.30am–noon, Sun 9.30am–2pm), just north of the market on the Anjuna road, you can make encashments against Visa cards; commission is one percent of the amount changed, plus Rs125 for the authorization phone call.

Books One of Goa's best book shops, The Oxford Bookstore, stands on the south side of town, directly opposite St Anthony's Chapel on the main Candolim road. Modern Book Palace, just off the beach road, stocks mainly titles on India and Goa, including a particularly good selection of bird field guides. Down in Gauro Waddo near *Gabriel's*, on the edge of Candolim, Café Literati (10am–7pm; closed Weds) has a more off-beat, bibliophile feel about it, with a great collection of paper- and hardbacks shelved in a converted Portuguese-era house.

Baga

BAGA, 10km west of Mapusa, is basically an extension of Calangute; not even the locals agree where one ends and the other begins. The only real difference between the two is that the scenery here is marginally more picturesque. Overlooked by a

▲ Fishing boats, Baga

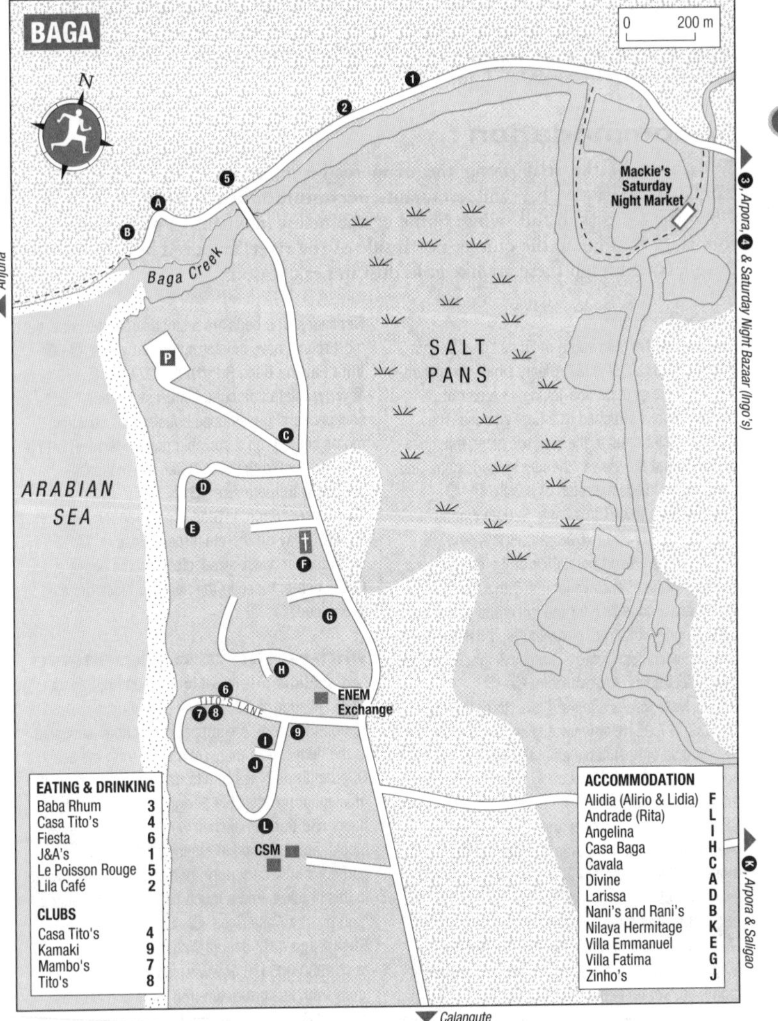

rocky headland draped in vegetation, a small tidal river flows into the sea at the top of the village, past a spur of soft white sand where ranks of brightly coloured fishing boats are moored.

Since the package boom, however, Baga has developed more rapidly than anywhere else in the state and today looks less like a Goan fishing village than a small-scale resort on one of the Turkish costas, complete with handbag dancers and bar brawls. The one things in its favour is that, as a consequence, its **nightlife** is far and away the most consistently full-on in Goa.

The **beach** itself is not for the faint-hearted. In front of an unbroken line of shacks, a shimmering mass of oiled, slowly basting flesh extends all the way to Candolim, sprawled on ranks of sunbeds stacked five or six rows deep in places.

Paragliders pulled into the air by noisy speedboats hang over the scene until the on-shore breezes die down at the end of the day, when the jet-skis and banana boats pack up and the stray cows move in to scour the sand for edible litter. So if you're looking for peace and quiet, forget it and head further north.

Accommodation

With most of the strip along the main road and its side lanes given over to handicraft boutiques, bars and restaurants, **accommodation** can be in short supply when the season's in full swing. Some of the nicest inexpensive guesthouses and rooms for rent lie on the quieter north side of the river, favoured by long-staying travellers, although these are like gold dust in peak season.

Inexpensive

Andrade (Rita) Just south of Tito's Lane, Saunta Waddo ⓣ0832/227 9087. Clean, simply furnished rooms, some of them sea-facing, in a pair of modern blocks attached to a family house. The slightly pricier ones to the rear are nicer, though you don't get the views. Friendly management, and close to the liveliest stretch of beach. ❸–❹

Angelina South of Tito's Lane, Saunta Waddo ⓣ0832/227 9145, or ⓣ9822/688084, ⓦwww.angelinabeachresort.com. Pick of the budget crop in this travellers' enclave just off Tito's Lane. The rooms are a good size for the price and well-maintained, with large, gleaming tiled bathrooms and big balconies. Owners Stanley & Preciosa D'Sa are perfect hosts. A/c available. ❸–❹

Divine Near *Nani's and Rani's*, north of the river ⓣ0832/227 9546, ⓦwww.indivinehome.com. Run by a couple of hospitable animal lovers, with rooms on the small side, if impeccably clean; some have attached shower-toilets, and there's a lovely upper terrace with sun-loungers and shades, presided over by a menagerie of animal finials on the rooftops. Complimentary wi-fi. Advance booking essential. ❹

Larissa Saunta Waddo ⓣ9823/269242. You could probably spot this day-glow, tangerine-coloured block from space. Thankfully its rooms are set up in more restrained style. They're huge for the price, impeccably clean, modern, have fridges and big, fat mattresses. Surveying the village from atop a dune, they're also right behind the beach, only a short stagger from the shacks. ❹

Nani's and Rani's North of the river (House #164) ⓣ0832/227 6313, ⓔjeshuafern@yahoo.com. A handful of red-tiled, whitewashed budget cottages in a secluded garden behind a huge colonial-era house. Fans, some attached bathrooms, well-water, outdoor showers and internet access. ❹

Villa Emmanuel *Calypso Hotel*, Saunta Waddo ⓣ0832/227 5667 or ⓣ9923/653514. You can't stay any closer to the beach than this double-storey block, run by local family Manuel and Meena Fernandes. The beds are a bit basic for the price, but most rooms have uninterrupted sea views. ❹–❺

Villa Fatima Baga Rd ⓣ0832/227 7418, ⓦwww.villafatima.com. Long-established backpackers' guesthouse boasting 32 attached rooms centred on a sociable garden terrace, with a nice big pool to the rear. Rates are reasonable, varying with room size. ❹

Zinho's 7/3 Saunta Waddo ⓣ0832/227 7383. Tucked away off the main road, close to *Tito's*. Seventeen modest-sized, clean rooms above a family home; those in the new a/c block are a bit overpriced. ❹–❺

Mid-range and expensive

Alidia (Alirio & Lidia) Baga Rd, Saunta Waddo ⓣ0832/227 6835, ⓔalidia@rediffmail.com. A compact resort hotel snuggled in the dunes, less than 1min walk from the beach. Offering three types of differently priced rooms, it's efficiently run, stylishly designed (with wooden floors and traditional shell windows in the newer block), and swathed in creepers and foliage. A gorgeous little curvi-form pool makes it great value in this bracket, and a much better deal all round than nearby *Casa Baga*. ❺–❻

Casa Baga 4/07 Saunta Waddo, ⓣ0832/241 6737 or ⓣ9960/605416 ⓦwww.casaboutiquehotels.com. With its corrugated-iron roofs and Balinese-inspired decor, this little boutique hotel is a curiously hybrid creature. While the location – only a stone's throw away from the sand – can't be faulted, the complex as a whole can feel oddly cramped. If you're tempted by its proximity to the beach, splash out on one of the 'luxury' (as opposed to the 'deluxe') rooms, which have wooden-floored verandas looking over the palm tops to the sea. There's also a small pool with a swim-up bar. Doubles from around Rs8000 ($180). ❾

Cavala Baga Rd ⓣ0832/227 7587 or 227 6090, ⓦwww.cavala.com. Modern hotel in tastefully traditional laterite, with a pool in a plot across the road surrounded by banana groves. The twin-bedded rooms have separate balconies front and back, the rear-side ones looking across open fields. Rooms range from simple non-a/c doubles to luxurious suites and are quiet despite the roadside location. 5–8

Nilaya Hermitage Arpora Bhati ⓣ0832/227 6793, ⓦwww.nilaya.com. Set on the crest of a hilltop 6km inland from the beach, with matchless views over the coastal plain, this ranks among India's most exclusive hotels, patronized by a very rich international jet set (Richard Gere, Giorgio Armani, Sean Connery and Kate Moss are all rumoured to have stayed here). The complex is a fantasy of rich Indian colours, fiddly ironwork and gilded pillars, opening onto a dreamy pool. Room tariffs include use of the steam room, gym and clay tennis court. Rooms from around $460 for two (or $700 over Christmas–New Year), including meals and airport transfers. 9

Eating and drinking

Nowhere else in the state offers such a good choice of quality **eating** as Baga. Restaurateurs – increasing numbers of them European expats or refugees from upper-class Mumbai – vie with each other to lay on the trendiest menus and most romantic, stylish gardens or terraces.

Baba Rhum Arpora ⓣ98220/78759. This funky French bakery-patisserie hidden deep in the expat enclave of Arpora, is a bit off the beaten track, but worth hunting out for its crumbly croissants, baguettes, pains au raisins, fruit salads, juices and perfect café au lait, served on heavy wood tables, with infectious World grooves playing in the background. You can lounge on a ground-floor terrace or on their shady roof space under floaty drapes. To find it, turn left off the main Calangute–Anjuna road when you see their signboard. Open 9am–3 or 4pm out of season, and through the evenings in Dec & Jan. Closed Sun.

Casa Tito's Opposite Ingo's Night Market, Arpora. Boutique-style restaurant in a stylishly renovated Portuguese *palacio*, filled with evocative memorabilia belonging to the Tito family. The menu is dominated by gourmet Mediterranean cuisine, served from a garden grill; it also functions as a lounge bar (see p.132). Most dishes Rs275–350.

Fiesta Tito's Lane ⓣ0832/227 9894, ⓦwww.fiestagoa.com. Baga's most sumptuously decorated restaurant enjoys a perfect spot at the top of a long dune, with sea views from the veranda of a 1930s house. Giant paper lanterns and an old fishing boat filled with scatter cushions set the tone. The contemporary Mediterranean food is as delectable as the decor. Try their carpaccio of beef for starters, followed by lasagne, ravioli or the succulent wood-baked pizzas (Rs250). Most starters and mains Rs300–400. Reservations recommended.

J&A's Anjuna Rd ⓣ0832/227 5274 or ⓣ9823/139488, ⓦwww.italyingoa.com. Authentic Italian food (down to the imported Parmesan, sun-dried tomatoes and olive oil) served in the gorgeous candle-lit garden of an old fisherman's cottage. There's an innovative range of salads and antipasti, a choice of sumptuous pasta dishes, wood-fired pizzas and tender steaks (with rosemary potatoes) for mains, though their signature dish, seafood lasagne, is hard to beat. For dessert, go for the melt-in-the-mouth hot chocolate soufflé. Most mains around Rs300–350; count on at least Rs1000 per head for three courses, plus drinks.

Le Poisson Rouge Baga Creek ⓣ0832/324 5800 or ⓣ9823/859276. The latest star addition to north Goa's gastronomic map, situated in a palm-shaded garden lit by pretty tea lights. Gregory Bazire, a second-generation chef from Normandy, adds a splash of Gallic panache to local ingredients and the results are *magnifique*. Try the golden fried Chapora calamari, served with basil hummus and a green coulis, followed by fragrant pomfret filet in anis-butter sauce, or asparagus rissotto. The menu changes every month or so, but usually features the chocolate mousse made with Keralan vanilla for desert. Most mains around Rs500. Advance reservation recommended.

Lila Café Baga Creek. Laid-back bakery-cum-snack-bar, run by a German couple who've been here for decades. Their healthy home-made breads and cakes are great, and there's an adventurous lunch menu featuring spinach à la crème, aubergine pâté and smoked water-buffalo ham. Open 8am–8pm.

Nightlife

That Baga's **nightlife** has become legendary in India is largely attributable to one club, **Tito's**. Lured by TV images of sexy dancewear and a thumping sound-and-light system, hundreds of revellers descend on its long narrow terrace each night

Saturday night bazaars

One of the few genuinely positive improvements to the north Goa resort strip over the past decade has been the **Saturday Night Bazaar**, held on a plot inland at Arpora, midway between Baga and Anjuna. Originally the brainchild of an expat German called Ingo, it's run with great efficiency and a sense of fun that's palpably lacking these days from the Anjuna flea market. The balmy evening temperatures and pretty lights are also a lot more conducive to relaxed browsing than the broiling heat of mid-afternoon on Anjuna beach.

Although far more commercial than its predecessor in Anjuna, many old Goa hands regard this as far truer to the original spirit of the flea market. A significant proportion of the stalls are taken up by foreigners selling their own stuff, from reproduction Indian pop art to antique photos, the latest trance party wear, hand-polished coconut shell art and techno DJ demos. There's also a mouthwatering array of ethnic food concessions to choose from and a stage featuring live music from around 7pm until midnight, when the market winds up. Admission is free.

A **competitor** in much the same mould – **Mackie's** – has opened nearby, closer to Baga by the riverside. Spurned by the expatriate designers and stallholders, this one is not quite as lively as its rival, though in recent years has made an effort to close the gap, with better live acts and more foreign stallholders.

to drink, shuffle about and watch the action, the majority of them men from other states who've come to Goa as an escape from the moral confines of life at home. For Western women, in particular, this can sometimes make for an uncomfortably loaded atmosphere, although since a recent face-lift (and a hike in door charges), *Tito's* seems to have put the era of Kingfisher-fuelled brawls behind it. New theme bars and clubs are also popping up each year, offering increasingly sophisticated alternatives.

For anyone who's been travelling around the rest of the country, Baga by night – complete with drunken karaoke, toga parties and all the garishness of a Saturday in British clubland – can come as an unpleasant shock. So, too, can the traffic congestion on Fridays and Saturdays; if you venture down here by motorbike on the weekend, park well away from Tito's Lane or you might find yourself literally jammed in until the small hours.

For more on the area's nightlife, see our accounts of Calangute (p.127) and Anjuna (p.137).

Bars and clubs

Casa Tito's Arpora, opposite Ingo's Night Market. Chic Italian gastro-lounge bar run by the *Tito's* nightclub crew as a homage to their father, in an old Portuguese-era house, with traditional furniture, family memorabilia, resident DJs, cocktails and gourmet food. A perfect post-Ingo's chillout spot.

Kamaki Tito's Lane. Big-screen sports and a state-of-the-art karaoke machine account for the appeal of this a/c, Brit-dominated bar just up the lane from *Tito's*. Rs200 cover charge sometimes applies.

Mambo's Tito's Lane. Large, semi-open-air pub with wooden decor and a big circular bar that gets packed out most nights in season with a lively, mixed crowd. Karaoke on Sunday is the big draw, though drinks cost well above average, and they slap on a Rs400 cover charge after 11pm, or when there's live entertainment. "Ladies Night", on Wednesday, means free entry and free drinks for women. From 8pm nightly.

Tito's Tito's Lane. ⓣ0832/227 5028 or ⓣ9822/765002. Occasional cabarets, fashion shows and guest DJs feature throughout the season at India's most famous nightclub. Red upholstery and uniformed waiters set the tone; music policy is lounge grooves till 11pm, and hip-hop, house, salsa and trance thereafter. See the noticeboard for Retro and other theme nights. Admission prices are Rs700 for men, which includes free drinks, and free for women (who also get free drinks). At Christmas, prices can soar to Rs1500 or more, depending on the attraction. Open 8–late Nov–Dec, and until 11pm out of season. Tues and Sat are busiest.

Anjuna

ANJUNA, the next sizeable village up the coast from Baga, was until a few years back the last bastion of alternative chic in Goa – where the state's legendary full-moon parties were staged each season, and where the Beautiful Set would rent pretty red-tiled houses for six months at a time, make trance mixes and groovy dance clothes, paint the palm trees flouro colours and spend months lazing on the beach. A small contingent of fashionably attired, middle-aged hippies still turn up, but thanks to a combination of the Y2K music ban (see p.143) and overwhelming growth in popularity of the flea market, Anjuna has seriously fallen out of fashion. Even the young Israeli hellraisers who inundated the village during the late 1990s – and were largely responsible for the government's crackdown on parties – have stopped coming.

As a consequence, the scattered settlement of old Portuguese houses and whitewashed churches, nestled behind a long golden sandy beach, nowadays resembles the place it was before the party scene snowballed.

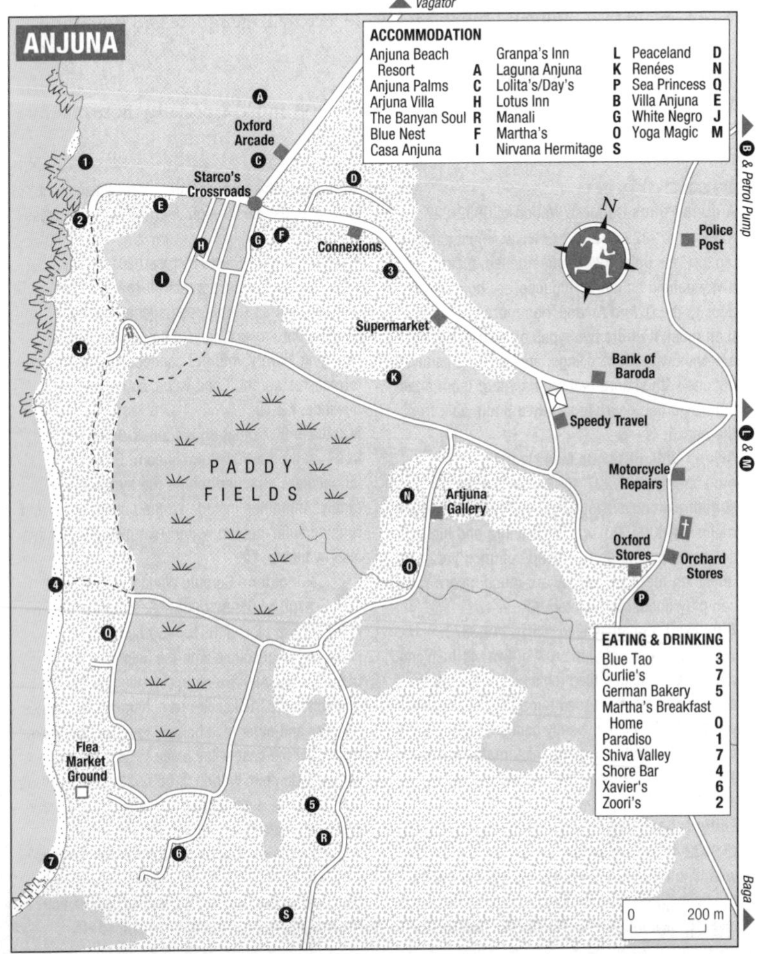

There are, however, two downsides to staying here. One is an enduringly druggy atmosphere. Levels of substance abuse, both among visitors and locals, remain exceptional, and the village suffers more than its fair share of dodgy characters. Just how seedy the scene revolving around Anjuna's shacks has grown became apparent in February 2008, after a British teenager, 15-year-old Scarlett Keeling, was raped and murdered. The other negative thing about the village – at least, if you're staying here – is the famous **flea market**. Every Wednesday, the beach and coconut groves at the south end of the beach get swamped with tourists and sellers from other resorts, forcing most of the resident tourist population north to neighbouring Vagator for the day.

Arrival

Buses from Mapusa and Panjim drop passengers at various points along the surfaced road across the top of the village, which turns right towards Chapora at the main crossroads by *Starco's*. If you're looking for a room, get off here as it's close to most of the guesthouses. The crossroads has a couple of small **stores**, a **motorcycle taxi** rank, and functions as a de facto village square and **bus stand**.

Accommodation

Visitors are spoilt for choice of **places to stay** in Anjuna, especially those on more flexible budgets.

Inexpensive

Anjuna Palms De Mello Waddo ⓣ0832/227 3268 or ⓣ9822/686817, ⓦwww.anjunapalms.co.uk. This little budget guesthouse, tucked away behind an old Portuguese-era house next door to the Oxford Arcade, has more character than most. It offers two types of rooms: larger, a/c ones with high ceilings; and more ramshackle options with shared bathrooms. All of them open onto a garden courtyard. Only a 5min walk from the beach. ❷–❸

Arjuna Villa 681/1 De Mello Waddo, 4th Lane ⓣ0832/227 4590 or 227 4591, ⓔgodfreymathia@hotmail.com. Pleasant budget rooms (Rs600–700) with tiled floors and high ceilings, opening on to a deep common veranda (those on the upper storey are much nicer). You can play floodlit badminton. ❸

Blue Nest Soronto Waddo ⓣ9763/063379. Jospah and Cecilia's little row of five old-fashioned rooms, with pitched tiled roofs and wood rafters, are close to the main road through the village, but you wouldn't know it. Neatly painted, they're large for the price and have good thick mattresses, as well as nice little tiled verandas looking onto woodland. ❸

Lolita's/Day's Behind Orchard Stores ⓣ9822/461615. A handful of simple, large rooms with high tiled roofs and attached shower-toilets, run by the affable Darryl Days. The pricier one has an air cooler, fridge and TV. Peaceful, despite its proximity to the road, and there's a relaxing roof terrace. Bookable through Joel's Mini Store across the road. ❹

Manali South of *Starco's* crossroads ⓣ0832/227 4421. Anjuna's most popular all-round budget guesthouse has simple rooms (shared toilets) opening onto a yard, fans, safe deposit, money-changing, library, internet connection and sociable terrace-restaurant. Good value, so book in advance. ❷–❸

Martha's 907 Montero Waddo ⓣ0832/227 4194, ⓔmpd8650@hotmail.com. Eleven immaculate attached rooms run by a friendly family. Amenities include kitchen space, fans and running solar-heated water. Two pleasant houses also available. ❹

Peaceland Soronto Waddo ⓣ0832/227 3700 or ⓣ9822/685255. Simple attached rooms in two blocks (Rs400–500), run by a charming local couple with the help of a pair of friendly dogs. All have high, clay-tiled roofs, mosquito nets, rucksack racks, hammocks, clothes hangers and other nice homely touches that make this easily the best-value place in its class. ❸

Renées Monteiro Waddo ⓣ0832/227 3405. This is a little gem of a guesthouse. Swathed in greenery, welcoming and family run, it holds only half a dozen rooms, most of them surprisingly spacious, with garden-facing balconies. A few have simple kitchenettes and fridges. It's a notch pricier than the competition, but worth the extra. ❹–❺

Mid-range

Anjuna Beach Resort De Mello Waddo ⓣ0832/227 4499, ⓔfabjoe@sancharnet.com. This place offers 32 spacious, comfortable rooms with balconies, fridges, attached bathrooms and solar-heated water in two concrete blocks ranged around a pool. Those on the upper floors are best. There's also a block of apartments for long-stayers; both are very good value, though the complex is showing signs of age. ❺–❻

The Banyan Soul Temb ⓣ9820/707283, ⓦwww.thebanyansoul.com. Leafy, designer chic on the quiet, southeastern fringes of the village. Shaded by an old banyan tree, the rooms are attractively decorated – though small for the price – and each has a private outdoor sitting area that's well screened from the neighbours. The German Bakery's just a skip away and owner Sumit is on site with help and advice. Some readers find this place a bit overpriced and boxed in; others love its tucked-away feel. ❻–❼

Granpa's Inn Gaun Waddo ⓣ0832/227 3270, ⓦwww.granpasinn.com. Formerly known as *Bougainvillea*, a lovely 200-year-old house set in half an acre of lush gardens, with a kidney-shaped pool and shady breakfast terrace. They offer three categories of rooms, all fully en suite: non-a/c standards; suites in the main house; and poolside (in a recently built chalet block built in traditional style, but with modern furnishings and private outdoor showers). Yoga on site (see p.139); and there's a billiards table. Very popular, so book well ahead. ❻–❼

Lotus Inn Zor Waddo ⓣ0832/227 4015, ⓦwww.lotusinngoa.com. On the leafy northern limits of Anjuna, tucked away down a maze of narrow lanes: eleven swish suites and six double rooms (on the small side for the Rs2000–3500 tariff), all with a/c and centred around a good-sized pool. They also host a trendy poolside Italian restaurant and barbecue parties on Sun. ❻–❼

Sea Princess 649 Goenkar Waddo, Dando ⓣ9890/449090. Simple guesthouse in a prime position in the middle of the beach, near the *Shore Bar*. The rooms are spacious, and all have bathrooms with dependable plumbing, but aren't as well maintained as they might be and suffer from the invasion of mosquitoes. Its main selling point is the location, right on the dunes. ❺

Villa Anjuna Near Anjuna beachfront ⓣ0832/227 3443, ⓦwww.anjunavilla.com. Modern, efficient resort hotel close to the beach, on the main road through the village. Amenities include a fair-sized pool and Jacuzzi. Popular with clubbers, as it's a short amble from *Paradiso* (so sometimes a little noisy at night). ❻–❼

White Negro 719 Praia de St Anthony, south of the village, near St Anthony's Chapel ⓣ0832/227 3326, ⓔdsouzawhitenegro@rediffmail.com. A row of twelve spotless back-to-back chalets catching the sea breeze, all with attached bathrooms, tiled floors, safe lockers and mosquito nets. Quiet, efficient and good value. ❺

Yoga Magic ⓣ0832/62 3796 or ⓣ9370/565717, ⓦwww.yogamagic.net. Innovative "Canvas Ecotel", offering low-impact luxury on the edge of Anjuna in Rajasthani hunting tents. The structures are all decorated with block-printed cotton, furnished with cushions, silk drapes, coir carpets and solar halogen lights, and colour-themed to correspond with the yogic chakras. Loos are of the biodegradable, non-smelly compost kind. They also have the even more luxurious (but only slightly more expensive) Maharaja and Maharani Suites in a wing of an adjacent stone house, with wooden doors, arched windows and shutters and beautiful curved walls. The king-size bed looks onto a veranda and a very sexy pool. Open mid-Nov to May. ❼

Expensive

Casa Anjuna 66 D'Mello Waddo ⓣ0832/227 4305, ⓦwww.casaboutiquehotels.com. Set in a converted 200-year-old colonial mansion, this exclusive small hotel has nineteen rooms, all of them fitted with handsome Indo-Portuguese-style four-posters, tapestries and textiles. The verandas are also pretty, as are the large pool and garden – a riot of frangipani, bougainvillea and alamanda flowers. Meals are served on what must be one of the loveliest roof terraces in India. Rs7000–13,000 ($157–292), rising to Rs12,000–18,000 ($270–405) over Christmas. ❾

Laguna Anjuna De Mello Waddo ⓣ0832/227 4305 or ⓣ9822/162111, ⓦwww.lagunaanjuna.com. Alternative boutique resort comprising 25 colourfully decorated, domed laterite cottages with wooden rafters and terracotta tiles, grouped behind a convoluted pool. While a bit shabby around the edges these days, it remains popular nonetheless, and there's also a restaurant, pool tables and bar. Doubles from $145 mid-season, rising to $335 for Christmas–New Year. ❾

Nirvana Hermitage Temb ⓣ0832/325 2850, ⓦwww.nirvanahermitage.com. A bungled attempt to replicate the designer style of the *Nilaya Hermitage*, with chalets and a large curviform pool wrapped around a west-facing hillside. It has a few too many rough edges for the tariffs, but the location, looking across the palm forest to the sea, is unrivalled in Anjuna. ❽–❾

The beach and flea market

The north end of Anjuna **beach**, just below where the buses pull in, is no great shakes by Goan standards, with a dodgy undertow and lots of even dodgier Kashmiris selling hash, as well as parties of whisky-filled daytrippers in constant attendance.

The vibe is much nicer at the far, southern end, where a pretty and more sheltered cove accommodates a mostly 20-something tourist crowd. A constant trance soundtrack thumps from the shacks behind it, cranking up to proper parties after dark, when **Curlies** and neighbouring **Shiva Valley** take turns to max their sound systems, hosting international DJs through the season. Chai ladies and food stallholders sit in wait on the sands, just as for the raves of old, but the party grinds to a halt at 10pm sharp.

The biggest crowds gather on Wednesdays, after Anjuna's **flea market**, held in the coconut plantation behind the southern end of the beach, just north of *Curlie's*. Along with the Saturday Night Bazaar at Arpora (see p.132), this is *the* place to indulge in a spot of souvenir shopping. Two decades ago, the weekly event was the exclusive preserve of backpackers and the area's seasonal residents, who gathered here to smoke chillums and to buy and sell party clothes and jewellery. These days, however, everything is more organized and mainstream. Pitches are rented out by the metre, drugs are banned and the approach roads to the village are choked all day with air-conditioned buses and Maruti taxis ferrying in tourists from resorts further down the coast. Even the beggars have to pay baksheesh to be here.

Each region of India is represented in the stalls. At one end, ever-diminishing ranks of Westerners congregate around racks of fluoro party gear and designer beachwear, while in the heart of the site, Tibetan jewellery sellers preside over orderly rows of turquoise bracelets and Himalayan curios. Most distinctive of all are the Lamani women from Karnataka, decked from head to toe in traditional tribal garb and selling elaborately woven multicoloured cloth, which they fashion into everything from jackets to money belts. Elsewhere, you'll come across

The Anjuna jinx

One reason Anjuna may have been spared the sprawling development that today blights most of Baga and Calangute is an old dictum prophesying **bad luck** for the owners of any construction with an upper storey. Every villager knows of the curse, and few, if any, have ignored it, despite the lucrative spread of concrete further down the coast. Express even the slightest scepticism and you'll be reminded of numerous cases.

No one knows where the curse originated. Less superstitious villagers suggest it may be derived from years of experience building on Anjuna's sandy soils. This, however, doesn't explain the bizarre runs of misfortune that appear to have dogged those who have erected "ground-plus-one" structures over the centuries.

Among the most notorious victims of the curse was one **Dr Manuel Albuquerque**, who in the early years of the twentieth century served as the personal physician of the Sultan of Zanzibar, Sayeed Khalifa 'bin Haruba. On being decorated with a special Golden Sword award for his long service, Albuquerque was asked by his employer what he would like as a gift of thanks for safeguarding the health of the royal household so devotedly. The doctor replied that he wanted to build a replica of the Sultan's palace in his native Goa, where he soon planned to retire. Permission was duly granted, and Albuquerque recruited a team of crack Zanzibari artisans to build his mansion, which boasted marble floors and was said to be crammed with ivory statues and Macao porcelain. However, Albuquerque's family, bedevilled by various misfortunes, bore no heirs and fell upon hard times, while the building, though still standing (just north of *Starco's* crossroads on the way to Vagator), now serves as a drug rehabilitation centre.

dazzling Rajasthani mirrorwork and block-printed bedspreads, Gujarati appliqué, Orissan palm-leaf manuscripts, pyramids of colourful spices and incense, sequined shoes and ayurvedic cures for every conceivable ailment.

What you end up paying for this exotic merchandise largely depends on your ability to **haggle**. Prices are sky-high by Indian standards. Be persistent, though, and cautious, and you can usually pick things up for a reasonable rate, except from the Westerner designers, who are not so fond of haggling.

Even if you're not spending, the flea market is a great place just to sit and watch the world go by. Mingling with the suntanned masses are bands of strolling musicians, mendicant sadhus and fortune-telling bulls. And if you happen to miss the show, rest assured that the whole cast reassembles every Saturday at Baga/Arpora's **night markets** (see p.132).

Eating and drinking

Responding to the tastes of its alternative visitors, Anjuna boasts a good crop of quality **cafés** and **restaurants**, many of which serve healthy vegetarian dishes and juices. If you're hankering for a taste of home, call in at the **Orchard Arcade** on the northern side of the village, which serves the expatriate community with a vast range of pricey imported delights.

For more restaurants in this area, see also "Eating" listings for Vagator and Chapora on p.142 and p.144.

Blue Tao On the main road through the village. An Italian-run "alternative health restaurant" that offers some of Goa's most delicious breakfasts (sourdough and wholemeal breads, herbal teas, *tahini* and spirulina spreads). In addition to a full menu of main courses (Rs175–250), they also do a tempting range of juices, including wheatgrass, ginseng and ayurvedic concoctions. Non-smoking and kid-friendly.

German Bakery South Anjuna, on the road to *Nirvana Hermitage* Ⓦ www.german-bakery.org. The one and only, original outlet of this much-copied wholefood café-restaurant, hidden away in a tree-shaded garden on the south side of the village, is Goa's ultimate travellers' hangout. Under old trees strung with Tibetan prayer flags and Pipli lanterns, you can order from an ever-evolving menu featuring such rarities as buckwheat porridge, cambucha tea and wheatgrass. For the less health conscious there's a full mains menu of Italian, Indian, Tibetan and seafood, and of course the bakery's famous cakes and coffee. Live music, dance and circus cabarets are frequent in season, and the place is wi-fi enabled.

Martha's Breakfast Home *Martha's* guesthouse, 907 Montero Waddo. Secluded, very friendly breakfast garden serving fresh Indian coffee, crepes, healthy juices, apple and cinnamon porridge, fruit salads with curd and – the house speciality – melt-in-the-mouth waffles with proper maple syrup.

Shore Bar Above the beach, midway down. Fantastic selection of food from amazing toasted *paneer* salads to traditional Goan fish dishes. There's also a good smattering of fusion food like calamari wraps. Great vibe, especially at sunset, although you might wish they'd turn the music down a bit.

Xavier's South Anjuna. Nestled in the palm forest just inland from the flea market ground, *Xavier's* has formed the hub of the south Anjuna alternative scene for decades, and is still going strong. Most people come for the seafood, kebabs, tikkas and tandoori dishes, but they also serve tasty Chinese and Italian, organic salads and delicious home-made pickles. Look for the sign on the left off the market lane.

Zoori's North end of the beach, next to *Paradiso* (see p.138). Chilled Israeli-run café-restaurant occupying a perfect spot on the clifftops – one of the most beautiful places in Goa for sunset, though the views outstrip the food. Open 10am–midnight.

Nightlife

Anjuna's far from the rave venue it used to be, but at least one big **party** is still held in the area around the Christmas–New Year full-moon period. For the rest of the season, techno heads have to make do with the rather shabby, mainstream

Paradiso, overlooking the far north end of Anjuna beach. Part owned by the government, this place epitomizes the new, more above-board face of Goa Trance. Presiding over a dance space surrounded by spacey statues of Hindu gods and Tantric symbols, visiting DJs spin trance for a mainly Indian and Russian crowd. *Paradiso* keeps to a sporadic timetable, but should be open most nights from around 10pm until dawn; admission charges are Rs300–700, depending on the night.

At the opposite end of Anjuna, **Curlie's** and **Shiva Valley** (see p.136) form the focus of a mini rave scene, with large, mixed crowds of both Indian and Western tourists gathering from sunset until 10pm. Some kind of "arrangement" has clearly been made with the local police here. Chillums and joints are smoked openly in and around the cafés, but arrests are commonplace along the paths and lanes behind. Be warned that rumours are rife of cops, or fake cops, extorting bribes and sexual favours from tourists caught in possession of illegal drugs. The death of 15-year-old Scarlett Keeling, whose body was found after she'd been raped and murdered in the dunes in 2008, showed just how dangerous the village's druggy underbelly can be.

Listings

Books On the floor above Oxford Stores, in southeast Anjuna, there's a small bookshop well stocked with new and secondhand titles.

Foreign exchange The *Manali* guesthouse and Oxford Arcade change money, but at poorer rates than you'll be offered down in Calangute market. The Bank of Baroda on the Mapusa Road will make encashments against Visa cards, but doesn't do foreign exchange. Local agents for Western Union are Connexions, east of *Starco's* (Ⓣ0832/227 74347).

Internet access *Manali* guesthouse and Space Ride, next to Speedy Travel.

Motorcycle repairs Anjuna's two motorcycle repair workshops are both up the road from the Oxford Stores. The smaller one, further back from the roadside, is more helpful. Fuel and some spares, such as inner tubes and spark plugs, can be bought from the store on the *Starco's* crossroads.

Pharmacy St Michael's Pharmacy, Soronto Waddo, near the *Starco's* crossroads, is open 24hr during the season.

Post office Just off the Mapusa Road, 1km inland.

Shopping The Oxford Arcade, just north of *Starco's* crossroads, is the area's largest supermarket, and stocks a huge range of imported foods, useful kit and Indian souvenirs.

Travel agents Connexions (Ⓣ & Ⓕ0832/227 74347), east of *Starco's* on the main Mapusa Road; Speedy Travel (Ⓣ0832/227 3266) lies between the post office and the *Rose Garden* restaurant.

Vagator

Barely a couple of kilometres of clifftops and parched grassland separate Anjuna from the southern fringes of its nearest neighbour, **VAGATOR**. Spread around a tangle of winding back lanes, this is a more chilled-out, undeveloped resort that appeals to a mix of young, backpacking party heads, and southern European beach bums who've been coming back for years. It's also the site of north Goa's two favourite party venues, the *Nine Bar* and *Hilltop*, around which a lively café scene has sprung up in recent years.

With the red ramparts of Chapora fort looming above it, Vagator's broad sandy **beach** – known as "**Big Vagator**" – is undeniably beautiful. However, a peaceful swim or sunbathe is out of the question here as it's a prime stop for bus parties of domestic tourists. A much better option, though one that still sees more than its fair share of day-trippers, is the next beach south. Backed by a steep wall of crumbling palm-fringed laterite, **Ozran** (or "Little") **Vagator beach** is actually a string of three contiguous coves. To reach them you have to walk from the bus

Yoga and holistic therapies in north Goa

North Goa ranks among the best places in the world to study **yoga** – as well as **massage** and **meditation**, not to mention more obscure therapies – with an unrivalled concentration of international teachers and centres. The Goan climate must take some of the credit for this, as must the proximity of the beach; fees are much lower than you'd pay back home, too. Below is a list of the established outfits. Pointers to individual teachers and courses appear in specific accounts.

Ashiyana Tropical Retreat Centre Junasa Waddo ⓦwww.ashiyana-yoga-goa.com. If you like your yoga retreats to be drop-dead gorgeous, look no further than here. Perched on the banks of the Mandrem River facing the sea from the middle of an old coconut *mand*, the centre offers world-class yoga, massage, meditation and satsang tuition – from resident and visiting teachers – with accommodation in beautifully designed Indonesian-style tree houses and eco lodges. All of them boast glorious sea views, and there's a funky wholefood-ayurvedic-veg restaurant on site (guests only). Daily and weekly rates include workshops.

Brahmani Centre In the garden of *Grandpa's Inn* (see p.135), Anjuna ⓦwww.brahmaniyoga.com. Offers drop-in yoga classes – mainly asthanga, with a few taster sessions in other styles, plus *pranayama* and *bhajan* devotional singing – by topnotch teachers. All levels of ability are catered for.

Kundalini Yoga Centre Girkar Waddo, Arambol ⓦwww.organickarma.co.uk (see p.155). Kundalini yoga (as taught by Yogi Bhajan) is a rarity in Goa, and this small rooftop garden in south Arambol is a great place to sample its trademark mix of posture (*asana*), breathing techniques (*pranayama*), chanting (mantra) and meditation practices, under the tutelage of expat British teacher Viriam Kaur.

Himalaya Yoga Valley Mandrem ⓣ98823/10709, ⓦwww.yogagoaindia.com. Nestled away in the peace of Mandrem, you can learn your backbends under the expert gaze of Yogacharya Lalit with drop-in classes, although their main focus is teacher training. This is their winter hideout; summer finds them in Dharamsala.

Purple Valley Centre Assagao ⓦwww.yogagoa.com. Purple Valley has accommodation for up to forty guests and what must be one of the loveliest yoga *shalas* (practice areas) in India. Their teachers include Nancy Gilgoff and Sharath Rangaswamy, grandson of the illustrious ashtanga guru, Shri K. Pattabhi Jois.

Raso Vai Ayurvedic Centre House No 162/2-A, on the road between Aswem and Morjim, nr *La Plage* ⓣ9850 973458, ⓦwww.rasovai.com. One of the best places to learn massage in Goa. As well as traditional ayurvedic treatments, they also offer their trademark fusion massages 'Ayurbalance' and 'Ayuryogic', which combines yoga stretches and massage.

Watsu Water Centre Assagao ⓣ9326/127020, ⓦwww.watsugoa.com. "Float into Bliss" runs the strapline of this innovative aqua therapy, which aims to restore the mind–body balance by stretching and relaxing in warm water. The centre's lovely, shaded pool is set in the garden of a private home.

park above Big Vagator, or drive to the end of the lane running off the main Chapora–Anjuna road (towards the *Nine Bar*), from where footpaths drop sharply down to a wide stretch of level white sand (look for the mopeds and bikes parked at the top of the cliff).

Long dominated by Italian tourists, the southernmost – dubbed "**Spaghetti Beach**" – is the prettiest, with a string of well-established shacks, at the end of which a face carved out of the rocks, staring serenely skywards, is the most prominent landmark. Relentless racquetball, trance sound systems and a particularly sizeable herd of stray cows are the other defining features.

Arrival and information

Buses from Panjim and Mapusa, 9km east, pull in every fifteen minutes or so at the crossroads on the far northeastern edge of Vagator, near where the main road peels away towards Chapora. From here, it's a one-kilometre walk over the hill and down the other side to the beach. *Bethany Inn*, on the north side of the village, has a **foreign exchange** licence (for cash and travellers' cheques) and efficient **travel agency** in the office on the ground floor. If you need medical attention, contact Dr Jawarhalal Henriques at Zorin, near the petrol pump in Chapora (☎0832/227 4308).

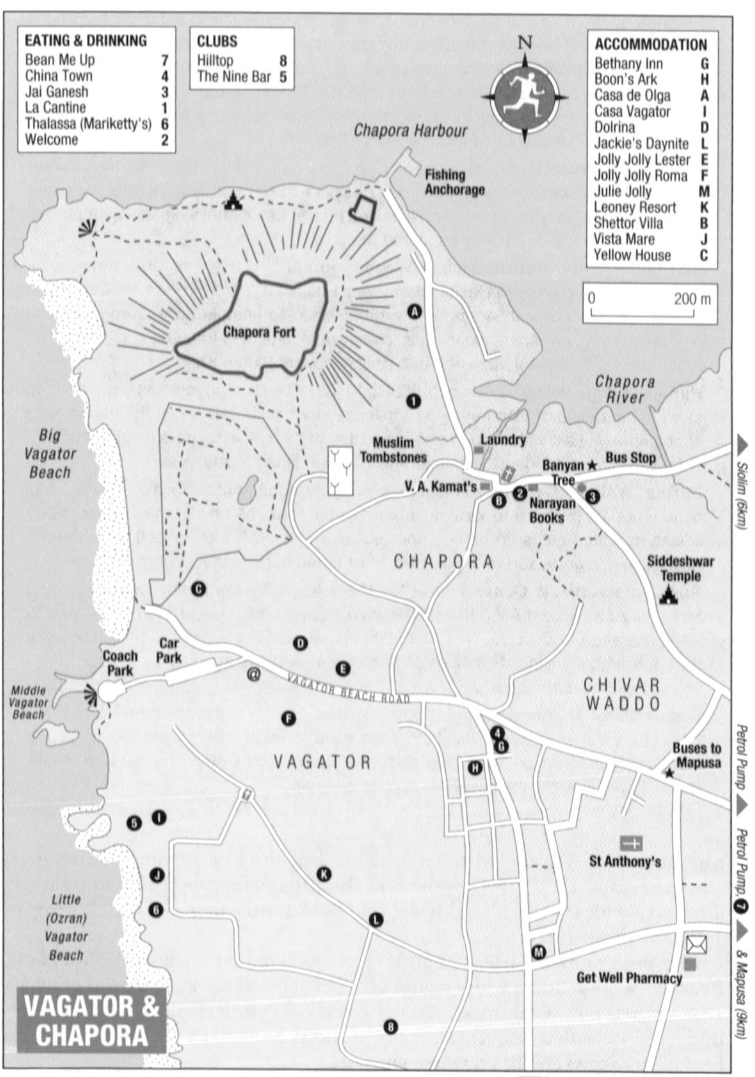

Accommodation

Accommodation comprises mostly family-run budget guesthouses hidden away in the lanes, and a string of pricey hut camps on the clifftop. As with everywhere else in this area, tariffs typically double at Christmas–New Year, when you'd be lucky indeed to find a bed anywhere at short notice.

Bethany Inn Just south of the main road ⓣ0832/227 3731, ⓦwww.bethanyinn.com. Eleven immaculate, self-contained rooms (four of them with a/c) with minibar fridges, balconies and attached bathrooms (Rs800); plus four additional a/c options in a new block, with big flat-screen TVs, larger balconies and more spacious tiled bathrooms (Rs1800). Tastefully furnished throughout, and efficiently managed by pair of young brothers from Pune. ❹–❺

Boon's Ark Near *Bethany Inn* ⓣ9822/175620, ⓦboonsark.com. Honest, clean, family-run place offering modern rooms with excellent beds, stone shelves, fridges and pleasant little verandas opening on a well-tended courtyard garden. Owners Peter and Jessie Mungu, also offer room service, money changing and bikes to rent. Great value. ❹

Casa Vagator 594/4 Ozran Vagator, behind *Nine Bar* ⓣ0832/241 6737 or ⓣ9960/605416, ⓦwww.casaboutiquehotels.com. New mini resort pitched at wealthy yuppy couples from Delhi and Mumbai. Surrounding an oval-shaped pool, it offers two kinds of rooms: the "deluxe" doubles (Rs7700/$173) share sit-outs and are far less inviting than the "luxury" options (Rs8800/$198), furnished with designer leather sofas and lovely polished granite floors. The big drawback here, though, is noise from the adjacent *Nine Bar* between 5 and 10pm. ❾

Dolrina Vagator Beach Rd ⓣ0832/227 3382, or ⓣ9822/980447. Nestled under a lush canopy of trees near the beach, Vagator's largest budget guesthouse is run by a friendly local couple and features attached or shared bathrooms, a couple of larger family rooms, sociable garden café, individual safe deposits and roof space. Single occupancy rates, and breakfasts is served in their atmospheric rear garden. ❷–❸

Jackie's Daynite Beach Rd ⓣ0832/227 4330, or ⓣ9822/133789. The best all-round budget place in the village, perfectly placed within easy reach of both the *Nine Bar* and *Hilltop*. Jackie De Souza has been running a café and shop here for more than thirty years, and recently added rooms behind. They're clean and great value, with solar hot water and sociable sit-outs facing a courtyard or garden terrace; often booked up, so reserve in advance. ❸–❹

Jolly Jolly Lester Vagator Beach Rd ⓣ0832/227 3620 or ⓣ9822/488536, ⓦwww.hoteljollygoa.com. Eleven agreeable doubles with tiled bathrooms, lockers and fresh towels provided, set in shady woodland and a garden lovingly protected by owners Lazarus and Remy from marauding monkeys. Small restaurant on site; single occupancy is possible. ❹

Jolly Jolly Roma Vagator Beach Rd ⓣ0832/227 3005 or ⓣ9822/488536, ⓦwww.hoteljollygoa.com. Very smart, good-sized chalet-style rooms with high ceilings, nice furniture and private verandas, again surrounded by a nice garden; they also offer laundry, exchange facilities and a small library. ❹–❺

Julie Jolly South side of the village ⓣ0832/227 3357, ⓦwww.hoteljollygoa.com. New complex built around a large (and kid-friendly) pool close to Ozran clifftop area. The rooms are on the small side, very Goan in their colour schemes, and don't have much outside sitting space, but they're immaculate and good value. ❺

Leoney Resort On the road to *Disco Valley* ⓣ0832/227 3634, ⓦwww.leoneyresort.com. Comfortable option, with swish "mock Portuguese" chalets and pricier (but more spacious) octagonal "cottages" on the sleepy side of the village, ranged around a very nice little pool. Restaurant, laundry, lockers, foreign exchange facilities and internet café on site. No advance bookings Dec–Jan. ❼–❽

Vista Mare Ozran clifftop ⓣ9822/120980. Lovely big rooms behind a (quiet-ish) restaurant on the clifftop, boasting king-size beds, spacious attached bathrooms, marble-topped tables and huge verandas. A top location and very good value. ❺

Yellow House Big Vagator ⓣ9822/125869. Henriquita Moniz and son Jubert recently renovated this guesthouse behind Big Vagator beach, which now looks better than ever after more than twenty years in business. It's peaceful and secluded, despite the proximity of the surf, and the rooms are neat and pleasantly furnished, though not all have outside sitting space (some open onto an internal gallery). Laundry available. ❹

Eating, drinking and nightlife

Vagator's travellers' scene has spawned a bumper crop of **restaurants**, as well as the usual rash of shacks down on the beach. With the exception of *Bean Me Up* and *Thalassa*, none are all that innovative, but they're a cut above the dives in Chapora bazaar.

The place for a sundowner is the **Nine Bar**, on the cliffs above Ozran beach, where big trance sounds attract a crowd for sunset, especially after the flea market (Wed). Admission is free, but drink prices are high and photography strictly prohibited. From late afternoon, punters drift between here and the nearby **Hilltop** bar, which has a pretty, circular dancefloor in a coconut grove, and heavy-duty PA. The palm trunks are painted regulation flouro colours, chai ladies ring the arena with their flickering kerosene lamps and freshly baked nibbles, foreign DJs do the honours on stage, and on Friday nights there's a colourful market where expat Westerners show off their creations. You could, in fact, be forgiven for thinking yourself back in the 1990s (precisely the effect intended) were it not for the Rs150 admission charge and security frisk on the way in.

Bean Me Up Near the petrol pump. India's one and only American-run tofu joint – the last word in Goan gourmet healthy eating. Design-your-own salads and fresh juices, or tuck into various tofu, tempeh and seitan combos steeped in creamy sauces, or pizzas from a real wood oven. Mains (Rs100–250) come with steamed spinach, fresh brown bread and hygienically washed greens; try their "cosmic sample platter" (a bit of everything served with brown rice). There's also a tempting range of vegan desserts.

China Town Chapora crossroads, next to *Bethany Inn*. This small roadside restaurant, tucked away just south of the main drag, is a perennially popular budget eating place, serving particularly tasty seafood dishes in addition to a large Chinese selection and all the usual Goa-style travellers' grub.

Thalassa (Mariketty's) Ozran clifftop ⓣ9850/033537. Corfu-born Mariketty started out selling *souvlakis* and kebabs from a hole-in-the-wall joint down in Chapora bazaar, and progressed to this clifftop taverna after middle-class foodies started joining the queues. *Thalassa* is now firmly established as one of the best restaurants in Goa. Unpretentious and hospitable, it serves honest, flavoursome and scrupulously authentic Greek cooking, against a backdrop of swaying palms and rippling ocean. The melt-in-the-mouth *souvlakis* are as good as ever, but for a full-on Hellenic feast, try the freshly baked moussaka or hearty lamb and feta stew (*kleftiko*). Mains around Rs250–300. Count on Rs650 for three courses, plus drinks.

Chapora

Huddled in the shadow of a Portuguese fort on the opposite, northern side of the headland from Vagator is **CHAPORA,** north Goa's main fishing port. The anchorage and boatyard below its red-walled citadel form the backbone of the village's economy, but there's always been a hard-drinking, heavy-smoking hippy tourist scene alongside it, revolving around the coffee shops and bars on the main street. Come here at sunset time and you'll see the "boom shankar brigade" out in full force, sipping banana lassis and toking on chillums under the banyan tree – a spectacle little changed in decades. For a brief period a few years back, Russian mafia types took over and forced the freaks out, but like migrating turtles they've returned to their old hangout in numbers undiminished by the recent changes in Goa. If this doesn't sound much like your bag, you'll probably be best off sticking to neighbouring Vagator.

The fort

Chapora's venerable old **fort** is most easily reached from the Vagator side of the hill (see map). The red-laterite bastion was built by the Portuguese in 1617 on the site of an earlier Muslim structure (whence the village's name – from Shahpura,

The dark side of the moon

Lots of visitors come to Goa expecting to be able to party on the beach every night, and are dismayed when the only places to dance turn out to be **mainstream clubs** they probably wouldn't look twice at back home. But the truth is that the full-on, elbows-in-the-air beach party of old, when tens of thousands of revellers would space out to huge techno sound systems under fluoro-painted palm trees, and chill out afterwards in the surf under massive full moons, is well and truly a thing of the past in Goa – thanks largely to the stern attitude of the local government.

Goa's coastal villages saw their first big raves back in 1960s with the influx of **hippies** to Calangute and Baga. Much to the amazement of the locals, the preferred pastime of these wannabe sadhus was to cavort naked on the sands together on full-moon nights, amid a haze of chillum smoke and loud rock music blaring from makeshift sound systems. The villagers took little notice of these bizarre gatherings at first, but with each season the scene became better established, and by the late 1970s the **Christmas and New Year parties**, in particular, had become huge events, attracting travellers from all over the country.

In the late 1980s, the local party scene received a dramatic shot in the arm with the coming of acid house and techno. Ecstasy became the preferred dance drug as the rock and dub-reggae scene gave way to rave culture, with ever-greater numbers of young clubbers pouring in for the season on charter flights. Goa soon spawned its own distinctive brand of psychedelic music, known as **Goa Trance**. Distinguished by its multilayered synth lines and sub-bass rhythms, the hypnotic style combines the darkness of hard techno with a brighter ambient edge. Cultivated by artists such as Goa Gill, Juno Reactor and Hallucinogen, the new sound was given wider exposure when big-name DJs Danny Rampling and Paul Oakenfold started mixing Goa Trance in clubs and on national radio back in the UK.

The **golden era** for Goa's party scene, and Goa Trance, was in the early 1990s, when big raves were held two or three times a week in beautiful locations around Anjuna and Vagator. For a few years the authorities turned a blind eye to the growing scene. Then, quite suddenly, the plug was pulled. For years, drug busts and bribes had provided the notoriously corrupt Goan cops with a lucrative source of baksheesh. But after a couple of drug-related deaths, a series of sensational articles in the local press and a decision by Goa Tourism to promote upmarket over backpacker tourism, the police began to demand impossibly large bribes.

Against this backdrop, the imposition during the run up to the Y2K celebrations of an **amplified-music ban** between 10pm and 7am sounded the death knell for Goa's party scene. A decade on, it has virtually disappeared, limited to a couple of established, above-board clubs – notably the *Nine Bar* and *Hilltop* in Vagator (see opposite), and *Paradiso* and *Curlie's* in Anjuna (see p.136). The occasional party does from time to time escape the notice of the local police (notably up in **Aswem**, at or around *Liquid Sky*; see p.150) but don't come to Goa expecting Ko Pha Ngan or Ibiza-on-the-Arabian-Sea.

"town of the Shah"). Intended as a border watchpost, it fell to various Hindu raiders during the seventeenth century, among them the Maratha chieftain Sambhaji, whose troops were, according to local legend, able to scale the precipitous walls with the aid of giant monitor lizards. Known as *ghorpad* in Konkani, these metre-and-a-half-long reptiles are said to be able to climb and support the weight of a man when wedged into a hole or between crenellations; they inflate themselves and will allegedly starve to death before relinquishing their grip.

The fortress was finally deserted by the Portuguese in 1892, after the territory's frontiers had been forced further north into the *Novas Conquistas* region. Today, it lies in ruins, although you can still see the heads of two tunnels that formerly provided supply routes for besieged defenders, as well as a scattering of Muslim **tombstones** ringed by an enclosure on the southern slopes of the hill, believed to be relics of pre-colonial days. However, the main incentive to climb up here is the superb **views** from the bastion's weed-infested ramparts, which look north across the estuary to Morjim.

Arrival and information

Direct **buses** arrive at Chapora three times daily from Panjim, and every fifteen minutes from Mapusa, with departures until 7pm. Most drop passengers at the old banyan tree at the far end of the main street, where the motorcycle pilots all hang out. Air, train, bus and catamaran **tickets** may be booked or reconfirmed at Soniya Tours and Travels, next to the bus stand.

Chapora also boasts a better-than-average general **store**: in addition to basic provisions, V.A. Kamat's, at the west end of the main street, stocks sun cream, postcards and other tourist essentials. Tiny Narayan Books, next door to *Baba Restaurant* on the main street, lends, sells and part-exchanges **secondhand books** in a range of languages.

Accommodation

By far the most (in fact, the only) congenial **place to stay** in Chapora is the *Casa de Olga* (Ⓣ0832/227 4355 or Ⓣ9822/157145; ❸), an immaculate, red-and-white-painted little guesthouse near the fishing anchorage. It's run with great efficiency and enthusiasm by a young couple called Edmund and Elifa. Their nicest rooms are the five in a new block to the rear, which are all en suite and have good-sized balconies. Cheaper and more basic is *Shettor Villa* (Ⓣ0832/227 3766 or Ⓣ9822/158154; ❷), off the west side of the main street. Half a dozen of its rooms, ranged around a sheltered backyard, come with fans and attached bathrooms; the other eighteen share shower-toilets.

Both places appear on our map on p.140.

Eating and drinking

Out on the road to the fishing anchorage, *La Cantine* is justifiably the most popular place in Chapora to **eat** these days. Run by an expat chef called Max, it serves healthy, home-cooked food – chickpea and pumpkin soup, beetroot tartare, pasta al forno and zucchini quiche – in a basic roadside shack. Otherwise, take your pick from the crop of inexpensive little cafés and restaurants lining the main street. The enduringly popular *Welcome*, halfway down, offers a reasonable selection of cheap and filling seafood, Western and veg dishes, plus relentless reggae and techno music and backgammon sets. *Jai Ganesh Café*, just up from the banyan tree, is the focal point of the tourist scene, where Chapora's resident Westerners watch the world go by over fresh-fruit juices and milkshakes. All of the above appear on the map on p.140.

Siolim

Although one of the state's largest villages, with a population of around 12,000, **SIOLIM**, like nearby Chapora, has been spared the tourist-led development that has ravaged the coastline around Calangute thanks to its distance from the beach. Spread under a rich canopy of palm trees, its collection of stunning colonial-era houses still exudes an air of Portuguese bourgeois prosperity. Siolcars love to

Siolim Zagor

While much of India has had to learn to live with the spectre of religious violence, Goa's Christians and Hindus manage to coexist peacefully in a spirit of mutual respect unsurpassed on the subcontinent. Emblematic of this communal harmony, and indeed of the richness of Goa's melting-pot culture in general, is Siolim's extraordinary **Zagor festival**, held on the first Sunday after Christmas.

Although ostensibly a Christian celebration, coinciding with the feast day of Nossa Senhora de Guia, the night-long event blends elements from both religions. It centres on a small Hindu shrine, housed under a *peepal* tree down a lane near the ferry ramp. This sacred spot is associated with an important local deity called **Zagoryo**, believed to be the guardian of the village dams (*bunds*) that hold the river off the rice paddy. During the festival, each household makes offerings to Zagor to give thanks and ensure the village is protected from flooding over the coming year.

The festivities, however, start with a sombre candle-lit **procession** through Siolim, in which an effigy of Zagor is carried around the various waddos of the village, stopping at wayside crosses and shrines along the way to receive offerings. Everyone then gathers at a *mand*, or sacred arena, in a Catholic house for a **dance drama**. The actors in this ancient ritual, assuming hereditarily assigned roles, are always drawn from two old Siolim families: the Shirodkars (Hindus) and D'Souzas (Catholics). At dawn, when the play is complete, Zagor is carried amid much pomp back to his shrine.

Traditionally, local satirists used to take over at this point, performing **zupatteos**, songs poking fun at politicians, priests and anyone else who deserved to be taken down a peg or two. These days, however, the culmination of Zagor tends to be a Konkani *tiatr* play.

Aside from being a model of religious tolerance, Zagor is a great spectacle and enormous fun. Few tourists participate, but foreigners are welcomed enthusiastically, to both the religious dance drama and the resolutely secular, *feni*-fuelled party that succeeds it.

remind you that their village has traditionally dominated the region's cultural and sporting life, having spawned a steady stream of soccer and hockey stars, as well as musicians (most recently pop supremo and film music composer Remo Fernandes; see p.296). Siolim's other boast is that it is the source of the world's best *feni* – a claim hotly contested by the residents of Palolem in the south.

Life in the village revolves around two centres of gravity. On its south side, at the foot of the road descending from Anjuna and Assagao, a busy little market area clusters around the crossroads in front of an ostentatiously Corinthian **Church of St Anthony**, one of the oldest Christian shrines in the region. The church's fame dates from the sixteenth century, when it was the scene of two miracles witnessed by the entire congregation. The second bazaar, known as **Tar**, lies five minutes' drive north, grouped around the concrete landing ramp on the Chapora River, from where the ferries (three per hour) chug back and forth to Chopdem. To do so, they have to navigate around the concrete supports of the massive new **road bridge** that nowadays carries most traffic across the river. En route, you can pull over to enjoy the views across the estuary.

Practicalities

The village has only one hotel, an elegantly converted *palacio* called *Siolim House* (Ⓣ0832/227 2138, Ⓦwww.siolimhouse.com; ⑨). Located just past the crossroads, a short way down the back (riverside) route to Chapora, the three hundred-year-old building used to belong to the governor of Macao, but fell into disrepair and was virtually derelict when its present London/Delhi-based owners acquired it. Today, the *palacio* numbers among the few hotels in the state that manage to recapture the period feel of the Portuguese era. Romantic, beautifully furnished rooms and suites are ranged around a pillared courtyard, individually styled and named after old colonial trading centres; they are priced at $134–158, rising to a range of $228–266 at Christmas. The more expensive ones are huge, with baths, gorgeous oyster-shell windows and four-poster beds. Mod cons have been kept to a minimum (no air-conditioning, minibars or televisions), but there's a twelve-metre pool in the garden, and an unobtrusive **restaurant** serving fine Goan food.

Pernem and the far north

Before the Portuguese annexed **Pernem**, Goa's northernmost *taluka*, in 1778, the Chapora River marked the border between old Christian Goa (the *Velhas Conquistas*) and wider Hindu India. The two-and-a-half centuries of colonial rule that preceded this acquisition, and that of the other marginal territories forming the so-called *Novas Conquistas* zone, ensured the divide was as much cultural as political, and even today the transition between the two is clearly discernible. Once across the river, most villages are grouped around brightly painted, colonnaded temples, the calendars in the provision stores sport images of Ganesh or Lakshmi rather than Our Lady, and the women tend to wear saris instead of dresses.

Until the road bridge was completed in 2002, the Chapora River also formed an effective check against the northward advance of mass tourism. Only a trickle of adventurous charter tourists used to venture across it via the old Siolim diesel ferry, leaving the spectacular beaches beyond the rivermouth wide open for the hippy refugees from the Baga-Calangute belt. **Arambol**, in the far north, was where most of them made for, and this large, mixed Christian-Hindu village remains a popular "alternative" resort frequented by long-staying budget travellers.

Aside from the magnificent stretch of virtually unbroken white sand that runs all the way from the Chapora River to Arambol, the main target for day-trips into Pernem is **Terekol Fort**, formerly the last outpost of Portuguese rule. Overlooking a tidal creek on the border with Maharashtra, its battlements enclose a fancy Parador-style Heritage Hotel where you can enjoy the wonderful backdrop of sea and sand over a beer or gourmet snack.

The last few years have also seen the hitherto empty beaches to the **south of Arambol** sprout a string of hut camps and small hotels. As yet, **Morjim**, **Aswem** and **Mandrem** remain fledgling resorts, but they're growing in size and sophistication year on year, and nowadays attract large numbers during the peak season period, primarily from Russia.

Travelling north from Siolim, the entry point to Pernem proper is the far side of the new road bridge at **Chopdem**. Head straight on for 200m or so until you arrive at a T-junction. A right turn here will take you along the quick route to Arambol; bear left, and you'll end up in Morjim.

Morjim

Viewed from Chapora fort, **MORJIM** appears as a dramatic expanse of empty sand sweeping north from a surf-lashed spit at the river mouth. Behind it, broken dunes are backed by palms and casuarina trees, sheltering a Hindu-Christian village which, because of its relative isolation, was where Goa's first **Russian tourists** made a beeline for back in the early noughties. Nowdays dubbed 'Mojimograd' by other foreign visitors, it's since become a resolutely Russian-only enclave, with hotels, guesthouses and rental villas controlled, if not owned outright, by Moscow mafiosi. A lot of sensational stories have appeared in the Indian media in recent years, reporting on the upscale prostitution and drug rackets run out of here. Although such reports do have a basis in truth, the majority of young sunseekers you see fizzing around Morjim on scooters are just regular, law-abiding holidaymakers. That said, the atmosphere in the guesthouses and restaurants can feel less than friendly, and most Western travellers find the experience of staying in Morjim a disconcerting one – not to mention eye-wateringly expensive – preferring to continue north to the more culturally mixed resorts of Aswem and Mandrem.

Morjim **beach** itself is dramatic and well worth at least a walk, especially early in the morning, when you'll see teams of fishermen hauling giant handnets from the surf. The spit at its southern end, opposite Chapora fort, is also a great birding hotspot: neither the local avian population, nor indeed the villagers who empty their bowels into the surf each morning, seem in the least deterred by the bizarre fitness routines practised by the Russians before breakfast.

Practicalities

Half a dozen **buses** per day skirt Morjim en route to Panjim, the first at 7am; heading the other way, you can pick up a direct bus from Panjim at 5pm, and there are frequent services from Mapusa via Siolim. They'll drop you on the main road, five minutes' walk from the beachfront area at **Vithaldas Waddo**.

Because of the unwelcoming Russian vibe, the **hotels and guesthouses** immediately behind the beach, in the dunes and along the beachfront road, are best avoided. There are, however, a couple of really nice options on the edges of Morjim. Facing the riverbank on the village's south side, *Jardin d'Ulysse* (Ⓣ9822/581928, Ⓔulyssemorjim@gmail.com; ④) is a charming Goan-French-run place comprising five "cottages" with tiled roofs, ochre-washed floors and kitchenettes. The piece de résistance here is a stylish, spacious penthouse room boasting both sunset and sunrise views over the bay. Down in the front garden, a small restaurant whips up an eclectic menu of steaks, scrumptious lasagna, Tibetan *momos* (filled dumplings steamed or fried) and salads for a mostly French and British clientele.

Even further from the brouhaha of Russian Morjim, hunt around the dunes on the opposite, north side of the village for magical *Ku* (Ⓣ9326/123570; ⑦–⑧), one of Goa's loveliest places to stay. Japanese and Balinese architecture inspired its design, rendered entirely in hardwood, bamboo and stone, using live trees as frame poles. There are just two rooms, divided by sliding screens, facing a magical garden and water path teeming with koi carp. At Rs3000–6000 depending on the time of year, the rates are restrained for somewhere that's been featured in glossy magazines worldwide.

If it's above your budget, consider calling by for a candle-lit meal at their **restaurant** ( ), prepared by host Marie in her open kitchen. The menu changes daily – expect something Asian and Spanish inflected, made from whatever was freshest in the market that day: green papaya salad, Vietnamese beef soup with lime, stir-fried tofu, veg couscous with homemade harissa, or snapper *a la plancha*. Count on Rs500–600 for three courses, with drinks extra.

The turtle wind

When a strong and steady on-shore breeze blows through the night in early November at Morjim, the locals call it a **turtle wind** because such weather normally heralds the arrival of Goa's rarest migrant visitors: **Olive Ridley marine turtles** (*Lepidochelys olivacea*).

For as long as anyone can remember, the spoon-shaped spit of soft white sand at **Temb**, the southern end of Morjim beach, has been the nesting ground of these beautiful sea reptiles. Each winter, a succession of females emerge from the surf during the night and, using their distinctive flippers, crawl to the edge of the dunes to lay their annual clutch of 105–115 eggs. Just under two months later, the fresh hatchlings clamber out and crawl blinking over their siblings to begin the perilous trek back to the water, guided into the sea by moonlight.

Little more is known about how these enigmatic creatures spend the rest of their long lives (turtles frequently live for over a century), but it is thought that the females return to the beaches where they were born to lay their own eggs. Some have been shown to travel as far as 4500 kilometres to do this.

Once a thriving species, with huge populations spread across the Pacific, Atlantic and Indian oceans, the Olive Ridley is nowadays **endangered**. Aside from a wealth of traditional predators (such as crows, ospreys, gulls and buzzards, who pick off the hatchlings during their dash for the sea), the newborns and their parents are vulnerable to a host of threats from humans. In Morjim, as in most of Asia, the eggs are traditionally considered a delicacy and local villagers collect them to sell in Mapusa market. Many (perhaps as many as 35,000 worldwide) are killed accidentally by fishermen each year, caught up in fine shrimp nets or attracted by squid bait used to catch tuna. Floating litter, which the hapless turtles mistake for jellyfish, has also taken its toll over the past two decades, as have tar balls from oil spills, which coat the animals' digestive tracts and hamper the absorption of food. The growth of tourism poses an additional danger: electric lights behind the beaches throw the hatchlings off course as they scuttle towards the sea, and sand compressed by sunbathers' trampling feet damages nests, preventing the babies from digging their way out at the crucial time.

In a bid to revive numbers, locals are employed by the Goa Forest Department to watch out for the females' arrival in November and to guard the nests after the eggs have been laid until they hatch. You'll see them camped under palm-leaf shades on the beach, with the nests fenced in and marked by red and green signs.

So far, the government-led **conservation attempt** has not proved all that effective. After an initial leap in hatchling figures, recent results have been mixed, which the Forest Department ascribes to an increase in tourist activity. The tracks of one female turtle which recently came ashore painted a disturbingly representative picture of the problems the animals face: after bumping into several sun loungers and deckchairs during the night, she collapsed from exhaustion and laid her eggs between two of the shacks lined up at the beach's southern end. Not that the shacks can be solely to blame for the decline: **Galjibag**, a deserted beach in the far south of Goa (see p.203), has experienced a similar drop in numbers over the past few seasons. It seems marine pollution and trawlers using illegal nets are the most likely culprits.

Watching the nesting turtles is an unforgettable experience, although one requiring a certain amount of dedication, or luck. No one knows for sure when an Olive Ridley female will turn up, but with a strong turtle wind blowing at the right time, the chances are good. Much more predictable are the appearances of the hatchlings, who emerge exactly 54 days after their mothers laid the eggs. If you ask one of the wardens looking after the nests, they can tell you when this will be.

Aswem

You could hardly call **ASWEM**, the next settlement north of Morjim, a village, let alone a resort. Enforcement of the Coastal Protection Zone (CPZ) planning law by the local village council has managed to hold at bay repeated attempts by developers to build behind the beach here, with the result that permanent structures are few and far between. However, the past few seasons have seen a belt of temporary hut camps and shacks spring up in the coconut *mand* backing the sand, and the place has started to feel quite crowded in December and January.

It's a much more wholesome scene than that holding sway around the headland to the south, though. Clean-living 30- and 40-something couples from northern Europe are the main demographic, increasing numbers of them with toddlers in tow, along with a sprinkling of old Goa hands who have outgrown, or given up on, Anjuna and Morjim. Aside from the recent Russian invasion, the main catalyst for this sudden upsurge in Aswem's popularity was the arrival a few years back of an incongruously chi-chi beach restaurant, *La Plage*, set up by a trio of French restaurateurs from Baga.

Arrival and information

Sporadic **buses** from Panjim and Mapusa cover the quiet stretch of road running parallel to the beach inland, from where a five-minute walk across the paddy fields brings you to the shacks and hut camps attached to them. The places listed below were the only ones we came across offering distinctive accommodation, and/or reasonable value for money; the rest of the camps were either too cramped for comfort, or absurdly overpriced, or both. Tourist facilities are thin on the ground in Aswem. Nearly everyone who stays rents a scooter from somewhere else to get to and around the area. The nearest internet access and shops are in Morjim, half an hour's plod south.

Accommodation

Leela Cottages near *La Plage* ⓣ9823/400055, ⓦwww.goaleela.com. Swish designer huts (all a/c) of various sizes and prices, grouped in a gated property under the palms only a stone's throw from the beach, but far enough away from the restaurants to remain peaceful and quiet (and free from cooking smells). The interiors are lovely, with French doors, muslin curtains and antique furniture collected from all over India by the young Gujarati owner. ❼–❽

Yab Yum ⓣ0832/ 224 7712, ⓦwww.yabyumresorts.com. A campus of beautiful domed structures made from palm thatch, mango wood and laterite, with curvy moulded concrete floors and walls, painted pale purple. Large and attractively furnished inside, the rooms have beds on platforms and comfy mattresses, glitter balls, paper lanterns and muslin drapes – though such alt-chic comes at quite a high price (Rs4800 per double or Rs5500 for suites). They also offer a handful of similarly stylish faux-Portuguese-era cottages, as well as a wooden deck for yoga and play teepee for the kids. Rates include breakfast. ❺

Yoga Gypsies ⓣ0832/645 3077 or ⓣ9326/130115. This spot, in the coconut plantation under the Ajoba temple just north of *La Plage*, is arguably the finest nook on the coast hereabouts, and Geordie Cathy Richardson has made the most of it, erecting five octagonal cottages made from dark mango wood on her plot. They're large, well spaced, have wrap-around verandas, and are naturally cross-ventilated, with quality beds and simple, relaxing decor. There are also two cliffside cottages for rent, a laid-back little restaurant, yoga space and a great lounge area looking through vegetation to the beach. ❼

Eating

Change Your Mind Just north of *La Plage*. Quality food – notably North Indian specialities – which won't dent your wallet. Also worth a visit is nearby *Pink Orange*, whose fusion menu fills their beach terrace each evening.

La Plage Aswem beach ⓣ9850/258543. Against a diaphanous backdrop of floaty white muslin and swaying palm trees, La Plage does a brisk trade in cool Gallic-Mediterranean snacks and drinks (chilled asparagus soup, mint lassis, Moroccan salads, fresh strawberries and cream), served by Nepali waiters in black *lunghis*. Their menu also features delicious char-grilled seafood and barbecued main courses; and don't miss the divine Bloody Mary with a coriander and mustard seed twist.

The Place *Liquid Sky* (see below), on the hilltop above Aswem beach. *The Place* takes itself a bit more seriously than most restaurants in the area, with chefs in proper hats toiling over hot grills in an open-sided kitchen. Bulgarian, Russian and Siberian specialities dominate a menu heavy on pork and veal, though there are plenty of veggie alternatives, and the baked fish in garlic butter and white wine with parsnips is consistently good. Most mains around Rs250.

Nightlife

La Plage is not the only Goa-chic outfit to have set up shop in Aswem. It's also the current home of the **Liquid Sky Collective**, an innovative electro party outfit pioneered by Belgian DJ Axailes (ⓦwww.myspace.com/axailes). With its beautiful "Lookout" dancefloor, sound-proofed interior space for post-10pm grooves and great music, the venue has established itself as the coolest in Goa. Keep your ear to the ground for their period boat parties down the Mandovi, co-organized with the **Arambol Experience** (ⓦwww.myspace.com/arambolexperience). Back down on the beach, *Shanti* also has a nice dancey vibe, with sets by international DJs.

Mandrem

From the far side of the creek bounding the edge of Aswem, a magnificent, and largely empty beach stretches north towards Arambol – the last undeveloped stretch of the north Goan coast. Whether or not **MANDREM** can continue to hold out against the rising tide of tourism remains to be seen, but for the time being, nature still has the upper hand here. Olive Ridley marine turtles nest on the quietest patches, and you're more than likely to catch a glimpse of one of the white-bellied fish eagles that live in the casuarina trees – their last stronghold in Pernem.

Information and getting around

A couple of small grocery stores, internet cafés and travel agents are on hand to provide essential services. But you'll have to rent a scooter, or walk for half an hour, to reach **Madlamaz-Mandrem**, the village's market hub, straddling the main road inland. Slap in the middle of it, **Parsekar Stores** holds an unrivalled stock of tourist-oriented food and drink – including muesli, olive oil, miso, Nilgiri cheese and natural cosmetics.

Accommodation

Most of the village's **accommodation** is tucked away inland at Junasa Waddo, where a handful of small guesthouses and hotels cater to a mixed, peace-and-quiet-loving crowd.

Dunes ⓣ0832/224 7219 or 224 7071, ⓦwww.dunesgoa.com. Huge "holiday village" of twin-bedded, yellow-painted leaf huts. They're a notch too close together for comfort and are brightly lit, so spoiling the aspect of the beach at night, but this is an efficiently run outfit that fills up in peak season. Pricier en suite is available. ❸–❺

Elsewhere ⓣ9326/020701 or ⓣ9820/037387, ⓦwww.aseascape.com. A collection of dreamy nineteenth-century villas on the quietest patch of dunes, with cobalt-blue interiors and uninterrupted sea views from their pillared verandas. Absolutely the last word in Goan beachside chic, and very exclusive – though at Côte d'Azur prices (from $900–2500 per week, depending on the house). See also *Otter Creek*, below. ❾

Mandala ⓣ9657/898021, ⓦwww.themandalagoa.com. Exquisitely painted murals adorn the buildings at *Mandala*, a "back-to-nature boutique resort" just upriver from the Ashiyana Retreat Centre (see p.139), where the theme is celebration of the natural world through art. You can opt to stay in the main house with all mod cons, or take one of the two-tier "touses" – designer tents with patios and lake views. It's close to the beach, but there's no direct road access. ❼

Otter Creek ⓣ022/2373 8757 or ⓣ9820/037387, ⓦwww.aseascape.com. You have to cross a rickety footbridge to reach these luxury tents, nestled on the riverbank just behind the dunes, in the thick of a coconut plantation. Each is fitted with a bamboo four-poster, bathroom, colour-washed sit-out and jetty on the river. Plus you get access to the same empty bit of beach as *Elsewhere* (see above). $410–1130 per week. ❾

Riva Resort ⓣ0832/224 7088 or 224 7612, ⓦwww.rivaresorts.com. The other big hut camp, further up the coast towards Arambol. This one's more upmarket, with swisher huts and higher rates (Rs600–2500 depending on the level of comfort). The site centres on a huge bar-restaurant that hosts DJ nights and has big-screen video. ❹–❻

Villa River Cat ⓣ0822/224 7928 or ⓣ9890/157060, ⓦwww.villarivercat.com. Quirky riverside hotel, screened from the beach by the dunes, with distinctive hippy-influenced decor and furniture. The sixteen rooms are all individually designed: mosaics, shells, devotional sculpture and hammocks set the tone. Some have balconies, and there's a great sunset roof terrace and rear garden for lounging in. Host Rinoo Seghal is an animal lover, so brace yourself for a menagerie of cats and dogs. Artists and musicians receive a ten percent discount. ❺–❼

Arambol (Harmal)

ARAMBOL (also called **Harmal**), 32km northwest of Mapusa, is by far the most populous village in the far north, and the area's main tourist hub. Traditionally a refuge for a hard-core hippy fringe, the village nowadays attracts a lively and eclectic mix of travellers, the majority of whom stick around for the season, living in rented rooms, hut camps and small houses scattered behind the magnficent white-sand beach. Hedonistic, well-heeled young Russians way outnumber the older, more alternative, spiritually inclined types from northern Europe who have long formed Arambol's mainstay. But the two groups rub along harmoniously enough, and the overall vibe here is inclusive and positive, with plenty of live music to enjoy in the evenings, lots of relaxed places to eat and drink, and more opportunities to learn new yoga poses and reshuffle your chakras than you could get through in several lifetimes, let alone a winter. Moreover, beach life is generally laid back too – except on weekends, when day-tripping drinkers descend en masse in SUVs from nearby Maharashtra.

Arrival and information

Taxis charge Rs1200 for the run from Dabolim airport to Arambol, and Rs350 for the thirty-minute trip from the nearest railhead at Tivim (Thivim). **Buses** to and from Panjim (via Mapusa) pull into the village every thirty minutes until noon, and every ninety minutes thereafter, at the small bus stop on the main road.

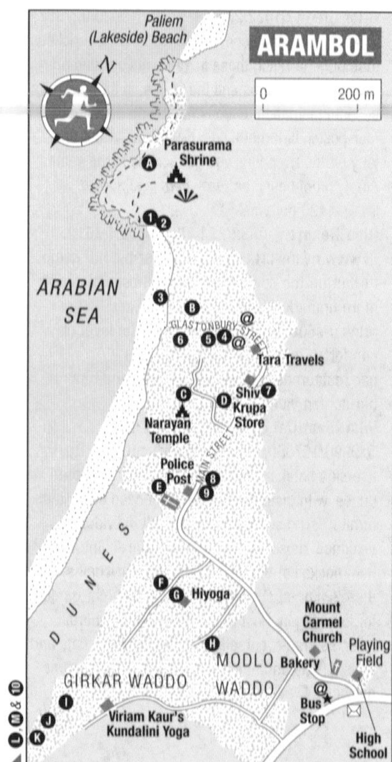

ACCOMMODATION		EATING & DRINKING	
Arun Huts	D	Double Dutch	8
Atman	L	Dreamland	9
Ave Maria	F	Eyes of Buddha	1
Famafa	B	Fellini's	6
God's Gift	J	Lamuella	7
Ivon's	I	Loeki's	4
Om Ganesh Cottages	A	Relax Inn	3
Pedro Driver	H	Rice Bowl	2
Phoenix Holiday Home	E	Sol e Luna	10
Piya	G	Sporting Heroes	5
Silver Sands	C	Surf Club	J
Surf Club	M		
Villa Pedro	K		

A faster private **minibus** service from Panjim arrives daily opposite the chai stalls at the beach end of the village.

The **post office** is on the east side of the village, beyond the big church. There are no ATMs, but several places in the village **change money** and do cash advances on debit and credit cards: try Delight, on the east side of the main road, and Tara Travel, directly opposite, where you can also reconfirm and book air tickets.

Accommodation

The cost of **accommodation** in Arambol has risen sharply over the past few seasons, reflecting the village's popularity with free-spending young Russians, but it's still nearly all pitched at budget travellers: no-frills, Goan-run guesthouses and expat-inspired hippy-chic predominate here rather than mainstream hotels. Beds tend to be in short supply come high season and houses virtually impossible to find unless you get here in October. A good area to start your hunt for a bed are **Modlo** and **Girkar Waddos**, south of the centre, both relatively peaceful with several family-run guesthouses, but be warned: you have to walk down the beach to get there (not such a great idea at night if you're female). The warren of narrow sandy lanes behind the north end of the beach, known as **Khalcha Waddo**, is busier, but – with the exception of those listed below – its guesthouses are uniformly cramped and grotty.

Arun Huts nr Narayan temple ⓣ9850/096468, ⓦarunhuts.arambolbeach.info. We loved this quirkly little hut camp, run by local beautician, Mrs Mala Singh, in the thick of Arambol village. Only 60m from the sea, it comprises two rows of neatly painted wood huts, fitted with decent mattresses, attached shower-toilets and fans. The whole earth-floored compound is smothered in banana trees, palms and flowers, and very atmospheric, especially in the evening. Good value. ❸

Atman Girkar Waddo ⓣ9881/311643, ⓦwww.atmangoa.com. Lovely bamboo and wood tree huts on the south side of the beach, prettily thatched and decorated with coco mats, colourful sari drapes, original fractal-flouro wall hangings, and bolsters on their spacious sit-out areas. Smiling Italian-Indian owners, Michaela and Sunil, also run a yoga space and small boutique, as well as a popular restaurant (see "Eating", p.154). A cut above the other hut camps on this stretch, though tariffs rise to Rs1500 in mid-Dec. ❺

Ave Maria 22 Modlo Waddo ⓣ0832/224 2974. Arambol's largest guesthouse offers well-kept budget rooms, with or without bathrooms, and a sociable rooftop restaurant in a three-storey modern building. Tricky to find: turn left onto a *kutcha* track where the main road through the south side of the village makes a sharp right bend. ❷

Famafa Khalcha Waddo ⓣ0832/229 2516, ⓦwww.travelingoa.com/famafa. Large, anodyne concrete place just off "Glastonbury Street"; popular mainly with Israeli backpackers, and correspondingly rowdy, but very close to the beach and great value for money. They don't take bookings and instead operate a 9am checkout so get here early for a room. ❷–❸

God's Gift 411, Girkar Waddo ⓣ0832/224 2391, ⓣ9923/427570. Variously priced, good-sized rooms in three-storey purple blocks; some have living space and kitchenettes. Not as good as *Ivon's* (the balconies are mostly tiny), but their rates are low and the proprietors friendly. Leaf huts opening onto a large yard soak up the overspill. ❹

Ivon's Girkar Waddo ⓣ0832/224 2672 or ⓣ9822/127398. The pick of the budget bunch: immaculately clean, tiled rooms, all with attached bathroom and fronted by good-sized tiled balconies opening onto the dunes or a well-groomed family compound. ❸

Om Ganesh Cottages In the cove between the village and Lakeside beach; book at the Om Ganesh stores on the main drag ⓣ0832/229 7614. Nicest of the "cottages" stacked up the cliffside just south of Lakeside beach. The sea views from their verandas are superb, but some may find the Israeli chillum scene in the nearby cafés a turn-off. Rates vary wildly according to demand, and advance booking (with a deposit) is all but essential by mid-season. ❺

Pedro Driver Modlo Waddo ⓣ9823/499090. Luminous purple place run by Sydney Fernandes and his family on the quiet southern edge of the village. Their neat rooms, which are fitted with gas hobs and have hot-water boilers, are dark, but large (plenty enough space for yoga), and the location's peaceful. ❸–❹

Phoenix Holiday Home Just off Main St, behind the chapel ⓣ9922/031961. This new place in the centre of Arambol is made of distinctively varnished red laterite stone. Pitched mainly at the Russian market, it's a smarter than average guesthouse, too, although the rooms are small for the price, and bathrooms only in closet partitions. The big plus here is the breezy rearside verandas, which look through the palm trees to the sea. ❺–❼

Piya Modlo Waddo ⓣ0832/224 2661. Well-run little budget guesthouse – the best fallback if nearby *Ave Maria* is full. Rock-bottom prices, and cheap roof huts for only Rs100. ❶–❷

Silver Sands 4-S Tara Ankush ⓣ0832/224 2648, ⓣ9923/667448. Huge, immaculately clean rooms with terracotta-tiled roofs and shining ceramic floors, overlooking the Narayan temple. The best ones are on the first storey of the newest block; cheaper budget options with shared bathrooms occupy the ground floor. Close to the beach and well maintained by resident owners, the Lavu family. ❷–❸

Surf Club Girkar Waddo ⓣ9850/554006, ⓔcontactus@surfclubgoa.com. Brit couple Phil and Maggie offer some of the nicest mid-scale rooms in north Goa, at a prime location on the far south side of Arambol beach. With high ceilings and comfy beds, they're well aired and light, and have lots of those homely touches (seagrass mats, shell lanterns and floaty white curtains). Ask for one on the upper floor – worth the extra for their fine sea views and breezes. Don't come here expecting peace and quiet in the evenings, though, as one of Arambol's most popular live music venues occupies the ground floor. ❹–❺

Villa Pedro Girkar Waddo ⓣ0832/224 2989. Warrenous, slightly scruffy but welcoming ten-room guesthouse, a stone's throw from the surf. It possesses plenty of local atmosphere, with pigs and kids running around, and crows hopping around the balconies, and its west-facing rooms look over a little chapel towards the beach. A pleasant and dependable budget choice. ❷

The village and beaches

Modern Arambol is scattered around a plot of high ground straddling the main coast road, where there's a market area clustered around a busy junction. From Mount Carmel Church, a bumpy lane runs downhill to a sharp right bend, beyond which the more traditional Christian and Hindu fishing quarter extends to the dunes, scattered under a canopy of palm trees. The main **beachfront** lies 200m further down a winding road lined cheek-by-jowl with clothes and bedspread stalls, travel agents, internet cafés and souvenir shops selling tourist knick-knacks – dubbed "Glastonbury Street" by Arambol's festival-savvy Brits.

Dozens of old wooden boats line up along the gently curving **main beach** – one of the most picturesque in south India. The best view of it is to be had from the crucifix and small **Parasurama shrine** on the hilltop to the north (see map on p.152 for route of the path), which is an especially serene spot at sunset time. After dark, when the hula-hoopers, fire jugglers and *bhajan* singers have turned homewards, the candles and fairy lights of the shacks illuminate the beachfront to magical effect.

Bathing is safe here during the daytime, but less inspiring than around the headland at **Paliem** or **"Lakeside" beach**, reached by following the track through a series of rocky-bottomed coves, emerging at a broad strip of soft white sand hemmed in by cliffs. Behind it, a small **freshwater lake** extends along the bottom of the valley into the jungle, lined with sulphurous mud, which, when smeared over the body, dries to form a surreal, butter-coloured shell.

Keep following the path around the back of the lake and you'll soon come to Paliem's famous **banyan tree**, a monster specimen with giant runners extending more than fifty metres – long a popular chillum smoking spot. Keen walkers can continue over the cliffs immediately north – Arambol's prime parascending venue – to reach Kerim beach (see p.156).

Eating and drinking

Thanks to its annually replenished pool of expatriate gastronomic talent, Arambol harbours a handful of unexpectedly good **restaurants** – not that you'd ever guess from their generally lacklustre exteriors. The village's alternative, western-European contingent cares more about flavours than fancy decor, and prices reflect this. Russians with money to splurge, meanwhile, tend to gravitate towards the fancier seafood joints spread along the beachfront, where the day's catch is displayed on cold trays for selection, then grilled alfresco in front of you. Prices can be eye-popping, so get a quote before you order. If you're on a rock-bottom budget stick to the "rice-plate" *dhabas* at the bottom of the village: *Sai Deep* has a devoted following, and serves copious fruit salads as well as thalis, and a good travellers' breakfast menu of pancakes, eggs and curd.

Double Dutch Main St, halfway down on the right (look for the yellow signboard). Spread under a palm canopy in the thick of the village, this laid-back café is the hub of alternative Arambol. Renowned for its melt-in-the-mouth apple pie, it also does a tempting range of home-baked buttery biscuits, cakes (Buddha's Dream's a winner), healthy salads and sumptuous main meals (from Rs175), including fresh buffalo steaks and the perennially popular "mixed stuff" (stuffed mushrooms and capsicums with sesame pesto).

Dreamland Near *Double Dutch*. This is where the local Western designers and people in the know go for good, strong coffee. To help calm the caffeine buzz, they also offer great paninis, crepes and cakes.

Eyes of Buddha North end of beach. Perennially popular travellers' hangout, occupying a perfect spot overlooking the main beach. It's renowned above all for its mountainous fruit-salad and curd breakfasts, and lunchtime salads, but they also do a great North Indian menu after sunset: try the succulent *paneer* and chicken kebabs with hot naan bread.

Fellini's "Glastonbury Street". Italian-run place serving delicious wood-fired pizzas (Rs100–175), and authentic pasta or gnocchi with a choice of over twenty sauces. It gets horrendously busy in season, so be here early if you want snappy service.

Lamuella Main St. Funky little roadside café, serving healthy breakfasts, toasties, hummus plates and filling salads during the daytime, as well as energizing juice combos and herb teas. After sunset you can order from a dinner menu featuring such delights as grilled kingfish on mushroom ravioli, Moroccan tagine and fish tempura – all freshly prepared and attractively presented; and there's chocolate fondant-ice cream for dessert. Most mains around Rs250.

Relax Inn North end of beach. Top-quality seafood straight off the boats and unbelievably authentic pasta (you get even more expat Italians in here than

at *Fellini's*). Try the *vongole* (clam) sauce. Inexpensive, but expect a wait as they cook to order.
Rice Bowl North end of beach. This place serves the best Chinese in Arambol, with a perfect view of the beach to match, and a pool table (Rs100/hr). Any of their tasty noodle dishes are safe bets, as are the Japanese and Tibetan specialities. Most mains Rs150–200.
Sole e Luna South end of beach. Real Italian home cooking – pasta-pesto, pizzas and cheesy bakes – served in Arambol's most colourful and funkily decorated shack, on low or high tables, with plenty of hammocks and coco-mat chill-out space. This place also makes a pleasant beach base during the day as it's quite a plod from the main strip further north.
Surf Club South end of beach. Most people come here for the music, but the *Surf Club* does some great food too, gleaned from British owner Maggie's culinary travels. Try the knock-out Tahitian raw tuna, Thai-style spiced cashew and chickpea croquets or the yummy honeybee chicken breast in cream sauce. Or if you're feeling you've over-indulged, one of the detox cocktails (the "potassium punch" gets our thumbs up). Most mains around Rs200.

Nightlife

Evenings in Arambol tend to revolve around the café-restaurants and whichever bar is hosting **live music**. Jam sessions and live bands alternate between *Loeki's*, just up from the beachfront, on Sunday and Thursday evenings, and *Sporting Heroes*. Standards vary with whoever happens to blow in, but there have been some memorable impromptu gigs held here over the past few seasons. Further down the beach, the *Surf Club* also hosts bands and occasional DJs in its bar-restaurant

Outdoor activities and holistic therapies

Posters pinned to palm trees and café noticeboards around Arambol advertise an amazing array of **activities**, from kite surfing to reiki. A good place to get a fix on what's happening are: the noticebaord at *Lamuella*; and *Double Dutch*'s "Bullshit Info" corner, which displays email addresses and meeting details for just about everyone who does anything – including their own popular *dokra* **bronze-casting** workshops, held annually each January.

For the adventurous, there's **paragliding** from the clifftops above Lakeside beach, run by a couple of German and British outfits who've been here for the best part of a decade, alternating between Goa and Manali. The cost of the flight includes all the equipment you'll need and full instruction. For more information, go to Arambol Hammocks, close to the *Rice Bowl* restaurant at the north end of the beach (see map).

Each season, an army of holistic therapists also offer their services and run courses in Arambol. Iyengar **yoga** teacher **Sharat** (Ⓦwww.hiyogacentre.com) holds five-day classes, as well as two-week intensives, in his studio in Modlo Waddo. Prospective students should sign up at the centre from 1–3pm; to find it, head for the *Priya* guesthouse (see map) and follow the 'HIYC' signs from there.

Viriam Kaur's yoga classes, held amid the leafy retreat of a rooftop garden in Girkar Waddo (see map, p.152), have attracted a strong following over the past few years – not least because it's among the few places in Goa where you can learn Kundalini yoga. Also trained in Western and ayurvedic massage, she and her partner, **Adam Divine**, offer individual sessions and training, as well as workshops and courses on chakra healing and other therapeutic techniques. Check out their website (Ⓦwww.organickarma.co.uk) for dates, contact details and rave reviews.

Finally, you can put your left leg in and shake it all about at **Temple of Dance** centre, in Girkar Waddo close to the Kundalini Rooftop Garden, which offers tuition in everything from bellydance to salsa, Bollywood and – *the* big Arambol craze of late – hula-hooping.

Terekol and Kerim beach

North of Arambol, the coast road winds to the top of a rocky, undulating plateau, then drops down through a swathe of thick woodland to join the Arondem River, which it then follows for 4km through a landscape of vivid paddy fields and coconut plantations dotted with scruffy red-brick villages. To reach **TEREKOL**, the northernmost tip of Goa, you can either take the **ferry** (every 30min from 6.30am to 9.30pm; 5min; Rs5) or – if it's low tide (when the service is suspended for three hours; to check tide times, phone the *Fort Tiracol*, see below) – pay one of the local fishermen Rs50–100 per head to take you across in his boat. Otherwise, you can backtrack 5km east down the main road to a second and more reliable ferry crossing: once on the far bank, follow the lane to the first village, turn left at the crossroads there and keep going for 10km via a winding route that takes you through the iron-ore mines.

Before you reach the jetty, however, keep your eyes peeled for a turning on the left (marked with white painting on the road surface), which leads across the fields to **Kerim beach**. Backed by a line of fir trees and straggly casuarinas, it shelves steeply and isn't the most picturesque stretch of sand in Goa, but is usually quiet (except at weekends, when jeep-loads of Maharashtrans picnic on it).

As you cross the river, Terekol's old **fort** comes into view on the north bank of the Arondem, marooned on a lonely hillside with the dusty smokestacks of the USHA iron-ore complex smouldering in the background. These days, it serves as a low-key luxury **Heritage Hotel**, *The Fort Tiracol* (see below). Non-residents are welcome to eat and drink at the restaurant and first-floor "lounge bar", on whose terrace they can enjoy authentic Goan cooking and one of the finest seascapes in southern India. If you're booked to stay in the hotel, note that they'll lay on a launch to get you across the river at low tide.

The fort was originally built by the Marathas at the start of the eighteenth century, but taken soon afterwards by the Portuguese, who held onto it more or less continuously until they were ousted by Nehru in 1961. Nothing much of any importance ever happened here, except in 1825, when the liberal Goan governor general, Dr Bernardo Peres da Silva, used it as a base for an armed insurrection against the Portuguese – the first of several such rebellions. The governor's own troops mutinied at the eleventh hour, however, and were massacred by their colonial overlords. Thereafter, Terekol disappeared into obscurity until 1954, when a band of Goan Gandhi-ites (*satyagrahas*) hoisted an Indian tricolour over the ramparts in defiance of Portuguese rule. Two of them were shot for their trouble: a plaque on the wall of the fort records the event.

Practicalities

The few visitors who venture up to Terekol tend to do so by motorbike or taxi, heading back at the end of the day to the relative comfort of Calangute or Baga. If you run out of fuel, it's useful to know that the nearest **petrol station** is at Arambol, though be warned that it frequently runs out of petrol and closes. One of GTDC's daily tours from Panjim (see p.68) comes up here, as does one daily Kadamba **bus** from Mapusa; alternatively, the 7am bus from Siolim pulls in at the Kerim ferry jetty an hour later. From the far bank, it takes ten minutes or so to reach the fort on foot.

Designed by the owners of the *Nilaya Hermitage*, **rooms** at the *Fort Tiracol* (Ⓣ0832/227 6793 or 02366 227631, Ⓦwww.nilaya.com/tiracol.htm; ⑨) start at $250 per night, which includes full board for two people. There are seven of them in total, all sparsely decorated in traditional Lusitanian ochre and white, with oxide floors, heavy wooden doors, wrought-iron furniture and gorgeous Indian textiles.

3

South Goa

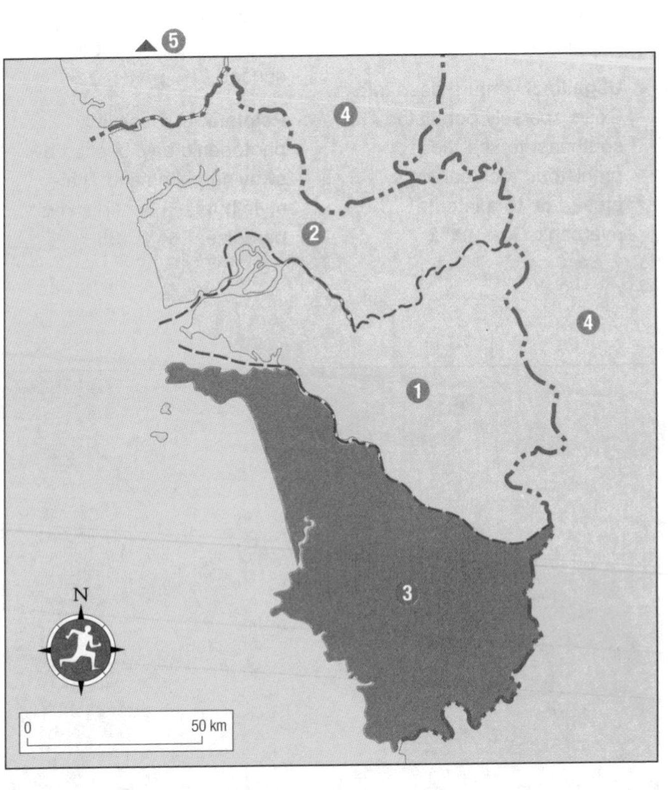

CHAPTER 3 Highlights

* **Menezes-Braganza House** Sumptuous eighteenth-century mansion in Chandor crammed with original furniture and antiques from the Portuguese heyday. See p.169

* **Palacio de Deão, Quepem** A rare chance to glimpse inside a perfectly restored, 200-year-old Indo-Portuguese mansion. See p.171

* **Usgalimal** Venture deep into Goa's sparsely populated southeast to see these prehistoric rock carvings, etched on to a laterite riverbank. See p.172

* **Shri Chandeshwar temple, Parvath** A panorama of the whole of the lush Salcete coast extends from this magical hilltop shrine. See p.172

* **Benaulim beach** The loveliest stretch of a 25-kilometre-long beach, where wooden outriggers provide shade. Best at sunset. See p.184

* **Palolem** An irresistibly photogenic bay, backed by swaying palms and Thai-style huts – a backpackers' paradise. See p.195

▲ Running with the water buffalo, Benaulim beach

3

South Goa

If you arrive by plane at Dabolim airport (see p.23), just outside the industrial city of **Vasco da Gama**, first impressions of south Goa can be unpromising. Once you're clear of the terminal, a parched laterite plateau stretches inland, scarred by the chimney stacks, agro-chemical plants and workers' slums of the Mormugao peninsula. Only after dropping down the flank of the headland towards the coast, past the hidden resort of **Bogmalo**, does the palm canopy reassert itself, spreading southwards in a lush belt that's edged by an expanse of shimmering sand and surf.

The string of villages and luxury hotel complexes lining 25-kilometre-long **Colva beach** marked the southernmost limit of tourism in Goa until a decade or so ago, when travellers started to explore the hilly coast beyond the **Cabo da Rama** headland. Crossing the *cabo* at **Karmali Ghat**, you find a superb vista opening up ahead over the tops of the cashew bushes to reveal a succession of exquisite sandy bays, sheltered by the forested slopes of the Sahyadri hills. The most beautiful of them all, **Palolem**, has over the past decade become a fully fledged backpackers' playground, attracting a greater number of tourists than anywhere else in the south.

With **Colva**, formerly the region's principal resort, patronized by domestic rather than foreign tourists, the European charter enclave has shifted south to **Cavelossim** and the farthest extremity of Colva beach, **Mobor**. In between, **Benaulim** remains a pleasantly uncrowded village with a distinctive Goan-Catholic atmosphere, despite the recent appearance of large Mumbai-owned time-share complexes amid its paddy fields. Even at the height of the season locals still well outnumber visitors and there's plenty of space on the vast beach, making this an ideal first footfall if you've just stumbled off the plane.

A ten-minute drive inland from Benaulim, south Goa's main market and transport hub is **Margao** – district headquarters of Salcete *taluka* – from where metalled roads fan west to the coast and east across fertile farmland to the Zuari River. Scattered over the plain around the town are dozens of picturesque villages, many harbouring colonial-era **country houses**. These, together with Margao market and the magical hilltop **Shri Chandeshwar temple**, provide the main focus for day-trips inland.

Staying in south Goa, you'll soon grow familiar with the distant wail of the **Konkan Railway** trains trundling up and down the coast. Along with the advent of low-cost flights, the line, completed only in 1997, has transformed the complexion of this formerly remote region, rendering it easily accessible to affluent, young, middle-class Indians from the metropolitan cities. With this new influx have come big developers' bucks and a new lease of life for the luxury hotels that punctuate the coastline. Staying in one of these, you'll be sharing the

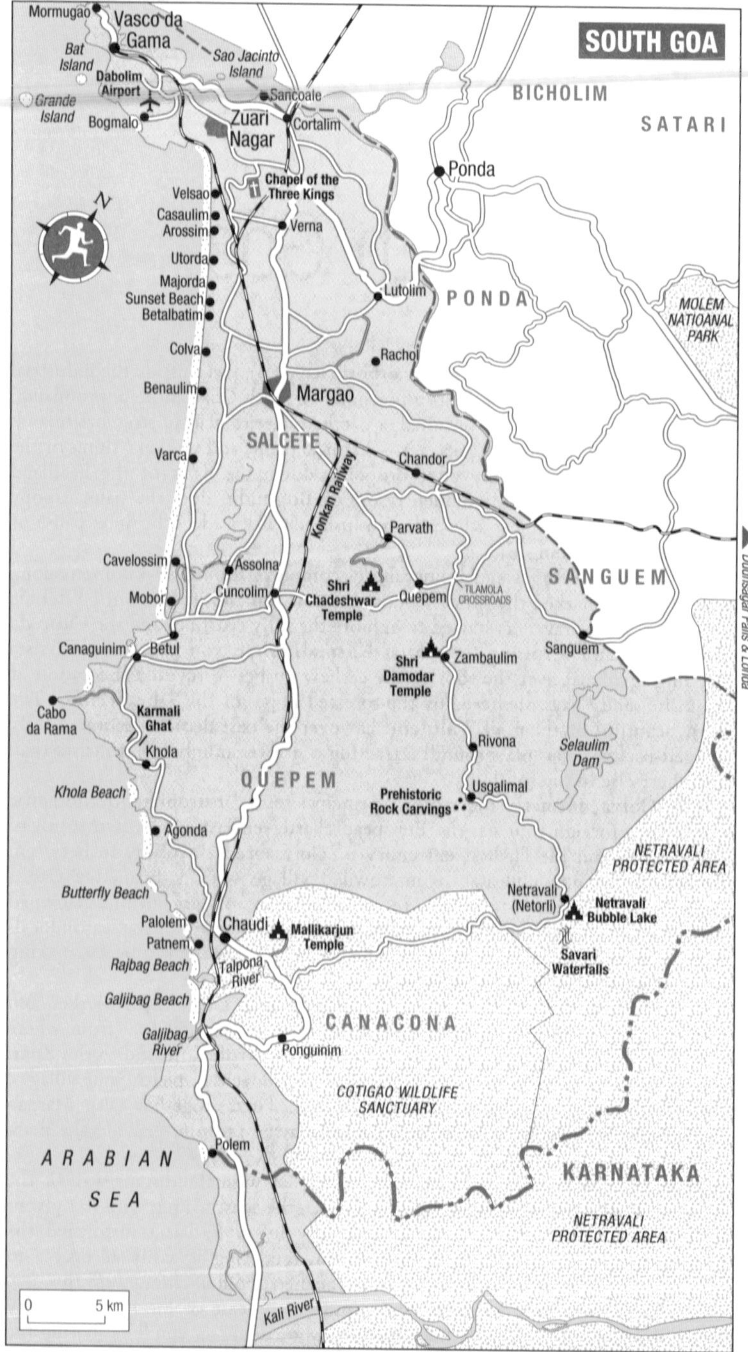
SOUTH GOA
Mormugao
Vasco da Gama
Bat Island
Sao Jacinto Island
Dabolim Airport
Grande Island
Bogmalo
Sancoale
Zuari Nagar
Cortalim
BICHOLIM
SATARI
Ponda
Chapel of the Three Kings
Velsao
Casaulim
Arossim
Verna
Utorda
Majorda
Sunset Beach
Betalbatim
Lutolim
PONDA
MOLEM NATIOANAL PARK
Colva
Rachol
Benaulim
Margao
SALCETE
Varca
Chandor
Konkan Railway
Parvath
Cavelossim
Assolna
Shri Chadeshwar Temple
Quepem
TILAMOLA CROSSROADS
SANGUEM
Mobor
Cuncolim
Dudhsagar Falls & Londa
Canaguinim
Betul
Sanguem
Shri Damodar Temple
Zambaulim
Cabo da Rama
Karmali Ghat
Khola
Rivona
Selaulim Dam
Khola Beach
QUEPEM
Usgalimal
Prehistoric Rock Carvings
Agonda
NETRAVALI PROTECTED AREA
Butterfly Beach
Netravali (Netorli)
Netravali Bubble Lake
Palolem
Chaudi
Mallikarjun Temple
Patnem
Savari Waterfalls
Rajbag Beach
Talpona River
Galjibag Beach
CANACONA
Galjibag River
Ponguinim
COTIGAO WILDLIFE SANCTUARY
Polem
ARABIAN SEA
KARNATAKA
NETRAVALI PROTECTED AREA
0 5 km
Kali River
Karwar, Mangalore & Gokarna

poolside with Delhi industrialists and honeymooning dot-com couples from Chennai, in addition to sun-seeking charter tourists from Russia, continental Europe and Britain.

Margao

MARGAO (sometimes spelt **Madgaon**), the capital of south Goa, is regarded as the state's second city, even though – with a population of around 85,000 – it's considerably smaller than Vasco da Gama, 30km northwest. Surrounded by fertile farmland, the town has always been an important agricultural market, and was once a major religious centre, boasting a university with a library of 10,000 books, and dozens of wealthy temples and *dharamsalas*; however, most of these were destroyed when the Portuguese absorbed the area into their *Novas Conquistas* during the seventeenth century. Today, Catholic churches still outnumber Hindu shrines, but Margao has retained a cosmopolitan feel, largely due to a huge influx of migrant labour from neighbouring Karnataka and Maharashtra.

If you're only in Goa for a couple of weeks and wonder what the rest of India is like, a morning here should suffice. Clogged solid with slow-moving traffic, the town centre – a hotch-potch of Portuguese-era municipal buildings and modern concrete blocks – simmers under a haze of petrol fumes and dust. The main reason most foreign visitors brave the melee is to shop in Margao's excellent **market**. While you're in town, it's also worth making time to visit the **Church of the Holy Spirit**, set in the heart of a run-down but picturesque colonial enclave to the north of the centre, and regarded as one of the finest specimens of Baroque architecture in Christian India.

Arrival, information and accommodation

Margao's train station, the only stop in Goa for most long-distance express services on the Konkan Railway, lies 3km east of the centre. Several principal **trains** pull into Margao at unsociable times of the night, but there's a 24-hour information counter (Ⓣ0832/271 2790) and a round-the-clock, pre-paid taxi and auto-rickshaw stand outside the exit. Taxis to Benaulim cost Rs250–300, auto-rickshaws Rs150–200. For details on ticket reservations, see "Listings" on p.165.

Arriving on long-distance government **buses**, you can get off either here or at the main **Kadamba (aka 'KTC') bus stand**, 3km further north, on the outskirts of town. This is also the departure point for interstate services to Mangalore, via Chaudi and Gokarna, and for non-stop services to Panjim. If you're just passing through Margao, local private buses can whisk you off to Colva and Benaulim from in front of the *Kamat Hotel*, on the east side of Margao's main square. Paulo Travel's deluxe coach to and from Hampi departs from a lot next to the *Nanutel Hotel*, one kilometre south of the Kadamba bus stand on Rua Padre Miranda.

GTDC's apathetic **information office** (Mon–Fri 9.30am–5.30pm; Ⓣ0832/222 2513) is inside the lobby of the GTDC *Margoa Residency*, on the southwest corner of the main square.

With Colva and Benaulim a mere twenty-minute bus ride away, there's no reason to stay in Margao, but if for any reason you do get stuck, try the good-value *Nanutel* (Ⓣ0832/270 0900–05, Ⓦwww.nanuindia.com; ❺–❻), a multistorey block north of the main square on Rua Padre Miranda. It's pitched at visiting businessmen, with 55 centrally air-conditioned rooms and a small pool.

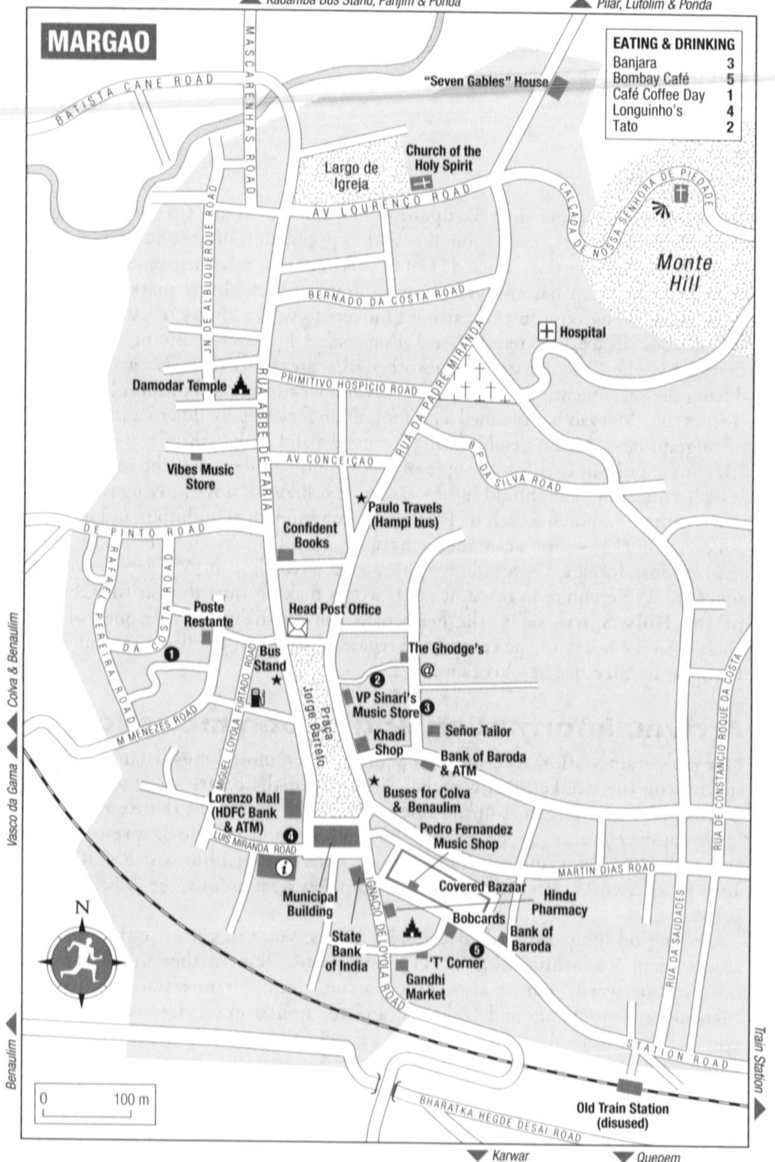

The Town

Margao's heart, the **Praça Jorge Barreto,** revolves around a hectic square with a threadbare Municipal Garden at its centre. On the south side, facing the park, stands the stalwart **Municipal Building**, a red-washed colonial edifice erected in 1905 which now houses the town library.

The congested streets south of the *praça* form Margao's **bazaar district**. Here, in a labyrinthine covered market, you'll find everything from betel leaves to baby clothes, all crammed into tiny stalls. When the syrupy thick air gets too stifling, explore the surrounding streets, among which is one given over to cloth merchants and tailors. Also worth checking out if you're looking to have clothes made is the excellent little government-run **Khadi Gramodyog** shop, on the southeast corner of the square (near the *Kamat* restaurant), which sells quality hand-spun cottons and raw silk by the metre, as well as ready-made traditional Indian garments.

The Largo de Igreja

A five-minute ride north of Praça Jorge Barreto, up **Rua Abbé de Faria,** lie the dishevelled remnants of Margao's **colonial quarter**. Once, this leafy suburb of Portuguese-era houses and tree-lined avenues must have been a peaceful enclave; nowadays, however, raucous traffic pours through on the main Panjim and Ponda roads, shattering the serenity of its central square, the **Largo de Igreja**.

Surrounded on three sides by some of the city's oldest residences, the square is dominated by the majestic **Church of the Holy Spirit (Espirito Santo)** (daily 6.30am–noon & 4–9pm), built in 1565 on the site of an ancient Hindu temple. The present structure, one of the finest examples of late Baroque architecture in Goa, dates from 1675, by which time the Jesuit seminary founded next door had been moved to a safer spot at Rachol. Forming a striking contrast with the brilliant red exposed brickwork of its side and rear walls, the church's white facade is flanked by a pair of square towers, each crowned by domes. The **interior**, entered via an ancient door on the south side, is equally impressive, with an elaborately carved reredos dedicated to the Virgin Mary, a gilded pulpit and an ornate stucco ceiling. As you leave, look out for the peacock motif moulded onto the wall of the north transept. This auspicious Hindu symbol, vehicle of Saraswati, the goddess of purification and fertility, would have been recognizable to new converts as they filed into church.

The monumental **cross** in the middle of the square, standing in the shade of a giant mango tree, also dates from the late seventeenth century. Mounted on a wedding-cake-confection pedestal, it is carved with images from the Easter story, among them Judas's bag of blood-money, a cockerel and a crown of thorns.

"Seven Gables" (Sat Banzam Gor)

Five minutes' walk northeast of Largo de Igreja, on the main Ponda road, stands one of Goa's grandest residences, "**Seven Gables**". The *palacio* originally sported a row of seven typically Goan high-pitched gables (whence its Konkani name, *Sat Banzam Gor*, which means "seven shoulders"). Now, only three of these remain, but the mansion – commissioned in 1790 by Sebastião da Silva, emissary and private secretary of the Portuguese viceroy – is still an impressive sight. Visits are not permitted, but no-one will mind you admiring the house's red Rococo-style facade from the roadside, with its oyster-shell windows, wrought-iron balconies and decorative scrollwork highlighted in limewash.

Monte Hill

For the best **views** of the town, head up the Calçada de Nossa Senhora de Piedade (Our Lady of Mercy), which winds from the crossroads immediately east of Largo de Igreja, to the top of **Monte Hill**. The small chapel overlooking the clearing at the end of the lane is always locked, but the fine views over Margao and Salcete's sand-fringed coastal plain make this ten- to fifteen-minute walk worthwhile. Blot out the modern concrete apartment blocks on the northern edge of town, and you can easily imagine what the old quarter, whose shaggy gardens and red-tiled rooftops spread from the foot of the hill, must have looked like two or three hundred years ago.

Eating and drinking

Even if you don't stay overnight, Margao does hold plenty of commendable **places to eat.**

Banjara De Souza Chambers. This swish basement restaurant is Goa's classiest North Indian joint outside Panjim, specializing in rich Mughlai and tandoori dishes. Tasteful wood and oil-painting decor, unobtrusive *ghazaal* background music, imported liquors and slick service. Most main courses are around Rs250.

Bombay Café Station Rd. Popular with office workers and shoppers for its cheap veg snacks, served on tin trays by young lads in grubby cotton uniforms. Handy pit stop for the market and open early for breakfast, though cramped.

Café Coffee Day Shop 18/19 Vasanth Arcade, nr Popular High School. India's answer to Starbucks has a super-cool a/c branch tucked away off the Municipal Gardens square, strategically placed to pull in local college kids. Aside from a perfect latte, it serves spicy savouries (such as mini-pizzas and salad wraps) and a very sinful "sizzling brownie", which will have chocoholics begging for loyalty cards.

Longuinho's Luis Miranda Rd. Relaxing, old-fashioned café serving a selection of meat, fish and veg mains, freshly baked savoury snacks, cakes and drinks. The food isn't up to much these days, and the 1950s Goan atmosphere has been marred by the arrival of satellite TV, but it's a pleasant enough place to catch your breath over a beer.

Tato Tucked away up an alley off the east side off Praça Jorge Barreto. The town's brightest and best South Indian café serves the usual range of hot snacks (including especially good samosas at breakfast time, and masala dosas from midday on). It gets a bit packed and overheated downstairs, but there's a cool a/c floor up the stairs where you can order wonderful thalis (for Rs60) and a range of North Indian dishes, as well as all the *udipi* nibbles dished up on the ground floor.

Listings

Banks There are plenty of ATMs dotted around the town centre: try HDFC, in the Lorenzo Mall, on the west side of Praça Jorge Barreto just up from *Longuinho's;* or the Bank of Baroda on the opposite side of the square. Bobcards office in the market sub-branch of the Bank of Baroda, on Station Rd, does Visa encashments. However, transactions can be time consuming.

Cashew nuts The Ghodge's, Shop #2, Varde Valaulikar Rd, near the *Tato* restaurant, sells export-grade Zantye's cashew nuts – the best brand available.

Cinema Goa's principal cinema, the Osia Multiplex (ⓣ0832/270 1717), out in the north of town near the Kadamba bus stand, screens Hollywood as well as Bollywood releases; tickets cost Rs80–120.

Hospitals South Goa's top hospital is the Apollo Victor, in the suburb of Malbhat (ⓣ0832/272 8888 or 272 6272, ⓦwww.apollovictorhospital.com).

Music shops Margao's best-stocked CD and cassette shop is Vibes, ten minutes' walk north of the main square off Rua Abbé de Faria; the shop is on Custodio Pinho Rd, left off the main drag (as indicated by a signboard). If they don't have what you're looking for, VP Sinari's, on the first floor of a new mall on the east side of the square (near the *Mabai* hotel), probably will. For cheap Konkani and Hindi pop compilations, check out the stalls in the market. Hohner and Gibson copy guitars, mandolins and other Indian-made musical instruments are on sale at Pedro Fernandes & Cia, in the bazaar on Station Rd (look for the sign above a doorway; the shop is up a flight of steps at the rear of the building).

Pharmacy Hindu Pharmacy, on J Ignacio de Loyola Rd, is the largest in town, with a huge range of traditional ayurvedic and homeopathic medicines, in addition to Western allopathic ones.

Post office The GPO (Mon–Sat 9.30am–1pm & 2–5.30pm) is at the top of the Municipal Gardens, although its poste restante is in a different building, 200m west on the Rua Diogo da Costa.

Tailors (Gents) Highly recommended is Señor Tailor (ⓣ0832/273 2243), off the southeast corner of the square, who specialize in suits and shirts.

Tea An excellent range of top-quality Indian tea – an ideal, lightweight present to take home – is sold loose at 'T' Corner Tea and Coffee Merchants, Gandhi Market. Try their fine-grade Nilgiri orange pekoe.

Train reservations Located 3km east of town at the main railway station, the Konkan Railway Company's reservation office (Mon–Sat 8am–4.30pm, Sun 8am–2pm) is divided between the ground and first floors; bookings for express services to Delhi are made at the hatch to the left of the main entrance. Tickets for trains to Mumbai and Kerala, in particular, are in short supply – so make your reservation as far in advance as possible, get here early in the day to avoid agonizingly long queues and bring a book. For more advice on booking train tickets, see p.260.

East of Margao

Dotted with wax-covered wayside shrines and whitewashed churches, the farming villages **east of Margao** form the heartland of Goa's Catholic belt. Nestled among them are some evocative old colonial-era monuments that can be visited on day-trips from the coast. Stately-home hunters should head for **Lutolim**, in the northeast of Salcete *taluka*, where some of Salcete's most elegant old family houses languish behind rambling gardens. A short detour further east on the way takes you to **Rachol**, site of a sixteenth-century Jesuit seminary. **Ponda** (covered in Chapter 1), Goa's main Hindu temple town, also lies just across the Zuari River from Lutolim, and is a worthwhile extension to this short foray north.

The area's remaining attractions are scattered to the southeast. Foremost among them is the famous Braganza-Perreira/Menezes-Braganza house at **Chandor**, renowned as Goa's most splendid mansion, whose subsiding walls harbour a hoard of eighteenth-century antiques. With your own transport, it's possible to head southeast into the hilly interior from there to see the Hindu temple at **Zambaulim** and **Rivona**'s ancient Buddhist hermitage en route to the

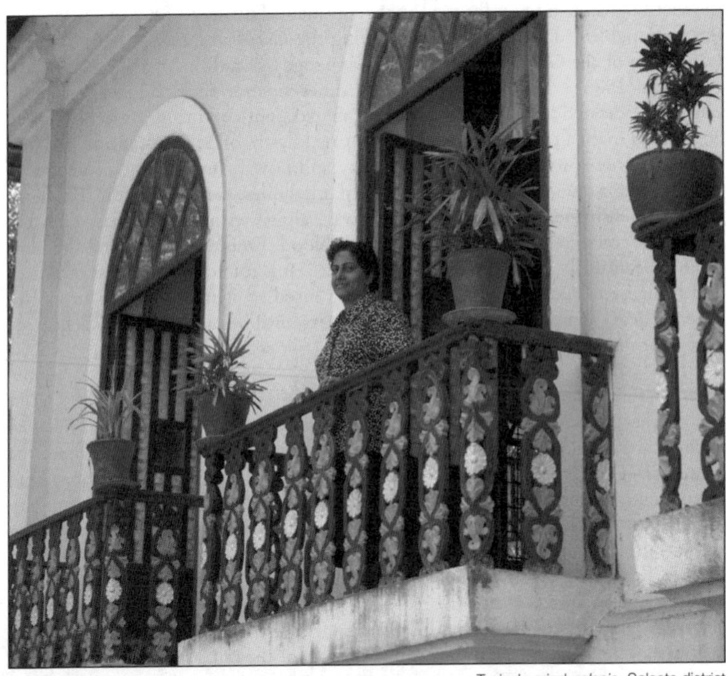

▲ Typical period *palacio*, Salcete district

remote **prehistoric rock-art** site at **Usgalimal**. Alternatively, loop south from Chandor to **Quepem**, home of the wonderful **Palacio de Deão**, where you can dine on the terrace of another magnificent Indo-Portuguese mansion, and then round off the day watching the sunset from the top of **Chandranath Hill**, near Parvath, with its sixteenth-century Shiva temple and superb panoramic views over the coast.

Rachol

The Catholic **seminary** at **RACHOL**, 7km northeast of Margao, rises proudly from the crest of a laterite hillock, surrounded by the dried-up moat of an old Muslim **fort** and rice fields that extend east to the banks of the nearby Zuari River. During the early days of the Portuguese conquests, this was a border bastion of the Christian faith, perennially under threat from Muslim and Hindu marauders. Today, its painstakingly restored sixteenth-century church and cloistered theological college lie in the midst of Goa's Catholic heartland. The seminary itself harbours nothing you can't see on a grander scale in Old Goa, but warrants a quick trip from the main road en route to Lutolim, 4km further north. Blue-painted Holy Family **buses** run here every hour or so from Margao's city bus stand, dropping passengers immediately below the church.

Rachol seminary

Rachol seminary was founded in 1580 by the Jesuits after its predecessor at Margao had been ransacked by the Muslims. The institution originally comprised a hospital and school for the poor, as well as the theological college; it also boasted one of India's earliest ever printing presses, installed by Father Thomas Stephens, the first Englishman to set foot in the subcontinent. During its 58 years of service, the press published sixteen books, including the *Christian Purana* (1616), the first translation of the Gospels into an Indian language (Marathi).

Built in 1576 – and renovated several times since – the seminary's splendid **church**, dedicated to St Ignatius Loyola, is in excellent condition. Its richly carved and gilded main altarpiece features a uniformed figure of St Constantine, the first Roman emperor to convert to Christianity and now revered as the protector of women against widowhood. Fragments of his bones, sent here from Rome in 1782, are enshrined near the main doorway, along with a small glass vial that originally contained a sample of the saint's blood. One reredos behind the altar holds a beautifully carved statue of the Infant Jesus, found on the coast of Africa and brought to Goa by a Jesuit priest, who installed it in his church in Colva, where it was reputed to have miraculous powers until being moved to Rachol (see p.166 for more on this story).

Rachol fort

Before the evangelization of Goa during the sixteenth century, Rachol hill was encircled by an imposing **fort**, built by the Muslim Bahmani dynasty that founded the city of Ela (Old Goa). Taken from the Sultan of Bijapur by the Hindu Vijayanagars in the fifteenth century, it was ceded to the Portuguese in 1520 in exchange for military help against the Muslims. One hundred cannons once nosed over the battlements, but when, during the late eighteenth century, the borders of the territory were pushed back further east into the *Novas Conquistas* area, these were redeployed and the fort eventually abandoned. Today, the red-, yellow- and white-stone archway that spans the road below the seminary is the only fragment left standing. You can, however, follow the course of the old **moat** around the base of the hill, along with the resident herd of water buffaloes.

Lutolim

Dotted around the tree-lined lanes of **LUTOLIM**, 10km northeast of Margao, are several of Goa's most beautiful colonial *palacios*, dating from the high watermark of the Portuguese empire, when this was the country seat of some of the territory's wealthiest *Goenkar* gentry. Lying just off the main road, the village is served by buses from Margao, which drop passengers on the square in front of a lopsided-looking church.

The cream of Lutolim's architecture lies within walking distance of here, nestled in the woods, or along the road leading south. However, residents don't tend to welcome casual visits. The only place set up to welcome tourists is the

The stately homes of Goa

The **stately homes of Goa** are scattered throughout its rural heartland and along the coastal belt of Salcete. Most date from the early eighteenth century, when the Portuguese were raking off handsome profits from their African colonies and the gold and gemstone trade with Brazil. However, their owners were not generally Europeans, but native Goans: wealthy merchants and high-ranking officials who were granted land as golden handshakes. Kept afloat by rent from their estates, these families weathered the decline of the empire to emerge as a powerful aristocracy, frequently intermarrying to preserve their fortunes. Many, however, had their estates confiscated and parcelled out to former tenants after Independence in 1961. Deprived of their chief source of income, some now struggle to maintain their rambling properties, living in one wing and selling off heirlooms to pay for renovation work on the others. In such cases, donations from visitors for the upkeep of the buildings are gratefully received.

The **architecture** of Goa's eighteenth-century stately homes was heavily influenced by European tastes, while remaining firmly rooted in a strong vernacular tradition. The materials and construction techniques mostly originated in India: red laterite for the walls and pillars, and local wood, overlaid with curved terracotta roof tiles from Mangalore (Karnataka). Many of the sumptuous furnishings, luxurious to the point of decadence, were imported: fine porcelain and silk came from China, Macao and Korea, cut glass and mirrors from Venice, chandeliers from Belgium and Germany and tapestries from Spain or Portugal. Some furniture was also shipped here, but most was fashioned by Goan craftsmen out of rare rosewood brought from Ceylon or Africa. Among the finest examples of the furniture-maker's craft – and a feature of most Goan mansions still – are the chapels used to celebrate Mass and important religious festivals. Looking more like giant cupboards than shrines, these elaborately carved **oratories** often contain gilded altars and ivory statues of saints.

The exteriors of the houses, too, incorporate several peculiarly Goan features. Most distinctive of these is the pillared porch, or **balcão**. Surmounted by a pyramidal roof and flanked by a pair of cool stone benches, this is where Goan families traditionally while away sultry summer evenings. In larger houses, the *balcão* opens onto a covered veranda that extends along the length of a colour-washed Classical facade, whose Rococo mouldings and pilasters are picked out in white. Another typical Goan trait, noted by the traveller François Pyrard in the early seventeenth century, is the use of **oyster shells** instead of glass for windows. The wafer-thin inside layer of the shells was cut into rectangular strips and fitted into wood frames to filter the glare of the Goan sun. Sadly, most have long since been replaced by glass, but you'll still come across them from time to time in more traditional villages, where the art of oyster-shell window-making survives. Goa's most famous stately homes are situated in Salcete villages such as **Lutolim** (see above), **Chandor** (site of the Braganza-Perreira/Menezes-Braganza house; see p.169) and **Quepem**, where the exquisitely restored Palacio de Deão (see p.170) should be top of your must-see list.

Casa Araujo Alvares (daily 9am–6pm; Rs125), a short way east of the village centre, opposite the main entrance to the Ancestral Goa exhibition (see below). Although evidently stripped of most of its antique furniture and fittings, the interior of this once dynastic seat conveys a sense of what life must have been like for the Goan aristocracy during the swansong of the Portuguese empire.

It also serves as the family home of the creator of the adjacent **Ancestral Goa exhibition** (daily 9am–6pm; Ⓦwww.ancestralgoa.com; Rs25), a model village showcasing Goan life as it was a hundred years ago, with various miniature houses representing the different occupations and social classes, from fisherfolk and fruit-wallahs in the market to the Portuguese colonial homes of the landowners. An additional attraction is a giant fourteen-metre sculpture of **Sant Mirabai**, which the site's creators, proudly quoting the *Limca Book of Records*, claim is the "longest laterite sculpture in India".

Practicalities

Lutolim is the site of a romantic heritage **guesthouse**, *Casa Susegad* (Ⓣ9850/473174, Ⓦwww.casasusegadgoa.com; ⓑ), located 1km or so down a winding lane from the village church. A cross between a British B&B and boutique hotel, it occupies a restored colonial-era mansion backing onto jungle, where langurs and exotic birdlife flit through the foliage. Hosts Carole and Norman offer only four crystal-coloured guest rooms, all of them air-conditioned, attached and filled with repro antique furniture and embroidered textiles collected on travels around India. The real plus of the house, though, is its garden pool, which you can walk straight into from your room; behind it, a shady path leads through the woods to a sunset terrace with views across the treetops. It's quite simply one of the loveliest places to stay in Goa, and the food gets rave reviews too.

That said, for proper Goan-Catholic fish-curry-rice plates and delicious fresh seafood, you won't do better than *Archie's* (Ⓣ0832/277 7065; closed Thurs), on the outskirts of Lutolim next to the main Margao–Ponda road. *Nostalgia*, a "Goa" theme **restaurant** signposted just off the main road nearby, is another commendable option in the area. Decked out with *azulejos* and Mario Miranda-esque murals, it's crammed with heritage clichés but fun nonetheless, and the food is scrupulously authentic. On a palm-shaded garden terrace, you can tuck into chicken *cafreal*, *ambotik* and fiery *xacuti*. For veggies there's *choulis ros*, a filling kidney-bean stew, and deliciously smoky *sanna*, steamed rice cakes flavoured with fresh *toddi*; most main courses are priced under Rs100.

Chandor

CHANDOR, 13km southeast of Margao, presides over Salcete's rice bowl hinterland, its tumbledown Indo-Portuguese houses ranged along tree-lined lanes, many of which sport a layer of fine red dust from the iron-ore trucks that thunder through. Between the late sixth and mid-eleventh centuries, the village was the site of ancient **Chandrapura**, capital of the Kadamba dynasty, which ruled the region until its conquest by the Vijayanagars in 1367. Known to medieval Arab cartographers as Zindabar, the city declined when the royal court decamped to Govapuri on the Zuari River in 1017, and crumbled completely after a sound sacking by the Muslim warlord Ghiyas-ud-din Tughluq three hundred years later.

Excavations carried out in Chandor in 1921, and more recently in 1999, revealed traces of a pre-Kadamba settlement in the north of the village (1km east of the square). The foundations of an ancient Shiva temple are believed to date from the third or fourth century AD, as does a copper donatory plaque unearthed in recent digs – the oldest piece of text ever discovered in Goa. This, and numerous fragments of 2000-year-old pottery, have been removed to the state archeological museum in Old Goa, but a solitary headless Nandi bull, garlanded and smudged with vermilion powder by local Hindus, still stands *in situ*.

Braganza-Perreira/Menezes-Braganza house

In addition to its uninspiring ancient remains, Chandor is famous in Goa for the huge stately home that sprawls across the south side of its church square. Fronted by a spectacular Portuguese-style facade, the **Braganza-Perreira/ Menezes-Braganza** house is a veritable museum of old furniture, paintings and porcelain, and makes Chandor one of the most rewarding day-trip destinations in South Goa. Visitors generally travel here by taxi or motorbike, but you can also get to Chandor by bus from Margao (8 daily; 45min). It's generally fine to turn up without an appointment (roughly: Mon–Sat 10am–noon & 3–6pm, Sun 3–6pm), but to ensure someone from the family is in to receive you, phone ahead (ⓣ0832/278 4227 or ⓣ9822/160009).

Although parts of the house date from the 1500s, when its owners were Hindus, most were built after the Braganza family had converted to Catholicism in the eighteenth century. Two separate wings were originally commissioned to accommodate the two sons and their wives. When no male heirs issued from either marriage, sons-in-law were drafted in for the daughters and granted inheritance rights on condition they adopt the Braganza title (hence the double-barrelled names). Descendants of both branches of the family still occupy their respective sides of the house but – if the contrasting condition of their homes is anything to go by – their fortunes have been divergent.

There are no fixed admission charges, but **donations** for the upkeep of the house are expected at both wings: Rs100 per head should be adequate for a short visit.

The east wing

The mansion's dilapidated **east wing** (on your left as you face the building) belongs to the Braganza-Perreira family. Gaping cracks to its rear indicate the extent to

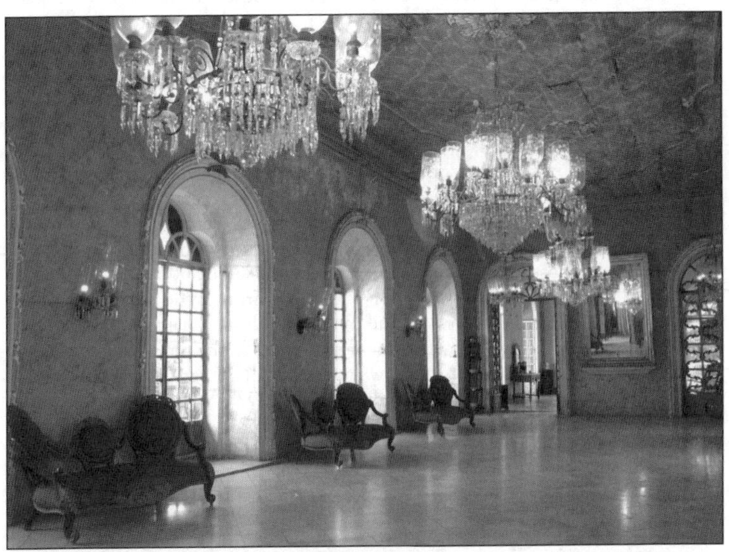

▲ The Great Salon, Braganza-Perreira/Menezes-Braganza house

which the house is in need of renovation; the long double-storeyed facade at the front, by contrast, is still in fine shape. Twenty-eight windows, each with its own wooden balustrades, flank the main entrance and were reputedly designed to catch the balmy zephyr breezes. Reached via a grand staircase, the top floor comprises a series of plush interconnecting salons, reception rooms, dining halls and the family's private chambers, ranged around a central courtyard; the ground floor, now empty, used to accommodate the kitchen and servants' quarters.

The grandest room in the house, if not in all of Goa, is the **Great Salon**, or ballroom. Sumptuous crystal chandeliers hang from its ceiling, decorated with floral motifs overlaid with a crisscross pattern of painted zinc netting, while the walls are beautifully marbled to match the floor and upholstery. Prominent among the pieces of furniture here is a pair of stately high-backed chairs, bearing the family crest, which were presented to the Braganza-Perreira household by King Dom Luís of Portugal.

The remaining rooms contain eighteenth-century furniture, much of it made from local *seeso* (martel wood), lacquered or inlaid with mother-of-pearl. You may, in addition, be shown the Perreira-Braganza's private **chapel**, among whose treasures number relics of the Cuncolim Martyrs, and, more precious still, St Francis Xavier's gold-and-diamond-encrusted fingernail, occupying pride of place on the main altar.

The west wing

The layout of the mansion's better-maintained **west wing**, belonging to the Menezes-Braganza family, mirrors that of its neighbour. Lovers of antiques, in particular, will drool over its superb collection of Chinese porcelain. Other highlights include several seventeenth- and eighteenth-century portraits of family members on glass, a pair of large ceramic elephants and a set of four matching conversation chairs, housed in the library. The five thousand or so leather-bound tomes shelved here were mostly collected by **Luis de Menezes-Braganza** (1878–1938), a famous journalist and freedom fighter, whose offspring also became involved in the independence struggle (the Menezes-Braganzas were one of the few wealthy Christian families in Goa actively to oppose Portuguese rule). Forced into exile in 1950, they returned twelve years later and were astonished to find their home untouched.

Fernandes House

An air of charismatic dilapidation hangs over the **Fernandes House**, on the south side of the village as you head towards Zambaulim. One of the oldest surviving *palacios* in Goa, its core is of pre-conquest Hindu origin, overlaid by later accretions. Sara Fernandes, the present owner, receives visitors in the wonderful **salon** that extends the length of the building's first floor, abutting a bedchamber containing its original, ornately carved four-poster.

The mansion's most outstanding feature – believed to be 500 years old – lies on the ground floor, accessed via a sinister trap door through the bottom of a false cupboard. Hidden in the bowels of the building below, a narrow passage fitted with disguised gun holes was where the family used to shelter when attacked by Hindu rebels and bandits. Visitors are welcome to call on Sara Fernandes any day of the week, but should telephone in advance (Ⓣ0832/278 4245). A **donation** of around Rs100 per head is expected.

Quepem

Until the Rei of Sundem granted the south of Goa to the Portuguese in the late eighteenth century, **QUEPEM**, today a small market town on the fringes of the state's iron-ore belt, was merely a forest outpost on a remote tributary of the Zuari River. In 1787, however, a high-ranking member of the Portuguese clergy and nobility, **Father José Paulo de Almeida**, built a country house here, which over time came to form the nucleus of a prisoner rehabilitation scheme. Released offenders were encouraged to settle and clear land for rice fields and palm groves; a market, hospital and churches followed, while José Paulo's residence, known as the **Palacio de Deão**, grew to become one of the most grandiose in the colony. From the 1830s, while fever and pestilence raged in Old Goa, it served as a retreat for the colony's viceroys, who would travel to it by boat down the Mandovi and Zuari.

Over the centuries, the Palacio, used most recently by the Church as a hostel for destitute women, fell into disrepair, but it has since been restored to its former glory by a couple from north Goa, Ruben and Celia Vasco da Gama. Ruben scoured libraries in Lisbon for original plans of the building and its garden, and what you see here is a faithful approximation of what the Palacio would have looked like in José Paolo's day, down to the furniture and fixtures – though it is very much a family home, too, with kids charging around the lofty salons and clambering over the carved wood furniture. The engaging guided **tour** (daily, except Fri 10am–6pm; ⓣ0832/266 4029; free) lasts around half an hour, winding up on the lovely rear terrace overlooking the river where, by prior arrangement, you can enjoy a copious Indo-Portuguese **lunch** (Rs450) – an experience not be missed.

Zambaulim and Rivona

Two historically significant religious sites – one Hindu, the other Buddhist – lie in the district of Sanguem, hidden in the foothills of the Western Ghats. Neither is of more than passing interest, but the road that leads to **Zambaulim** and **Rivona**, winding through the picturesque Pareda valley, makes a pleasant detour from Chandor, 10km northwest. Self-reliant travellers with their own transport may also want to press on further south into Sanguem *taluka* to visit Goa's most enigmatic archeological site – the prehistoric rock art at **Usgalimal**.

ZAMBAULIM, 10km south of Chandor, is renowned throughout Goa for its **Shri Damodar temple** – an important Hindu pilgrimage centre rebuilt in the 1950s and 1960s. The *Shivalingam* enshrined inside is associated with a well-known legend in which the son of a wealthy local landowner and his bride were murdered on their wedding day by a gang of thugs hired by a jealous suitor. A temple was erected in Margao to mark the tragedy, but this was pulled down by the Portuguese to make way for their Church of the Holy Spirit. The *lingam*, however, was smuggled to this out-of-the-way spot, where it is still revered beside an image of Lakshminarayan.

A small rice-farming hamlet 3km further southeast along the road from Zambaulim, **RIVONA** is the site of a pair of ancient rock-cut caves hidden in the wooded hills behind the settlement. Nicknamed the **Pandava caves**, these served as cells for a small community of Buddhist monks in the seventh century, who carved them from a slab of overhanging laterite. To find the site, follow the road through Rivona until it sweeps into a sharp bend; a signpost marked "Shri Sansthan Gokarn" points left up a dirt track. The main opening to the caves is next to a small stepped well and ablutions tank. Flanked by a sixteenth-century bas-relief of the Hindu monkey god Hanuman, the doorway leads, via a low-roofed tunnel, to the cells.

The Usgalimal rock carvings

In 1993, archeologists scouring Sanguem *taluka* for traces of prehistoric settlement hit the jackpot at **Usgalimal**, 6km south of Rivona, when local villagers led them to a bend in the River Kushawati where a rock shelf of laterite was covered in spirals, lines, images of bulls and human figures. The carvings are now thought to date from the Upper Paleolithic or Mesolithic eras, between twenty and thirty thousand years ago, which makes this one of the most important prehistoric sites in western India.

If you are tempted to look for them, be prepared for a bit of an adventure: the site, hidden behind an old iron-ore mine, lies a fair way from the coast, along winding backroads that are punctuated with few settlements. The directions below, however, should get you there. Coming from Chandor, head south through Zambaulim and Rivona, continuing on beyond the hamlet of **Colomba**, until you see the round, green and red ASI (Archeological Survey of India) sign on the roadside. This points the way (to the right) along a dirt track that skirts an ore heap and, later, a giant flooded pit, before dropping downhill towards a large areca plantation. The carvings can be seen on the uneven shelf of rock lining the near bank. If you're having trouble, ask a local for the *fatrar koree-lee cheetra*, ("rock carvings" in Konkani).

Spread over an area of 500 square metres, the rock art comprises around one hundred distinct figures, mostly figurative depictions of animals – zebu bulls, bison, deer and antelope. Some show wound marks, or have spears and harpoons stuck in their sides; others are of the X-ray type, showing anatomical details. Alongside the animals are a number of less distinct human figures, the most impressive of which is a "dancing woman", shown with her left arm resting on her hip and her leg raised. Other female forms have small figures next to them which archeologists think represent placentas or babies.

The best-preserved and most striking of all the carvings, though, are the shapes dubbed as **triskelions** – circular mazes of seven concentric furrows, roughly 15cm wide and 2–3cm deep, centred on what could be symbolically rendered cobra heads. Archeologists have speculated they might have been used for time measurement.

The Shri Chandeshwar (Bhutnath) temple

Blistering out of the coastal plain 12km southeast of Margao, the semicircular ridge of **Chandranath Hill** is crowned with the famous **Shri Chandeshwar** (or **Bhutnath**) **temple** – a perfect spot to wind up trips into the interior of Goa. Affording superb sunset views over the surrounding plains and coast, the shrine, reached via a narrow, winding forest road, has, according to ancient Sanskrit inscriptions, stood on this magical spot for nearly 2500 years, ever since a large meteorite landed here. However, the present building, dedicated to Shiva, is comparatively modern, dating from the late 1600s. The only part of the building that is definitely a vestige of the distant past is its cavernous inner sanctum, hollowed from a rock around which the site's seventeenth-century custodians erected a typically Goan-style structure, capped with a red-tile roof and domed sanctuary tower. A wild-eyed golden Chandeshwar, Shiva as "Lord of the Moon", is the presiding deity. His consort, Parvati, and elephant-headed son, Ganesh, are housed in small niches to the rear, reached via a circumambulatory passage which you should walk around in a clockwise direction.

You'll need your own **transport** to get to the Shri Chandeshwar temple, as there are no buses up the hill. Travelling from Margao, look for a right turn across the fields about a kilometre beyond the main Chandor junction (marked by a yellow sign in Marathi).

Vasco da Gama and around

VASCO DA GAMA (commonly referred to as "Vasco"), 29km by road southwest of Panjim, is the hub of Goa's petrochemical and iron-ore industries, as well as its principal port. Drawn here by the prospect of employment in the neighbouring boatyards or Zuari Agro fertilizer plant, a sizeable proportion of the town's 150,000-strong population live in slum encampments on the outskirts, while the centre is marred by the storage tanks of a large oil refinery. In short, this is no place to spend time if you can help it. With the state's principal railhead now moved to Margao, the only conceivable reason you might end up here is by getting lost on the way to or from the airport. If you've time to kill, jump in a taxi or auto-rickshaw and head off 8km southeast to Bogmalo beach, on the opposite of the Mormugao peninsula.

Sao Jacinto, Sao Antonio and Sancoale

Connected to the shore by a causeway, **SAO JACINTO**, a wooded islet 7km east of Vasco da Gama, is marked by a little whitewashed **chapel**, whose stone steps double up as a landing stage for the island's tiny population of *toddi* tappers. Beginning at the hamlet just beyond it, you can follow a path through the trees to a clearing at the top of the hill. An old **lighthouse** stands at the opposite end of the clearing from where the track drops down to Sao Jacinto village: an easy round walk of fifteen to twenty minutes.

A little over 1km further west along the coast road sits another tiny islet, **SAO ANTONIO**, joined to the shore by a narrow isthmus of land. Time your visit to coincide with low tide on Sunday afternoon and you'll be treated to one of the great spectacles of the Zuari, when hundreds of locals gather to forage for clams, submerged up to their waists in muddy water. As befits all the best Goan get-togethers, Sao Antonio's Sunday **clam hunt** is accompanied by much drunkenness and shouting. Afterwards, everyone sloshes home along the road to cook up their haul in a big *pulao*, flavoured with stone-ground chilli *rechead* and *toddi* vinegar.

When Jesuit missionary priests first reached Goa in 1560, their landfall lay a little way west of Sao Antonio at the hamlet of **Sancoale**. This historic occasion was commemorated with the construction of a magnificent church, **Nossa Senhora de Saude** (Our Lady of Health), completed in 1566 on the site of an earlier Hindu temple. Only a fragment of the facade is left standing, but it's a supremely elegant chunk, embellished with the decorative panels and fancy plasterwork typical of early Christian-Goan architecture. A red Archeological Survey sign flags the turning off the main road.

Bogmalo

A snug bay of yellow sand enfolded by steep, wooded cliffs, **BOGMALO** is a little hidden gem clinging to the south side of the Mormugao headland, just below Dabolim. With its surf and picturesque views of São Jorge Island, the resort certainly photographs well. But what brochure images fail to convey, and rarely mention, is the proximity of one of India's busiest naval bases and civil airports immediately to the north – as well as the smoke stacks of the nearby fertilizer plant. But if you can handle the periodic scream of low-flying jets, and unsettling air pollution gauges on the approach roads, this makes a pleasant enough base. The sand is clean and not too crowded, the water generally safe for swimming, and there are plenty of places to eat, drink and shop.

Diving at Bogmalo

Bogmalo boasts one of Goa's few **dive** schools where you can do PADI-approved Open Water diving courses. Operating out of *Joet's Guest House*, at the far end of the beach (see below), British-run Goa Diving also offers guided dives to shipwreck sites and coral beds off the coast and tuition for more advanced qualifications. The only potential drawback of diving here is the visibility, which fluctuates wildly from 20m to 2m. For this reason, the firm also runs overnight trips to Pigeon Island in neighbouring Karnataka, where conditions are better and marine life abundant. Prices range from Rs2000 for a one-tank guided dive, to Rs20,000 for the three-day PADI Open Water course. For more information, contact Goa Diving, House #145P, Chapel Bhat, Chicalim, near Bogmalo (ⓣ0832/255 5117 or ⓣ9822/100380), or visit ⓦwww.goadiving.com).

Halant beach

Just around the headland from Bogmalo, **HALANT BEACH** can be reached by turning left off the road just past the airport; 3km later you arrive at a secluded tidal cove that's locked in a peculiarly Goan time warp. It's not such a great place to bathe, the sand being brown and silty, but the little bar behind it has plenty of local atmosphere, and if you follow the blobs of melted candles up the steps from the car park, cross the railway line and head through the coconut *mand* at the top of the hillside, you'll be rewarded with a wonderful view over Colva beach, stretching south to the horizon.

Accommodation

As Bogmalo is primarily a package tourist destination with small, family-run hotels (the majority of them given over to British charter companies), walk-in **accommodation** is very limited and best booked ahead.

Bogmallo Beach Resort overlooking the cove ⓣ0832/253 8222, ⓦwww.bogmallobeachresort.com The favourite haunt of Bollywood movie makers and flight crews, this used to be one of Goa's top hotels but these days is showing signs of wear and tear. Its big selling point is its location, which the pool, sundeck and upper-floor rooms make the most of, to spectacular effect. A double room in season will set you back just under Rs7000 per night. ⑧

Coconut Creek Behind *Joet's* ⓣ0832/253 8100 or 0832/253 8090, ⓔcoconutcreek@dataone.in. Ten beautifully designed, double-storey chalets grouped around a lagoon-shaped pool, with hammocks strung between the trees, in a well-shaded walled compound. Run with great efficiency by the same British-Goan family that own nearby *Joet's*, it offers two types of room: standard a/c ones on the ground floors, and non-a/c ones on the upper storeys. The latter are only slightly less expensive, and are naturally ventilated using high-pitched, tiled roofs, Venetian blinds and sliding windows. Prices on are the steep side for walk-in clients (around Rs6000 per night for a double in season), but discounts are offered for stays of a week or more. The poolside restaurant, with its Brit-oriented menu, gets mixed reviews. ⑧

Joet's Guest House Far end of beach ⓣ0832/253 8036. Smart, efficient little guesthouse, with sunny rooms slap on the beach, though it's invariably booked by returning customers. Non-residents are welcome to eat in their breezy restaurant, which serves excellent seafood and hosts a local crooner on Friday evenings after sunset. ⑤–⑥

Sarita Guest House Bogmalo beach ⓣ0832/255 5965. Well-furnished, comfortable rooms and terrace bar-restaurant. You're more likely to find a vacancy here than at nearby *Joet's*, and it's much less pricey. ④–⑤

Tanisha Chicolna Waddo, Bogmalo village ⓣ0832/648 3681 or ⓣ9764/268445. Hidden away in the trees 10–15min from the beach is this small block of four furnished apartments, owned by British expat, Richard. Opening onto a little plunge pool, they're clean, modern, with a/c and kitchenettes; ask for one on the upper floor, which pitched roofs and more outside sitting space. Discounts for longer stays. ⑥

The sinking of the Ehrenfels

Mormugao Bay, the natural harbour at the mouth of the Zuari estuary, was the scene of one of the most bizarre and audacious episodes of World War II, immortalized in the Hollywood film *Sea Wolves*, starring Roger Moore, David Niven and Gregory Peck, and by James Leasor's rip-roaring account, *The Boarding Party*.

Following the outbreak of hostilities in 1939, one Italian and four German ships made a dash for Goa – at that time the nearest neutral port in the Arabian Sea. The vessels anchored in Mormugao harbour, safe in the knowledge that the Allies would not dare jeopardize their relationship with Portugal by making an armed attack. While most of the Axis crews sat out the last years of the war on board, the radio operator of the 7752-ton *Ehrenfels* was kept busy with a transmitter hidden in the engine room, broadcasting details of Allied shipping movements to U-boats prowling the coast. This information, gleaned from an extensive network of agents all over India, was causing catastrophic losses for the Allies: 46 ships were sunk in the Arabian Sea in less than six weeks.

Eventually, the British traced the transmissions to the *Ehrenfels*, but were unable to intervene because of a potential political backlash (it was feared that any discovery of Allied troops in Goa might be deemed a violation of the colony's neutrality, provoking the Portuguese to side with Germany). The solution to this dilemma, devised by the top-secret Special Operations Executive (SOE), reads like a script from an old Ealing comedy. The five Italian and German ships were to be stolen or sunk by a team of veteran civilians recruited from the ranks of the Calcutta Light Horse, a gentlemen's regiment that was more a social club than a fighting unit. If captured, these men – a motley crew of middle-aged company directors, accountants, tea planters and jute merchants – could feasibly claim the raid was a drunken prank conceived while on leave in the Portuguese territory.

After a crash course in basic commando skills, the fourteen men were dispatched by train to Cochin (Kochi), on the southwest coast of India. There they met up with a SOE officer and a plastic-explosives expert who, together with a hastily assembled Bengali crew, had sailed from Calcutta in an old mud-dredger called *Little Phoebe* – the only seaworthy tub not already requisitioned by the British navy. Meanwhile, another member of the Calcutta Light Horse was covertly organizing diversions that would lure the German crews ashore on the night of the attack. These included a ritzy reception at the Portuguese governor's residence for the officers, and, for the rest of the crews, a week of complimentary hospitality in Mormugao's brothels, paid for by the British secret service.

The raid went off smoothly. As *Little Phoebe* chugged into Mormugao Bay during the small hours of March 9, 1943, its crew, clutching Sten guns and with faces blackened, could hear music and raucous laughter drifting across the water. Using long bamboo ladders, they crept aboard the *Ehrenfels* and began to dismantle its anchor chains. However, the Germans, who had been half-expecting an assault, set off incendiary devices and kerosene bombs. During the ensuing commotion, valves in the ship's sides were opened and its holds flooded, though not before the raiders had destroyed the radio room. Keeping close to the shore to avoid the Portuguese searchlights, *Little Phoebe* slipped out of the harbour, as the five Axis ships burned in its wake, having been scuppered by their crews.

Newspaper reports the next day claimed that German and Italian sailors had set fire to their own ships in desperation at their internment in Goa. No one knew the true cause of the sinkings until years later. Four of the Germans involved in the *Ehrenfels* incident raised enough money after the war to salvage their old ship and retired in Goa on the proceeds. One, known to everyone in Panjim simply as "Fritz", married a local woman and opened a clock and camera repair shop in the capital, where he worked until his death in 1997.

Confirmed Goa enthusiasts should try to track down a video copy of *Sea Wolves*, less for the wooden acting and low-budget pyrotechnics than the evocative location scenes shot in and around Panjim in the early 1980s.

Eating and drinking

What the resort lacks in places to stay, however, it makes up for in **bars** and **restaurants**. Most of the shacks dotted along the beach depend on a steady trickle of refugees from the *Bogmallo Beach Resort* (see p.174) and have whacked up their prices accordingly. The *Full Moon*, outside the main hotel entrance, takes the lion's share of the overspill. Its menu of mainly seafood and chicken dishes, including locally caught tiger prawns and lobster, is predictably expensive. The *Sea Cuisine*, prettiest of the places further along the sand, offers identical dishes and prices, but tends to be less crowded, while further up the beach still, *Joet's*, decked out in cheerful blue and white mosaic, occupies a prime spot and dishes up moderately priced seafood from its breezy terrace, mostly to 50-something British package tourists. *Coconut Creek*'s Brit-oriented, poolside terrace restaurant is pretty but pricey, and gets mixed reviews.

Colva beach

Spectacular **COLVA BEACH**, 6km west of Margao, constitutes the longest unbroken stretch of white sand in the state, spanning 25km from the Mormugao peninsula in the north to Cabo da Rama (Cape Rama) in the south. Lined by a deep band of coconut plantations, it sweeps south to the horizon, seemingly empty save for an occasional rank of wooden outriggers or a fleet of trawlers bobbing in the middle of the bay. However, appearances from a distance can be deceptive. Closer up, the beach reveals itself to be backed by a string of resorts and walled five-star complexes, interconnected by a network of lanes that feed onto a busy north–south artery.

Colva, at the middle of the beach, is the area's main tourist trap, sucking in the lion's share of southern Goa's domestic tourist trade. Its rash of hotels and beach bars peters out further north, but erupts again at **Betalbatim**, continuing in an all-but unbroken line through the villages of **Majorda**, **Utorda**, **Cansaulim** and **Velsao**. With the scar of the Zuari Agro Chemical plant to the north, however, this top end of the beach is less appealing than the section **south of Colva**, where **Benaulim** holds the area's best-value accommodation, most of it overlooking paddy fields and coconut groves. Further south still, the largely empty beach features a series of jarring cultural juxtapositions, as fishing settlements stand cheek-by-jowl with a string of mega-luxurious resorts. The most intrusive of these occur around **Varca**, **Cavelossim** and **Mobor**, where a long spit of soft white sand noses into the Assolna estuary, forming a natural border between Salcete and Quepem *talukas*.

Although a couple of **buses** each day run from Vasco da Gama along the coast road to Colva village (via Dabolim airport), the most straightforward way to approach Colva beach is through **Margao**, from where regular buses and a busy fleet of auto-rickshaws and taxis service most of the coastal settlements. Having found your feet, you can get around the area by rented **bicycle**. The hard sand exposed at low tide supports heavy Indian cycles, allowing you to make the most of the (rapidly shrinking) hawker-free stretches between resorts.

Colva

A hot-season retreat for Margao's moneyed middle classes since long before Liberation, **COLVA** is the oldest and largest – but least appealing – of south Goa's resorts. Its leafy outlying *waddos* are pleasant enough, dotted with colonial-era *palacios* and ramshackle fishing huts, but the beachfront is dismal: a lacklustre

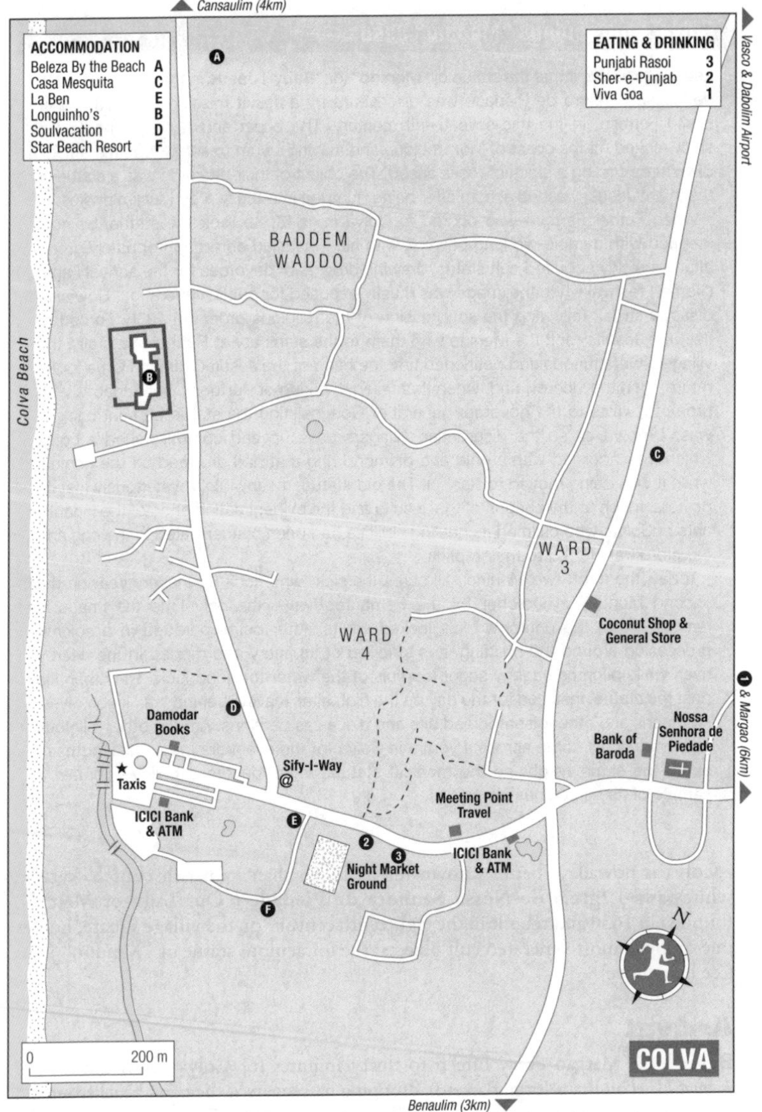

collection of concrete hotels, souvenir stalls and fly-blown snack bars strewn around a bleak central roundabout. Each afternoon, busloads of visitors from out of state mill around here after a paddle on the crowded foreshore. The ambience is not improved by heaps of rubbish dumped in a rank-smelling ditch that runs behind the beach, nor by the stench of drying fish wafting from the nearby fishing village. If, however, you steer clear of this central market area, and stick to the cleaner, greener outskirts, Colva can be just about bearable. Swimming is relatively safe (the local lifeguards are more for show than anything else), while the sand, at least away from the beachfront, is clean.

Colva's miraculous "Menino" Jesus

Local legend has it that the statue of **"Menino"** (or **"Baby"**) **Jesus** in the church of Igreja de Nossa Senhora de Piedade was discovered by a Jesuit missionary, Revd Father Bento Ferreira, in the mid-seventeenth century. The priest and his party had been shipwrecked off the coast of Mozambique and, having swum to safety, spotted a flock of vultures circling a stack of rocks ahead. The object of their attention was a statue of the Infant Jesus, washed ashore after being dumped into the sea by Muslim pirates.

When Father Ferreira was posted to Colva in 1648, he took the statue, by now credited with miracle-working powers, with him. Installed on an appropriately grand altar, it quickly acquired cult status, drawing crowds of devotees for the annual *Fama* ("fame") festival when the image was ritually exposed for public veneration. However, disaster struck following the suppression of the religious orders in 1836. Forced to flee, the Jesuits took the Menino with them to the seminary at Rachol. Naturally, the villagers were furious and petitioned first the head of the Jesuit Order in Rome for its return, then the viceroy, and, when that failed, the king of Portugal, Dom João V, who promptly wrote to the governor general of Goa insisting the statue be sent back. It wasn't, however, so the disgruntled villagers gave up and commissioned a copy, which they adorned with a gold and diamond ring that had dropped off the original while it was being moved to Rachol. The old statue, meanwhile, mysteriously lost its powers, much to the chagrin of the Jesuits and the evident satisfaction of the inhabitants of Colva, who claimed its healing abilities had been concentrated in the ring and therefore transferred to their replica.

Today, the mark-two Menino still cures the sick, who flock here every year on the second Monday in October for the **Fama festival** – the only time the image is removed from the church's triple-locked vaults. After being paraded in a solemn procession around the building, it is stripped of its finery and dipped in the nearby river, while pilgrims eagerly scoop cupfuls of the water for good luck. They then file past the statue, installed for the day on the high altar, leaving behind wax limbs, eyes, stomachs and other disembodied bits and pieces as petitions. Among other religious souvenirs you'll come across if you're in Colva for the event are *medidas*, lengths of string the same height as the magical statue, which devotees believe contain a sample of its miraculous properties.

Colva is nowadays better known for its beach than its parish church, yet the whitewashed **Igreja de Nossa Senhora de Piedade** ("Our Lady of Mercy"), founded in 1630 and rebuilt in the eighteenth century on the village square, houses one of Goa's most venerated cult objects: the miraculous statue of "Menino" Jesus (see box above).

Arrival

Buses leave Margao every fifteen to thirty minutes for Colva (from outside the *Kamat Hotel* on Praça Jorge Barreto), dropping passengers at the main beachfront and at various points along the main road. The thirty- to forty-minute trip costs virtually nothing, but can be a real endurance test towards the end of the day when the conductors pack on punters like sardines. Far better to take an **auto-rickshaw** for Rs150, or hail a **taxi** (Rs250). Marutis line up on the north side of the beachfront, next to the public toilets, and outside all of the upmarket resort hotels.

Accommodation

Colva's **acommodation** is generally much pricier than that on offer in neighbouring Benaulim, though you're nearly always guaranteed vacancies.

Beleza By the Beach Thondo Waddo ⓣ0832/278 1300 ⓣ9765/023024, ⓦwww.belezagoa.com. Colva's smartest hotel: a campus of ten stylish, spacious villas set in the dunes on the north side of the village. You can rent one large room (Rs5000) or the whole unit (Rs12,500). Comforts comparable to a five-star (big pool, exclusive beach access, wi-fi, terrace restaurant, spa, gym, DVD library) but much better value, and the location is as peaceful as Goa gets. ❽

Casa Mesquita 194 Vasco Rd, Ward 3 ⓣ0832/278 8173. Large rooms in a fading old colonial-style house, with rickety four-poster beds (if you're lucky) but no fans or attached shower-toilets. Mosaic-floored verandas add to the Old World atmosphere. A touch grubby and melancholic, but cheap and full of period atmosphere. ❷

La Ben On the beach road ⓣ0832/278 8040, ⓦwww.laben.net. Neat, clean and good value at this price, though better known for its rooftop restaurant. ❹

Longuinho's North of the beachfront ⓣ0832/278 8067, ⓦwww.longuinhos.net. The oldest resort in south Goa, with lawns opening straight onto the beach, though now showing signs of wear. Most rooms have a/c and sea views, and there's a shabby pool and in-house travel agent; the "standard" options are decidedly frayed, but the "deluxe" ones, in a more recently renovated wing, are better. ❻

Soulvacation ⓣ0832/278 8144 or ⓣ9810/684948, ⓦwww.soulvacation.in. Pretentiously chic resort, decked out entirely in white, with ludicrously high tariffs for its two different kinds of rooms (from $180–203/215–248 high/peak season). Patronized mostly by wealthy metropolitan Indians. ❾

Star Beach Resort Near the Night Market Ground ⓣ0832/278 8166 or 278 0092, ⓦwww.starbeachresortgoa.com. Spacious a/c rooms (four different types) – not all of them with balconies – grouped around a large pool and ayurvedic health centre. ❹–❺

Eating and drinking

When the season is in full swing, Colva's beachfront sprouts a row of large seafood **restaurants** on stilts, some of them extremely ritzy. The prices in these places are top-whack, but the portions are correspondingly big and standards high. There is also a string of good-value, popular **Indian places** lining the road to the beach.

Punjabi Rasoi Between the beachfront and church. Pure veg North Indian food, including cheap lunch-time thalis, served on a no-frills roadside terrace.

Sher-e-Punjab Between the beachfront and church. Offshoot of the popular Panjim Punjabi joint, serving an exhaustive menu of inexpensive, deliciously spicy Indian food. Butter chicken is their signature dish, but there are plenty of tasty vegetarian options too, and their naan bread is the best in the village.

Viva Goa South Colva. Innocuous-looking place on the backroad to Sernabatim, just south of the roundabout, serving three (and only three) fantastic Goan dishes: pomfret *caldin*, ox-tongue roast and chicken *cafreal*. The rest of the menu is best avoided.

North of Colva: Betalbatim to Velsao

North of Colva, the sand stretches for 12km to meet the Mormugao peninsula, overshadowed by the pressurized storage tanks of Zuari Agro's giant fertilizer plant. Seepages from this complex, dubbed by Goan green groups as "an industrial time bomb", caused ground-water pollution and the death of tonnes of fish here during the mid-1970s; its presence overlooking one of the world's most beautiful beaches is a continued source of controversy.

Another debate rages over the line of luxury hotels spreading inexorably across the dunes and paddy fields in the area. The profile of the big five-stars, however, seems to have inadvertently shielded the countryside immediately inland from other kinds of development, with the result that once out of sight of the holiday complexes, you find yourself in a pleasantly uncongested, traditional belt that will appeal greatly to anyone seeking peace and quiet within walking distance of the beach.

The other reason to venture up here is to hunt out the splendid old **palacios** belonging to the region's *Goenkars*, or landlords, built during the Portuguese era – a couple of which have been converted into heritage guesthouses.

Betalbatim

BETALBATIM lies only twenty minutes' walk up the beach from Colva but the contrast couldn't be more marked. Although the main market area, clustered around a crossroads inland, can be busy at certain times of day, the beach to the west sees fewer visitors than any other stretch in this area. Only on Sundays, when local courting couples and bus loads of picnickers descend on a patch of casuarina trees to the southwest of the village known as "**Lovers Beach**", can you expect much action. Signposted from the main road, the other noteworthy landmark is *Martin's Corner*, south Goa's most popular restaurant.

Practicalities

The homeliest and most atmospheric **place to stay** hereabouts is *Manuelina,* at 4, Thond Waddo (Ⓣ9422/455500; ❷–❸), with very large, very good-value attached rooms and an airy communal veranda looking onto atmospheric woodland. They also offer a pleasant self-catering apartment, equipped with a small kitchen and spare bedroom. Further up the scale, *Coconut Grove*, in Rabn Waddo (Ⓣ0832/288 0123, Ⓦwww.coconutgrove.in; ❽–❾) offers a campus of pretty pastel-coloured chalets set amid landscaped grounds right behind the beach, with a large curviform pool. Rooms start at around Rs5200. Also in Rabn Waddo, *Royal Orchid* (Ⓣ0832/288 4400, Ⓦwww.galaxyresortgoa.com; ❾) is a stylish beachside resort set in five acres of lawns, and recently the subject of a minimalist-designer makeover. You can choose between three kinds of room: the suites are way the nicest, with their own Jacuzzis, private plunge pools and sea views. A popular feature here is the sunken bar in the large overflow pool, and staffed kids' play area. Prices start from $240 (Rs11,000).

Patronized by droves of foreign tourists and Indian glitterati in season, *Martin's Corner*, in Bin Waddo (Ⓣ0832/288 0765, Ⓦwww.martinscornergoa.com), is *the* place to **eat in Betalbatim**. It's the brainchild of Mrs Carfina Pereira, who started out cooking fish curry and choriço-sausage baps for local taxi drivers, while their passengers were off eating inferior food for ten times the price in nearby hotels. The secret soon got out, however, and today she presides over one of the most acclaimed restaurants in the region, frequented most famously by cricketing hero, Sachin Tendulkar (who has a holiday house in the village). Seafood and chicken dishes are the main specialities. Goan highlights include fish *caldin* and chicken *cafreal*. If you're splashing out, go for the lobster in garlic-butter sauce. It's open for lunch and dinner; no reservations necessary. Karaoke Wednesdays and Saturdays; live cover bands nightly from 8pm. Most mains Rs175–200.

Majorda and Utorda

Some of Salcete's grandest Indo-Portuguese houses huddle under the palm canopy enveloping the main road through **MAJORDA** and its neighbour to the north, **UTORDA**. Among the many forgotten architectural gems worth seeking out in Majorda is the double-storeyed **Casa dos Piedade Costas**, next to the main road at the Utorda end of the village. Dating from the early seventeenth century when the more austere, so-called "châ" ("plane") school of architecture predominated, the house enfolds an inner courtyard, entered via a side doorway that enabled the Portuguese ladies to pass through and dismount from their palanquins without being seen. Attached to this is an early seventeenth-century chapel, facing a well and an ornamental cross. You can experience a particularly elegant example of this kind of architecture from the inside by spending a night at the *Vivenda Dos Palhaços* hotel (see below).

A broad, clean and relatively quiet stretch of white sand, the **beach** is reached via a tangle of winding lanes and makeshift wooden bridges spanning occasional stagnant creeks.

Accommodation

The bulk of the **accommodation** here tends to be in luxury resorts scattered across the sun-bleached paddy fields and dunes, where Russian charter tourists account for most of the business.

Alila Diwa Goa 48/10 Adao Waddo, Majorda ⓣ832/274 6800, ⓦwww.alilahotels.com. The latest addition to this area's panoply of mega five-stars and more architecturally inspiring than most, with Goan-style pitched tile roofs, high ceiling columns, verandas and quiet courtyards. Everything's state-of-the-art, down to the wood-lined loft rooms, 40" plasma screens and palm trees growing out of basins in the huge infinity pool. From $270. ⓽

Casa Ligorio near the *Kenilworth*, Utorda ⓣ0832/275 5405, ⓦwww.casaligorio.com. A welcoming, recently built guesthouse on three floors. Extremely neat and as well furnished as a star hotel, but at lower rates. The rooms all have a/c, mosquito screens and large balconies, and there's a relaxing garden to laze in. ⓺

Majorda Beach Resort Majorda ⓣ0832/275 4871, ⓦwww.majordabeachresort.com. One of India's most opulent resort hotels, boasting indoor and outdoor pools, tennis and squash courts, a sauna, health club, large sun terrace and billiards room. From $270. ⓽

Sand Dunes Gonsua Waddo, Majorda ⓣ0832/288 1413 or ⓣ9850/456767, ⓦwww.sanddunes.8k.com. A welcome budget option, comprising a row of fourteen heavy canvas tents, furnished with fans and proper beds, right behind the beach in 3000 square metres of lawns; there's also a restaurant and small dancefloor on site. Good value for this area. ⓷

Vivenda Dos Palhaços Costa Waddo, Majorda ⓣ9881/720221, ⓦwww.vivendagoa.com. Blending Indo-Portuguese elegance and boutique chic with touches of the British Raj, this charming heritage guesthouse in a quiet cul-de-sac occupies a converted, 100-year-old *palacio*. It's beautifully furnished, and run with considerable joie de vivre by brother and sister team, Simon and Charlotte Hayward, descendants of the family responsible for that quintessential Indian truck driver's tipple, Haywards 2000. Pantagruelian dinners are served on a rustic wooden dining table, and there's a very pretty, stepped pool to the rear if you can't manage the 20min walk to the beach. Rooms from $140–215. ⓼–⓽

Eating

For topnotch seafood straight off the boats, and served on an incomparably lovely sandy terrace next to the beach, head for *Zeebop By The Sea* on Utorda beachfront, beyond the *Kenilworth* (ⓦwww.zeebopbythesea.com). The cooking is simple, Goan-style "grilled with butter-garlic sauce", but prices are sky high – reflecting the restaurant's proximity to the *Kenilworth* and *Hyatt* five-stars, and the number of Bollywood stars and Russians with bulging wallets who come here. A more sophisticated, and even pricier, option is *Fusion* (ⓣ0832/288 1694 or ⓣ9890/064833), nearby on the lane leading to the *Majorda Beach Resort*. Grilled seafood and steaks are the thing here, turned out to perfection by Brazilian chef-patron, Neel Souza. House specialities include a fragrant crab gratin and *salpicão* salad for starters, with beef medallions or prawns in white wine sauce for mains, and creamy chocolate sorbet cake to round off. Allow Rs1500–2000 per head for three courses. No credit cards.

Arossim, Cansaulim and Velsao

At the far north end of Colva beach, **AROSSIM**, **CANSAULIM** and **VELSAO** feel a little more in the thick of things than villages further south – due in no small part to the smoking hulk of the Zuari Agro plant on a nearby hilltop, and proximity of the airport, only a twenty-minute drive away. Trains rumble through regularly on the Vasco branch line, too, but impinge very little on the high-walled exclusivity of places like the *Park Hyatt*, the most luxurious of several swanky resort complexes sited here. Unless you're staying in one of these, you're unlikely to venture to this extremity of the beach, although might consider doing so if you're passionate about old Goan houses and furniture.

In a 200-year-old *palacio* in Arossim (next door to *Casa Andrade*, see below), **The Treasure** is a smart showroom specializing in expensive Indo-Portuguese furniture and cut-glass chandeliers – most of it reproduction, and far too heavy to take home on the plane, but good for a browse.

A short drive further north, languishing in the palm groves midway between **Cansaulim** and **Velsao**, stands precisely the kind of mansion where such furniture would not look out of place. The **Casa dos Roldão de Souza** (aka "Maison Rodesa") is reached by turning left (west) under a low railway bridge (look for the "Horizon Beach Resort" sign, and then the first right shortly after). Built at the beginning of the twentieth century, the house's handsome yellow, white and blue facade features unique window surrounds which, despite their misleadingly jazzy star-shaped arches, are thought to take their cue from sixteenth-century Manueline architecture.

Another recommended sidetrip in this area takes you up a steeply curving lane from Velsao to the **Chapel of the Three Kings** (Reis Magos), signposted off the main airport road, from where the view south over the treetops extends over the entire length of Colva beach – a mesmerizing spectacle at sunset.

Practicalities

For a rare opportunity to stay in a proper ancestral Indo-Portuguese house without denting your wallet, head to *Casa Andrade*, House No 194, Arossim (Ⓣ0832/275 4147, Ⓦwww.casaandradegoa.com; ❸–❺). Recent renovation work has left very few original features intact in the south wing, where the six large, smartly furnished guest rooms are all attached, ceramic-tiled and fully air-conditioned. But if you value atmosphere over comfort, ask for a cheaper, scruffier room in the more basic, as yet untouched north wing. If you'd rather stay on the beach, *Horizon Beach Resort* in Velsao (Ⓣ0832/275 4923, Ⓦwww.horizonbeachresortgoa.com; ❻) is one of the few purpose-built resort complexes hereabouts to have made any concessions to local architecture, featuring traditional tiled roofs and typically 1950s Goan motifs. The pleasant rooms have a fresh yellow and white colour scheme and are ranged around a nice pool, set amid attractive gardens. Arrosim beach, meanwhile, boasts one of Goa's flagship luxury resorts, the *Park Hyatt Goa* (Ⓣ0832/272 1234, Ⓦwww.goa.park.hyatt.com; ❾). Its 251 rooms and thirteen suites are designed in elegant Indo-Portuguese *pousada* style, with pitched tiled roofs, wooden beams and lathe-turned pillars. Some of the rooms have their own "secret gardens" where you can enjoy a private shower outside, and the pool is the largest in India. A state-of-the-art spa complex, Thai massage parlour and superb watersports facilities are also on offer. From $240–2700 (Rs11,000–125,000) per night.

South of Colva: Benaulim

The predominantly Catholic fishing village of **BENAULIM** lies in the dead centre of Colva beach, scattered around the coconut groves and paddy fields, 7km west of Margao. Two decades ago, the settlement had barely made it onto the backpackers' map. Nowadays, though, affluent holidaymakers from metropolitan India come here in droves, staying in the huge resort and time-share complexes

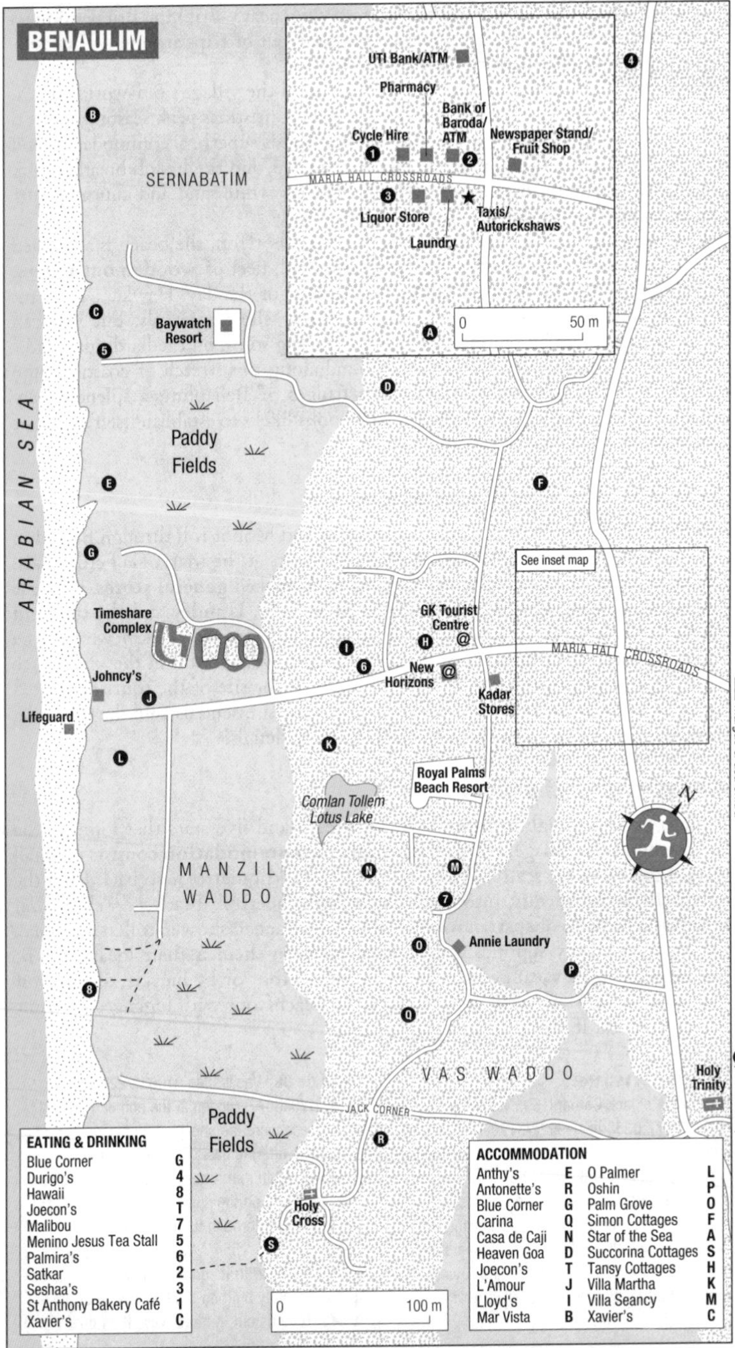
BENAULIM
Colva, Majorda, Betalbatim, Velsao & Airport
UTI Bank/ATM
Pharmacy
Bank of Baroda/ ATM
Cycle Hire
Newspaper Stand/ Fruit Shop
MARIA HALL CROSSROADS
Liquor Store
Taxis/ Autorickshaws
Laundry
0 50 m
SERNABATIM
Baywatch Resort
ARABIAN SEA
Paddy Fields
See inset map
Timeshare Complex
GK Tourist Centre
New Horizons
MARIA HALL CROSSROADS
Kadar Stores
Margao & Goa Chitra
Johncy's
Lifeguard
Royal Palms Beach Resort
Comlan Tollem Lotus Lake
MANZIL WADDO
Annie Laundry
VAS WADDO
Holy Trinity
T, Cavelossim, Mobor & Palolem
JACK CORNER
Paddy Fields
Holy Cross
0 100 m
EATING & DRINKING
Blue Corner G
Durigo's 4
Hawaii 8
Joecon's T
Malibou 7
Menino Jesus Tea Stall 5
Palmira's 6
Satkar 2
Seshaa's 3
St Anthony Bakery Café 1
Xavier's C
ACCOMMODATION
Anthy's E
Antonette's R
Blue Corner G
Carina Q
Casa de Caji N
Heaven Goa D
Joecon's T
L'Amour J
Lloyd's I
Mar Vista B
O Palmer L
Oshin P
Palm Grove O
Simon Cottages F
Star of the Sea A
Succorina Cottages S
Tansy Cottages H
Villa Martha K
Villa Seancy M
Xavier's C

mushrooming on the outskirts, while long-staying, heavy-drinking Brit pensioners and 30-something European couples taking time out of trips around the subcontinent make up the bulk of the foreign contingent.

Benaulim's rising popularity has certainly dented the village's old-world charm, but time your visit well (avoiding Diwali and the Christmas peak season), and it is still hard to beat as a place to unwind. The seafood is superb, accommodation and motorbikes cheaper than anywhere else in the state, and the **beach** breathtaking, particularly around sunset time, when its brilliant white sand and churning surf reflect the changing colours to magical effect.

Shelving away almost to Cabo da Rama on the horizon, the beach is also lined with Goa's largest, and most colourfully decorated, fleet of **wooden outriggers**, and these provide welcome shade during the heat of the day. Hawkers, itinerant masseurs and fruit-wallahs appear at annoyingly short intervals, but you can usually escape them by renting a bike and pedalling south on the hard tidal sand.

Conventional sights are thin on the ground along this stretch of coast, though one exception stands out on the eastern fringes of Benaulim: a splendid new ethnographic museum, **Goa Chitra**, which looks likely to establish itself as one of Goa's foremost cultural attractions.

Arrival and information

Buses from Margao, Colva, Varca, Cavelossim and Mobor roll through Benaulim every fifteen to thirty minutes, dropping passengers at the Maria Hall crossroads. Ranged around this busy junction are two well-stocked **general stores**, a couple of locals' café-bars, a **bank (with ATM)**, **pharmacy**, **laundry** and the **taxi and auto-rickshaw rank**, from where you can pick up transport 2km west to the beach, or back into Margao. For details of **motorcycle rental** in the village, see p.189. A second crossroads, 500m further west, is the site of the tourist-oriented Kadar Stores **mini-market**, the best source of tourist essentials, and the two main **internet** places. See "Listings" on p.189 for more details.

Accommodation

Aside from the unsightly time-share complexes and five-stars that loom in the fields around the village, most of Benaulim's **accommodation** consists of small budget guesthouses, scattered around the lanes a kilometre or so back from the beach. Most fall firmly into the "cheap and cheerful" bracket – clean, but featureless annexes of spartan rooms with fans, attached shower-toilets and small balconies; the only significant difference between them is their location. The best way to find a vacancy is to hunt around on foot or by bicycle, although if you wait at the Maria Hall crossroads or the beachfront with luggage, someone is bound to ask if you need a room.

Inexpensive

Antonette's Jack Corner, 1695 Vas Waddo ⓣ0832/277 0358 or ⓣ9922/312984. Next to a crossroads where all the local fishermen and lads hang out, but in an otherwise peaceful corner of the village, with simple but clean rooms, the best of them to the rear of the building looking over the fields. Well-stocked fridges with beers and bottled water on the upstairs landing. Owner Geraldo Rodrigues is exceptionally friendly and helpful. ❶

Casa de Caji Vas Waddo ⓣ0832/227 0028 or ⓣ9822/986547. Hidden at the end of a quiet side lane, these were the cheapest rooms we found in Benaulim, offering basic comforts (shared shower toilets and thin mattresses), but in a clean, pleasant setting. Those on the upper storey, south side, have tranquil views through the trees. ❶

Lloyd's 1554/A Vas Waddo ⓣ0832/277 1492. With its garish yellow exterior, this place, recently built on the beach side of the village, stands out in more ways than one. The

Green Benaulim

The massive blocks of holiday accommodation sprouting in Benaulim's outlying paddy fields will have a dramatic impact if, and when, they ever fill up. But for the time being the kind of tourism predominating here – with visitors staying mostly in local, family-run guesthouses, and eating in Goan-owned shacks rather than oversized resorts – has to be some of the most sustainable and mutually beneficial in the state. Moreover, the village has stolen a march on others in the region when it comes to establishing its **green credentials**.

Set up in 2000, the **Benaulim Environmental Trust** (BET) was created to help protect the local environment, preserve its natural resources and promote awareness of green issues in the wider community. As part of its attempt to promote eco-tourism among visitors, the association has produced an excellent little booklet entitled *The Benaulim Green Book*, which, apart from giving a rundown of local flora, fauna and walking and cycling trails, highlights numerous ways visitors can minimize the impact of their stay. One of these is to ensure your refuse gets recycled.

In spite of inadequate waste-disposal provision by the local municipality, a wide range of materials are processed by an unofficial system of waste pickers, who collect paper, cardboard, plastics, glass bottles and metal for sorting at three **recycling stations** on the eastern outskirts of Benaulim, near the Goa Chitra museum (see opposite) – the *Benaulim Green Book* (available at shops around the village; Rs25) has a map showing you precisely where they are. Alternatively, check at your guesthouse to find out whether it arranges for waste to be collected by the recyclers. For more info, contact BET's Tony Correia-Afonso on ⓣ0832/272 2062.

rooms are really big for the price, with high ceilings, quality beds and fans, plus neat mozzie screens over the windows. And they offer variously sized appartments upstairs (❺) for longer stays. ❸

O Palmar Beach Rd ⓣ0832/277 0631, ⓔopalmar@sanchar.net. A row of weathered, sea-facing chalets with their own verandas opening onto a patch of dunes. They're a bit gloomy and plagued by cafe noise in the evenings, but very close to the beach and good value. ❸

Oshin Mazil Waddo ⓣ0832/277 0069, ⓔinaciooshin@rediffmail.com. Large complex set well back from the road. Opening on to leafy terraces, its rooms are spacious and clean, with attached bathrooms and balconies; those on the top floor afford views over the tree tops. A notch above most places in this area, and good value, but quite a walk from the beach. ❸–❹

Simon Cottages Sernabatim ⓣ0832/277 0581. Perennially among the best budget deals in Benaulim, in a quiet spot at the unspoilt north side of the village and with huge rooms on three storeys, all with shower-toilets and verandas, opening onto a sandy courtyard. ❷

Succorina Cottages 1711/A Vas Waddo ⓣ0832/277 0365. Small but immaculate rooms in a jazzily decorated, pinkhouse, 1km south of the crossroads in the fishing village, offering glimpses of the sea across the fields from large first-floor sit-outs. A perfect place to get away from the tourist scene, and a 5min walk from the quietest stretch of beach. Telephone bookings accepted by hosts Sebby and Succorina. ❷

Villa Martha near the 'Lotus Lake', off Beach Rd ⓣ0832/227 1429 or ⓣ9850/962115. A couple of very pleasant first-floor rooms and furnished appartments overlooking the lake. Family run, only a 10min walk from the beach and you get the use of gorgeous little sitting areas under the palms. ❸–❹

Mid-range and expensive

Anthy's Sernabatim ⓣ0832/277 1680, ⓔanthysguesthouse@rediffmail.com. Nicely furnished rooms right on the sea, with tiny bathrooms and breezy verandas – though you pay through the nose for the location. ❺

Blue Corner Sernabatim. Popular hut camp on the beach, run by an enthusiastic young crew themselves led by hospitable owner, Raj. Large palm-leaf structures with fans, mosquito nets, attached shower-toilets and plywood sitouts. Quiet and secure, and the bar-restaurant is one of the most happening places on the beach in the evenings. ❹

Carina Tamdi-Mati, Vas Waddo ⓣ0832/277 0413, ⓦwww.carinabeachresort.com. Large, somewhat lackadaisical mid-scale hotel in a tranquil location on the south side of Benaulim, with a pool, garden and bar-restaurant. Some rooms have a/c. 5

Heaven Goa 1 Sernabatim, ⓣ0832/275 8442 or ⓣ9890/698202, ⓦwww.heavengoa.in. Run by a welcoming Swiss-Keralan couple, Karin & Sunil, this new-ish block of a dozen or so rooms occupies a plum spot, ten minutes back from the sea beside a lily pond alive with frogs, egrets and water buffalo. The rooms are spacious and well set up (with wood shelves, mosquito nets, shiny tiled floors and balconies overlooking the water). Expert ayurvedic massages are offered; and they bake fresh pizzas in a wood oven, too. Excellent value for money in this bracket. 4

Joecon's 1795 Cal Waddo ⓣ0832/277 0077, ⓦwww.joeconsbeachresort.com. New, Goan-owned resort complex near the *Taj Exotica*, built on a seemingly grand scale, but holding only 35 rooms facing lawns and a big curvy pool. Luxurious for the price and close to the beach. Generous discounts for longer stays. 9

L'Amour Beach Rd ⓣ0832/277 0404, ⓦwww.lamourbeachresort.com. Benaulim's oldest hotel comprises a comfortable thirty-room cottage complex; its chalets (some a/c) are spacious and cool, with ceramic tiled floors and little verandas opening onto a central garden. Reasonable rates, but avoid the rooms on the first floor of the main block, which get horribly hot. 3–5

Mar Vista Sernabatim ⓣ0832/278 8612, or ⓣ9422/875685. Row of pretty, primrose-coloured chalet rooms fronted by a long, Goan-style pillared veranda. It's right on the dunes looking straight out to sea – an idyllic spot, well away from the neighbouring charter hotels, and reasonably priced given the location. 4–5

Palm Grove Tamdi-Mati, 149 Vas Waddo ⓣ0832/277 0059, ⓦwww.palmgrovegoa.com. Secluded hotel surrounded by beautiful gardens, offering three classes of mostly a/c rooms, the newest block very luxurious indeed. A bike ride back from the beachfront, but very pleasant, and the management is helpful. 5–6

Star of the Sea Vas Waddo ⓣ0832/277 0134 or ⓣ9823/238108. Large, smart and very comfortably furnished charter-style rooms in a three-storey block, boasting comfy beds, quiet a/c units and balconies overlooking a pool to the rear. Quite a plod from the beach, but good value. 5

Tansy Cottages Beach Rd ⓣ0832/277 0574, ⓔtansycottages@yahoo.in. Not a great location and the shocking green paintwork is hard to live with, but the rooms here are some of the nicest lower-mid-range options in Benaulim: they're a generous size, with tiled floors and new attached bathrooms. 4

Villa Seancy Vas Waddo ⓣ0832/227 0496 or ⓣ9822/108453. This is a sound choice if you want to extend your stay. Hostess Percy Rodrigues offers half a dozen modern apartments, equipped with kitchenettes, large bedrooms and balconies, close to the centre of the village – the nicest of them on the upper floors. Bargain rates, too. 4

Xavier's Sernabatim ⓣ0832/277 1489, ⓔjovek@sanchar.net. Well-maintained, large rooms ranged around a lovely garden, virtually on the beach but within walking distance of the village centre. All rooms have private terraces and low-slung cane chairs to lounge on, and the local owners, who have been here for decades, are genuinely hospitable. A peaceful, well-managed and perfectly situated option. 5

The Village

According to Hindu mythology, Goa was created when the sage Shri Parasurama, Vishnu's sixth incarnation, fired an arrow into the sea from the top of the Western Ghats and ordered the waters to recede. The spot where the shaft fell to earth was known in Sanskrit as *Ba-na-li* ("the arrow has come"), later corrupted by the Portuguese to 'Benaulim'. Local Hindus assert the exact site of its landfall was the sweet-water lake at the centre of the village, the **Comlan Tollem**, formerly famed for its lilies and lotus blooms. The remnants of the tank survive, replenished after each monsoon, and are still an important source of water for the second rice crop of the year, *vaingonn*. It's still a bucolic site, and great place for bird- and buffalo-spotting, in spite of the resorts creeping along its banks: to get there, follow the track from the main beach road towards *Villa Martha* guesthouse (see map, p.183).

It was to catalogue the kind of farming methods and implements formerly used to harvest and process rice at spots such as the Comlan Tollem that the **Goa Chitra** museum (Tues–Sun 9.15am–6pm, last tour 5.15pm; ⓣ0832/657 0877, ⓦwww.goachitra.com; Rs300) was created a few years back. Set against a backdrop of a working organic farm, the exhibition comprises a vast array of antique Goan agricultural tools and artefacts, ranging from giant cooking pots and ecclesiastical robes to tubas and sugar-cane presses. The idea is to promote appreciation of the region's traditional agrarian lifestyle – but this is no dull inventory. Each of the 4,000 objects on display tells its own compelling story, showing how Goans from various backgrounds used to grow their food, care for their livestock, prepare meals, medicines, and religious rituals – a world of traditional knowledge and skills fast disappearing today.

To get to Goa Chitra by bike or motorcycle, head east from Maria Hall crossroads towards Margao, and take the first turning on your left at a fork after 1.5km. When you reach the T-junction ahead, turn sharply right; the museum lies another 500m on your right.

Dhirio

The spectacle of large, sleek, well-fed water buffalo bulls being led on strenuous jogs along Benaulim beach (see p.158 and lifes a beach colour section for photo) is as definitive of the village as its painted fishing boats. But what few tourists realize is that the spectacle forms part of an illegal **bloodsport** of which this corner of Salcete is the heartland. **Dhirio** – bullfighting – has been practised here ever since the early Portuguese era. Unlike its Iberian cousin, however, in the Goan version the bulls fight each other rather than a strutting matador – a sight no less anathema to local Hindus and animal rights activists, who, in the mid-1990s, managed to bring about a total ban on the sport.

Since then, *dhirio* has been driven underground, or more precisely to remote clearings in the palm cover well away from main roads, resorts and disapproving Brahmin eyes. But it is still followed as passionately as ever by local Catholic men, some of whom put a great deal of time, effort and money into building up their prize bulls, which they name after boxers, screen icons and mythological heroes. Rich mixtures of fortifying grains and herbs are fed to the animals ahead of big bouts, for which they're trained long and hard on the beach. Dips in the surf and oil massages also form part of the build-up.

An animal's success in the ring is as much down to psychology as strength. Many fights are over even before they start, with a bull turning tail when it first comes face to face with opposition. The least sign of reluctance, however, is usually nipped in the bud by a stern yank of the testicles from the trainer, which is usually enough to drive the bulls into a closing charge.

Bouts between well-matched animals can last for hours. With horns locked, the beasts struggle to force each other backwards, blood oozing from gashes on their necks. Eventually, though, one of them throws in the towel and makes a desperate dash for the exit, sending the crowd scurrying for safety.

It's rare an animal is seriously hurt or killed. Even so, we don't recommend you seek out a *dhirio* meet – the sport is as dangerous to onlookers as it is an ordeal for the poor old bulls, and attending can technically lead you into trouble with the law (although in reality local police are bribed to stay away). Bullfights are, nonetheless, an essential part of the local Goan-Catholic scene, and an extraordinary one in a country where cow-slaughter remains, in some regions at least, a capital offence.

Eating and drinking

Benaulim's proximity to Margao market, along with the presence of a large Christian fishing community, means its **restaurants** serve some of the tastiest, most competitively priced seafood in Goa. The largest and busiest shacks flank the beachfront area, where *Johncy's* catches most of the passing custom. However, you'll find better food at lower prices further along the beach, at places which seem to change chefs annually; the only way to find out which ones offer the best value for money is to wander past and see who has the most customers. An enduring favourite is *Domnick's*, whose garrulous owner hosts bonfire parties one night per week (traditionally on Thursdays), featuring a live band; prices here are on the high side. *Pedro's* on the beachfront is marginally better value and also puts on gigs, mostly on Saturday nights.

Blue Corner Sernabatim. Great little beachside joint specializing in seafood and authentic Chinese. House favourites include "fish tomato eggdrop soup", scrumptious "dragon potatoes" and, best of all, their "super special steak". Also featured on their eclectic menu are tasty Italian dishes, sizzlers and, for homesick veggies, a pretty good cauliflower cheese. Most mains Rs150–250.

Durigo's Sernabatim, 2km north of Maria Hall crossroads on the outskirts of Colva. This is the locals' favourite place to eat, serving traditional Goan seafood of a kind you rarely find in the shacks: try their tasty mussels, lemonfish (*modso*) or barramundi (*chonok*), marinated in spicy, sour *rechead* sauce and pan-fried in millet. Some may find the atmosphere a bit rough and ready (though the service is unfailingly polite), in which case follow the example of the village's middle classes and order a takeout.

Hawaii South end of beach. Nadia and Vinod from Himachal Pradesh have run this welcoming little shack for a nearly a decade, and can claim one of the most loyal clienteles in the village, most of whom come for the Italian dishes, prepared with home-made pasta, fresh herbs, olive oil and proper cheese. The prawn lasagna and moussaka also get the thumbs up, and they do a zingy, fresh-mint *mojito*. During the day, extra large backgammon sets and a dedicated kids' play area are additional attractions. Mains Rs120–160.

Joecon's 1795 Cal Waddo ☎0832/277 0077, near *Taj Exotica*. *Joecon's* started life as the most popular shack on Colva beach but has since graduated to swanky new premises on the southern fringes of Benaulim. It's the ritziest restaurant in the village, but the food is old-school: snapper, mullet, sea bass, kingfish and pomfret pan-fried or baked in a proper wood-fired oven. Prices are as high as you'd expect for somewhere right outside a Russian-dominated resort hotel, but the owner has his own trawler so freshness is guaranteed. Live music most evenings.

Malibou Vas Waddo, near *Palm Grove*. Cosy little corner café-restaurant that's also a popular late-night drinking spot, hosting regular cabarets (from crooners to Rajasthani troubadours). Attentive service, fresh seafood, and there's a tandoor to bake pomfret and kebabs. Mains from Rs175–225.

Menino Jesus Tea Stall Sernabatim. If you've ever wondered what beach shacks were like thirty years ago, check this place out. It's where the local rickshaw drivers refuel on spicy fish-curry-rice plates, piping hot slices of millet-fried mackerel and *bhaji pao* for only Rs50. Rough and ready, but the food's delicious, and the sea view perfect.

Palmira's Beach Rd ☎0832/277 1309. Benaulim's best breakfasts: wonderfully creamy and fresh set curd, copious fruit salads with coconut, real espresso coffee, warm local bread (*bajri*) and the morning paper. For a light lunch, try their delicious prawn toast or tomato or ginger-carrot soups.

Satkar Maria Hall crossroads. No-frills locals' *udipi* canteen that's the only place in the village where you can order regular Indian snacks – samosas, masala dosas, hot pakoras and spicy chickpea stew (*channa*) – at regular Indian prices.

Seshaa's/St Anthony Bakery Café Maria Hall crossroads. A local institution, *Seshaa's* is a gloomy and rather cramped lads' café that's great for pukka Goan *channa bhaji* and, best of all, deliciously flaky veg or beef patties. On the opposite side of the road, *St Anthony Bakery Café* is equally popular (especially in the mornings) serving the same local grub, but is less male-dominated – and its patties come straight out of the ovens.

Xavier's Sernabatim. Host Jovek's mum, Maria, does most of the masala preparation and cooking for this breezy beachside restaurant, so the Goan dishes – prawn vindaloo, fish *caldin* and a knock-out *chouriço* chilli-fry are top notch. Less spicy alternatives include a particularly tasty lemon rice. Facing one of the most tranquil stretches of the beach, the terrace is most atmospheric at night, with the waves crashing in only a few feet away.

Listings

Bicycles Bikes cost around Rs100/day to rent; there are outlets at Maria Hall crossroads and elsewhere around town. If you're intending to stay for a long time, it might be worth buying one. Several cycle shops in Margao sell standard Indian-style Hero models for Rs2500–3000; you can expect to resell it for half the original price.

Foreign exchange Bank of Baroda has a (temperamental) ATM on Maria Hall; the UTI one around the corner on the main road is a bit more dependable. For changing currency, try GK Tourist Centre, at the crossroads in the village centre, and New Horizons, diagonally opposite. It's often worth comparing rates at the two.

Internet access GK Tourist Centre and New Horizons (Rs40/hr).

Laundry Annie Laundry, opposite Palm Grove, offers an inexpensive same-day service.

Motorcycle rental Signs offering motorbikes for rent are dotted along the lane leading to the sea: rates are standard at Rs175–200 in season, rising to double or triple that over Christmas. Local boys will try to get you to pay them to fill your bike up in Margao, but invariably pocket half of the money in the process, so you're advised to do it yourself (Margao's main petrol pump is on the west side of the Praça Jorge Barreto – see map, p.183). The other scam is to charge you for a full tank that only has a couple of litres in.

Shopping Kadar Stores, at the crossroads in the middle of the village, is well stocked with tourist essentials.

Travel agents International and domestic flights can be booked, altered or reconfirmed at the highly efficient New Horizons (ⓣ0832/277 1218, ⓔdokl@goatelecom.com), opposite the GK Tourist Centre. They also have access to special train quotas on the Konkan Railway, although you have to book in person for these.

South of Benaulim

South of Benaulim, the main road, running parallel with Colva beach, passes through a string of small settlements dominated by large churches. Bumpy back lanes peel west at regular intervals, winding across rice fields where enormous blocks of serviced apartments and time-shares have started to rise incongruously on the outskirts of fishing hamlets, while rows of luxury resort hotels punctuate the beach. By the time you reach **Cavelossim**, gateway to the package enclave and trawler anchorage of **Mobor**, the palm cover has all but petered out, and the pale green profile of the Sahyadri Hills beckons to the southeast.

Cavelossim and Assolna

Unless you're booked into one of the big resorts or are following the more tranquil coast road south in preference to the Margao–Chaudi highway (NH-17), there's little reason to venture into the far southwest corner of Salcete *taluka*. Away from the beach, the scenery is flat and monotonous and, once you've reached **CAVELOSSIM**, 11km south of Colva, blighted by new building sites and ugly resorts. A short way beyond the village's picturesque church **square**, however, a narrow lane veers left (east) across an open expanse of paddy fields to the delightful Cavelossim–Assolna **ferry crossing** (every 20min, with last departures at 8.30pm from Cavelossim and 8.45pm from

Assolna; Rs2), near the mouth of the Sal River. Make the trip at low tide, and you'll probably see scores of men wading up to their necks in the water, collecting clams, mussels and oysters from the river silt.

Turn left when you disembark from the ferry, and a winding lane will lead you to the middle of **ASSOLNA** bazaar, lining the main Margao–Karnataka highway. The village holds a well-preserved collection of colonial-era mansions (though none of them are officially open to visitors).

The most congenial place to stay in this area is the *Hotel Dona Sa Maria*, in Tamborim Waddo (ⓣ0832/274 5290 or 274 5673, ⓦwww.donasamaria.com; ❸), on the outskirts of Cavelossim. Singposted off the main road, it's a laid-back little hotel with helpful staff, a good-sized pool, restaurant and friendly family atmosphere. Owner Serafin recently installed a fantastic recycling plant in the garden to process waste from the hotel – a model of its kind.

Mobor

The tract of rolling dunes backing the southern limits of Colva beach come to an abrupt end at **MOBOR**. Tapering into the Sal estuary, this remote spit of sand serves Goa's largest concentration of purpose-built luxury resorts, pitched as much at wealthy Indian clients as northern European and Russian tourists. Great controversy attended the development in its early days, but the environmentalists seem to have given up trying to stem the rising tide of concrete, which now includes air-conditioned shopping malls and fast-food outlets. Whatever the rights or wrongs of individual cases, few would deny that the sprawling campuses – complete with golf courses, enormous pools and, in one case, a monumentally kitsch mock sailing ship – do nothing to enhance the area's natural beauty.

Set against a backdrop of receding hills, the beach itself is largely screened from the resorts by the few surviving trees. A row of large shack restaurants and sunbeds lines up beneath them, with their owners laying on firework parties on alternate nights in season to attract punters, but otherwise life here is mellow given the potential number of tourist beds in the area.

Accommodation

Dona Sylvia In the middle of Mobor village, opposite the shopping mall ⓣ0832/287 1321, ⓦwww.donasylvia.com. A huge charter hotel with 176 rooms, mostly attractive two-storey cottages in traditional Goan style, grouped around a pool. Double rooms from $678 (Rs30,000) for a minimum stay of three nights. ❾

Gaffino's ⓣ0832/287 1441 or 287 1430, ⓦwww.gaffinos.com. The smallest of Mobor's hotels is a friendly family-run place: sixteen immaculate rooms (with river views), and a small restaurant. Great value considering the cost of other accommodation in the area. ❺

Haathi Mahal ⓣ0832/287 1101, ⓦwww.haathimahal.com. The newest of Mobor's resorts is geared squarely for domestic tourists, although it does boast an "authentic Cornish pub". Tariffs start around $192 (Rs8500) per double. ❾

Holiday Inn Resort Near the *Leela* hotel ⓣ0832/287 1303, ⓦwww.holidayinngoa.com. Formulaic four-star with 170 luxury rooms and suites, two restaurants, a coffee shop, tennis court, gym and pool. Very near the beach. Rooms from $270–430 (Rs12,000–19,000) per night. ❾

The Leela ⓣ0832/287 1234, ⓦwww.leelagoa.com. This massive resort was, until the *Hyatt* and *Taj Exotica* appeared further north, the most luxurious hotel in the state. Set amid 45 acres of gardens, it's often block-booked up by Russian mafiosi, with facilities including seven multi-cuisine restaurants, a huge pool, casino and unrivalled sports facilities. Golf carts take you to your chalet. Worth calling in just to see the antique Chola bronzes, textiles and wood sculpture in the lobby. From $270–1470 (Rs12,000–65,000). ❾

Sao Domingo's ⓣ0832/287 1629 or ⓣ9822/153527, ⓦwww.saodomingosgoa.com. Spruce, family-run place near the river, made of marble with 29 large, light, cool and pleasantly furnished rooms opening onto separate balconies. Good value. ❺

Canacona

Ceded to the Portuguese by the Rei of Sundem in the Treaty of 1791, Goa's far south – **Canacona** *taluka* (from the Kannad for "forest full of bison") – was among the last parts of the territory to be absorbed into the Portuguese colony, and has retained a distinctly Hindu feel: multicoloured *tulsi* plant pots stand outside its red-tiled houses, and all of the villages have small colonnaded temples. The area also boasts some outstanding scenery. Set against a backdrop of the jungle-covered **Sahyadri Hills** (part of the Western Ghat range), a string of pearl-white coves and sweeping **beaches** indents its coastline, enfolded by laterite headlands and colossal piles of black boulders.

The finest of them is **Palolem**, whose beautiful curved bay supports a tourist scene that's more full-on than anywhere else in south Goa. Opinion tends to be divided over whether the village has been irrevocably spoilt by the volume of visitors it receives these days, but the beach alone is worth the trip down here, especially at sunset time. A more peaceful alternative lies a twenty-minute drive north at **Agonda**, a village whose economy remains firmly rooted in its traditional fishing and *toddi*-tapping economy, despite the recent arrival of the **Konkan Railway**, which since 1997 has connected this formerly remote corner of Goa with Mumbai and South India by fast express trains. The region's other main transport artery is the NH-17, which cuts through the middle of the district headquarters, **Chaudi**. Bus services between here and Margao are frequent, but off the highway you'll need a motorcycle to get around – it's a good idea to rent one further north and drive it down here as few are available on the spot.

Travelling south in a taxi or with your own transport, the best route to follow is not the NH-17 – a perilous undertaking even on quiet days – but the backroad winding along the coast via Assolna and the scruffy fishing settlement of **Betul**, from where a bumpy road climbs a series of laterite headlands. The Portuguese carved out a border post on the tip of the most prominent of these, **Cabo da Rama**, the ruined ramparts of which provide fine views back up the coast.

Cabo da Rama

Cabo da Rama ("Cape Rama"), the long bony finger of land that juts into the sea at the south end of Colva Bay, takes its name from the hero of the Hindu epic, the *Ramayana*, who, along with his wife Sita, holed up here during his exile from Ayodhya – one of several such sacred sites in central and southern India. This one, however, is more grandiose than most, commanding spectacular views north over the length of Colva beach, and down the sand-splashed coast of Canacona. The easily defensible promontory was crowned by a **fort** centuries before the Portuguese wrested it from the local Hindu rulers in 1763. They erected their own citadel soon after, but this now lies in ruins, lending to the headland a forlorn, world's end feel.

A circular, green and red Archeological Survey signpost marks the turning for Cabo da Rama off the coast road, 5km east. If you're travelling by **bus** from Margao (4–5 daily; 1hr 30min), you'll be dropped outside the fort's gatehouse. Once inside, either turn right and scale the battlements, where a crumbling turret still houses a couple of rusty old Portuguese cannons, or else head straight on past the chapel, swathed in colourful bougainvillea bushes, towards the west end of the peninsula. Until 1955, the bastion housed a prison; now its only habitable building is a lonely government observation bungalow, occupied from time to time by scientists from Dona Paula's Institute of Oceanography.

From the bungalow a steep path passes through a gap in the boundary walls to a narrow ridge, eventually emerging from the wooded bluff beyond at the windswept tip of the cape. The sea views from this serene spot are superb, taking in a remote bay to the north where, a few years back, a team of Italian developers illegally erected a boutique hotel on the clifftops. They made the mistake, however, of denying access to fishermen from the village. After an indignant local priest organized a protest march to draw attention to the development, Congress Party leader, Sonia Gandhi, took up the cause: a demolition order was issued soon after. Nothing but the foundations of the hotel now remain and the sands are still blissfully empty on weekdays – though be warned that large, noisy groups of picnickers descend at weekends.

The one and only **place to stay and eat** at Cabo de Rama is *Anshoy's* bar (Ⓣ0832/267 6259; ❷), 3km before the fort on the roadside. Facilities are basic, but John and his wife are very welcoming hosts, serving tasty *chouriço* sausage baps and fresh thalis made with local *rawa*-fried mackerel for next to nothing.

Agonda

Local opposition to tourism in Goa has never been so vehement as it was in **AGONDA** back in the mid-1980s, when a consortium led by Rajiv Gandhi (son of the then prime minister, Indira) tried to build a resort hotel and golf course in the palm groves behind the south end of the village beach. Fearing the development would jeopardize their traditional livelihoods, local *toddi* tappers threatened violent protest, daubing anti-tourist slogans on rocks in the bay. As a consequence, the big hotel was never completed (you can still see its decaying remnants in the woods) but it's taken more than 25 years for the villagers to put the episode behind them and fully embrace the global economy.

The resulting level of under-development comes as a pleasant surprise after the chaos reigning elsewhere in Goa. Accommodation here is in small-scale, mostly family-run guesthouses and hut camps, the restaurant scene is relatively unsophisticated, and the clientele easygoing and health-conscious. Granted, you don't get a dreamy brake of palm trees as a backdrop, but since the Boxing Day tsunami the beach seems to have lost its menacing undertow and the sand is as clean as any in the state. Moreover, the surrounding hills and forest are exquisite.

The smart money says Agonda could all too soon go the way of its neighbours to the south (several large hut-camp owners have recently purchased leases on land here in anticipation of a mass exodus from Palolem) but for the time being the village deserves to be high on the hit list of anyone seeking somewhere quiet and wholesome, with enough amenities for a relaxing holiday, but still plenty of local atmosphere.

Arrival and information

Four **buses** run daily between Agonda and Chaudi (departing Chaudi 8.30am, 9.00am, 3.30pm & 4.30pm), and two run all the way to and from Margao (departing Agonda 6.15am & 2.30pm). Most services stop at the junction on the main Palolem road, 1km east (you can usually find a rickshaw for the trip into the village), but a couple go as far as the church in the centre of Agonda, which stands near the middle of the beach. From there, a surfaced lane extends left (south), leading to most of the pukka-built hotels and guesthouses. In the other direction, a second tarmac lane heads north, soon degenerating into a dirt track which runs behind an unbroken row of hut camps to a small footbridge over the river, at the far end of the beach.

True Value Travel Agency, a couple of hundred metres north of the church, and Shri Kaushik (opposite the bakery, also just north of the church) provide **cash withdrawals** on credit and debit cards, as well as train, bus and flight **ticketing**, and broadband **internet** access. The nearest **ATMs** are in Chaudi, 10km south.

Accommodation

Tariffs are on a par with those of Palolem and Patnem, though dropping dramatically if the season is slack. Few places accept advance bookings so you'll probably have to plod around to find somewhere that suits, or else phone ahead from the comfort of a café table (though note that mobile coverage tends to be patchy hereabouts).

Abba's Glory Land Doval Kazan ⓣ0832/264 7822. This place offers well-made bamboo and plywood beach huts on the roadside at the north end of the beach, but their four rooms, set back under the palms, are what get our vote. With high roofs and stone-tiled floors, they're spacious and cool, opening onto a narrow shared veranda. Restaurant noise could be a problem in high season. ❸

Bioveda Doval Kazan ⓣ9422/388982, ⓦwww.bioveda.in. Luxurious huts with attached bathrooms opening onto the beach. A thirty-second skip from the surf and roofed with paddy thatch, they're attractively set up, cool and comfortable, and equipped with quality beds, split-cane blinds and lots of other homely touches. The welcoming British-Keralan owners, Sunil and Fiona, also run an excellent little ayurvedic centre on site where you can enjoy detox programmes, authentic treatments and massages by qualified male and female staff. Advance booking possible via their website. ❺

Chattai Doval Kazan ⓣ9423/812287, ⓦwww.chattai.co.in. One of Agonda's more stylish options, comprising a dozen or so well-spaced huts that wouldn't look out of place in an Amazon rainforest. They're right on the beach behind a little bar area, and roomier than most, with pitched jute roofs, well-aired bathrooms, quality mattresses and mozzie nets. Advance booking possible through the website. ❺

Chris-Joana near the Church ⓣ0832/264 7306 or ⓣ9421/155814, ⓔbelu_miranda5@yahoo.in. Smart new house on the roadside just south of St Anne's Church. Its bargain-priced rooms are clean, light and airy, and have decent beds. Go for one on the rear side, overlooking the rooftops and creek to coconut plantations; the front ones get warm in the afternoons. ❸

Dersy's South end of the beach, on the roadside ⓣ0832/264 7503. Very clean and cosy rooms, with tiled floors and good-sized bathrooms. Those on the first floor (front side) have a common sea-facing veranda that catches the breezes; you can lie in bed and hear the waves crashing only 100m away. They also run a couple of rows of (rather overpriced) beach huts on the opposite side of the lane. ❷

Dunhill Resort South end of beach ⓣ9822 685138, ⓦwww.goyam.in. Prettily painted and furnished red-tiled bungalows, facing an earth-floored courtyard just across the road from the beach. The interiors are luxurious (especially the beds) – more like proper star hotel rooms that beach chalets – and the place is run with matchless efficiency by the *Goyam & Goyam* team of Palolem's *Dropadi* (see p.199) fame. ❼

Fatima South side of beach, next to *La Dolce Vita* ⓣ0832/264 7477 ⓣ9423/332888. Very good value budget guesthouse offering spacious, squeaky-clean attached rooms with shiny tiled floors, bucket of hot water and sea views from the upper floor, plus there's a friendly Great Dane the size of a horse. Best of the cheapies. ❸

H2O South of St Anne's Church ⓣ421/152150 or ⓣ9423/836994, ⓦwww.h2oagonda.com. Currently the hippest of the camps on the beach – and the most pricey, charging upwards of Rs5000 per night in season for a plywood chalet right on the sand. Painted black, the tiled huts are styled with shocking pink and turquoise-coloured drapes and quilts; each has a semi-open-air bathroom and veranda with low sofas and bolsters. There's also a similarly snazzy café-restaurant adjacent. ❽

Jardim A Mar Doval Kazan ⓣ9420/820470, ⓦwww.jardim-a-mar.com. Professionally run "palm-tree-garden resort", offering budget rooms and pricier beachside huts, nicely decorated with Rajasthani quilts and blockprint throws, grouped around a sandy plot only a stone's throw from the surf. Partly German-owned, it has a slicker feel than most of the competition. ❺

Mahnamahnas Vall Waddo ⓣ421/152158, ⓦwww.agondabeach.com. Great-value, double-storey plywood huts with proper tiled roofs, and big bathrooms on the ground floor, plus hammocks strung on large balconies boasting uninterrupted sea views. The camp is German-owned and accepts advance bookings online. ❹

Maria Paulo Just north of *Dersy's* towards the church ⓣ0832/264 7606, ⓦwww.mariapauloagonda.com. This modern pink building on the roadside – look for the "Welcome Aboard" life ring – is a bigger and slightly more anonymous guesthouse than the others in the village, which some might prefer. Six large, cool marble-floored rooms, all with quality beds and mozzie nets; the pricier ones have generous verandas. ❸–❹

Palm Beach Lifestyle Resort Behind *Dersy's* ⓣ0832/264 7783 or ⓣ9422 450380, ⓦwww.palmbeachgoa.com. Simple but very pleasant, terracotta-coloured chalets, ranged over terraces under a coconut plantation. They all have attractive wood floors, comfy mattresses and sea views from raised decks. Far better value than comparable places on the beach. ❹

Secret Garden Doval Kazan ⓣ0832/264730, ⓣ9421/152054. At the far north end of the beach next to *Chattai*, the *Secret Garden* is more ramshackle than most of the camps in Agonda, but has a special edge. The owners have lived here for four generations and have allowed a screen of vegetation to grow up between the plot and the beach, making it more secluded, quiet and private. There are only four simple huts (the top-most one with a view to die for from its terrace), plus a couple of cottage-style rooms. Especially recommended for families. ❸–❹

Eating and drinking

Agonda's **restaurants** are as much hangouts as places to eat. Most are furnished with relaxing cane chairs, pretty lanterns and lounge areas with bolsters, and are on or near the beach – the excellent *Greek Place* being the notable exception. Standards of cooking (and, alas, hygiene) vary wildy from year to year in many beachside places, mainly because the staff are predominantly untrained Nepalis and Assamese from poor mountain villages who work here for the season.

Arabian Nights Near *Jardim A Mar. Arabian Nights* hosts a popular daily BBQ each evening with fresh grilled seafood and tasty steaks (from Rs250), rounded off with a slice of their famous banoffee pie.

Cuba Set well away from the village houses, this beachside café runs a late bar that serves as Agonda's unofficial party place.

Dunhill's Goyam & Goyam South of the church. Same owners as *Dropadi* and *Goyam & Goyam* in Patnem (see p.199 & p.202), and the same great service, with wide selection of fabulous North Indian food and fresh fish. Most mains around Rs150.

Greek Place Opposite St Anne's Church. Proper Greek café on a secluded roadside terrace in the centre of Agonda, where you can order scrumptious *souvlaki* (Rs100–140) and proper *horiatiki* salads with real feta (Rs180) to a background of rembetiko music. Owners Kosmas and Maria make this a friendly, fun and very Hellenic little hangout.

Jardim A Mar Doval Kazan. A café-restaurant that ticks all the boxes: it's slap on the sand, well shaded (under palms and a Ladakhi parachute), with comfy cane chairs, hammocks and silk cushions scattered on lounge mats. And it's a great breakfast spot, churning out fresh fruit juices, proper coffee, grilled baguettes and, the house speciality, rice pudding, as well as a popular all-day menu.

Madhus North side of beach. For years, the best tandoori outfit on the beach: great for fresh local fish and Indian dishes alike. It's inexpensive and always busy, so get there early. Most mains only Rs100.

Khola Beach

Just around the headland to the north of Agonda lies one of Goa's most secluded and beautiful beaches, **Khola**. Until a Vasco-based outfit erected a tent camp at the north end of the cove a few years back, this was one of the state's best-kept secrets, but it now serves as a bolt hole for mostly Russian charter tourists based further north, who stay as part of mini-packages. The camp's owners aggressively discourage non-residents from crossing the coconut plantation behind the beach, but you're entitled to walk through if you wish.

Alternatively, book into the idyllic *Dwarka Eco Beach Resort* (Ⓣ9823 377025, Ⓦwww.dwarkagoa.com; ❽) at the opposite (southern) end of the cove. Set up by a photographer who discovered the site while recce-ing a fashion shoot, the resort consists of ten paddy-thatch cabins clustered under palm groves on the edge of a freshwater lagoon, which you cross by means of a rickety wooden footbridge. The huts themselves, mounted on laterite bases, are simply furnished in natural materials, with diaphanous muslin curtains and little balconies where you can sip cocktails reclined on bent-cane chairs. If you came to Goa in search of the proverbial palm-fringed idyll, this is probably the nearest you'll get. Tariffs start at around Rs4500 per double hut per night, inclusive of all meals.

Khola is most easily accessed via an unsurfaced track that peels south off the main Agonda–Cabo da Rama road at the village of Khola, 7km north of the turning for Agonda. Anyone staying at the *Dwarka* resort can arrange to be met by the owner on the roadside.

Palolem

Nowhere else in peninsular India conforms so closely to the archetypal image of a paradise beach as **PALOLEM**, 35km south of Margao. Lined with a swaying curtain of coconut palms, the bay forms a perfect curve of golden sand, arcing north from a giant pile of boulders to a spur of the Sahyadri Hills, which tapers into the sea draped in thick forest. Palolem, however, has become something of a paradise lost over the past decade. It's now Goa's most popular resort, deluged from late November by legions of long-staying tourists, and busloads of day-trippers from Karnataka and beyond. Visitor numbers become positively overwhelming in peak season, when literally thousands of people spill across a beach backed by an unbroken line of shacks and Thai-style hut camps.

Basically, Palolem in full swing is the kind of place you'll either love at first sight or want to get away from as quickly as possible. If you're in the latter category, try smaller, less frequented **Patnem** beach, a short walk south around the headland, where the shack scene is more subdued and the sands marginally emptier.

Arrival

Regular buses to Palolem from Margao stop at the end of the lane leading from the main street to the beachfront. Frequent **buses** run between Margao and Karwar (in Karnataka) via the nearby market town of Chaudi (every 30min; 2hr), 2km southeast across the rice fields. The last bus from Palolem to Chaudi/Margao leaves at around 4.30pm; check with the locals for the precise times, as these change seasonally. Chaudi is also the nearest **railhead** to Palolem; the station lies a short way north of the main bazaar. **Rickshaws** charge Rs75–100, taxis Rs150–200 for the ride to the beach.

▲ Palolem bay

Accommodation

The local municipality's strict enforcement of a rule banning new concrete construction in Palolem (it went so far as to bulldoze without warning the entire resort a few years back) has ensured that most of the village's accommodation consists of simple palm-leaf **huts** or "tree houses". Apart from the more snazzily setup places listed below, there's very little difference between the camps: check into the first that takes your fancy and reconnoitre the rest of the beach at leisure when you've found your feet.

Bhakti Kutir Far southern end of the beach, on the hill dividing Palolem from Colom ⓣ0832/264 3469 or 264 3472, ⓦwww.bhaktikutir.com. Environmentally friendly, Indian-village-style "back-to-nature cabañas" equipped with Western amenities (including compost toilets), set amid mature gardens 5min walk from the south end of Palolem beach, on the headland above the fishing village. They're beautifully situated, discreet and sensitively designed to blend with the landscape. The double-storey units, aimed at families, offer more space, and there's a quality ayurvedic healing, yoga and massage centre on site. ❼–❽

Ciaran's Camp Middle of the beach ⓣ0832/264 3477, ⓦwww.ciarans.com. Luxury coir and coconut-wood huts ranged around a neatly kept tropical garden, only 20m from the beach. Each has stone-tiled floors, mosquito nets, quiet fans, hammocks, plump cushions and good-sized bathrooms; the pricier ones boast roof-level sundecks, daybeds to laze on and sea views. A breezy spot slap on the beachfront, and better run than most. ❽

Cozy Nook North end of the beach, near the island ⓣ0832/264 3550, ⓦwww.cozynookgoa.com. One of the most attractive set-ups in the village, comprising 25 bamboo huts (sharing seven toilets, but with good mattresses, mosquito nets, safe lockers and fans) opening onto the lagoon on one side and the beach on the other – an unbeatable spot, which explains the higher than average tariffs. ❻

Dream Catcher North end of the beach behind *Cozy Nook* ⓣ0832/647 0344 or ⓣ9822/137446,

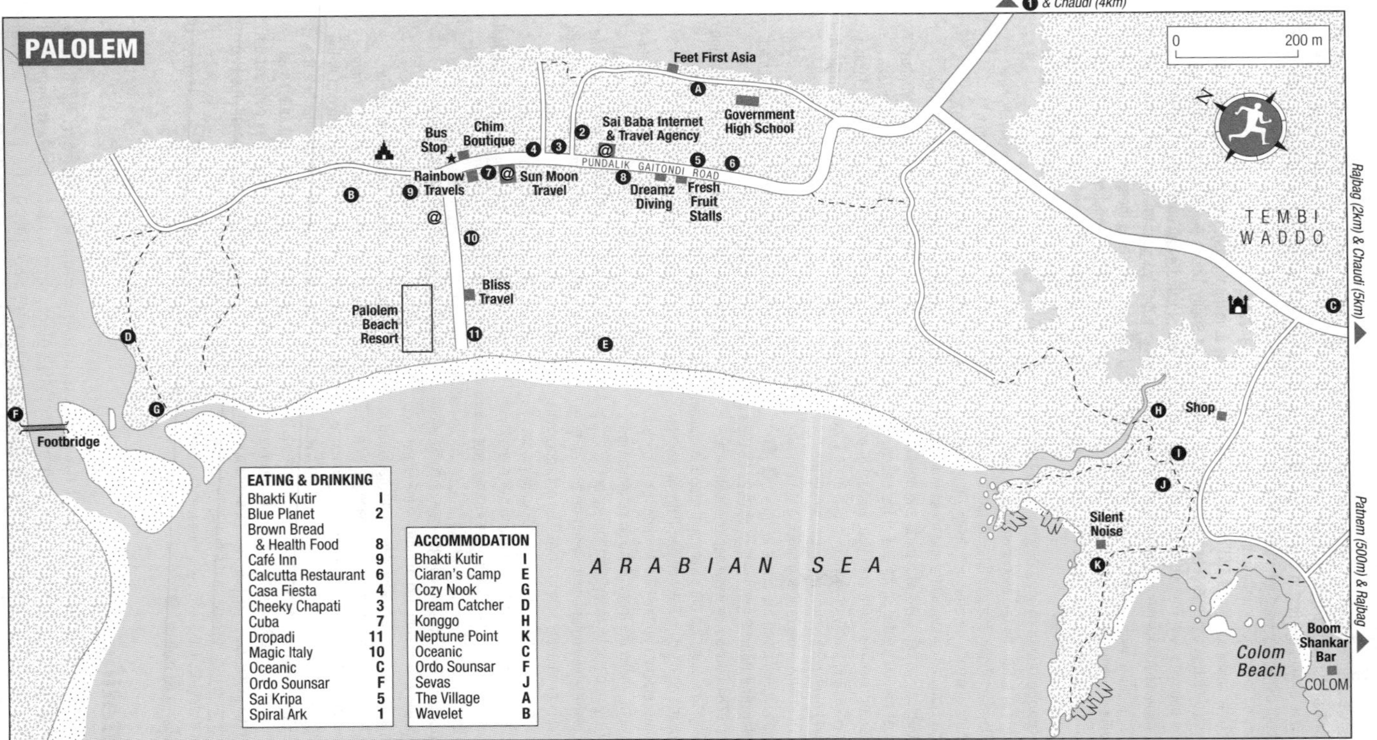

PALOLEM
1 & Chaudi (4km)
Rajbag (2km) & Chaudi (5km)
Patnem (500m) & Rajbag
0 200 m
N
Feet First Asia
Government High School
Sai Baba Internet & Travel Agency
Bus Stop
Chim Boutique
PUNDALIK GAITONDI ROAD
Rainbow Travels
Sun Moon Travel
Dreamz Diving
Fresh Fruit Stalls
Bliss Travel
Palolem Beach Resort
Footbridge
TEMBI WADDO
Shop
Silent Noise
ARABIAN SEA
Colom Beach
Boom Shankar Bar
COLOM
EATING & DRINKING
Bhakti Kutir I
Blue Planet 2
Brown Bread & Health Food 8
Café Inn 9
Calcutta Restaurant 6
Casa Fiesta 4
Cheeky Chapati 3
Cuba 7
Dropadi 11
Magic Italy 10
Oceanic C
Ordo Sounsar F
Sai Kripa 5
Spiral Ark 1
ACCOMMODATION
Bhakti Kutir I
Ciaran's Camp E
Cozy Nook G
Dream Catcher D
Konggo H
Neptune Point K
Oceanic C
Ordo Sounsar F
Sevas J
The Village A
Wavelet B

Ⓦwww.dreamcatcher.in. Walter and Jackie, the British-Keralan couple who run *Dreamcatcher*, were among the first in Goa to realize that if you built bigger plywood huts than the competition, styled them individually with Indian textiles, pretty coloured drapes and mozzie nets, you could charge a packet – and that people would be happy to pay. They've since pushed the philosophy to its most extreme limits yet, with some ultra-luxurious, Keralan-style "mini wood villas" overlooking the river. The large, 50-hut site includes a large yoga *shala* and ayurvedic health spa. ❻–❼

Konggo Ourem Ⓣ9422 059217 or Ⓣ9764 267511. Run by the welcoming Claire and Dominic Pinko, *Konggo* has the most interesting huts currently on offer in Palolem, ingeniously constructed around cliffs and rocks in a beautiful tropical garden alive with birds and butterflies, just behind the far south end of the beach. The larger ones (Rs1500) are huge, with long, deep decks, and plenty of room in which to do yoga and even cook your own meals, while the bathrooms have proper plumbing. And they're good value given the prime location. ❹–❺

Neptune Point South Palolem Ⓣ9822 584968 or Ⓣ9764 686555, Ⓦwww.neptunepoint.com. *Neptune* occupies the sweet spot atop the boulder headland dividing Palolem and Patnem, and its huts, stacked up the hillside under giant coconut palms, make the most of the stupendous views. They're basic by today's standards, but comfortable enough, and having the sea on three sides is a unique selling point. The only downside is the *Silent Noise* disco and movie evenings (see p.200), held on the premises twice weekly, which bring in big crowds. Rates treble over Christmas and New Year. ❹–❺

Oceanic Tembi Waddo Ⓣ0832/264 3059, Ⓦwww.hotel-oceanic.com. Ten minutes' walk inland from the beach (and also reachable via the backroad to Chaudi), *Oceanic* is owned and managed by a resident British couple, its marble-floored rooms stylishly designed, fresh, cool and relaxing, with large mosquito nets, block-printed bedspreads and bedside lamps. Mango branches grow alluringly through the upper terrace. There's also a pool on a forested patio behind, and a quality restaurant, plus it's child-friendly, with cots, monitors and pool alarms on request. ❼

Ordo Sounsar Far northern end of Palolem beach, on the far side of the creek (look for the rickety footbridge to the right as you head for the island) Ⓣ9822/488769 or Ⓣ9422 639497, Ⓦwww.ordosounsar.com. Run by a hospitable brother-and-sister team, Serafin and Shelly, this is Palolem's most idyllic hut camp, tucked away on the tranquil side of the river, which you get to via a rickety wooden footbridge. The huts themselves are a generous size, comfortably furnished and well spaced, with great sitouts to lounge on and funky thatched roofs; and there's a sociable bar and excellent restaurant. ❹–❺

Sevas Far southern end of the beach, on the hill dividing Palolem from Colom Ⓣ0832/264 3977 or Ⓣ9422/065437, Ⓦwww.sevaspalolemgoa.com. A cheaper, less sophisticated version of *Bhakti Kutir*, but beautifully done all the same, and the site is peaceful. The "ethnic" cabañas have traditional rice-straw roofs, mud-and-dung floors, hygienic squat-style loos and bucket baths. They also offer massages and yoga classes, and there's a pleasant restaurant serving very good thalis for Rs125–150. ❸–❹

The Village House #196, near Government High School Ⓣ0832/264 5767 or Ⓣ9960 487627, Ⓦwww.villageguesthousegoa.com. This British-run boutique guesthouse, on the fringes of Palolem, a 10min walk from the beach, is the most comfortable and stylish place to stay in the area. Furnished with four-posters and vibrant silk bed covers, it's wi-fi-enabled; a/c rooms are large – and the designer bathrooms palatial. A shady rear garden serves as a common breakfast area, and you can take your drinks out onto the veranda in the evenings. ❼

Wavelet Palolem village Ⓣ0832/264 3451, Ⓦwww.waveletbeachresort.com. Ceramic tiled rooms in a modern three-storey block, situated near the lane running from the main junction in the village to the far north end of the beach. Not exactly the kind of architecture that enhances the village's natural feel, but it's an out-of-the-way spot and some may consider the comfort and security a good trade-off. It's also good value. ❸

Eating

Palolem's **restaurants** reflect the cosmopolitan make-up of its visitors. Each year, a fresh batch of innovative, ever more stylish places opens, many of them managed by expats. For those on tight budgets, there also are a couple of cheap and cheerful local **tea shops** along the road running parallel with the beach – the *Sai Kripa* serves filling breakfasts of *pao bhaji*, fluffy bread rolls, omelettes and chai for next to nothing, while the *Calcutta Restaurant* dishes up piping hot *parathas* and chapatis in the morning, and rice-plate meals at lunchtime.

Bhakti Kutir Far southern end of the beach, on the hill dividing Palolem from Colom. Laid-back terrace café-restaurant with rustic wooden tables and an Indo-European fusion menu: sunny tomato and mozzarella salad (with fresh basil), fish from the bay and North Indian vegetarian dishes, all made with local and organically produced ingredients.

Blue Planet Just off Pundalik Gaitondi Rd, ⓦwww.blueplanet-café.com. Organic, veggie-vegan place located a stone's throw from the main drag, turning out healthy, balanced and tasty meals to Palolem's health-conscious contingent. Their spinach lasagna, served with baby corn, dry tomato, stir fry and green salad, is the house favourite, but the pumpkin cheese burger with cumin potatoes isn't far behind; and they do a great selection of juices, herbal teas and non-dairy milks.

Brown Bread & Health Food Pundalik Gaitondi Rd. Not exactly the funkiest name on the strip, but the breakfasts served in this clean, friendly café are copious and delicious. The croissants come straight out of the oven (try one filled with sprouted mung beans and cheese), and their pineapple pancakes pull in hungry souls from far and wide. The not-so-healthy cakes aren't bad, either.

Café Inn Pundalik Gaitondi Rd. By far the best coffee in Palolem, made with a proper Italian coffee machine by an Israeli duo. They get packed out for breakfast, and have a small but eclectic menu of meals and snacks (including yummy cream-cheese sandwiches), with a fully a/c, wi-fi-enabled caféteria – a first for the area. The best reason to come here, though, is the legendary coffee slush. Open daily 10am–11pm.

Casa Fiesta Pundalik Gaitondi Rd. Popular place on the main drag, offering an eclectic menu of world cuisine: hummus, Greek salad, wood-baked pizzas, Mexican specialities and fish *pollichatu* mains (mostly under Rs200) come with delicious roast potatoes.

Cheeky Chapati Pundalik Gaitondi Rd. Rustic, dark-wood furniture sets a Robinson Crusoe tone at this Brit-owned, Brit-oriented restaurant in the village centre, where you can tuck into proper Sunday roast each week from 7pm. The rest of the time, specialities include monster cooked breakfasts with all the trimmings (including cafetières of hangover-busting fresh coffee), chapati wraps, crunchy salads and a focused menu of main meals dominated by seafood (mostly around Rs250). Scrabble and Jenga sets are on hand for the twitchy fingered.

Dropadi Beachfront. This place enjoys both a top location and Palolem's best Indian chef, who specializes in rich, creamy Mughlai dishes and tandoori fish. Go for the superb *murg makhini* or crab masala with spinach. Most main courses are in the range Rs150–400.

Magic Italy Beach Rd. On the busy approach to the seafront, this is South Goa's number-one Italian restaurant, serving home-made ravioli and tagliatelle, along with scrumptious wood-fired pizzas (Rs150–250).

Oceanic Tembi Waddo. Chilled terrace restaurant, set well back from the beach but worth the walk for the better-than-average food and background music (the owner is an ex-Womad sound man). North and South Indian dishes are the chef's forte (especially *dum aloo* Kashmiri and butter chicken), but there're also great red and green Thai curries, tempting desserts (including lemon-and-ginger cheesecake and banoffee pie) and coffee liqueur. Many people head here for lunch and a dip in the pool, then stay on for a sundowner.

Ordo Sounsar Far northern end of Palolem beach (for directions see under "Accommodation"). With most places using previously frozen fish instead of fresh these days, this laid-back restaurant, on a terrace in a hut camp of the same name, is something special. Seasonal Goan seafood and vegetarian dishes are their specialities: pomfret stuffed with green chilli; papaya curry in coconut juice; green-pea *xacuti*; prawn *balchao*; shark *ambotik*; white cabage in lime dressing – all made with the choicest and freshest ingredients. Count on Rs300–400 for two courses.

Spiral Ark Agonda Rd. Delightful fair-trade deli and terrace café serving fresh, wholesome juices, salads, soups, home-made breads, cakes and organic thalis on the terrace of an old Portuguese-era house. It's a 10min ride from the beach area, but worth the effort, and you can browse their gorgeous shop afterwards (see p.200).

Drinking and nightlife

As with everywhere else in Goa, the ubiquitous 10pm amplified music ban is strictly observed in Palolem, although one crew has found a way of circumventing the rule. Hosted by *Neptunes Point* at the far south end of the bay, the **Silent Noise** collective stages weekly **headphone parties** on Saturday nights (9pm–4am; Rs400), where the music is broadcast digitally to individual headsets instead of through PAs. You've a choice of different house, electro and big beats mixes on three separate channels, synced with live AV screens, lights and lasers, and of course there's a dreamy view through the palm trees of India's most beautiful beach. Native American tepees are also on hand as chillout space, along with massage chairs and the usual rank of traditional chai ladies, with their hot, spicy tea and fresh samosas. The vibe is genuinely relaxed and fun – a far cry from the heavier dance venues of north Goa. For details of forthcoming programmes, and sample mixes, go to Ⓦwww.silentnoise.in.

In addition, the same site (featured on our map on p.197) screens movies on Wednesdays, which you can watch while enjoying a *mojito* from *Neptune Point's* bar. For a full-on pub experience, try *Cuba* on the main street, which has a full-size pool table, big-screen TV showing live football matches and a great range of cocktails. A handful of **bar-restaurants** stage popular open-mic and music performances, among them *Laguna Vista* in Colom (see p.202), where you can enjoy live Indo-French fusion on Friday nights. Other than that, lounging in beachside cafés takes up most visitors' evenings.

Shopping

Palolem's main drag is lined with stalls and shops selling the usual range of cheap cotton clothes and Kashmiri handicrafts, but for something a little more stylish, check out **Chim** (Ⓦwww.chimshop.com), at the end of the road leading to the beach, which sells pretty, Indian-inspired designer clothes, beachwear and accessories. **Spiral Ark** (Ⓦspiralark.com), 2km northeast of Palolem on the Agonda road, is a wonderful Aladdin's Cave of natural, handmade items sourced from tribal communities in the region and beyond – elegant Indian clothes made from organic cotton, funky toys, art objects and devotional curios, all displayed to great effect in a Portuguese-era house. Look out for occasional "farmers' markets"; the emporium also hosts a pleasant terrace café and deli (see p.199).

Outdoor activities

For those who tire of the beach, a handful of **outdoor** firms operate out of Palolem, offering guided trips into local landscapes which most tourists don't even know exist. French-run Goa Jungle Adventures (Ⓦgoajungle.free.fr) runs **canyoning** expeditions through hidden river gorges to spectacular waterfalls – as well as treks to natural swimming sites. Rates range from Rs1500–1800 per half-day, including all equipment. Working from the *Sea Shells Guest House* in Palolem, **Dreamz Diving** (Ⓣ9326/113466, Ⓦwww.dreamzdiving.com) are the people to contact if you're in search of a scuba adventure. Their PADI-qualified instructors offer guided dives to sites around Pigeon Island, down the coast at Murudeshwar, Karnataka, in much clearer waters than you get around Palolem. Dives range from $60 for a one-tank outing, to $400 for an Open Water course. A full rundown of services appears on the company's website.

Finally, **Goa Sailing** (Ⓣ9850/458865, Ⓦwww.goasailing.com) has three 15-foot Prindle Catamarans for hire – by the hour (Rs1250), half-day (Rs3000) or full day (Rs4000). They come with a fully qualified instructor, but can be taken out solo if you can demonstrate competence. Some wonderfully remote beaches are hidden away down the coast and this is the best (and in a few cases, the only) way to reach them.

Listings

Doctor Dr Sandheep, at the private Dhavalikar Hospital (Ⓣ0832/264 3147), 2km out of Palolem at Devabag on the road to Agonda, just before *Spiral Ark*.
Foot care Foot specialist Alecz Mullany (Ⓦwww.feetfirstasia.com) magics away cracked heels and in-growing toenails from a small clinic near *The Village* guesthouse (see map, p.198).
Foreign exchange Several agents in Palolem are licensed to change money; LKP Forex in the *Palolem Beach Resort* (see map, p.197) offer competitive rates. Sai Baba International, Sun Moon Travel and Rainbow Travels on the main street all do cash advances against Visa and Mastercards. The nearest ATM (for Visa and Mastercard withdrawals) is in Chaudi.
Internet cafés Bliss Travel, on the left near the main entrance to the beach; Rs40/hr for the village's fastest broadband lines. Go armed with an extra layer – the a/c's fierce.
Pharmacy Palolem's main pharmacy is 1km out of the village on the Chaudi road, to your right just after the Agonda turning. It's closed on Sundays, but out of hours you can call at the pharmacist's house immediately behind the shop.
Tarot readings Ujalah (Orly) Ⓣ9049/912907.
Telephones Bliss Travel (see under "Internet" above) is one of the few surviving IST/STD places in Palolem with a reliable connection.

Colom

A stony path threads its way through the boulders and *toddi* groves at the south end of Palolem beach to the Hindu hamlet of **COLOM**, clustered around the rocky shore of two palm-shaded coves. Several families here rent out huts and rooms to travellers, and there are a handful of small cafés – the most famous of them the legendary *Boom Shankar* bar – but these are the only discernible trickle-down from Palolem. This idyllic state of affairs, however, looks set to change. In 2009, Colom's ancestral landlady, Dona Maria de Lourdes Figueiredo de Albuquerque, sold off her landholding here to a consortium of Russian developers, who immediately tried to evict residents from the headland overlooking the cove. A violent standoff ensued, which ended with the Russians backing down, but it's unlikely such wealthy interests can be held off indefinitely. The consequences of a luxury resort being built in the midst of this poor fishing community can only be guessed at. So enjoy it while you can.

Practicalities

Tucked away in the woods at the top of a low rise as you enter Colom, *Tree Shanti* (Ⓣ0832/264 4460 or Ⓣ9923/795290; ❻–❼) is a small family **guesthouse**, run by a feisty couple of sisters, Gita and Sarita Komarpunt. They have five comfortable, red-tiled cottages and four spacious rooms (all with big bathrooms), set in a leafy garden swathed in forest. It's a fun place to stay, with a friendly atmosphere that's a world away from Palolem's hut camps. Another popular option nearby is the *Boom Shankar* bar (Ⓣ0832/264 4035; ❷–❸), on the southern edge of Colom, where the path rounds the headland to Patnem. The attached rooms are simply furnished, but clean, with lots of lounging space and fine views across the cove. They can also help you find longer-term rentals in houses dotted around the headland behind.

Boom Shankar itself does a great range of **food** – including its perennially popular fresh mozzarella and tomato salads – and, with a rear terrace overlooking the bay and gorgeous views, is the perfect place for a sundowner. Just up the track on the right, *Bocado de Cardinales* rustles up heavenly tapas, great fish dishes and more-ish cocktails – but watch your alcohol intake as there is a very tempting clothes and textile boutique on the premises too. Also worth checking out in the village is *Laguna Vista*, which does classy food and live music (Friday evenings only), when DJ Axailles sings along with Indian classical musicians.

Patnem

A string of small hut camps and shacks line the sand at **PATNEM**, just south of Colom, but the scene here is altogether more subdued than Palolem. The beach, curving for roughly a kilometre to a steep bluff, is broad, with little shade, and shelves quite steeply at certain phases of the tide, though the undertow rarely gets dangerously strong. Most of the foreign tourists who stay here tend to do so for months on end, rather than weeks, dabbling in holistic therapies, yoga and massage between lengthy sessions in the excellent cafés nestled behind the beach. It's far from a secret, but remains about as close to peaceful and quiet as this stretch of coast gets these days.

Accommodation

Goyam Towards the north end of the beach ⓣ9822/685138 or ⓣ9890/877844; ⓦwww.goyam.net. Luxury, double-storeyed wooden bungalows painted pretty pastel colours. Partly screened by casuarina trees, each is smartly furnished and fitted with bathrooms, mosquito nets and swings on sea-facing balconies; those at the front are the village's number-one des reses, and thus invariably booked up months in advance. ❼

Home Middle of the beach ⓣ0832/264 3916, ⓦwww.homeispatnem.com. A chic little Swiss-British-run guesthouse, comprising an annexe of attached rooms under Mangalorean tiles, pleasantly decked out with textiles, coconut mats, lampshades and other touches to justify their hefty tariffs. ❺–❻

Namaste Middle of the beach ⓣ9850/477189. Among the string of budget traveller camps in Patnem, is a dependable, lively budget option, run by the amiable Satay. Rates in the range from Rs700–1500 depending on size and comfort of the bamboo hut, time of year and how far back you are from the sand; all have individual shower-toilets. ❹–❺

Papaya's Middle of the beach ⓣ9923/079447, ⓦwww.papayasgoa.com. A delightfully green oasis, where water is recycled to keep the plants in their prime. The eco-huts have breezy little sitouts, shaggy palm-frond fringes made from locally sourced materials, and the power comes from solar panels. ❺–❻

Parvati Middle of the beach ⓣ9822/189913, ⓦwww.parvatihuts.in. A cut above your average hut camp, offering spacious, circular bamboo huts, each with a good-sized bathroom, Western-style toilet and shower, safe locker and mozzie net. The best value in this category, it's set in a leafy garden smothered in hibiscus plants – and has a more chilled vibe than most of the neighbours. ❹–❺

Eating

It's a safe bet you'll spend a few hours each day in one or other of the sandy floored **shack-cafés** lining Patnem beach, among which the following stand out.

Bora Dista Café Harmonic Healing Centre (see opposite). Up on the rocks overlooking the beach, this laid-back café boasts the most extensive views of any hereabouts, and serves up healthy foods as well as a few treats, though it's open only until 4.30pm.

Goyam North end of the beach. This swanky beachside restaurant, an off-shoot of the popular

Dropadi in Palolem, does superb seafood prepared in rich North Indian style: crab *makhini* and tandoori sea bass (Rs350–400) are their signature dishes.
Home Middle of the beach. Patnem's nicest beach café, serving mezes, freshly baked bread, Swiss röstis, fresh salads (from around Rs150), proper Lavazza espresso and wonderful desserts (banoffee pie, warm apple tart with fresh cream, chocolate and walnut cake). It's a particularly pleasant option for breakfast, with Chopin playing over the sound system and sparrows chirping in the palms.
UTI (United Tastes of India) Set back from the beachfront. South Indian dosas and *iddlis*, complete with chatni and spicy *samber*, are *UTI's* speciality, but they also rustle up big portions of traditional North Indian fare, including tasty *palak paneer* and veg makanwalla, which hungry punters shovel in with fluffy naan breads and chapatis.

Holistic therapies

The **Harmonic Healing & Eco Retreat Centre** (Ⓣ9822/512814, Ⓦwww.harmonicingoa.com), on the headland to the north of Patnem, is the place to come if you need to sort out your body and soul. Wrapped in greenery with panoramic views of the beach, the centre hosts daily yoga and pilates classes, as well reiki initiations, energy balancing and Thai massages from internationally acclaimed teachers. They even offer lessons in Bollywood dance and classical Indian singing – all against one of the most spellbinding panoramas in Goa. Drop-in sessions cost around Rs250; one-to-one treatments come in at Rs1000/1500 for 60/90 minutes. You can save money by investing in a Harmonic membership card, or splurge on a have-it-all "Pamper Day" (Rs5000), entitling you to two yoga classes and a two-hour treatment, plus breakfast, lunch and afternoon tea in their suitably chilled-out clifftop café.

Rajbag and Talpona

At low tide, it's possible to wade around the bottom of the steep-sided headland dividing Patnem from neighbouring **RAJBAG**, another kilometre-long sweep of white sand. Sadly, the remote feel of this wonderful, windswept beach has been entirely submerged by the massive five-star *Lalit Goa* (Ⓦwwww.ichotelsgroup.com; ⑨) erected on the land behind it – much to the annoyance of the locals, who campaigned for four years to stop the project.

South of Rajbag, the Talpona River can be crossed via a hand-paddled ferry, which usually has to be summoned from the far bank (fix a return price in advance and only pay once you've completed both legs of the trip, as the boatmen are rumoured to have been holding wealthy tourists from the *Lalit* to ransom by refusing to paddle them back unless they hand over huge "tips"). Once across, a short walk brings you to **Talpona Beach**, backed by low dunes and a line of straggly palms.

Galjibag

One of Goa's least known shorelines, **GALJIBAG**, 16km south of Chaudi, can be reached on foot if you continue south from Talpona across a low headland. Alternatively, heading south on the NH-17, take a right turn after the large double-river bridge. The approach to the beach, fringed by wispy casuarina trees, hugs the south bank of the Talpona River, passing a string of Hindu hamlets and a railway bridge. The village, sandwiched between two estuaries, is devoid of tourist facilities, and its tranquil beach refreshingly unspoilt. It is also one of only three remote spots in Goa where the rare **Olive Ridley marine turtle** (see box, p.148) nests. Villagers have traditionally harvested the eggs laid in the sand by the females, who return each year in early November to the same spot, but the Forest Department now strictly protects the turtles from poaching in an attempt to arrest their decline. During the breeding season you'll see their nests fenced off and marked with flags. Nevertheless, the number of hatchlings has been in sharp decline for the past two or three winters: the sudden drop, a Goa-wide phenomenon, is thought to have been caused by intensive trawler fishing off-shore.

As reward for having walked all the way here, treat yourself to a fish thali at *Surya's Café*, nestled under the casuarinas at the far southern end of Galjibag Beach. The eponymous Surya works as a chef at the *Lalit* these days, so his young cousin takes orders while his mother rustles up fresh mackerel, kingfish, pomfret and oysters, straight out of the nets, over a smoky wood fire behind. The food is bursting with traditional flavours, and inexpensive.

The Mallikarjun temple

Few non-Hindu visitors make it to the **Mallikarjun temple**, 7km northeast of Chaudi (look for the signpost off the NH-17). Yet this small Shiva shrine is one of Goa's oldest – not that you'd know it from the outside, which is awash with concrete and garish pink paint. Its interior, however, has largely escaped heavy-handed renovation. Some of the finest surviving art is to be found in the assembly hall, or *mandapa*, whose stocky wooden pillars writhe with sculpted musicians, dancers and floral motifs. At the far end, an elaborately embossed door jamb opens onto the inner sanctum, where a *Shivalingam* with a metallic mask is enshrined.

The inland route to Rivona: Netravali

A few kilometres beyond the turn-off for the Mallikarjun temple, a Forest Department checkpoint on the left of the NH-17 marks the start of what is arguably **Goa's most scenic road**. Taking you through pockets of fragrant forest into the heart of the mountains, it penetrates the jungle wilderness separating Canacona from Quepem *taluka*, eventually joining up with the main road to Rivona. With a motorbike, you can use it to reach the extraordinary **Stone Age rock carvings** at Usgalimal (see p.172), and then press on north via the Gopinath temple, with its famous **"Bubble Lake"** towards Rivona, Tilamola and Chandor, where the main road connects the interior with Margao and the coastal highway. This circuit makes a memorable drive, but don't under-estimate the remoteness of some of the terrain: the *ghat* section, in particular, is rough in places and a long way from the nearest village. Check your location regularly with any woodcutters, forest wardens or cattle herders you meet along the way, and take along plenty of water, plus a litre or two of spare fuel.

From the Forest Department checkpoint and turning off NH-17 south of Mallikarjun, the road crosses open cultivated land before passing through a couple of villages to begin the climb, via a series of sharp switchbacks, into the mountains. By the time you reach the pass, the jungle – and profusion of bird and insect life – is impressive, while odd gaps in the tree cover reveal wonderful panoramas over the hidden valleys on the far side of the hills.

Once at the pass, you're officially in the buffer zone of the **Netravali Wildlife Sanctuary**, a recently created reserve which, along with the neighbouring Mhadei Wildlife Santuary, protects 420 square kilometres of densely forested country. In October 2009, poachers were arrested north of here near Mhadei with a tiger carcass; a live adult female with cub has also been spotted in the area in recent years. You're very unlikely to see a big cat from the road, but stand a good chance of sighting giant squirrels and hornbills as you descend the rough terrain to a second forest checkpoint.

Shortly after, look out on your right for the pinky-orange **Gopinath temple**, near the village of **Netravali (Netorli)**. The shrine, a largely modern structure with ancient carved Kadama pillars inside, is renowned throughout Goa for the adjacent temple bathing tank, Budbudyanchi Tali, better known as the "Bubude Tali" or "Bubble Lake". Hang around on the laterite steps surrounding the murky green tank for long enough and you'll notice spooky little bubbles rising to the surface – the subject of numerous local legends. The other reason to stop here is for the one-hour trek to the nearby **Savari waterfalls**, an idyllic local picnic spot deep in the jungle to the south of Netravali where you can swim in natural pools at the foot of a spectacular cascade. A clear path leads to the site, and there are stepping stones across the four streams encountered along the way, but you'll need local guidance to find the start of it.

From Netravali, the winding road continues northwest through the remote Pareda Valley towards the sinuous Kushawati River, in the heart of Goa's iron-ore mining zone, which it eventually approaches on the outskirts of **Usgalimal** village – close to the site of the prehistoric rock carvings featured on p.172. Keep heading north for another 13km and you'll reach the Tilamola crossroads, where a left turn will take you back towards Margao.

Cotigao Wildlife Sanctuary

The **Cotigao Wildlife Sanctuary**, 10km southeast of Chaudi, was established in 1969 to protect a remote and vulnerable area of forest lining the Goa–Karnataka border. Best visited between October and March, Cotigao is a peaceful and scenic park that makes a pleasant day-trip from Palolem, 12km northwest. Encompassing 86 square kilometres of mixed deciduous woodland, the reserve is certain to inspire tree lovers, but less likely to yield many wildlife sightings: its tigers and leopards were hunted out long ago, while the gazelles, sloth bears, porcupines, panthers and hyenas that allegedly lurk in the woods rarely appear. You do, however, stand a good chance of spotting at least two species of monkey, a couple of wild boar and the odd gaur (the primeval-looking Indian bison), as well as plenty of exotic birdlife.

Any of the buses running south on the NH-17 to Karwar via Chaudi will drop you within 2km of the gates. However, to explore the inner reaches of the sanctuary, you really need your own transport. The wardens at the reserve's small **Interpretative Centre** at the gates, where you have to pay your entry fees (Rs5, plus Rs100 for a car, Rs50 for a motorbike; Rs50 for a camera permit) will show you how to get to a 25-metre-high treetop watchtower, overlooking a **waterhole** that attracts a handful of animals around dawn and dusk. You can also stay here at a rather unprepossessing little room (Rs250 per night), in the compound behind the main reserve gates. Food and drink may be available by prior arrangement, and there's a shop at the nearest village, 2km inside the park.

Polem

A stone's throw from the state border, **POLEM**, 30km south of Chaudi, is Goa's southernmost beach, and sufficiently secluded to have been overlooked even by the sand-hopping hippies heading between Goa and Gokarna in Karnataka. The hundred-metre strip of smooth white sand, enfolded by a pair of rocky headlands, is immaculate and unspoilt, and visited regularly by dolphins and white-bellied fish eagles. However, it's not the most welcoming of places, possibly because the principal source of income for the villagers is smuggling and illegal liquor. Westerners sunbathing and swimming can expect a frosty reception from the locals.

It is possible to get to within striking distance of Polem by **bus** from Panjim, Margao or Chaudi: catch any service heading south down NH-17 to Karwar (every 30min), and get off 2km before the border at the *Milan Bar* (you'll know you've overshot the turning if you see a petrol station on the left). The owner of this roadside café will show you the path leading across the paddy fields to Polem, a pleasant fifteen-minute walk.

Across the Goa-Karnataka border

If you're heading **south from Goa** towards Jog Falls or the Hindu pilgrimage town of Gokarna (covered in Chapter 4, p.223), you'll have to cross the state border at a road barrier a short way before the river bridge, near the town of Karwar. For travellers on buses, or in cars, this is a straightforward procedure; you probably won't even have to fill in the requisite form. Anyone who is crossing into Karnataka on a rented motorbike, however, can expect some **hassle from the police**. The standard routine is to take your passport, scrutinize it with a very stern face, and then inform you that you can't continue south because of some directive from Panjim. Of course, this is all a ploy to extract baksheesh, and like it or not, you'll probably have to shell out at least Rs100 to continue. Curiously enough, the cops are honest when it comes to recognizing you on the return trip, and will politely wave you through the barrier after you sign the ledger in their office.

Around Goa

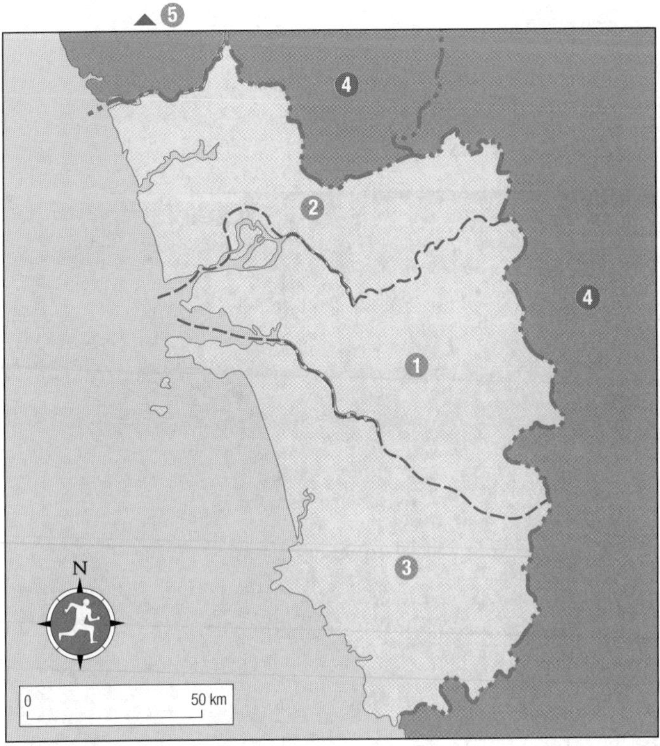

CHAPTER 4

Highlights

* **Sawantwadi** Travel north of Goa through the remote forests of Maharashtra to visit a maharaja's palace where ageing artisans paint beautiful packs of Indian playing cards. See p.212

* **Jog Falls** India's highest waterfalls, set high up in the Western Ghat mountains. See p.222

* **Gokarna** Bustling Hindu pilgrimage town with heaps of atmosphere, close to a string of lovely beaches. See p.223

* **Hampi** Ruined palaces, wild monkeys, hilltop temples and a serene riverine setting combine to create one of Asia's most memorable destinations. See p.242

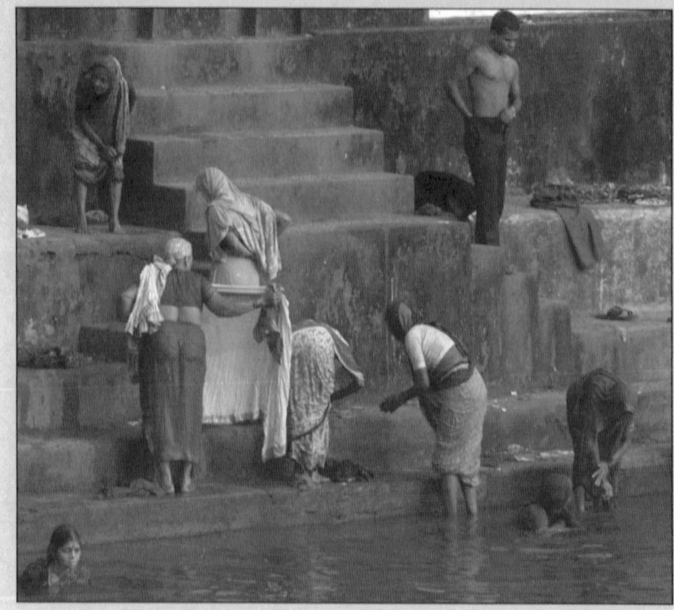

▲ Ritual ablutions at Kooti Tirtha Kund, Gokarna

4

Around Goa

Goa's towns and coastal resorts may induce a certain culture shock when you first arrive, but they are far from representative of the rest of the country, and many visitors are tempted across the state border into neighbouring **Maharashtra** and **Karnataka**, beyond the limits of Portuguese colonial influence, for a taste of the "real" India. Even if you're only here for two weeks, it's perfectly feasible to do this. Indeed, a foray through the forests of southern Maharashtra, across the Western Ghats to the **Deccan plateau**, or south down the lush **Konkan coast** may well provide some of the most vivid experiences of your trip. And don't let the prospect of long overland journeys deter you. A number of southwest India's most exotic sights lie a mere day's drive from Goa, set amid landscapes that differ wildly from the palm groves and paddy fields of the coast. Moreover, travelling to them can be fascinating, yielding glimpses of everyday life in both remote, rural villages and the cities just beyond Goa's eastern border.

The single greatest incentive to venture away from the beaches has to be the extraordinary ruined city of **Vijayanagar**, better known as **Hampi**. Situated eight hours by train east of the coast, this vast archeological site harbours the remains of palaces, temples and bazaars dating from the fifteenth and sixteenth centuries, when it was the capital of a huge Hindu empire – among the largest and most powerful in Asia in its heyday. The city was destroyed by Muslim armies in 1565, but enough finely carved stone buildings survive to occupy visitors for days. Hampi's setting is impressive too: an otherworldly jumble of smooth boulders, piled in colossal heaps around the banks of the Tungabhadra River, with banana plantations and rice paddies cutting swathes of green through the rocky terrain. People travel the length of India to see Hampi, and few visitors from Goa return disappointed.

The other obvious target for a trip out of state is the Hindu pilgrimage town of **Gokarna**, 154km south of Margao, which harbours a couple of major Hindu temples and plenty of attractive vernacular architecture. Most of the backpackers who travel here, however, do so to laze on the exquisite beaches to the south, some of which are still only accessible on foot or by boat.

If you are making the trip to Gokarna, it's worth taking a detour through the hills and forests of the Ghats to **Jog Falls**, the highest waterfalls in India. Tourist facilities and public transport services in the adjacent village are minimal (most Indians visit only for the day), but the scenery is dramatic and the road trip across the mountains an adventure.

Finally, from Goa's northernmost enclave, Terekol, you can head further north into Maharashtra to visit the market town of **Sawantwadi**, where local craftsmen and women make traditional Hindu playing cards, or *ganjifa*, in the ceremonial

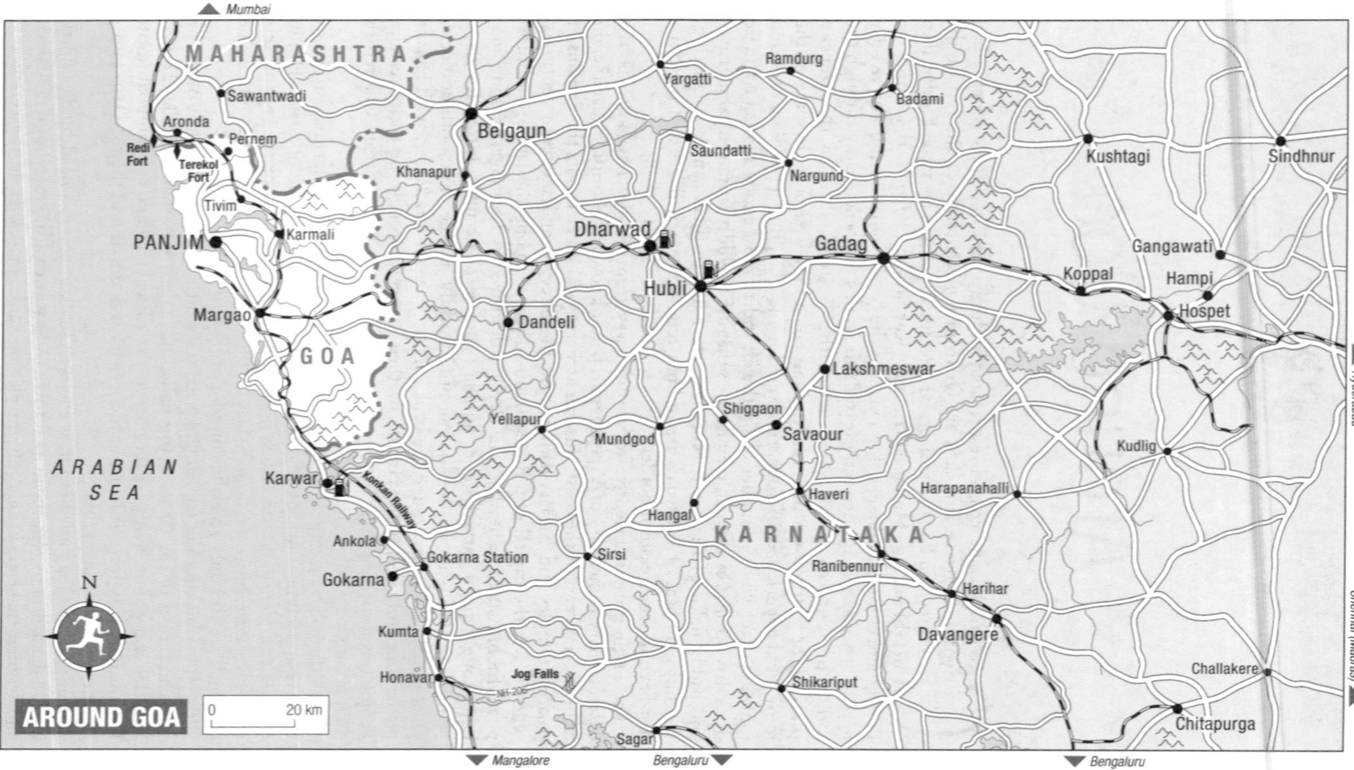

AROUND GOA
Mumbai
Hyderabad
Chennai (Madras)
Bengaluru
Bengaluru
Bengaluru
Mangalore
MAHARASHTRA
GOA
KARNATAKA
ARABIAN SEA
N
0 20 km
Sawantwadi
Aronda
Pernem
Redi Fort
Terekol Fort
Tivim
Karmali
PANJIM
Margao
Belgaun
Khanapur
Dharwad
Hubli
Dandeli
Yellapur
Mundgod
Karwar
Konkan Railway
Ankola
Gokarna Station
Gokarna
Kumta
Honavar
Jog Falls
NH-206
Sagar
Sirsi
Hangal
Shiggaon
Savaour
Haveri
Lakshmeswar
Gadag
Yargatti
Ramdurg
Saundatti
Nargund
Badami
Kushtagi
Sindhnur
Gangawati
Koppal
Hampi
Hospet
Kudlig
Harapanahalli
Ranibennur
Harihar
Davangere
Shikariput
Challakere
Chitapurga

Durbar Hall of a faded maharaja's palace. On the way, **Redi Fort**, just across the border, gives you a taste of what this coast must have looked like before the advent of tourism.

Travelling up the coast to Sawantwadi, or in the other direction between Goa and Gokarna, is straightforward, with fast and regular services on the Konkan Railway from Pernem, Tivim (Thivim), Karmali, Margao and Chaudi. Running in tandem with the rail route, the coastal highway is also well served by buses from towns in Goa – as is the main eastbound road artery crossing the Western Ghats to **Hospet**, the nearest sizeable town to Hampi.

Into Maharashtra: Redi Fort and Sawantwadi

Put off by the spectre of iron-ore workings on the horizon, hardly anyone ever ventures **north of Terekol Fort**, but once clear of the industrial zone, the road empties, the forest and cashew bushes return, and the coastal scenery becomes magnificent. Only half an hour's ride from the Goan border, **Redi Fort** is an atmospheric first stop – an old ruin perched on a cliff above jungle-backed beaches. From there, you can press on northwards to **Sawantwadi**, where the local maharaja's palace supports one of India's last guilds of traditional playing-card painters.

To cover the routes described here you'll need your own transport – though Sawantwadi can also be reached via the **Konkan Railway**.

Redi Fort

Originally built by the Marathas in the sixteenth century and later remodelled by the Portuguese, **REDI FORT** rests on a bluff above a tidal creek, looking out to sea and north up the Maharashtran coast. Entered via a series of fortified gateways, its upper citadel is enclosed by high ramparts which you can clamber up to in several places. Strangled by giant creepers, tubers and tree roots, it's a charismatic old structure that sees few visitors, beyond the troupe of langur monkeys patrolling the walls.

The Hermitage

A tropical **fruit farm** with accommodation for paying guests provides a wonderfully rustic base from which to explore one of the remotest, and rarely visited, corners of the **Western Ghat mountain range**. Called *The Hermitage* (☎9242/623020, Ⓦwww.thehermitageguesthouse.com; ❼), the property lies a long, bone-jarring trip into the forest from Goa, the last two hours of it along unsurfaced jeep tracks. Hosts David and Morvarid Fernandez moved here from the city in the early 1980s to cultivate *chikoo*, mango, coconut and pepper; they now also produce coffee, tea and cocoa, as well as various medicinal plants. Their guest accommodation, all made from local materials to traditional designs, is in bamboo stilt huts and rammed earth cottages (with attached bathrooms and Western-style toilets). The food is old-school, wholesome Parsi and Anglo-Indian fare.

This is a fabulous area for **trekking**, and the family offer a wide choice of guided walks of various lengths, as well as excursions to forgotten forts, waterfalls, remote tribal villages and wildlife spotting sites. Transport to *The Hermitage* from Goa can be arranged on request, or you can get there under your own steam with a combination of train and taxi; full details are posted on their website.

The quickest and most direct route from Terekol itself is to turn right in the village instead of continuing uphill to Terekol fort, and then follow the road over the hill behind, through the USHA pig-iron plant. After three kilometres or so, this road drops down to a junction where you should turn left. Alternatively, it's possible to avoid the dreadful stretch through the industrial complex by crossing the Arondem River 4km east of Kerim–Terekol. From the ferry jetty on the far bank, a couple of easy kilometres bring you to **Aronda** village; head through the bazaar and take the second turning left, which brings you on to a good road leading for 6km west to Redi (the first left leads back to Terekol).

Sawantwadi

SAWANTWADI, 20km north of the Goan border, was the former capital of the Bhonsale dynasty, who ruled this remote corner of Maharashtra for more than three hundred years before the dissolution of princely privileges by the Indian government in the 1950s and 1960s. Surrounded by forest, it's now a bustling market town with a population of 40,000, many of whom trade coconuts, cashews and betel produced in the surrounding woods.

Aside from the lively bazaar in the town centre, the main incentive to travel up here is to visit the Bhonsales' nineteenth-century **palace**, still inhabited by the local rani, and famous as a centre for the manufacture of traditional Indian playing cards, or **ganjifa**. A British-style pile built of local stone, it stands in the centre of town, next to a circular lake. Arriving from the south, you'll come to a fork in the road when it reaches this lake. Take the road off to the right, and after a couple of hundred metres you'll see the palace gates on your right.

The *ganjifa* workshop (daily except public holidays 8.30am–1.30pm & 2.30–5.30pm; Rs50; Ⓣ02363/272010, is in the old **Durbar Hall** to the rear of the building. Surrounded by old weapons, hunting trophies, a bust of Queen Victoria and the silver throne made for the last raja's coronation in 1947, half a dozen men and women are all that survive of the town's once thriving *ganjifa* industry. Up until the end of the nineteenth century, several families were employed in manufacturing cards, but by 1959, when the maharaja decided to revive the art form, only one man could be found who still made *ganjifa* (at a rate of two packs per year). Most of what is made here today is exported for sale in other parts of the country or abroad; the sheer amount of time needed to paint a full pack puts the cards beyond the pocket of most Indians.

Ganjifa

Unlike their counterparts in Western countries, different types of **ganjifa** packs come in different-sized suits: eight (known as "Moghul", or *Changkanchan* in Konkani); nine (*Navagraha*, after the "nine planets" frequently enshrined in Hindu temples); ten (*Dasavatara*, after the god Vishnu's "ten incarnations"); twelve (*Rashi*, after the signs of the zodiac); and even sixteen or twenty-four in the eastern Indian state of Orissa. The mythological and astrological themes also provide the subject matter for the *ganjifa*'s rich decoration, meticulously hand-painted according to designs that have been passed down through generations.

A set of *ganjifa* makes a beautiful, and affordable, souvenir. Painted in vibrant reds, saffrons and blues, the cards feature ocean-churning tortoises, man-lions, sacred boars, dwarves, axe-wielding or elephant-headed gods, princes and winged griffons, to name but a few of the designs drawn from Hinduism's pantheon. In Sawantwadi, sets start at Rs1200.

Photographs of *ganjifa* appear on the website of the International Playing Card Society at Ⓦwww.pagat.com/ipcs/pattern/.

A small **gallery** on the ground floor of the palace outlines the history of Sawantwadi *ganjifa* and their revival, with a collection of old photographs that vividly evoke the last days of the Raj. Upstairs, you can browse a wide selection of expertly made painted wood objects and other affordable souvenirs.

Spurred on by the success of the palace's efforts, other local artisans have followed suit, and the Chitarli Gully bazaar running uphill from the opposite shore of the lake is crammed with the brightly painted toys, wooden fruit and other knick-knacks traditionally given as presents in this area.

Practicalities

Sawantwadi lies around 25km northeast of Redi: from the fort, return to the main Terekol road, turn left, and continue north for 2km until you reach **Shiroda**, where you pick up a road winding northeast for 22km.

On the **Konkan Railway**, it takes a little under half an hour to reach Sawantwadi from north Goa; the railway station is situated 8km from the centre; auto-rickshaws are on hand to ferry passengers to and from town. With rail services conveniently timed for returning to Goa, there's no reason to stay in the town, but you might want to **eat**. The best option is the vegetarian thali restaurant in the modern, multistorey building at the bottom of Chitarli Gully bazaar (its sign is in Mahrahti, but as it's virtually the only restaurant in the area, it's easy to locate).

Hospet

HOSPET, a busy, dusty market town 375km east of Margao, is of little interest except as a springboard for the ruined city of Vijayanagar (Hampi), 13km northeast. If you want somewhere fairly comfortable to sleep, it makes sense to stay here and catch a bus or taxi out to the ruins the following morning. Otherwise, find a room in Hampi itself, where the setting more than compensates for the basic facilities.

Arrival

The most stress-free and economical way to reach Hospet from Goa is the four-times-weekly **train** service from **Margao**. The Vasco–Howrah Express (#8048) departs every Tuesday, Thursday, Friday and Sunday at 8.15am, arriving just over six hours later. Travelling in the opposite direction (#8047), it leaves Hospet on Mondays, Wednesdays, Thursdays and Saturdays at 6.30am, arriving (in theory at least) in Margao at 1.45pm (journey time 7hr 15min). Note, however, that as this latter train originates in Calcutta, a day and a half away, it more often than not pulls in late – and occasionally not at all – leaving you little option but to take a bus or taxi back to Goa.

Train fares range from Rs200 for a seat in an ultra-basic, crowded second-class compartment to Rs675 for second-class air-conditioned – the most comfy option. **Tickets** can be bought on the day at either point of departure. Arrive at Margao by at least 7.30am, as the "queues" are invariably more like rugby scrums.

Hospet's **railway station** is 1500m north of the centre. At the main entrance, you'll probably be greeted by a volley from rickshaw-wallahs wanting to take you to Hampi (Rs80–100), but the road there is badly pot-holed, making the twenty- to thirty-minute trip a lot more comfortable (and quicker) by local bus. These leave roughly every half-hour from the long distance **bus stand**, 250m south of the train station down MG (Station) Road (jump on a cycle-rickshaw for Rs15), and drop you off at Hampi Bazaar.

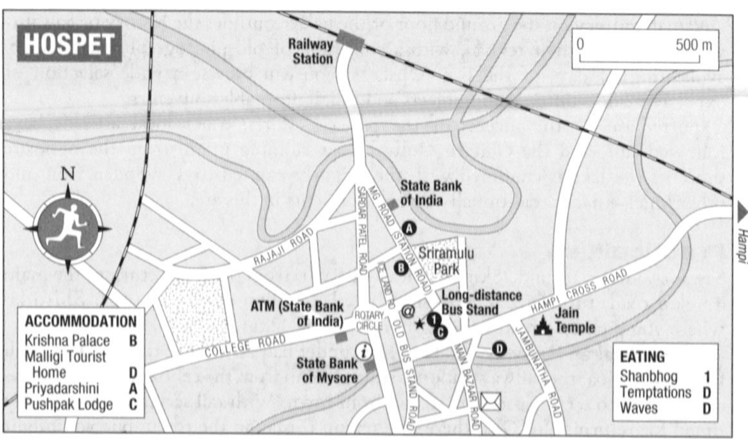

Given the low cost and convenience of the train, you'd have to be a bit of a masochist to want to do the Goa–Hospet trip by **bus**. Two or three clapped-out government services leave **Panjim's** Kadamba stand (platform 9) each morning for Hospet, the last one at 10.30am. Brace yourself for a long, hard slog; all being well, it should take nine or ten hours, but delays and breakdowns are frustratingly frequent. **Tickets** should be booked at least one day in advance at the hatches in the KSRTC (Kadamba State Road Transport Company) bus stand, Panjim.

You can also travel between Goa and Hampi on a **night bus from Margao**, complete with pneumatic suspension and sleeper berths. The service, operated by Paulo Travels (Ⓦwww.paulotravels.com), leaves from next to the *Nanutel Hotel* on Rua da Padre Miranda, at 7pm, arriving at 5.30am the next morning. Tickets cost Rs600.

Getting to Hospet/Hampi by **taxi** may sound like the softest option – but it isn't. The road trip takes much longer than the train, and can be a lot more stressful and tiring. Fares vary wildly: count on paying Rs1500–1750 for each day your driver stays with you, which includes meals, overnight charges and fuel.

Information

The **tourist office** at the Rotary Circle (Mon–Sat: June–March 10am–5.30pm; April & May 8am–1.30pm; Ⓣ08394/228537) offers limited information and sells tickets for KSTDC tours. You can **exchange** travellers' cheques and cash at the State Bank of Mysore (Mon–Fri 10.30am–2.30pm & Sat 10.30am–12.30pm), next to the tourist office, and cash only at the State Bank of India (same hours) on MG (Station) Road. Full exchange facilities are available at the *Malligi Tourist Home* (see opposite), while Cybernet (Rs40/hr), near the bus stand, can get you online.

Accommodation and eating

Many of the hotels have good **dining rooms**, but in the evening, the *Malligi*'s upscale though affordable indoor restaurant, *Temptations*, and its terrace *Waves* bar serve good tandoori and chilled beer. *Shanbhog*, an excellent little *udipi* restaurant next to the bus station, is a perfect pitstop before heading to Hampi, and opens early for breakfast.

Krishna Palace MG Rd ⓣ08394/294300, ⓦwww.krishnapalacehotel.com. Snazzy new central a/c, hotel, with smartly furnished rooms and an ostentatious lobby. Popular with high-end tour groups. ❼–❽

Malligi Tourist Home 6/143 Jambunatha Rd, 2min walk east of MG Rd (look for the signs) and the bus stand ⓣ08394/228101, ⓦwww.malligihotels.com. Recently refurbished with several blocks of luxurious a/c rooms and suites separated by manicured lawns, the *Malligi* also has a large outdoor swimming pool (Rs50/hr for non-residents), plus billiards and massage facilities, in addition to a small bookshop, internet access, and an efficient travel service. ❼

Priyadarshini MG Rd ⓣ08394/228838. Large and bland, but spotless and decent value, especially the a/c rooms (some with balconies). There are also two good on-site restaurants: the veg *Naivedyam* and, in the garden, the excellent non-veg *Manasa*, which has a bar. ❺

Pushpak Lodge MG Rd ⓣ08394/421380. With basic but clean attached rooms, this is the best rock-bottom lodge in town, conveniently located right by the bus stand. ❷

Hampi (Vijayanagar)

The ruined city of **Vijayanagar**, "the City of Victory" (also known as **HAMPI**, the name of a local village), spills from the south bank of the Tungabhadra River, littered among a surreal landscape of golden-brown granite boulders and leafy banana fields. According to the *Ramayana*, the settlement began its days as Kishkinda, ruled by the monkey kings Vali and Sugriva and their ambassador, Hanuman. The weird rocks – some balanced in perilous arches, others heaped in colossal, hill-sized piles – are said to have been flung down by their armies in a show of strength.

Between the fourteenth and sixteenth centuries, this was the most powerful Hindu capital in the Deccan. Travellers were astonished by its size and wealth, telling tales of markets full of silk and precious gems, beautiful bejewelled courtesans, ornate palaces and joyous festivities. However, in the second half of the sixteenth century, the dazzling city was devastated by a six-month Muslim siege. Only stone, brick and stucco structures survive the ensuing sack – monolithic deities, crumbling houses and abandoned temples dominated by towering *gopuras* – as well as the sophisticated irrigation system that channelled water to huge tanks and temples.

Thanks to the Muslim onslaught, most of Hampi's monuments are in disappointingly poor shape, seemingly a lot older than their four or five hundred years. Yet the serene riverine setting and air of magic that lingers over the site, sacred for centuries before a city was founded here, make it one of India's most extraordinary locations. Mainstream tourism has made little impact: along with bus-loads of Hindu pilgrims and sadhus who hole up in the more isolated rock crevices and shrines, most visitors are budget travellers en route to or from Goa. Many find it difficult to leave, and spend weeks chilling out in cafés, wandering to whitewashed hilltop temples and gazing at the spectacular sunsets.

The **best time to come** to Hampi, weather-wise, is from late October to early March, when daytime temperatures are low enough to allow long forays on foot through the ruins. It does start to get busy over Christmas and New Year, however, and from early January for a month or so the site is invaded by an exodus of (mostly Israeli) travellers from Goa, so if you want to enjoy Hampi at its best, visit outside high season.

Some history

The rise of the **Vijayanagar empire** seems to have been a direct response, in the first half of the fourteenth century, to the expansionist aims of Muslims from the north, most notably Malik Kafur and Mohammed-bin-Tughluq. Two Hindu brothers from

Andhra Pradesh, Harihara and Bukka, who had been employed as treasury officers in Kampila, 19km east of Hampi, were captured by the Tughluqs and taken to Delhi, where they supposedly converted to Islam. Assuming them to be suitably tamed, the Delhi sultan despatched them to quell civil disorder in Kampila, which they duly did, only to abandon both Islam and allegiance to Delhi shortly afterwards, preferring to establish their own independent Hindu kingdom. Within a few years they controlled vast tracts of land from coast to coast. In 1343, their new capital, Vijayanagar, was founded on the southern bank of the Tungabhadra River, a location long considered sacred by Hindus. The city's most glorious period was under the reign of **Krishna Deva Raya** (1509–29), when it enjoyed a near monopoly of the lucrative trade in Arabian horses and Indian spices passing through the coastal ports.

Thanks to its natural features and massive fortifications, Vijayanagar was virtually impregnable. In 1565, however, following his interference in the affairs of local Muslim sultanates, the regent Rama Raya was drawn into a battle with a confederacy of Muslim forces, 100km away to the north, which left the city undefended. At first, fortune appeared to be on the side of the Hindu army, but there were as many as 10,000 Muslims in their number, and loyalties may well have been divided. When two Vijayanagar Muslim generals suddenly deserted, the army fell into disarray. Defeat came swiftly; although members of his family fled with untold hoards of gold and jewels, Rama Raya was captured and suffered a grisly death at the hands of the sultan of Ahmadnagar. Vijayanagar then fell victim to a series of destructive raids, and its days of splendour were brought to an abrupt end.

The site

Although spread over 26 square kilometres, the ruins of Vijayanagar are mostly concentrated in two distinct groups: the first lies in and around **Hampi Bazaar** and the nearby riverside area, encompassing the city's most sacred enclave of temples and *ghats*; the second centres on the **royal enclosure** – 3km south of the river, just northwest of **Kamalapuram** village – which holds the remains of palaces, pavilions, elephant stables, guardhouses and temples. Between the two stretches a long boulder-choked hill and a swathe of banana plantations, fed by ancient irrigation canals.

Most people prefer to tour the site on foot or bicycle, setting out from Hampi Bazaar. After a look round the soaring **Virupaksha temple**, work your way east along the main street and riverbank to the beautiful **Vitthala temple**, and then back via the **Achutharaya** complex at the foot of Matanga Hill. From here, a dirt path leads south to the royal enclosure, but it's easier to return to the bazaar and pick up the tarred road, calling in at **Hematuka Hill**, a group of pre-Vijayanagar temples, en route.

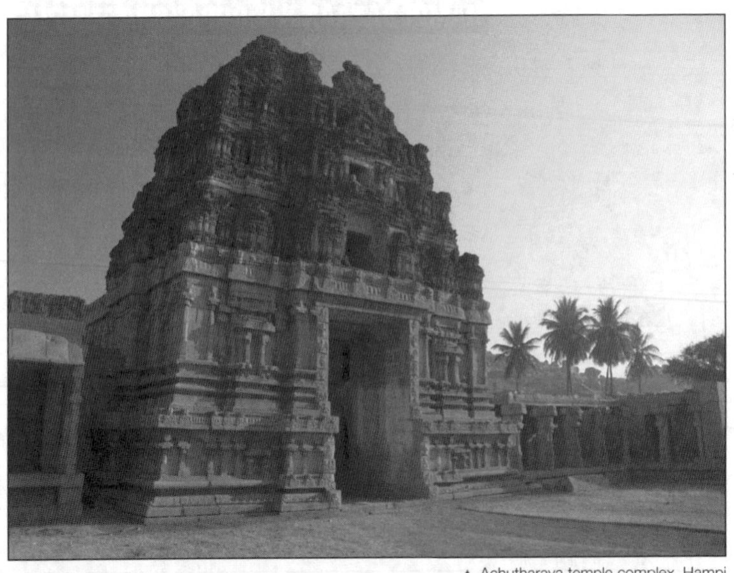

▲ Achutharaya temple complex, Hampi

Hampi Bazaar and the Virupaksha temple

Lining Hampi's long, straight main street, **Hampi Bazaar**, which runs east from the eastern entrance of the Virupaksha temple, you can still make out the remains of Vijayanagar's ruined, columned bazaar, partly inhabited by today's lively market. Families of squatters live in many of the crumbling 500-year-old buildings.

Dedicated to a local form of Shiva known as Virupaksha or Pampapati, the functioning **Virupaksha temple** (daily 8am–12.30pm & 3–6.30pm; Rs2) dominates the village, drawing a steady flow of pilgrims from all over South India. Also known as **Sri Virupaksha Swami**, the complex (open to non-Hindus) consists of two courts, each entered through a towered *gopura*.

A colonnade surrounds the inner enclosure, usually filled with pilgrims dozing and singing religious songs. On entering, if the temple elephant is around, you can get her to bless you by placing a rupee in her trunk. In the centre, the principal shrine is approached through a *mandapa* hallway whose carved columns feature rearing animals. Rare Vijayanagar-era paintings on the ceiling include aspects of Shiva, a procession with the sage Vidyaranya, the ten incarnations of Vishnu and scenes from the *Mahabharata*.

The sacred **ford** in the river is reached from the Virupaksha's north *gopura*; you can also get there by following the lane around the impressive temple **tank** and past *Shanti Guest House*. A *mandapa* overlooks the steps that originally led to the river, now some distance away. Both a small **motor boat** and *putti* (circular rush-basket **coracle**) ply this part of the bank, ferrying villagers to the fields and tourists to the increasingly popular enclave of **Virupapuragadda**. The road left through the village eventually loops back towards the hilltop Hanuman temple, about 5km east, and on to **Anegondi** – a recommended round walk: turn left at the first fork; right at the T junction, and then keep on the main surfaced road, ignoring the turning on left, for around 1km until you see steps leading to Hanuman temple on the right-hand side.

Matanga and Hemakuta Hills

The place to head for sunrise is the boulder hill immediately east of Hampi Bazaar. From the end of the main street, an ancient paved pathway winds up a rise, at the top of which the magnificent Tiruvengalanatha temple is revealed. The views improve as you progress up **Matanga Hill**. At the summit, a small stone temple provides an extraordinary vantage point. Be warned, however, that over the years there have been a number of **muggings** early in the morning along this path, and that you're advised to walk in a group.

Rising from the west end of Hampi Bazaar, **Hemakuta Hill** is dotted with pre-Vijayanagar temples that probably date from between the ninth and eleventh centuries (late Chalukya or Ganga). Aside from the architecture, the main reason to clamber up here is to admire the **views** of the ruins and surrounding countryside. Looking across the boulder-covered terrain and banana plantations, the sheer western edge of the hill is Hampi's number-one sunset spot, attracting a crowd of blissed-out tourists most evenings, along with a couple of entrepreneurial chai-wallahs and little boys posing for photos in Hanuman costumes.

The riverside path to Vitthalla temple

To reach the **Vitthala temple** (daily 8am–4pm; $5 [Rs10]; ticket also valid for the Lotus Mahal on the same day) from the village, walk east along the length of Hampi Bazaar. Fifty metres or so before the end, a path on the left, staffed at regular intervals by conch-blowing sadhus and an assortment of other ragged mendicants, follows the river past the *Shiv Moon* café (see p.222). Beyond at least four Vishnu shrines, the paved and colonnaded **Achutya Bazaar** leads due south to the **Tiruvengalanatha temple**, whose beautiful stone carvings – among them some of Hampi's famed erotica – are being restored by the ASI. Back on the main path again, make a short detour across the rocks leading to the river to see the little-visited waterside **Agni temple**; next to it, the Kotalinga complex consists of 108 (an auspicious number) tiny *linga*, carved on a flat rock. As you approach the Vitthala temple, to the south is an archway known as the **King's Balance**, where the rajas were weighed against gold, silver and jewels to be distributed to the city's priests.

Although the area around the Vitthala temple does not show the same evidence of early cult worship as Virupaksha, the ruined bridge to the west probably dates from before Vijayanagar times, while the bathing *ghat* may be from the Chalukya or Ganga period. As the temple itself has fallen into disuse, however, it seems that the river crossing (*tirtha*) here hasn't enjoyed the same sacred significance as the Virupaksha site. Now designated a World Heritage Monument by UNESCO, the temple was originally built for Vishnu, who according to legend was too embarrassed by its ostentation to live there.

The open *mandapa* features slender monolithic granite **musical pillars** which were constructed so as to sound the notes of the scale when struck. Today, due to vandalism and erosion from being repeatedly beaten, heavy security makes sure that no one is allowed to touch them. Guides, however, will happily demonstrate the musical resonance of other pillars on an adjacent structure. Outer columns sport characteristic Vijayanagar rearing horses, while friezes of lions, elephants and horses on the moulded basement display sculptural trickery – you can transform one beast into another simply by masking one portion of the image.

In front of the temple, to the east, a stone representation of a wooden processional **rath**, or chariot, houses an image of Garuda, Vishnu's bird vehicle. Now cemented, at one time the chariot's wheels revolved.

Anegondi and the Hanuman temple

With more time, you can head across the Tungabhadra to **ANEGONDI**, a village set amid the remains of an old fortress town predating Vijayanagar that's littered with the remains of ancient temples and shrines. The most pleasant way to cross is by *putti*, a circular rush-basket coracle traversing the river 1500m east of the Vitthala temple; the *puttis*, which are today reinforced with plastic sheets, also carry bicycles. Though a bridge had been constructed at this point, it subsequently collapsed and there are no plans to rebuild.

Another worthwhile detour is the hike up to the tiny whitewashed **Hanuman temple**, perched on a rocky hilltop north of the river, from where you can enjoy superb views over Hampi, especially at sunrise or sunset. The steep climb up to it takes around half an hour. From here it's possible to loop back to Virupapuragadda following the route described on p.218 in reverse.

The southern and royal monuments

The most impressive remains of Vijayanagar, the city's **royal monuments**, lie some 3km south of Hampi Bazaar, with a couple of interesting monuments en-route. The first of these, a walled **Krishna temple complex** to the west of the road, dates from 1513. Although dilapidated in parts, it features some fine carving and shrines. Hampi's most photographed monument stands just south of the Krishna temple in its own enclosure. Depicting Vishnu in his incarnation (*avatar*) as the Man-Lion, the monolithic **Narashima** statue, with its bulging eyes and crossed legs strapped into yogic pose, is one of Vijayanagar's greatest treasures.

Further south in the royal enclosure itself, surrounded by impressive **stone walls**, landmark monuments include the fifteen-metre-square **Queen's Bath**, where women from the royal household would bathe and relax in a beautiful pavilion, and the **Mahanavami-Dibba** or "House of Victory", a twelve-metre pyramidal structure built to commemorate a successful campaign in Orissa. From here the king watched the magnificent parades, music and dance performances, martial arts displays, elephant fights and animal sacrifices that celebrated the ten-day Dusshera festival famed throughout the land. Carved reliefs decorate the sides of the platform.

The two-storey **Lotus Mahal** (daily 8am–4pm; $5 [Rs10]; ticket also valid for the Vitthala temple on the same day), a little further north and part of the **zenana enclosure**, or women's quarters, was designed for the pleasure of Krishna Deva Raya's queen: a place where she could relax, particularly in summer. Displaying a strong Indo-Islamic influence, the pavilion is open on the ground floor, whereas the upper level (no longer accessible by stairs) contains windows and balcony seats. A moat surrounding the building is thought to have provided water-cooled air via tubes.

Beyond the Lotus Mahal, the **Elephant Stables**, a series of high-ceilinged, domed chambers entered through arches, are the most substantial surviving secular buildings at Vijayanagar – a reflection of the high status accorded to elephants, both in ceremonies and in battle.

Worth a look at the end of your tour of the royal enclosure is the small **Archeological Museum** (daily except Fri 10am–5pm; free) at Kamalapuram. Among the sculptures, weapons, palm-leaf manuscripts and painting from Vijayanagar and Anegondi, the highlight is a superb scale model of the city, giving an excellent bird's-eye view of the entire site.

Arrival and information

Buses from Hospet terminate close to where the road joins the main street in Hampi Bazaar, halfway along its dusty length. A little further towards the Virupaksha temple, the **tourist office** (daily except Fri 10am–5.30pm;

Ⓣ08394/241339) can put you in touch with a **guide** for Rs800 per day but not much else.

Rented **bicycles** are available from stalls near the lodges (Rs10/hr, Rs40–50/day). Pedal bikes can be hard work on the bumpy roads so consider a motorized two-wheeler. The Raju stall, round the corner from the tourist office, has **motorbikes** and **scooters** for hire (around Rs150/day). Sneha Travels, whose main office is at D131/11 Main St (daily 9am–9pm; Ⓣ08394/241590), can **change money** (albeit at lowish rates) and advance cash on credit cards. They can also book tickets for planes, trains and **sleeper coaches** to Goa and Gokarna, though you have to pick them up from Hospet (see p.213). Note, too, that whatever you are told, the Gokarna bus involves a transfer at Ankola in the wee hours. It's better to hop on one of three early-morning express trains from Hospet to Hubli (last one at 8am; 2hr), from where you can catch a bus to Gokarna (5.5hr) or nearby Ankola (4.5hr), saving both time and money.

Accommodation

Hampi Bazaar remains the best **place to stay** for access to the sites, choice of restaurants and other facilities. There are no fancy hotels but around forty guesthouses of varying size and calibre. Some travellers, especially Israelis, prefer to stay across the river in **Virupapuragadda**, which is fast developing and has caught up in price. Prices are pretty low most of the year apart from the Christmas to mid-February peak, when they at least double.

Hampi Bazaar

Archana Towards the river from village centre Ⓣ08394/241547, Ⓔaddihampi@yahoo.com. The best rooms here are in the river-facing block, which has shared balconies with swinging baskets and a roof terrace. ❷

Garden Paradise Far northeast end of village Ⓣ08394/652539. Five attached and seven non-attached huts in an excellent riverside location, with a chilled-out restaurant area. ❶

Gopi Centre of village Ⓣ08394/241695, Ⓔkirangopi2002@yahoo.com. One of the more established places, offering small, simple rooms, as well as free yoga classes to residents. ❶–❷

Hampi Boulders Narayanpet, Bandi Harlur Ⓣ08539/265939 or 9448/034202. Overlooking a bend in the Tungabhadra River, this small, quirky resort hotel is the best upscale option in the area – though you need a bit of a sense of adventure to enjoy it. Access is via coracle (water levels permitting) and 6-km trudge down a dusty lane, or else by a 30min (20km) car ride from Hampi Bazaar. Once you're there, the sense of isolation is complete. Accommodation comes in two grades of cottage, moulded around giant boulder outcrops, with palms, mango trees and brakes of bamboo for shade, and a lookout platform from which to savour the views. Service can be hit-and-miss (though it's always affable), and the meals are so-so Indian buffets, but for atmosphere and location *Hampi Boulders* can't be beaten; and they have a natural rock-cut swimming pool. Doubles from $110–220 (Rs5000–10,000). ❾

Kiran Beside the river Ⓣ08394/204159, Ⓔgowdakiran96@yahoo.co.in. The basic rooms here are compact but clean enough, and there are fine views of the river and temple from its rooftop restaurant. ❶

Shanti Guest House Just north of the Virupaksha temple Ⓣ08394/241568. This is a real favourite, comprising a dozen or so twin-bedded rooms arranged on two storeys around a leafy inner courtyard. It's basic (showers and toilets are shared) but spotless, and all rooms have fans and windows. ❶

Sudha Northeast end of village Ⓣ94810/42336. One of the nicest, friendliest places to stay. The rooms have been renovated and some of the new ones are spacious for Hampi. Plus there's a Tibetan restaurant on the roof. ❶–❸

Vicky's 100m north of tourist office Ⓣ08394/241694. Small clean rooms, some attached. Friendly, and popular for its rooftop restaurant. ❷

Across the river

Goan Corner 500m inland and east of boat crossing, Virupapuragadda Ⓣ09448/718951. Large complex set amid paddy fields and rocks with a range of rooms and huts, some attached bathrooms, and lively restaurant. ❶–❷

 **Mowgli** Far west end of main road, Virupapuragadda ⓣ08394/329844, ⓔhampimowgli@hotmail.com. A range of rooms with comfy sitouts and private balconies, some boasting fantastic views, as well as a welcoming restaurant, set against a gorgeous paddy and river backdrop. The best value place in Viru – so book ahead. ❶–❹

Sai Plaza Virupapuragadda ⓣ08533/287017, ⓔsantoshgvt@yahoo.com. These fifteen bungalows enclosing an attractive courtyard garden are relaxed and welcoming. The restaurant has delicious lassis and sandwiches, and excellent views across the river. ❶

Sunny Virupapuragadda ⓣ08533/287005. Nicely landscaped gardens with brightly painted bungalows and a row of compact rooms. The *Sheesh Besh* restaurant is a popular hangout. ❶–❷

Umashankar Lodge Virupapuragadda ⓣ08533/287067. Cosy, popular spot with small but clean attached rooms – the upstairs ones rather overpriced – and set round a leafy courtyard. ❶–❷

Eating

Hampi has a plethora of traveller-oriented **restaurants**. Many of the most popular are attached to guesthouses in the Bazaar or Virupapuragadda. As a holy site, the whole village is supposed to be strictly vegetarian and alcohol-free but one or two places bend the rules. There are no such restrictions on the other side of the river.

Laughing Buddha Virupapuragadda. Good for meat dishes such as schnitzel and has a generally relaxed atmosphere. Films shown every evening.

Mango Tree 300m beyond sacred ford. Wonderfully relaxed riverside hangout on a series of stone terraces, though it can be plagued by flies during the day.

New Shanti On the path from Virupaksha temple down to the river. Best known for its delicious cakes and breads but also does standard Indian and Continental dishes.

Ravi's Rose East end of Main Bazaar. Small rooftop joint specializing in traveller-friendly food, though they can do spicier dishes to order. Good sound system and lassis.

Shiv Moon Riverside path, east of the Main Bazaar. A pleasant place to break the journey to or from the Vitthala temple, serving pastas and standard curries.

Sri Sangameshwar Main Bazaar. One of the more genuine Indian places, where you can get the best thalis and masala dosas, as well as the odd Western snack.

Suresh On the path from Virupaksha temple down to the river. Established joint which specializes in tuna, Goan dishes and *momos* (Tibetan dumplings).

Trishul On the lane down from the tourist office. Offers one of Hampi's widest menus, featuring chicken, tuna, lasagne, pizza and desserts such as scrumptious apple crumble. Beer also occasionally available.

Jog Falls

Hidden in a remote, thickly forested corner of the Western Ghats, **Jog Falls**, 240km northeast of Mangalore, are the highest **waterfalls** in India. These days, however, they are rarely as spectacular as they were before the construction of a large dam upriver, which impedes the flow of the River Sharavati over the sheer red-brown sandstone cliffs. Still, the surrounding scenery is gorgeous, with dense scrub and jungle carpeting sparsely populated, mountainous terrain. The views of the falls from the opposite side of the gorge are also impressive, unless, that is, you come here during the monsoons, when mist and rain clouds envelop the cascades. Another reason not to come here during the wet season is that the extra water and abundance of leeches at this time make the otherwise excellent **hike** to the valley floor a trial; if you can, head up here between October and January. The trail starts just below the bus park and winds steeply down to the water, where you can enjoy a refreshing dip. The whole patch opposite the falls has been landscaped, with its own impressive entrance gate and attractively designed reception centre.

Practicalities

Buses from Panjim run to Jog across the Ghats via the recently constructed NH-206 to **Honavar** (4–6 daily; 2hr 30min). The **tourist office** (Mon–Sat

10am–1.30pm & 2.30–5.30pm), upstairs at the new reception centre, opens rather erratically but can supply information on transport and vehicle rental.

Accommodation in the settlement is limited and largely a KSTDC monopoly (ⓣ08186/244732); it runs the ugly concrete *Mayura Sharavathi* (❸), whose vast rooms are old-fashioned but comfortable with good views, and the humbler *Tunga Tourist Home* nearer the reception centre, with basic attached doubles (❷) and a Rs100 dorm. On the opposite side of the road the Karnataka Power Corporation also lets out four comfy air-conditioned rooms (ⓣ08186/244742; ❹) when available, as does the Shimoga District PWD *Inspection Bungalow* (ⓣ08186/244333; ❸), whose air-conditioned rooms are nicely situated on a hillock about 400m west. The youth hostel (ⓣ08186/244251; ❶), ten minutes' walk down the Shimoga road, is very basic and tatty.

Apart from the KSTDC *Mayura* canteen next to the *Tunga Tourist Home*, which offers the usual adequate but uninspiring fare, the only other **food** options are at the enclave of small chai stalls and shops that have been relocated to the reception centre – *Hotel Rashmita* is the best of the bunch.

Gokarna

Among India's most scenically situated pilgrimage sites, **GOKARNA** (Gokarn) lies between a broad white-sand beach and the verdant foothills of the Western Ghats, six hours north of Mangalore by bus. This compact little coastal town – a Shaivite centre for more than two millennia – remained largely "undiscovered" by Western tourists until the early 1990s, when it began to attract dreadlocked and didgeridoo-toting neo-hippies fleeing the commercialization of Goa. Though now firmly on the tourist map, the town offers a more vivid taste of Hindu India than anywhere else in the region: shaven-headed Brahmins sit crosslegged on their verandas murmuring Sanskrit verses, while pilgrims (who still far outnumber the foreigners) file through a bazaar crammed with religious paraphernalia to the sea for a holy dip.

Arrival and information

From Goa, the fastest and most convenient way to travel down the coast to Gokarna is via the **Konkan Railway**. At 2.25pm, train #KR1 Dn leaves Margao, passing through Chaudi (listed as "Canacona" on timetables) at 3.05pm en route to Gokarna, where it arrives around an hour and a half later. The station lies 9km east of Gokarna town itself, but a minibus (Rs60 per head) and a couple of beaten-up taxis (Rs300–400) are on hand to shuttle tourists into town. The locals walk 1km to the main road and wait for regular buses (Rs5) there. Heading back to Goa, #KR2 Up departs at 10.22am, arriving in Chaudi (Canacona) at 11.34am and Margao at 1pm. As this is classed as a passenger service, you don't have to buy tickets in advance; just turn up at the station fifteen to thirty minutes before the departure time and pay at the regular ticket counter. However, it is always a good idea to check timings in advance, through any tourist office, travel agent or the KRC's website (ⓦwww.konkanrailway.com).

Buses take as much as two and a half hours longer to cover the same route. Catch any of the services that run between Goa and Mangalore, and jump off either at Ankola, or at the Gokarna junction on the main highway, from where frequent private minibuses and *tempos* run into town. Alternatively, a direct service leaves Margao's interstate stand in the north of town daily at 1pm. If you're planning to travel here **from Hampi**, it's worth knowing that, in addition to a daily government bus, Paulo Travels operates a night service (see p.214). However, it'll drop

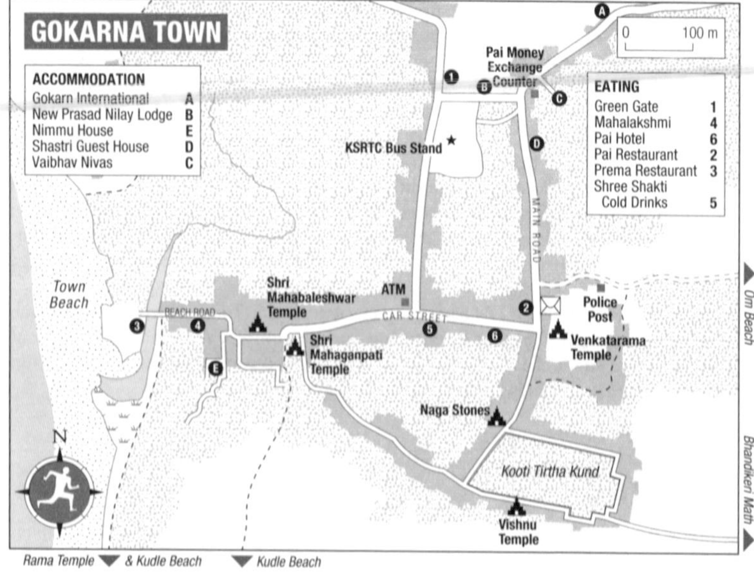

you in Ankola in the middle of the night, leaving you to the rickshaws. The KSRTC **bus stand** is 300m from Car Street and within easy walking distance of Gokarna's limited accommodation.

You can **change money** at the *Om Hotel* near the bus stand but the best rates to be had are at the Pai STD booth on the road into town near the bus stand, one of several licensed dealers. There are a couple of ATMs, including Karnataka Bank's, opposite the bus stand. **Joya Tours and Travels**, behind the bus stand and opposite *Ram Dev Lodge*, will book **train tickets** and **provide cash** on MasterCard and Visa for a two-percent fee. Numerous **internet** places (all Rs40/hr) are dotted along Car Street and even on the beaches. **Bicycles** are available for rent from a stall next to the *Pai Restaurant*, for Rs5 per hour or Rs50 for a full day. Auto-rickshaws and taxis cost Rs100–150 to Om Beach. The **post office** is at the east end of Car Street, above a small produce market. Just east of the beach, a small, well-stocked **bookstore**, Sri Radhakrisna, contains good Indian, spiritual and fiction sections. If you need a **doctor**, English-speaking Dr Shastri (ⓣ08386/256220) is highly recommended by long-stay visitors.

Accommodation

Gokarna town has a couple of bona fide **hotels** and some simple **guesthouses** – none of them approaching Goan standards of cleanliness and comfort, but adequate for a night or two. After staying in the village for a couple of days, however, many visitors strike out for the **beaches** where – in addition to the new **luxury resorts** – there are dozens of rough-and-ready hut camps

Gokarn International On the main road into town ⓣ08386/256622, ⓔhotelgokarn@yahoo.com. Popular mid-scale place in a four-storey block on the edge of town, offering a good-value range, from no-frills singles to deluxe, carpeted a/c doubles. The better ones have balconies overlooking the palm tops. Restaurant and bar on the premises. ❷–❹

Gokarn International Beach Resort Kudle Beach ⓣ08386/257843, ⓔhotelgokarn@yahoo.com. Set back from the sands in its own small garden, this compact, modern hotel offers comfortable mid-price rooms with small kitchenettes and verandas, some of them sea-facing. ❹

Namaste Northwest end of Om Beach ⓣ08386/257141. One of the more popular beach options, with well-built attached rooms. Each has a different theme: in one, everything is round (including the bed); another resembles a rustic log cabin. Phone and internet connection on site, along with a pleasant, shaded restaurant. ❷–❸

New Prasad Nilay Lodge On lane near the KSRTC bus stand ⓣ08386/257135. Very clean budget place with helpful management. The pricier rooms have cable TV and balconies. ❶–❷

Nimmu House Gokarna town, just south of main road, towards Kudle beach ⓣ08386/256730, ⓔnimmuhouse@yahoo.com. The foreign backpackers' favourite: double rooms in the attractive modern block are well maintained and have decent mattresses, but avoid the grungier old wing. Many upper rooms have balconies with fine beach and sea views and there's a peaceful yard to sit in. ❶–❹

Om Beach Resort 1.5km east of town ⓣ0944/857 9395, ⓦwww.ombeachresorts.com. Despite the name, this campus of a dozen colonial-style chalets is actually near Gokarna town – high on a sun-blasted hilltop, a good 45min (shadeless) walk to the beaches. It was conceived primarily as an ayurvedic health spa, so there are qualified doctors on site, along with acclaimed Keralan masseurs. Rates from $100–150 (Rs4600–7000) per night (full board); details of spa packages appear on their website. ❼

Seabird Resort 1.5km east of town, just across the road from the *Om Beach Resort* ⓣ08386/257689. Marooned high up on the hilltop above Gokarna town, but a good-value option, with choice of modern a/c or non a/c, all opening onto private sitouts. The views over the scrubby slopes are great and there's a multi-cuisine restaurant and small pool. ❻

Shastri Guest House 100m east of the bus stand ⓣ08386/256220, ⓔshastriguesthouse@gmail.com. Tucked behind the Shastri Clinic on the main road, this quiet place offers some attached rooms and rock-bottom single rates. Only Rs50 more in high season. ❶

SwaSwara Above Om beach ⓣ0484/301 1711, ⓦwww.swaswara.com. The first luxury resort in Gokarna, offering beautifully designed wooden villas spread over terraces on a hillside overlooking the bay. There's a pool, yoga dome and an ayurvedic treatment centre, all set in extensive gardens. Minimum five-day stay, all-inclusive packages cost €1680 per villa. ❾

Vaibhav Nivas Off the main road, less than five minutes from the bus stand ⓣ08386/256714. Friendly, cheap and deservedly popular guest-house pitched at foreigners, with a rooftop café-restaurant; all rooms are attached. ❶

The Town

Gokarna **town**, a hotchpotch of wood-fronted houses and red terracotta roofs, is clustered around a long L-shaped bazaar, its broad main road – known as **Car Street** – running west to the town beach, a sacred site in its own right. Hindu mythology identifies it as the place where Rudra (another name for Shiva) was reborn through the ear of a cow from the underworld after a period of penance. Gokarna is also the home of one of India's most powerful *Shivalingams* – the **pranalingam** – which came to rest here after being carried off by Ravana, the evil king of Lanka, from Shiva's home on Mount Kailash in the Himalayas.

The *pranalingam* resides in Gokarna to this day, enshrined in the medieval **Shri Mahabaleshwar temple**, at the far west end of the bazaar. It is regarded as so auspicious that a mere glimpse of it will absolve a hundred sins, even the murder of a Brahmin priest. Local Hindu lore also asserts that you can maximize the *lingam*'s purifying power by shaving your head, fasting and taking a holy dip in the sea before *darshan*, or ritual viewing of the deity. For this reason, pilgrims traditionally begin their tour of Gokarna with a walk to the beach, guided by their family *pujari*. Next, they visit the **Shri Mahaganpati temple**, a stone's throw east of Shri Mahabaleshwar, to propitiate the elephant-headed god Ganesh. Between the two, check out the splendid **rath**, or chariot, that stands at the end of the bazaar next to the Mahaganpati temple. During important festivals, notably Shiva's "birthday", **Shivratri** (Feb), deities are installed inside this colossal carved-wood cart and hauled by hand along Car Street, accompanied by

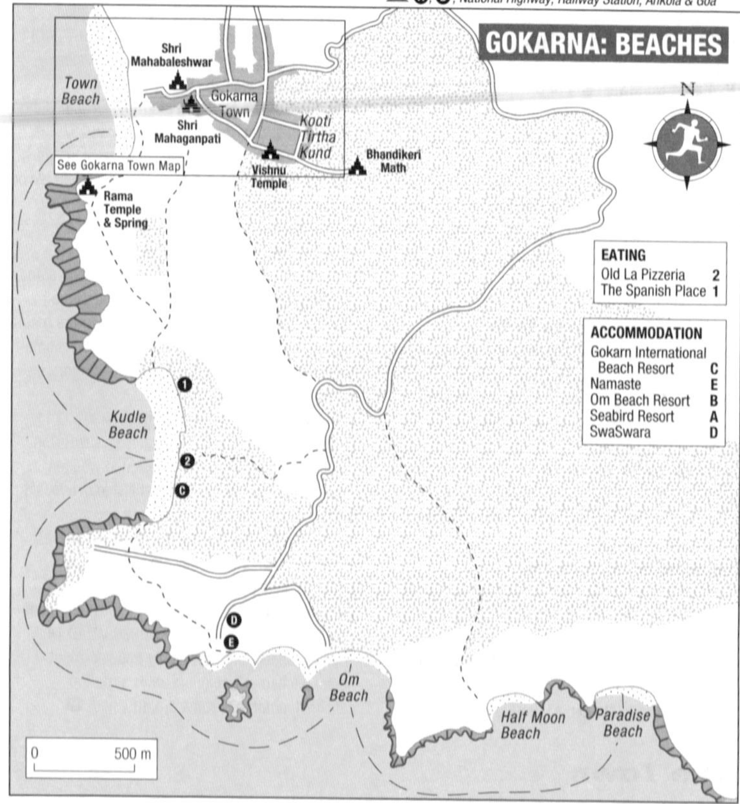

drum bands and watched by huge crowds. Sadly, owing to some insensitive behaviour by a minority of foreigners (Israeli girls dressed in party clothes), tourists are now banned from the Mahabaleshwar temple, though you can usually visit the Mahaganpati.

East of Car Street and the bazaar, **Kooti Tirtha Kund** is a large, rectangular water tank surrounded by sacred *ghats* where pilgrims perform ritual ablutions. It is believed to have been created by Vishnu's mount, the winged gryphon, Garuda. Vishnu performed penance here after he'd vanquished the thousand-armed demon Banasura. Early in the morning, pilgrims come to the tank to bathe, wash their clothes and carry out funerary rituals for recently deceased relatives, consigning sandalwood ash and *pinda* (balls of barley, ghee and coconut) to the water. On the south side of the tank, a white-painted temple is the most important *vaishnava* shrine in Gokarna, and a prominent call on the pilgrims' circuit. Also worth a look is the collection of carved *naga* (snake) worship stones stacked under the peepal tree on the opposite, northwestern corner of Kooti Tirtha. Liberally dusted with turmeric powder and red *kum kum*, ancient cobra deities such as these are a common feature of popular South Indian worship, and are associated with female ritual activities.

The beaches

Notwithstanding Gokarna's numerous temples, shrines and tanks, most Western tourists come here for the beautiful **beaches** situated south of the more crowded town beach, beyond the lumpy laterite headland that overlooks the town. You can reach them either on foot, or by jumping in one of the fishing boats that leave periodically through the day from the main town beach – prices range from Rs50 to 150 per head, depending on the number of passengers and how well you can haggle.

To pick up the footpath, head along the narrow alley opposite the south entrance to the Mahaganpati temple, and follow the path uphill from the south end of the town beach, past the Rama temple and spring. After twenty minutes, you drop down from a rocky plateau to **Kudle beach** – a wonderful kilometre-long sweep of golden-white sand sheltered by a pair of steep-sided promontories. The palm-leaf chai stalls and seasonal **cafés** that spring up here during the winter offer some respite from the heat of the midday sun, and very basic **accommodation** in bamboo shacks.

It takes around twenty minutes to hike over the headland from Kudle to the exquisite **Om beach**, so named because its distinctive twin crescent-shaped bays resemble the auspicious Om symbol. The advent of a dirt road from town means the coves are now frequented by a more diverse crowd than the hard-core hippy fringe whose exclusive preserve it used to be. For the time being, hammocks, palm-leaf huts and chai stalls still dominate the palm groves behind, though they're fast being overshadowed by the luxury "eco" resorts sprouting on the hillsides above. Set up to emulate Keralan-style Ayurveda spas, these places compete for the custom of wealthy health-conscious tourists with their Panchakarma clinics, yoga *shalas* and obligatory thatched roofs (hiding decidedly un-eco-friendly constructions).

It's unlikely the concrete mixers will – at least in the next few years – reach Gokarna's two most remote beaches, which lie another twenty- to forty-minute walk over the hill. **Half Moon** and **Paradise** beaches are, despite the presence of one or two simple bamboo-hut guesthouses and cafés, mainly for intrepid sun-lovers happy to pack their own supplies. If you're looking for near-total isolation, these are your best bet.

Eating

Gokarna town offers a good choice of **places to eat**, with a string of busy joints along Car Street and the main road. Look out for the local sweet speciality *gadbad* – several layers of different ice creams mixed with chopped nuts and chewy dried fruit.

There are also plenty of simple shack cafés out on the beaches, serving the usual traveller-oriented grub. Be warned, however, that these places may not apply the same standards of hygiene as do Goan shacks – incidents of food poisoning are all too common among foreigners staying at the leaf huts on the beaches.

Green Gate *Om Hotel*, near the KRSTC bus stand. The *Om Hotel*'s pleasant upstairs courtyard restaurant offers a range of Mexican, Italian and Israeli dishes, as well as fish and sizzlers. The snack bar downstairs is a male-dominated, dimly lit drinking den, though it serves spicy chicken tikka and other north-Indian-style non-veg food. Most mains Rs150.

Mahalakshmi Beach road. Delicious, carefully prepared veg food – Indian, Western and Chinese – served on a snug rooftop terrace close to the beach. Long waits, but the cooking's worth it. Try their marvellous home-made pesto and pasta, or creamy *malai kofta* (spicy vegetable dumplings steeped in rich gravy). Most mains under Rs150.

Old La Pizzeria Kudle Beach. A few tables on the sand and a cosy atmosphere within make this one of the better beach dining spots. Most people come for the wood-baked pizzas (Rs100–120) but they do a range of other Italian specialities and health foods, as well as generous portions of standard traveller-oriented food.

Pai Hotel Car St. A favourite meeting spot for travellers, this tiny joint has excellent, inexpensive veg snacks and delicious milky coffee.

Pai Restaurant Main Rd. Topnotch local *udipi* place close to the market. Its filling rice-and-veg thalis, served daily from 11.30am, are the best budget meals in Gokarna, and they do crispy masala dosas, *iddli-wada-sambar,* teas and coffees at all hours. Open until late.

Prema Restaurant Near the beach end of Car St. Standard traveller-friendly menu of pasta, superb toasted English muffin sandwiches, and the biggest *gadbad* in town.

Shree Shakti Cold Drinks Car St. Tasty home-made peanut butter and fresh cheese, both made to American recipes, the latter served with rolls, garlic and tomato. Also available are filling toasties, ice cream and creamy lassis.

The Spanish Place North-central Kudle Beach. Good pasta, sandwiches, sweets and creamy lassis in a relaxed atmosphere.

Mumbai

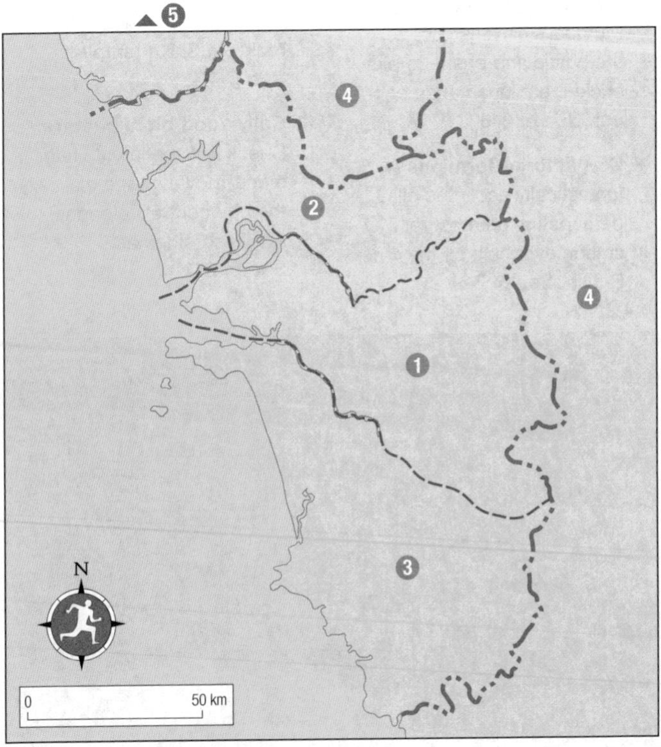

CHAPTER 5

Highlights

* **The Gateway of India** Mumbai's defining landmark, and a favourite spot for an evening stroll. See p.242
* **Chhatrapati Shivaji Museum** A fine collection of priceless Indian art, from ancient temple sculpture to Mughal armour. See p. 245
* **Maidans (parks)** Where Mumbai's citizens escape the hustle and bustle to play cricket, eat lunch and hang out. See p. 246
* **CS (Victoria) Terminus** A fantastically eccentric pile, perhaps the greatest railway station ever built by the British. See p. 249
* **Haji Ali's Tomb** Mingle with the crowds of Muslim worshippers who flock to the island tomb of Sufi mystic Haji Ali to listen to *qawwali* music on Thursday evenings. See p. 251
* **Elephanta Island** Catch a boat across Mumbai harbour to see one of ancient India's most wonderful rock-cut Shiva temples. See p. 253
* **Bollywood blockbusters** Check out the latest Hindi mega-movie in one of the city centre's gigantic Art-Deco cinemas. See p. 257

▲ CS (Victoria) Terminus

5

Mumbai

Ever since the opening of the Suez Canal in 1869, the principal gateway to the Indian subcontinent has been **MUMBAI (Bombay)**, the city Aldous Huxley famously described as "the most appalling… of either hemisphere". Travellers tend to regard time spent here as a rite of passage to be survived rather than savoured. But as the powerhouse of Indian business, industry and trade, and the source of its most seductive media images, the Maharashtran capital can be a compelling place to kill time. Whether or not you find the experience enjoyable, however, will depend largely on how well you handle the heat, humidity, hassle, traffic fumes and relentless crowds of India's most dynamic, Westernized city.

First impressions of Mumbai tend to be dominated by its chronic **shortage of space**. Crammed onto a narrow spit of land that curls from the swamp-ridden coast into the Arabian Sea, the city is technically an island, connected to the mainland by bridges and narrow causeways. In less than five hundred years, it has metamorphosed from an aboriginal fishing settlement into a megalopolis of over sixteen million people – one of the biggest urban sprawls on the planet. Being swept along broad boulevards by endless streams of commuters, or jostled by coolies and hand-cart pullers in the teeming bazaars, you'll continually feel as if Mumbai is about to burst at the seams.

The roots of the population problem and attendant poverty lie, paradoxically, in the city's enduring ability to create **wealth**. Mumbai alone generates one third of India's tax income, its port handles half the country's foreign trade, and its movie industry is the biggest in the world. Symbols of prosperity are everywhere: from the phalanx of office blocks clustered on Nariman Point, Maharashtra's Manhattan, to the expensively dressed teenagers posing in Colaba's trendiest nightspots.

The flip side to the success story is the city's much-chronicled **poverty**. Each day, an estimated five hundred economic refugees pour into Mumbai from the Maharashtran hinterland. Some find jobs and secure accommodation; many more end up living on the already overcrowded streets, or amid the squalor of some of Asia's largest slums, reduced to rag-picking and begging from cars at traffic lights.

However, while it would definitely be misleading to downplay its difficulties, Mumbai is far from the ordeal some travellers make it out to be. Once you've overcome the major hurdle of finding somewhere to stay, you may begin to enjoy its frenzied pace and crowded, cosmopolitan feel.

Some history

Mumbai originally consisted of seven **islands**, inhabited by small Koli fishing communities. In 1534, Sultan Bahadur of Ahmedabad ceded the land to the **Portuguese**, who subsequently handed it on to the English in 1661 as part of the Portuguese Infanta Catherine of Braganza's dowry for her marriage to Charles II.

Mumbai or Bombay?

In 1996, Bombay was renamed **Mumbai**, as part of a wider policy instigated by the right-wing Maharashtran nationalist Shiv Sena Municipality to replace names of any places, roads and features in the city that had connotations of the Raj. The Shiv Sena asserted that the British term "Bombay" derived from the Marathi title of a local deity, the mouthless "Maha-amba-aiee" (Mumba Devi for short). In fact, historians are unanimously agreed that the Portuguese, who dubbed the harbour "Bom Bahia" ("Good Bay") when they first came across it, were responsible for christening the site and that the later British moniker had nothing to do with the aboriginal Hindu earth goddess.

The name change was widely unpopular when it was first imposed, especially among the upper and middle classes, and non-Maharashtran immigrant communities, who doggedly stuck to Bombay. Some fifteen years on, however, "Mumbai" (and "Mumbaikars", referring to the city's inhabitants) seems to have definitively taken root with the dotcom generation and even outgrown the narrow agenda of its nationalist originators – just as "Bombay" outlived the Raj.

Bombay's safe harbour and strategic commercial position attracted the interest of the **East India Company**, based at nearby Surat, and in 1668 a deal was struck whereby they leased Bombay from Charles for a pittance.

Life for the English was not easy, however: "fluxes" (dysentery), "Chinese death" (cholera) and other diseases culled many of the first settlers, prompting the colony's chaplain to declare that "two monsoons are the age of a man". Nevertheless, the city established itself as the capital of the flourishing East India Company, attracting a diverse mix of settlers including Goans, Gujarati traders, Muslim weavers and the business-minded Zoroastrian Parsis. The cotton crisis in America following the Civil War fuelled the great Bombay **cotton boom** and established the city as a major industrial and commercial centre, while the opening of the Suez Canal in 1869 and the construction of enormous docks further improved Bombay's access to European markets and ushered in an age of mercantile self-confidence embodied by the grandiloquent colonial-Gothic buildings constructed during the governership of **Sir Bartle Frere** (1862–67).

As the most prosperous city in the nation, Bombay was at the forefront of the **Independence** struggle; Mahatma Gandhi used a house here, now a museum, to co-ordinate the struggle through three decades. Since Independence (in 1948), Mumbai has prospered as India's commercial capital and the population has grown tenfold, to more than sixteen million, although the modern city has also been plagued by a deadly mixture of **communal infighting** and outside **terrorist attacks**. Tensions due to the increasing numbers of immigrants from other parts of the country, and the resultant overcrowding, have fuelled the rise of the extreme right-wing Maharashtran party, the **Shiv Sena**, founded in 1966 by Bal Thackery, a self-confessed admirer of Hitler. Thousands of Muslim Mumbaikars were murdered by Hindu mobs following the destruction of the Babri Masjid in Ayodhya in 1992–93, while in March 1993, ten massive retaliatory **bomb blasts** killed 260 people. The involvement of Muslim godfather Dawood Ibrahim and the Pakistani secret service was suspected, and both Ibrahim and the Pakistanis have been linked with subsequent atrocities. These include the bomb blasts in August 2003, which killed 107 tourists next to the Gateway of India; the subsequent explosions in July 2006, when coordinated bomb blasts simultaneously blew apart seven packed commuter trains across the city; and, most dramatically, the horrific attacks of **November 26, 2008**, during which a group of rampaging gunmen ran amok across the city, killing 172 people.

Despite these setbacks, Mumbai has prospered like nowhere else in India as a result of the country's ongoing **economic liberalization**. Following decades of stagnation, the textiles industry has been supplanted by rapidly growing IT, finance, healthcare and back-office support sectors. Whole suburbs have sprung up to accommodate the affluent new middle-class workforce, with shiny shopping malls and car showrooms to relieve them of their income. Even so, corruption in politics and business has drained away investment from socially deprived areas. Luxury apartments in Bandra may change hands for half a million dollars or more, but an estimated seven to eight million people (just under fifty percent of Mumbai's population) live in slums with no toilets, on just six percent of the land.

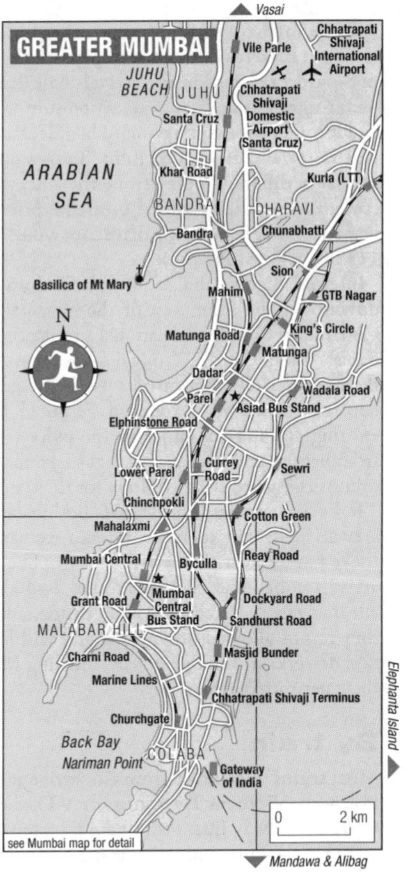

Arrival and information

Unless you arrive in Mumbai by train at **Chhatrapati Shivaji Terminus** (formerly Victoria Terminus), be prepared for a long slog into the centre. The international and domestic **airports** are way north of the city, and ninety minutes or more by road from the main hotel areas, while from **Mumbai Central** railway or **bus station**, you face a laborious trip across town.

By air

Mumbai's busy **international airport**, **Chhatrapati Shivaji** (30km north; Ⓦwww.csia.in), is divided into two terminals, one for Air India flights (terminal 2C) and the other for foreign airlines (terminal 2B). All of the domestic airlines also have offices outside the main entrance. The arrivals concourse houses a 24-hour State Bank of India exchange facility and ATM, India Tourism and MTDC tourist information counters and car rental kiosks, while a handy 24-hour **left luggage** "cloakroom" is located in the car park nearby. There's also an **Indian Railways booking office** (terminal 2B; daily 8am–1pm & 2–8pm) – very useful if you know your onward destination, since it could save you a long wait at the reservation offices downtown. If you're on one of the few flights to land in the afternoon or early evening – by which time most hotels tend to be full – it can be worth paying on the spot for a room at the **accommodation booking desk** in the arrivals hall. All of the domestic airlines have offices outside the main entrance.

While many of the more upmarket hotels, particularly those near the airport, send out **courtesy coaches** to pick up their guests, most people make use of the **pre-paid taxi** desk in the arrivals hall. Fares are slightly higher than the normal meter rate, but at least you can be sure you'll be taken by the most direct route and it might save you having to haggle. Fares are Rs355 (or Rs455 a/c) to Colaba, Rs165 (or Rs210 a/c) to Juhu. Taxi-wallahs sometimes try to persuade you to stay at a different hotel from the one you ask for. Don't agree to this; their commission will be added onto the price of your room. Alternatively, if you want to book a car with driver for your arrival, try RNK Travels (Ⓣ022/2437 1112, Ⓦwww.rnk.com)

Internal flights land at Mumbai's **domestic airport** (26km to the north of downtown and 2km west of the international airport); technically this is part of Chhatrapati Shivaji international airport, though it's still widely referred to by its old name, "Santa Cruz". Terminal 1A handles Air India, Indian Airlines and Kingfisher flights, while all other carriers use Terminal 1B. "Note that if you're taking a flight departing from newly opened Terminal 1C, you'll still have to check in at the existing counters in either of the older terminals". If you're transferring directly from here to an international flight take the free "fly-bus" that shuttles every fifteen minutes between the two; look for the transfer counter in your transit lounge.

India Tourism and the MTDC both have 24-hour **information counters** in the arrivals hall, and there's a foreign exchange counter and accommodation desk tucked away near the first-floor exit. The official "Pre-Paid" taxi counter on the arrivals concourse charges around Rs400 to Colaba. Don't be tempted by the cheaper fares offered by touts outside, and avoid **auto-rickshaws** altogether, as they're not allowed downtown and will leave you at the mercy of unscrupulous taxi drivers on the edge of vile-smelling Mahim Creek, the southernmost limit of their permitted area.

By train

Most trains to Mumbai from Goa arrive at **Chhatrapati Shivaji Terminus** or **CST** (formerly **Victoria Terminus**, or **VT**), the main railway station at the end of the Central Railway line. From here it's a ten- or fifteen-minute ride to Colaba; taxis queue at the busy rank outside the south exit, opposite the new reservation hall.

Some trains from Goa arrive at more obscure stations. If you find yourself at **Dadar** or, worse, still, **Kurla** station, just south of the domestic airport, jump in a cab rather than trying to cram into either a suburban train or bus.

By bus

Nearly all interstate **buses, including services from Goa,** arrive at **Mumbai Central Bus Stand**, a stone's throw from the railway station of the same name. Government services use the main Maharashtra State Road Transport Corporation (MSRTC) stand itself; private ones operate from the roadside next to Mumbai Central railway station, two minutes' walk west on the opposite side of busy Dr AN Marg (Lamington Road). To get downtown, either catch a suburban train

Malaria warning

Due to the massive slum encampments and bodies of stagnant water around the **airports**, both the international and domestic terminals are major **malaria** black spots. Clouds of mosquitoes await your arrival in the car park, so don't forget to smother yourself with strong insect repellent before leaving the terminal.

from Mumbai Central's local platform, over the footbridge from the mainline, or take a cab at the rank in front of the station.

Information

The best source of **information** in Mumbai is the excellent **India Tourism** (Mon–Fri 9am–6pm, Sat 9am–2pm; ⓣ022/2207 4333 or 4334, ⓔindiatourism@mtnl.net.in) at 123 M Karve Rd, opposite Churchgate Station's east exit, with exceptionally helpful staff and lots of free maps and brochures.

For detailed **listings**, the most complete source is Mumbai's *Time Out* (ⓦwww.timeoutmumbai.net). Alternatively, check out the "Metro" page in the *Indian Express* or the "Bombay Times" section of the *Times of India*. All are available from street vendors around Colaba and downtown.

City transport and tours

Gridlock is the norm during peak hours, and you should brace yourself for long waits at junctions if you take to the roads by taxi, bus or auto. Local **trains** get there faster, but can be a real endurance test even outside rush hours.

Trains

Mumbai's local **trains** carry an estimated 6.1 million commuters each day between downtown and the sprawling suburbs in the north – half the entire passenger capacity of Indian Railways (see box, p.236). Services depart every few minutes from roughly 5am until midnight, stopping at dozens of small stations (for main routes, see map, p.233). Carriages remain packed solid virtually the whole time, with passengers dangling precariously out of open doors to escape the crush, so start to make your way to the exit at least three stops before your destination. Peak hours (approximately 8.30–10am & 4–7pm) are the worst of all. Women are marginally better off in the "ladies carriages"; look for the crowd of colourful saris and *salwar kameezes* grouped at the end of the platform.

Buses

BEST (ⓣ022/2285 6262, ⓦwww.bestundertaking.com) operates a **bus** network of labyrinthine complexity, covering every part of the city. You can check routes and bus numbers on their website; recognizing bus numbers in the street, however, can be more problematic, as numerals are written in Marathi (although in English on the sides). Aim, wherever possible, for the "Limited" ("Ltd") services, which stop less frequently, and avoid rush hours at all costs. Tickets are bought from the conductor on the bus.

Taxis and car rental

With rickshaws banished to the suburbs, Mumbai's ubiquitous black-and-yellow **taxis** are the quickest and most convenient way to nip around the city centre. In theory, all should have meters and a current "tariff card" (to convert the amount shown on the meter to the correct fare); in practice, particularly at night or early in the morning, many drivers refuse to use them. If this happens, either flag down another or haggle out a fare. As a rule of thumb, expect to be charged Rs10 per kilometre after the

Rail records

The suburban rail network in Mumbai is officially the busiest on the planet. No other line carries as many passengers, nor crams them into such confined spaces. At peak times, as many as 4700 people may be jammed into a nine-carriage train designed to carry 1700, resulting in what the rail company, in typically jaunty Mumbai style, refers to as "Super-Dense Crush Load" of 14–16 standing passengers per square metre. Not all of these actually occupy floor space, of course: ten percent will be dangling precariously out of the doors.

The busiest stretch, a sixty-kilometre segment between Churchgate terminus and Virar in north Mumbai, transports nearly 900 million people each year – that's 255 million passengers per kilometre, the highest of any rail network in the world. **Fatalities** are all too frequent: on average, 3500 die on the rail network annually, from falling out of the doors, crossing the tracks or because they're hit by overhead cables while riding on the roof.

The daily ordeal of commuting has its own distinct culture, with regulars forming life-long friendships that might never extend beyond the carriage. People look out for each other, sharing newspapers and saving seats for their "train friends" in the comfiest spots out of the sun. In *Maximum City*, Suketu Mehta describes how latecomers who are forced to sprint up the platform to catch their train will always find helping hands extended from the open doors, and space miraculously made where none existed before:

"And at the moment of contact, they do not know if the hand that is reaching for theirs belongs to a Hindu or Muslim or Christian or Brahmin or Untouchable or whether you were born in this city or arrived this morning or whether you live in Malabar Hill or Jogeshwari; whether you're from Bombay or Mumbai or New York. All they know is that you're trying to get to the city of gold, and that's enough. Come on board, they say. We'll adjust."

minimum fare of around Rs20, plus a small sum for heavy luggage (Rs5–10 per article). The latest addition to Mumbai's hectic roads is the **Cool Cab** (Ⓣ022/2216 4466, Ⓦwww.citycoolcab.in), blue taxis with air-conditioning and tinted windows; rates are around forty percent higher than in a normal cab.

Cars with drivers can be rented per eight-hour day (Rs1200–1500 for a non-a/c Ambassador, upwards of Rs1500 for more luxurious air-conditioned cars) through any good travel agent (see p.262).

Boats

Ferryboats regularly chug out of Mumbai harbour, connecting the city with the far shore and some of the larger islands in between. The most popular with visitors is the **Elephanta Island** launch (see p.253), which departs from the Gateway of India (see p.242), as do frequent boats to **Mandawa Jetty**, for Alibag, the transport hub for the rarely used **coastal route south**.

Tours

A number of operators around the Gateway of India offer whistlestop **one-day city tours** by bus (around Rs150, not including admission charges) – an inexpensive but usually very rushed way to cram Mumbai's tourist highlights into a single day. The MTDC runs one-hour **after-dark tours** on an open-top bus (weekends 7pm & 8.15pm; upper deck Rs120, lower deck Rs150) of Mumbai's illuminated landmarks. Tours are bookable at the MTDC kiosk near the Gateway, which is also where they leave from.

A more leisurely alternative, focusing mainly on period buildings and colonial history, is to go on one of the excellent guided walks organized by architects Abha Bahl and Brinda Gaitonde of **The Bombay Heritage Walks** (Ⓦwww.bombayheritagewalks.com). The two-hour walks (Rs1500 for up to three people; Rs500 per additional person) are offered mainly at weekends, though weekday evening walks can sometimes be arranged depending on availability. Advance bookings essential on Ⓣ022/2369 0992 or Ⓔinfo@bombayheritagewalks.com. Another possibility is **Mumbai Magic** (Ⓦwww.mumbaimagic.com), which offers a range of interesting walking and driving tours delving into various aspects of the city ranging from colonial architecture to Jewish heritage. Finally, **Reality Tours and Travels** runs compelling trips out to the huge Dharavi shantytown – see the box on p.252 for more details.

Accommodation

Finding **accommodation** at the right price when you arrive in Mumbai can be a real problem. Budget travellers, in particular, can expect a hard time finding decent but affordable accommodation. The best budget places tend to fill up by noon, which can often mean a long trudge in the heat with only an overpriced fleapit at the end of it, so you should really phone ahead as soon as (or preferably well before) you arrive. Prices in upmarket places are especially high for India; state-imposed "**luxury tax**" (currently ten percent), and "**service charges**" levied by the hotel itself further bump up bills; both add-ons are included in the price symbols used in the following reviews.

Colaba and Kala Ghoda

A short ride from the city's main commercial districts, railway stations and tourist office, **Colaba** makes a handy base, and is where the majority of foreign visitors head first. The streets around the Gateway of India are chock-full of accommodation, and the area also offers more in the way of food and entertainment than neighbouring districts. The hotels below are marked on the map of Colaba on p.244, except for the *Taj President*, which is shown on the map on pp.238–239.

Budget

Aga Bheg's & Hotel Kishan Ground, 2nd & 3rd floors, Shirin Manzil, Walton Rd Ⓣ022/2284 2227. Muslim-run pair of budget guesthouses on different floors of the same building. Rooms (some with a/c) are a bit shabby, although a passable fallback if you can't get into any of the places below. ❹–❺

Lawrence 3rd floor, 33 Shri Sai Baba Marg (Rope Walk Lane), off K Dubash Marg, behind *TGI's* Ⓣ022/2284 3618 or 6633 6107. Close to the Jehangir Art Gallery, this is arguably south Mumbai's best rock-bottom choice, with five well-scrubbed doubles (plus two singles and two triples) with fans, and not-so-clean shared shower-toilets; breakfast included. Advance booking essential. ❸

Red Shield Red Shield House, 30 B Behram Marg (Mereweather Rd), near the *Taj* Ⓣ022/2284 1824, Ⓔredshield@vsnl.net. Ultra-basic bunkbeds (Rs225) in cramped, stuffy dorms (lockers available), or larger good-value doubles (some with shared bath, some with a/c). Rates include breakfast and lunch, served in a sociable canteen. Maximum one-week stay. ❹

Sea Shore 4th floor, 1-49 Kamal Mansion, Arthur Bunder Rd Ⓣ022/2287 4237. Among the best budget deals in Colaba, although the sea-facing rooms with windows are much nicer than the airless cells on the other side, and baths are all common. Management is friendly and there's a free, safe baggage store. There are also slightly cheaper, wooden-partitioned rooms (shared bath only) at the less salubrious *India* (Ⓣ022/2283 3769; ❸) in the same building. ❸–❹

Mid-range

Ascot 38 Garden Rd Ⓣ022/6638 5566, Ⓦwww.ascothotel.com. One of the oldest and most comfortable small hotels in Mumbai, updated with

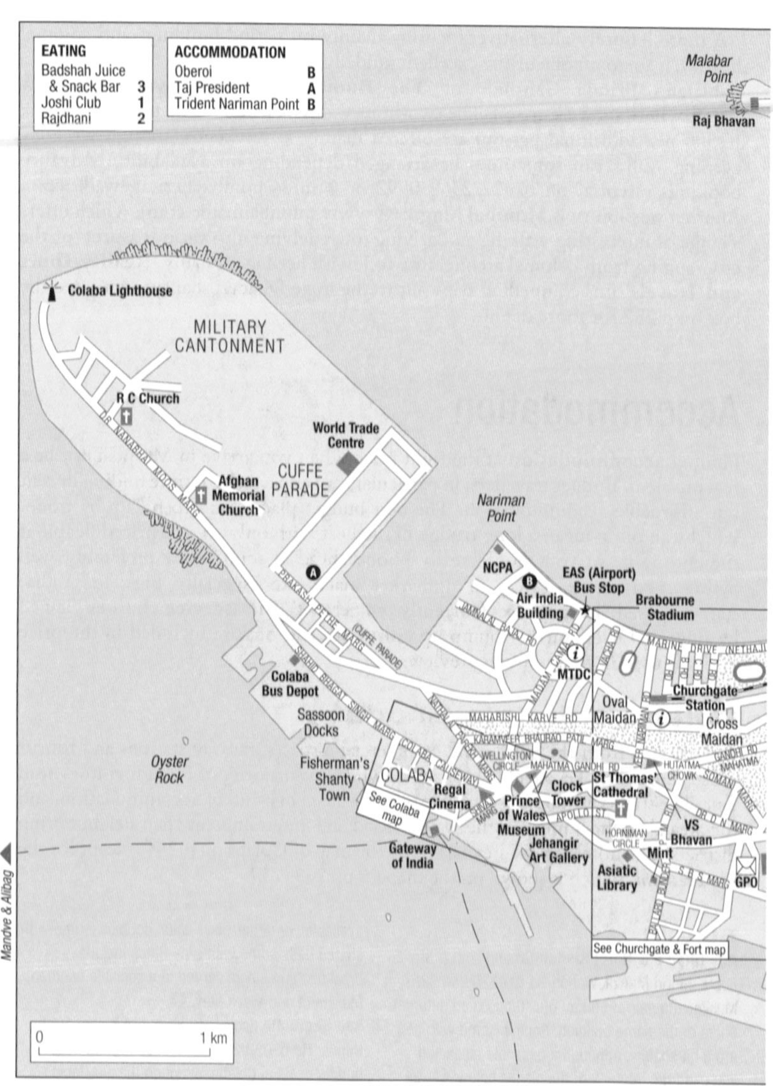

contemporary glass-and-marble designer interiors and spacious modern rooms. 8–9

Bentley's 17 Oliver Rd ⓣ022/2284 1474, ⓦwww.bentleyshotel.com. Dependable old Parsi-owned favourite in five different colonial tenements, all on leafy backstreets. Rooms (with optional a/c for Rs300 extra) are quiet, secure and spacious, if a little worn, though the overall shabbiness isn't compensated for by the rates, which are higher than you'd expect for the level of comfort. 6

Godwin Jasmine Building, 41 Garden Rd ⓣ022/2287 2050, ⓦwww.mumbainet.com/hotels/godwin. Top-class three-star with large, international-standard rooms and great views from upper floors (ask for #804, #805 or #806). 8

Moti International 10 Best Marg ⓣ022/2202 1654, ⓔhotelmotiinternational@yahoo.co.in. Quiet and friendly hotel in a characterful old colonial building. Rooms are cosy and clean, and all come with a/c, fridge and TV. Good value. 6

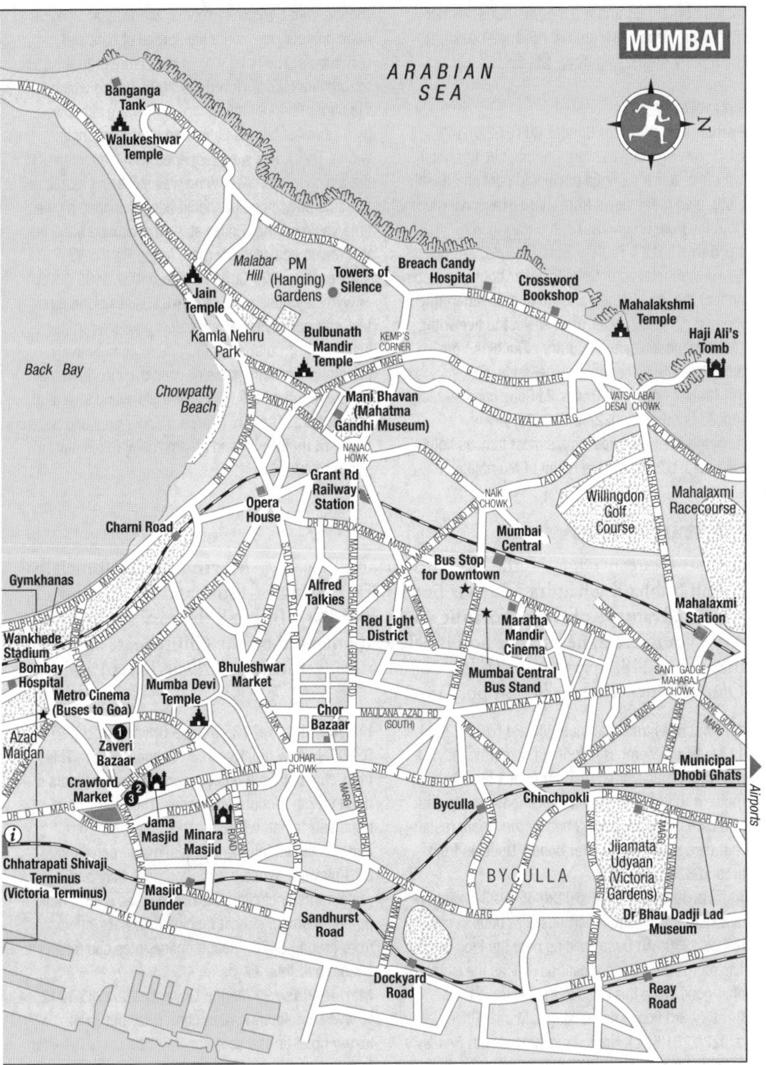

Sea Palace Kerawalla Chambers, 26 PJ Ramchandani Marg (Apollo Bunder) ⓣ022/2284 1828, ⓦwww.seapalacehotel.net. Comfortable, well-maintained hotel at the quiet end of the harbour front. All rooms are a/c but sea views cost extra. Breakfast and light meals are served on a sunny terrace at the front. ⑦–⑧

Strand PJ Ramachandani Marg (Apollo Bunder) ⓣ022/2288 2222, ⓦwww.hotelstrand.com. Deservedly popular mid-scale option on the seafront that's nicely situated and efficiently run. Rooms are old-fashioned but comfortable, with fine harbour views from the more expensive ones. *Hotel Harbour View* (ⓣ022/2282 1089, ⓦwww.viewhotelsinc.com; ⑦), on the top two floors of the same building, is very similar. ⑦

YWCA 18 Madam Cama Rd ⓣ022/2202 5053, ⓔywcaic@mtnl.net.in. Relaxing, secure and quiet hostel (open to men as well as women) with spotless attached rooms. Rates include breakfast and a generous buffet dinner – a bargain for south Mumbai. Advance booking (by money draft) obligatory. ❻–❼

Luxury

Fariyas 25, off Arthur Bunder Rd ⓣ022/6141 6141, ⓦwww.fariyas.com. Compact luxury hotel with five-star trimmings (including pool and health club), plus great views from more expensive rooms. Doubles from around Rs10,930 ($240). ❾

Gordon House 5 Battery St ⓣ022/2289 4400, ⓦwww.ghhotel.com. Chic designer boutique place behind the Regal cinema. Each floor is differently themed: "Scandinavian" (the easiest to live with), "Mediterranean" and "Country". Doubles from around $360; discounts at weekends. ❾

Taj Mahal Palace & Tower PJ Ramchandani Marg (Apollo Bunder) ⓣ022/6665 3366, ⓦwww.tajhotels.com. Perhaps India's most famous hotel (see map, p.244) and the haunt of Mumbai's *beau monde*, with 546 luxury rooms, shopping arcades, a huge outdoor pool and a big spread of bars and restaurants. The hotel was at the centre of the terrorist attacks of November 2008, during which the upper floors of the *Palace* wing were set ablaze by a series of bombs detonated by the terrorists within. The *Tower* wing reopened within a month of the attacks; the *Palace* wing was still being rebuilt at the time of writing but should have reopened by the time you read this. Prices start from around $250 in the *Tower*, considerably more in the *Palace*. ❾

Taj President 90 Cuffe Parade ⓣ022/6665 0808, ⓦwww.tajhotels.com. Modern, business-oriented five-star occupying a seventeen-floor skyscraper just south of Colaba. A much more competitively priced option than its sister concern, the *Taj Mahal Palace & Tower*, though lacking old-world style and atmosphere. There is a large outdoor pool and an adjacent multi-gym and steam room. Rates start at around $400. ❾

Marine Drive

At the western edge of the downtown area, swanky **Marine Drive** (officially Netaji Subhash Chandra Marg) is lined with a string of four- and five-star hotels taking advantage of the panoramic views over Back Bay and the easy access to the city's commercial heart. The hotels below are marked on the Churchgate and Fort map on p.248, apart from *Trident Nariman Point* (formerly *Hilton Towers*) and the *Oberoi*, which are marked on pp.238–239.

Ambassador Veer Nariman (VN) Rd ⓣ022/2204 1131, ⓦwww.ambassadorindia.com. Recently renovated four-star with smart (albeit bland) modern rooms and a choice location close to sea and cafes. The revolving *Pearl of the Orient* restaurant (see p.256) is another bonus. Doubles from around $260. ❾

Astoria Jamshedji Tata ⓣ022/6654 1234, ⓦwww.astoriamumbai.com. Smart business hotel in refurbished 1930s Art Deco building near the Eros cinema. The rooms are nowhere near as ritzy as the lobby but offer good value this close to the centre. ❽–❾

Bentley 3rd floor, Krishna Mahal, Marine Drive ⓣ022/2281 5244. Not to be confused with *Bentley's* in Colaba (see p.238), this small, friendly guesthouse is across town on the corner of D Rd/Marine Drive, near the cricket stadium. The marble-lined a/c rooms are clean and comfortable for the price, though most share shower-toilets. Rates (from Rs1650) include breakfast. ❺

Chateau Windsor 5th floor, 86 Veer Nariman (VN) Rd ⓣ022/6622 4455, ⓦwww.chateauwindsor.com. Impeccably neat and central, with unfailingly polite staff and a selection of attractively renovated modern rooms. Very popular, so reserve well in advance. ❼–❽

Intercontinental 135 Marine Drive ⓣ022/3987 9999, ⓦwww.mumbai.intercontinental.com. This ultra-chic boutique hotel is currently one of India's most stylish modern addresses. The rooms have huge sea-facing windows and state-of-the-art gadgets (including 42-inch plasma screens and DVD players), while the rooftop pool, bars and restaurants (including the *Dome* – see p.257) rank among Mumbai's most fashionable. Rack rates from around $475, though online rates can be almost half this. ❾

Marine Plaza 29 Marine Drive ⓣ022/2285 1212, ⓦwww.hotelmarineplaza.com. Ritzy but small luxury hotel on the seafront, with the usual five-star facilities and a (pseudo) Art Deco atrium lobby topped by a glass-bottomed rooftop pool. Rooms from around $560. ❾

Oberoi Nariman Point ⓣ022/2232 5757, ⓦwww.oberoihotels.com. One of the focal points of the November 2008 terrorist attacks, the *Oberoi* was closed for rebuilding at the time of writing, though is scheduled to reopen in the near future. Enjoying a prime spot overlooking Back Bay, the hotel is traditionally the first choice of business travellers to the city – lacking the heritage character of the *Taj Mahal Palace & Tower*, but with fine views from its

The Portuguese legacy

Portugal governed Goa for 451 years, and while only a vestigial population still speak Portuguese, the legacy of their former colonizers persists in countless other ways. Nor are these merely the superficial elements of Goan society: the whitewashed church fronts, the liquor ads, or the silky Latinate dresses glimpsed from taxi windows. In fact, nearly every aspect of life in the state still carries traces of Portuguese rule, this despite a steady dilution through nearly five decades as part of the Indian Republic.

The Great Salon, Menezes-Braganza house, Chandor ▲

Palacio interior, Colva ▼

Palacios

Upper-class Goan-Catholic families who voluntarily converted from Hinduism in the sixteenth century were not only rewarded with plum positions in the colony's administration. They also benefited handsomely from trade in gold, gemstones and opium. Profits from the boom financed the construction of splendid mansions, or **palacios**, whose architecture blended indigenous, climate-friendly design sense with the fashionable European motifs of the day. Approached via sweeping staircases and pillared verandas with moulded stone seats (*balcoes*), their facades, whether Neoclassical, Baroque or Art Deco, enclosed interiors stuffed with the spoils of empire: Macau porcelain, Belgian crystal, Venetian mirrors and lustrous, elaborately carved rosewood furniture.

After Liberation in 1961, many *palacios* lapsed into **decline** as their owners decamped to the Portuguese "motherland", leaving their ancestral seats in the charge of less well-off relatives who couldn't afford to maintain them. Engulfed by overgrown gardens, and with their roofs degenerating with each monsoon, literally thousands survive in a state of semi-dereliction. Some especially beautiful ones close to the coast have in recent decades been renovated to serve as heritage hotels or "lifestyle stores". But by far the most interesting specimens are those still inhabited by descendents of their original owners, living in splendid, aristocratic poverty.

Two particularly resplendent specimens that are open to the public are the Menezes-Braganza house in Chandor, South Goa (see p.169), and the Palacio de Deão, in Quepem – the latter even hosts lunches of wonderful Indo-Portuguese cuisine (see opposite).

Indo-Portuguese cuisine

The elderly cooks who work in the kitchens of Goa's stately homes today are repositories of a **gastronomic tradition** every bit as hybrid as the local architecture. It was through Goa that the Portuguese first introduced to the subcontinent potatoes, tomatoes, papaya, pineapple, cashews, guava, pumpkin and – not least of all – chillies. Along with European preparation methods, these were soon adapted to local tastes, while pungent south Indian spices were, for the first time, added to meats such as beef and pork. The most famous Goan dish has to be vindaloo – derived from the wine (*vinho*) and garlic (*alho*) marinades Portuguese sailors used to preserve their meat. Into this the Goans infused palm-sap vinegar and coconut milk, paprika, pepper, and other hot spices to create a distinctively, sour-tasting curry still eaten today.

Thanks to the Portuguese, cakes and baking are also still very much part of the Goan scene today. Bakeries all over the state prepare both typically European iced sponges and the like, as well as older, more traditionally Goan treats, invented when local cooks starting adding eggs – Portuguese style – to their mixtures of coconut milk and *jaggery* (raw sugarcane).

The most ubiquitous Portuguese culinary legacy of all, however, is the humble bread roll, or **pao**. The first sound most people hear in the morning is the bakery boy's cycle horn as he pedals through the lanes with a basket of fresh rolls. These will be used to soak up breakfast bowls of spicy *bhaji* stews, made from chickpeas and little cubes of potato. Later in the day, hungry children and husbands returning home may be handed a *pao* stuffed with reviving slices of eye-watering Goan sausage, called *chouriço* after its (much milder) Portuguese namesake.

▲ Vindaloo

▼ *Pao*

Fontainhas, Panjim ▲

Fontainhas

Nowhere else in the state has retained as much old-world Lusitanian atmosphere as **Fontainhas**, a dozen or so blocks of colour-washed nineteenth-century lanes on the eastern side of the state capital, Panjim. Strolling through them you'll still hear neighbours chatting in Portuguese from balconies festooned with geraniums, and fados played on scratchy violins through open oyster-shell windows. Portuguese grants have helped spruce the quarter up, and its picturesque, neatly painted housefronts have sprouted pretty *azulejo* labelled with names like Maria do Rosario, Ribeiro de Santana and Cantinho dos Afonsos.

Church of the Holy Spirit, Margao ▼

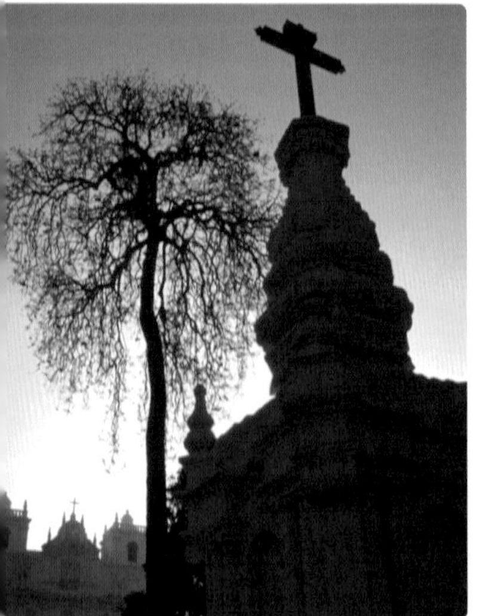

Five places to experience Indo-Portuguese Goa

▸▸ **Church of the Holy Spirit,** Margao (see p.163). Local Catholics turn out in all their finery for mass on Sunday morning, spilling into the adjacent square.

▸▸ **Rachol Seminary** (see p.166). Where young Goan men are prepared for the priesthood, amid sombre eighteenth-century surroundings.

▸▸ **Calizz**, Candolim (see p.119). A wonderful folk museum showcasing the region's architectural heritage, furniture and cuisine.

▸▸ **Feast of St Francis Xavier**, Old Goa (see p.88). Christians flock from all over India to worship at the glass-sided tomb of "Goencho Sahib" on his saint's day – a highly charged event, and the most important religious festival for Goan Catholics.

▸▸ **Carnival**, Panjim (see p.75). A typically Portuguese pre-Lenten bash, celebrated with great gusto, float processions and lots of beer drinking in the state capital.

Carnival, Panjim ▼

soaring tower and an atmosphere of glittering opulence throughout. ❾

Sea Green/Sea Green South 145 Marine Drive ⓣ022/6633 6525, ⓦwww.seagreenhotel.com & 145-A Marine Drive ⓣ022/6633 6535, ⓦwww.seagreensouth.com. Jointly owned and enduringly popular pair of seafront hotels. Decor is old-fashioned going on shabby, and rates are quite high, although the sweeping bay views from front-facing rooms partly compensate. ❼

Trident Nariman Point (formerly the *Hilton Towers*) Nariman Point ⓣ022/6632 4343, ⓦwww.tridenthotels.com. Sitting next to the *Oberoi* (see opposite) on Nariman Point, the *Trident* suffered slight damage during the 2008 attacks but reopened shortly afterwards. It's currently the city's premier business hotel, with full five-star facilities and trimmings, including a gigantic lobby and sea views from its pool. Doubles from around $250. ❾

Around Chhatrapati Shivaji (Victoria) Terminus

The area immediately around **CST** (VT) station and the nearby GPO, though fairly central, has little to recommend it, although there are a couple of decent mid-range and a few more upmarket options. CST (VT) itself also has upmarket **retiring rooms** (❺), although these can't be booked in advance, so you'll have to take pot luck. The following are all marked on the Churchgate and Fort map on p.248.

City Palace 121 City Terrace, Walchand Hirachand Rd ⓣ022/2261 5515, ⓦwww.hotelcitypalace.net. Large and popular hotel bang opposite the station. Economy rooms are tiny and windowless (almost like in a capsule hotel), but have a/c and are perfectly clean. Deluxe rooms higher up the building are larger and have bird's-eye views. ❺–❻

Grand 17 Shri SR Marg, Ballard Estate ⓣ022/6658 0506, ⓦwww.grandhotelbombay.com. Characterful old British-era three-star out near the old docks, nicely refurbished and with well-equipped rooms at competitive rates. ❼–❽

Oasis 276 Shahid Bhagat Singh Marg ⓣ022/3022 7886, ⓦwww.hoteloasisindia.in. Very well placed for CST station, and the best-value budget option in this area: rooms (all attached; some a/c) have good beds, clean linen and TVs. It's worth splashing out on a top-floor "deluxe" room as they offer better views. ❺

Residency 26 Rustom Sidhwa Marg, off DN Rd T022/2262 5525, ⓦwww.residencyhotel.com. Great little mid-range hotel, close to the best shopping areas. Its variously priced rooms (all with safe and wi-fi) offer unbeatable value, especially the no-frills "standard" options, though you'll have to book at least a couple of weeks ahead to get one. ❻

Juhu and around the airports

Hotels in the congested area around the international **airport** cater predominantly for transit passengers and business executives. Nearly all the hotels below have courtesy buses to and from the terminal building, or at worst can arrange for a car and driver to meet you. If you can face the thirty-minute drive across town and afford the first-world room tariffs, head for the beachside suburb of **Juhu**, one of the city's most upmarket addresses.

Hyatt Regency Airport Rd, Andheri (East) ⓣ022/6696 1234, ⓦwww.mumbai.regency.hyatt.com. Ancient Hindu precepts on architecture and design were incorporated into this ultra-luxurious five-star, right next to the airport. The results are impressive, and a notch more stylish than the competition, with floor-to-ceiling windows, rain showers and dark marble floors. From around $200. ❾

ISKCON Guesthouse Juhu Church Rd, Juhu ⓣ022/2620 6860, ⓦwww.iskconmumbai.com (follow the "Guest House" link on left-hand menu). Idiosyncratic hotel run by the International Society for Krishna Consciousness. Rooms (some with a/c) are very large for the price, though certain restrictions apply (no alcohol, meat or caffeine may be consumed on the premises). Forty days' advance booking recommended. ❻

JW Marriott Juhu Tara Rd, Juhu ⓣ022/6693 3000, ⓦwww.marriott.com. Palatial five-star complex with five opulent restaurants, three pools (one of them filled with treated salt water), a topnotch spa and blocks of luxury rooms looking through landscaped grounds to the beach. From around $300. ⑨

Lotus Suites Andheri Kurla Rd, International Airport Zone, Andheri (East) ⓣ022/2827 0707, ⓦwww.lotussuites.com. An "Eco-Four-Star at Three-Star prices" is how this environment-friendly hotel describes itself, designed using energy-saving materials and with "green" trimmings such as jute slippers and recycling bins in the rooms. A very comfortable option for under $150 if you book online. ⑧

Midland Jawaharlal Nehru Rd, Santa Cruz (East) ⓣ022/2611 0414, ⓦwww.hotelmidland.com. Dependable two-star with well-furnished twin-bedded rooms. Rates (from Rs4400) include courtesy bus and breakfast. ⑦

Orchid 70-C Nehru Rd, Vile Parle (East) ⓣ022/2616 4040, ⓦwww.orchidhotel.com. Award-winning "Eco-Five-Star", built with organic or recycled materials and using low-toxin paints. Every effort is made to minimize waste of natural resources, with a water-recycling plant and "zero garbage" policy. Rooms from around ⑧

The City

Nowhere reinforces your sense of having arrived in Mumbai quite as emphatically as the **Gateway of India**, the city's defining landmark. Only a five-minute walk north, the **Prince of Wales Museum** should be next on your list of sightseeing priorities, as much for its flamboyantly eclectic architecture as for the art treasures inside. The museum provides a foretaste of what lies in store just up the road, where the cream of Bartle Frere's Bombay – the **University** and **High Court** – line up with the open maidans on one side and the boulevards of **Fort** on the other. But for the fullest sense of why the city's founding fathers declared it Urbs Prima in Indis, you should press further north still to visit the **Chhatrapati Shivaji Terminus (CST)**, the high-water mark of India's Raj architecture.

Beyond CST lie the crowded bazaars and Muslim neighbourhoods of **central Mumbai**, at their liveliest and most colourful around **Crawford Market** and **Mohammed Ali Road**. Possibilities for an escape from the crowds include an evening stroll along **Marine Drive**, bounding the western edge of downtown, or a boat trip out to **Elephanta**, a rock-cut cave on an island in Mumbai harbour containing a wealth of ancient art.

Colaba

At the end of the seventeenth century, **Colaba** was little more than the last in a straggling line of rocky islands extending to the lighthouse that stood on Mumbai's southernmost point. Today, the original outlines of the promontory (whose name derives from the Koli fishermen who first lived here) have been submerged under a mass of dilapidated colonial tenements, hotels, bars, restaurants and handicraft emporia. If you never venture beyond the district, you'll get a very distorted picture of Mumbai; even though it's the main tourist enclave and a trendy hang-out for the city's rich young things, Colaba has retained the sleazy feel of the port it used to be.

The Gateway of India and the Taj hotel

Commemorating the visit of King George V and Queen Mary in 1911, India's own honey-coloured Arc de Triomphe was built in 1924 by George Wittet, the architect responsible for many of the city's grandest constructions. Blending indigenous Gujarati motifs with high Victorian pomp, it was originally envisaged as a ceremonial disembarkation point for passengers alighting from the P&O steamers, although nowadays the only boats bobbing about at the bottom of its stone staircase are the launches that ferry tourists across the harbour to Elephanta Island (see p.253).

▲ The Gateway of India

Directly behind the Gateway, the older hotel in the **Taj Mahal Palace & Tower** complex (see p.240) stands as a monument to local pride in the face of colonial oppression. Its patron, the Parsi industrialist J. N. Tata, is said to have built the old *Taj* as an act of revenge after he was refused entry to what was then the best hotel in town, the "whites only" *Watson's*. The ban proved to be its undoing. *Watson's* disappeared long ago, but the *Taj* still presides imperiously over the seafront. Lesser mortals are allowed in to experience the tea lounge, shopping arcades and vast air-conditioned lobby – all now fully renovated after being gutted by fire and explosions during the terror attacks of November 26, 2008, when the hotel was besieged by extremist Islamist gunmen.

Colaba Causeway and Sassoon Docks

Reclaimed in the late nineteenth century from the sea, the district's main thoroughfare, **Colaba Causeway** (as this stretch of Shahid Bhagat Singh Marg is known), leads south towards the military cantonment. Few tourists stray much further down it than the claustrophobic hawker zone at the top of the street, but it's well worth doing so, if only to see the neighbourhood's earthy **fresh produce market**, a couple of blocks south of the Strand cinema. From here, return to the main road and turn left to reach the gates of Mumbai's wholesale seafood market, **Sassoon Docks**. The quaysides are at their liveliest immediately before and after sunrise, when coolies haul the night's catch in crates of crushed ice over gangplanks, while Koli women cluster around the auctioneers. The stench, as overpowering as the noise, comes mostly from bundles of one of the city's traditional exports, **Bombay duck** (see box, p.245). Note that **photography** is strictly forbidden as the docks are adjacent to a sensitive navy area.

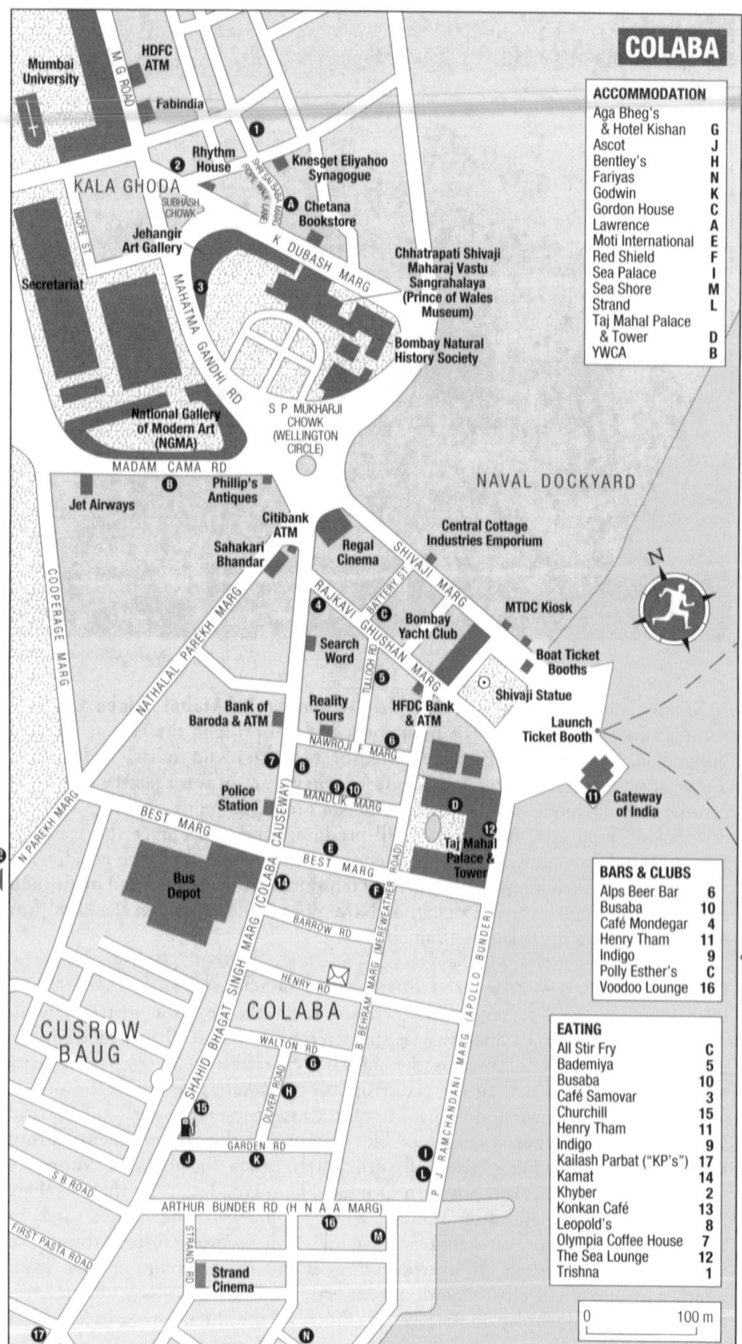

COLABA
ACCOMMODATION
Aga Bheg's & Hotel Kishan G
Ascot J
Bentley's H
Fariyas N
Godwin K
Gordon House C
Lawrence A
Moti International E
Red Shield F
Sea Palace I
Sea Shore M
Strand L
Taj Mahal Palace & Tower D
YWCA B
BARS & CLUBS
Alps Beer Bar 6
Busaba 10
Café Mondegar 4
Henry Tham 11
Indigo 9
Polly Esther's C
Voodoo Lounge 16
EATING
All Stir Fry C
Bademiya 5
Busaba 10
Café Samovar 3
Churchill 15
Henry Tham 11
Indigo 9
Kailash Parbat ("KP's") 17
Kamat 14
Khyber 2
Konkan Café 13
Leopold's 8
Olympia Coffee House 7
The Sea Lounge 12
Trishna 1
Mumbai University
HDFC ATM
Fabindia
M G ROAD
Rhythm House
Knesget Eliyahoo Synagogue
KALA GHODA
SUBHASH CHOWK
Chetana Bookstore
Jehangir Art Gallery
K DUBASH MARG
HOPE ST
Secretariat
MAHATMA GANDHI RD
Chhatrapati Shivaji Maharaj Vastu Sangrahalaya (Prince of Wales Museum)
Bombay Natural History Society
National Gallery of Modern Art (NGMA)
S P MUKHARJI CHOWK (WELLINGTON CIRCLE)
MADAM CAMA RD
Phillip's Antiques
Jet Airways
NAVAL DOCKYARD
Citibank ATM
Sahakari Bhandar
Regal Cinema
Central Cottage Industries Emporium
SHIVAJI MARG
BATTERY ST
MTDC Kiosk
COOPERAGE MARG
NATHALAL PAREKH MARG
RAJKAVI GHUSHAN MARG
Bombay Yacht Club
Search Word
TULLOCH RD
Boat Ticket Booths
Shivaji Statue
Bank of Baroda & ATM
Reality Tours
HFDC Bank & ATM
Launch Ticket Booth
NAWROJI F MARG
Police Station
MANDLIK MARG
Gateway of India
N PAREKH MARG
BEST MARG
CAUSEWAY
Taj Mahal Palace & Tower
Bus Depot
(COLABA
BARROW RD
(MEREWEATHER ROAD)
HENRY RD
SHAHID BHAGAT SINGH MARG
B BEHRAM MARG
COLABA
CUSROW BAUG
WALTON RD
OLIVER ROAD
P J RAMCHANDANI MARG (APOLLO BUNDER)
GARDEN RD
S B ROAD
ARTHUR BUNDER RD (H N A A MARG)
FIRST PASTA ROAD
STRAND RD
Strand Cinema
Elephanta Island
Mandawa & Alibag
0 100 m

Bombay duck

Its name suggests some kind of fowl curry, but **Bombay duck** is actually a fish – to be precise, the marine lizard fish (*Harpalon nehereus*), known in the local dialect of Marathi as *bummalo*. How this long, ribbon-like sea creature acquired its English name no one is exactly sure, but the most plausible theory holds that the Raj-era culinary term derives from the Hindustani for mail train, *dak*. The nasty odour of the dried fish is said to have reminded the British of the less salubrious carriages of the Calcutta–Bombay *dak* when it pulled into VT after three days and nights on the rails, its wooden carriages covered in the stinking mould that flourished in the monsoonal humidity.

A kilometre or so further south, the **Afghan Memorial Church of St John the Baptist** – built as a memorial to the British victims of the First Afghan War – wouldn't look out of place in Worcester or Suffolk. If the door is unlocked, take a peep inside at the battle-scarred military colours and memorials to officers killed in various campaigns on the Northwest Frontier.

Kala Ghoda and around

Immediately north of Colaba, **Kala Ghoda** ("Black Horse") district is named after the large equestrian statue of King Edward VII that formerly stood on the crescent-shaped intersection of MG Road and Subhash Chowk. Flanked by Mumbai's principal museum and art galleries, the neighbourhood has in recent years been relaunched as a "cultural enclave" – as much in an attempt to preserve its many historic buildings as to promote the contemporary visual arts that have thrived here since the 1950s. Fancy stainless-steel interpretative panels now punctuate the district's walkways, and on Sundays in December and January, the **Kala Ghoda Fair** sees portrait artists, potters and *mehendi* painters plying their trade in the car park fronting the Jehangir Art Gallery.

Chhatrapati Shivaji Museum

The Prince of Wales Museum of Western India, or **Chhatrapati Shivaji Maharaj Vastu Sangrahalaya** as it was renamed by the Shiv Sena (daily except Tues 10.15am–6pm; Rs300 [Rs25], camera Rs200, video Rs1000 – no tripods or flash), ranks among the city's most distinctive Raj-era constructions. It stands rather grandly in its own gardens off MG Road, crowned by a massive white Mughal-style dome, under which one of India's finest collections of paintings and sculpture is arrayed on three floors. The building was designed by George Wittet, of Gateway of India fame, and stands as the epitome of the hybrid **Indo-Saracenic** style – regarded in its day as an "educated" interpretation of fifteenth- and sixteenth-century Gujarati architecture, mixing Islamic touches with typically English municipal brickwork.

The foreigners' ticket price includes an **audio tour**, which you collect at the admissions kiosk inside, though you'll probably find it does little to enhance your visit. The heat and humidity inside the building can also be a trial. For a break, the institutional tea-coffee kiosk in the ground-floor garden is a much less congenial option than the *Café Samovar* outside (see p.254), but to exit the museum and re-enter (which you're entitled to do) you'll have to get your ticket stamped in the admissions lobby first. A number of galleries were closed for renovation at the time of writing, so certain exhibits might have moved around a bit by the time you read this.

The **Key Gallery** in the central hall of the **ground floor** provides a snapshot of the collection's treasures, including the fifth-century AD stucco Buddhist figures unearthed by archeologist Henry Cousens in 1909. The main **sculpture room** on the **ground floor** displays other fourth- and fifth-century Buddhist artefacts, mostly from the former Greek colony of Gandhara. Important Hindu sculptures include a seventh-century Chalukyan bas-relief depicting Brahma seated on a lotus and a sensuously carved torso of Mahisasuramardini, the goddess Durga, with tripod raised ready to skewer the demon buffalo.

The main attraction on the **first floor** has to be the museum's famous collection of **Indian painting**. More fine medieval miniatures are housed in the recently inaugurated **Karl & Meherbai Khandalavala Gallery**, on the renovated east wing of this floor, along with priceless pieces of Ghandaran sculpture, Chola bronzes and some of the country's finest surviving examples of medieval Gujarati woodcarving.

Indian **coins** are the subject of the new **House of Laxmi Gallery**, also in the east wing, while the **second floor** showcases a vast array of Oriental ceramics and glassware. Finally, among the grisly **weapons** and pieces of armour stored in a small side-gallery at the top of the building, look out for the cuirass, helmet and jade dagger which the museum only recently discovered belonged to no less than the Mughal emperor Akbar.

Kala Ghoda art galleries

Technically in the same compound as the Prince of Wales Museum, though approached from further up MG Road, the **Jehangir Art Gallery** (daily 11am–7pm; free) is Mumbai's longest-established venue for contemporary art, with five small halls specializing in twentieth-century arts and crafts from around the world. You never know what you're going to find – most exhibitions last only a week and exhibits are often for sale.

On the opposite side of MG Road, facing the museum and Mukharji Chowk, stands the larger **National Gallery of Modern Art** (NGMA; Tues–Sun 11am–6pm; Rs150 [Rs10]; Ⓦwww.ngmaindia.gov.in), showcasing a mix of permanent and temporary exhibitions on three storeys and charting the development of modern Indian art from its beginnings in the 1950s to the present day. The installations, in particular, tend to be a lot more adventurous than those you'll find in the Jehangir across the road.

Around Oval Maidan

North of Kala Ghoda stretches the breezy green **Oval Maidan**, where impromptu cricket matches are held almost every day. Some of the city's finest Victorian piles flank the eastern side of the maidan, offering a good taste of what travel writer Robert Byron described as the city's "architectural Sodom" (adding, "Indian, Swiss chalet, French chateau, Giotto's tower, Siena cathedral & St Peter's are to be found altogether in almost every building"). Just north of here lies the characteristically ostentatious **High Court**, described in 1903 by Indian civil servant G.W. Forrest as "a massive pile whose main features have been brought from Venice, but all the beauty has vanished in transhipment".

Across AS D'Mello Road from the High Court are two major buildings belonging to **Mumbai University** (established 1857), which were designed in England by Sir Gilbert Scott, architect of the Gothic extravaganza that is London's St Pancras railway station. Funded by the Parsi philanthropist Cowasjee "Readymoney" Jehangir, the **Convocation Hall** greatly resembles a church. The **library** is topped by the 79.2-metre-high **Rajabhai Clock Tower**, which is said to have been modelled on Giotto's campanile in Florence and which formerly chimed tunes such as *Rule Britannia* and *Home Sweet Home*.

Dabawallahs

Mumbai's size and inconvenient shape create all kind of hassles for its working population – not least having to stew for over four hours each day in slow municipal transport. One thing the daily tidal wave of commuters does not have to worry about, however, is where to find an inexpensive and wholesome home-cooked lunch. In a city with a wallah for everything, it will find them. The members of the **Nutan Mumbai Tiffin Box Suppliers Charity Trust (NMTSCT)**, known colloquially, and with no little affection, as "**dabawallahs**", see to that. Every day, around 4500 to 5000 *dabawallahs* deliver freshly cooked meals from 175,000 to 200,000 suburban kitchens to offices in the downtown area. Each lunch is prepared early in the morning by a devoted wife or mother while her husband or son is enduring the crush on the train. She arranges the rice, dhal, *subzi*, curd and *parathas* into cylindrical aluminium trays, stacks them on top of one another and clips them together with a neat little handle. This **tiffin box**, not unlike a slim paint tin, is the lynchpin of the whole operation. When the runner calls to collect it in the morning, he uses a special colour code on the lid to tell him where the lunch has to go. At the end of his round, he carries all the boxes to the nearest railway station and hands them over to other *dabawallahs* for the trip into town. Between leaving the wife and reaching its final destination, the tiffin box will pass through at least half a dozen different pairs of hands, carried on heads, shoulder-poles, bicycle handlebars and in the brightly decorated handcarts that plough with such insouciance through the midday traffic. Tins are rarely, if ever, lost – a fact recently reinforced by the American business magazine, *Forbes*, which awarded Mumbai's *dabawallahs* a 6-Sigma performance rating, the score reserved for companies who attain a 99.9 percentage of correctness. This means that only one tiffin box in 6 million goes astray, in efficiency terms putting the illiterate *dabawallahs* on a par with bluechip firms such as Motorola.

If, like Richard Branson and Bill Clinton, you'd like to watch them close up, contact the NMTSCT via its website, ⓦwww.mydabbawala.2com, and look for the link to their "Day With a Dabbawala" scheme.

Fort

East of Oval Maidan stretches **Fort** district, site of Mumbai's original British settlement and first fort – hence the name. This is still the commercial hub of the southern city and a great area for aimless wandering, with plenty of old-fashioned cafés, department stores and street stalls crammed in between the stately Victorian piles.

At the heart of the district lies the spacious **Horniman Circle**, conceived in 1860 as the centrepiece of a newly-planned Bombay by the then municipal commissioner, Charles Forjett, on the site of Bombay's "Green". Later, the space served as a cotton market and parade ground. Flanking the east side of the circle, the impressive **Town Hall** on Shahid Bhagat Singh Marg was among the few buildings in Mumbai that pleased Aldous Huxley: "(Among) so many architectural cads and pretentious bounders," he wrote in 1948, "it is almost the only gentleman." The Doric edifice, dating from 1833, was originally built to house the vast collection of the **Asiatic Society Library**, still open to the general public (Mon–Sat 10am–7pm). Save for the addition of electricity, little has changed here since the institution was founded. Inside reading rooms lined with wrought-iron loggias and teak bookcases, scholars pour over mouldering tomes dating from the Raj. Among the ten thousand rare and valuable manuscripts stored here is a fourteenth-century first edition of Dante's *Divine Comedy*, said to be worth around US$3 million, which the Society famously refused to sell to Mussolini. Visitors are welcome but should sign in at the head librarian's desk on the ground floor.

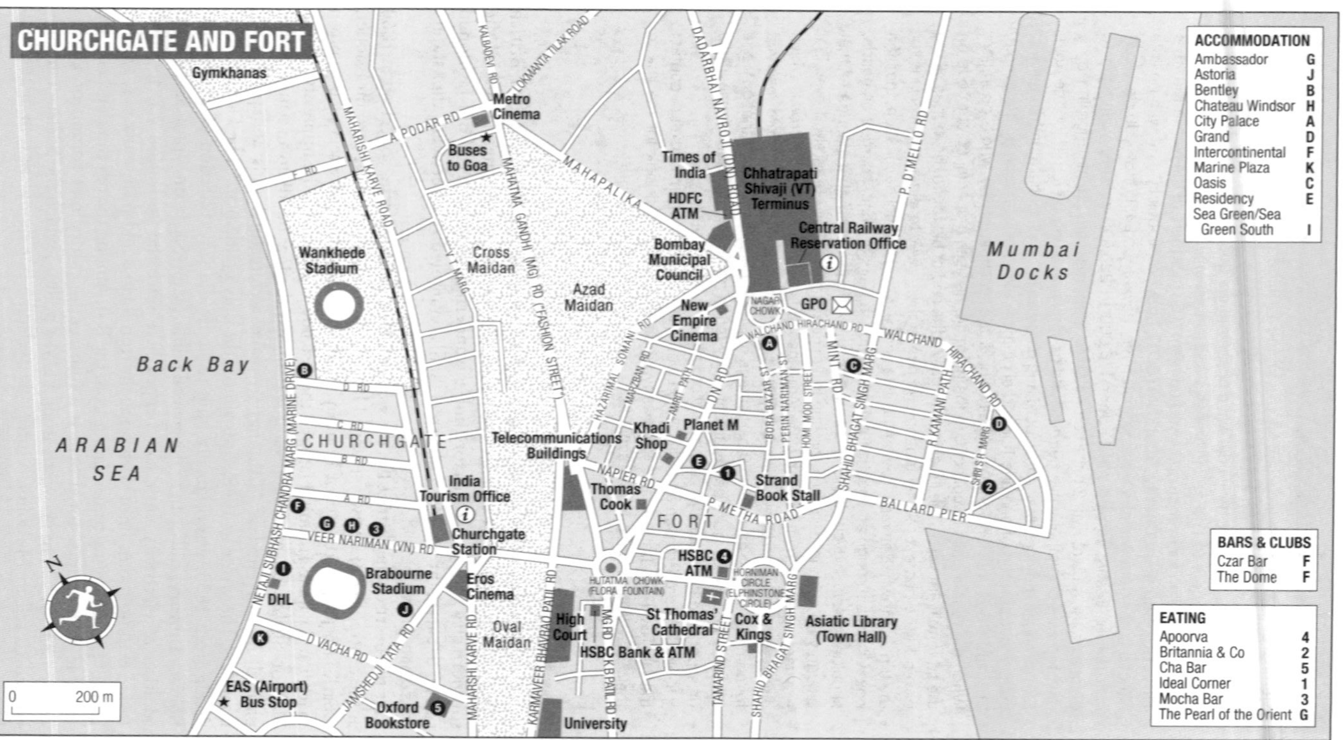
CHURCHGATE AND FORT
ACCOMMODATION
Ambassador G
Astoria J
Bentley B
Chateau Windsor H
City Palace A
Grand D
Intercontinental F
Marine Plaza K
Oasis C
Residency E
Sea Green/Sea Green South I
BARS & CLUBS
Czar Bar F
The Dome F
EATING
Apoorva 4
Britannia & Co 2
Cha Bar 5
Ideal Corner 1
Mocha Bar 3
The Pearl of the Orient G
Gymkhanas
Metro Cinema
Buses to Goa
Times of India
HDFC ATM
Chhatrapati Shivaji (VT) Terminus
Central Railway Reservation Office
Mumbai Docks
Wankhede Stadium
Cross Maidan
Azad Maidan
Bombay Municipal Council
New Empire Cinema
GPO
Back Bay
ARABIAN SEA
CHURCHGATE
FORT
Telecommunications Buildings
Khadi Shop
Planet M
Strand Book Stall
Thomas Cook
India Tourism Office
Churchgate Station
Brabourne Stadium
Eros Cinema
DHL
Oval Maidan
High Court
HSBC ATM
St Thomas' Cathedral
Cox & Kings
Asiatic Library (Town Hall)
HSBC Bank & ATM
University
EAS (Airport) Bus Stop
Oxford Bookstore
MAHARISHI KARVE ROAD
A PODAR RD
KALBADEVI RD
LOKMANYA TILAK ROAD
DADARBHAI NAVROJI (DN) ROAD
MAHAPALIKA
MAHATMA GANDHI (MG) RD ("FASHION STREET")
V T MARG
P. D'MELLO RD
NAGAR CHOWK
WALCHAND HIRACHAND RD
MINT RD
SHAHID BHAGAT SINGH MARG
R KAMANI PATH
SHRI S R MARG
BALLARD PIER
BORA BAZAR ST
PERIN NARIMAN ST
HOMI MODI STREET
DN RD
HAZARIMAL SOMANI RD
MARZBAN RD
AMRIT PATH
NAPIER RD
P METHA ROAD
HUTATMA CHOWK (FLORA FOUNTAIN)
HORNIMAN CIRCLE (ELPHINSTONE CIRCLE)
TAMARIND STREET
MG RD
K B PATIL RD
KARMAVEER BHAVRAO PATIL RD
MAHARSHI KARVE RD
JAMSHEDJI TATA RD
D VACHA RD
VEER NARIMAN (VN) RD
NETAJI SUBHASH CHANDRA MARG (MARINE DRIVE)
D RD
C RD
B RD
A RD
F RD
N
0 200 m

Just west of Horniman Circle lies small, simple **St Thomas' Cathedral** (daily 7am–6pm), reckoned to be the oldest British building in Mumbai, blending classical and Gothic styles. After the death of its founding father, Governor Aungier, the project was abandoned; the walls stood 5m high for forty-odd years until enthusiasm was rekindled in the second decade of the eighteenth century. It was finally opened on Christmas Day, 1718, complete with the essential "cannon-ball-proof roof". In those days, the seating was divided into useful sections for those who should know their place, including one for "Inferior Women". The whitewashed and polished brass-and-wood interior looks much the same at it did in the eighteenth century. Lining the walls are memorial tablets to British parishioners, many of whom died young, either from disease or in battle.

Chhatrapati Shivaji Terminus (Victoria Terminus)

Inspired by St Pancras Station in London, F.W. Stevens designed **Victoria Terminus**, the most barmy of Mumbai's buildings, as a paean to "progress". Built in 1887 as the largest British edifice in India, it's an extraordinary amalgam of domes, spires, Corinthian columns and minarets that was succinctly defined by the journalist James Cameron as "Victorian-Gothic-Saracenic-Italianate-Oriental-St Pancras-Baroque". In keeping with the current re-Indianization of the city's roads and buildings, this icon of British imperial architecture has been renamed **Chhatrapati Shivaji Terminus (CST)**, in honour of the famous Maratha warlord. The new name is a bit of a mouthful, however, and locals mostly still refer to it as **VT** (pronounced "vitee" or "wee-tee").

Few of the two million or so passengers who fill almost a thousand trains every day notice the mass of decorative detail. A "British" lion and Indian tiger stand guard at the entrance, and the exterior is festooned with sculptures executed at the Bombay Art School by the Indian students of John Lockwood Kipling, Rudyard's father. Among them are grotesque mythical beasts, monkeys, plants and medallions of important personages. To minimize the sun's impact, stained glass was employed, decorated with locomotives and elephant images. Above it all, "Progress" stands atop the massive central dome.

Crawford Market and the bazaars

Crawford (aka Mahatma Phule) **Market**, ten minutes' walk north of CST, is an old British-style covered bazaar dealing in just about every kind of fresh food and domestic animal imaginable. Before venturing inside, stop to admire the **friezes** wrapped around its exterior – a Victorian vision of sturdy-limbed peasants toiling in the fields, designed by Rudyard Kipling's father, Lockwood, as principal of the Bombay School of Art in 1865. The **main hall** is still divided into different sections: pyramids of polished fruit and vegetables down one aisle, sacks of nuts or oil-tins full of herbs and spices down another. Around the back of the market, in the atmospheric wholesale wing, the pace of life is more hectic. Here, noisy crowds of coolies mill about with large reed-baskets held high in the air (if they are looking for work) or on their heads (if they've found some).

The streets immediately **north of Crawford Market** and west of **Mohammed Ali Road** form one vast bazaar area, dominated by the domes and minarets of the chintzy white **Jama Masjid**, or "Friday Mosque" (c.1800).

Marine Drive and Chowpatty Beach

Netaji Subhash Chandra Marg, better known as **Marine Drive**, is Mumbai's seaside prom, an eight-lane highway with a wide pavement built in the 1920s on reclaimed land. The whole three-kilometre stretch – still often referred to by

▲ Chowpatty Beach

Mumbaikars as the "Queen's Necklace" after the row of lights which illuminates its spectacular curve at night – is a favourite place for a stroll; the promenade next to the sea has uninterrupted views virtually the whole way along, while the peeling, mildewed Art Deco apartment blocks on the land side remain some of the most desirable addresses in the city.

Chowpatty Beach, at the top of Marine Drive, is another Mumbai institution. On evenings and weekends, Mumbaikars gather here in large numbers – not to swim (the sea is foul) but to wander, sit on the sand, munch kulfi and *bhel puri*, get their ears cleaned and gaze across the bay while the kids ride a pony or a rusty Ferris wheel. Once a year in September the **Ganesh Chathurthi** festival draws gigantic crowds as idols, both huge and small, of the elephant-headed god Ganesh are immersed in the sea.

A ten-minute walk north from the middle of Chowpatty Beach along Pandita Ramabai Marg, **Mani Bhavan**, at 19 Laburnum Rd (daily 9.30am–6pm; free, with optional donation), was Gandhi's Bombay base between 1917 and 1934. Set in a leafy upper-middle-class road, the house has now been converted into a permanent memorial to the Mahatma. The lovingly maintained polished-wood interior is crammed with historic photos and artefacts – the most disarming of which is a friendly letter to Hitler suggesting world peace.

Malabar Hill

Its brow bristling with gigantic skyscrapers, the promontory enfolding Chowpatty Beach at the north end of Back Bay has been south Mumbai's most desirable neighbourhood almost since the city was founded. The British were quick to see the potential of its salubrious breezes and sweeping sea views, constructing bungalows at the tip of what was then a separate island – the grandest of them the Government House, originally erected in the 1820s and now the seat of the serving governor of Maharashtra, **Raj Bhavan.**

Although none of Malabar's landmarks can be classed as unmissable, its Hindu shrines and surviving colonial-era residences form an interesting counterpoint to the modernity towering on all sides. Bal Gangadhar Kher Marg (formerly Ridge Road) is the district's main artery. You can follow it from Mumbai's principal **Jain Temple** (see map, pp.238–239), with its mirror-encrusted interior dedicated to Adinath, all the way to the tip of the headland, where the famous **Walkeshwar Temple** stands as the city's oldest Hindu shrine surviving *in situ*. According to the *Ramayana*, Rama fashioned a *lingam* out of sand to worship Shiva here, which over the centuries became one of the Konkan's most important pilgrimage centres. Today's temple, erected in 1715 after the original had been destroyed by the Portuguese, is of less note than the **Banganga Tank** below it – a rectangular lake lined by stone *ghats* and numerous crumbling shrines.

North of Malabar Hill

The centre of Mumbai, beyond Malabar Hill, is mostly made up of working-class neighbourhoods: a huge mosaic of dilapidated tenements, markets and industrial eyesores left over from the Victorian cotton boom. For relief from the urban cauldron, residents travel west to the seashore to worship at the **Mahalakshmi Temple** (if they're Hindus) or the island **tomb of Haji Ali** (if they're Muslims).

Buses #83, #124 or #132 will take you from Colaba to Haji Ali, within a stone's throw of the Mahalakshmi Temple. Buses #124 and #153 continue from here to the *dhobi ghats*, or alternatively catch the train to nearby Mahalakshmi station direct from south Mumbai.

Mahalakshmi Temple and Haji Ali's tomb

Mahalakshmi Temple, just off Bhulabhai Desai Road, is approached via an alley lined with stalls selling spectacular floral offerings and devotional pictures. Gifts for Mumbai's favourite *devi*, **Lakshmi**, goddess of beauty and prosperity – the city's most sought-after attributes – pile so high that the temple *pujaris* run a money-spinning sideline reselling them. While you're here, find out what your future holds by joining the huddle of devotees pressing rupees onto the rear wall of the shrine room. If your coin sticks, you'll be rich.

Occupying a small islet in the bay just north of the Mahalakshmi is the mausoleum of the Muslim saint, Afghan mystic **Haji Ali Bukhari**. The tomb is connected to the mainland by a narrow concrete **causeway**, only passable at

The Towers of Silence

High on Malabar Hill, screened from prying eyes by a high wall and dense curtain of vegetation, stand the seven **Towers of Silence**, where the city's dwindling Zoroastrian community (better known as Parsis) dispose of their dead. Pollution of the four sacred elements (air, water, earth and, holiest of all, fire) contradicts the most fundamental precepts of the 2500-year-old Parsi faith, first imported to India when Zoroastrians fled from Sassanid Persia to escape Arab persecution in the seventh century. So instead of being buried or cremated, the bodies are laid out on top of open-topped, cylindrical towers, called *dokhmas*, for their bones to be cleaned by **vultures** and the weather. The remains are then placed in an ossuary at the centre of the tower.

Recent decades have seen a sharp decline in the number of Parsis choosing this traditional funerary rite, one reason for which is the disappearance of India's vultures – a result of their exposure to the anti-inflammatory drug, Diclofenac, which is fed to cattle and therefore found in the carcasses on which the birds more commonly feed. Solar panels have instead been installed in the towers, to use the sun's rays to dispose of the corpses; captive vultures are being considered as another solution.

The Towers of Silence are strictly closed to visitors.

low tide. When not immersed in water, its entire length is lined with beggars supplicating passers-by and chanting verses from the Qu'ran. The site is a great place to head for on Thursday and Friday evenings, when large crowds gather around the headland to watch the sunset and listen to live **qawwali** music. Non-Muslims are welcome, but you'll need to keep well covered up (a headscarf should be worn by women). The entire complex was undergoing major **renovations** at the time of writing, but these should have finished by the time you read this.

Mahalakshmi dhobi ghats

On the face of it, the idea of going out of your way to ogle Mumbai's dirty washing sounds like a very perverse pastime. If you're passing, however, the **municipal dhobi ghats**, near Mahalakshmi suburban railway station, are a sufficiently memorable spectacle to break a trip across town to see. Washing from all over the city is brought here each morning to be soaked in concrete vats and

Dharavi: the £700 million slum

Flying into Mumbai airport, your plane's undercarriage will almost skim the corrugated-iron rooftops of the vast shantytown spread across the middle of one of **India's largest slums**. Sprawling over 550 acres, **Dharavi**'s maze of dilapidated shacks and narrow, stinking alleyways is home to more than a million people. An average of 15,000 of them share a single toilet. Infectious diseases such as dysentery, malaria and hepatitis are rife; and there aren't any hospitals.

Despite the poverty, Dharavi has been described by the UK's *Observer* newspaper as "one of the most inspiring economic models in Asia": hidden amid the warren of ramshackle huts and squalid open sewers are an estimated 15,000 single-room factories, employing around a quarter of a million people and turning over a staggering £700 million (US$1.4 billion) annually. The majority of small businesses in Dharavi are based on **waste recycling** of one kind or another. Slum residents young and old scavenge materials from across the city and haul them back in huge bundles to be reprocessed. Aluminium cans are smelted down, soap scraps salvaged from schools and hotels are reduced in huge vats, leather reworked, disused oil drums restored and discarded plastic reshaped and remoulded. An estimated ten thousand workers are employed in the plastics sector alone. Ranging from Rs3000–15,000 per month, wages are well above the national average, and though Dharavi may not have any health centres, it does hold a couple of banks, and even ATMs.

As India's largest and most iconic slum, Dharavi has also found an unlikely niche in the history of Indian and international **cinema**. The district provided many of the settings for Mira Nair's seminal portrait of the city, *Salaam Bombay!*, and has also featured in numerous other Bollywood and Tamil flicks from the 1970s onwards. Dharavi's defining moment of celluloid fame, however, came in 2009 with Danny Boyle's multiple Oscar-winning **Slumdog Millionaire**. The slum provided many of the film's locations, as well as several of its leading child actors.

You can visit Dharavi yourself by joining one of the "**Slum Tours**" run by Reality Tours and Travels out of Colaba. Tickets for these engaging guided trips cost Rs400 (including transport), or you can also opt for a longer and more comfortable version with an a/c car for Rs800. For more details, contact Krishna Pujari on ⓣ022/2283 3872, or ⓣ9820/822253, check out ⓦwww.realitytoursandtravel.com, or just drop in at their booking office (Mon–Fri 10.15am–8.35pm, Sat 10.15am–3.45pm) off Colaba Causeway (SBS Marg), in Akber House on Nawroji Fardonji Marg, opposite the *Laxmi Vilas Hotel* (see map, p.244 – enter Akber House via the passageway through S. S. S. Corner next to the *New Apollo Restaurant*; the office is on the first floor, reached via the Unique Business Service Centre).

thumped by the resident *dhobis*. A trickle of curious foreign tourists gathers on Mahalakshmi road bridge for this uniquely Indian photo opportunity.

By far the easiest way to get to Mahalakshmi is to jump on a suburban train from Churchgate. Emerging from the station, turn left and follow the road over the rail tracks – the *ghats* will be below you on your left (the hawkers from the nearby slums who work the spot will show you the way). Alternatively, catch bus #124 from Colaba.

Elephanta

An hour's ride northeast across Mumbai harbour from Colaba, the island of **Elephanta** offers the best escape from the seething claustrophobia of the city – as long as you time your visit to avoid the weekend deluge of noisy day-trippers. Populated only by a small fishing community, it was originally known as **Gherapura**, the "city of Ghara priests", until the island was renamed in the sixteenth century by the Portuguese in honour of the carved elephant they found at the port. Its chief attraction is its unique **cave temple**, whose massive **Trimurti** (three-faced) **Shiva sculpture** is as fine an example of Hindu architecture as you'll find anywhere.

Half-hourly boats set off from the Gateway of India (daily 9am–2.30pm; returning from Elephanta noon to 5pm; book through the kiosks near the Gateway of India); note that boats may be cancelled due to adverse weather conditions during the monsoon. **"Deluxe" boats** (Rs120 return) include a thirty-minute tour with a government guide – ask for your guide at the cave's ticket office on arrival. **Ordinary ferries** (Rs100 return) don't include the guided tour and are usually more packed. There's also a **tourist tax** of Rs5 payable on arrival. Cool drinks and souvenir stalls line the way up the hill, and, at the top, the MTDC *Chalukya* restaurant offers substandard food and warm beer, served on a terrace with good views out to sea. If you don't want to walk up the 120 steps to the caves there's a miniature train up from the jetty (Rs8 return). Note that you cannot stay overnight on the island and that the caves are closed on Mondays.

The cave

Elephanta's impressive excavated eighth-century **cave** (Tues–Sun 9.30am–5pm; Rs250 [Rs10]), covering an area of approximately 5000 square metres, is reached by climbing more than one hundred steps to the top of the hill, lined by souvenir and knick-knack stalls. Inside, the massive columns, carved from solid rock, give the deceptive impression of being structural. To the right as you enter, note the panel of **Nataraj**, Shiva as the cosmic dancer. Though spoiled by the Portuguese who, it is said, used it for target practice, the panel remains magnificent: Shiva's face is rapt, and with one of his left hands he removes the veil of ignorance. Opposite is a badly damaged panel of Lakulisha, Shiva with a club (*lakula*).

Each of the four entrances to the simple, square main **shrine** – unusually, it has one on each side – is flanked by a pair of huge fanged *dvarpala* guardians (only those to the back have survived undamaged), while inside a large *lingam* is surrounded by coins and smouldering joss left by devotees. Facing the northern wall of the shrine, another panel shows Shiva impaling the demon Andhaka, who wandered around as though blind, symbolizing his spiritual blindness. The panel behind the shrine on the back wall portrays the marriage of Shiva and Parvati, but the cave's outstanding centrepiece is its powerful six-metre bust of **Trimurti**, the three-faced Shiva, whose profile has become almost as familiar to Indians as that of the Taj Mahal.

From Cave 1 you can follow a paved path around the north flank of the hillside past a string of other, unfinished excavations, which exemplify how the caves were originally dug out and carved. If you've the stamina, follow the dirt path that leads from the end of the paved trail beyond these to the summit of Elephanta Hill, a stiff hike of fifteen minutes. At the top you'll be rewarded with an encounter with a couple of rusting Portuguese cannons and a magnificent view back over Mumbai harbour to the distant city beyond.

Eating

Mumbai is crammed with interesting **places to eat**. The cafés, bars and restaurants of **Colaba** encompass just about the full gamut of gastronomic possibilities, while a short walk or taxi ride north, **Kala Ghoda** and **Fort** are home to some of the best cafés and restaurants in the city, including its last traditional Parsi diners, whose menus (and sometimes decor as well) have changed little in generations.

Phone numbers have been given where we recommend you reserve a table. Beware of service charges levied on your bill by some of the more expensive places.

Colaba and Kala Ghoda

Except where noted, all the following are shown on the map on p.244.

All Stir Fry *Gordon House Hotel.* Cool modern restaurant specializing in build-your-own wok meals using a selection of fresh veg, meat, fish, noodles and sauces, flash-cooked in front of you. The satay and dim sum are particularly good. Rs420 for unlimited servings.

Bademiya Behind the *Taj Mahal Palace & Tower* on Tulloch Rd. Legendary Colaba kebab-wallah serving delicious flame-grilled chicken, mutton and fish steaks, as well as veg alternatives, wrapped in paper-thin, piping hot *rotis*, from benches on the sidewalk. Rich families from uptown drive here on weekends, eating on their car bonnets, but there are also little tables and chairs if you don't fancy a takeaway.

Busaba 4 Mandlik Marg ⓣ022/2204 3779. Sophisticated bar-restaurant specializing in Far Eastern cuisine – Thai, Korean, Burmese, Vietnamese and Tibetan staples, with exotic salads (green mango and glass noodle). One of *the* places to be seen (if you can't quite afford to eat at *Indigo* next door). Mains Rs350–550.

Café Samovar Jehangir Art Gallery, MG Rd ⓣ022/2284 8000. Very pleasant, peaceful semi-alfresco café opening onto the museum gardens, with plenty of à la carte choices (prawn curry, *roti* kebabs and fresh salads, and dhansak). They also serve delicious chilled guava juice and beer. Daily except Sun 11am–7.30pm.

Churchill 103 Colaba Causeway. Tiny Parsi diner, with a bewildering choice of dishes, including salads, pastas and burgers, mostly meat-based and served in mild sauces alongside a blob of mash and boiled veg – ideal if you've had your fill of spicy food. No alcohol. Main Rs210–275.

Henry Tham Dhanraj Mahal, CST Rd, Apollo Bunder, Colaba ⓣ022/2202 3186, ⓦwww.henrytham.com. Within spitting distance of the

Street food

Mumbai is renowned for distinctive street foods – especially **bhel puri**, a quintessentially Mumbai masala mixture of puffed rice, deep-fried vermicelli, potato, crunchy *puri* pieces, chilli paste, tamarind water, chopped onions and coriander. More hygienic, but no less ubiquitous, is **pao bhaji**, a round Portuguese-style bread roll served on a tin plate with griddle-fried, spicy vegetable stew, and **kanji vada**, savoury doughnuts soaked in fermented mustard and chilli sauce. And if all that doesn't appeal, a pitstop at one of the city's hundreds of **juice bars** probably will. There's no better way to beat the sticky heat than with a glass of cool milk shaken with fresh pineapple, mango, banana, *chikoo* (small brown fruit that tastes like a sweet pear) or custard apple. Just make sure they hold on the ice – which may be made with untreated water.

Gateway of India, this swanky restaurant serves up excellent contemporary-style Chinese food, including good dim sum and lunchtime set menus.

Indigo 4 Mandlik Marg ⓣ022/6636 8999, ⓦwww.foodindigo.com. One of the city's most fashionable restaurants, for once deserving the hype, and specializing in superb international and modern European cooking with an Indian twist (Kerala oysters with saffron ravioli, for example). Mains from around RS600. Reservations essential.

Kailash Parbat ("KP's") 1 Pasta Lane, near the Strand cinema. Uninspiring on the outside, but the breakfast *aloo parathas*, pure veg nibbles, hot snacks and sweets (across the road) are worth the walk. A Colaba institution – try their famous *makai-ka* (corn) *rotis*.

Kamat Colaba Causeway. Friendly little eatery serving unquestionably the best South Indian breakfasts in the area, as well as the usual range of southern snacks (*iddli*, vada, *sambar*), delicious spring dosas and (limited) thalis for Rs60–150. The best option in the area for budget travellers with big appetites.

Khyber opposite Jehangir Art Gallery ⓣ022/2267 3227. Opulent Arabian Nights interior and uncompromisingly rich "Northwest Frontier" cuisine. The chicken tikka is legendary, and their tandoori dishes and kebab platter are superb too. Mains Rs240–425.

Konkan Café *Taj President Hotel*, Cuffe Parade (see map pp.238–239) ⓣ022/6665 0808. Just the place to push the boat out: a sophisticated five-star hotel restaurant serving fine regional cuisine from coastal Maharashtra, Goa, Karnataka and Kerala. You can choose from their thali platters (Rs845–1045) or go à la carte: butter-pepper-garlic crab is to die for. Quite simply some of the most mouth-watering South Indian food you'll ever eat.

Leopold's Colaba Causeway. A Mumbai institution for decades, *Leopold's* is the number-one hangout for India-weary Western travellers, who continue to cram onto its small tables for bland, overpriced Indian, Continental and Chinese tourist fare – despite (or perhaps because of) the fact that the café was one of the leading targets of the 2008 terror attacks (staff will show you the bullet holes in the walls, now discreetly hidden behind pictures). Expect to queue. Mains Rs150–300; beer Rs200.

Olympia Coffee House Colaba Causeway. *Fin-de-siècle* Irani café with marble tabletops, wooden wall panels, fancy mirrors and a mezzanine floor for women. Waiters in Peshwari caps and *salwar kameezes* serve melt-in-the-mouth kebabs and delicious curd-based dips. It gets packed out at breakfast time for cholesterol-packed mutton masala fry, which regulars wash down with bright orange chai. A quintessential (and inexpensive) Bombay experience. Mains Rs60–100.

The Sea Lounge *Taj Mahal Palace & Tower*. Gorgeously atmospheric 1930s-style lounge café on the first floor of the *Taj*, with fine Gateway and harbour views – good for coffee and cake (from around Rs600) or a sumptuous breakfast (Rs1000). Daily 7am–midnight.

Trishna 7 Sri Sai Baba Marg (Ropewalk Lane), Kala Ghoda ⓣ022/2261 4991. Visiting dignitaries and local celebs, from the president of Greece to Bollywood stars, have eaten in this dimly lit Mangalorean. There are wonderful fish dishes in every sauce going, including the signature butter-pepper-garlic crab (around Rs700–800) and superb pomfret stuffed with green masala (Rs490), plus cheaper North Indian standards (from Rs200). Very small, so book in advance.

Churchgate and Fort

Except where noted, all the following are shown on the map on p.248.

Apoorva SA Brelvi Rd ⓣ022/2287 0335. Popular Mangalorean, hidden up a sidestreet off Horniman Circle (look for the tree trunk wrapped with fairy lights). The cooking's completely authentic and the seafood – simmered in spicy coconut-based gravies – comes fresh off the boat each day. Try their definitive Bombay duck, *surmai* (kingfish) in coconut gravy or sublime prawn gassi, served with perfect sanna and appams. Mains Rs100–475. Licensed.

Britannia & Co Shri SR Marg, Ballard Estate. Quirky little Parsi restaurant, famous as much for its quaint period atmosphere as its wholesome Irani food. Most people come for the sublime "berry pulao" (chicken, mutton or vegetable), made with deliciously tart dried berries imported from Tehran (Rs200, but portions are gigantic). For afters, there's the house "caramel custard". One of the city's unmissable eating experiences. Open 11.30am–3.30pm.

Cha Bar Oxford Bookstore, 3 D Vacha Rd, Churchgate. Chic a/c café at the back of downtown's top bookshop serving an exhaustive range of single-estate speciality teas, from Kashmiri *kawa* to Ladhaki butter tea, plus coffees, sandwiches, wraps and cakes.

Ideal Corner 12 F/G Hornby View, Gunbow St ⓣ022/2262 1930. Another Parsi café with a cult following, dishing up delicious home-made specialities like *kchchidi* prawn, lamb dhansak, chicken *farcha* and legendary *lagan* custard. Most mains Rs50–75. Mon–Sat 9am–4.30pm.

Mocha Bar Veer Nariman (VN) Rd. Chilled terrace café where swarms of south Mumbai bratpackers pose over speciality coffees, tapas, panini, wraps and crepes (or puff on hookah pipes in the smoking area at the back). Very much the zeitgeist.

The Pearl of the Orient *Ambassador Hotel*, Veer Nariman (VN) Rd ⓣ022/229 1131. Revolving Oriental restaurant in this faded four-star hotel. The cooking's nothing special (and expensive at around Rs1000 for three courses), but the views over the city are extraordinary.

Crawford Market and the central bazaars

The following three places are shown on the map on pp.238–239.

Badshah Juice and Snack Bar Opposite Crawford Market, Lokmanya Tilak Rd. Mumbai's most acclaimed *falooda* joint also serves delicious kulfi, ice creams and dozens of freshly squeezed fruit juices. The ideal place to round off a trip to the market, though expect to have to queue for a table.

Joshi Club 31-A Narottamwadi, Kalbadevi Rd ⓣ022/2205 8089. Also known as The Friends Union Joshi Club, this eccentric thali canteen serves what many aficionados regard as the most genuine and tasty Gujarati–Marwari meals in the city, on unpromising Formica tables against a backdrop of grubby walls. Rs95 buys you unlimited portions of four vegetable dishes, dhals and up to four different kinds of bread, with all the trimmings (and banana custard). Finding it requires some effort: walk or catch a cab to the bottom of Kalbadevi Rd (opposite the Metro cinema; see map, pp.238–239); head north across Vardhaman Chowk, and continue up Kalbadevi Rd for 5min until you see a signboard on your right for "Bhojanalaya", below a first-floor window.

Rajdhani Sheikh Memon St. Outstanding, eat-till-you-burst Gujarati thalis. Very cramped and more expensive than usual (Rs250, or Rs299 for the "Special" Sun lunch), but they don't stint on quality. Closed Sun evening. It's on the road leading to the Jama Masjid (approaching from Crawford Market cross the road by the entrance and turn right past the Lokmanya Tilak Marg Police Booth).

Bars and nightlife

Colaba Causeway is the focus of the travellers' social scene but if you want to sample the pulse of the city's **nightlife**, venture up to Bandra and Juhu, where the nightclub scene remains the most full-on in India. Tiny, skin-tight outfits that show off razor-sharp abs and pumped-up pecs are very much the order of the day, especially in venues frequented by Bollywood's movers and shakers – and the pretty young things desperate to break into the industry. Dominated by *filmi* pop mixes, the music is far from cutting edge by the standards of London or New York, but no one seems to mind. Dancefloors get as rammed as a suburban

Performing arts in Mumbai

Mumbai is a major centre for traditional **performing arts**, attracting the finest **Indian classical musicians** and **dancers** from all over the country. Frequent concerts and recitals are staged at venues such as Bharatiya Vidya Bhavan, KM Munshi Marg (ⓣ022/2363 0224), the headquarters of the international cultural (Hindu) organization, and the National Centre for the Performing Arts, Nariman Point (NCPA; ⓦwww.ncpamumbai.com).

For more contemporary **live music**, the leading venue is Blue Frog, in North Mumbai at D/2 Mathuradas Mills Compound, NM Joshi Marg, Lower Parel (ⓣ022/4033 2300, ⓦwww.bluefrog.co.in), opened in late 2007 and recently named by the UK's *Independent* newspaper as one of the world's top live music venues. Performances are staged inside a huge old warehouse in Mumbai's former mill district, showcasing leading Indian and international live music acts and DJs – anything from rock to hip-hop.

For **theatre**, head out to the Prithvi Theatre (ⓣ022/2614 9546, ⓦwww.prithvitheatre.org) on Juhu Church Road, a small but lively venue focusing mainly on Hindi-language theatre, along with some English productions.

Bollywood

The home of the Hindi blockbuster, the "all-India film", is Mumbai, famously known as **Bollywood**, and visitors to the city should have ample opportunity to sample its delights, traditional or otherwise. To make an educated choice, buy *Time Out Mumbai* magazine, which contains extensive **listings** and reviews. Alternatively, look for the biggest, brightest hoarding, and join the queue. Seats in a comfortable air-conditioned cinema cost Rs120–200, or less if you sit in the stalls (not advisable for women).

Of the two hundred or so **cinemas**, only a dozen or so regularly screen **English-language** films. The most central and convenient are the gloriously ArtDeco halls dating from the twilight of the Raj: the Regal in Colaba; the Eros opposite Churchgate station; and the Metro at Dhobi Talao junction – the latter was recently converted into a state-of-the-art multiplex. Down on Nariman Point, near Express Towers, the Inox (Ⓦwww.inoxmovies.com) is another big multi-screen venue, built only a few years ago in retro Mumbai Art Deco style.

commuter train and the cover charges are astronomical. Door policies and dress codes tend to be strict ("no ballcaps, no shorts, no sandals"), and, in theory, most clubs have a "couples-only" policy – they charge per couple on the door (with a portion of the entrance cost redeemable at the bar). In practice, if you're in a mixed group or don't appear sleazy you shouldn't have any problems. At the five-star hotels, entry can be restricted to hotel guests and members.

Bars

Alps Beer Bar Nawroji F Marg, Colaba, behind *Taj Mahal Palace & Tower* (see map, p.244). Slightly down-at-heel but quiet alternative to the queues and crowds of nearby *Leopold's* and *Café Mondegar*, with the cheapest beer in Colaba plus a bit of food including curries, steaks and sizzlers.

Aurus Nichani House, Juhu Tara Rd, Juhu Ⓣ022/6710 6666, Ⓦwww.dishhospitality.com. Sexy beachside hang-out, boasting a funky bar-restaurant inside and a relaxing terrace overlooking Juhu Beach, backed up with good international fusion cuisine and a wide-ranging wine and cocktail list. Boasts its fair share of Bombabes and celebs, though the entry policy is usually less snooty than other places hereabouts.

Busaba 4 Mandlik Marg, Colaba (see map, p.244). Downstairs from the swanky *Busaba* restaurant (see p.254), this chic, dimly lit bar serves up a good selection of Australian, South African and New World wines, plus single malts, cool cocktails and a decent range of international beers.

Café Mondegar Colaba Causeway (see map, p.244). Draught and bottled beer (imported and Indian) and deliciously fruity cocktails are served in this small café-bar. The atmosphere is very relaxed, the music tends towards cheesy rock classics and the clientele is a mix of Westerners and local students; murals by a famous Goan cartoonist give the place a cheerful ambience. There's also a big menu of average Indian, Chinese and Continental food. Expect to queue to get in.

Czar Bar *Hotel Intercontinental*, 135 Marine Drive (see map, p.248). Trendy vodka bar with chic, minimalist decor, clever lighting and over forty brands on offer (from Rs400), plus a full range of other drinks and cocktails. Music is lounge until around 11pm, then picks up. Quiet on weekday nights, but popular at weekends. Daily 5.30pm–1.30am.

The Dome *Hotel Intercontinental*, 135 Marine Drive (see map, p.248). This cool rooftop bar is easily south Mumbai's most alluring spot for a sundowner. Plush white sofas and candle-lit tables surround the eponymous domed rotunda and a very sexy raised pool, while the views over Back Bay make even the sky-high drink prices feel worth it. Daily 5.30pm–1.30am.

Henry Tham Dhanraj Mahal, CST Road, Apollo Bunder, Colaba (see map, p.244). Downstairs from the excellent Chinese restaurant (see p.255), this small but kicking bar is currently the preferred haunt of south Mumbai's beautiful people, boasting excellent cocktails and one of the city's best house soundtracks.

Indigo 4 Mandlik Rd, Colaba (see map, p.244). Attached to the fashionable *Indigo* restaurant (see p.255), this is the coolest hang-out in Colaba, with funky, stripped-bare decor, frequented by young media types and would-be wine buffs.

Olive 4 Union Park Rd, Pali Hill (between Juhu and Bandra). Nowhere pulls in Bollywood's A-list like *Olive*. If you want to rub shoulders with Hrithik, Abhishek and Aishwarya, Preity and Shilpa, this is your best bet, though dress to kill – and come armed with a flexible wallet. While basically just a pretext to crowd-watch, the food is fine gourmet Mediterranean.

Vie Lounge 102 Juhu Tara Rd, Juhu ⓣ022/2660 3003, ⓦwww.vie.co.in. Chilled-out Ibiza-style beach bar overlooking Juhu Beach, with resident and visiting DJs and an excellent cocktail list, plus a decent selection of seafood and Cajun cuisine.

Wink *Taj President*, 90 Cuffe Parade ⓣ022/6665 0808, ⓦwww.tajhotels.com (see map, pp.238–239). Classy Asian-style lounge bar, with one of the city's best drinks lists, including a superb selection of speciality cocktails. A good place for a quiet drink early on, though the DJ gradually ramps up the volume as the evening progresses, with full-on club beats by the end of the night.

Zenzi 183 Waterfield Rd, Bandra West ⓣ022/5643 0670, ⓦwww.zenzi-india.com. Chic Dutch-owned bar-restaurant, decorated in contemporary Asian Balinese-cum-Thai style, with a choice of restaurant (dishing up classy pan-Asian cuisine), bar, posy DJ lounge and a breezy open-air terrace upstairs. Usually quiet before 11pm, but often gets rammed with glamorous locals later on.

Nightclubs

Enigma *JW Marriott Hotel*, Juhu Tara Rd. If you want to see what Hindi film stars and hip young Indian millionaires do for kicks, this is the place to come: the sexiest outfits, latest Bolly-bhangra mixes, most gorgeous decor and stiffest entrance cost (from Rs800–Rs2500 per couple depending on the night).

Polly Esther's *Gordon House Hotel*, Battery St, Colaba (see map, p.244). Retro club with brightly coloured 70s/80s decor and waiters wearing ludicrous fluoro-coloured Afro wigs. Live music, hip-hop, Bollywood and retro on different nights. Rs900–1200 per couple. Open Wed–Sun.

Squeeze 5th Rd, Khar, Bandra. Bandra's funkiest nightspot is aptly named: it's packed seven nights a week, and bursting at the seams on weekends, when the music's less dominated by Hindi pop than elsewhere. Admission around 1500 per couple.

Voodoo Lounge Arthur Bunder Rd, Colaba (see map, p.244). This cavernous but delightfully louche little dive off Colaba Causeway plays host to Mumbai's one and only gay club, from 9pm on Sat (it's dead and depressing the rest of the week). The atmosphere's restrained by Western standards, but welcoming and sociable for both gay and straight men and women, though most of the punters do come to cruise. Admission Rs300/head.

Shopping

Mumbai is a great place to shop, whether for last-minute souvenirs or essentials for the long journeys ahead. If you're after a small, lightweight gift, try the decent range of Assam, Nilgiri and (especially) Darjeeling black and green teas at Central Cottage Industries Emporium, 34 Shivaji Marg, near the Gateway of India in Colaba.

Antiques, clothes and handicrafts

The **Chor Bazaar** area, and Mutton Street in particular, is the centre of Mumbai's **antique trade**. Another good, if much more expensive, place is **Phillip's** famous antique shop, opposite the Regal cinema in Colaba. Brass, bronze and wood Hindu sculpture, silver jewellery, old prints and aquatints form the mainstay of its collection.

For **traditional Indian clothes**, look no further than the Khadi shop (signed "Mumbai Khadi Gramodyog Sangh") at 286 Dr DN Road, near the Thomas Cook office. As Whiteaway & Laidlaw, this rambling Victorian department store used to kit all the newly arrived *burra-sahibs* out with pith helmets, khaki shorts and quinine tablets. These days, its old wooden counters and shirt and sock drawers stock dozens of different hand-spun cottons and silks, sold by the metre or made up as vests, *kurtas* or block-printed *salwar kameezes*. Other items include the ubiquitous white Nehru caps, *dhotis*, Madras-check *lunghis* and fine brocaded silk saris.

Regionally produced **handicrafts** are marketed in assorted state-run emporia at the World Trade Centre, down on Cuffe Parade, and along Sir PM Road, Fort. The quality is consistently high – as are the prices, if you miss out on the periodic holiday discounts. The same goes for the **Central Cottage Industries Emporium**, 34 Shivaji Marg, near the Gateway of India in Colaba, whose size, central location and big range of inlaid furniture, wood- and metalwork, miniature paintings, jewellery, toys, clothing and textiles make it the single best all-round place to hunt for souvenirs. **Mereweather Road** (now officially B Behram Marg), directly behind the *Taj Mahal Palace & Tower*, is awash with Kashmiri handicraft stores stocking overpriced papier-mâché pots and bowls, silver jewellery, woollen shawls and rugs. Avoid them if you find it hard to shrug off aggressive sales pitches.

Music and bookshops

For **cassettes and CDs** a good first stop is Rhythm House, on Subhash Chowk opposite the Jehangir Art Gallery. This is a veritable Aladdin's cave of classical, devotional and popular music from all over India, with a reasonable selection of Western rock, pop and jazz, as well as DVDs of classic and contemporary Hindi movies. A ten-minute walk further north along Dr DN Road in Fort, Planet M also has a good stock of music CDs and DVDs. Mumbai likewise has a good range of English-language **bookshops** and bookstalls, the most convenient being Nalanda, in the *Taj Mahal Palace & Tower*; the Oxford Bookstore, at Apeejay House, 3 Dinsha Vacha Rd, Churchgate; and Search Word, on Shahid Bhagat Singh Marg (Colaba Causeway).

Sports

In common with most Indians, Mumbaikars are crazy about **cricket**. Few other spectator sports get much of a look-in, although the **horse racing** at Mahalakshmi draws large crowds on Derby days. Previews of all forthcoming events are posted on the back pages of the *Times of India*, and in *Time Out Mumbai*.

Cricket

Cricket provides almost as much of a distraction as movies in the Maharashtran capital, and you'll see games in progress everywhere, from impromptu sunset knockabouts on Chowpatty Beach to more formal club matches in full whites at the gymkhanas lined up along Marine Drive. In south Mumbai, **Oval Maidan** is the place to watch local talent in action, set against a wonderfully apt backdrop of imperial-era buildings. Something of a pecking order applies here: the further from the path cutting across the centre of the park you go, the better the wickets and the classier the games become.

Pitches like these are where Mumbai's favourite son, **Sachin Tendulkar**, cut his cricketing teeth. The world's most prolific batsman in both test and one-day cricket still lives in the city and plays regularly for its league-winning club side at the **Brabourne Stadium**, off Marine Drive. A kilometre or so further north, 45,000-capacity **Wankhede Stadium** is where major test matches are hosted, amid an atmosphere as intense, raucous and intimidating for visiting teams as any in India.

Getting to Goa

Easily the best-value way to travel the 500km from Mumbai to Goa is by **plane** – prices often compare favourably with the cost of the same journey via the **Konkan Railway**, which has two departures daily. Whatever your budget, think twice before attempting the hellish overnight **bus** journey.

By air

Around fifteen flights leave daily from Mumbai's domestic airport for Goa's Dabolim airport (code GOI). Flights are currently operated by Jet Airways, JetLite, Kingfisher, IndiGo, SpiceJet, Go Air, Indian Airlines and Air India. One-way fares start from around Rs2000; check Ⓦwww.expedia.co.in and Ⓦwww.travelocity.co.in for latest deals, or the websites of the airlines themselves (see p.22) for special offers and promotions.

Demand for seats can be fierce around Diwali and Christmas/New Year, when you're unlikely to get a ticket at short notice. At other times, one or other of the carriers should be able to offer a seat on the day you wish to travel – though perhaps not at the lowest fares. If you didn't pre-book when you purchased your international ticket, check availability with the airlines as soon as you arrive; tickets can be bought directly from their airport ticket desks, their downtown offices, if they have one (see opposite), through any reputable travel agent in Mumbai (bearing in mind that an agent may charge you the dollar fare at a poorer rate of exchange than that offered by the airline company), by phone or direct via the internet (though note that some low-cost airlines refuse payments by credit or debit cards not registered in India).

By train

The **Konkan Railway** line runs daily express trains from Mumbai to Margao in Goa (Rs300 for non-air-conditioned sleeper class; Rs800-1100 for a/c). However, these services are not always available at short notice from the booking halls at CST and Churchgate and you may want to **book tickets online** before you leave home. This can be done from ninety days in advance right up to four hours before the scheduled departure time – most easily, though the website Ⓦwww.cleartrip.com, which

The Indian cricket season runs from October to February. Tickets for big games are almost as hard to come by as seats on commuter trains, but foreign visitors can sometimes gain preferential access to quotas through the Mumbai Cricket Association's offices on the first floor of Wankhede.

Horse racing and horseriding

The **Mahalakshmi Racecourse**, near the Mahalakshmi Temple just north of Malabar Hill, is the home of the **Royal Western India Turf Club** – a throwback to British times that still serves as a prime stomping ground for the city's upper classes. Race meets are held twice weekly, on Wednesdays and Saturdays between November and March, and big days such as the 2000 Guineas and Derby attract crowds of 25,000. Entrance to the public ground is by ticket on the day. Seats for the colonial-era stand, with its posh lawns and exclusive *Gallops Restaurant* are, alas, allocated to members only. Race cards are posted in the sports section of the *Times of India* and at Ⓦwww.rwitc.com.

On non-race days, the Mahalakshmi ground doubles as a riding track. Temporary membership of the **Amateur Riding Club of Mumbai**, another bastion of elite Mumbai, entitles you to use the club's thoroughbreds for classes. Full details on how to do this, along with previews of forthcoming club **polo** matches, are posted at Ⓦwww.arcmumbai.com.

charges Rs100 per ticket to process purchases; major foreign credit cards are accepted. The site also handles **tatkal tickets**, which – for an extra charge of Rs75–150 – buy you access to a premium late-availability quota, released only two days before the train departs. In addition, Indian Railways maintains a small **tourist quota** of seats on Konkan services, but you'll have to apply in person at the reservations halls at CST/Churchgate, as neither the Indian Railways official site (very unreliable and best avoided) nor the more efficient, aforementioned cleartrip site are permitted to sell seats on this quota. Don't, whatever you do, be tempted to travel "unreserved" class on any Konkan service, as the journey as far as Ratnagiri (roughly midway) is overwhelmingly crushed. The most convenient services (all departing from CST) are the Konkan–Kanya Express (#0111; daily 11.05pm; 11hr 45min), the Jan Shatabdi (#2051; daily 05.10am; 9hr). Other services leave from more obscure stations to the north of Mumbai, which would involve a long taxi or suburban train ride from downtown, but may be worth considering if seats on the CST departures are not available.

By bus

The Mumbai–Goa bus journey ranks among the very worst in India. Don't believe travel agents who assure you it takes thirteen hours. Depending on the type of bus you get, appalling road surfaces along the sinuous coastal route make sixteen to eighteen hours a more realistic estimate.

Fares start at around Rs250 for a push-back seat on a beaten-up Kadamba (Goan government) or MSRTC coach. Tickets for these services are in great demand in season with domestic tourists, so book in advance at Mumbai Central. Quite a few **private overnight buses** (around a dozen daily) also run to Goa, costing from around Rs250 for no-frills buses up to Rs1000 for swisher air-conditioned Volvo coaches with berths (which bizarrely you may have to share). Tickets should be booked at least a day in advance through a reputable travel agent (see p.262), or direct through the bus company. The largest operator for Goa is Paulo Travels (Ⓦwww.paulotravels.com); tickets can be booked by phone on Ⓣ0832/663 7777 or online.

Listings

Airlines, domestic Air India, Air India Building, Nariman Point Ⓣ1800/227722; Air India Express, Air India Building, Nariman Point Ⓣ022/2279 6330; GoAir Ⓣ1800 222111; Indian, Air India Building, Nariman Point Ⓣ01800/180 1407; IndiGo Airlines, Ⓣ099/1038 3838 or 1800 180 3838; Jet Airways, B1, Amarchand Mansion, Ground Floor, Madam Cama Road, Colaba Ⓣ022/3989 3333; Jet Lite Ⓣ1800/223020; Kingfisher 241/242, Ground Floor, Nirmal Building, Nariman Point Ⓣ022/6649 9393; SpiceJet Ⓣ1800/180 3333.

Airlines, international See p.22 for airline websites. Air France, 201/B Sarjan Plaza, 2nd Floor, 100 Dr. Annie Besant Road, Worli Ⓣ1800/110055; Air India, Air India Building, Nariman Point Ⓣ022/2548 9999 or 1800/227722; British Airways Ⓣ08925/77470; Cathay Pacific, 2 Brady Gladys Plaza (2nd Floor), 1/447 Senapati Bapat Marg, Lower Parel Ⓣ022/6657 2222; Emirates, 3 Mittal Chambers, Ground Floor 228, Nariman Point Ⓣ0224 097 4097; Gulf Air, Maker Chambers V, Ground Floor, Nariman Point Ⓣ1800/221122; Jet Airways, B1, Amarchand Mansion, Ground Floor, Madam Cama Road, Colaba Ⓣ022/3989 3333; KLM, 201/B, Sarjan Plaza, 100 Annie Besant Road, Worli Ⓣ0124/272 0273; Kuwait Airways, 902N Nariman Bhavan, 9th Floor, Nariman Point Ⓣ022/66555655; Lufthansa, Express Towers, 4th Floor, Nariman Point Ⓣ022/6630 1940; Qantas Airways, 4th Floor, Rear Wing, Sunteck Centre, 37-40 Subhash Road, Vile Parle (East) Ⓣ022/2200 7440; Qatar Airways, Bajaj Bhavan, Nariman Point Ⓣ022/4456 6000; Singapore Airlines, *Taj Mahal Palace & Tower*, Apollo Bunder, Colaba Ⓣ022/2202 2747; South African Airways, Podar House, 10 Marine Drive Ⓣ022/2284 2237;

Thai Airways, Mittal Tower A Wing, Ground Floor 2A, Nariman Point ⓣ022/6637 3737.
Airport enquiries Chhatrapati Shivaji international airport ⓣ022/2681 3000, ⓦwww.csia.in; Chhatrapati Shivaji (Santa Cruz) domestic airport ⓣ022/2626 4000, ⓦwww.csia.in.
Ambulance ⓣ101 for general emergencies; but you're nearly always better off taking a taxi. See also Hospitals, below.
Banks and currency exchange The most convenient place to change money when you arrive in Mumbai is at the State Bank of India's 24hr counter in Chhatrapati Shivaji international airport. Rates here are standard but you may have to pay for an encashment certificate – you may need to produce this if you intend to buy tourist-quota train tickets or an Indrail pass at the special counters in Churchgate or CST (VT) stations. There are dozens of ATMs dotted around the city – see the various maps in the guide for precise locations. All the major state banks downtown change foreign currency (Mon–Fri 10.30am–2.30pm, Sat 10.30am–12.30pm); some (eg the Bank of Baroda) also handle credit cards and cash advances. Thomas Cook's big Dr DN Road branch (Mon–Sat 9.30am–7pm; ⓣ022/6160 3333), between the Khadi shop and Hutatma Chowk, can also arrange money transfers from overseas.
Consulates and high commissions Note that most of India's neighbouring states, including Bangladesh, Bhutan, Burma, Nepal and Pakistan, only have embassies in New Delhi and/or Kolkata (Calcutta). All of the following are open Mon–Fri only: Australia, 16th Floor, 36 Maker Chambers 6, Nariman Point (ⓣ022/6669 2000, ⓦwww.utsavaustralia.in); Canada, 41/42, 4th Floor Maker Chambers VI, Nariman Point (ⓣ022/2287 6027); Republic of Ireland, Kamanwalla Chambers, 2nd Floor, Sir PM Road, Fort (ⓣ022/6635 5635); South Africa, Gandhi Mansion, 20 Altamount Rd (ⓣ022/2389 3725); United Kingdom, Naman Chambers, C/32 G Block, Bandra Kurla Complex, Bandra (East) (ⓣ022/6650 2222, ⓦukinindia.fco.gov.uk); USA, Lincoln House, 78 Bhulabhai Desai Rd (ⓣ022/2363 3611, ⓦmumbai.usconsulate.gov).
Hospitals The best hospital in the centre is the private Bombay Hospital, New Marine Lines (ⓣ022/2206 7676, ⓦwww.bombayhospital.com), just north of the government tourist office on M Karve Rd. Breach Candy Hospital (ⓣ022/2367 1888, ⓦwww.breachcandyhospital.org) on Bhulabhai Desai Rd, near the swimming pool, is also recommended by foreign embassies.
Internet access There are surprisingly few places to get online in Mumbai. A couple of cramped 24hr places (Rs40/hr) can be found in Colaba on Nawroji F Marg. If you have your own computer, wi-fi access is available at many of the city's more upmarket hotels and at local branches of the Barista coffee-shop chain (there's a branch next to the Regal Cinema in Colaba).
Left luggage There's a left-luggage office at CST (VT) Station (Rs12/day). Anything left here, even rucksacks, must be securely fastened with a padlock and can be left for a maximum of one month.
Police The main police station in Colaba (ⓣ022/2285 6817) is on the west side of Colaba Causeway, near the crossroads with Best Marg.
Postal services The GPO (Mon–Sat 9am–8pm, Sun 9am–4pm) is around the corner from CST (VT) Station, off Nagar Chowk. The parcel office (10am–4.30pm) is behind the main building on the first floor. Packing-wallahs hang around on the pavement outside. DHL (ⓣ022/2850 5050) has eleven offices in Mumbai, the most convenient being the 24hr one under the *Sea Green Hotel* at the bottom of Marine Drive.
Travel agents The following travel agents are recommended for booking domestic and international flights, and long-distance private buses where specified: Cox and Kings India, 16 Bank St, Fort ⓣ1800/221235, ⓦwww.coxandkings.co.in; Sita World, 11th Floor, Bajaj Bhavan, Nariman Point; Thomas Cook, 324 Dr DN Road, Fort ⓣ022/6160 3333, ⓦwww.thomascook.co.in.

Contexts

Contexts

History 265

The religions of Goa 278

Environmental issues in Goa 283

Natural history 287

Goan music and dance 295

Books 299

History

For most of the twentieth century, Goa's isolated position, separated from the rest of the subcontinent by jungle-covered mountains and tidal rivers, ensured it remained relatively detached from the influences that moulded modern India. This was, however, not always the case. Long before the Portuguese annexed the region at the beginning of the sixteenth century, the thriving Hindu city that flourished here on the Konkan belt (near the site of subsequent European settlement) was exposed to a wealth of outside influences, brought along with the caravans of spices, silk and precious stones from the interior and with shiploads of horses from Arabia. Interaction over hundreds of years between the local merchants and their counterparts across Asia gave rise to a highly heterogeneous culture with diverse and far-reaching roots – a defining feature of the region's history since prehistoric times.

Pre- and early history

According to Hindu mythology, **Goa** was originally created by **Parasurama**, the sixth incarnation of Vishnu (one of the Hindu trinity) following his victorious war with the *Kshatriya* warrior caste. As a reward for his victory, the god is said to have been granted the right to claim land where his Brahmin caste could live forever in peace. The territory would be defined by seven arrows fired from a mountaintop into the sea around South India. From the spots where they fell, the waters are said to have receded to form the Brahmin homeland, known as Parasurama Kshetra ("Parasurama's Country"). One of these seven regions, midway down the west coast, was Govarashtra.

Historians have long interpreted this origin myth as some kind of transmission from ancient times, probably the period between 12,000 and 10,000 BC, when – as the presence of burnt shells and marine fossils in the red Goan soil confirms – a massive elevation of the coastal strip seems to have taken place. The Parasurama story could well refer to the intensive reclamation, drainage work and forest clearance carried out in the wake of these geological upheavals (*parasurm* means "axe") by the first farmers of the Konkan – migrants from the interior who were being displaced by the expansion from the northwest of the Aryan tribes.

Any notion that these first settled agriculturalists were Goa's aboriginal inhabitants, however, was firmly scotched in the 1990s by a series of dramatic **archeological discoveries**. Believed to date from the Upper Palaeolithic era (100,000–10,000 BC), the extraordinary rock carvings at **Usgalimal**, together with scattered stone implements recently unearthed in the hills around the headwaters of the Zuari River, near Dudhsagar Falls, prove the existence of a much older hunter-gatherer population.

Knowledge of farming techniques was imported by immigrants from the interior – either Aryans or those societies fleeing them – around 600 BC, but the first solid historical record of the region dates from three centuries later, when Goa formed a distant southwest province of the mighty **Mauryan empire**, based at Magadha in the Ganges Valley. Having filled the power vacuum that ensued from the break-up of Alexander the Great's empire in northwest India, the Mauryans expanded south to annex the Konkan coast, which Ashok, the second and greatest of the Mauryan emperors, renamed **Aparanta Desh**, or "Beyond the End". He also dispatched a Buddhist missionary of Greek origin, Dharmarakshita, to evangelize the locals. Based at rock-cut cave-temples positioned at junctions of the region's main trade routes, they preached the Buddhist doctrine of non-violence, encouraging the local tribes to give up blood sacrifice. Literacy and the use of the plough quickly took root as a result of their efforts, but the wider religious mission met with little success: when the empire collapsed after Ashok's death in 232 BC, Brahmanical Hinduism reasserted itself as the region's predominant religion.

The Hindu Golden Age

For the next seven hundred years, a succession of powerful **Hindu dynasties** held sway over Goa from their capitals elsewhere in India, installing puppet governors and exacting tribute from them in exchange for military protection. However, while the Bhojas, Silharas, Pallavas, Chalukyas and Rashtrakutas wrestled for control of South India and the Deccan Plateau, a home-grown dynasty emerged in Goa itself. Having declared independence from the Pallavas in 420 AD, the **Kadambas** gradually came to dominate the region, forging marital alliances with their powerful neighbours and founding a royal family that would endure well into the next millennium.

In 973, when the Kadambas' old allies and overlords, the Chalukyas, finally defeated their arch rivals, the Rashtrakutas, the Goan kings took this as their cue to oust the latter's governors from the capital, **Chandrapura** (see p.168), which they invaded by placing a fleet of ships side by side to form a bridge across the Zuari. Shortly afterwards, they shifted northwest to Govapuri on the banks of the river. Blessed with a deep harbour, the new Kadamba capital was perfectly placed to profit from the thriving maritime trade between the Malabar coast, Arabia and the Hindu colonies in Southeast Asia.

The move soon paid off. Within a decade, the Kadambas had amassed a fortune from the shipments of spices and horses that passed through their port, ploughing huge sums into civic building and the construction of exquisite stone temples throughout the kingdom, which by the reign of Jayakeshi II (1104–48) extended from just north of present-day Mumbai to the Malabar coast, and inland as far as the modern city of Belgaum. As a symbol of his might, the king adopted the figure of a roaring lion as his crest (an image that nowadays adorns the sides of vehicles owned by the state bus company, Kadamba Transport).

Muslim merchants from East Africa and Arabia were also encouraged to settle, and they added to the splendour by erecting mosques and villas in the capital. It was only a matter of time before such opulence attracted the attention of Muslim raiders who, during the eleventh and twelfth centuries, were pouring across India from the northwest in ever greater numbers. The old alliance with the Chalukyas had thus far protected Goa from Muslim incursions, but when the last ruler of the dynasty died in 1198, the kingdom lay exposed and vulnerable to attack from the Deccan.

Muslim invasions

The first **Muslim raids** on Goa took place late in the **tenth century**, orchestrated by the warlord Mahmud of Ghazni from Delhi. Directed mainly at the Kadambas' temples, which housed most of the region's treasure, the incursions grew more frequent and destructive as the twelfth and thirteenth centuries progressed, culminating with the excesses of **Ala ud-din Khalji**, the sultan of Delhi, and Muhammed Tughluq. Successive sackings of Govapuri reduced it to ruins, and the beleaguered Kadambas were forced to flee to their former capital at Chandrapura. This, too, was eventually destroyed, although not before Govapuri had been rebuilt.

The spirit of religious tolerance that prevailed between Goa's Arab merchants and their Kadamba hosts (even during the Muslim raids of the medieval era) vanished almost overnight in 1350 with the arrival of the **Bahmanis**. Driven by a new religious fanaticism, the invaders instigated a systematic persecution of the Hindus, smashing up temples and murdering priests. Many of the most sacred deities were smuggled to the safety of the interior, but nearly all of the ornately carved shrines were destroyed: only one – the tiny **Mahadeva Mandir** at **Tambdi Surla** in central Goa, hidden in the forests at the foot of the Western Ghats – has survived (see p.102).

This first period of Bahmani rule was short-lived, for in 1378, the Hindu **Vijayanagar** kings swept into the region across the Ghats from their capital at Hampi on the Deccan Plateau. Exacting revenge for the earlier slaughter of their co-religionists by the Bahmanis, they massacred the Muslim inhabitants of the Goan capital, which the invaders occupied until it was counterattacked nearly a century later in 1470. This time the Bahmanis made sure of victory by launching a massive two-pronged invasion, with a vast army from the east and a navy of 120 warships from the sea.

The city they conquered, however, had already lapsed into decline. Blocked by silt, its once thriving harbour had been left high and dry, forcing the Bahmanis to move to a more convenient location further north on the banks of the Mandovi River. Known as **Ela**, this new capital, erected on the site of a Hindu religious centre founded by the Vijayanagars, would soon become the wealthiest city on India's southwest coast.

The transformation of Ela from sleepy sacred site to prosperous port was masterminded by the **sultans of Bijapur**, who succeeded the Bahmanis in 1490. The rapidly expanding horse trade with Arabia enabled their first leader, **Yusuf 'Adil Shah**, to embark on a major building spree. During his short twenty-year rule, the sultan erected a huge mosque and a grand fort-palace overlooking the Mandovi, as well as a two-storey summer palace for his harem further upriver at a village called Pahajani.

The Portuguese discoveries

With the Moors ousted from the Iberian peninsula and Christendom established in the North African port of Ceuta in 1415, the crusading **European superpowers** began to seek fresh pastures in which to exercise their proselytizing zeal. The Americas, recently discovered by Columbus, provided the Spanish with potentially rich pickings, while the rival Portuguese turned their sights towards the African Gold Coast and beyond. Their initial goal had been to spread Christianity and locate the mythical Christian ruler Prester John, whom the Portuguese hoped would aid them in their quest against Islam in Africa. Later, however, the lure of cheap silk, pearls and spices overshadowed other motives, particularly after Bartolemeu Dias rounded the Cape of Good Hope in 1488, making a route across the Indian Ocean at last seem within reach. If this route could be opened up, it would bypass the much slower trans-Asian caravan trail, threatening the old Venetian-Muslim monopoly on Indian luxury goods and providing direct access to the spice islands of the Philippines – all of which meant potentially vast profits for any nation able to maintain maritime dominance.

As a result, the Portuguese were quick to throw their Spanish rivals off the scent, informing them that the Cape lay a good ten degrees further south than it did. This ruse made the voyage around the tip of Africa seem a lot less viable as a short cut to the spiceries, and contributed in no small part to the **Treaty of Tordesillas** of 1494, in which the Spaniards relinquished any claims to territories east of a dividing line set at 370 leagues west of the Cape Verde Islands, off the coast of West Africa.

Once rights to the world's seas had been carved up between the two Iberian nations, the way was open for the Portuguese to capitalize on their earlier efforts along the rim of the Indian Ocean. Aside from Dias' pioneering expedition, several secret voyages, of whose existence historians have only recently learned from old naval records, probed up the east coast of Africa. The scene was thus set for the entry of **Vasco da Gama**, whose **1498** voyage from Lisbon to Calicut, on the west coast of India, marked the beginning of the colonial era. On his second and third expeditions, both marred by bloody encounters with his African and Indian hosts, Da Gama established permanent trade stations that would, in the course of the coming century, become the first European colonies in India. Before this was possible, however, the Portuguese would have to assert their control of the Indian Ocean's seaways. Since Da Gama's first crossing, the Europeans had been universally detested in East Africa and South Asia because of the atrocities they inflicted on local populations, and the major powers of southern India were eager to settle accounts.

The battle of Diu

To counter the Portuguese naval threat in the Indian Ocean, the Ottoman Turks spent nearly a decade building a fleet of twelve ships at the head of the Red Sea. The Zamorin of Calicut, whose capital had been cannonaded and subjects mercilessly terrorized by Da Gama and subsequent Portuguese traders, also wished to give the Christians a bloody nose, and sent a hundred light vessels north to join the Turks. Together they closed in on the Portuguese at Chaul (midway between modern Goa and Mumbai) in 1508, where a small fleet under the command of Dom Lourenço Almeida, son of the so-called viceroy of the *Estado da India*, was sheltering. In the ensuing engagement, the Portuguese flagship was sunk and its commander killed; the rest of the fleet limped south.

When news reached Almeida senior of his son's death, the viceroy swore revenge, but a year elapsed before he came within firing distance of the Muslim fleet at **Diu**, a strategically important island at the mouth of the Indus delta. From here, shipping to and from the textile-rich region of Gujarat could be controlled, as could trade into the Persian Gulf. As they prepared for battle, both sides must have known that whoever won would dominate the Indian Ocean for many years to come.

In the event, the superior firepower and manoeuvrability of the Portuguese ships prevailed, and the Muslim navy was squarely routed. To impress their triumph upon the local people, the Portuguese indulged in a characteristically gratuitous bout of bloodletting; whenever the fleet approached a town or city, prisoners taken in the battle were decapitated and their heads and limbs fired at close range.

Albuquerque and the conquest of Goa

Eleven years after Da Gama's first arrival in India, the Battle of Diu had ensured Portuguese control of the South Asian sea trade. This monopoly was maintained in a variety of ways. In addition to attacking and looting any Muslim ships, which the Christians considered fair game, they also decreed that anyone wishing to trade in the Indian Ocean carry a special permit, or **cartaz**, for which merchants had to pay large sums. As the decade progressed, however, it became clear that some kind of permanent enclave was required from which to administer the huge volume of trade passing through Portuguese control. A site was needed for warehouses and sanatoriums where sick sailors could recuperate and ships could be repaired in dry docks.

The man who would oversee the creation of Portugal's first colony was not Francisco de Almeida, the victorious commander at the Battle of Diu and India's first viceroy, but his bitter rival, **Alfonso de Albuquerque**, whom Almeida rightly suspected had been earmarked by Lisbon for his job. A veteran of anti-Islamic crusades, Albuquerque had cut his teeth in North Africa and was as famous for his loathing of Muslims as for the strength of his own religious convictions. During Almeida's rule as viceroy, he kept a low profile, preferring to secure footholds on the African coast rather than the Indian. But after a string of exceptional military successes, notably in Muscat in 1507 and Hormuz the following year, he confronted the viceroy and demanded a transfer of power. Almeida was understandably incensed by this, and promptly incarcerated Albuquerque, until the latter was liberated by an emissary from Lisbon. The envoy, **Fernando Countinho**, had also brought with him instructions from the royal council that Albuquerque should capture the then Muslim port of Goa and establish a bastion there, while Coutinho himself was commanded to take Calicut, long a thorn in the side of Portuguese domination in the Indian Ocean. Together the two led a force south; both were nearly killed in the attack on Calicut, but slipped away to fight another day in Goa, where Turkish survivors of the Battle of Diu had allegedly taken refuge. Aside from mopping up the remnants of a potentially troublesome fleet, the engagement would also fulfil Albuquerque's orders from Lisbon. When it emerged that the local overlord was fighting a war on the opposite side of his kingdom, and that Goa was thus poorly defended, the attack was launched.

The battle for Ela

The depleted Muslim garrison at Panaji fort was unprepared for the onslaught by the better-armed Europeans, and capitulated without a fight. However, while the Portuguese were wondering what to do with their new acquisition, the chief minister and regent of the newly enthroned 13-year-old sultan of Bijapur, Ismail 'Adil Shah, ordered a massive counteroffensive. Albuquerque and his soldiers held out for a couple of weeks, but were eventually pushed back to the mouth of the Mandovi River, where, hemmed in by cannon-fire from Panaji fort and with supplies of food and water dwindling, they remained for three months, their only escape route blocked by heavy monsoon seas.

The storms eventually subsided and the Portuguese were able to retreat. Seeing this as a chance to slip back to Bijapur, the sultan and his ministers also withdrew, but left Goa inadequately defended, not suspecting that Albuquerque would attempt another assault with his impoverished force. The wily Portuguese commander, however, was able to galvanize his troops and mount a ferocious second attack on the city on November 25, 1510, St Catherine's Day, which, this time, resulted in a decisive victory. The European soldiers swarmed through **Ela**, routing the Muslims and strengthening defences against the inevitable Bijapuri backlash. In his treatment of the survivors, Albuquerque, furious that the Muslim population of Goa had aided the 'Adil Shah's army in its attempt to retake the city, demonstrated the same predilection for atrocity he had so often shown in Morocco and East Africa.

Work on fortifying the city progressed at an extraordinary pace and was completed by the time Albuquerque left Goa in 1513 to attack ports in the Red Sea and Persian Gulf. But the hitherto indefatigable commander suffered a bitter defeat at Aden, where he lost most of his soldiers in an ill-conceived siege, and found the establishment of a fort at Hormuz – his last significant contribution to the Portuguese empire in Asia – too much for his exhausted body. Leaving Hormuz in the care of his cousin, Albuquerque set sail for Goa knowing that his life was drawing to an end. The death blow came when, still moored in Panaji harbour, he received the news that another governor had been appointed in his absence. Apparently he said to himself, "Old man, oh for your grave! You have incurred the king's displeasure for the sake of his subjects, and the subjects' displeasure for the sake of the king!"

The 'Adil Shah launched a counterattack four years after Albuquerque's death, but to no avail. Ela was by then securely under Portuguese control, and would remain so for another 450 years.

Conversion to Christianity

The zeal with which the Portuguese had seized Ela from the Muslims did not subside after the conquest. Rather, it was channelled in another direction: the **dissemination of Christianity**, which both justified the colonial enterprise and endowed it with the air of a religious crusade.

Ela's Muslims fled from the city in 1510, but a large contingent of Hindus remained (Portugal's alliance with the Bijapuris' enemies, the Vijayanagars, had ensured their safety), and it was towards them that the first Christian **missionaries**, representatives of the Franciscan Order invited by the king of Portugal, directed their attention when they arrived. Under Albuquerque's administration, the Church was relatively tolerant, relying on persuasion rather than force to claim converts. The governor also encouraged his soldiers to marry local women in the knowledge that the children of such alliances would be raised as Christians.

Such tactics proved effective but were deemed too liberal by Goa's first vicar general, whose arrival in 1532 signalled the start of a markedly more oppressive regime. Supported by the zealous, newly arrived **Jesuits**, he passed a law in 1541 ordering the closure of all Hindu temples. This was followed four years later by the outlawing of collective worship of idols and the exiling of all Brahmin priests. The proclamation also sparked off an orgy of iconoclasm, with more than 350 shrines plundered and razed across the territory.

Worse was to follow. In 1559, idols were banned from private houses, and the following year, the Tribunal of the Holy Office, better known as the **Inquisition**, descended on Goa to weed out anyone who dared deviate from the dogma of the Roman Catholic Church. Imprisoned in the dungeons of the 'Adil Shah's former palace, suspects were subjected to appalling tortures that culminated in spectacular **autos da fé**, literally "acts of faith", when they would have to publicly recant their heresy before being condemned – usually to death or slavery (a fuller account of the Goan Inquisition appears in the box on p.100).

However, even two hundred years of the Inquisition failed to eradicate Hinduism altogether. A large number of deities were smuggled into the Portuguese-free zone in the middle of the state, where they were enshrined in secret temples, tended by priests in exile and worshipped by devotees under cover of darkness, who risked their lives to pray. Many of these temples still exist in Goa, hidden in the woods and valleys of Pernem, Satari, Sanguem and Canacona *talukas*.

"Goa Dourada"

By the time the Inquisition arrived in Goa in 1560, the territory's Golden Age was already in full swing. Situated at the nexus of Asia's most prosperous trade routes, the city of Old Goa raked in vast profits from the shipment of spices to Europe and of Arabian horses into the subcontinent, earning for it the nickname "**Goa Dourada**", or "Golden Goa". Taxes levied on the movement of goods through its port financed a prolific **building boom**, as dozens of splendid churches and cathedrals were erected in the capital – monuments worthy of Goa's role as the headquarters of Christianity in Asia.

Lured by the seemingly inexhaustible supply of heathen souls to save, representatives of various **religious orders** began to pour in to staff these lavish buildings, accompanied by an even greater deluge of **immigrants**. During the colony's heyday, an estimated 2500 people left Portugal each year, causing a chronic shortage of workers in the mother country and precipitating a recession there that would contribute in no small part to Goa's eventual decline. Many Portuguese emigrants perished during the sea voyage, but enough survived to swell the city's population to around 300,000 – bigger than either London or Lisbon at that time, in spite of appalling **epidemics** that regularly swept through the city. The permanent population was further boosted by a transient contingent of soldiers, sailors and traders who came to seek their fortune.

Littered around the more salubrious suburbs of Asia's largest metropolis were the elegant villas and grand colonial residences of its **hidalgos**, or Portuguese nobility. The lifestyle enjoyed by this wealthy elite was, in spite of the Church's high profile, famously decadent. Accounts by contemporary travellers – notably the Frenchman François Pyrard, who visited Goa after being shipwrecked in the Maldives in 1608 – describe the unbridled debauchery that prevailed among Goa's aristocracy. Sexual mores were notoriously lax, with prostitution and adultery rife among both the upper and lower classes. Pyrard even claimed that wealthy women of the colony regularly used to drug their husbands with an extract from the hallucinogenic *datura* plant: in small quantities, the substance induced sleep and memory loss, allowing them to facilitate their adulterous liaisons undetected.

When reports of this decadence finally filtered back to Lisbon, King Dom João III dispatched a party of young Jesuit priests to remedy the situation. Among them was **Francis Xavier** (see p.88), the most successful missionary of his day, who used the city as a base for his evangelical missions to the Malabar coast (modern day Kerala). The saint's body, which for centuries remained miraculously free from signs of decomposition, is today enshrined in Old Goa's **Basilica of Bom Jesus**, the most magnificent of Goa's churches and spiritual heart of Roman Catholicism in India.

Decline

The writing was on the wall for Goa long before the source of its wealth – total control of Asia's booming maritime trade – ran dry in the seventeenth century. The roots of the colony's **decline** lay in its ill-chosen location. Situated amid low-lying swampland, the city swarmed with malaria-carrying mosquitoes. In addition, outbreaks of cholera and typhoid were common, spread by the sewage that swilled through the streets during the rains. **Epidemics** plagued the city from the start, and by the late 1600s, its population had plummeted to less than a tenth of its previous peak. The Mandovi River had also begun to silt up, and ships were finding it increasingly difficult to dock at the quayside.

Politics also played their part in the colony's demise. The first blow was struck by the sultans of Bijapur. After Adil Shah's death in 1557, his son, Ali, negotiated an alliance between the region's five main Muslim nations against the Hindu Vijayanagars. This bore fruit eight years later when the Muslim coalition defeated their arch adversaries at the **Battle of Talikota**. The sack of the Hindu capital lasted for six months and furnished the attackers with enough booty to erect some of India's finest Islamic monuments in Bijapur. Squabbles over the loot subsequently divided the Muslim league, although the Ahmednagar and Bijapuri dynasties stuck together to launch a combined attack on Goa in 1570: a fleet blockaded the port, while a massive army encircled the city itself, defended by a force of fewer than one hundred Portuguese soldiers and black slaves. The attack, however, failed. Bogged down in Goa's swamps, the invaders eventually succumbed to cholera and were forced to retreat after a year-long siege.

Further threats to Goa's survival followed as the struggle between European powers for trade supremacy in the region intensified. Foremost among the challengers to Portuguese maritime hegemony were the **Dutch**, whose lighter and more manoeuvrable ships easily outsailed the old-fashioned, ungainly Portuguese galleons. Mercantile rivalries were given an added edge by religious differences: determined not to allow Asia to be carved up by the proselytizing Roman Catholics, the Protestant Dutch systematically whittled away at Portugal's Oriental colonies, while pepper-smuggling **privateers** found it increasingly easy to slip through the net cast by the Portuguese navy in the Indian Ocean.

With its trade monopoly broken, its port blocked by silt, its administration in tatters and its population decimated by disease, Goa was well and truly on its last legs by the end of the seventeenth century.

The Maratha Wars and Novas Conquistas

Meanwhile in the Deccan, a formidable new challenge to European ambitions in India was taking shape. From their homeland in the Northwestern Ghats, the Hindu **Marathas**, led by the indomitable and militaristic chieftain **Shivaji**, were proving a thorn in the side of the mighty Mughal emperors, who ruled most of Northern India at this time. For years, the Portuguese watched the skirmishes between these two native powers from the wings, but when Shivaji sacked the Mughal stronghold of Surat in 1664, both sides petitioned the Portuguese for support, and the viceroy found himself on the brink of involvement in the conflict.

He avoided commitment on this occasion, but was outmanoeuvred a couple of years later when a Mughal army massed on the Goan border and demanded safe passage through the territory, which it was reluctantly granted. This provided the ambitious new Maratha chief **Sambhaji**, Shivaji's son, with precisely the excuse he needed to attack the Portuguese trading post of Chaul, a short way south of British Bombay. The Portuguese responded by attacking Ponda, recently seized by the Marathas from the neighbouring raja, but the offensive failed, with disastrous consequences for the Portuguese. No sooner had they retreated towards the Goan capital than the opposing Hindu army surged forward in an attack to annex chunks of Bardez and Salcete.

Outflanked and with no hope of reinforcements, the viceroy decided to appeal to God for help. Hurrying to the Basilica of Bom Jesus, he opened up the tomb of St Francis Xavier and placed inside it his viceregal regalia, putting the fate of the colony in the miracle-working hands of its patron saint. His faith proved well founded. Within days, the Mughals appeared on the border, forcing the Marathas to beat a hasty retreat.

War between the Hindu rebels and their Muslim overlords kept the two sides busy for the next couple of decades, but Goa found itself in the firing line again in 1737. The Marathas, led this time by Sambhaji's son, **Shapu**, were besieging **Bassein**, a major Portuguese fort and coastal settlement north of Bombay. In order to waylay any potential Portuguese reinforcements, he also mounted a diversionary raid on Goa, seizing Margao and encircling the bastion at Rachol. Had Shapu realized just how weak the Goans had become since the last war, he would no doubt have pressed on to take the capital. However, fierce resistance at Bassein led him to overestimate the defensive capacity of his Portuguese adversaries, and the Maratha leader opted for a truce. The **Treaty of May 1739** ceded control of Portugal's northern provinces (including Bassein but not Daman) to the Hindus, in exchange for the complete withdrawal of Maratha forces from Goa. In addition, the Portuguese agreed to pay a hefty sum in **compensation**. This, coming in the wake of other territorial losses and financial setbacks inflicted by its European rivals, totally impoverished the territory, whose capital now lay virtually deserted and in ruins.

The Maratha surrender let the Portuguese off the hook, but the latter found the humiliation hard to stomach and tried to regain the provinces lost in the treaty of 1739. However, both the Marathas and the British, who had gained a number of important footholds on India's west coast (among them a couple of former Portuguese possessions), proved too powerful. Instead, Portugal sought to enlarge Goa as a way of boosting morale and compensating for their recent defeats. Bicholim and Satari, two rural districts to the east of Mapusa, were assimilated in 1780–81, and Pernem in the far north later that decade. Finally, in 1791, the raja of Sunda handed over Ponda, along with Sanguem, Quepem and Canacona in the south. These acquisitions, known as the **Novas Conquistas** (New Conquests), were quickly integrated with the older-established districts of Tiswadi, Bardez and Salcete – the **Velhas Conquistas** (Old Conquests) that formed a buffer zone around the capital – and the frontiers of modern Goa were finally fixed.

The rise of Panjim and the Independence Movement

The **nineteenth century** was a period of great flux in Goa. Money was still trickling in from the gold and ivory trade with East Africa, but the capital had lapsed into irreversible decay, eclipsed by Portugal's more recently established colony of Brazil. When the French Abbé Cottineau visited Goa in 1822, he found only churches marooned in rubble and jungle, while Richard Burton, in his 1850 travelogue *Goa and the Blue Mountains*, remarked that the city was a scene of "utter destitution", its population "…as sepulchral-looking as the spectacle around them".

Disease and the decline of the empire had taken their toll, but the demise of the once proud metropolis was hastened by the departure of its few remaining inhabitants to a more salubrious site further west along the Mandovi.

At the start of the nineteenth century, **Panjim** was a small fishing settlement of around two hundred houses, with a decrepit Muslim fort, a handful of chapels and churches and the 'Adil Shah's former summer palace presiding over its waterfront. However, its healthy position and proximity to both the open sea and the remains of Old Goa city made it an obvious candidate for the site of the colony's new capital. **Dom Manuel de Portugal e Castro**, Panjim's founding father and viceroy between 1827 and 1835, is the man widely credited with the city's metamorphosis. He ordered the levelling of dunes and the draining of swamps around the town to create additional land for building, and oversaw the construction of the impressive administrative blocks that still stand in the centre today. By the mid-nineteenth century, Panjim had become a bustling town of tree-lined avenues and leafy seaside suburbs.

As its size increased, so too did disenchantment with direct rule from Lisbon. Calls for Goa to be made a republic or be absorbed into British India were echoed in Portugal, which at this time was divided by civil war. The mounting distrust culminated in a **coup** attempt by the Goan military, which was unsuccessful but led to the appointment of Dom Manuel de Portugal e Castro as new governor. Yet even the former viceroy was unable to stave off the series of further mutinies by the army that resulted in the bloody "**massacre of Gaspar Dias**", when, on May 4, 1835, the fort at Gaspar Dias was destroyed by rebel soldiers and the regiment posted inside it slain.

When the dust settled after the mutiny, the Portuguese remained in power, although drastic measures were now clearly required if the rising tide of disenchantment in Goa was to be stemmed. Frustration with Portuguese rule was felt most keenly by the Hindus, who were still treated as second-class citizens by the administration. Iniquitous colonial laws (some of which were introduced as late as 1910) denied them access to government jobs and positions of influence, even though many of the colony's most prosperous merchants and businessmen were Hindu.

Prominent politicians had successfully publicized Goa's plight in Europe, but it was through the local press that the fledgling **freedom movement** found its wings. In spite of stringent censorship laws, the newly created newspapers provided a platform for the separatists, whose ideas found favour among both the educated classes at home and influential Goan expatriates in Bombay.

However, after Portugal had itself been declared a republic in 1926, Goa's independence struggle sustained a major setback. For the next 46 years, Portuguese foreign policy was to be laid down by the right-wing dictator **Salazar**. Staunchly pro-colonial, he refused to relinquish control of Goa or Portugal's remaining possessions in Africa and Southeast Asia, even though the impoverished mother country could scarcely provide for itself, let alone prop up its flagging foreign territories.

Portugal's economic woes had another important **social consequence** for Goa. Throughout the twentieth century, hundreds of thousands of Goans were forced out-of-state and overseas – to Bombay, Bangalore and the Portuguese colonies in Africa – in search of work. Many men from poorer, low-caste fishing families also took jobs in the merchant marine and on cruise liners – a tradition that endures to this day among coastal communities.

Meanwhile, India's national independence struggle gathered momentum, culminating in the **British withdrawal** of 1947. Inevitably, the end of the Raj intensified demands for Portugal to quit Goa. Inspired by Gandhi's philosophies of non-violent resistance, a dozen or more groups formed to agitate for Goan independence, but these failed to establish a unified front, riven by petty rivalries and political feuding. Nevertheless, hundreds of *satyagrahas* ("freedom fighters") were imprisoned, tortured, shot or exiled to Africa and Portugal through the 1950s in Goa, as the Portuguese dictator struggled to shore up his rapidly crumbling hold over the colony.

Liberation

Outraged by reports of atrocities in Goa, India's first prime minister, **Jawaharlal "Pandit" Nehru**, openly encouraged civil disobedience in the colony. In March 1961, he sent a message of support to independence campaigners, denouncing Portuguese rule and urging Goans to fight "unremittingly" for liberation. Later, ostensibly in response to a build-up of Portuguese forces in the region, a massive movement of troops and battleships was ordered around Goa's borders. The previous year, India's prestige had received a bloody nose after China's invasion of Ladakh, in the Himalayas, and with an election pending, Nehru was in need of a foreign policy success to bolster his popularity.

Salazar, meanwhile, desperately tried to whip up international condemnation of India's claim on Goa by lobbying world leaders. But foreign powers were determined not to become embroiled in a conflict and kept their distance.

In the end, it was Salazar who gave Nehru the pretext he needed to invade, when Portuguese troops stationed at Anjediv Island (10km south of Goa) opened fire on Indian fishing boats. One month later, on December 17, 1961, Indian forces finally entered Goa and the other remaining Portuguese enclaves in India, Daman and Diu. Mounted in defiance of a United Nations resolution (subsequently vetoed by the Soviet Union), "**Operation Vijay**" met with only token resistance from the 1800 Portuguese troops stationed in the colony, with barely a shot fired on either side.

The offensive was heralded as an act of heroic "**liberation**" by India, but met with a more ambivalent response in Goa itself. Many feared assimilation would result in a drop in the relatively high standards of living in the territory. The influx of immigrant workers from poorer states, as well as the army of troops and bureaucrats that descended from Delhi, also made Goans more acutely aware of how different they were from their neighbours.

Centuries of divide-and-rule politics from the Portuguese had the effect of accentuating social divisions rather than cultural similarities. To both colonizers and the colonized, Goa felt more like a conglomeration of separate communities – Hindus, Christians, Muslims and dozens of castes and sub-castes – than a culturally homogeneous region. Notions of a definable "Goan identity" were thus either nebulous or, in the case of the Portuguese-speaking elite, based on the hackneyed, outdated image of "Goa Dourada" promoted by its European rulers. Now, however, with the Portuguese Raj replaced by an army of moustachioed troops and bland bureaucrats from distant Delhi, fears mounted that a merger with the mother country might result in a loss of cultural identity.

The road to statehood

Recognizing Goa's cultural and historical distinctiveness, the Indian government immediately designated the former colony a **Union Territory**, with semi-independent status and its own ruling body, or Legislative Assembly. Within two years, Goa boasted its own popularly elected government, headed by the millionaire mining magnate, D.B. Bandodkar.

During the first two decades after liberation, sweeping **economic changes** transformed life in the territory beyond recognition, as it metamorphosed from a traditional colonial society to an industrial capitalist one. But the issue that most preoccupied the new leader and his electorate at this time was merger – the debate over whether or not to join the neighbouring state of Maharashtra.

In 1963, the ruling party, the **Maharashtrawadi Gomantak** (or MGP), came to office on a pro-merger platform, asserting that "Goan culture" was in essence a colonial myth and Konkani no more than an inferior dialect of Maharati; it also attacked the power of the upper-caste *goenkars* by championing rights of the lower, landless castes. In opposition, the **United Goan Party** (UGP) stood vehemently against assimilation with Maharashtra, advocating greater autonomy and a more inclusive, less caste-based realpolitik.

These two parties dominated the fiercely fought campaign that preceded the **Opinion Poll** of January 16, 1967, when Goans were asked to vote for or against merger. After three days of intense nail-biting, a crowd of 25,000 gathered outside the Menezes Braganza Institute in Panjim to learn that 54 percent of the population had voted in favour of remaining a Union Territory. When it came to declaring their hand, Goa's Hindus had, contrary to the pundits' predictions, preferred the status quo. Integration with Maharashtra would have meant becoming a remote corner of a huge state, hence significantly fewer job opportunities and reduced government investment. Goa's liberal liquor laws, too, would have disappeared overnight, depriving tens of thousands of *toddi* tappers of their traditional livelihoods. In the end, it was probably these factors, rather than ideological ones, which swayed the day.

The pro-Goan lobby had triumphed by only a slim margin, but it was enough to bury the merger issue once and for all. After Bandodkar's death in 1973, when he was succeeded as chief minister by his daughter, **Shashikala Kakodkar**, the MGP found itself increasingly marginalized. Six years later, in the elections of 1979, it finally lost out to the Congress Party, which has remained in power in Goa more or less until the present day.

In the 1980s, the status of **Konkani**, the language spoken by the majority of Goans but not that of government or education, formed the primary focus of debate over the territory's future. Spearheaded by the Konkani Porjech Avaz (KPA), campaigners agitated for it to be upgraded to an official language. The movement boiled over into riots in December 1986, provoking political upheavals and, two months later, the announcement from Delhi of the eagerly awaited Official Language Bill.

Indian states are drawn primarily along linguistic lines; thus the step from official language status to full-blown statehood is a small one. Calls for Goa to be made the twenty-fifth state in the Republic of India soon came to dominate editorials in the notoriously emotive local press. As one commentator wrote at the time, "Konkani is the soul of the red soil of Goa. Statehood will be the body which will provide a home for the soul." The landmark decision was finally made on **May 31, 1987**, giving permanent acknowledgement from the central government to the region's distinct cultural identity.

Recent history

For the past twenty years, political life in the fledgling state has been dogged by **chronic instability**. No fewer than sixteen chief ministers have held power since 1990, the majority of them over shaky, opportunistic coalitions, cobbled together during periods of post-electoral deal-cutting. As a result, policymaking was for much of the time rendered near impossible, while **corruption** steadily eroded the fabric of public life.

Among the main beneficiaries of the ongoing chaos have been the right-wing Hindu nationalists, the **Bharatiya Janata Party** (BJP), which won a majority of the seats in the Goan State Legislature in 2000. During his five years in power, the BJP chief minister, **Manohar Parrikkar**, became popular among urban, middle-class voters – not least for his makeover of Panjim's esplanade and for securing the capital as venue for the prestigious International Film Festival of India. Even so, Congress managed to regain power in 2004, accelerating the power struggle between the two rival parties. A series of high-profile defections and sackings soon followed, and within months the situation had degenerated into a full-on fiasco, as scenes of unbridled rowdiness in the State Legislature at Alto Porvorim brought the reputation of Goan politics to a new low.

Eventually, after a succession of no-confidence votes, New Delhi decided to step in and declare **President's Rule**. The ignominy dominated national headlines at the time, until fresh elections could be held in June 2005, when Congress won four out of the five seats, and Pratapsingh Rane was declared chief minister.

Communal riots between Hindus and Muslims in 2006, sparked in the iron-ore mining town of **Sanvordem** by plans to erect a new mosque, demonstrated the extent to which the political unrest in Goa had fostered the rise of right-wing religious parties. Amid the inquiries that followed, the only certainty to have emerged was that, far from being an isolated incident, Sanvordem was part of a growing trend of anti-Muslim violence in Goa largely orchestrated by pro-Marathi, BJP Hindu nationalists.

The state has always been proud of its communal harmony, but whether this can hold in the face of rising tensions elsewhere in India remains in question. Goa today no longer stands aloof from the mainstream of national life, as it did under Portuguese rule. After the **terror attacks** on **Mumbai** in **November 2008**, its tourist hot spots were on red alert, with armed troops patrolling the Anjuna flea market and sniffer dogs dispatched to nightclubs such as Tito's.

Fears over the pace of change on the coastal strip have also started to dominate public life and the media. A sudden influx of wealthy **Russians** and Indian **property developers** from Delhi and Mumbai since 2003 has provoked a backlash from the government, with a state-sponsored land grab of expatriate property. Hundreds of resident Europeans spuriously accused of illegally buying land have had their assets confiscated since 2007, and have fled home. A series of high-profile attacks on and by foreigners – notably the murder in 2008 of British teenager Scarlett Keeling – has done little to improve the state's image abroad. Meanwhile, as ever-improving infrastructural links with the rest of India render Goa's borders more porous, the survival of the region as a culturally distinct entity continues to hang in the balance.

The religions of Goa

Three great religions – Hinduism, Christianity and Islam – are represented in Goa, and they play a vital part in the everyday lives of the population. Indeed, some religious festivals, like Diwali and Christmas, have become elevated to such a stature that they are among the region's main cultural events, while temples and churches provide a focus for social as well as devotional life.

Roughly speaking, **Christian** Goa encompasses the centre of the state: the coastal region of Tiswadi, Salcete and Bardez *talukas*. Known as the *Velhas Conquistas*, or Old Conquests, this area is still littered with whitewashed churches and wayside crosses, and its older houses are very much in the Portuguese mould. The **Hindu** heartland lies in the hilly interior around the town of Ponda, and in parts of the north and south of the state, known as the *Novas Conquistas*, or New Conquests, which retained a more obviously Indian feel. Despite being the religion of the region's rulers for a few centuries, **Islam** has declined in Goa, with only a small remaining community.

Though politics in the state have been increasingly hijacked by communal interests over the past decade or so, violence is still relatively rare. Incidents such as those in Sanvordem in March 2006 (see p.276) are unusual enough to dominate the news for months. For the most part Hindus, Christians and Muslims live in a spirit of mutual tolerance – even, on occasions, participating in each others' religious festivals (Hindu and Christian neighbours, for example, commonly exchange sweets – *mithai* – for Diwali and Christmas). The two major faiths have also taken on many common traits: Goan temples incorporate features of Italian Renaissance architecture, while Christian worship frequently has the devotional air of Hindu rituals, with garlanded icons and prayers sung in Konkani.

Hinduism

The product of several millennia of evolution and assimilation, **Hinduism** was the predominant religion in Goa long before the arrival of Christianity, and is today practised by two-thirds of the region's population. Although underpinned by a plethora of sacred scriptures, it has no single orthodoxy, prophet, creed or doctrine, and thus encompasses a wide range of different beliefs. Its central tenet is the conviction that human life is an ongoing series of rebirths and reincarnations (*avatars*) that eventually leads to spiritual release (*moksha*). An individual's progress is determined by **karma**, very much a law of cause and effect, where negative decisions and actions impede the process of upward incarnations, and positive ones, such as worship and charitable acts, accelerate it. A whole range of deities is revered, which on the surface can make Hinduism seem mind-bogglingly complex, but with a loose understanding of the *Vedas* and *Puranas* – the religion's most influential holy texts – the characters and roles of the various gods and goddesses become apparent.

Castes in Hinduism

Every Hindu is born into a rigid social class, or **varna** (literally "colour", but sometimes referred to as **caste**), each with its own specific rules and responsibilities. In descending hierarchical order, the four *varnas* are: Brahmins, known as *Bamons* in

Konkani (priests and teachers); *Kshatriyas*, or *Chardos* (rulers and warriors); *Vaishyas* (merchants and cultivators); and *Shudras* (menials). Members of the first two classes, known as "twice-born", are distinguished by a sacred thread worn from the time of initiation, and are granted full access to religious texts and rituals; members of the fourth *varna* are occasionally excluded from some of India's most sacred shrines. Below all four categories, groups whose jobs involve "polluting" – coming in contact with dirt or death – such as undertakers, sweepers or leather workers, were traditionally classified as **Untouchables**, later renamed, following the campaign of Mahatma Gandhi, as *Harijans*, or "Children of God". Discrimination against this lowest stratum of society, called *Chamars* in Goa, is now a criminal offence, but "Untouchability" is by no means a thing of the past.

Within the four main *varnas* exist numerous sub-categories which usually, though no longer necessarily, denote a person's occupation. Each has a set place in the complex and rigid social hierarchy of Hinduism. In Goa, for example, members of the *Chardo* caste may be *borem munis* (literally "good people") or *sokol munis* ("low people"), while *Shudras* could be *shetkamti* (agricultural workers), *dhobis* (clothes washers), *dorjis* (tailors) or *render* (*toddi* tappers), depending on the traditional work undertaken by their family. As a rule, it is possible to ascertain a person's caste from their surname, but sub-caste is expressed through many other factors too: such as which part of a village a person's family comes from, what roles they play in temple rituals and even what they eat and wear.

While it is certainly true that caste divisions are less marked in Goa than most other parts of India (in some states, such as Bihar and Rajasthan, inter-caste violence has taken on civil-war proportions), they remain influential, particularly in villages. For example, landowners (*Goenkars*) are invariably *Bamons*, or high *Chardos*, while the people who work their fields in exchange for a share of the rice harvest are nearly always *Shudras*. Government jobs have also tended to be taped up by *Bamons*, traditionally more literate and better educated than the lower castes, although the Delhi-imposed job-reservation system – wherein sought-after positions, in both the civil service and government, are allocated according to quotas – has enabled greater representation for members of the so-called "Scheduled and Other Backward Castes" (SOBCs) in politics and public life.

Temples

That said, post-Independence egalitarianism has had little impact in **Hindu temples**, whose ritual life and finances remain firmly in the control of the *Bamons*. Known as *devuls* or *mandirs* ("houses of God") in Konkani, Goan temples are the homes of deities (**devtas**) on earth and as such are the focal point of communal worship. Ranging from simple stones to solid-gold statues, the cult objects inside them are worshipped not as mere symbols of divine power, but as actual embodiments of a particular god or goddess. The buildings in which they are enshrined also vary in scale and splendour according to how important the *devta* is: some are modest concrete affairs, while others are soaring multicoloured piles crammed full of finery.

The culmination of worship, or **puja**, is always the moment of **darshan**, or ritual viewing of the deity. After ringing a bell in front of the shrine, the worshipper steps forward, salutes the god or goddess (sometimes by prostrating him- or herself), and presents an offering of fruit, incense, flowers or money to the temple priest (*pujari*). They are then given a spoonful of holy water (*tirtha*) and *prasad* – food (usually a sugary bonbon) – that has been blessed by the deity. Meanwhile, the bare-chested Brahmin priests busy themselves with the daily round of readings and rituals: waking, bathing, dressing and garlanding the *devta*, chanting Sanskrit texts and smearing vermilion paste (*tilak*) on the foreheads of worshippers.

Non-Hindus are welcome to **visit** Goan temples, but you're expected to observe a few simple conventions. The most important of these is to dress appropriately: women should keep their shoulders and legs covered, while men should wear long trousers or *lunghis*. Always remove your shoes at the entrance to the main hall (not the courtyard), and never step inside the doorway to the shrine, which is strictly off limits to everyone except the *pujaris*. **Photography** is nearly always prohibited inside the temple but allowed around the courtyard. Finally, if there is a passage (*pradakshena*) encircling the shrine, walk around it in a clockwise direction. Small donations are welcomed by the priests; Rs20–50 will suffice.

A more detailed account of Goan temples, including their historical background and a rundown of their chief architectural features, appears on p.98.

Christianity

Roman Catholicism was imposed on Goa by the Portuguese in the sixteenth century, spread by missionaries, and zealously upheld by the dreaded Inquisition, which weeded out heretics and ruthlessly persecuted any converts deemed to have lapsed into "pagan" ways. The Inquisition's chief weapons were the infamous *autos da fé*, or "acts of faith", in which individuals suspected of heresy were tortured and, if found guilty, burnt at the stake. In later years, Hindus and Muslims were allowed to practise their religions openly, but by this time Christianity had firmly taken root, albeit in a form that retained too many indigenous traits to meet with Portuguese approval.

Today, just under a third of the total population is Christian, and the state trains priests and nuns in its seminaries and convents for service throughout India. At the head of the Catholic hierarchy in the region is the **Archbishop of Goa**, whose whitewashed palace stands at the top of Altinho Hill in the capital, Panjim; below him come the parish priests.

The spiritual heart of Christianity in Goa is the **Basilica of Bom Jesus** in Old Goa, which houses the sacred relics of **St Francis Xavier** – the region's patron saint. Every ten years, his corpse, which for centuries remained miraculously incorrupt, is exposed for public veneration: an event witnessed by tens of thousands of pilgrims. His annual saint's day in December also attracts huge crowds. Francis Xavier was against Indians entering the clergy, but his opposition was ultimately ignored, and the region's church has long been staffed by native Goans, some of whom are even in line for canonization.

On Sundays families flock to Mass togged out in their best clothes. Saints' days celebrating the patron saint of the village church also draw large congregations, as do the numerous religious festivals held around the state. As you'll see if you come

Our Lady of Health Vailankani

Even more prominent in the popular iconography of Christian Goa than St Francis Xavier is **Our Lady of Health Vailankani**, whose name and image you'll see displayed on buses and taxis everywhere. Goans who wish to make a special plea for divine intercession – to help overcome a serious illness, for example – will often travel to Our Lady's church, two or three days' long drive southeast in distant Tamil Nadu. The shrine was established in the early 1600s following a series of apparitions and miracles, and still attracts millions of worshippers each year, many of them Hindu and Muslim. Our Lady's mass appeal, however, displeases some of the clergy, who fear her popularity has begun to eclipse that of Jesus in the hearts of many Catholic Goans.

across one, these, and more routine church services, have a uniquely Goan atmosphere: violinists accompany the hymn singing, garlands adorn the Madonnas and high altars, and Mass is said in Konkani.

The most spectacular **Goan churches** are located in Old Goa, whose grandiose 400-year-old cathedrals have earned UNESCO World Heritage status. However, several other equally impressive buildings lie in less frequented parts of the state. Most are left open and can be visited freely, but in more out-of-the-way villages you may have to ask the local priest to unlock the doors for you. It goes without saying that you should dress respectfully when visiting churches, and it's also appropriate to leave a small donation for the upkeep of the building when you leave.

Caste in Goan Christianity

Among the more notable differences between Goan Christianity and that practised by its former colonial overlords is the persistence of **caste**. During the religious persecution of the sixteenth and seventeenth centuries, Hindus faced a stark choice between conversion and escape across the border. Many took their temple deities and fled, but many more – including a significant number of those at the top of the social hierarchy, who were permitted to keep their land and wealth if they converted – stayed, exchanging their Indian surnames for Latin ones like Gomes and Barbosa. In Catholicism, where worship is largely communal, revolving around sharing of the Eucharist, the old Hindu concepts of pollution had no place and were quickly relinquished. However, belief in the importance of high and low birth persisted. This may have been because such ideologies sat comfortably with the Portuguese insistence on nobility and *pureza de sangue*, or "blood purity", which was jealously guarded by the European colonizers.

Today, caste remains a fundamental basis of social life for Goan Christians (even though few will readily admit to the fact). The same basic *varna* divisions apply, with former *Bamons* (Brahmins) and *Chardos* at the top, and *Shudras* at the bottom. Greater occupational mobility since Independence has meant the lines between them may be blurred, but it is rare to find a parish priest or landowner (*Goenkar*) who's not from a *Bamon* or *Chardo* family, or a share-cropping field-worker who isn't a *Shudra*.

Caste distinctions and status are preserved in numerous ways, most obviously through endogamous marriage (ie marrying only within one's caste), but also by adherence to a variety of less conspicuous customs. Writing of life in a small village in Salcete *taluka*, the anthropologist Rowena Robinson describes how caste among Christians in her study area was discernible through table manners and taste in music, diet and dress, with higher-caste families tending towards the European ways of their former rulers. *Chardo* women, for example, always wore *vistid* (dresses), whereas *Shudra* women mostly dressed in traditional *kepod*, or saris.

Among Goan Christians, however, the social hierarchy is most dramatically apparent in the life of the local parish church, particularly those occasions when the whole community comes together to worship or celebrate feasts, saints' days and marriages. During Sunday services, it is customary for higher-caste families to sit in the front pews of the church and lower-castes to stand at the back, while the *passe* celebration on Good Friday tends to be completely dominated by *Bamon* and upper *Chardo* families. In virtually all Christian villages, lower-caste people are also excluded from membership of the **fabrica** association, which oversees the maintenance of the church buildings, properties and finances. In addition, each church has its own **confrarias**, literally "brotherhoods", which organize feast days; needless to say, the *Chardos* and *Goenkars* join one *confraria*, running the most important festivals, while the *Shudras' confraria* organizes the minor feasts.

Charismatic Christianity

Since the early 1980s, **charismatic Christianity** has been on the increase in Goa and you may well encounter large open-air services held on specially erected stages. Focusing on teachings from the New Testament, charismatics believe that the power of the Holy Spirit can be accessed through prayer and used to heal or expel evil forces. Worship is far less formal and passive than conventional Christianity, with lots of singing and dancing, and incidents of spirit possession or speaking in tongues. One interesting aspect of the movement is that its congregations tend to be drawn from predominantly *Shudra* and other low-caste families, perhaps as a backlash against their exclusion from more mainstream Christianity – a notion vehemently rejected by most charismatic priests, who do not acknowledge caste in any form.

Islam

Islam was brought to Goa in the eleventh century by Arab merchants, who played a pivotal role in maritime trade along the Malabar coast south of Goa. Encouraged by local Hindu rulers, wealthy Muslims erected mosques and put down roots in the region, practising their religion freely. However, this period of peaceful coexistence came to an abrupt end in the thirteenth century with the arrival from the northwest of marauders from Delhi and the Deccan. By the fourteenth century, an intolerant brand of Islam was in the ascendant, as the raiders made permanent settlements, forcing out the Hindus, whom they regarded as heathen idol-worshippers. The Bahmani conquests of the mid-1300s finally brought Goa under Muslim rule, with Hindu temples razed and their deities banished to the relatively inaccessible foothills of the Western Ghats.

While Hinduism weathered the religious persecution of the Portuguese era, Islam petered out almost completely in Goa, and today only a vestigial Muslim community remains. Distinguished by their half-beards and skullcaps on men, and by enveloping veils called *burqas*, or long shirts and pyjama trousers known as *salwar kameez* on women, most live in and around Ponda, where the state's main mosque, the Safa Masjid, is located.

Environmental issues in Goa

Impeded for decades by a near-bankrupt colonial administration, the pace of development in Goa has increased exponentially since Liberation in 1961. Both light and heavy industries have mushroomed, tourism has boomed, and the state's population has more than doubled – all of which have placed an enormous burden on the state's fragile natural environment. Deforestation, mining, sand extraction, overfishing, water use and tourism-related pollution all remain virtually impervious to central control. Goa's green activists, though small in number, have achieved remarkable success in bringing the environmental debate to the public, but the task they face is an uphill one.

Water

The most contentious environmental issue in Goa is the use and abuse of **water**. As affluence increases and the population continues to rise, augmented by immigrants from neighbouring states and an ever-growing annual deluge of foreign visitors, water is becoming increasingly scarce: in many coastal villages, wells often run dry by late February. The problem is compounded by **pollution** from industrial plants and mines, and by **deforestation** of the interior, which interferes with the state's river systems.

Goa receives around two and a half metres of rain during the annual monsoon – more than double the national average. Yet the dry season is regularly accompanied by **droughts** affecting tens of thousands of villagers (and, increasingly, urban residents too). The main reason the wells and irrigation ducts dry up is that an estimated eighty percent of the annual rainfall flows straight into the sea. The response to the problem by the Indian government in the 1970s was to commission a series of **dams** at the foot of the Western Ghats to regulate the flow of water to the densely populated coastal plain. However, as is often the case with such large-scale engineering projects in India, the benefits reaped from the schemes have thus far proved scant reward for the huge sums of money invested in them, not to mention the displacement of thousands of villagers. The **Selaulim Dam**, begun in south Goa in 1972 and long the *bête noire* of the Goan green lobby, exemplifies the potential drawbacks of dam-building as a response to the region's water problem. Plagued by financial setbacks and political scandals, the project necessitated the clearance of seven square kilometres of virgin forest – exacerbating water shortages by causing soil erosion and an eventual drop in rainfall – and the relocation of 643 families, many of whom had to endure substandard housing and soil that was too poor to farm. Another criticism of the dam is that its water was pumped to luxury resorts and a chemical plant on the coast years before it arrived in the towns of south Goa, while water promised to local farmers has yet to materialize.

Among the few beneficiaries of water shortages in Goa are the "**peddlars**", private hauliers who tap communal wells and transport their contents in tankers to villages where the supply has been exhausted. Writs have been served to prevent this trade, but few peddlars have so far been brought to book: water transportation is so lucrative during the dry season that most can easily afford to pay off the local police.

The **lowering of water tables** on the coast, which has allowed many wells to become polluted with salt water, is frequently cited by the government as a reason

Khazans

The saline flood plains lining Goa's tidal estuaries – a fertile patchwork of paddy fields and palm groves known as **khazans** – are the linchpin of the region's lowland economy. Rice, fruit and vegetables all grow in profusion on its soils, and salt, fish and shells for the production of limewash are obtained from waterlogged areas.

Lying well below sea level, *khazans* are maintained by a complex system that has altered little over the past few millennia. The first lines of defence are the impenetrable **mangrove swamps** growing along the edges of Goa's estuaries, backed where necessary by sturdy laterite walls. Behind these, a grid of **bunds** – embankments made from mud, straw and areca poles – protects the fields, while sluice gates operate like valves to regulate the flow of water onto and off the land. As salt water kills off most crops, retention of fresh monsoon flood waters is essential for cultivation.

Stable for centuries, the fragile ecology of the *khazans*, which comprise 180 square kilometres of Goa's coastal plain, is now under **threat** from a variety of sources. Large tracts of wetland have been drained and built on as urbanization gathers pace in the state, bringing with it increased amounts of sewage. Other causes of **pollution** include chemicals swept down from the iron-ore mines by streams, and oil swilled out of ships' bilges in the estuaries. The Konkan Railway has also carved a great red scar down the coastal plain, causing flooding. However, the greatest potential risk to the *khazans* is posed by **poor land management**. A gradual breakdown in the indigenous *communidades* system of land tenure has led to increasingly widespread neglect of the ditches and sluice gates, and even their wilful destruction. Landless peasants not engaged in rice production have been known to dynamite dykes illegally so that the fields behind them may be used for more lucrative (but ecologically unsustainable) fish or prawn farming, a practice dubbed as "**bund busting**".

The consequences of destroying the *khazans* are not only environmental. Flooded, polluted land is the perfect breeding ground for the *Culex vishnui* mosquito, carrier of the deadly disease Japanese encephalitis, which killed nearly one hundred people during the 1992 monsoons and may well have been what wiped out the population of Old Goa two hundred years ago.

to build more dams. Yet there has been little evidence that such projects actually alleviate the problem. In many cases, the promises of short-term financial gain for local companies or politicians turns out to be the real motive.

Tourism

Around two-and-a-half million tourists visit Goa each year, fifteen percent of them from abroad. The result of so many people concentrated into a narrow strip along the coast during the winter has had a dramatic impact on the local environment. Construction has boomed – much of it illegal, or beyond the control of the authorities – while little or no provision has been made for the disposal of the waste generated, causing huge build-ups of plastic rubbish. Innumerable trees have been felled to make way for hotels, vast quantities of ground water tapped to supply resorts (causing dry-season shortages in many places) and hitherto natural, wild places colonized by seasonal hut camps or shack restaurants.

Despite the powerful Coastal Protection Zone law, which forbids the construction of any permanent structure within a band of 200 metres from the high-tide line, the Goan government has proved a toothless tiger when it comes to stopping unplanned development along its shoreline. There are many things, however, you as an individual can do to help minimize the impact of your stay.

One of the main ones is to **avoid plastic water bottles and bags**, which as yet cannot be recycled in Goa, or else buy 5-litre containers instead of .75-litre bottles. See p.36 for advice on how to eliminate plastic bottle use altogether by sterilizing water. Sturdy, reusable shopping bags are available everywhere.

Industry

Goa is a predominantly rural state, but thirteen pockets of heavy industry have sprung up over the past three decades, posing in some instances a serious threat to the environment and well as bringing potential health risks for local people. The oldest-established and most controversial is the **Zuari Agro Chemical Fertilizer Plant** (**ZAC**) on the Dabolim plateau, near the airport. Overlooking the north end of beautiful Colva beach, the factory first made headlines in the mid-1970s when toxic chemicals found their way into the water table and ocean, decimating fish populations and raising fears about the plant's overall safety.

ZAC has since been modernized, but its productive capacity has increased enormously and environmentalists remain concerned about the risk of ammonia and other toxic gases escaping from its old-fashioned and poorly maintained storage tanks. In addition, emissions from the factory's chimney stacks are said to have affected the health of villagers nearby (ZAC, of course, vehemently denies this but continues to rotate staff lodged in the northeast side of the plant – downwind of the stacks – to more salubrious quarters every two years). Meanwhile, tanker trucks carrying loads of lethal chemicals routinely use local roads.

Mining

Head into the hilly heart of Goa and you're bound to encounter a couple of open-cast **ore mines**. Forming gigantic red gashes across the landscape, these colossal industrial eyesores generate half of India's iron-ore exports and more foreign currency than all of Goa's hotels and restaurants put together: around ten percent of the state's GDP. In the past, ninety percent of the ore went to Japan (which funded the industry to begin with), but China's demand for steel has made it the main importer these days. Unfortunately, the mines also inflict untold damage on the region's ecology, causing **soil erosion** on a massive scale, destroying extensive tracts of forest and farmland, and leading to chronic **health problems** for local people.

The roots of the environmental problems lie in the nature of open-cast mining itself. To extract one tonne of ore, you have to dig up between two and three times that amount of surplus earth; the thirteen million tonnes of iron and manganese ore that Goa exports every year leave around forty million tonnes of rock and soil waste in their wake, most of which gets dumped in massive heaps around the edges of the mines. With the onset of the monsoons, rainwater drains the slag heaps of their finer soil and flushes it into streams and rivers. These then clog up with silt, causing frequent floods in low-lying, rice-cultivating areas: paddy fields ruined for decades by slicks of red mud are nowadays a common sight in and around mining areas.

Mining companies in Goa have consistently ducked their environmental responsibilities, but they may in the future be forced to clean up their act or face bankruptcy. Some Goan rivers have silted up to such an extent over the past few decades that the barges which transport the ore to Mormugao harbour, at the head of the Zuari estuary near Vasco da Gama, are only able to operate in the period after the rains, when water levels are highest (which explains why, if you stand on Candolim beach in October, the horizon is dominated by lines of floodlit dredgers and ore transport ships). Several mines have to shut down towards the end of the dry season. Spurred on by the example of a few large operators, the industry is now madly planting its tips with trees in an attempt to forestall the rate of the erosion. Such initiatives were given a further spur in 2005, when India's Supreme Court ruled that all mines failing to adhere to environmental laws would be shut down.

Fishing

Between 40,000 and 50,000 Goans are directly dependent on fishing for a livelihood, the majority of them families who work in wooden outriggers or small fibreglass boats. Despite the introduction of outboard motors, their methods remain traditional and low-tech. This is particularly true of the hand-net fishermen you'll see on many Goan beaches, who join together in teams of twenty or thirty to haul in giant U-shaped nets laid in the shallows. Once landed, the catch is divided up according to each family's stake in the net (called a *rampon* in Konkani) and the sardines, mackerel and other smaller fish (used as fertilizer for coconut trees) are gathered by the women in baskets to be carried home.

Yields from this kind of fishing have diminished sharply over the past two or three decades, principally because of competition from larger, more modern and better-equipped trawlers. Ironically, these were introduced in the 1970s with large government subsidies aimed at boosting the protein intake and living standards of disadvantaged coastal communities. In fact, few poor fishing families could afford the hefty down-payment required to secure the government loans, which were instead picked up by wealthy business people, politicians and industrialists. They, over time, have made huge profits, benefiting from grants by foreign governments and manufacturers eager to sell boats and engines, and obtain a cheap source of fish.

The results of this economic revolution have been three-fold: first, an increase in the price of fish (which is now largely beyond the pockets of most Goans); secondly, the virtual destruction of in-shore fishing as a viable livelihood; and thirdly, greater marine pollution. To combat such problems, Hindu and Christian in-shore fishermen from across the state got together and formed a union, the **Goenchea Ramponkarancho Ekvott** (or Goan Handnet Fishermen's Union). After much heated debate and occasional armed clashes between union members and trawler owners, a law was passed in the 1980s limiting the trawlers' fishing grounds to beyond a five-kilometre exclusion line.

However, the fishing limit was never enforced and continues to be routinely ignored. The root of the government's inability to uphold the law and protect the rights of poor fishermen lies in the fact that most representatives in the Goan State Legislature are firmly in the pockets of the trawler owners (if not trawler owners themselves). Just how ineffectual the law really is when set against such a powerful lobby was underlined in July 2000 when the High Court – responding to data on fish spawning supplied by the National Institute of Oceanography – imposed a blanket ban on mechanized fishing during the monsoon period. The decision, however, was effectively overturned only the following day by the State Legislature, which passed a bill prohibiting the court from ruling on the matter again.

Natural history

In spite of increased pressures on the rural landscape, Goa remains a state of beautiful and varied scenery with its own abundant and distinct flora and fauna. Many species have been hunted out or squeezed eastwards over the past fifty or so years, but enough survive to make a trip into the countryside worthwhile. Walking on less frequented beaches or through the rice fields of the coastal plain, you'll encounter dozens of exotic birds, while the hill country of the interior supports an amazing variety of plants and trees. The majority of Goa's larger mammals keep to the dense woodland lining the Karnatakan border, where three nature sanctuaries afford them some protection from the hunters and loggers who have wrought such havoc in this fragile forest region over the past few decades.

Geography

Rarely in India do you find such a wide range of different landscapes packed so tightly, or wilderness areas situated so close to modern towns and resorts, as in Goa. Broadly speaking, the state may be divided into three major **habitats**: the low-lying coastal plain, the laterite plateau country of the midland region, and the lush, forest-cloaked hills of the Western Ghats. Crammed into a fifty-kilometre-wide strip, these different terrains form a closely integrated ecosystem sustained by a tangle of rivers and tributaries meandering westwards into the Arabian Sea.

The **Western Ghats** (from the Sanskrit word for "sacred steps") are Goa's most important topographical feature. Running parallel to the coast at a mean elevation of between 900m and 1200m, the sheer mountains, which extend along the entire length of peninsular India, impede the path of the monsoon rain clouds as they sweep in from the southwest. The moist deciduous forest draped over their flanks thus acts like a giant sponge, soaking up the rainwater on which the region depends and channelling it down to the plains. **Deforestation** of this sparsely populated region – home to over 3500 different varieties of flowering plants (almost a third of India's total) and a rich assortment of mammals, birds, reptiles and insects – is a worsening problem: without the trees to modulate the flow of water, flooding and soil erosion are spoiling crops and destroying centuries-old irrigation systems.

From the foot of the Ghats, steep-sided **laterite plateaux** extend west, covered in scrub and savannah grasslands. Although the soil in this midland region is thin, the floors and sides of the many well-watered valleys are important agricultural zones, carpeted with fragrant cashew trees (the source of Goa's main cash crop) and areca groves. This is also the home of the state's largest **spice plantations**, as well as its lucrative iron- and manganese-ore mines, which form gigantic trenches of red against the green and yellow backdrop.

The majority of Goa's inhabitants live on the 105-kilometre-long **coastal strip**, whose fertile rice fields and coconut groves, together with a thriving fishing industry, provide the bulk of the region's food. The epicentre of the region's industry and tourism, this is also the most ecologically vulnerable area of Goa. Demand for new building space and the shift away from traditional subsistence farming methods have led to the drainage of wetlands and the destruction of many **mangrove swamps**, while the threat of pollution from chemical plants, power stations and tourist resorts looms ever larger.

Land settlement and usage

Most of the farmable land these days is given over to the production of **rice** or **coconuts**. The region's two main crops formerly met subsistence needs, but following the sudden surge in population caused by the arrival of the Portuguese, huge amounts of grain had to be imported from elsewhere in India. This forced the colonial administration to intensify production, which it did by introducing new farming methods (including high-yielding – but disease-prone – strains of rice) and a more strictly organized system of land tenure. The **communidades** system, originally devised by the Saraswat Brahmins during the fifth century AD but refined under the Portuguese, placed control of all land not owned privately into the hands of the local villagers, who collectively granted the rights to farm it to the highest bidders. Proceeds from these auctions were then used to pay government taxes and maintain community properties (such as temples), while anything left over was divided up evenly among the male villagers. The replacement after Independence of the *communidades* with the *panchayat*, or council system – a brainchild of the British – is often cited as a cause of environmental degradation in rural areas. With former *communidades* land now owned by the state, local villagers lack the incentive to protect it from unscrupulous developers.

Crops

Goa's main staple, **rice**, is grown in paddy fields (*cantors*) right across the coastal strip and on patches of flat ground, known as *molloi*, between the laterite plateaux in the middle of the state. Two different crops are planted: *sorondio* is sown during the monsoon in June and harvested in November, and *vangana* is cultivated during the dry season between October and February using irrigation water stored in reservoirs and ponds. Each stage of the process involves days sloshing around in thick mud or being bent double under blazing sunshine. Without such toil, though, many thousands of Goans would go hungry: rice is the mainstay of the rural economy, providing a livelihood for the state's landless sharecroppers and subsistence farmers.

Coconut cultivation, along with fishing, is the main moneymaker in many coastal villages. The principal derivative of this ubiquitous plant is its sap, or *toddi* – used to distil the local liquor, *feni* – but other parts are put to good use, too. The *copra* oil squeezed from the young nuts is used for cooking or sold to soap and cosmetic manufacturers; the coarse hair surrounding the shell produces fibre for rope, coirmatting and furniture upholstery; dried palm fronds make baskets, brooms and thatch; while the wood from fallen trees is used to make rafters for houses.

Further inland, you'll come across clusters of spindly palm trees. More delicate than their coconut cousins, **areca trees** – the source of betel nuts that are ground and chewed by millions of Indians as *pan* – require constant irrigation and plenty of shade. Finally, alongside these are often planted fruit trees, most commonly mango (*ambo*), jackfruit (*ponos*), and cashews (*cazu*), whose fruit (which grows separately from the nut), produces a strong-smelling juice that Goans use to make *feni*.

Flora

Goa supports more than 3500 species of flowering **plants** – 27 percent of India's total – as well as countless lower orders of grasses, ferns and brackens. The greatest floristic diversity occurs in the Western Ghats, where it is not uncommon to find one hundred or more different types of trees in an area of one hectare. Many were introduced by the Portuguese from Europe, South America, Southeast Asia and Australia, but there are also a vast number of indigenous varieties which thrive in the moist climate.

Along the coast, the **coconut (aka *toddi*) palm** predominates, forming a near-continuous curtain of lush foliage. Spiky **spinifex** also helps bind the shifting sand dunes behind Colva and Calangute beaches, while casuarina bushes form striking splashes of pink and crimson during the winter months.

In the towns and villages of central Goa, you'll encounter dozens of beautiful **flowering trees** that are common in tropical parts of India but unfamiliar to most Europeans and North Americans. The **Indian laburnum**, or cassia, throws out masses of yellow flowers and long seed pods in late February before the monsoons. This is also the period when **mango** and **Indian coral** trees are in full bloom; both produce bundles of stunning red flowers.

Among the most distinctive trees that grow in both coastal and hill areas is the stately **banyan**, which propagates by sending out shoots from its lower branches. The largest-known specimen, recorded in neighbouring Maharashtra, had a staggering circumference of 577m. The banyan is also revered by Hindus and you'll often find small shrines at the foot of mature trees. Another tree regarded as sacred by Hindus (and by Buddhists, because Buddha is believed to have attained enlightenment beneath one), is the **peepal**, which has distinctive spatula-shaped leaves. Temple courtyards often enclose large peepals, usually with strips of auspicious red cloth hanging from their lower branches.

Tree lovers and botanists should not miss an opportunity to visit the **Western Ghats**, which harbour a bewildering wealth of flora, from flowering trees and plants to ferns and fungi. These are among Asia's densest rainforests. Sheltered by a leafy canopy that can rise to a height of twenty metres or more, buttressed roots and giant trunks tower above a luxuriant undergrowth of brambles, creepers and bracken, interspersed with brakes of bamboo. Common tree species include the **kadam**, **sisso** or martel, **kharanj** and **teak**, distinguished by its straight, bare trunk and broad leaves. There are dozens of representatives of the *Ficus*, or fig, family too, as well as innumerable (and ecologically destructive) **eucalyptus** and **rubber** trees, planted as cash crops by the Forest Department.

Mammals

During a fact-finding expedition to Goa in the 1970s, the eminent Indian naturalist Salim Ali complained the only animal he saw was a lone leopard cat lying dead at the roadside. For although the state harbours more than fifty species of **mammals**, visitors to the coast are unlikely to spot anything more inspiring than a monkey or tree squirrel. Most of the exciting **animals** have been hunted to the point of extinction, or else have fled into neighbouring Karnataka. The few that remain roam the dense woodland lining the Western Ghats, in the sparsely populated far east, glimpsed only by forest-dwelling tribespeople or enthusiasts prepared (and equipped) to spend several days and nights trekking through the jungle. Even so, it's nice to know they are still there, and if Goa's three **wildlife sanctuaries** are adequately protected over the coming decade, populations stand a strong chance of recovering.

One animal you definitely won't come across is the tiger, which has been completely hunted out. However, several kinds of **big cat** survived the depredations of the colonial era. Among the most adaptive and beautiful is the **leopard** or panther (*panthera panthus*), known in Konkani as the *bibto vag*. Prowling the thick forests of Sanguem and Canacona *talukas*, these elusive cats prey on monkeys and deer and occasionally take domestic cattle and dogs from the fringes of villages. Their distinctive black spots make them notoriously difficult to see amongst the tropical foliage, although their mating call (reminiscent of a saw on wood) regularly pierces the night air in remote areas. The **leopard cat** (*Felis bengalensis*), or *vagati* in Konkani, is a miniature version of its namesake, and more common.

Viewing wildlife in Goa

Of the state's main wildlife parks, the **Bhagwan Mahaveer Sanctuary**, 56km east of Panjim (see p.101), harbours the most impressive scenery and diverse fauna, with the **Cotigao Sanctuary** in south Goa (see p.205) coming a close second. **Bondla** (see p.100), near Ponda in central Goa, is more a zoo than wildlife park – a depressing spectacle of small cages and enclosures – although the variety of birdlife in this area can be astonishing. Ornithologists should also make time to take in the **Salim Ali Sanctuary** on Chorao Island (see p.91), a short way upriver from Panjim, where mangrove swamps and mudflats teem with waders and other water birds.

The **best time of year** for viewing wildlife is immediately after the monsoons, between October and January, when water levels are still high and temperatures cool enough for hiking. During the rainy season – roughly late June to September – off-track transport is frequently disrupted by flooding, and the larger reserves are closed to visitors. If you plan to do any serious wildlife-spotting, bring with you a pair of sturdy waterproof shoes or boots, a set of binoculars and a good field guide (those available in Goa are not so great; recommended titles are listed on p.302).

Sporting a bushy tail and round spots on soft buff or grey fur, it's about the same size as a domestic cat and lives around villages, picking off chickens, birds and small mammals. Another cat with a penchant for poultry, and one which Goan villagers occasionally keep as a pet if they can capture one, is the docile **Indian civet** (*Viverricual indica*), or *katanoor*, recognizable by its lithe body, striped tail, short legs and long pointed muzzle.

Wild cats share their territory with a range of other mammals unique to the subcontinent. One you've a reasonable chance of seeing is the **gaur**, or Indian bison (*Bos gaurus*), known in Goa as the *govo redo*. These primeval-looking beasts, with their distinctive sleek black skin and knee-length white "socks", forage around bamboo thickets and shady woods. The bulls are particularly impressive, growing to an awesome height of two metres, with heavy curved horns and prominent humps.

With its long fur and white V-shaped bib, the scruffy **sloth bear** (*Melursus ursinas*), or *bhalu*, ranks among the weirder-looking inhabitants of Goa's forests. Sadly, it's also very rare, thanks to its predilection for raiding sugar-cane plantations, which has brought it into direct conflict with humans. Sloth bears can occasionally be seen shuffling along woodland trails, but you're more likely to come across evidence of their foraging activities: trashed termite mounds and chewed-up ants' nests. The same is true of both the portly **Indian porcupine** (*Hystix indica*), or *sal*, which you see a lot less often than the mounds of earth it digs up to get at insects and cashew or teak seedlings, and the **pangolin** (*Manis crassicaudata*), or *tiryo*, a kind of armour-plated anteater whose hard grey overlapping scales protect it from predators.

Full-moon nights and the twilight hours of dusk and dawn are the times to look out for **nocturnal animals** such as the **slender loris** (*Loris tardigradus*). This shy creature – a distant cousin of the lemur, with bulging round eyes, furry body and pencil-thin limbs – grows to around twenty centimetres in length. It moves as if in slow motion, except when an insect flits to within striking distance, and is a favourite pet of Goa's forest people. The **mongoose** (*Herpestes edwardsi*) is another animal sometimes kept as a pet. Rudyard Kipling's "Rikitikitavi", known in Konkani as the *mongus*, keeps dwellings free of scorpions, mice, rats and other vermin. It will also readily take on snakes, which is why you often see it writhing in a cloud of dust with king cobras during performances by snake charmers.

Late evening is also the best time for spotting **bats**. Goa boasts four species, including the **fulvous fruit bat** (*Rousettus leshenaulti*), or *vagul* – so-called because it gives off a scent resembling fermenting fruit juice – **Dormer's bat** (*Pipistrellus dormeri*), the very rare **rufous horse-shoe bat** and the **Malay fox vampire** (*Magaderma spasma*), which feeds off the blood of live cattle. **Flying foxes** (*Pteropus gigantus*), the largest of India's bats, are also present in healthy numbers. With a wingspan of more than one metre, they fly in cacophonous groups to feed in fruit orchards, sometimes falling foul of electricity cables on the way: frazzled flying foxes dangling from live cables are a common sight in the interior of Goa.

Other species to look out for in forest areas are the **Indian giant squirrel** (*Ratufa indica*), or *shenkaro*, which has a coat of black fur and red-orange lower parts. Two and a half times larger than its European cousins, it lives in the canopy, leaping up to twenty metres between branches. The much smaller **three-striped squirrel** (*Funambulus palmarum*), or *khadi khar*, recognizable by the three black markings down its back, is also found in woodland. However, the **five-striped palm squirrel** (*Funambulus pennanti*) is a common sight all over the state, especially in municipal parks and villages.

Forest clearings and areas of open grassland around Molem and Cotigao are grazed by four species of **deer**. Widely regarded as the most beautiful is the **cheetal** (*Axis axis*), or spotted axis deer, which congregates in large groups around waterholes and salt licks, occasionally wandering into villages to seek shelter from its predators. The plainer buff-coloured **sambar** (*Cervus unicolor*) is also well represented, despite succumbing to diseases spread by domestic cattle during the 1970s and 1980s. Two types of deer you're less likely to come across, but which also inhabit the border forests, are the **barking deer** (*Muntiacus muntjack*), or *bhenkaro*, whose call closely resembles that of a domestic dog, and the timid **mouse deer** (*Tragulus meminna*), or *pisoi*, a speckled-grey member of the *Tragulidae* family that is India's smallest deer, growing to a mere thirty centimetres in height. Both of these are highly secretive and nocturnal; they are also the preferred snack of Goa's smaller predators: the **striped hyena** (*Hyaena hyaena*), or *yeul*, **jackal** (*Canis aureus*) or *colo*, and **wild dog** (*Cuon alpinus*), or *deucolo*, which hunts in packs.

Long-beaked **dolphins** are regular visitors to the shallow waters of south Goa's more secluded bays and beaches. They are traditionally regarded as pests by villagers, who believe they eat scarce stocks of fish. However, this long-standing antipathy is gradually eroding as local people realize the tourist-pulling potential of the dolphins: Palolem beach, in Canacona, is where you're most likely to see one, although dolphin-spotting boat trips also operate out of Colva.

Finally, no rundown of Goan wildlife would be complete without some mention of **monkeys**. The most ubiquitous species is the mangy pink-bottomed **macaque** (*Macaca mulatta*), or *makad*, which hangs out anywhere scraps may be scavenged or snatched from unwary humans: temples and picnic spots such as Dudhsagar Falls in the Western Ghats are good places to watch them in action. The black-faced **Hanuman langur**, by contrast, is less audacious, retreating to the trees if threatened. It's much larger than the macaque, with pale grey fur and long limbs and tail. In forest areas, the langur's distinctive call is an effective early-warning system against big cats and other predators, which is why you often come across herds of cheetal grazing under trees inhabited by large colonies.

Reptiles

Reptiles are well represented in the region, with more than forty species of **snakes, lizards, turtles** and **crocodiles** recorded. The best places to spot them are not the interior forests, whose dense foliage makes observation difficult, but open cultivated areas: paddy fields and village ponds provide abundant fresh water, nesting sites and prey (frogs, insects and small birds) to feed on.

Your house or hotel room, however, is where you are most likely to come across Goa's most common reptile, the **gecko** (*Hemidactylus*), which clings to walls and ceilings with its widely splayed toes. Deceptively static most of the time, these small yellow-brown lizards will dash at lightning speed for cracks and holes if you try to catch them, or if an unwary mosquito, fly or cockroach scuttles within striking distance. The much rarer **chameleon** is even more elusive, mainly because its constantly changing camouflage makes it virtually impossible to spot. They'll have no problem seeing you, though: independently moving eyes allow them to pin-point approaching predators, while prey is slurped up with their fast-moving, forty-centimetre-long tongues. The other main lizard to look out for is the **Bengal monitor**. This brown speckled reptile looks like a refugee from *Jurassic Park*, growing to well over a metre in length. It used to be a common sight in coastal areas, where they basked on roads and rock, but as monitors are often killed and eaten by villagers, they have become increasingly rare.

The monsoon period is when you're most likely to encounter **turtles**. Two varieties paddle around village ponds and wells when water is plentiful: the **flap-shell** (*Lissemys punctata*) and **black-pond** (*Melanochelys trijuga*) turtles, neither of which is endangered. Numbers of **marine turtles** (*Lepidochelys olivacea*), by contrast, have plummeted over the past few decades because villagers raid their nests when they crawl onto the beach to lay their eggs. This amazing natural spectacle occurs each year in Morjim and Galjibag, supervised by local wardens employed by the Forest Department to stamp out poaching. For more on Goa's **Olive Ridley** marine turtles, see box, p.148.

An equally rare sight nowadays is the **crocodile**. Populations have dropped almost to the point of extinction, although the Cambarjua Canal near Old Goa, and more remote stretches of the Mandovi and Zuari estuaries, support vestigial colonies of **saltwater** crocs, which bask on mudflats and river rocks. Dubbed "salties", they occasionally take calves and goats, and will snap at the odd human if given half a chance. The more ominously named **mugger crocodile**, however, is harmless, inhabiting unfrequented freshwater streams and riversides around Devil's Canyon, near Molem (see p.101).

Snakes

There are 23 species of **snake** in Goa, ranging from the gigantic **Indian python** (*Python molurus*, or *har* in Konkani) – a forest-dwelling constrictor that grows up to four metres in length – to the innocuous **worm snake** (*Typhlops braminus*) or *sulva*, which is tiny, completely blind and often mistaken for an earthworm.

The eight **poisonous snakes** present in the region include India's four most deadly species: the cobra, the krait, the Russel's viper and the saw-scaled viper. Though these are relatively common in coastal and cultivated areas, even the most aggressive will slither off at the first sign of an approaching human. Nevertheless, ten thousand Indians die from snake bites each year, and if you regularly cut across paddy fields or plan to do any hiking, it makes sense to familiarize yourself with the following four or five species just in case: their bites nearly always prove fatal if not treated immediately with anti-venom serum, available at most clinics and hospitals.

Present in most parts of the state and an important character in Hindu mythology, the **Indian cobra** (*Naja naja*), or *naga*, is the most common of the venomous species. Wheat-brown or grey in colour, it is famed for the "hood" it unfurls when confronted and whose rear side usually bears the snake's characteristic spectacle markings. Its big brother, the **king cobra** (*Naja hannah*), or *Raj nag*, is much less often encountered. Inhabiting the remote forest regions along the Karnatakan border, this beautiful brown, yellow and black snake, which grows to a length of four metres or more, is very rare, although the itinerant snake charmers that perform in markets occasionally keep one. Defanged, they rear up and "dance" when provoked by the handler, or are set against mongooses in ferocious (and often fatal) fights. The king cobra is also the only snake in the world known to make its own nest.

Distinguished by their steel-blue colour and faint white cross-markings, **kraits** (*Bungarus coerulus*), locally known as *kaner* or *maniar*, are twice as deadly as the Indian cobra: even the bite of a newly hatched youngster is lethal. **Russel's viper** (*Viperi russeli*), or *mandol*, is another one to watch out for. Distinguished by the three bands of elliptical markings that extend down its brown body, the Russel hisses at its victims before darting at them and burying its centimetre-long fangs into their flesh. The other common poisonous snake in Goa is the **saw-scaled viper** (*Echis carinatus*), or *phurshem*. Grey with an arrow-shaped mark on its triangular head, it hangs around in the cracks between stone walls, feeding on scorpions, lizards, frogs, rodents and smaller snakes. *Phurshems* also hiss when threatened; they produce the sound by rubbing together serrated scales located on the side of their head. Finally, **sea snakes** (*Enhdrina schistosa*), called *kusada* in Konkani, are common in coastal areas and potentially lethal, although rarely encountered by swimmers as they lurk only in deep water off the shore.

Harmless snakes are far more numerous than their killer cousins and frequently more attractive. The beautiful **golden tree snake** (*Chrysopelea ormata*), or *kalingin*, for example, sports an exquisitely intricate geometric pattern of red, yellow and black markings, while the **green whip snake** (*Dryhopis nasutus*), or *sarpatol*, is stunning parakeet-green with a whip-like tail extending more than a metre behind it. The ubiquitous **Indian rat snake**, often mistaken for a cobra, also has beautiful markings, although it leaves behind it a foul stench of decomposing flesh. Other common non-poisonous snakes include the **wolf snake** (*Lycodon aulicus*), or *kaidya*, the **Russel sand boa** (*Eryx conicus*), or *malun*, the **kukri snake** (*Oligodon taeniolatus*), or *pasko*, the **cat snake** (*Boiga trigonata*), or *manjra* and the **keelbacks** (*Natrix*).

Birds

You don't have to be an aficionado to enjoy Goa's abundant **birdlife**. As you travel around the state, breathtaking birds regularly flash between the branches of trees or appear on overhead wires at the roadside.

Thanks to the internationally popular brand of Goan beer, the **kingfisher** has become the state's unofficial mascot: it's not hard to see why the brewers chose it as their logo. Three common species of kingfisher frequently crop up amid the paddy fields and wetlands of the coastal plains, where they feed on small fish and tadpoles. With its enormous bill and pale green-blue wing feathers, the **stork-billed kingfisher** (*Perargopis capensis*) is the largest and most distinctive member of the family, although the **white-throated kingfisher** (*Halcyon smyrnensis*) – which has iridescent turquoise plumage and a coral-red bill – and the **common kingfisher** (*Alcedo althis*), identical to the one frequently spotted in northern Europe, are more alluring.

Other common and brightly coloured species include the green, blue and yellow **bee-eaters** (*Merops*), the stunning **golden oriole** (*Oriolus oriolus*) and the **Indian roller** (*Coracias bengalensis*), famous for its brilliant blue flight feathers and exuberant aerobatic mating displays. **Hoopoes** (*Upupa epops*), recognizable by their elegant black-and-white tipped crests, fawn plumage and distinctive "*hoo…po… po*" call, also flit around fields and villages, as do **purple sunbirds** (*Nectarina asiatica*), and several kinds of bulbuls, babblers and drongos (*Dicrurus*), including the fork-tailed black drongo (*Dicrurus macrocercus*) – a year-round resident that can often be seen perched on telegraph wires. If you're lucky, you may also catch a glimpse of the **Asian paradise flycatcher** (*Tersiphone paradisi*), which is widespread in Goa and among the region's most exquisite birds: males of more than 4 years of age sport a thick black crest and long silver-white streamers, while the more often seen females and young males are rufous colour.

Goa's paddy fields, ponds and saline mudflats are teeming with **water birds**. The most ubiquitous of these is the snowy white **cattle egret** (*Bubulcus ibis*), which can usually be seen wherever there are cows and buffalo, feeding off the grubs, insects and other parasites that live on them. The **great egret** (*Casmerodius albus*) is also pure white, although lankier and with a long yellow bill, while the third member of this family, the **little egret** (*Egretta garzetta*), sports a short black bill and, during the mating season, two elongated feathers from the nape of its neck. Look out too for the mud-brown **Indian pond heron** (*Ardeola grayii*), colloquially known as the "**paddy bird**", India's most common heron. Distinguished by its pale green legs, speckled breast and hunched posture, it stands motionless for hours in water waiting for fish or frogs to feed on.

The hunting technique of the beautiful **white-bellied sea eagle** (*Haliaeetus leucogaster*), by contrast, is truly spectacular. Cruising twenty to thirty metres above the surface of the water, this black and white osprey swoops at high speed to snatch its prey – usually sea snakes and mackerel – from the waves with its fierce yellow talons: an everyday sight in the more secluded coves of south Goa. More common birds of prey such as the **brahminy kite** (*Haliastur indus*), recognizable by its white breast and chestnut head markings, and the **black kite** (*Milvus migrans*), a dark brown kite with a fork tail, are widespread around towns and fishing villages, where they vie with raucous gangs of **house crows** (*Corvus splendens*) for scraps.

Other birds of prey to keep an eye open for, especially around open farmland, are the white-eyed buzzard (*Butastur teesa*), the oriental honey buzzard (*Pernis ptilorhyncus*), the black-shouldered kite (*Elanus caeruleus*) – famous for its blood-red eyes – and shikra (*Accipiter badius*), which closely resembles the European sparrowhawk.

The region's **forests** may have lost many of their larger animals, but they still offer exciting possibilities for birdwatchers. One species every enthusiast hopes to glimpse while in the woods is the magnificent **hornbill**, of which three species have been spotted in the region: the **Malabar grey hornbill** (*Ocyceros griseus*), with its blue-brown plumage and long curved beak, is the most common, although the Malabar pied hornbill (*Anthracoceros coronatus*), distinguished by its white outer tail feathers, often flies into villages in search of fruit and lizards. The magnificent **great hornbill** (*Buceors bicornis*), however, is more elusive, limited to the forest areas around Molem and Canacona where it may occasionally be spotted flitting through the dense canopy. Growing to 130 centimetres in length, it has a black-and-white striped body and wings, and a huge yellow beak with a long curved casque on top.

Several species of **woodpecker** also inhabit the interior forests, among them three types of flameback woodpecker: the black-rumped flameback (*Dinopium benghalense*), with its crimson crown and bright splashes of yellow across its rear side, is the one casual birdspotters are most likely to come across, being common not just in forests, but in gardens, coconut groves and hotel grounds too. To see some of Goa's rarest birds, however, there are few places better than the Cotigao sanctuary (see p.205), which is one of the last remaining strongholds of the **white-bellied woodpecker** (*Dryocopus javensis*). In spite of its bright red head and white rump, this shy bird is more often heard than seen, making loud drumming noises on tree trunks between December and March.

Another bird whose call is a regular feature of the Goan forest, particularly in teak areas, is the wild ancestor of the domestic chicken – the **jungle fowl**. Its most common representative is the **grey** or **Sonnerat's jungle fowl** (*Galolus sonneratii*), which has darker plumage scattered with yellow spots and streaks inhabit; its clearings, and is most often seen scavenging for food on the verges of forest roads.

Goan music and dance

With reggae and techno blaring out of so many beach bars, you'd be forgiven for thinking Goa's music and dance scene started with the invention of the synthesizer. However, the state boasts a vibrant musical tradition of its own: a typically syncretic blend of East and West that is as spicy and distinctive as the region's cuisine. You won't hear the calypso-like rhythms of Konkani pop or haunting Kunbi folk songs at the full-moon parties, though. Rooted in village and religious life, Goan music is primarily for domestic consumption, played at weddings, temple festivals, harvest celebrations, as an accompaniment to popular theatre and, most noticeably, on the crackly cassette machines of local buses.

Devotional music and dance

Devotional music and dance have played an important part in Hindu temple worship in Goa for at least a thousand years. Traditionally, wealthier temples employed permanent groups of musicians to regale the deity and participate in the annual *Yatra* processions. Accompanied by the harmonium, *tabla* and other percussion instruments, singers led the performances, which were usually held in the hall in front of the shrine, or in a special musicians' tower (*naubhat khanna* or *sonddio*) erected above the main entrance to the temple precinct. For important festivals, the congregation would also assemble in front of the sanctum to intone devotional songs, known as **kirtans** and **bhajans**. Traditional temple musicians can still be heard in performances at weekly *pujas* and annual *yatras* in temples such the as Shri Mahalasa in central Goa (see p.95), where drumming and the piercing tones of the double-reeded *shennai* (a kind of oboe) regal the gods on their processions around the precincts' inner courtyards.

Folk music and dance

Wander into almost any Hindu village on the eve of an important *puja*, particularly around harvest time after the monsoons, and you'll experience Goan roots music and dance at its most authentic. The torchbearers of the region's thriving **folk tradition** are the Kunbi class of landless labourers, most often seen bent double in rice paddies, the women with garish cotton saris tied *dhoti*-style around their legs. Agricultural work – planting, threshing and grinding grain, raking salt pans and fixing fishing nets – provides the essential rhythms for Konkani songs, known as **Kunbi geet.**

More rehearsed performances take place during the Hindu month of Paush (late Feb), when groups of women gather in the village square-cum-dance ground (*mannd*) to sing *dhalos* and *fugdis*. The singing may run over seven or more nights, culminating with outbreaks of spirit possession and trances.

The most famous Goan folk song and dance form, though, has to be the **mando**. Originally, this slow and expressive dance (whose name derives from the Sanskrit *mandala*, meaning circular pattern) was traditionally performed in circles, but these days tends to be danced by men and women standing opposite each other in parallel lines, waving fans and coloured handkerchiefs. *Mandos* gather pace as they progress and are usually followed by a series of **dulpods**, quick-time tunes whose lyrics are traditionally satirical, exposing village gossip about errant housewives, lapsed priests and so on. *Dulpods*, in turn, merge into the even jauntier rhythms of **deknis**, bringing the set dances to a tumultuous conclusion.

The basic rhythmic cycles, or *ovis*, of Goan folk songs were exploited by early Christian missionaries in their work. Overlaid with lyrics inspired by Bible stories, many were eventually assimilated into the local Catholic tradition: today, the *mando*, for example, is usually danced by Christians on church *festas* and wedding days. It also became the favourite dance of the Goan gentry, who, dressed in ball gowns and dinner suits with fans and flamboyant handkerchiefs, used to perform it during the glittering functions held in the reception rooms of the territory's top houses.

Fados

The most European-influenced of all the Goan folk idioms is the **fado**. Rendered in a turgid mock operatic style, these melancholic songs epitomize the colonial predilection for nostalgia or longing for the home country, known in Portuguese as *saudades*. Ironically, though, few *fadistas* actually laid eyes on the fabled lights of Lisbon or Coimbra they eulogized in their lyrics, and today the *fado* is a dying art form. However, a couple of renowned folk-singers, notably the band leader **Oslando** and singer-guitarist **Lucio Miranda**, invariably include a couple of old *fado* numbers on their albums. Lucio, the greatest living exponent of the form, also gives the odd performance in the five-star hotels around Panjim.

Remo

Ask anyone in Goa to name you a famous Goan and they'll probably say "**Remo**". The state's most acclaimed musician, singer-songwriter and local hero, Remo Fernandes is unknown in the West but enjoys megastar status among India's young English-speaking middle classes. The secret of his success is his eccentric flair for **fusion**. Dressed in a cotton *dhoti* and twelve-hole Doc Martens, Remo blends Western rock with traditional Indian sounds, spiced up with South American rhythms and overscored by punchy issues-based lyrics. He's also staunchly proud of his Goan heritage, and is as happy crooning *fados* and Konkani folk tunes at local *festas* as performing electric sets in the concert halls of Delhi and Mumbai.

Born in 1953 in the picturesque riverside village of Siolim, near Chapora in north Goa, Remo's earliest musical influence was his father's collection of Portuguese, Latin-American and Goan records. A spell with a college rock band in Mumbai during the 1970s, followed by a couple of years hitching around Europe and North Africa, added new ingredients to this musical melting pot, and in 1980 he founded the ground-breaking fusion band Indiana, whose extravagant stage costumes and hybrid style would later become hallmarks of the Goan's own career.

Remo's big break, though, came in 1983 with the release of his first solo album, *Goan Crazy*. Recorded and mixed at his family home in Siolim, its multicultural sound and acerbic social commentary showcased Remo's talents as a multi-instrumentalist and lyric writer, finally bringing him to the attention of Mumbai's movie moguls and record companies. A series of hit film scores and a major record deal followed, culminating in his two best-selling albums, *Pack That Smack* and *Bombay City*, which both shot straight to the top of the rock/pop charts.

Then, just at the point when Remo's career looked set to go from strength to strength, tragedy struck. In the monsoons of 2000, three members of his "troupe" – two musicians from the backing band and his personal assistant – were killed in a car accident while on tour in the North Indian city of Kanpur.

Remo's stage appearances were cancelled in the wake of the tragedy, but a decade on he is performing regularly again. Among his most notable recent gigs was a 2005 appearance in Dubai with rock legends Jethro Tull.

Recommended albums

Virtually every musical street stall in Goa stocks a representative selection of **CDs** by Goan artists. The "Golden Oldies" of Chris Perry, Lorna and Alfred Rose form the backbone of a wonderful series released on the Saregama label in 2005 and 2006. Most are still available in Goan music shops, and abroad via download sites and online stores.

Alfred Rose *Goa's Musical Hero* (Saregama). Twenty classic Konkani hits recorded at the height of Rose's career between 1966 and 1977.

Chris Perry *Golden Hits (*Saregama*)*. This gives more of a flavour of the legendary early-1970s era of Konkani pop than any other Chris Perry compilation, with classics such as Lorna's "Red Rose" (the best-loved Goan tune of all time) and the infectiously funky "Mog Boom Boom Boom" by Babs Peter. There's also a track marking the brief period in the early 1970s when one of Hindi cinema's greatest ever crooners, Mohammed Rafi, recorded a handful of Konkani film songs.

Gavana *Cantando em Goa* (Viagem Dos Sons). The only *conjunto* still using exclusively acoustic instruments, Gavana was formed to preserve traditional Goan music and dance, and this album is their richest offering to date, with an engaging cross-section of *deknis*, *dulpods*, *mandos* and *saudades*-inspired Konkani classics. It comes with handsomely illustrated cover notes, giving background on the songs as well as translations of the lyrics. Sadly, the album is harder to come by than the less exciting *Souvenir* trio of audio cassettes (of which number three is the best).

Lorna *Lisboa* (Saregama). One of several greatest hits compilations by the undisputed queen of Konkani music, drawn from her classic Sixties and Seventies big band repertoire rather than the less easy-on-the-ear comeback albums of recent years.

Various Artists *Noman Noman Tuka Goa!* (Saregama). The pick of Saregama's recent crop of compilations, featuring early 1970s hits by Lorna, Mohammed Rafi, Chris Perry, Alfred Rose, Usha Mangueshkar and other stars. Aside from the waltzy title track, landmark golden oldies covered include "Maria", a famous duet with Lorna and Rafi in fine voice, and one of the best Konkani song intros ever, in "Noxibac Roddtam".

Konkani pop

Rave music aside, most of the sounds you hear around Goa these days are either *filmi* hits from the latest blockbuster Hindi movies, or a mish-mash of folk tunes and calypso rhythms known as **Konkani pop**. Backed by groups of women singers and fanfaring mariachi-style brass sections, Konkani lead vocalists croon away with the reverb cranked up against a cacophony of electric guitar and keyboard accompaniment.

Konkani pop is best experienced live (the costumes tend to be as lurid as the music), but if you don't manage to get to a gig, every kerbside cassette-wallah stocks a range of popular tapes. World-music aficionados should definitely check out a couple of CDs or cassettes to sample the surreal blend of musical influences. Underpinning the Portuguese-style melodies are conga-driven African and Caribbean rhythms, Brazilian syncopations and almost Polynesian-sounding harmonies; the only part of the world that Konkani pop doesn't sound like it comes from is India.

The Sixties and Seventies marked the golden era of Konkani popular music, when band leaders like **Chris Perry** (aka "the Man with the Golden Trumpet" and "King of Cha Cha Cha") first started arranging Goan songs with the kind of jazz and dance influences picked up while gigging in five-star hotels and cruise-liner ballrooms. It was Chris Perry who first discovered **Lorna**, whose voice would become the hallmark of Konkani music worldwide. Born in Bombay, in 1946, the "Goan Nightingale" first fronted Perry's 24-piece band at the age of 15, touring clubs and hotels across India. Recordings of songs composed by her mentor around this time have become the "Golden Oldies" of the Konkani repertoire, adored by generations of Goans, especially those marooned away from their loved ones in the Gulf. Lorna's voice, while retaining a hint of light-hearted mischief, is charged with just the kind of melancholic yearning with which homesick expats the world over identify. However, quite suddenly, at the height of her fame in the mid-1970s, a personal tragedy catapulted Lorna into premature retirement and a long depression that would deprive Goans of her voice for nearly three decades. Only in 1996, after musical director Ronnie Monsarate coaxed her back into the studio, did she start singing again. Since then, Lorna has churned out dozens of hit albums, and continues to perform both in Goa and for adoring audiences in the Gulf and beyond.

The other iconic voice of Konkani song is that of **Alfred Rose**, another Bombay-born singer who became famous in the 1960s as a bandleader (of the legendary "Rosebud Swing Band") and an actor in musical theatre. Credited with the release of the first ever Konkani music cassette, Rose, from Aldona near Mapusa, recorded many hit movie soundtracks as well as the Konkani classics that earned for him the nickname of Goa's "Melody King". His death in 2003 was mourned by the entire state, Hindus and Christians alike.

Books

There's a surprising dearth of books on Goa, particularly when you consider the reams of printed matter devoted to regions of India formerly colonized by the British. Most titles are either specialist tomes on history and architecture, or else travelogues that feature accounts of short sojourns in the territory.

While many of the titles listed below are stocked by high-street bookshops in Western countries, those published in India tend only to be available in Goa itself, usually at a fraction of what they would cost back home. The Other India Bookstore in Mapusa (above Mapusa Clinic; ⓣ0832/226 3306, ⓦwww.otherindiabookstore.com) is the best-stocked bookshop in the state, and offers an efficient online mail order service. Where books are out of print, they are annotated o/p. Titles marked ⁂ are particularly recommended.

History, society and architecture

Mário Cabral e Sá *Legends of Goa* (India Book House, Mumbai). After David Tomory's *Hello Goodnight* (see p.301), this is the most engaging book to have come out of Goa for years: a compendium of curious historical snippets drawn from across the centuries, handsomely packaged in hardback and featuring illustrations by the famous Goan cartoonist Mario Miranda.

Helder Carita *Palaces of Goa*. An encyclopedic, richly illustrated overview of civil Indo-Portuguese architecture in Goa, by the world's foremost authority on the subject. The only reason you'd want to buy it, however, are for Nicholas Sapieha's sumptuous photographs; the text is frustratingly incoherent and repetitious and offers little help as a field guide.

Charles Dellon *L'Inquisition de Goa*. The only surviving first-hand account of the Goan Inquisition, by a French traveller who experienced it in the seventeenth century. Dellon's chilling narrative, in this French edition illustrated with the original engravings, was the *Papillon* of its day, and remains a shocking indictment of the genocide perpetrated by the colonial clergy – at least, if you can read French (its English translation is out of print and extremely rare).

José Nicolau da Fonseca *Sketch of the City of Goa* (Asian Educational Services, New Delhi). A detailed overview of Goan history and society, compiled as part of the British Imperial Gazetteer in 1878. The typically Victorian "Statistical Account of the Territory" has become historical material in its own right, but the description of Old Goa remains the best of its kind ever published. AES's facsimile edition comes with copies of the original fold-out illustrations.

Richard Hall *Empires of the Monsoon*. This wide-ranging account of colonial expansion into the Indian Ocean is more erudite and compellingly written than most, tracing the web of trade connections that bound Africa, Europe and India from the fifteenth century onwards. Among its many highlights is a particularly vivid description of Vasco da Gama's voyages (in all their brutality) and Albuquerque's subsequent founding of Goa.

Koshy, Pandit & Mascarenhas *The Houses of Goa* (Architecture Anonymous, New Delhi). Only its hefty price tag puts this layman's guide to Goa's stately homes beyond the reach of casual readers. The prose, though a bit flowery and heavily reliant on sycophantic anecdote, is far more accessible than Helder Carita's, and the photos are top-class. The one real gripe is that the images aren't captioned, so you can't work out where half the places are, which renders the book redundant as a guide.

Robert Newman *Of Umbrellas, Goddesses & Dreams* (Other India Press, Delhi). A selection of scholarly essays on Goan culture and society, by an American anthropologist who's been studying the state since the late 1970s. Most of the pieces focus on religion – notably vision cults, church and temple festivals and Hindu–Christian crossovers – with engaging forays into the Konkani issue, fishing controversy and tourism. The writing's packed with insights, but you have to wade through a fair bit of repetitious academic prose to find them.

M.N. Pearson *The Portuguese in India*. A concise academic history of the Lusitanian empire in the subcontinent, from Vasco da Gama to Salazar. Conceived as a distillation of historical research in the field, it includes a wealth of amazing statistics relating to trade and military matters, contextualized by sharp insights into Portuguese society across the centuries.

José Pereira et al. *India and Portugal: Cultural Interactions* (Marg Publications, India). The cultural legacy of five centuries of Portuguese contact is presented in this copiously illustrated hardback. Subjects covered range from the evolution of church architecture to furniture, dance, dress and cuisine, with scores of colour photos and facsimiles of rare sixteenth-century engravings to justify its hefty price tag.

Rowena Robinson *Conversion, Continuity and Change: Lived Christianity in Southern Goa*. An anthropological monograph drawing on fieldwork in a Salcete village, which the author contextualizes with excerpts from a wide range of historical sources. If you can deal with the academic jargon, this makes a fascinating read, putting paid to any notion that caste disappeared with conversion to Christianity.

Elaine Sanceau *Indies Adventure: the Amazing Career of Alfonso de Albuquerque*. A lengthy but highly readable biography of Goa's first Portuguese governor, who wrested the territory from its former Muslim overlords in 1510.

Georg Schurhammer *Francis Xavier: His Life and Times*. A definitive biography of Goa's wandering patron saint, including a graphic rundown of the amputations inflicted on his corpse (see p.88).

Sunil Sethi *Indian Interiors*. In its three-hundred-page odyssey around India, this sumptuously illustrated coffee-table book pulls back the curtains on five Goan homes, ranging from the eighteenth-century Casa de Braganza in Chandor to a humble beach shack occupied by a couple of foreign expats. You also "see" inside the highly coloured, terrazzo-floored suites of the *Nilaya Hermitage* hotel at Arpora, diamond tycoon Jimmy Gadzar's monumentally kitsch pad at Fort Aguada and the Deshprabhus' stately home at Pernem.

Robert Sewell *A Forgotten Empire* (reprinted in facsimile by Asian Educational Services, New Delhi). A concise history of the Vijayanagars, supplemented by the translated chronicles of Domingo Paes and Fernao Nuniz, two Portuguese travellers who visited the royal city at the height of its splendour. Essential reading if you want to get to grips with the history behind Hampi's ruins.

Manohar Shetty (ed.) *Ferry Crossing: Short Stories From Around Goa*. This anthology of Goan fiction, put together by a local poet and widely available in the state, comprises broadly themed short stories woven around the local landscape and people. Translated from Konkani, Marathi and Portuguese, none is what you might call world class, but they offer fresh perspectives on Goan life, particularly the impact of modernization on villages.

Guide books

Maurice Hall *Window on Goa: A History and Guide*. Published posthumously, this widely available work, completed during the author's retirement after a career as a steel engineer in India, was clearly a labour of love. Covering every conceivable site of historic interest, it offers a concise, highly readable background on all aspects of Goan life, brought to life by dozens of colour photographs.

Anthony Hutt *Goa: A Traveller's Historical and Architectural Guide*. A detailed overview of Goa's past and present, with accounts of the main monuments and illustrations, and a good index. Ideal if you want to deepen your understanding of the region without getting tangled in nit-picking academic prose.

Travel writing

R.F. Burton *Goa and the Blue Mountains* (Asian Educational Services, New Delhi). One of the Victorian era's most acclaimed traveller-adventurer-anthropologists, Burton was but a lowly young army officer on sick leave when he wrote this, his first book, in 1847. As an account of Portuguese Goa it's pretty lame, but if you can ignore all the bigotry and racist asides about "*mestiço* mongrel men", it has its moments (the most infamous being an attempt to abduct a beautiful orphan from a Goan convent, which went wrong when the perpetrators – among them a thinly disguised Burton – carried off the abbess by mistake).

Gita Mehta *Karma Cola*. Satirical look at the psychedelic 1970s freak scene that winds up, appropriately enough, at the Anjuna flea market. Now somewhat dated, but with some hilarious anecdotes and many a telling observation on the excesses of spiritual tourism in India.

Jerry Pinto (ed.) *Reflected in Water: Writings on Goa*. A wide-ranging compilation of pieces culled from books spanning five centuries, from travel essays by the likes of William Dalrymple, Graham Greene and David Tomory, to more impressionistic, literary and historical articles on various aspects of local life, past and present, by eminent Goans. Full of insight and elegantly written observation – a must for any interested visitor to the region.

François Pyrard *Voyage to the East Indies, the Maldives, the Moluccas and Brazil* (Hakluyt Society, India). Albert Gray's translation of the famous French chronicler's travelogue includes a vivid first-hand description of the Portuguese colony during its decadent heyday. Goa was Pyrard's first port of call after he was shipwrecked in the Maldives in 1608.

David Tomory *Hello Goodnight*. An upbeat account of Goa through the ages, enlivened with experiences and encounters distilled from over thirty years of visiting and reading about the region. It's all in here: from Albuquerque to Wendell Rodrick, and Jungle Barry to the *Nine*

Bar, crammed into 23 chapters of poppy prose that faithfully captures Goa's essential quirkiness. Some will find it short on analysis, but the book's depiction of contemporary tourist culture, in particular, is spot on.

Wildlife and the environment

Claude Alvares (ed.) *Fish Curry and Rice: A Citizens' Report on the Goan Environment* (Ecoforum, India). The most thorough overview of Goan green issues ever compiled in a single volume, giving a region-by-region rundown of the state's natural habitats, followed by articles outlining the principal threats to the environment from tourism, transport policy, changes in local farming practices and a host of other eco evils.

Grimmet & Inskipp *Birds of Southern India*. The bird-lovers' bible: a beautifully organized, written and illustrated 240-page field guide listing every species known in South India. It's a tailored, region-specific version of the heftier *Pocket Guide to the Birds of the Indian Subcontinent* by the same authors (Helm), which lists all 1300 species spotted in South Asia.

Insight Guides *Indian Wildlife*. An excellent all-round introduction to India's wildlife, with scores of superb colour photographs, features on different animals and habitats, and a thorough bibliography.

Kamierczak and Van Perlo *A Field Guide to the Birds of the Indian Subcontinent*. Less popular than Grimmet and Inskipp's competing guide, but just as thorough, expertly drawn and well laid out, with every species named.

P. Killips *A Guide to the Flora and Fauna of Goa* (Orient Longman, Hyderabad). A seventy-page field guide, illustrated with amateur photos but listing all the common species of palms, flowering trees, butterflies, reptiles, mammals, insects and beach creatures.

Romulus Whitaker *Common Indian Snakes*. A detailed and illustrated guide with all the Goan species included.

Language

Language

Konkani 305

Konkani words and phrases 305

Food and drink terms 307

Glossary of Hindi and Konkani words 310

Konkani

Konkani, an Indo-Aryan offshoot of Sanskrit that took root in the region more than two thousand years ago, is the mother tongue of most Goans, spoken by virtually all of its native inhabitants. Only in 1978, however, was it recognized by Delhi as more than a minor dialect, and another fourteen years elapsed before the Indian government, bowing to popular opinion, named it the state's official language. However, **Marathi**, the language of Goa's politically and economically powerful neighbour, Maharashtra, remains the principal medium of primary education.

Although the two languages are closely related, the debate over which to use in government has aroused strong feelings over the years – most notably during the run-up to Delhi's decision to rubber-stamp Konkani, which divided the regional press and sparked off violent confrontations between rival groups. The issues at stake, however, have far less to do with which language is more universally understood than with the politics and notions of regional identity. Those Goans who wanted their children taught in Marathi also tended to favour merger with Maharashtra, whereas the pro-Konkani lobby believed the state would be better off with greater autonomy.

An added complication has been the lingering presence of **Portuguese**. Only a tiny number of Goans still speak the former colonial mother tongue, but they tend to be from a well-educated, politically influential elite. The only places you're likely to hear it spoken in the street are the neighbourhood of Fontainhas, Panjim, which remains solidly pro-Portuguese, and in the stately homes of the Velhas Conquistas – though of course, innumerable words from the former colonial mother tongue have crept into Konkani.

India's official national language, **Hindi**, has a place in Goa, too, largely thanks to the increasing number of settlers from the north of the country and the popularity of "Bollywood" movies. However, the language of higher education, law and the quality press is **English**, which is so prevalent in the resorts that you can easily get by without a word of Konkani or Marathi. Even fluent English speakers, though, will be flattered if you attempt a few words of their native tongue.

The lists of words and phrases below are intended as an aid to meeting people and travelling independently around more off-the-beaten-track areas of the state, where English is less commonly spoken. Konkani has no official script of its own (Christians tend to use Roman, and Hindus write with Devanagiri), so we've transcribed the expressions phonetically.

Konkani words and phrases

Meeting people

hello/good morning/ good evening	dio boro dees diun
what is your name?	tu chay nau kitay?
my name is (David)	majay nau (David)
where do you come from?	tu koyee-sau yat-ee?
I come from …	mau zo gao …
how are you (male)?	kos-o-asaee?

how are you (female)?	kos-hey-am?
thank you	dio boray korunc
Happy Christmas	Kooshal bhooreet Natala
Happy Holi	Holi moobarak
may I take your photograph?	au eek foto kardum?
yes/no	hoee/na
good	borem
I am tired	aoo tsod tokla
I am happy	aoo tsaud kooshi
I love Goa	maka Goeya boray lakta
I understand a little Konkani	maka toree Konkani sazmata
I speak a little Konkani	aoo toree Konkani oolayta
goodbye	miochay

Getting around and finding accommodation

where can I catch the bus to (Calangute)?	(Calangute) bus ko-ee tamta?
does this bus go to (Calangute)?	Ee Calangute bus?
when does the bus leave?	bus kitley-anc so-ta?
have we arrived in (Candolim)?	(Candolim) poh-lay?
how much to (Anjuna)?	kitlay pot-ollay (Anjuna)?
how many kilometres is i t to (Calangute)?	(Calangute) kitley pois asa?
turn left/right	dai-an/ooj-an wot
drive more slowly!	sossegarde solay!
do you have a room/ house to rent?	tu jay shee room/ gora asa?

Eating and drinking

I am hungry	maka bhook lagleah
I am thirsty	maka taan lagleah
water	oodak
no ice	barf naka
no sugar	shakhar naka
not spicy	makha tikh naka
the food is good	jon boray ha

Shopping

how much?	kitlay?
too expensive!	ekdtom ma-araog!
I don't want it	maka naka tem
I'll take this	haon hem khatan
have you got another one?	aslem aneek assa

Families

father	pai (Christian), bapui (Hindu)
mother	maee (Christian), avoi (Hindu)
grandmother	shamai
grandfather	shapai
daughter	dhoo
son	phoot
wife	bhai
husband	ghoo
male/female cousin	primo/prima
older adults (polite)	tia (female)/tio (male)

Time and days

now	at-ants
today	atz
yesterday	kal
tomorrow	falyam

morning	sakal
afternoon	donpara
evening	sanz
night	rat
Monday	Somar
Tuesday	Munglar
Wednesday	Boodhwar
Thursday	Virestar
Friday	Sookarar
Saturday	Shenvar
Sunday	Aee-tar

Other useful words

beach	prayia
cave	bhuher
church	igroz
coconut	nal
doctor	daktar
hill	dongoor
moon	tsondrim
palm tree	mard
river	wow
road	rosto
sea	doria
sun	wot
temple	day-vool
tender coconut	adzar
village	ga

Numbers

1	ek
2	dohn
3	teen
4	char
5	pants
6	soh
7	saht
8	ahrt
9	nou
10	dha
20	vees
30	tees
40	cha-ees
50	po-nas
100	chem-bor
150	dher-chen
200	dho-chen
1000	ek-azar
2000	dhon-azar

Note: A hundred thousand is a *lakh* (written 1,00,000); ten million is a *crore* (1,00,00,000). Millions, billions and the like are not in common usage.

Food and drink terms

Goan dishes and cooking terms

ananas	pineapple
apa de camarao	prawn pie with a crisp rice-flour crust
balchao	a preserve of rich red-chilli sauce
bazlele	fried
bharli vaangi	stuffed aubergines (eggplant)
bibo upkari	cashews cooked with spices
cabedala	pungent pork dish
cafreal	spicy fried chicken or fish
caja	cashew nut
caldo verde	Portuguese potato and cabbage
chanyacho ros	dried peas prepared with dry-roasted coconut and whole spices

chouriço	small red pork sausages flavoured with *feni*, *toddi* vinegar and chillies; known as *lingiss* in Konkani
feijoada	butter-bean stew; often with chunks of chouriço
gur	coconut sugar
keli	banana
kishmar	dried and powdered shrimp
leitao	roast suckling pig; originally a speciality of Coimbra, Portugal
nal	coconut
neeshtay	fish
neeshtaychi corri	fish curry water
pilau	Basmati rice stewed in stock and flavoured with whole spices and saffron
rechad	a hot red-chilli paste, mainly used to flavour fish
rechado	stuffed with rechad
sorpatel	pickled pork seasoned with hot spices; eaten at Christmas and marriage feasts
taanoo	rice
tamari bhaji	a red-spinach dish with onions, chillies and grated coconut
tel	cooking oil
toddi	palm sap vinegar or wine
vindaloo	pork or chicken marinated in an extra-hot and sour curry sauce
xacuti	a fiery sauce for meat made with lemon juice, nuts, coconut milk and lots of red chillies

Seafood

bangra	mackerel
bodorn	tuna
ching-go	lobster
chonok	barramundi
dzob or **shenanio**	mussels
eison	kingfish
gobro	rockfish
paloo	bream
kooli	crab
mandkin	kalamari (squid)
modso	lemon fish
mori	shark
pomflit or **pitorshi**	pomfret
shewter	mullet
sulta	tiger prawns
tamso	snapper

Dishes from other regions

biriyani	rice with saffron or turmeric, whole spices and meat (sometimes vegetables), and often hard-boiled egg; mild
cutlet	minced meat or vegetables fried in the form of a flat cake
jalfrezi	with tomatoes and green chilli; medium hot
jeera	cumin; a masala so described will usually be medium hot
keema	minced lamb
korma	braised in yoghurt sauce with almonds; mild

malai kofta balls of minced vegetables in a rich spicy sauce

pilau rice, lightly spiced and pre-fried

rogan josh red lamb curry; a classic Mughlai dish; medium hot

sambar tangy vegetable and lentil soup with asa foetida and tamarind

subje white-coconut chutney served with most South Indian dishes

tarka da split orange lentils cooked in a masala of turmeric, fried garlic and onions

Breads and pancakes

batura soft deep-fried white bread that traditionally accompanies *channa* (chick peas)

chapati unleavened bread made with mixed white and whole wheat flour, dry-baked on a flat griddle

dosa crispy rice pancake

iddli steamed rice cake usually served with *sambar*

***kunechi poee** pitta-like unleavened bread, often baked or dry-fried in the shape of a butterfly

nann/naan white leavened bread baked in a clay oven (*tandoor*)

***pao** or **poee** soft and crusty Portuguese-style white bread rolls

papadam crisp, thin chick-pea-flour cracker, deepfried or grilled

paratha wholewheat bread made with butter and griddle-fried; tastes like a chewy pancake and is often stuffed with vegetables or meat

puri soft white-dough bread that puffs up and crispens when deep-fried in oil

roti a loosely used term; often just another name for chapati, though it should be thicker, chewier and baked in a *tandoor*

***sanna** traditional crumpet-like bread rolls made with rice flour, sugar and partially fermented *toddi*

uttapam griddle-fried, rice-batter pancake, speckled with holes and soft in the middle; often prepared using onions

wada or **vada** deep-fried doughnuts made from lentil flour

* Goan terminology; all other bread and pancake terms above refer to North or South Indian cuisine.

Cakes and desserts

alebele rice-flour pancakes stuffed with grated fresh coconut

batica coconut cake

bebinca a ten-layer, cholesterol-filled Christmas cake made with egg yolks, coconut milk and sugar

bolinhas small, round and crumbly rice-flour cakes

culculs tiny shell-shaped biscuits

dodol jaggery and coconut water, reduced to a fudge-like slab with roasted coconuts and cashews

mangada mango jam

neuros half-moon-shaped stuffed pastries

Glossary of Hindi and Konkani words

argashallas pilgrims' hostels in Hindu temples

ashram religious institution built around a spiritual or political leader (guru)

avatar reincarnation of Hindu god on earth, in human or animal form

azulejos white ceramic tile hand-painted in blue and yellow: a traditional Portuguese art form

balcão deep veranda of Goan villas with stone benches where residents relax during siesta and in the evening

beedis tiny Indian cigarettes hand-rolled in brown eucalyptus leaves and tied with cotton thread. The aroma they give off is one of India's quintessential smells

bhel puri a typical Mumbai masala mixture of puffed rice, deep-fried vermicelli, potato, crunchy puri pieces, chilli paste, tamarind water, chopped onions and coriander

brahmapuri Hindu religious centre

Brahmins caste made up of priests and teachers

burqa enveloping black veil worn by Muslim women

cadeirinha or **palkhi** traditional Indo-Portuguese sedan chair with two seats facing each other

caravela Portuguese galleon with a triangular sail derived from the Arab dhow

chai Indian tea; usually boiled with lots of milk and sugar

charas cannabis resin (hashish)

chowkidar watchman/caretaker

darshan ritual viewing of a deity or saint; receiving religious teachings

deep stambhas lamp tower positioned outside Hindu temples – a feature introduced to Goa by the Marathas

deepmal lamp tower (see above)

devta deity

devul temple

dhaba roadside food stall selling local dishes

dharamsala rest house for pilgrims

dhobi man or woman who washes clothes

dhoop thick pliable block of strong incense

dhoti white ankle-length cloth worn by men, tied around the waist, and hitched up through the legs

dwarpalas guardian deities; in Goa, these feature on the embossed silver doors flanking the temple shrine rooms

feni clear liquor distilled from cashew fruit or coconut sap (*toddi*)

festa Christian feast day connected with a patron saint

filmi popular Hindi movie music

garbhagriha sanctum or shrine room of a Hindu temple

gaur Indian bison

ghat literally "step"; usually refers to the Sahyadri Hills lining the Goan border

ghor house

goenkar (or **gaunkar**) high-caste landowner

gopura ornamental gateway to a temple enclosure, surmounted by a multi-tiered tower (often decorated with statues)

gram roasted maize, sold on streets all over India

Harijans literally "Children of God" a term introduced by Mahatma Gandhi to designate those outside, or below, the four principal Hindu castes

hidalgos Portuguese nobles

igreja church

kott fort

Kshatriyas the second-highest caste, made up of rulers and warriors

kum kum finely ground, brightly coloured powder (usually scarlet) used to mark the forehead of deities in *puja*, and on the parting of married women

langur black-faced monkey

lingam phallic symbol in places of worship representing the god Shiva

lunghi male garment: long wraparound cloth worn tucked in at the waist flowing down to the ankles.

macheela old Portuguese sedan chair, similar to a *cadeirinha*

maidan large open space or field

mandapa assembly hall tacked onto the front of a temple, often with many pillars

mandir temple

mestiço Portuguese name for a person of mixed Indian–European parentage

mihrab niche in the wall of a mosque indicating the direction of prayer (to Mecca). In India, the *mihrab* is normally in the west wall

moksha spiritual release from the cycle of rebirth

mundkar tenants, usually of low caste

nacre rectangles of polished fish scales (often referred to as "oyster shells") traditionally used instead of glass to make windows

naubhat khanna musicians' gallery in a Goan temple

Novas Conquistas the "New Conquests" area of Goa: Pernem, Satari, Canacona and Sanguem *talukas*, acquired by the Portuguese in the eighteenth century

palacio Indo-Portuguese-style stately home

pariwar devta family *devta*, or deity

pradakshena circumambulatory passage around a temple shrine

puja worship

pujari priest

rath processional temple chariot

sala/Shala reception room or hall in a *palacio*

salwar-kameez long shirt and pyjama trousers worn by women and Muslim men

sanyasin religious devotee

satyagrahas Goan Ghandhi-ites: non-violent protesters against colonial occupation

sesso martel wood

shikhara temple tower or spire

shivalingam see *lingam*

Shudras the lowest of the four castes, designating menial workers

sonddios galleries for storing musical instruments in temples

sossegarde a typically Goan expression, meaning "laid-back"

swami Hindu holy man

taluka administrative district

tiatr (or **khel-tiatr**) popular Konkani theatre

tilak vermilion paste smeared on the forehead by Hindu worshippers

tirtha literally "crossing place", where the temporal world and divine realms meet, as in a temple bathing pool or sacred river confluence

tulsi vrindavan ornamental pot (*vrindavan*) containing the sacred shrub *tulsi*, a variety of basil, representing a former mistress of Vishnu

vahana the vehicle of a deity; the bull Nandi is Shiva's *vahana*

Vaishyas third-highest of the Hindu castes, made up of tradesmen

Velhas Conquistas the Old Conquests area of Goa: Bardez, Tiswadi and Salcete *talukas*

waddo ward, or area of a village

wallah/walli suffix implying occupation or purveyor of something, eg rickshaw-wallah (rickshaw driver), flower-walli (lady flower-seller)

Travel store

Travel

Andorra The Pyrenees, Pyrenees & Andorra Map, Spain
Antigua The Caribbean
Argentina Argentina, Argentina Map, Buenos Aires, South America on a Budget
Aruba The Caribbean
Australia Australia, Australia Map, East Coast Australia, Melbourne, Sydney, Tasmania
Austria Austria, Europe on a Budget, Vienna
Bahamas The Bahamas, The Caribbean
Barbados Barbados DIR, The Caribbean
Belgium Belgium & Luxembourg, Bruges DIR, Brussels, Brussels Map, Europe on a Budget
Belize Belize, Central America on a Budget, Guatemala & Belize Map
Benin West Africa
Bolivia Bolivia, South America on a Budget
Brazil Brazil, Rio, South America on a Budget
British Virgin Islands The Caribbean
Brunei Malaysia, Singapore & Brunei [1 title], Southeast Asia on a Budget
Bulgaria Bulgaria, Europe on a Budget
Burkina Faso West Africa
Cambodia Cambodia, Southeast Asia on a Budget, Vietnam, Laos & Cambodia Map [1 Map]
Cameroon West Africa
Canada Canada, Pacific Northwest, Toronto, Toronto Map, Vancouver
Cape Verde West Africa
Cayman Islands The Caribbean
Chile Chile, Chile Map, South America on a Budget
China Beijing, China, Hong Kong & Macau, Hong Kong & Macau DIR, Shanghai
Colombia South America on a Budget
Costa Rica Central America on a Budget, Costa Rica, Costa Rica & Panama Map
Croatia Croatia, Croatia Map, Europe on a Budget
Cuba Cuba, Cuba Map, The Caribbean, Havana
Cyprus Cyprus, Cyprus Map
Czech Republic The Czech Republic, Czech & Slovak Republics, Europe on a Budget, Prague, Prague DIR, Prague Map
Denmark Copenhagen, Denmark, Europe on a Budget, Scandinavia
Dominica The Caribbean
Dominican Republic Dominican Republic, The Caribbean
Ecuador Ecuador, South America on a Budget
Egypt Egypt, Egypt Map
El Salvador Central America on a Budget
England Britain, Camping in Britain, Devon & Cornwall, Dorset, Hampshire and The Isle of Wight [1 title], England, Europe on a Budget, The Lake District, London, London DIR, London Map, London Mini Guide, Walks In London & Southeast England
Estonia The Baltic States, Europe on a Budget
Fiji Fiji
Finland Europe on a Budget, Finland, Scandinavia
France Brittany & Normandy, Corsica, Corsica Map, The Dordogne & the Lot, Europe on a Budget, France, France Map, Languedoc & Roussillon, The Loire, Paris, Paris DIR, Paris Map, Paris Mini Guide, Provence & the Côte d'Azur, The Pyrenees, Pyrenees & Andorra Map
French Guiana South America on a Budget
Gambia The Gambia, West Africa
Germany Berlin, Berlin Map, Europe on a Budget, Germany, Germany Map
Ghana West Africa
Gibraltar Spain
Greece Athens Map, Crete, Crete Map, Europe on a Budget, Greece, Greece Map, Greek Islands, Ionian Islands
Guadeloupe The Caribbean
Guatemala Central America on a Budget, Guatemala, Guatemala & Belize Map
Guinea West Africa
Guinea-Bissau West Africa
Guyana South America on a Budget
Holland see The Netherlands
Honduras Central America on a Budget
Hungary Budapest, Europe on a Budget, Hungary
Iceland Iceland, Iceland Map
India Goa, India, India Map, Kerala, Rajasthan, Delhi & Agra [1 title], South India, South India Map
Indonesia Bali & Lombok, Southeast Asia on a Budget
Ireland Dublin DIR, Dublin Map, Europe on a Budget, Ireland, Ireland Map
Israel Jerusalem
Italy Europe on a Budget, Florence DIR, Florence & Siena Map, Florence & the best of Tuscany, Italy, The Italian Lakes, Naples & the Amalfi Coast, Rome, Rome DIR, Rome Map, Sardinia, Sicily, Sicily Map, Tuscany & Umbria, Tuscany Map, Venice, Venice DIR, Venice Map
Jamaica Jamaica, The Caribbean
Japan Japan, Tokyo
Jordan Jordan
Kenya Kenya, Kenya Map
Korea Korea
Laos Laos, Southeast Asia on a Budget, Vietnam, Laos & Cambodia Map [1 Map]
Latvia The Baltic States, Europe on a Budget
Lithuania The Baltic States, Europe on a Budget
Luxembourg Belgium & Luxembourg, Europe on a Budget
Malaysia Malaysia Map, Malaysia, Singapore & Brunei [1 title], Southeast Asia on a Budget
Mali West Africa
Malta Malta & Gozo DIR
Martinique The Caribbean
Mauritania West Africa
Mexico Baja California, Baja California, Cancún & Cozumel DIR, Mexico, Mexico Map, Yucatán, Yucatán Peninsula Map
Monaco France, Provence & the Côte d'Azur
Montenegro Montenegro
Morocco Europe on a Budget, Marrakesh DIR, Marrakesh Map, Morocco, Morocco Map,
Nepal Nepal
Netherlands Amsterdam, Amsterdam DIR, Amsterdam Map, Europe on a Budget, The Netherlands
Netherlands Antilles The Caribbean
New Zealand New Zealand, New Zealand Map

DIR: Rough Guide **DIRECTIONS** for short breaks

Available from all good bookstores

Nicaragua Central America on a Budget
Niger West Africa
Nigeria West Africa
Norway Europe on a Budget, Norway, Scandinavia
Panama Central America on a Budget, Costa Rica & Panama Map, Panama
Paraguay South America on a Budget
Peru Peru, Peru Map, South America on a Budget
Philippines The Philippines, Southeast Asia on a Budget,
Poland Europe on a Budget, Poland
Portugal Algarve DIR, The Algarve Map, Europe on a Budget, Lisbon DIR, Lisbon Map, Madeira DIR, Portugal, Portugal Map, Spain & Portugal Map
Puerto Rico The Caribbean, Puerto Rico
Romania Europe on a Budget, Romania
Russia Europe on a Budget, Moscow, St Petersburg
St Kitts & Nevis The Caribbean
St Lucia The Caribbean
St Vincent & the Grenadines The Caribbean
Scotland Britain, Camping in Britain, Edinburgh DIR, Europe on a Budget, Scotland, Scottish Highlands & Islands
Senegal West Africa
Serbia Montenegro Europe on a Budget
Sierra Leone West Africa
Singapore Malaysia, Singapore & Brunei [1 title], Singapore, Singapore DIR, Southeast Asia on a Budget
Slovakia Czech & Slovak Republics, Europe on a Budget
Slovenia Europe on a Budget, Slovenia
South Africa Cape Town & the Garden Route, South Africa, South Africa Map
Spain Andalucía, Andalucía Map, Barcelona, Barcelona DIR, Barcelona Map, Europe on a Budget, Ibiza & Formentera DIR, Gran Canaria DIR, Madrid DIR, Lanzarote & Fuerteventura DIR Madrid Map, Mallorca & Menorca, Mallorca DIR, Mallorca Map, The Pyrenees, Pyrenees & Andorra Map, Spain, Spain & Portugal Map, Tenerife & La Gomera DIR
Sri Lanka Sri Lanka, Sri Lanka Map
Suriname South America on a Budget
Sweden Europe on a Budget, Scandinavia, Sweden
Switzerland Europe on a Budget, Switzerland
Taiwan Taiwan
Tanzania Tanzania, Zanzibar
Thailand Bangkok, Southeast Asia on a Budget, Thailand, Thailand Map, Thailand Beaches & Islands
Togo West Africa
Trinidad & Tobago The Caribbean, Trinidad & Tobago
Tunisia Tunisia, Tunisia Map
Turkey Europe on a Budget, Istanbul, Turkey, Turkey Map
Turks and Caicos Islands The Bahamas, The Caribbean
United Arab Emirates Dubai DIR, Dubai & UAE Map [1 title]
United Kingdom Britain, Devon & Cornwall, Edinburgh DIR England, Europe on a Budget, The Lake District, London, London DIR, London Map, London Mini Guide, Scotland, Scottish Highlands & Islands, Wales, Walks In London & Southeast England
United States Alaska, Boston, California, California Map, Chicago, Colorado, Florida, Florida Map, The Grand Canyon, Hawaii, Los Angeles, Los Angeles Map, Los Angeles and Southern California, Maui DIR, Miami & South Florida, New England, New England Map, New Orleans & Cajun Country, New Orleans DIR, New York City, NYC DIR, NYC Map, New York City Mini Guide, Oregon & Washington, Orlando & Walt Disney World® DIR, San Francisco, San Francisco DIR, San Francisco Map, Seattle, Southwest USA, USA, Washington DC, Yellowstone & the Grand Tetons National Park, Yosemite National Park
Uruguay South America on a Budget
US Virgin Islands The Bahamas, The Caribbean
Venezuela South America on a Budget
Vietnam Southeast Asia on a Budget, Vietnam, Vietnam, Laos & Cambodia Map [1 Map],
Wales Britain, Camping in Britain, Europe on a Budget, Wales
First-Time Series FT Africa, FT Around the World, FT Asia, FT Europe, FT Latin America
Inspirational guides Earthbound, Clean Breaks, Make the Most of Your Time on Earth, Ultimate Adventures, World Party
Travel Specials Camping in Britain, Travel with Babies & Young Children, Walks in London & SE England

ROUGH GUIDES Don't Just Travel

Computers Cloud Computing, FWD this link, The Internet, iPhone, iPods & iTunes, Macs & OS X, Website Directory
Film & TV American Independent Film, British Cult Comedy, Comedy Movies, Cult Movies, Film, Film Musicals, Film Noir, Gangster Movies, Horror Movies, Sci-Fi Movies, Westerns
Lifestyle Babies & Toddlers, Brain Training, Food, Girl Stuff, Green Living, Happiness, Men's Health, Pregnancy & Birth, Running, Saving & Selling Online, Sex, Weddings
Music The Beatles, The Best Music You've Never Heard, Blues, Bob Dylan, Book of Playlists, Classical Music, Heavy Metal, Jimi Hendrix, Led Zeppelin, Nirvana, Opera, Pink Floyd, The Rolling Stones, Soul and R&B, Velvet Underground, World Music
Popular Culture Anime, Classic Novels, Conspiracy Theories, Crime Fiction, The Da Vinci Code, Graphic Novels, Hidden Treasures, His Dark Materials, Hitchhiker's Guide to the Galaxy, The Lost Symbol, Manga, Next Big Thing, Shakespeare, True Crime, Tutankhamun, Unexplained Phenomena, Videogames
Science The Brain, Climate Change, The Earth, Energy Crisis, Evolution, Future, Genes & Cloning, The Universe, Weather

For more information go to www.roughguides.com

NOTES

Small print and Index

A Rough Guide to Rough Guides

Published in 1982, the first Rough Guide – to Greece – was a student scheme that became a publishing phenomenon. Mark Ellingham, a recent graduate in English from Bristol University, had been travelling in Greece the previous summer and couldn't find the right guidebook. With a small group of friends he wrote his own guide, combining a highly contemporary, journalistic style with a thoroughly practical approach to travellers' needs.

The immediate success of the book spawned a series that rapidly covered dozens of destinations. And, in addition to impecunious backpackers, Rough Guides soon acquired a much broader and older readership that relished the guides' wit and inquisitiveness as much as their enthusiastic, critical approach and value-for-money ethos.

These days, Rough Guides include recommendations from shoestring to luxury and cover more than 200 destinations around the globe, including almost every country in the Americas and Europe, more than half of Africa and most of Asia and Australasia. Our ever-growing team of authors and photographers is spread all over the world, particularly in Europe, the US and Australia.

In the early 1990s, Rough Guides branched out of travel, with the publication of Rough Guides to World Music, Classical Music and the Internet. All three have become benchmark titles in their fields, spearheading the publication of a wide range of books under the Rough Guide name.

Including the travel series, Rough Guides now number more than 350 titles, covering: phrasebooks, waterproof maps, music guides from Opera to Heavy Metal, reference works as diverse as Conspiracy Theories and Shakespeare, and popular culture books from iPods to Poker. Rough Guides also produce a series of more than 120 World Music CDs in partnership with World Music Network.

Visit www.roughguides.com to see our latest publications.

Rough Guide credits

Text editor: Brendon Griffin
Layout: Ankur Guha
Cartography: Swati Handoo
Picture editor: Mark Thomas
Production: Rebecca Short
Proofreader: Jennifer Speake
Cover design: Nicole Newman, Dan May, Chloë Roberts
Photographer: David Abram
Editorial: **London** Andy Turner, Keith Drew, Edward Aves, Alice Park, Lucy White, Jo Kirby, James Smart, Natasha Foges, Róisín Cameron, James Rice, Lara Kavanagh, Emma Beatson, Emma Gibbs, Kathryn Lane, Monica Woods, Mani Ramaswamy, Harry Wilson, Lucy Cowie, Alison Roberts, Eleanor Aldridge, Ian Blenkinsop, Joe Staines, Matthew Milton, Tracy Hopkins, Ruth Tidball; **Delhi** Madhavi Singh, Lubna Shaheen, Jalpreen Kaur Chhatwal
Design & Pictures: **London** Scott Stickland, Dan May, Diana Jarvis, Nicole Newman, Sarah Cummins, Emily Taylor; **Delhi** Umesh Aggarwal, Ajay Verma, Jessica Subramanian, Pradeep Thapliyal, Sachin Tanwar, Anita Singh, Nikhil Agarwal, Sachin Gupta
Production: Liz Cherry, Louise Daly, Erika Pepe
Cartography: **London** Ed Wright, Katie Lloyd-Jones; **Delhi** Rajesh Chhibber, Ashutosh Bharti, Rajesh Mishra, Animesh Pathak, Jasbir Sandhu, Karobi Gogoi, Deshpal Dabas, Lokamata Sahu
Online: **London** Faye Hellon, Jeanette Angell, Fergus Day, Justine Bright, Clare Bryson, Aine Fearon, Adrian Low, Ezgi Celebi; **Delhi** Amit Verma, Rahul Kumar, Narender Kumar, Ravi Yadav, Debojit Borah, Rakesh Kumar, Ganesh Sharma, Shisir Basumatari
Marketing & Publicity: **London** Liz Statham, Jess Carter, Vivienne Watton, Anna Paynton, Rachel Sprackett, Laura Vipond; **New York** Katy Ball; **Delhi** Aman Arora
Digital Travel Publisher: Peter Buckley
Reference Director: Andrew Lockett
Operations Assistant: Becky Doyle
Operations Manager: Helen Atkinson
Publishing Director (Travel): Clare Currie
Commercial Manager: Gino Magnotta
Managing Director: John Duhigg

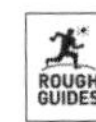

Publishing information

This eighth edition published November 2010 by
Rough Guides Ltd,
80 Strand, London WC2R 0RL
11, Community Centre, Panchsheel Park, New Delhi 110017, India
Distributed by the Penguin Group
Penguin Books Ltd,
80 Strand, London WC2R 0RL
Penguin Group (USA)
375 Hudson Street, NY 10014, USA
Penguin Group (Australia)
250 Camberwell Road, Camberwell, Victoria 3124, Australia
Penguin Group (NZ)
67 Apollo Drive, Mairangi Bay, Auckland 1310, New Zealand
This paperback edition published in Canada in 2010. Rough Guides is represented in Canada by Tourmaline Editions Inc., 662 King Street West, Suite 304, Toronto, Ontario, M5V 1M7
Cover concept by Peter Dyer.
Typeset in Bembo and Helvetica to an original design by Henry Iles.
Printed in Singapore

328pp includes index
A catalogue record for this book is available from the British Library
ISBN: 978-1-84836-562-9

1 3 5 7 9 8 6 4 2

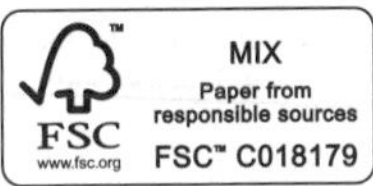

Help us update

We've gone to a lot of effort to ensure that the eighth edition of **The Rough Guide to Goa** is accurate and up-to-date. However, things change – places get "discovered", opening hours are notoriously fickle, restaurants and rooms raise prices or lower standards. If you feel we've got it wrong or left something out, we'd like to know, and if you can remember the address, the price, the hours, the phone number, so much the better.

Please send your comments with the subject line "**Rough Guide Goa Update**" to mail@roughguides.com. We'll credit all contributions and send a copy of the next edition (or any other Rough Guide if you prefer) for the very best emails.

Have your questions answered and tell others about your trip at www.roughguides.com

Acknowledgements

David Abram would like to thank: Viriam Kaur for her invaluable Arambol dispatches; Shelly, Teresa, Royston and Willy at the Casa Sea Shell in Candolim, for their kind hospitality during Cyclone Phyan; Fiona Jeffry for the lowdown on Agonda; and to all the guesthouse owners, hoteliers, restaurateurs and expat layabouts who took time to bring me up to speed on their respective patches: Mariketty in Vagator, Virendra in Calangute, Axel and Lucie in Arambol, Joanna Thornycroft in Lutolim, Simon Hayward in Majorda, Jazz KoKo and Fiona Spiral in Palolem. This guide relies heavily, and unashamedly, on local knowledge.

In the UK, thank you to editor Brendon Griffin, who tidied up this new, slimmer, more information-packed edition with unfailing good humour from the depths of the snowy Scottish Borders; and to Nick Edwards and Gavin Thomas for supplying Karnataka and Mumbai updates respectively.

The maps in this book were all updated using a hand-held GPS device – thank you to the clever people at Garmin for inventing it, and the MapSource software, and to our long-suffering cartographer in Delhi, Swati Handoo, for deciphering the results; their efforts have helped create the most accurate set of plans of Goa ever published.

Last, but by no means least, thank you to partner VM, who cared for our two small sons, Morgan and Aeris, back home in the cold while I was away researching, and without whom this book could not have been written.

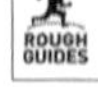

Readers' letters

Thanks to all the readers who have taken the time to write in with comments and suggestions (and apologies if we've inadvertently omitted or misspelt anyone's name):

Sam Athol-Murray; Barry Atkinson; Louise Attwood; Kathryn Barley; Chris Baumann; Peter Castro; Bill Clark; Malcolm Clark; William Darling; Lydia Dawson; Ann Day; Marie Fenyes; Sharon "Shazbaz" Foxwell; Suzie Goldring; Stuart Graham; Rob Head; Helen Holding; Ardella Hones; Beryl Jackson; Peter Jacques; Libby Jellie; John Kehoe; Sonia Khan and John Hendry; Judith and Bill Landles; Tim Pearson, Pedro de Porto; Berl Peck; Mark Perrott; Henry Pfeifer; Erika Shantz; Carol Whitmore; Bob Wiggins; Jackie Williams; Hans Dieter Schmitt; Rev Fr Ynte de Groot.

Photo credits

All photography by David Abram © Rough Guides except the following:

Introduction

Family separating a catch © Joe Lasky/Getty Images
Little Vagator Beach © Franck Guiziou/Hemis/Axiom
Flower garland being made © Andrea Pisolesi/Getty Images
Women carrying baskets © Art Wolfe/Getty Images
Nuns outside church © Paul Miles/Axiom
Coconut picker © Rick Strange/Alamy

Things not to miss

07 Goan food © Nicholas Pitt/Getty Images
12 Spice plant © Travel Ink/Getty Images
13 Usgalimal carvings © David Abram

Life's a beach colour section

Sunset over Mandarem © Helder Filipe/Alamy
Vagator Beach © Andrea Pistolesi/Getty Images

The Portuguese legacy colour section

St Francis of Assisi Church © Michele Falzone/Getty Images
Vindaloo © Bon Appetit/Alamy
Pao © Bon Appetit/Alamy
Fontainhas © Simon Reddy/Alamy
Church of the Holy Spirit © Rawdon Wyatt/Alamy
Carnival © Ladi Kirn/Alamy